Youth Violence

Youth Violence

Edited by Michael Tonry
and Mark H. Moore

Crime and Justice
A Review of Research
Edited by Michael Tonry

VOLUME 24

The University of Chicago Press, Chicago and London

This volume was prepared under Grant Number 95-IJ-CX-0035 awarded to the
Castine Research Corporation by the National Institute of Justice, U.S. Department
of Justice, under the Omnibus Crime Control and Safe Streets Act of 1968 as
amended. Points of view or opinions expressed in this volume are those of the editors
or authors and do not necessarily represent the official position or policies of the U.S.
Department of Justice.

The University of Chicago Press, Chicago 60637
The University of Chicago Press, Ltd., London

© 1998 by The University of Chicago
All rights reserved. Published 1998
Printed in the United States of America

ISSN: 0192-3234

ISBN: 0-226-80845-9 (cloth)
ISBN: 0-226-80846-7 (paper)

LCN: 80-642217

Library of Congress Cataloging-in-Publication Data

Youth violence / edited by Michael Tonry and Mark H. Moore.
   p. cm.—(Crime and Justice, ISSN 0192-3234; v. 24)
   Includes bibliographical references and index.
   ISBN 0-226-80845-9 (cloth).—ISBN 0-226-80846-7 (pbk.)
   1. Juvenile deliquency—United States. 2. Problem youth—United
States. 3. Violent crimes—United States. I. Tonry, Michael H.
II. Moore, Mark Harrison. III. Series: Crime and Justice (Chicago,
Ill.): vol. 24.
HV9104.Y6857   1998
364.36'0973—dc21   98–29200
                                       CIP

Contents

Preface

Something extraordinary seemed to be happening to American teenagers in 1995 when this volume was conceived. Violent crimes by and against young people appeared to be skyrocketing; sharp annual increases in both had occurred for a half dozen years; and the national media, a handful of academics, and many public officials were trumpeting the arrival of a new class of "superpredators."

Those phenomena were especially striking because they occurred at a time when overall violent and property crime rates were falling, when property crime rates by young people also were falling, and when debates were breaking out among public officials over who could rightly claim credit for the good news. Something had happened, however, journalists and others claimed, that made a subset of young people, mostly disadvantaged minority residents of inner cities, especially dangerous and incorrigible and likely to prey on other Americans for years to come.

In retrospect, what sociologists call a "moral panic" had set in. Had we but known it, youth violence rates had peaked in 1993; the 1994 police data showing a decline from the peak, a decline that has continued every year since, did not become available until late in 1995. Thus youth violence had been in decline for nearly two years when concern about it reached its height. By 1997, Shay Bilchik, administrator of the federal Office of Juvenile Justice and Delinquency Prevention, was writing, "While we hear an awful lot of talk about predators, even of a generation of juvenile superpredators, it is simply not true. . . . Talk of superpredators is tabloid journalism that distorts the facts."

It is good news that the short-lived epidemic of youth violence has subsided and that few people continue to speak of "superpredators," but it remains true that young people commit a disproportionate share of violent crimes that blight their victims', their communities', and their own lives.

For all their sakes, and not least the disadvantaged young people who have led lives that make gang involvement, illegal gun use, and violence seem sensible things to do, a decent society would want to understand the causes of youth violence and develop social policies that make its incidence less likely and its effects less damaging.

This volume distills accumulated learning from several mountains of research on the causes, correlates, courses, and consequences of youth violence. It includes work by qualitative and by quantitative researchers and by people of many disciplines working within diverse research communities and traditions. We hope readers will find it a comprehensive and thoughtful overview of current knowledge and its implications.

This is the ninth thematic volume in the *Crime and Justice* series, and its development followed a now well-marked course. The editors drafted a prospectus for the volume that was discussed at a small planning meeting in Washington, D.C., attended by representatives of the National Institute of Justice and other government agencies, members of the series' editorial board, and the editors. Papers were commissioned from leading scholars.

Drafts were discussed at a research conference in Washington attended by the writers, NIJ and OJJDP staff, and senior scholars of relevant expertise. Readers' reports were solicited on each paper. Informed by those processes, the editors provided detailed guidance to writers concerning preparation of final versions. Long-suffering and remarkably patient writers prepared final drafts, and now the volume has appeared.

Volumes such as this one could not exist but for support and effort from many people. We are grateful to the National Institute of Justice and its director, Jeremy Travis, for providing financial support, and to Mary Graham, Communications Division director and project monitor for *Crime and Justice*, for her unfailingly cheerful and efficient help. Others attended the midcourse conference—Barbara Allen-Hagen, Alfred Blumstein, Steven Edwards, Denise Gottfredson, Mary Graham, Darnell Hawkins, Philip Heymann, Sally Hillsman, Joan Hurley, Sara Ingersoll, Lois Mock, Carol Petrie, Winnie Reed, Jack Riley, Lawrence Sherman, Jeremy Travis, Jim Trudeau, Christy Visher, and Jane Wiseman—and the papers and the volume are the better for the discussions and disagreements that occurred there.

Anonymous reviewers provided written comments on early drafts. The writers, of course, are the book. We are grateful to them all. Whether, however, the fruits justify the labors, readers will decide for themselves.

Michael Tonry
Mark H. Moore

Mark H. Moore and Michael Tonry

Youth Violence in America

For a decade now, the United States has been besieged by an epidemic of youth violence. At a time when the overall crime rate has been stable or falling, violence committed by and against youth rose sharply during the late 1980s and early 1990s. Both frightened and disheartened, society wants to understand what is happening to its young people.

Predictably, some widely held conceptions—formed more by compelling anecdotes circulated through popular culture than by academic research—have emerged to explain the nature and causes of the problem. One common idea, for example, is that the epidemic of youth violence is caused by the escalation of ordinary adolescent disputes to lethal violence as a consequence of the ready availability of guns. Other common explanations include a demographic shift that increased both the absolute number and proportion of youth in the overall population; a change in economic opportunities that made prospects for upward mobility among disadvantaged youth seem increasingly remote; a collapse of community and family structures that in earlier times provided informal social controls and channeled young men toward productive careers; the disappearance of African-American men from the nation's hard-pressed ghettos because of penal policies that place unprecedented numbers in prison; the emergence of gangs as an alternative to family and community that tended to support, even demand, violence from their members; an epidemic of crack cocaine use that not only under-

Mark H. Moore is Daniel and Florence V. Guggenheim Professor of Criminal Justice Policy and Management at the John F. Kennedy School of Government, Harvard University. Michael Tonry is Sonosky Professor of Law and Public Policy at the University of Minnesota Law School.

1

mined community and family structures, but also created an environment in which a capacity for violence had economic as well as expressive value; a general enabling culture that seemed to glorify violence and fighting as a way of controlling situations or settling disputes; and a ready supply of exceptionally dangerous semiautomatic guns.

Closely related to these understandings are predictions about the future and what needs to be done now to stem the rising violence. Some scholars have warned that the United States faces a coming wave of "superpredators" as an "echo baby boom"—raised under particularly adverse conditions—reaches peak offending ages (Gest and Pope 1996). To deal with this threat, the country is advised to develop more effective preventive interventions, to end leniency toward juvenile thugs, and dramatically to increase prison capacity to lock up the superpredators (DiIulio 1995, 1996; Fox 1996).

There is to be sure another side of the story. The projected plague of superpredators was based on straight-line projections of the unprecedented increase in juvenile violence and, like most extraordinary trends, it did not continue. In retrospect, there may have been an element of hysteria (or ideology run amok) in the assumption that upsetting trends would continue forever (Zimring and Hawkins 1998). As Shay Bilchik, administrator of the federal Office of Juvenile Justice and Delinquency Prevention, has written, "Talk of superpredators is tabloid journalism that distorts the facts" (Bilchik 1997, p. 5). Youth violence nonetheless remains a serious and pressing national problem.

Unfortunately, the academic capability to illuminate the nature of the problem and the range of possible solutions is limited. Available data on criminal offenses allow tolerably accurate observations of the size, scale, and directions of youth violence and the epidemic's historical uniqueness. But the data are far too gross, and statistical methods far too weak, to offer either powerful explanations of the past or precise predictions about the future. Similarly, our ability to offer practical advice about interventions is limited. Having theories about causes of youth violence that are consistent with available evidence offers some guidance about interventions: namely, rely on the interventions that seem to reach the important causes of the problem. But knowledge of causes is too imprecise to be confident about the value of attacking one cause rather than another. And even if the relative importance of the causes was clear, there might not be instruments that could reach the cause reliably at an acceptable price. Working the problem from the other end—namely, trying interventions and seeing whether they work—has not yet produced unequivocal results. In sum, experience is accumulating faster than knowledge, and that limits the capacity of academic social scientists to offer useful policy advice.

Nonetheless, the purpose of this volume is to help the process of comprehending the problem and policy challenges of youth violence by engaging academic researchers in serious efforts to describe and explain the epidemic, and to devise plausibly effective means for combating it. Inevitably, the work is partial and many conclusions are provisional. The aim, then, is not to be comprehensive and definitive, but to get something into the world that can speed up the rate at which we learn from our own experience. Toward this end, we have assembled essays that describe recent trends in youth violence, develop and test some of the principal theories that might help to explain it, and offer advice about what interventions would be both just and practically useful.

I. An Epidemic of Youth Violence?

The opening line of this essay introduces our subject: understanding and responding to an "epidemic of youth violence." We thought hard before presenting the subject in these terms. It is a conventional enough phrase, of course. Public health researchers who first documented and drew attention to the phenomenon of youth violence have made it so. Yet, we recognize its inflammatory aspects. All three words have powerful normative connotations as well as precise, denotative meanings. Thus, framing the problem as an epidemic of youth violence risks distortion of both our understanding of the phenomenon and our capacity to act prudently to deal with it.

A. Violence

Consider, first, the word "violence." Ordinarily, violence refers to physical trauma or injury: something is violent if flesh has been torn or bones have been broken. But violence also suggests (and particularly in this context) that the trauma has not just occurred accidentally; it has been inflicted. After all, the epidemic of youth violence is an epidemic not only of youthful wounds; it is also an epidemic of youthful offending. In this sense, the violence is not only in the effects on the victim, but also in the heart of the attacker. This is not to say, of course, that the victim is necessarily wholly innocent, or the attacker wholly evil. In many cases, labeling one youth the victim may mean nothing more than that he was the one lying on the floor at the end of the fight. The youth labeled the attacker may, for one reason or another, have felt obliged to fight (see E. Anderson, in this volume). The word violence can also refer to the psychological trauma that comes from being frightened, or threatened, or consistently terrorized. It certainly is not difficult to imagine that psychological trauma is an important consequence of violence. And, one can imagine using the word violence to refer not to particular acts or consequences but to a more general climate in which violent acts occur often enough to make the fear of such acts omnipresent.

Indeed, this last meaning of the word violence may in many ways be the most important, for one of the worst consequences of youth violence is that children and their caretakers become afraid and demoralized. It may also be that the common occurrence of violence itself becomes a cause in sustaining or expanding overall levels of violence. This could occur if, for example, each act of violence became an act that had to be avenged in some way. It could also occur if fear of violence caused people to arm themselves and adopt hypersensitive and vigilant stances toward the conduct of others. And it could occur if violence so demoralized and weakened the sources of formal and informal social control that an area was essentially abandoned to those who were most capable in the use of violence. In such cases, we might well describe a neighborhood as a violent place. Elijah Anderson's evocative essay offers a particularly vivid image of how the context and feel of a neighborhood changes from one of safety and security to one of violence in just a few blocks, even though there is no immediate evidence of violence taking place.

At the core of the concept of violence is physical trauma inflicted by one person on another. That is mostly what the writers in this volume mean, seek to measure, and try to understand. But to comprehend fully both the consequences and the causes of youth violence, it is important to keep in mind the wider meanings that embrace psychological trauma, and the neighborhood conditions as well as the individual incidents.

B. Youth

Consider, next, the word "youth." It can be given a specific meaning by attaching ages to it—say, twelve to eighteen. But, once again, there is an additional meaning. The idea of a youth means someone who is unformed and still developing. If it is true that youths (even those who have committed violent acts) are unformed and still developing, then just and effective responses to violent acts committed by them are different from those for a more mature person. Franklin Zimring has noted elsewhere (Zimring and Hawkins 1998), and reasserts in his essay in this volume, that youths have a special status in society—one that reduces their criminal culpability for any given act, and increases our practical interest in making investments in their development that can restore them to a healthy developmental process. Thus characterizing violence as being committed by youths implicitly suggests a different response than if it were adult violence, or drug violence, or gang violence.

The difficulty is that the underlying characteristic that makes youth violence different as a matter of justice and practical interest (namely, the lack of maturity and judgment that would expose the offender to the rigors of an adult criminal justice system) is only imperfectly correlated with age. It is even less well correlated with the seriousness of an offense. Many people looking at an eighteen-year-old who has just sprayed a street with a MAC-10 in retaliation for the wounding of a friend, would find it hard to see the youth behind the reckless attacker. It would be easier if the offender were fourteen; easier still if the fourteen-year-old had closed his eyes and squeezed off one shot from an old Colt revolver in a desperate but misguided effort to become accepted into a neighborhood gang. Yet, it is quite possible that the eighteen-year-old, too, has an unformed character and is in the grip of powerful external forces that compel him to engage in the kind of behavior that makes him a dangerous offender in the eyes of the general population. And it is important both to justice and to the future life of the young offender to be able to determine whether he is youthful in materially important ways.

C. Epidemic

Consider, finally, the word "epidemic." The public health community has brought this word into common usage. But when public health specialists use the word, they have a specific technical meaning in mind. They mean that a particular health problem (in this case, injury caused by violence) is above the expected level. The expectation could have been set by past trends, or by past trends within particular demographic groups, or by past trends within population groups possessing certain "risk factors" for the health condition. Thus an epidemic of youth violence means nothing more than that more trauma is inflicted by violent episodes in the youth population than in the past.

What is important is that public health practitioners do not ordinarily mean by the use of the term epidemic that there is some contagious mechanism operating that tends to spread the problem from one person to another. There could be such a mechanism operating. And that could be the reason for the unexpectedly high levels of the health problem. But whether there are contagious mechanisms at work is a matter to be investigated, not assumed.

This is important because, again, some important imagery goes along with the idea of epidemics. Further, these ideas are influential in shaping policy responses. It is not hard to imagine various ways in which youth violence could be contagious in the sense that one incident creates conditions favorable to another incident occurring. For example, if a strong cultural norm existed among youth that violent incidents had to be avenged in some way, each violent act could become the occasion for another. Or, if one youth arrived in town with the orientation and skills to create a gang, it could be that the gang culture could spread quickly. The gang style could become culturally influential—"in" or "cool." Or, it could become necessary for self-defense to become a member of a gang.

If youth violence can be characterized as an epidemic with some contagious mechanisms operating, then many concepts linked to the control of more traditional contagious disease epidemics seem relevant. For example, it becomes sensible to think about "primary preventive efforts" designed to change the general environment to one that is less supportive of the epidemic; or "secondary preventive efforts" designed to reduce risk factors for particular populations that are at high risk of either offending or being victimized; and "tertiary preventive efforts" designed to minimize the bad consequences of the violence when it occurs. It also becomes important to think about ways to eliminate or confine some of the contagious elements—for example, the gun dealer who is willing to supply youthful offenders with semiautomatic weapons, or the charismatic gang leader who helps to spread a culture of violence.

Again, for the most part, the word epidemic is used here only in the narrow, technical sense: a higher-than-expected level of youth violence compared with past historical experience. But there may be some contagious mechanisms at work to produce nonlinear increases and decreases in levels of violence among youth, and some of the conceptual apparatus of the public health world may be useful in imagining responses that could be made.

II. Has There Been an Epidemic of Youth Violence?

Has the United States experienced an epidemic of youth violence? The answer, established by Cook and Laub (in this volume), is almost certainly yes. By triangulating several different, imperfect sources of data, they convincingly show that all forms of youth violence increased significantly in the late eighties and early nineties, and that homicide (as one particularly serious form of violence) increased particularly dramatically. They also show that while violence has remained concentrated in the demographic group that has long been most victimized—namely, young, African-American men—the degree of concentration lessened as the epidemic has gotten worse. In short, the violence seems to have spread to Hispanic, Caucasian, and Asian males as well as to African-Americans. It also leaped the gender gap and began increasingly to involve girls as well as boys.

Although Cook and Laub make it clear that the United States has experienced an important epidemic of youth violence, they also provide additional facts that help keep this phenomenon in perspective. For example, they note that despite the increases in youth violence and youth homicide, youth violence never amounts to a large proportion of the overall burden of violence in the United States. The main action remains with adults. In their words, youth violence remains a sideshow (albeit an important one) in the overall pattern of violence the country experienced in the late eighties and early nineties.

They also note important descriptive facts about the epidemic that suggest possible explanations of causes. They observe, for example, that while the rates at which youth commit violent offenses and are themselves victimized by violent offenses tend to increase together, giving credence to the imagery of youth killing youth, a close look at whom youth are victimizing, and who is victimizing youth tells a somewhat different story. Youth are victimizing people older than their age cohorts as well as people within them. And they are being victimized by offenders older than their age cohorts as well as offenders within them.

Cook and Laub also observe that increases in youth violence occurred contemporaneously in several different age cohorts—those entering the teenage years, those in the middle, and those maturing out of the teenage years. This suggests that something happened all at once to all youth rather than slowly to one cohort at a time.

Cook and Laub also show (as do Fagan and Wilkinson, in this volume) that guns figure much more prominently in youth violence and

homicides than they did before. Indeed, it is precisely the gun homicides that add the increment of violence that constitutes the epidemic.
This does not necessarily mean, of course, that a shift in the availability
of weapons caused the epidemic to occur. But it does seem that a ready
supply of weapons was at least an important enabling condition for the
epidemic to occur and become as prevalent as it did.

So, the evidence indicates that the United States has experienced an
important epidemic of youth violence. The epidemic remained concentrated in urban, minority, male populations, but the degree of concentration diminished as the overall level of violence rose. The epidemic occurred simultaneously in all age groups within the twelve- to
eighteen-year-old youth cohort, and became more pronounced in the
late eighties and early nineties than in the mid-eighties. The share of
the violence that involved guns increased dramatically.

III. Explaining the Epidemic of Youth Violence

Given that an epidemic of youth violence occurred, what caused it?
Unfortunately, there are too many plausible explanations and not
enough facts to discriminate among them. But a number of hypotheses
have been offered and they can be assessed in light of research findings
now available.

A. Age Is Destiny

Consider, first, the simplest demographic account. In this account,
there was an increase in the absolute level of youth violence, and an
increase in the share of all violence that could be attributed to youth,
simply because the absolute size and share of the population that was
youthful went up during the period 1985–95. It is true that the absolute size and share of youth in the U.S. population increased in this
period as the echo baby boom began to make its appearance. It is also
true that this would naturally have led to absolute increases in levels
of youth violence, and to youth violence becoming a larger share of
violence overall.

What actually happened, however, was that offending and victimization rates within the youth cohorts increased during this period to historically unprecedented levels. It was not just that there were more
youths as an absolute number and as a share of the general population:
they were offending and being victimized at higher levels than ever before. So, the increase came both from there being more youth and
from the existing youth offending and being victimized more than

other cohorts. And it is this second fact—the increase in offending and victimization rates within the cohort—that requires special explanation.

This could conceivably be explained as a function of the number of youth in the overall population. It could be, for example, that as the ratio of youth to mature adults within a population changes, important changes occur within the youth cohort. Their numbers may strain the capacity of adults to supervise. Or, they may be able to dictate more of the cultural style through sheer force of numbers. Something of the sort may well have happened in the mid- to late sixties as the first baby boom generation hit their teenage years (Wilson and Herrnstein 1985, pp. 425–30). And it could be happening again now as their children reach their teenage years.

But this explanation depends not on the simple account that relatively fixed rates of offending and victimization by age explain rates of violent crime in terms of changes in the age distribution of the population. It is, instead, one that depends on changing rates of offending and victimization as a function of the ratios of demographic groups and the effects of these different ratios on cultural style.

B. Risk Factors Are Destiny

Consider next a somewhat more sophisticated demographic account that seeks to explain the epidemic of youth violence in terms of characteristics of the circumstances under which contemporary youth were raised. The most important such characteristics are those that are known to be "risk factors" for violent offending or victimization. The idea is that the increased level of youth violence can be explained by pointing to the increased adversity of the conditions under which children were raised. If more youth than ever before were being raised in families that were poor and female-headed, or marked by substance abuse and family violence, or lacking in required parenting skills and effective male role models, then rates of youthful offending and victimization might rise simply because more youth were exposed to known risk factors for violence.

This is certainly a plausible explanation. There is lots of evidence to suggest that conditions within poor families in urban areas were worsening at the time that the young, violent offenders and victims of the late eighties and early nineties were going through important developmental stages in the mid- to late seventies and early eighties (W. J. Wilson 1987). The worsening conditions could have caused any particular cohort to become more violent as more individuals faced community and family conditions that increased their likelihood of becoming violent offenders. Such mechanisms could have planted the time bomb that exploded in the late eighties.

But several things cast doubt on this story. For one thing, the period in which conditions in the inner cities were becoming most desperate seemed to come later than the mid- to late seventies (W. J. Wilson 1996). Of course, that may mean that the worst is yet to come. Indeed, some have made precisely that prediction on precisely this basis (DiIulio 1995, 1996; Fox 1996). But, it could also mean that even this refined demographic prediction is wrong: that there is, in fact, a great deal of variability in rates of youthful victimization and offending that cannot be accounted for by demographic or background characteristics of offenders.

It also seems significant that the increase in youthful offending happened quite suddenly, and within all age groups at the same time. This general pattern is more consistent with a story of a sudden change that affected everyone at the same time than with a story that emphasizes the gradual erosion of family and community structures that interact with each child's individual developmental trajectory in adverse ways. On balance, then, it seems better to understand the worsening conditions within poor inner-city families as conditions that enabled the epidemic to occur and to spread widely rather than as a precise cause of the particular timing and shape of the epidemic as it actually occurred.

C. An Entrenched, Intensifying, and Spreading Culture of Violence

If demographic changes cannot account for the sudden increase in youth violence, how about the emergence of a more or less pervasive culture of violence? There are lots of interesting possibilities here. One possible culprit is TV and movie violence that works on young minds exposed to it. Another is a culture that celebrates violence expressed in sports, and that encourages violence as a means of parental discipline or the resolution of childhood disputes. In this view, youth have been socialized into violence from an early age, and it should not be surprising that they engage in it when they become teenagers.

The difficulty with these broad cultural explanations is that, like the demographic explanations, they seem most plausible as accounts of how certain enabling conditions might be created rather than an explanation of why the epidemic occurred when and where it did. The generation that reached teenage years in the mid-eighties and nineties was among the first to be exposed to a steady diet of violence on TV, and that conceivably could account for the apparently strong period effect. But even so, some more geographically and spatially local factors must be added to explain why the epidemic occurred when and where it did. That can be done without leaving the world of "cultural" explanations.

Cultural influences are usually envisioned as very broad, pervasive, and enduring phenomena that grind powerfully and widely, but slowly. But culture also operates in a different way—as style or fashion or fads. In this conception, cultural changes happen quickly and locally, and then spread, and die out. Elijah Anderson's essay (in this volume), for example, provides a vivid picture of a local culture that makes it important for individuals to respond to violence with violence. What his account does not reveal is how long the culture he describes has existed, and how strong and pervasive it is. But it is possible that this particular culture is not necessarily deeply rooted—that it emerged from relatively recent changes in objective circumstances.

If culture is seen in this way, then it is easy to imagine cultural trends that could operate to produce quickly spreading violence among teenagers who might be particularly vulnerable to such trends. One possibility is that the culture of violence was not produced by TV or corporal punishment by parents, but by the more recent, more local, and altogether more frightening emergence of violent, street-level crack markets. If teenagers grew up in neighborhoods dominated by drug violence, and if they experienced it closely not only as witnesses, but also as victims and as individuals recruited to the trade, then the culture of violence has a local meaning and specificity that makes it a more plausible contender as an explanation for increased violence. The culture of violence could be imagined to have been established and spread through the agency of gangs that provided justifications for violence, training in its use, and occasions in which to use it. The gang ideology could have been spread through "gangsta rap." Alternatively, a culture that was hypersensitive to "dissing," and that called on every young male to assert his manhood through violence if offended, could have been produced and generated by the spread of a prison culture to a local neighborhood as young fathers and older brothers returned from prison, having learned there that the only way to avoid victimization was through constant vigilance, and a willingness to respond to attacks with immediate retaliation.

The E. Anderson and Fagan and Wilkinson essays in this volume testify to the potential importance of cultural supports for violence.

The Hagedorn essay in this volume explains why gangs might have emerged, but also sees youth violence as importantly connected to gangs. So, it may be that there are important cultural explanations for the epidemic of youth violence—particularly if there are both society-wide cultural features that move slowly and local cultures that can move more quickly, and local cultural forces are understood to include the potential impact of crack markets, gangs, and the return of older males from prison.

D. A Concomitant of the Crack Epidemic

Consider, next, the hypothesis that the epidemic of youth violence came as a concomitant to the epidemic of crack cocaine use (Hage-dorn, in this volume). This hypothesis seems to hit closer to the mark. The crack epidemic occurred at times and places where the epidemic of youth violence occurred. And the crack epidemic can plausibly be connected to youth violence through several mechanisms.

One story is of violence emerging from the supply side of the market. In this story, demonstrating a capacity for violence is an important asset to anyone selling drugs in an illegal market. The violence is important to ensure discipline within drug dealing organizations, to ensure that customers pay, and to enhance one's competitive position. Youth are potentially attractive candidates for involvement since they are cheap, loyal, and easily intimidated, and do not face the same harsh penalties that would fall on adults. Thus drug entrepreneurs have incentives to recruit youth into drug selling, which necessarily involves them in violence. Surges of violence are likely elements of such a story: fights for territory and competitive advantage would break out, and killing by one trafficking group would have to be avenged quickly by counterattacks.

A second story would focus more on demand-side violence. In this conception, kids using cocaine would be more inclined to engage in violence either because the cocaine intoxication made them more likely to commit violence, or because they engaged in violence to get money to buy cocaine.

The difficulty with both these stories is that the violence actually committed by youth does not seem to be that closely linked either to cocaine dealing or to cocaine use (Fagan and Wilkinson, in this volume). The data that link particular acts of violence to drug use is not particularly powerful (Fagan 1990). There is more ambiguity in research findings relating violence to drug dealing, but such relations as exist appear to be part of a complex mix of gangs, guns, drugs, and subcultural norms (E. Anderson, in this volume; Hagedorn, in this volume). Drug-related violence in any case accounts for only a small proportion of violent events involving youth. Gang-related violence is far more common, and there have been epidemics of youth violence in places such as Chicago even without an epidemic of crack cocaine use. So, the crack epidemic might explain some of the important upsurge in youth violence, but not all or even most of it.

E. An Increased Supply of Lethal Guns to Youth

It is also tempting to find the explanation for increased violence among youth in the supply of guns. After all, as Fagan and Wilkinson show, the increase in gun homicides among youth is very dramatic. Indeed, if youth gun homicides are subtracted from all the other homicides, what is left is the "normal," or "expected," level of youth homicide. Thus it seems that gun homicides have changed in the world, and it is the availability of weapons that has made the difference.

At a superficial level, this logic seems compelling. And there is no doubt that the ready availability of weapons may be one important enabling condition that allowed the epidemic of youth violence to become widespread and virulent. But again, to explain the sudden upsurge in youth violence in terms of gun availability requires either a supply-side theory that claims that there was an important change in the availability of guns to kids, or a demand-side theory that there was a sudden change in the desire of youth to own, carry, and use weapons.

The supply-side case is difficult to make. The aggregate stock of guns, built on years of manufacture and sale, is pretty large, and has probably not changed dramatically. There may have been some important changes in the flow of weapons, and this flow may have become more differentially available to youth than it has in the past, but this effect is difficult to pin down.

The demand-side case is easier to make. It is easy to imagine that as youth have encountered more dangerous conditions on the streets and in school, and as their culture has been changed by crack markets, gangs, and the influence of prison culture spread by older males, more kids have found it prudent as well as stylish to acquire, carry, and use guns. Moreover, it is not hard to imagine that if guns are more immediately available to and more on the minds of kids, that the level and especially the seriousness of violent attacks among youth would increase. In this sense, the ready availability of weapons is an important cause of the epidemic of youth violence. But when searching for the policy implication of that conclusion, it is important to recognize that interventions could be focused either on the supply of guns to youth or on the demand for guns by youth, and it is not obvious which would have the greater payoff.

F. Toward a Synthesis

Thus the causes of the epidemic remain somewhat elusive. There are too many different plausible explanations. Consequently, everyone has a favorite explanation. That usually corresponds to a person's favorite villain and to their favorite target for intervention—usually chosen on grounds other than the importance of that variable in causing the epidemic, or the ease with which that variable can be attacked through policy interventions.

What may be more important and more striking, however, is the common effort to explain the epidemic of youth violence through a simple additive model, in which the primary objective is to find the single variable that explains most of the variance. The effort succeeds if others can be persuaded that specific risk factors for violent offending are important—a culture of violence, guns, gangs, or crack markets. The effort succeeds if others can be persuaded that a single variable is the most important cause because the scientific goal is to produce the most parsimonious account of the phenomenon of interest, and the policy goal is to identify the single variable that should be the focus of an intervention.

But the world is seldom modeled as a linear, additive model. Things are more dynamic than this. It is not hard to imagine a different model that hypothesizes the existence of enabling conditions that might or might not lead to epidemics of youth violence if other more uncertain local events occur. What is hard is proving these alternative hypotheses and estimating the key parameters in a dynamic model. Following David Farrington's theoretical efforts (in this volume), here is one story.

Imagine a world in which kids are growing up in a particular environment. One part of that environment could be considered "background" in the following senses: it happened to them in the past; it was an aggregate condition that operated on them more or less continuously, but in any case persistently; effects of exposure to these conditions have accumulated within them as certain propensities or dispositions, or personality, or character. These propensities differ from one person to another. They are more or less durable.

Another part of the environment could be considered "foreground"; it is what individuals see immediately and more distantly in front of them. The environmental factors immediately in front of them are opportunities or challenges or threats. The environmental factors in the more distant foreground are the images of their possible futures. The foreground viewed by individual kids has structural properties in the sense that it has stable aggregate features known more or less perfectly. But the foreground environment from the point of view of an individual seems fortuitous and idiosyncratic. It produces somewhat randomly a wide variety of particular, short-lived features such as opportunities and challenges. These interact with individual propensities to produce bits of behavior. Some of these bits of behavior are violent. A feedback loop converts these bits of behavior into an individual's past experience and, through that, to continuity or change in propensities. Thus background environments have shaped individual propensities toward violence; and foreground environments create challenges and opportunities. The two working together over time produce certain levels of violence, and certain propensities toward violence within the population.

Now add the idea that the bits of behavior that emerge shape the environment of others. They constitute challenges and opportunities. They shape people's views of what is normal and expected. One person's behavior can affect others via the mechanisms of creating specific opportunities and challenges, via affecting more general views, via setting examples. There can be various escalating and dampening effects. This is the abstract image of a model that gives standing to many different kinds of factors in producing observed aggregate levels of violence.

A simple, more concrete story is consistent with this abstract model and fits recent experience. In the late seventies and early eighties, the social and economic structure of many urban neighborhoods began to collapse under a variety of economic and social pressures. Small merchants shut down and moved away; employment dwindled. Under the economic pressures, families broke apart. Social services could not fill the gaps. Children grew up under increasingly adverse conditions. These are the structural factors that produced conditions ripe for an epidemic.

In response to these conditions, some youth joined gangs in search of affiliation and security. The gangs produced fears and rivalries that caused other gangs to form and more kids to join the gangs. The infrastructure of gangs increased the number of potential conflicts.

An epidemic of crack cocaine hit the already troubled areas. The epidemic exploded families and communities still further. But the epidemic also created an economic opportunity for the community. Some of the youth gangs that already existed began selling cocaine. Other kids not previously involved in gangs began to participate in drug-selling enterprises. To protect themselves from external attack and internal betrayal, the drug-dealing gangs armed themselves.

The arming of both drug-dealing and non-drug-dealing gangs produced both dangerous conditions on the street and a cultural style that encouraged many other kids to arm themselves in response. The large supply of available guns made it possible for youths to arm themselves once it became important and stylish to do so. The arming of youth, in turn, made conflicts much more lethal. And, since there were now many more potential conflicts among gangs and others than there had once been, society experienced an epidemic of youth violence.

Note that what is important in this story is not just the worsening of aggregate social conditions, but also a response to that situation that seems to feed on itself. It is the growth of gangs that begets other gangs and produces both arming and conflicts. It is the crack epidemic spreading from one user to another that further erodes informal social control and creates incentives for illicit drug dealing that spawns its own rivalries and violence. It is the widespread availability of weapons that allows the increased gang and drug-dealing activity to become very dangerous. And it is that danger that causes new gangs to form and more kids to join gangs or arm themselves in self-defense. These mechanisms seem different—more explosive, but also more superficial and vulnerable to intervention—than the deep structural factors. These could be called the "epidemic" factors.

IV. How to Intervene?

Given this tentative understanding of the causes of the epidemic of youth violence, what sorts of interventions might make sense? To answer that question persuasively requires understanding of more than the causes of the epidemic. Concrete ideas about policies and programs must be developed that could in principle, or have in practice, reached the causes and produced the desired effects. A normative framework must be constructed for use in evaluating proposed interventions that not only recognizes the benefits of the initiative in terms of reduced violence, but also keeps track of the costs of the efforts (in terms both of money and diminished freedom), and anticipates unexpected but important side effects. Finally, it is necessary to try to determine whether a particular proposal could be adopted and reliably implemented in the political and institutional setting in which it was being proposed. These are all additional requirements of effective policy analysis that go beyond the usual requirements of social science to identify cause-and-effect relations. We cannot offer a complete policy analysis here, but some parts of that analysis have been attempted by writers of essays in this volume

A. The Normative Framework

Consider, first, the normative framework that is used (explicitly or implicitly) to guide the design and evaluation of policy interventions. The obvious goal is to reduce the level and seriousness of youth violence: that is the social benefit to be sought. Yet this goal does not define all the dimensions of public value that are plausibly at stake. To the extent that the interventions rely on public funds to pay for improved parenting classes, or enhanced quality and security in public schools, then society becomes interested in ensuring that these costs are minimized or, more precisely, that the effect of any given expenditure on reducing youth violence is maximized. This defines the familiar utilitarian framework of cost-benefit or cost-effectiveness analysis.

In discussing youth violence, however, these utilitarian concerns are only part of the normative framework for assessing particular interventions. Often, in designing interventions, society is equally concerned with issues of justice and fairness. These issues arise partly because public money is being allocated. When that is true, those who spend the money must be able to show that funds were distributed fairly as well as efficiently and effectively. But concerns about justice and fairness arise even more prominently when public authority is engaged in responding to youth violence. We do not often think of "spending" public authority; that is what is done when rules are established governing student conduct in and around schools, when youth curfews are established, and when youths who have carried weapons or committed violence are subjected to criminal prosecution. When these things are done, the question must be answered whether such interventions are fair and just as well as whether they are effective.

Sometimes, these different normative frameworks are linked to particular political ideologies. Some, for example, might say that concerns for the "hot button" issues of justice and retribution are commonly linked with right-wing political views on crime. Concerns for cost-effectiveness, demonstrated effects, and the disciplined balancing of ends and means, by contrast, are often linked to the rational, scientific approach that characterizes the Left's political stance. Yet, a little reflection reveals that there is both a Left and a Right utilitarian conception of how best to respond to youth violence, and a Left and a Right justice approach to youth crime.

The Right/utilitarian approach to youth violence emphasizes the important role of deterrence and the development of consistent and consistently enforced rules of conduct. The Left/utilitarian approach emphasizes the importance of primary prevention efforts and rehabilitation programs when things have gone wrong. The Right/justice approach emphasizes the concept of youth accountability for criminal offenses, and refuses to compromise on the question of criminal culpability for offenses. The Left/justice approach emphasizes the idea that children have rights to social conditions that give them a reasonable chance to develop. It follows, then, that if society fails to ensure a chance for healthy development, it would be unjust for society to hold young people strictly accountable for their failure to develop as society demands.

Understanding these basic normative frameworks is important for two reasons. First, analytically, they can be used to assess the value of particular policy interventions—all things considered. This requires switching from one normative framework to another, accepting each as a plausible guide to just and effective action. A second use, however, is exactly the opposite of the first. It often seems that the frameworks are used to decide among competing policy interventions without further examination or reflection. If one starts with a conviction that the appropriate normative framework to use in assessing youth violence policies is the Right/justice view, then one is inclined to favor the toughening of the juvenile justice system as the best and most appropriate response to youth violence. If, however, one starts with a conviction that the right way to evaluate policies is the Left/justice view, then one is apt to conclude that the best policy interventions are those that focus public resources on the conditions that lead to the development of youthful offenders.

B. The Strategic Choices

The important ideas about how to intervene to stop the epidemic of youth violence appear in the essays in this volume by Howell and

Hawkins, D. Anderson, Fagan and Wilkinson, Zimring, and Feld. Different spirits animate these essays. In an important sense, the first three are animated by a search for preventive effectiveness. The last two also are interested in preventive effectiveness, but in a world where the interventions must meet tests of justice and fairness as well as effectiveness. This should not be surprising. The first three are interested in mounting interventions that do not depend on criminal laws and the institutions of the criminal justice system. The last two are interested in interventions explicitly rooted in agencies of the criminal justice system—namely, the juvenile justice system.

Howell and Hawkins offer an authoritative march through a variety of programs designed to prevent youth violence. The programs could be considered primarily primary or secondary prevention programs in that they seek to reach youth before they have reached crime-prone ages, and individual youths before they have committed offenses. A particular strength of their essay is that these programs are considered in light of a particular theory of conditions that might expose children to a greater risk of committing violence: namely, individual factors that increase the likelihood of violent offenses (roughly the same factors inventoried by Farrington); the bonding or connection of kids to social institutions such as adults, parents, community, and school (these factors are also considered important by Farrington); and the existence of clear standards of conduct that are consistently enforced over time and across institutions that exercise some oversight of the kids. In addition, the essay makes the point and keeps us conscious of the important fact that while some kids tend to persist in violence, many kids will engage in some violence at some stage, but then desist. Thus the mere fact of violence in a youth's history need not portend a sustained commitment to violence in the future.

While the Howell and Hawkins essay reviews many individual programs that have been undertaken to prevent youths from becoming involved in violent offending, it concludes that the effective prevention of youth violence probably does not depend on the development and implementation of any one program. Instead, the authors argue that the promising lines of attack depend crucially on a more generalized process of community mobilization, within which a variety of different programs targeted on different risk factors might be created and sustained. Their argument is that community mobilization as a process is important in preventing youth violence: because it is a necessary condition to ensure a steady supply of resources—money, public support, volunteer effort—to sustain the portfolio of programs that the initiative identifies; because communities differ from one another and therefore require somewhat different mixes of programs; and because a united, committed community is a powerful force that is greater than the effects of any particular set of programs.

This observation is welcome for many reasons, not least because it draws attention to the important question of where the resources and energy for intervening will come from and the question of what programs might work. It also recognizes that resources and energy will be forthcoming only when those who are asked to provide the resources believe in the effort. And finally, it recognizes that the places and people from which the resources and energy are needed include informal institutions such as families, PTAs, and other community-based actors in addition to government agencies. So, if we are to prevent youths from becoming involved and staying involved in violence, we will have to rely on many different programs, shaped in portfolios designed to both meet local problems and respond to local concerns and capabilities, and supported by some combination of private and public resources organized through networks mobilized by concern for the problem.

This perspective leads quite naturally to D. Anderson's essay on schools. It instructs that schools play three importantly different roles in controlling the epidemic of youth violence. First, as educational institutions, they presumably can affect the dispositions and capabilities of kids. Schools can serve not only as springboards for future success of kids (their primary function), but also as platforms for launching more specific programs designed to shape students' views of and reliance on violence as a method for adjudicating disputes (an additional purpose they may have to take on in a world in which the epidemic of youth violence rages).

Second, as places where kids spend a great deal of their time, schools can become arenas within which violence occurs or is controlled. A great argument rages about the best way to produce reliable security in schools; specifically, whether it is best produced by concentrating on providing quality education and fair but firm governance of the school environment, or whether special security measures such as weapons detection equipment, police in schools, or regular searches of lockers are required. Anderson does not and cannot resolve this great debate, but he does cast doubt on the idea that a school is a hopeless hostage to the community in which it finds itself. In his view, schools have both the responsibility and the capability to become "safe havens" for kids in otherwise violent environments.

Third, as community institutions, schools can provide the physical places and the social networks that could begin the process of mobilizing a community as a whole against violence. In short, for the kinds of community mobilizations that Howell and Hawkins think are most important in preventing youth violence, schools are at least important parts of the mobilization effort, and might, on some occasions, emerge at the leading edge.

Fagan and Wilkinson take a different approach to prevention. One strand that runs through their essay is the suggestion that the ready availability of weapons plays a key role in shaping the epidemic of youth violence. Zimring also urges that this is an important factor fueling the epidemic of youth violence. The compelling piece of evidence is that the increase in youth homicide is accounted for almost exactly by the increase in homicides committed with guns. It is also significant that youths more commonly possess and carry guns than in the past. It is tempting, therefore, to treat guns—and particularly the semiautomatic weapons that have proved particularly attractive—as a "vector" in the epidemic of youth violence. If guns were not available, then the epidemic would not have spread so far, or been so lethal. If the availability of guns could now be suppressed, the extent and virulence of the epidemic could be stemmed. This view seems strongly held by Fagan and Wilkinson and by Zimring.

This is a very different idea of prevention than the ideas offered by Howell and Hawkins. They view the important predisposing condition for the epidemic of youth violence as the existence of young people either disposed, or insufficiently hostile, to the use of violence as a means to acquire wealth or status, as a vehicle for self-expression, or as a device for resolving disputes: the key objective of prevention efforts must be to reduce the pool of those susceptible to using violence. They may also believe that it is an important matter of justice that children be provided with opportunities to grow up well. Fagan and Wilkinson, however, treat the availability of weapons as a key contributing factor. Instead of focusing on the disposition of youth to engage in violence, they focus on the availability of a particular "criminogenic commodity." This could, arguably, hold out the hope that we need not succeed in the expensive, arduous, chancy, long-run task of keeping youths on healthy developmental trajectories to prevent youth violence; it would be an important step if we could reduce the availability of weapons to children.

Unfortunately, even though the task of reducing weapons availability to youths seems technically straightforward, it is by no means easy to accomplish. A vast stock of weapons is already available and there is strong political opposition to reducing it significantly. Perhaps more importantly, the task of keeping weapons from youths may end up involving the same wide set of actors and policy instruments as is required to achieve the larger goal of keeping kids on favorable developmental trajectories. It is necessary for communities to decide that they want to achieve this goal of reducing gun availability to kids (and local communities might well disagree on the urgency of that goal). Then it is necessary for a variety of actors to act on the responsibilities implied by that goal: for parents to take on the responsibility of locking up their own weapons and monitoring their children's weapons carrying; for regulatory agencies to demand that gun dealers live up to their civil responsibilities to refuse to sell guns to children or their agents; and for criminal justice agencies to enforce laws against illegal sales, carrying, and distribution. Politically and bureaucratically speaking, then, keeping guns from children may be every bit as demanding a task as ensuring that children follow favorable developmental trajectories. Even this, therefore, may require the community mobilization that Howell and Hawkins recommend.

It should be striking to readers of this volume that we have proceeded this far in examining interventions to control the epidemic of youth violence and have not yet mentioned the institutions that many think should be most centrally involved: the juvenile justice system. The reason for this is that those writing for this volume see little connection between the juvenile justice system and the epidemic of youth violence. At best, it is seen as a set of institutions that responds more or less justly and more or less effectively to specific instances of youthful violent offending. To both Zimring (in this volume) and Feld (in this volume), the juvenile justice system is too reactive to be very preventive, and neither particularly effective nor particularly just in the way it responds to individual incidents.

Both Zimring and Feld see great difficulties in the trends forcing the juvenile justice system to act more like the adult criminal justice system. By focusing attention primarily on the seriousness of the offense rather than on the persistence of offending as the basis for deciding whether cases stay in juvenile court or are exposed to the rigors of adult prosecution, a key idea in juvenile justice is undermined. That key idea is that youths have less well-formed intentions and characters than adults. That implies that, as a matter of justice, it is wrong to hold youths accountable for their crimes in the same way as for adults. It also means, as a matter of practical concern, that there might be a greater opportunity to intervene in the future development of youths than would be true for adults. If we understand that some youths commit violence even though their commitment to violence may not be deep or sustained, the inability of the juvenile justice system to note and respond to this difference reduces both the justice and the efficacy of the system as a device for handling youth violence.

What the Feld and Zimring essays point to is the importance of remaking our images of the juvenile justice system. If the juvenile justice system is to be nothing more than a criminal court for children, then it adds little to our overall social capacity to deal with youth violence. But what is the alternative? One important idea might be to see the juvenile justice system as less outside the system of community mobilization that Howell and Hawkins envision than Zimring and Feld seem to view it. After all, the juvenile court controls a potentially important community asset: namely, the right to use the authority of the state to exercise control over youthful offenders and (perhaps) those private and public actors who are responsible for their care. This asset may be more valuable when it is held in reserve rather than used directly, but it may be part of the apparatus that helps form a consistent set of expectations for youth, and it may also help mobilize some of the resources needed in individual cases to deal with some of the individual factors that are disposing youth to violence, such as mental illness or violence within the family. That might be particularly effective if the court acts in concert with community-based social service organizations to help children and their caretakers meet their obligations to stay on successful developmental paths. In short, it may be that the juvenile court could become an important instrument of youth policy as well as youth violence policy. That is implicit in the court's current jurisdiction if not in its current focus or capabilities.

V. Where to Go from Here

To those who want answers about what to do about youth violence, this volume may seem a bit discouraging. A great deal is known about the factors that expose youth to violence, but we are not sure that these risk factors are the only ones that generated the epidemic of youth violence. It may be that these simply create a larger or smaller pool of those susceptible to being caught up in an epidemic, but do not alone determine how broadly the epidemic will spread, how long it will last, or its ultimate virulence.

There is some evidence about programs that have produced some preventive impacts but, for both practical and theoretical reasons, effective prevention probably does not depend on nationally mandating and funding any particular program. Instead, it depends on mobilizing local communities to define and deal with problems. In some ways, that is a quite appealing idea, but there is the problem that some of the nation's hardest-hit communities may lack the capacity to rally themselves to deal with the intense local epidemic of youth violence. It is also discouraging to learn how crippled and uncertain are two social institutions that should be on the front line of the battle: namely, schools and the juvenile justice system.

Sadly, the epidemic of youth violence may continue. Given the toll, we cannot fail to act. But given our uncertainty about causes and effective interventions, we must proceed with less precision and confidence than we would like. This need not be disabling. Indeed, it can be liberating. But one of the important features of the current situation is that it may very well reverse what is ordinarily thought to be the correct relationship between research and action.

In a well-ordered world, the relationship between research and action is clear: research provides both the technical basis and political legitimacy for action. It tells us what to do. It offers assurances that we are acting neither recklessly nor dangerously. But what is the relationship between action and research in a messy world in which urgent problems require action and the available knowledge is incomplete? Here, responses must be more experimental, and more collaborative.

Researchers have to offer their best knowledge and ideas, but recognize that their knowledge is limited and that they must be as uncertain as everyone else is about what will happen with any particular intervention. That increases rather than reduces the pressure to be clear about why one thinks a particular intervention might work, and to gather information not only about whether the intervention seemed to produce a result, but also whether it operated in ways that were not anticipated. Thus there is urgency for both process and outcome evaluations of interventions to be made.

Researchers have to be more collaborative with communities and the government agencies they support, for three simple reasons. First, given that researchers' knowledge is limited, the difference between expert knowledge and lay knowledge is less than in some other policy realms, and there may be important substantive ideas to be learned from, or developed in partnership with, communities and their operational agencies. Second, given uncertainty about the consequences of proposed actions, communities must share the risks and consent to avowedly uncertain initiatives. Third, given that the implementation of many initiatives depends on actions taken by communities and agencies, it is important that they come to understand and agree with reasons why a particular intervention, or a particular portfolio of interventions, is being undertaken.

We conclude, then, with the idea that in dealing with the epidemic of youth violence, researchers must be part of the community mobilization that Howell and Hawkins recommend. They cannot guide or direct that activity. Nor should they stay aloof from it. They must enter into the partnership with a commitment to use their skills to ensure that the doing is well-considered, and also to ensure that we learn while doing. That, in contrast to the traditional call for more research and more restraint in policy action until the research can be completed, is what we recommend in dealing with the pressing problems of youth violence.

REFERENCES

Anderson, David C. In this volume. "Curriculum, Culture, and Community: The Challenge of School Violence."

Anderson, Elijah. In this volume. "The Social Ecology of Youth Violence."

Bilchik, Shay. 1997. "Making a Difference." *Juvenile Justice* 4(2):2–8.

Cook, Philip J., and John H. Laub. In this volume. "The Unprecedented Epidemic in Youth Violence."

DiIulio, John. 1995. "The Coming of the Super-Predators." *Weekly Standard* (November 27), p. 23.

———. 1996. *How to Stop the Coming Crime Wave*. New York: Manhattan Institute.

Fagan, Jeffrey. 1990. "Intoxication and Aggression." In *Drugs and Crime*, edited by Michael Tonry and James Q. Wilson. Volume 13 of *Crime and Justice: A Review of Research*, edited by Michael Tonry and Norval Morris. Chicago: University of Chicago Press.

Fagan, Jeffrey, and Deanna L. Wilkinson. In this volume. "Guns, Youth Violence, and Social Identity in Inner Cities."

Farrington, David P. In this volume. "Predictors, Causes, and Correlates of Youth Violence."

Feld, Barry C. In this volume. "Juvenile and Criminal Justice Systems Responses to Youth Violence."

Fox, James. 1996. *Trends in Juvenile Violence: A Report to the United States Attorney General on Current and Future Rates of Juvenile Offending*. Boston: Northeastern University Press.

Gest, Ted, and Victoria Pope. 1996. "Crime Time Bomb." *U.S. News and World Report* (March 25), p. 28.

Hagedorn, John M. In this volume. "Gang Violence in the Postindustrial Era."

Howell, James C., and J. David Hawkins. In this volume. "Prevention of Youth Violence."

Wilson, James Q., and Richard J. Herrnstein. 1985. *Crime and Human Nature*. New York: Simon & Schuster.

Wilson, William Julius. 1987. *The Truly Disadvantaged*. Chicago: University of Chicago Press.

———. 1996. *When Work Disappears: The World of the New Urban Poor*. New York: Knopf.

Zimring, Franklin E. In this volume. "Toward a Jurisprudence of Youth Violence."

Zimring, Franklin E., and Gordon Hawkins. 1998. *Youth Violence*. New York: Oxford University Press.

Philip J. Cook and John H. Laub

The Unprecedented
Epidemic in Youth Violence

ABSTRACT

The epidemic of youth violence that began in the mid-1980s has been
demographically concentrated among black male youths: the homicide-
commission rate for this group increased by a factor of about 4.5. A
number of patterns stand out: one of every four or five serious crimes of
violence, and one of ten homicides, are committed by juveniles who are
less than age eighteen; the proportion of arrests for violent crimes,
however, that involved juveniles (20 percent) was about the same in 1994
as in 1965. A decline in the adolescent population has been balanced by
an increase in rates of arrest. Youths kill more often than they are killed,
and there is a great deal of crossover killing (in both directions) between
adolescents and older people. The claim that the explosion in youth
violence can be attributed to "superpredators," with each cohort having
greater prevalence of such fiends than the last, does not accord well with
available data. There is a clear indication of increased gun availability
during the epidemic: every category of homicide, as well as other violent
crimes, exhibited an increase in gun use. While the sizes of successive
youth cohorts are increasing and will continue to do so for the foreseeable
future, that is not a sound basis for predicting that the volume of youth
violence will also increase.

A decade ago, we published a precursor to this essay titled "The (Surprising) Stability of Youth Crime Rates" (Cook and Laub 1986). We

Philip J. Cook is the ITT/Sanford professor of public policy and economics, Sanford
Institute of Public Policy, Duke University. John H. Laub is professor of criminology
and criminal justice at the University of Maryland and visiting scholar at the Henry A.
Murray Research Center, Radcliffe College. Cook acknowledges the support of the
Sloan Foundation. Karen Price, Kristin Goss, Chris Kenaszchuk, and Roni Mayzer pro-
vided extensive research assistance. Gary Thompson and Geof Gee managed the data
and statistical programming. The authors are grateful for suggestions from Alfred
Blumstein, Francis Cullen, Don Kates, Jr., Melissa Sickmund, Daniel Webster, and
Franklin Zimring.

documented the "stability" in the arrest statistics since the early 1970s and argued that it was a "surprise" given the secular decline in the quality of family life and parental resources devoted to socializing children. Unfortunately, the potential for trouble has now been realized. While the adolescent arrest rate for property crimes has remained quite stable since we remarked on this phenomenon, there has been an explosion in the rates at which adolescents commit and are victimized by serious crimes of violence. The increase was concentrated among black males: between 1984 and 1993, the homicide-victimization rate more than tripled for thirteen- to seventeen-year-old adolescents, and the homicide-commission rate increased by a factor of 4.5, reaching levels with no precedent in this century. This increase is all-the-more remarkable given that homicide rates for victims over twenty-five were declining during this period (Blumstein 1995; Fox 1996).

In this essay, we document the recent trends in violent crime for juveniles and young adults and make some effort to explain what happened. The effects of increased violence rates by youths have been somewhat muted by the decline in number of teenagers between 1975 and 1990; that trend has now been reversed, and several criminologists have spelled out the scary implications. For example, one report suggests that "If trends continue as they have over the past 10 years, juvenile arrests for violent crime will more than double by the year 2010" (Snyder, Sickmund, and Poe-Yamagata 1996, p. 15).

While we cannot deny the logic of this claim, the volatility of youth-violence rates makes predictions of any sort highly uncertain. The run-up has been more akin to an outbreak of some contagious disease than to a conventional secular trend. That characterization provides room for optimism since epidemics tend to be self-limiting. And, as it turns out, the most recent data indicate that the surge of violence has reversed. For example, homicide arrest rates peaked for ten- to seventeen-year-olds in 1993 and had declined 23 percent by 1995 (Butterfield 1996; Snyder 1997).

The essay is organized as follows. Section I describes and discusses sources of data for measuring trends in youth violence. Section II then analyzes the role of juveniles in the overall societal burden of criminal violence, finding that one out of every four or five serious crimes of violence (and just one in ten homicides) is committed by a juvenile. Section III provides documentation on trends in arrest rates since the 1960s; other than the overall trends, we find an interesting change in the demographic composition of juvenile arrests, with both the black-white and male-female arrest ratios dropping sharply since 1968, from about eleven to below six. Thus violence, or at least arrests for violent offenses, has become somewhat less concentrated in traditional high-violence groups.

Sections IV–VI focus on homicide rates. First, we develop a new indicator, a "homicide-commission rate," primarily based on FBI data. We demonstrate that the commission rate follows the same time pattern as the better-known victimization rate, but in all years, the commission rates exceed the victimization rates for adolescents and young adults. We then document an unexpected phenomenon with respect to age: there is a great deal of crossover killings (in both directions) between adolescents and young adults. Only a minority of adolescent victims are killed by adolescents, and a majority of the victims of adolescent killers are adults. (Indeed, a majority of victims are five or more years older than their adolescent killers.) In that sense "they" are not killing each other, as is commonly supposed.

Section V explores two hypotheses concerning the explosion in lethal youth violence: first, each successive cohort is becoming more morally impoverished and vicious; and, second, youths have become more involved with guns, and hence their violent encounters have become more lethal. The former hypothesis does not account for the intertemporal patterns as well as the latter; for example, the upsurge in killings in the mid-1980s was abrupt and involved a number of different age cohorts simultaneously. Thus the impetus appears to be environmental and sudden, not what would be expected from a secular deterioration in the moral character of kids. The second hypothesis, however, is clearly correct, at least with respect to its premise. The increase of gun carrying and use in violent crime is pervasive during this period and includes most types of homicides (not just gang and drug related) as well as robbery.

In Section VI, we briefly explore the extent to which the annual count of youth homicides can be predicted on the basis of demographic trends. Since 1968, the ups and downs of youth homicides have had very little to do with the size of the relevant population; in fact, the correlation is negative. The prediction that the volume of youth violence is likely to increase as a result of the ongoing increase in the number of youths seems plausible, but the volatility of youth homicide is so great as to make predictions of any kind very chancy.

I. Data Sources

Our focus is on the serious violent crimes of rape, robbery, aggravated assault, and criminal homicide. The Federal Bureau of Investigation (FBI) has tabulated crimes known to the police in these categories as part of the Uniform Crime Reporting Program (UCR) since 1930. The FBI provides police agencies with definitions of each of these categories in an effort to standardize reporting.

"Murder and nonnegligent manslaughter" (which we refer to as "criminal homicide" or simply "homicide") is the willful killing of one person by another, excluding homicides that are legally justifiable. "Negligent" or "accidental" homicides, such as death caused by reckless driving, are excluded from the count.

"Forcible rape" ("rape") is carnal knowledge of a female by force or threat and against her will. This category includes attempts; it excludes statutory rape without force.

"Robbery" is theft or attempted theft by force, violence, or threat. It includes muggings and stickups; it excludes purse snatches, picked pockets, and other thefts from the person that have no violent element.

"Aggravated assault" is an unlawful attack for the purpose of inflicting severe bodily injury. It includes unarmed attacks that result in broken bones and other serious injuries together with attacks with guns and other lethal weapons whether or not injury is actually inflicted. Less serious assaults, such as the typical fist fight, are classified as "simple assaults."

These four categories make up the violence portion of the FBI's Crime Index, a social indicator that also includes the property crimes of burglary, larceny, motor vehicle theft, and arson. In the analysis of crime trends presented below, we sometimes follow the FBI's lead and report on the combined total of Index crimes. In the case of the four violent crimes, this total count is numerically dominated by aggravated assault and robbery; homicide and rape account for less than 10 percent.

For these four types of crime, the UCR is not the only source of data on national trends. Since 1973, the National Crime Victimization Survey (NCVS) has provided national estimates for rape, robbery, and aggravated assault, using definitions very similar to the UCR definitions. And in the case of criminal homicide, the National Center for Health Statistics' Vital Statistics Program has produced national estimates for most of the century. We briefly review the salient aspects of these sources below.[1]

---

[1] For a general overview of these data sources, see O'Brien (1985), and for a detailed discussion of the complexity of measuring violent offending and victimization, see Reiss and Roth (1993, esp. app. B).

A. Uniform Crime Reports Data

Uniform Crime Reporting data are compiled from tabulations provided by law-enforcement agencies, either directly to the FBI or through a state agency.[2] The ultimate source of these data is crimes made known to the police, usually as a result of reports received from victims or witnesses and then confirmed by police investigation. Since a majority of rapes, robberies, and aggravated assaults are never reported to the police, the UCR greatly underestimates the true total. For our purposes, however, the total is less important than the trend. If the fraction of crimes that is "known" remains constant over time, then the proportional changes in reported crime rates will be equal to the proportional changes in actual crime rates. But there are reasons why this fraction may have been trending upward over the past few decades: such innovations as 911 and community policing may increase the fraction of crimes that are reported to the police, while increased centralization and computerization of data collection within law-enforcement agencies may reduce administrative "slippage" in crime recording. However, citizen reporting could decline if, for example, fear of retaliation from offenders has become more widespread.

Further difficulties arise given that our objective is measuring not trends in overall violence but trends in *youth* violence. The UCR reported-crimes data do not include information on the age of the perpetrators or victims. For that reason, we use arrest data rather than crime reports, thereby introducing new sources of potential error.[3] Recorded arrests are not a representative sample of crimes known to the police, let alone actual crimes committed. Whether one or more arrests are made (and recorded) for a particular crime depends on the

[2] Some agencies do not submit crime data or do so only sporadically. Further, the number of agencies reporting data for arrest statistics is less than the number of agencies reporting crimes known to the police. Over the years, the FBI has changed its procedures for including agency reports. Prior to 1973, the FBI collected data from police agencies annually. In 1974, monthly reports were implemented. The result was that agencies that submitted as few as six monthly reports for the year were included in the annual reports. During the 1980s, the FBI modified their procedures once again. From 1982 to the present, only those agencies that report data for the full twelve months are included in the annual reports. Finally, special reports produced by the Uniform Crime Reporting Program, such as the report on age- and race-specific arrest rates (FBI 1993), include data from all police agencies that provide twelve months of data, even though these data may have been submitted after the deadline for the annual report (personal communication with Patricia Radway of the FBI, August 16, 1996).

[3] Criminologists have long recognized that crime reports tend to be a better representation of the underlying volume of crime for index purposes than statistics that are more heavily influenced by the practices of the criminal justice system, such as arrests or court dispositions (Sellin 1931).

operating procedures of the relevant agency, the cooperativeness of the victim, the skill of the perpetrator, and a host of other factors.[4] Further, law-enforcement agencies have been less faithful about submitting arrest data to the FBI than they have about crime-report data. Given fluctuations in the number of agencies reporting age-specific arrest data and the occasional omission of major cities or whole states, Zimring has suggested that making year-to-year comparisons in youth violence is a "hazardous occupation" (Zimring 1979, p. 88).

Despite the evident problems with these data, criminologists continue to use them in studying trends and patterns in crime (for a recent example, see LaFree and Drass 1996). Indeed, there is some evidence that arrest data provide reasonably accurate measures of the relative rates of offending by age, sex, and race (see, e.g., Hindelang 1978, 1981; Blumstein et al. 1986). Our view is that the arrest data have some value but that it is best to compare arrest trends with other trend information whenever possible. The NCVS provides one important alternative for measuring nonlethal violence.

B. National Crime Victimization Survey

Initiated in 1973, the National Crime Victimization Survey is an ongoing survey designed to measure the extent of personal and household victimization in the United States. Interviews are conducted at six-month intervals with respondents twelve years of age and older who live in residential housing units in the United States. The NCVS is the only national data source that allows individual-level analyses of victims and their experiences across a variety of crime categories. And unlike the UCR, the NCVS measures crimes whether or not they come to the attention of the police and are properly recorded. These two characteristics make the NCVS a rich source of information on the nature and extent of criminal victimization and victims of crime in the United States.[5]

NCVS data provide estimates of victimization rates for youths. In

---

[4] It has long been suggested that these factors may include the age, sex, race, and social class of the suspects; see Hindelang, Hirschi, and Weis (1981), for an extended discussion of this issue.

[5] A logical alternative would be to interview a national sample concerning the crimes they have committed. The National Youth Survey, for example, interviewed a national probability sample of 1,725 youth ages eleven to seventeen concerning their drug use and delinquency (see Elliott, Huizinga, and Ageton 1985). The data collection for this longitudinal survey began in 1977, and individuals were reinterviewed for nine waves (see Elliott 1994).

addition, for face-to-face crimes of violence, the NCVS may be used to assess the commission rates by particular age groups, since respondents are asked to report on the age, race, and sex of their assailant. We use these data to assess the trends and patterns in violent offending.

Of course, the NCVS data are not problem free. They exclude data on homicide and on crimes with victims younger than age twelve. More importantly, the sampling frame excludes people who are homeless or in hospitals, prisons, and other institutions. Hard-to-reach populations, such as those who lack a fixed address or are rarely at home, are underrepresented (Loftin and Mercy 1995). Probably as a result of these sampling problems, the NCVS underestimates the number of gunshot victims by a factor of three (Cook 1985a).

Response error also infects NCVS results. Inaccurate reports result in part from memory problems (Skogan 1981, pp. 15–22).[6] Other sources of underreporting are embarrassment and fear, common in victims of rape and crimes involving family members. Such crimes are often not reported to NCVS interviewers, even in cases where they were reported to the police (see Skogan 1981). Finally, the accuracy of victims' reports regarding the age and other characteristics of their assailants is questionable and largely untested (see Laub 1987 for more details).

We make some use of the NCVS data in what follows, primarily as a check on trends measured from arrest data. But the "gold standard" in measuring crime trends is homicide data.

C. Homicide

Criminal homicides are almost always known to the police, and a large majority of homicides result in arrests. Hence both the homicide counts and the homicide arrest statistics are more reliable than for other types of violent crime. Further, uniquely in the case of homicide, there is an alternative to arrest statistics for estimating the demographic characteristics of offenders: Most law-enforcement agencies submit Supplementary Homicide Reports to the FBI, including de-

---

[6] The NCVS estimates appear to be remarkably sensitive to how the survey questions are asked. The NCVS interview schedule was redesigned recently, with changes in the screening questions for possible victimizations and new "short cues" to jog the memories of the respondents about a wide range of incidents and activities. The new estimates for crimes such as rape and assault are considerably larger than estimates using the old interview format (Bureau of Justice Statistics 1996a).

tailed information from the police investigation. The demographic characteristics of the killer may be known and recorded in the Supplementary Homicide Reports, even if there is no arrest.

An entirely separate source of data on homicides is provided by the National Center for Health Statistics through the Vital Statistics Program. Reports by coroners and medical examiners on the characteristics of victims and the type of weapon are compiled into national rates that serve as a check on the police statistics (see Cantor and Cohen 1980).

Homicide is of course the most serious of the violent crimes and hence of great interest in its own right. It is also valuable as a check on trends in aggravated-assault statistics, since there is good reason to believe that homicide and aggravated assault should exhibit similar patterns.[7] When NCVS and UCR data indicate quite different trends (as they do in the case of aggravated assault over the last two decades), we find more credible the series that most closely matches the intertemporal pattern for homicide.

Ultimately, the usefulness and validity of particular crime series depends on the purposes for which they are used. We begin by assessing trends in the burden of juvenile violence on law enforcement and society at large, a task for which arrest statistics are relatively well suited.

II. The Burden of Juvenile Violence

The society-wide effect of the recent epidemic of youth violence has been muted by the decline in the youth population. Between 1975 and 1990, the population in the high-crime ages of thirteen to seventeen declined by 21 percent; between 1985 and 1990 (a time of rapidly escalating homicide rates per capita among teenagers), the decline was 10 percent. That downward demographic trend has since been reversed, and the ever larger cohorts of the next decade are the basis for the scary projections offered by criminologists (Fox 1996)—a matter we return to in a subsequent section. Here we focus on the contribution of youths to the overall violence problem during the last three decades.

The most readily available measures of the youth "burden" derive from the arrest statistics compiled by the FBI. These data are tabulated by demographic characteristics and crime type and hence provide a

---

[7] The difference between aggravated assault and homicide may be just a matter of luck—whether or not the bullet strikes a vital organ. While not uncontroversial, the close logical and statistical relationship between the two crimes has been extensively documented. See, e.g., Zimring (1972) and the review in Cook (1991).

convenient indicator of the extent to which different groups commit particular crimes. And since arrests constitute the "input" for the courts and corrections systems, arrest statistics provide a direct indicator of the portion of the criminal justice system's workload accounted for by youths. In what follows, we not only analyze some of the important patterns in the arrest data but also take a look at the NCVS data on the perceived characteristics of assailants in personal crimes.

Working with data requires a precise definition of the age group of interest. We adopt eighteen as our dividing line. Eighteen is the age by which most youths have left high school and are expected to take on a greater degree of autonomy with respect to their parents. In most states, eighteen is the age at which arrestees are routinely processed within the criminal courts rather than the juvenile courts. And as a practical matter for our purposes here, some of the tables of arrest data in the FBI's annual report *Crime in the United States* group arrestees according to whether they are less than age eighteen or not.

For some measures, we also need a minimum age, and have chosen thirteen. While children under thirteen are occasionally arrested for violent crime, that is a relatively rare event.[8] Our focus, then, is on "juveniles" (less than age eighteen) and sometimes "adolescents" (ages thirteen to seventeen).

A. Arrests

Figure 1 depicts the proportion of arrests for each of the FBI's Index crimes that involve juveniles. In 1994, about one in six arrestees for homicide, rape, and aggravated assault were juveniles. Juvenile arrests for robbery are twice that, constituting one-third of all arrests. When all arrests for serious crimes of violence are combined, juveniles made up one-fifth of the total. As shown in this figure, the next-older group, ages eighteen to twenty-four, accounts for a somewhat larger portion of violence arrests (27 percent). The median age of those arrested for violent crimes is a youthful twenty-five.

As it turns out, the proportion of arrests for serious violent crime in 1994 that involve juveniles is about average for the preceding thirty years: as shown in figure 2, juveniles constituted the same fraction of the violence arrest volume—20 percent—in 1965 as in 1994. (This fraction was somewhat above twenty during the 1970s and below dur-

---

[8] In 1994, just 1.5 percent of the arrestees for serious violent crime were less than thirteen years old (FBI 1995, p. 229).

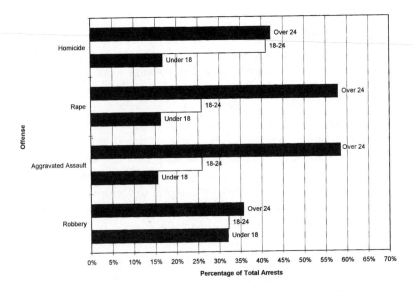

Fig. 1.—Age of arrestees for violent offenses, 1994. Source: Bureau of Justice Statistics (1997).

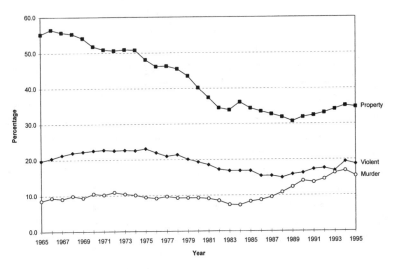

Fig. 2.—Arrests for juveniles under age eighteen (percentage of total). Sources: Bureau of Justice Statistics (1986, 1990); FBI (1966–96).

ing the 1980s.) By contrast, the percentage of Index property-crime arrests involving juveniles has declined throughout most of this period (also shown in fig. 2), dropping from 50 percent in the early 1970s to a low near 30 percent in 1990.

So where is the epidemic of youth violence in these pictures? The only hint in figure 2 comes from the percentage of arrests for criminal homicide. After a long plateau at around 10 percent, the juvenile share of homicide arrests started climbing in the mid-1980s, reaching 17 percent by 1994. For other violent crimes, however, the law-enforcement burden posed by juvenile arrests has not in recent years been especially high by historical standards.

An alternative measure of "burden" is the percentage of crimes cleared by arrest, which is also tabulated by the FBI. This measure indicates the likelihood that a police investigation of a crime will result in the arrest of one or more juveniles. For all four types of serious violent crime, juveniles figure less importantly in crimes-cleared-by-arrest statistics than they do in the arrest rates. One reason is simply that youths are more likely than adults to have accomplices in their crimes: as Zimring has pointed out, kids do crime, like they do most everything, in groups (Zimring 1981). As a result, there are often multiple arrests of juveniles for the same crime.

In 1994, the percentage of crimes cleared by arrest in which those arrested were juveniles was about 10 percent for homicide, 13 percent for aggravated assault, 14 percent for rape, and 20 percent for robbery.[9] While these statistics suggest that juveniles constitute a rather minor portion of the violent-crime problem, it is noteworthy that their relative importance has been growing since the late 1980s and that for all four types of crime the percentage is higher in 1994 than in 1975 (or any year between)—despite the decline in the size of the relevant population since then (Snyder, Sickmund, and Poe-Yamagata 1996, pp. 18–19).

B. Victimization Data

The National Crime Victimization Survey (NCVS) provides information on the demographic characteristics of perpetrators based on re-

---

[9] These statistics include relatively few cases in which the clearance was by "exceptional means"—the suspect was not arrested because the complainant refused to cooperate with police or because the suspect was dead.

TABLE 1

Juvenile Perpetrators in Serious Violent Crime:
Percentage of Victimizations, 1975–94

Period	FBI Data, Crimes Cleared by Juvenile Arrests as a Percentage of All Crimes Cleared	NCVS Data, Victimizations in Which Perpetrators are Less than Age 18	
		Excluding Unknowns	Percentage of All Victimizations
1975–79	12	20	17
1980–84	10	18	15
1985–89	9	17	14
1990–94	13	23	18

Source.—FBI data is from *Crime in the United States* (1976–95). Unpublished NCVS data was provided by Michael Rand, Bureau of Justice Statistics.

Note.—NCVS = National Crime Victimization Survey. Percentages are for the crimes of rape, robbery, aggravated assault, and (for the FBI statistics only) criminal homicide. The NCVS statistics are based on respondents' reports of the age of the perpetrators.

spondents' reports. Table 1 displays some results for the period 1975–94. Since the number of NCVS respondents who report a serious violent crime (aggravated assault, robbery, and rape) is quite small in any one year, we combine the data into five-year intervals. The pattern that emerges from these tabulations generally conforms to the pattern in the clearance-by-arrest statistics, also shown in this table.

We report NCVS results with and without the cases in which the respondent was unable to provide information on the age of the perpetrator. Both series indicate a somewhat greater involvement by juveniles in serious violent crime than is indicated by the crimes-cleared-by-arrest statistics.[10] The general pattern evident in all three series is one in which the 1980s had lower values than the late 1970s or the 1990s.

C. Conclusion

Juveniles commit a small fraction of the serious crimes of personal violence: one out of every four or five of the nonlethal crimes and just

---

[10] The difference is primarily for aggravated assault. A possible explanation is that aggravated assaults committed by juveniles are less likely to be reported to the police (and hence to result in a clearance by arrest) because they tend to be less serious than those committed by adults.

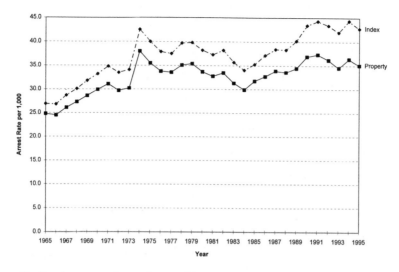

Fig. 3.—Arrest rates for youths ages thirteen to seventeen per 1,000 population, FBI Index crimes. Sources: Bureau of Justice Statistics (1986); FBI (1966–96); U.S. Bureau of the Census (1990, 1993); U.S. Department of Commerce (1966–96).

one out of ten homicides. These fractions are actually higher now than during the 1980s, reflecting the reversal of the long decline in the size of the adolescent population together with an increase relative to adults in crime-commission rates.

According to FBI figures, the volume of serious violent crimes (reported to the police) increased by 40 percent between 1985 and 1994. Juveniles accounted for one-quarter of that increase (Snyder, Sickmund, and Poe-Yamagata 1996, p. 20). Thus the epidemic of youth violence is real, but it is by no means the whole story.

III. Youthful Offending Rates

In the mid-1970s, the Index-crimes arrest rate for adolescents ages thirteen to seventeen was about forty per 1,000; in the 1990s, it was virtually the same at forty-three per 1,000. In the intervening years, as shown in figure 3, the arrest rate for Index crimes dipped somewhat, but what is most remarkable about this time series is its stability. It seems to contradict the widespread impression that kids are behaving badly these days in comparison with, say, a generation ago. What's more, it seems to contradict our understanding of what *makes* kids behave badly; stable arrest rates are not what one expects to find in the face of deteriorating family life, increasing poverty rates, and a gener-

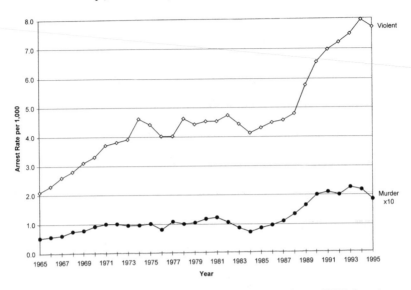

Fig. 4.—Arrest rates for youths ages 13 to 17 per 1,000 population, FBI Index crimes of violence. Sources: Bureau of Justice Statistics (1986); FBI (1966–96); U.S. Bureau of the Census (1990, 1993); U.S. Department of Commerce (1966–96).

ally reduced presence of parents in the lives of children (Cook and Laub 1986).[11]

For certain crimes, however, including the violent crimes in the FBI Index, the long period of stability is over. As shown in figure 4, the adolescent arrest rate for homicide abruptly doubled during the late 1980s, while their arrest rate for other violent crimes began a steep climb in 1989 after a long static period. (These increases are scarcely noticeable in the overall arrest rate for Index crimes, since the vast majority of Index arrests are for property crimes.)[12] So while it does not appear that kids are committing more burglaries and thefts, they are most certainly committing more assaults and robberies than in the 1970s and 1980s.

This conclusion receives support from the NCVS data. As before, we estimated juvenile involvement in violent crimes by five-year inter-

[11] During these twenty years, for example, the percentage of children living with both parents declined from 81 to 72 percent while the percentage of children living in poverty (and with mothers working) increased. For a detailed assessment of the changes in children's lives over the last fifty years, see Hernandez (1994).

[12] In 1994, there were 898,300 Index-crime arrests for those under age eighteen. Just 150,200, or 17 percent, were for one of the violent crimes.

TABLE 2

Juvenile Perpetrators in Serious Violent Crime, Rates per 1,000:
NCVS Data, 1975–94

Period	Commission Rate by Perpetrators Ages 12–17, No. of Crimes (Thousands)/No. of Youths (Millions) = Rate per 1,000	
	Excluding Unknowns	Apportioning Unknowns
1975–79	505/25.0 = 20.2	599/25.0 = 24.0
1980–84	449/22.3 = 20.1	540/22.3 = 24.2
1985–89	376/21.0 = 17.9	464/21.0 = 22.1
1990–94	573/20.9 = 27.4	721/20.9 = 34.5

Source.—Unpublished NCVS data was provided by Michael Rand, Bureau of Justice Statistics.

Note.—NCVS = National Crime Victimization Survey. All statistics are for the crimes of rape, robbery, and aggravated assault. The NCVS statistics are based on re-spondents' reports of the age of the perpetrators. Crimes in which there are multiple perpetrators are counted as one.

vals. Table 2 reports the results as a rate per 1,000 juveniles ages twelve to seventeen. The sharp increase during the 1990s corresponds to the arrest-rate pattern.

Figure 5 provides a broader context for the recent run-up in adolescent violence by depicting the age profiles of violence arrest rates for males in 1985 and 1994.[13] During this nine-year period, the largest increases (both proportionally and absolutely) have been for the youngest, those ages thirteen to eighteen. But the upward shift has not been limited to teenagers: arrest rates increased by 40 percent for men in their twenties and 62 percent for men in their thirties. The bulk of these increases is for the crime of aggravated assault, which, as we pointed out above, is the usual precursor to criminal homicide.

But the age profiles for *homicide* offenders tell a somewhat different story. As with other violent crimes, homicide arrest rates increased sharply for the youngest cohorts (especially thirteen to eighteen) between 1985 and 1994. Those in their early twenties exhibited smaller

[13] These arrest rates are adjusted for population coverage of the arrest data received from the FBI, which was 81 percent in 1985 and 80 percent in 1994. The 1985 data are taken from the FBI's *Age-Specific Arrest Rates and Race-Specific Arrest Rates for Selected Offenses, 1965–1992.* Arrest counts for 1994 are from *Crime in the United States, 1994* (FBI 1994) while population estimates are from the *Statistical Abstract of the U.S.* (U.S. Department of Commerce 1966–96).

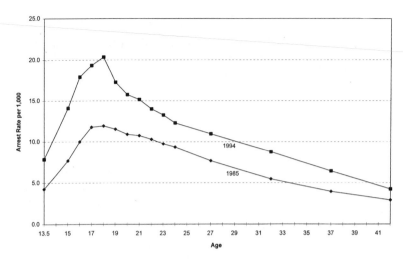

Fig. 5.—Age profiles and violence arrest rates of males, 1985 and 1994. Sources: FBI (1966–96, 1993). Coverage rate is 80 percent, and arrest rates have been adjusted accordingly.

increases. The surprise comes from the fact that the homicide arrest rates for those age twenty-five and over actually have declined since 1985 (Blumstein 1995; Fox 1996). Thus we have the paradox for older cohorts of large increases in aggravated assault coupled with decreases in the most serious outcome of aggravated assault, homicide. Our conjecture is that the increases in adult arrests for aggravated assault are not the result of changes in offending but rather police practice with respect to making arrests (and classifying these arrests for UCR purposes) in domestic-violence cases. This conjecture fits the facts for California.[14] In any event, for youths there is no paradox: All arrest rates are moving up together.

A. Sex and Race

Arrests for violent crime are highly concentrated with respect to sex and race. In 1994, boys constituted 86 percent of juvenile violence arrestees, six times as many as girls. With respect to race, half of all juvenile violence arrests were of blacks, implying an arrest rate over five

[14] Allan Abrahamse of the RAND Corporation has demonstrated this result in unpublished work based on data from the California Bureau of Criminal Statistics.

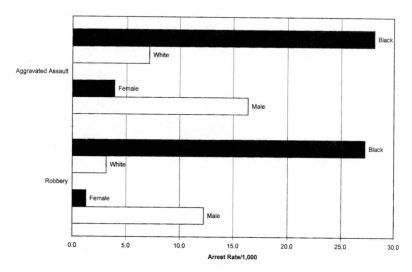

Fɪɢ. 6.—Arrest rates for aggravated assault and robbery of arrestees under age 18, 1994. Source: FBI (1966–96). Coverage rate is 80 percent, and arrest rates have been adjusted accordingly.

times as high as for whites. Figure 6 depicts 1994 arrest rates by race and sex for the two most common of the violent crimes, robbery and aggravated assault. Both race and sex disparities are especially great for robbery.

While these differences are large, they were still larger in earlier years; juvenile arrest rates have become more uniform across sex and race categories. Figure 7 depicts an interesting but little-remarked pattern, that arrest rates for black juveniles declined sharply relative to those for white juveniles in the early 1970s, from a ratio of eleven or so to a ratio of about six, and have dropped still further during the 1990s (see MacKellar and Yanagishita 1995). There was also an abrupt decline in the male-female arrest ratio around 1970, and a secular decline since 1978. This trend has been quite steep during the 1990s; violence arrests for juvenile girls increased 48 percent between 1990 and 1994, compared with just a 23 percent increase for boys.[15]

[15] FBI (1994, p. 224). See also Poe-Yamagata and Butts (1996). The downward trend in the male-female ratio appears to contradict the conclusion of Steffensmeier and Allan (1996) that there has been little narrowing of the gender gap over the last three decades. But it is possible to partially reconcile our conclusion with theirs. While we are looking at total arrests for violent crimes, Steffensmeier analyzes the different crime types separately. As it turns out, during the 1980s, the downward trend in the arrest ratio was primarily the result of a changing composition of violent-crime arrests. The male-female arrest ratio for aggravated assault is the same in 1975 as in 1990 and also was little

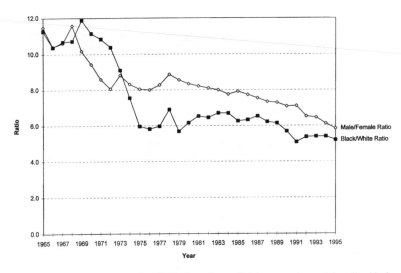

Fig. 7.—Arrest rate ratios for FBI Index crimes of violence: males and females, blacks and whites, arrestees under age 18. Sources: FBI (1966–96, 1993); U.S. Department of Commerce (1966–96).

B. Conclusion

From both FBI and NCVS data, it appears that adolescents committed violent crimes at a substantially higher rate during the first half of the 1990s than in previous decades.

Half of juvenile violence arrests are of blacks, despite the fact that whites outnumber blacks six-to-one. White or black, most of the violent crime is committed by males. But these race and sex differences are only half as large as they were during the 1960s. Thus violent offending, or at least arrests for violent offending, is less concentrated demographically now than previously.

IV. Homicide Victims and Offenders

For a variety of reasons, it is worth taking a separate look at criminal homicide. In recent years, it is the escalation of youth homicide (rather than of robbery or rape) that has focused public attention on the epidemic of youth violence. For our purposes, it is also relevant that the

changed for robbery during this period, but the aggravated-assault arrest rate grew more rapidly than the robbery arrest rate during this period. Since the male-female ratio is lower in aggravated assault than in robbery, the overall ratio for violent crime is trending downward. But this change in composition is not the whole story. The sharp downward trends before 1975 and after 1990 are exhibited by robbery and assault separately, as well as for all violent crime types combined. For confirmation, see Austin (1993).

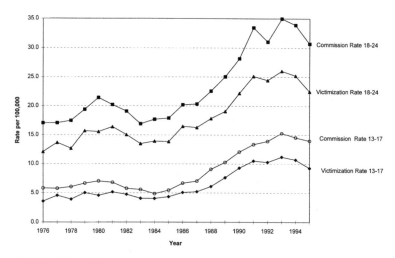

Fig. 8.—Homicide-commission and victimization rates, ages thirteen to seventeen and eighteen to twenty-four. Sources: FBI (1976–95); National Center for Health Statistics (1976–95); U. S. Department of Commerce (1966–96). Adjusted for unknowns and adjusted for underreporting by police using vital statistics. The adjustment information is available from Cook on request.

data on homicide are more complete and accurate than data are on other crimes of violence.

There are two sources of detailed data on homicide. The Supplementary Homicide Reports (SHR) data compiled by the FBI from law-enforcement agencies provide information on individual homicides, including what is known about the victim, the killer or killers, and the circumstances. Because some agencies fail to send in these reports, the SHR only captures 80–90 percent of all homicides (see the appendix, table A1).[16] The other source, the mortality data from the National Center for Health Statistics' Vital Statistics Program, includes individual records on *all* of the known homicides each year compiled from medical examiners' reports. These data are useful as a check on the SHR but lack information on circumstances of the homicides and characteristics of the killers.

Figure 8 depicts the trend in homicide-commission rates and victimization rates for males in two age groups: adolescents (ages thirteen to seventeen) and young adults (ages eighteen to twenty-four). The commission rates are not based on arrests but rather are based on the SHR

[16] This percentage has been declining in recent years, from about 95 percent in the late 1970s to just 80 percent in 1991.

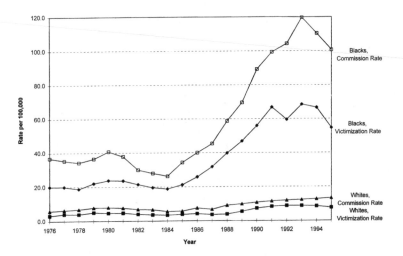

FIG. 9.—Homicide-commission and victimization rates for black males and white males ages thirteen to seventeen. Sources: FBI (1976–95); National Center for Health Statistics (1976–95); U.S. Department of Commerce (1966–96). Adjusted for unknowns and adjusted for underreporting by police using vital statistics. The adjustment information is available from Cook on request.

data concerning demographic characteristics of suspects. (We have adjusted these statistics for missing data.)[17] There are several notable patterns evident from this graph: both series depict the unprecedented increase in homicide-commission rates that occurred during the late 1980s and early 1990s; and the trends for victimization and commission are remarkably similar with respect to both timing and amplitude, although the rates of commission are consistently higher than the rates of victimization. The similarity is evident for both of the age groups.

Figure 9 depicts the victimization and commission rates for the younger age group, males only, for whites and for blacks. Figure 10 provides the same information for the age group eighteen to twenty-four. For both age groups, the same patterns are evident as in figure 8.

[17] Data are missing for two reasons: Some law-enforcement agencies did not submit their SHR data to the FBI, and some of the homicide reports that were submitted included no information on the killer—presumably because the investigation had failed to yield an arrest or even a description. We correct for the failure to report by use of the National Center for Health Statistics' Vital Statistics Program data as explained in the appendix, table A1. We then correct for missing data on unsolved homicides by inflating each year's rates according to the following assumption: The percentage of unsolved homicides with victims of a particular age in which someone from thirteen to seventeen years old was the killer is the same as the percentage of solved homicides with victims of that age. (We make the same assumption about killers ages eighteen to twenty-four.)

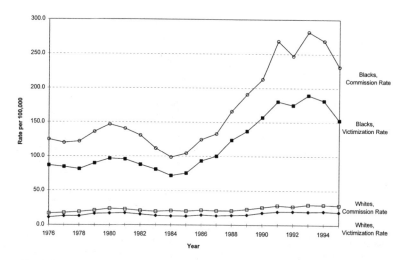

F IG. 10.—Homicide-commission and victimization rates for black males and white males ages eighteen to twenty-four. Sources: FBI (1976–95); National Center for Health Statistics (1976–95); U.S. Department of Commerce (1966–96). Adjusted for unknowns and adjusted for underreporting by police using vital statistics. The adjustment information is available from Cook on request.

In addition, the race differences shown in these figures are interesting. The increase in black-youth homicide commission and victimization began three years earlier (1985) than for white youth (1988) and was greater both proportionately and in terms of the absolute count. Again, the close parallel between commission and victimization is evident for each group.

As an aside, we note that by 1993 the homicide-commission rate had grown to 120 in 100,000 for black males ages thirteen to seventeen and to 280 per 100,000 for those ages eighteen to twenty-four—extraordinarily high rates. (The cumulative homicide-commission rate implied by these numbers is nearly 2.5 percent between the ages of thirteen and twenty-four.) These unique data provide a check on the more common measure, the arrest rate. We note that the commission rates tend to be higher than the arrest rates.[18] Further, the black-white ratio is higher in the commission rates than the arrest rates.

Given similar trends between killing and being killed, it is somehow

[18] Note that more than one youth may be arrested for any given homicide, whereas our procedure for estimating the commission rate has the effect of limiting the number of killers to the number of victims. In cases where the SHR included more than one suspect, we assigned the case to the oldest.

TABLE 3

Age Patterns of Homicide Victimization and Commission:
SHR Data, 1994

Age of Killer (Years)	Percent Distribution of Victims Ages 13–17*	Age of Victim (Years)	Percent Distribution of Killers Ages 13–17†
<13	.5	<13	5.8
13–17	37.2	13–17	25.9
18–24	47.2	18–24	30.0
>24	15.2	>24	39.4
N	1,036	N	1,489

Source.—FBI, Supplementary Homicide Reports (1994).

Note.—SHR = Supplementary Homicide Reports. Excludes homicides not reported by local police agencies to the FBI as part of the SHR. Excludes negligent manslaughter and justifiable homicide. The total percent distribution for victims is 100.0 and for killers is 100.0.

* For 535 victims ages 13–17, there were no suspects listed. In cases where there was more than one suspect, the killing was assigned to the oldest of those listed.

† For 8 of the cases in which the oldest suspect was from 13–17 years old, the age of the victim was unknown.

natural to conclude that "they" are killing each other. But the truth is that most adolescent homicide victims are killed by people older than seventeen, and most of the victims of adolescent killers are also older than seventeen.

Table 3 provides the details based on 1994 data. For adolescent victims, fewer than half are killed by juveniles. More precisely, just 38 percent of the homicides in which the ages of the killers are known were committed by killers who were less than eighteen. In 47 percent of cases involving adolescent victims, the suspects were eighteen to twenty-four years old, and in another 15 percent, the suspects were older than twenty-four.

In the reverse direction, we see from table 3 that only about one-quarter of the victims of juvenile killers are themselves juveniles; three-quarters are age eighteen or over, and most of those are age twenty-five or older.

More details are provided in table 4 (illustrated in fig. 11) and table 5. Starting with all homicide victims ages thirteen to seventeen, we see in the first of these tables that most of the suspected killers were older than the victims and a majority were at least three years older than the victim. In 1985, a relative low point in youth homicide rates, half of

TABLE 4

Age Relationship between Victim and Killer for Homicide Victims Ages 13–17, Unknown Relationships Excluded

	Percent of Homicide Victims		
	1985	1991	1995
Killer older than victim	81	80	78
Killer three or more years older than victim	63	56	55
Killer five or more years older than victim	50	39	35

SOURCE.—FBI, Supplementary Homicide Reports (1985, 1991, 1995).

NOTE.—SHR = Supplementary Homicide Reports. For 1985 and 1991, the oldest perpetrator was selected to represent the killer in cases of multiple offenders. In 1995, the SHR reported only one perpetrator for each homicide. Excludes homicides not reported by local police agencies to the FBI as part of the SHR. Excludes negligent manslaughter and justifiable homicide.

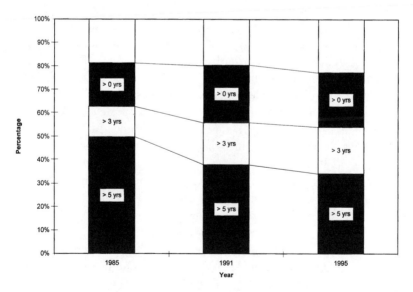

FIG. 11.—Killer's age minus victim's age for homicide victims ages thirteen to seventeen. Sources: FBI (1976–95); U.S. Department of Commerce (1966–96). Adjusted for unknowns and adjusted for underreporting by police using vital statistics. The adjustment information is available from Cook on request.

TABLE 5

Age Relationships between Victim and Killer for Killers Ages 13–17, Unknown Relationships Excluded

| | Percent of Killers | | |
	1985	1991	1995
Killer younger than victim	76	77	79
Killer three or more years younger than victim	63	63	63
Killer 5 or more years younger than victim	53	52	53

SOURCE.—FBI, Supplementary Homicide Reports (1985, 1991, 1995).

NOTE.—SHR = Supplementary Homicide Reports. For 1985 and 1991, the oldest perpetrator was selected to represent the killer in cases of multiple offenders. In 1995, the SHR reported only one perpetrator for each homicide. Excludes homicides not reported by local police agencies to the FBI as part of the SHR. Excludes negligent manslaughter and justifiable homicide.

the killers were at least five years older than the victims; that declined to 39 percent in 1991 and 35 percent in 1995, indicating that the age gap, while surprisingly large, tended to be smaller during the peak years of the 1990s than previously.

No such trend is evident when we consider the ages of the victims of adolescent killers. Table 5 indicates that most adolescent killers select older victims, and half select victims who are at least five years older. The pattern is virtually identical in the three years, despite the enormous changes in the underlying homicide rates reflected there.

What can be learned from these age patterns in homicide? We find them surprising, since we began this analysis with an image of juvenile violence in which the homicides, like the fistfights, largely involved age peers. After all, for better or worse high-school-aged kids tend to associate with other kids their age, both in and out of school. But the lesson of the data is that a large percentage of the adolescents at lethal risk have conflicts that extend outside their age cohort. It seems important to ascertain what activities engender these contacts and conflicts, such as drug dealing, gang activity, or individual arguments.[19] While

[19] Violent crime is not the only risky activity in which teenagers are involved with adults. A recent study found that at least half of the babies born to teenage girls ages

this issue is beyond the scope of this essay, some answers are found in other contributions to this volume.

V. Is It the Kids or the Guns?

Going back at least to the 1960s, commentators have sought to explain the increasing rates of violent crime in terms of the changing character of youths (Cook 1985*b*). It seems plausible: If youths are committing more homicides, does that not suggest that they are more vicious than earlier cohorts? But of course there is an alternative sort of explanation for the recent run-up in violence. Rather than a change in the intrinsic character of the youths, there may be something about the current social, economic, or physical environment that is more conducive to lethal violence than in previous years. It is not that they are more vicious but that their circumstances promote an intensification of conflict. For example, some commentators have pointed to the introduction of the crack-cocaine trade in the mid-1980s as providing the resources and motivation for many young men to obtain and begin carrying guns (Blumstein 1995). Below we sketch some of the evidence on these two explanations.

A. Increasing Viciousness

Adolescents are both killing and being killed at rates that are substantially higher than at any previous time in the twentieth century.[20] In some respects, it is also true that the primary socializing mechanism—supervision by parents and other adult family members—has attenuated to an extraordinary extent, as suggested by the prevalence of illegitimacy, single-parent households, lack of adult supervision after school, and so forth (Panel on High-Risk Youth 1993, chap. 2; Hernandez 1994). For most children, television is now the predominant socializing influence, and the message of many television shows encourages violent solutions to everyday problems (Coie and Dodge

---

fifteen to seventeen were fathered by adults age twenty or older (Landry and Forrest 1995).

[20] Throughout the early decades of the twentieth century, there was a sustained rise in violent crime that ended in the early 1930s. Following a thirty-year decline, another increase began in 1965. National homicide rates were higher in 1980 than in the 1920s (Gurr 1981). Good historical data on juvenile violence as distinguished from adult violence are scarce, but what we have suggests that for most of the century teenage involvement in homicide was relatively less than in the late 1980s. For example, Hoffman (1925, p. 43) reports for males a fourfold difference in the homicide-victimization rate for those ages twenty to twenty-nine compared with those ages five to nineteen for the period 1908–12.

1998). These trends make plausible the possibility that cohorts of children growing up in such circumstances will be more violence prone than in an earlier day when the family environment for children was healthier.

John DiIulio has referred to the new generation of juvenile criminals as "superpredators" and argued that "today's bad boys are far worse than yesteryear's and tomorrow's will be even worse than today's" (Bennett, DiIulio, and Walters 1996, pp. 26–27). The result is that "America is now home to thickening ranks of juvenile 'super-predators'—radically impulsive, brutally remorseless youngsters, including ever more preteenage boys, who murder, assault, rob, burglarize, deal deadly drugs, join gun-toting gangs, and create serious communal disorders" (p. 27). The underlying cause of the superpredator phenomenon is "'moral poverty'—children growing up without love, care, and guidance from responsible adults" (p. 59). In this view, the growing rate of youth homicide is the result of secular change in character.

DiIulio's explanation attributes the epidemic of youth homicide to what demographers call a cohort effect, as opposed to a period effect. But the data on homicide-victimization rates for nonwhite males suggest that it is the period rather than the cohort that is to blame. Consider the cohort of nonwhite males ages fifteen to nineteen in 1990, which given its very high rate of homicide involvement in that year does indeed appear exceptionally vicious. But in 1985, this same cohort (then ages ten to fourteen) experienced a homicide-victimization rate that was the *lowest* for any cohort in that age group (ages ten to fourteen) since the 1960s. The next oldest cohort (ages twenty to twenty-four in 1990) followed the same pattern: their homicide-victimization rate was relatively high compared with earlier cohorts in that age range but this cohort had also experienced relatively low homicide rates in its younger years (MacKellar and Yanagishita 1995). So these cohorts do not exhibit a sustained high level of lethal violence, but rather their homicide-victimization rates moved up together from ordinary levels for their respective ages in 1985 to extraordinarily high levels in 1990.

The assertion that the socialization of children is increasingly inadequate or perverse fails to take account of other patterns in the crime statistics as well. For example, the deterioration in family life noted above has been proceeding for over a generation. Yet for most of that period, adolescents experienced a far lower homicide rate (of both commission and victimization) than in the early 1990s. There is no steady downhill progression where each cohort is more deadly than the last. Indeed, as shown in figure 8 above, the youth-homicide rate dropped during the early 1980s before beginning its upward rush. And the most recent data on homicide arrests indicate large declines in juvenile involvement between 1993 and 1995 (Snyder 1997).

When the epidemic began, it was not limited to the youngest cohorts: adolescent homicide rates turned up at the same time as young-adult homicide rates (Blumstein 1995). The turning point was 1984 for black males, and a few years later for white males (figs. 9 and 10). That the upturn occurred simultaneously for different cohorts suggests that the cause was a change in the environment rather than any change in the character of new cohorts.

While females are exposed to the same trends in family life and popular culture as males, white girls and young women have for the most part stayed clear of lethal violence. Further, at the same time that youth-homicide rates have been escalating, there has been a decline in the number of family members killed by youths. A general increase in viciousness would presumably not have spared the family.

If there is in fact increasing "moral poverty," then we would expect large increases in all types of crime. But property crime does not follow this pattern. While there was some increase in property-crime arrest rates for adolescents after 1984, the increase was only sufficient to restore the rates to the level they had reached in the mid-1970s.

These observations tend to favor a period-based explanation for the volatility of youth-homicide rates. Something happened in the mid-1980s that had the effect of triggering a rush to the most violent end of the spectrum of possibilities.

B. Increasing Gun Use

The leading explanation for why youth-homicide rates began increasing in the mid-1980s is the introduction of crack cocaine and, in particular, the conflict that attended its marketing (Reiss and Roth 1993; Blumstein 1995; Cork 1997). The timing is about right, and this explanation fits in other respects as well. Young black males, whose homicide rates started increasing before other groups, were the primary purveyors of crack in most cities, and hence they were on the front lines in the battles over territory and control. However, the introduction of crack is not a complete explanation, since the killing has continued long after these conflicts have quieted. Some commentators have resolved this apparent contradiction by speculating that the crack

violence has been contagious; the initial surge induced changes in attitudes and behavior that had the effect of causing the violence to
perpetuate itself and spread. For many youths, the response to the increased threat of violence was to carry a gun or join a gang for self-
protection, while adopting a more aggressive interpersonal style (Anderson 1994; Blumstein 1995; Gladwell 1996; Hemenway et al. 1996;
Wilkinson and Fagan 1996).

Guns are of central importance in this account. The drug trade has
provided dealers with the financial means and the incentive, as well as
the connections, that facilitate their access to black-market sources of
guns. The same fears that promote gun acquisition have also encouraged street youths to carry their guns when they go out in public. Since
guns are a more deadly instrument than knives or fists and relatively
easy to use, the result has been an increased lethality or intensification
of violence among youths. This problem has been further exacerbated
by a change in the mix of guns on the street, with an infusion of large-
calibre pistols replacing revolvers (Wintemute 1996; Koper 1997).
After the drug wars quieted, the guns and the fear remained, and so
did the killing.

This account seems plausible, but the available evidence is not sufficiently detailed to provide a real test. One thing is sure: the increase
in youth homicide during the late 1980s was accomplished by the use
of guns, just as it had been in earlier epidemics. Figure 12 demonstrates that gun homicide has been more volatile than nongun homicide. Notice that for male killers in both age groups, nongun-homicide
rates have been relatively steady since 1976, while gun-homicide rates
dropped in the early 1980s and climbed to new heights in the late
1980s. *All* of the epidemic increase in killing by adolescents and young
adults in the late 1980s was accomplished with firearms.

Figure 13 depicts male-victimization data going back to 1968, which
provides further illustration of the differential volatility. The first wave
of juvenile violence in this period occurred between 1968 and 1974,
and the increases for gun homicides were substantially larger than nongun homicides. The same is true for the second cycle, 1976–80. Finally, dramatic differences emerge in gun- and nongun-homicide rates
during the third cycle, 1985–94. Gun-homicide-victimization rates
more than doubled while nongun-victimization rates remained virtually flat.

What explains this pattern? Gun-homicide rates may be volatile because gun use is typical of certain types of homicides (gang and drug

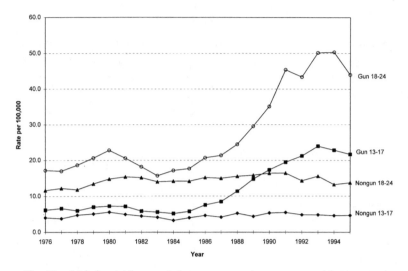

Fig. 12.—Male homicide-commission rate, gun and nongun, ages thirteen to seventeen and eighteen to twenty-four. Source: FBI (1976–95).

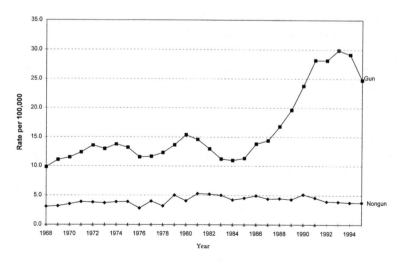

Fig. 13.—Male homicide-victimization rates, gun and nongun, ages thirteen to twenty-four. Sources: National Center for Health Statistics (1976–95); U.S. Bureau of the Census (1990, 1993); U.S. Department of Commerce (1966–96).

TABLE 6

Changes in the Proportion of Homicides with Guns for Male Killers
Ages 13–24: SHR Data, 1982–85 and 1990–92

	Percent of All Homicides		Percent with Guns	
Circumstances	1982–85 (1)	1990–92 (2)	1982–85 (3)	1990–92 (4)
Family and inti-mates	15.5	10.4	52.0	55.3
Felony type	23.6	27.7	53.5	73.1
Brawls and argu-ments	34.4	33.5	56.6	73.6
Gang related	2.8	8.3	78.9	90.5
Other known cir-cumstances	8.7	9.5	50.3	69.8
Unknown cir-cumstances	8.6	10.6	56.8	77.6
All circumstances	100.0	100.0	54.7	72.3
N	16,219	16,401	. . .	. . .

Source.—FBI, Supplementary Homicide Reports (1982–85, 1990–92).
Note.—SHR = Supplementary Homicide Reports. Excludes homicides not reported by local police agencies to the FBI. Excludes manslaughter by negligence and justifiable homicide.

related, e.g.) that tend to be relatively volatile. Alternatively, gun use may be driven in part by the availability of guns on the street, which in turn may tend to be volatile. In effect, the question is whether the pattern of gun use over time is best explained by the mix of circumstances or by access to guns. We now explore these two possibilities.

The Supplementary Homicide Reports include items on the relationship between victim and killer and the circumstance that motivated the killing. In columns 2 and 3 of table 6, we indicate the prevalence of gun use for each of a number of categories of homicide. The statistics are for all cases in which there was a suspect from thirteen to twenty-four years old, for two periods: 1982–85 and 1990–92.[21] Some homicides are more likely to involve guns than others, and the pattern is consistent in the two periods; of our categories, homicides involving

[21] When there was more than one suspect, we included the homicide if the oldest was in the age range from thirteen to twenty-four. In some cases, there were two suspects of the same age who differed with respect to race or sex: We classified those cases according to the characteristics of the first suspect listed.

family members are the least likely to involve guns, while gang-related homicides are most likely.

If the pattern of gun use over time is the result of changing access, then the percentage of homicides within each category should also vary. If general availability increases, for example, then we expect the gun percentage in gang-related homicide, felony homicide, and family homicide to all go up as well. However, if the overall gun-use percentage varies only as a result of a changing mix of circumstances, then the circumstance-specific gun-use percentages will not exhibit a common trend.

As it turns out, the extraordinary increase in gun use during recent years is apparent in most all types of homicide. The last two columns of table 6 tell the story. In this table, we compare two periods: 1982–85, when both the homicide rate and use of guns was at a relatively low level, and 1990–92, when both were at a high point. The overall use of guns increased from 55 percent to 72 percent, and gun use increased for each of the six circumstance categories. The mix of circumstances also changed, with family killings declining and gang killings increasing—a pattern that contributed to the overall increase in the gun percentage. But that change only contributes 4.1 points of the 17.7 percentage-point increase in gun use.[22] It appears that gun possession was much more widespread among violence-prone youths in the early 1990s than in the early 1980s.

We find confirmation for this conclusion from statistics on robbery, a crime committed primarily by youths.[23] In the NCVS, the percent of armed robbery victimizations in which the perpetrator used a gun (rather than a knife or some other weapon) increased from 33 percent in 1985 to 47 percent in 1992. Of armed robberies known to the police, the percent with a gun grew from 60 to 67 percent during that period (Maguire and Pastore 1996, p. 345). Further supporting evidence comes from the arrest statistics for weapons offenses, which are predominantly the result of illegal possession or carrying of firearms. Adolescent arrest rates were static during the 1970s and early 1980s,

---

[22] If the gun-use percentage had been the same for each of the SHR's categories in the later period as in the earlier, then the overall percent with guns in the later period would have been 58.8 percent (compared with the actual percentage in the earlier period of 54.7 percent). In making this calculation, we use the SHR's twenty-five circumstance categories of homicides with one exception: We separate out all homicides in which the victim and killer were related or intimate and treat them as a separate circumstance.

[23] In 1993, for instance, 62 percent of robbery arrests were of people under age twenty-five.

but then began climbing steeply and doubled between 1985 and 1993 (Greenfeld and Zawitz 1995).[24] Finally, Blumstein and Cork (1996) have demonstrated that the percentage of adolescent suicides committed with guns began increasing in the late 1980s, suggesting a general increase in availability.

C. Conclusion

While it is natural to judge individual character by observed behavior, it is wiser to first inquire as to the circumstances. So it is for entire cohorts as well. While recent cohorts of youths have committed homicides at unprecedented rates, we should not be too quick to condemn them as exceptionally "vicious" or otherwise character flawed. In fact, the evidence suggests that the tragically large increases in youth homicide in recent years have resulted more from a change in juveniles' circumstances than a sudden change in character. The cycle initiated by the crack wars may tell much of the story: Young men became increasingly fearful of each other and turned to guns and gangs for protection, which had the collective effect of widening the killing fields and engendering still greater fear. Whether this account is accurate remains to be tested. What is clear from the evidence presented here is that more and more violence-involved youths turned to guns during this period. The result has been a tragic intensification of violence.

VI. Predicting Youth Violence

What does the future hold with respect to juvenile violence? In our previous review of youth-crime trends (Cook and Laub 1986) we observed that despite the long period of stability beginning in the early 1970s, there was a potential for rapid change; after all, juvenile arrest rates for Index crimes had increased by 30 percent between 1966 and 1971. Our caution has proven justified given the experience with youth violence since the mid-1980s. The volatility documented in Section IV suggests that making confident predictions is a fool's game.

Fox (1996) and other commentators have drawn our attention to the "demographic time bomb"—the anticipated increase in crime and violence resulting from the upward trend in the population of adolescents and young adults. But while there is no doubt that the youth population is increasing and will continue upward through 2010 and beyond,

---

[24] The highest arrest rate is for eighteen-year-olds, which reached 1.0 percent in 1993. But sixteen- and seventeen-year-olds are close behind.

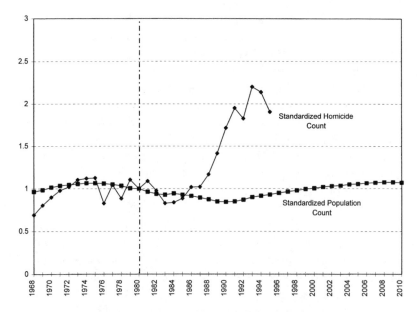

Fig. 14.—Standardized homicide-victimization count, ages thirteen to seventeen. Sources: National Center for Health Statistics (1976–95); U.S. Bureau of the Census (1997); U.S. Department of Commerce (1966–96).

that information is of little help in predicting violence rates. Figure 14 depicts the adolescent population and adolescent homicide count since 1968, both normalized to 1980. There is little relationship between these two lines; in fact, the correlation between population and homicide counts is *negative* for this period.[25] The effects of the increasing adolescent population (shown in this figure through 2010) on the volume of lethal violence are likely to be swamped by changes in victimization and commission rates. The same conclusion applies to the young-adult population as well.

Since the intertemporal "action" in youth violence lies with changes in the per capita rate of violence rather than changes in the number of youths, our ability to predict is limited by our understanding of the determinants of this rate. While we know quite a bit about the socioeconomic circumstances into which tomorrow's adolescents are being born and have some reason to believe that those circumstances matter in determining lethal-violence rates (Land, McCall, and Cohen 1990),

[25] The correlation is negative because the high homicide rates of the late 1980s and early 1990s occurred during a period when the adolescent population was relatively low.

the volatility of the homicide rate suggests the futility of this line of inquiry as a basis for confident projection. The magnitude of the changes since 1984 should keep us humble.

Labeling the late-1980s increase in youth homicide an "epidemic" evokes the thought that it may have been the result of some contagion, a self-generating process where violence begot violence. Such processes do not necessarily produce volatility but have that potential if initial conditions push the rate above some threshold or "tipping point" (Gladwell 1996). Understanding the positive-feedback mechanisms that appear to play a role in youth violence, and how they might be limited or reversed, is the goal of ongoing research by a number of scholars.

Even if the future is dim, the recent past is becoming clearer. What we have attempted to demonstrate is how unique (in historical context) and devastating the epidemic has been and to describe some of the characteristics of this surge in lethal violence. It has been sharply delimited with respect to sex and has involved blacks more than whites. Adolescents as a group exhibited the biggest proportional increase in homicide commission and victimization, but the biggest absolute change was for young adults, and there was a good deal of cross fire between these two age groups. All of the increase in homicide rates was with guns, and it appears to be changing access and use of guns, rather than a change in the character of the youths, that best accounts for their increased involvement in lethal violence. These findings are cues to a deeper understanding of the contagion.

The youth-homicide rates turned down after 1993, and there is hope that we are returning to more normal levels. Gaining better understanding of what went wrong and what reversed that process is of paramount importance.

TABLE A1

Missing Data in the SHR

Year	SHR Count	VS Mortality Count	Ratio: VS/SHR
1976	16,605	19,293	1.16
1977	18,032	19,699	1.09
1978	18,714	20,232	1.08
1979	20,591	22,202	1.08
1980	21,860	24,052	1.10
1981	20,053	23,439	1.17
1982	19,483	22,073	1.13
1983	18,672	19,922	1.07
1984	17,260	19,510	1.13
1985	17,543	19,628	1.12
1986	19,257	21,462	1.11
1987	17,963	20,896	1.16
1988	17,971	21,871	1.22
1989	18,952	22,658	1.20
1990	20,273	24,614	1.21
1991	21,676	26,355	1.22
1992	22,716	24,706	1.09
1993	23,180	25,725	1.11
1994	22,084	24,547	1.11
1995	20,060	22,297	1.11

SOURCES.—FBI, Supplementary Homicide Reports (1976–95). Unpublished National Crime Victimization Survey data was provided by Michael Rand, Bureau of Justice Statistics.

NOTE.—SHR = Supplementary Homicide Reports. VS = vital statistics. The VS counts exclude justifiable homicide as well as deaths where homicide, accident, or suicide could not be discerned.

REFERENCES

Anderson, Elijah. 1994. "The Code of the Streets." *Atlantic Monthly* (May), pp. 81–94.

Austin, Roy L. 1993. "Recent Trends in Official Male and Female Crime Rates: The Convergence Controversy." *Journal of Criminal Justice* 21:447–66.

Bennett, William J., John J. DiIulio, and John P. Walters. 1996. *Body Count: Moral Poverty and How to Win America's War against Crime and Drugs.* New York: Simon & Schuster.

Blumstein, Alfred. 1995. "Youth Violence, Guns, and the Illicit-Drug Industry." *Journal of Criminal Law and Criminology* 86:10–36.

Blumstein, Alfred, Jacqueline Cohen, Jeffrey A. Roth, and Christy A. Visher, eds. 1986. *Criminal Careers and Career Criminals.* Washington, D.C.: National Academy Press.

Blumstein, Alfred, and Daniel Cork. 1996. "Linking Gun Availability to Youth Gun Violence." *Law and Contemporary Problems* 59(1):5–24.

Bureau of Justice Statistics. 1986. *Sourcebook of Criminal Justice Statistics, 1985.* Washington, D.C.: U.S. Government Printing Office.

———. 1990. *Sourcebook of Criminal Justice Statistics, 1989.* Washington, D.C.: U.S. Government Printing Office.

———. 1997. *Criminal Victimization in the United States, 1994.* Washington, D.C.: U.S. Government Printing Office.

Butterfield, Fox. 1996. "After 10 Years, Juvenile Crime Begins to Drop." *New York Times* (August 9), pp. 1, A25.

Cantor, David, and Lawrence Cohen. 1980. "Comparing Measures of Homicide Trends: Methodological and Substantive Differences in Vital Statistics and the Uniform Crime Report Time Series (1933–1975)." *Social Science Research* 9:121–45.

Coie, John D., and Kenneth A. Dodge. 1998. "Aggression and Anti-social Behavior." In *Handbook of Child Psychology*, 5th ed., vol. 3, *Social, Emotional, and Personality Development*, edited by N. Eisenberg and W. Damon. New York: Wiley.

Cook, Philip J. 1985a. "The Case of the Missing Victims: Gunshot Woundings in the National Crime Survey." *Journal of Quantitative Criminology* 1:91–102.

———. 1985b. "Is Robbery Becoming More Violent? An Analysis of Robbery Murder Trends since 1968." *Journal of Criminal Law and Criminology* 76:480–89.

———. 1991. "The Technology of Personal Violence." In *Crime and Justice: A Review of Research*, vol. 14, edited by Michael Tonry. Chicago: University of Chicago Press.

Cook, Philip J., and John Laub. 1986. "The (Surprising) Stability of Youth Crime Rates." *Journal of Quantitative Criminology* 2:265–77.

Cork, Daniel. 1997. "Crack Markets and the Diffusion of Guns among Youth." Pittsburgh, Pa.: Carnegie-Mellon University, Heinz School of Urban and Public Affairs.

Elliott, Delbert. 1994. "Serious Violent Offenders: Onset, Developmental Course, and Termination." *Criminology* 32:1–21.

Elliott, Delbert, David Huizinga, and Suzanne Ageton. 1985. *Explaining Delinquency and Drug Use.* Beverly Hills, Calif.: Sage.

Federal Bureau of Investigation. 1966–96. *Crime in the United States.* Washington, D.C.: U.S. Government Printing Office.

———. 1976–95. Supplementary Homicide Reports [machine-readable data file].

———. 1993. *Age-Specific Arrest Rates and Race-Specific Arrest Rates for Selected Offenses, 1965-1992.* Washington, D.C.: U.S. Government Printing Office.

Fox, James Alan. 1996. *Trends in Juvenile Violence.* Washington, D.C.: U.S. Department of Justice, Bureau of Justice Statistics.

Gladwell, Malcolm. 1996. "The Tipping Point." *New Yorker* (June 3), pp. 32–38.

Greenfeld, Lawrence A., and Marianne W. Zawitz. 1995. *Weapons Offenses and Offenders*. Washington, D.C.: U.S. Department of Justice, Bureau of Justice Statistics.

Gurr, Ted Robert. 1981. "Historical Trends in Violent Crimes: A Critical Review of the Evidence." In *Crime and Justice: An Annual Review of Research*, vol. 3, edited by Michael Tonry and Norval Morris. Chicago: University of Chicago Press.

Hemenway, David, Deborah Prothrow-Stith, Jack M. Bergstein, Roseanna Ander, and Bruce P. Kennedy. 1996. "Gun Carrying among Adolescents." *Law and Contemporary Problems* 59(1):39–54.

Hernandez, Donald J. 1994. "Children's Changing Access to Resources: A Historical Perspective." *Social Policy Report: Society for Research in Child Development* 8:1–23.

Hindelang, Michael J. 1978. "Race and Involvement in Common Law Personal Crimes." *American Sociological Review* 43:93–109.

———. 1981. "Variations in Sex-Race-Age-Specific Incidence Rates of Offending." *American Sociological Review* 46:461–74.

Hindelang, Michael J., Travis Hirschi, and Joseph G. Weis. 1981. *Measuring Delinquency*. Beverly Hills, Calif.: Sage.

Hoffman, Frederick L. 1925. *The Homicide Problem*. Newark, N.J.: Prudential.

Koper, Christopher. 1997. *Gun Density versus Gun Type: Did More Guns or More Lethal Guns Increase Homicides in Dallas, 1980–1992?* Final Report submitted to the National Institute of Justice, Washington, D.C.

LaFree, Gary, and Kriss A. Drass. 1996. "The Effect of Changes in Intraracial Income Inequality and Educational Attainment on Changes in Arrest Rates for African Americans and Whites, 1957 to 1990." *American Sociological Review* 61:614–34.

Land, K., P. McCall, and L. Cohen. 1990. "Structural Covariates of Homicide Rates: Are There Any Invariances across Time and Space?" *American Journal of Sociology* 95:922–63.

Landry, David J., and Jacqueline Darroch Forrest. 1995. "How Old Are U.S. Fathers?" *Family Planning Perspectives* 27:159–65.

Laub, John H. 1987. "Data for Positive Criminology." In *Positive Criminology*, edited by Michael R. Gottfredson and Travis Hirschi. Newbury Park, Calif.: Sage.

Loftin, Colin, and James A. Mercy. 1995. "Estimating the Incidence, Causes, and Consequences of Interpersonal Violence for Children and Families." In *Integrating Federal Statistics on Children: Report of a Workshop*. Washington, D.C.: National Academy Press.

MacKellar, F. Landis, and Machicko Yanagishita. 1995. *Homicide in the United States: Who's at Risk?* Washington, D.C.: Population Reference Bureau.

Maguire, Kathleen, and Ann L. Pastore, eds. 1996. *Sourcebook of Criminal Justice Statistics—1995*. Washington, D.C.: U.S. Department of Justice, Bureau of Justice Statistics.

National Center for Health Statistics. 1976–95. Mortality detail files [machine-readable data file].

O'Brien, Robert M. 1985. *Crime and Victimization Data*. Beverly Hills, Calif.: Sage.

Panel on High-Risk Youth. 1993. *Losing Generations: Adolescents in High-Risk Settings.* Washington, D.C.: National Academy Press.

Poe-Yamagata, Eileen, and Jeffrey A. Butts. 1996. *Female Offenders in the Juvenile Justice System.* Washington, D.C.: Office of Juvenile Justice and Delinquency Prevention.

Reiss, Albert J., Jr., and Jeffrey A. Roth, eds. 1993. *Understanding and Preventing Violence.* Washington, D.C.: National Academy Press.

Sellin, Thorsten. 1931. "The Bias of a Crime Index." *Journal of Criminal Law and Criminology* 22:335–56.

Skogan, Wesley G. 1981. *Issues in the Measurement of Victimization.* Washington, D.C.: U.S. Department of Justice, Bureau of Justice Statistics.

Snyder, Howard N. 1997. *Juvenile Arrests, 1995.* Juvenile Justice Bulletin. Washington, D.C.: Office of Juvenile Justice and Delinquency Prevention.

Snyder, Howard N., Melissa Sickmund, and Eileen Poe-Yamagata. 1996. *Juvenile Offenders and Victims: 1996 Update on Violence.* Washington, D.C.: Office of Juvenile Justice and Delinquency Prevention.

Steffensmeier, Darrell, and Emile Allan. 1996. "Gender and Crime: Toward a Gendered Theory of Female Offending." *Annual Review of Sociology* 22:459–87.

U.S. Bureau of the Census. 1990. Current Population Reports. Series P-20, Population Characteristics.

———. 1993. Current Population Reports. Series P-20, Population Characteristics.

———. 1997. Data available from "National Population Projections" online at http://www.fedstats.gov/population/natproj.html.

U.S. Department of Commerce, Economics and Statistics Administration, Bureau of the Census. 1966–96. *Statistical Abstract of the United States.* Washington, D.C.: U.S. Government Printing Office.

Wilkinson, Deanna L., and Jeffrey Fagan. 1996. "The Role of Firearms in Violence 'Scripts': The Dynamics of Gun Events among Adolescent Males." *Law and Contemporary Problems* 59(1):55–90.

Wintemute, Garen. 1996. "The Relationship between Firearm Design and Firearm Violence." *Journal of the American Medical Association* 275(22):1749–53.

Zimring, Franklin E. 1972. "The Medium is the Message: Firearm Calibre as a Determinant of Death from Assault." *Journal of Legal Studies* 1:97–124.

———. 1979. "American Youth Violence: Issues and Trends." In *Crime and Justice: An Annual Review of Research,* vol. 1, edited by Norval Morris and Michael Tonry. Chicago: University of Chicago Press.

———. 1981. "Kids, Groups and Crime: Some Implications of a Well-Known Secret." *Journal of Criminal Law and Criminology* 72:867–85.

Elijah Anderson

The Social Ecology of Youth Violence

ABSTRACT

This essay, largely drawn from Elijah Anderson's forthcoming book, *Code of the Street*, offers an ethnographic representation of the workings of the code of the street in the context of the trying socioeconomic situation in which the inner-city black community finds itself, as jobs have become ever more scarce, public assistance has increasingly disappeared, and frustration has been building for many. The material presented here was gathered through many visits to various inner-city families and neighborhood settings, including carry-outs, laundromats, taverns, playgrounds, and street corners. In these settings, Anderson conducted in-depth interviews with adolescent boys and girls, young men (some incarcerated, some not), older men, teenage mothers, and grandmothers. The structure of the community, and that community's extreme poverty, which is in large part the result of structural economic change, will be seen to interact in a way that facilitates the involvement of so many maturing youths in the culture of the streets, in which violence and the way it is regulated are key elements.

A clarifying note on methodology is perhaps in order for those unfamiliar with the ethnographic method. Ethnography seeks to paint a conceptual picture of the setting under consideration, by observation and in-depth interviews. The researcher's goal is to illuminate the social and cultural dynamics that characterize the setting by answering such questions as "How do the people in the setting perceive their situation?" "What assumptions do they bring to their decision making?"

Elijah Anderson is professor of sociology, Department of Sociology, University of Pennsylvania. This essay draws heavily on his *Code of the Street*, to be published in 1999 by W. W. Norton & Co. Use here is by permission of Norton.

"What behavior patterns result from their choices?" "What are the social consequences of those behaviors?" An important aspect of the ethnographer's work is that it be as objective as possible. This is not easy since it requires researchers to set aside their own values and assumptions as to what is and is not morally acceptable—in other words, to jettison the prism through which they typically view a given situation. By definition, one's own assumptions are so basic to one's perceptions that seeing their influence may be difficult. Ethnographic researchers, however, have been trained to look for and recognize underlying assumptions, their own and those of their subjects, and to try to override the former and uncover the latter. I have done my best to do so in the text that follows.

Adults who have grown up in inner-city neighborhoods understand the requirements of the code of the street and the necessity that their children understand them as well. The story of the inner-city black community, in Philadelphia as elsewhere, is at heart one of profound isolation—economic, physical, and social. In its simplest form the story is familiar—slavery, emancipation, migration to cities for opportunities in industrial and menial work. There they competed with European immigrants and faced significant racial discrimination. Segregation and ghettoization resulted and became institutionalized. The civil rights movements and the 1960s civil disorders followed, and, in response, the system opened up somewhat. Affirmative action resulted in a growing black middle class. A split developed between the working class and the middle class. Deindustrialization, the global economy, and other factors eliminate the manufacturing jobs that once provided working-class employment in the city. White people follow the jobs out of the city. Black people are prevented from moving because of housing discrimination and from commuting because of lack of public transit. As local neighborhoods become perceived as "black," the remaining white people leave, city services decline, and police and other institutions abdicate their responsibility to protect residents and property. The neighborhoods develop a "second-class" status. Eventually there is a concentration of poor blacks, as middle-class blacks join the white residents in fleeing the area. In addition, social welfare is being eliminated and many job-training programs have been terminated, further exacerbating so many of the conditions alluded to above. Then, in the absence of family-sustaining jobs and the lack of hope for the future in ghetto neighborhoods, the drug trade and the underground economy move in and proliferate, providing opportunity where the wider economy provides none.

The historic social isolation of the black community in the United States contributes to the sense of alienation in these neighborhoods. The idea has circulated since the time of slavery that the wider system is against them, that the white authorities have a "plan" for the subjugation of black people, if not the annihilation of the black community. Today drugs, guns, and the persistent poverty of the inner city are seen by the most alienated residents of these economically compromised communities as part of a plan to destroy them.

Because of these factors, in the inner-city black community people have a strong sense that they are "on their own," that in matters of personal defense they must take primary responsibility. In this context the code of the street provides a set of prescriptions and proscriptions for behavior. It affects the exchange of goods and services and indicates a social status system. It provides a certain order in places where law has failed and, in that sense, might be called a "people's law." It is a cultural adaptation to a situation where other institutions and "codes" have failed. It involves give-and-take, reciprocity, and payback. To grow up in this inner-city community is to be affected by that culture.

Almost everyone in poor inner-city neighborhoods is struggling financially and therefore feels a certain distance from the rest of America, but there are degrees of alienation, captured by the labels "decent" and "street." Residents use these labels as judgments on themselves or others. People of both orientations often coexist in the same extended family. There is also a great deal of "code-switching": a person may exhibit both decent and street orientations, depending on the occasion. Decent people, especially young people, put a premium on the ability to code-switch. They share many of the "decent" middle-class values of the wider society, but know that the open display of such values carries little weight on the street: it does not provide the emblems that say "I can take care of myself." So they develop a repertoire of behaviors that provide that security. Those who are street, having had less exposure to the wider society, may have difficulty code-switching. They are strongly imbued with the code of the street and either do not know the rules for decent behavior or may see little value in displaying such knowledge.

At the extreme of the street group are those who can be called "hard-core street." People making up this class are often profound casualties of the social and economic system. Not only do they lack a decent education, they also lack an outlook that allows them to see far beyond their present circumstances in the most positive sense. Moreover, they tend to be alienated and angry.

Overall, members of this group are among the most desperate and alienated people of the city. For them, all people and situations are best thought of as "having a trick to them," and in most situations the effort is geared to not being "caught up in the trick bag." To them, it is important to see all persons and situations as part of life's obstacles; they are things to subdue, or to "get over." One gets over by developing an effective "game" or "game plan," setting oneself up in a position to prevail by outsmarting others. In line with this, one must always be wary of his counterparts, suspecting that they are involved with him only for what they can get out of the situation.

In this world, the competition is intense. It is a competition in which "winners" totally dominate "losers," and losing is a fate that is worse than death. So one must be on one's guard constantly. Other people are not to be trusted, partly because there is so much at stake but also because everyone else is understood to be so very needy.

Usually, these are the people who are identified as the "criminal element." They not only engage in criminal activity but teach their children to do so as well, at times starting with stealing and shoplifting. In some parts of the community there are whole families that have been in trouble with the law. Mom was a crack addict. Dad was a drug dealer who is now incarcerated. He taught brothers Joe and Tom how to steal cars. The whole family is living a checkered life. The moral code of the wider society has no authority for them, and of course they have no moral authority for that society. And when members of the wider society look at the ghetto, they tend to stereotype the community, unable or unwilling to see the differences, distinctions, and human complexities of the lives the residents are leading.

I. Down Germantown Avenue

Germantown Avenue is a major Philadelphia artery that goes back to colonial days. Eight and a half miles long, it links the northwest suburbs with the heart of inner-city Philadelphia. It traverses a varied social terrain as well. Germantown Avenue provides an excellent cross-section of the social ecology of a major American city. Along this artery live the well-to-do, the middle classes, the working poor, and the very poor. The story of Germantown Avenue with its wide social and class variations can serve in many respects as a metaphor for the whole city. This essay about the "code of the street" begins with an introduction to the world of the streets, by way of a tour down Germantown Avenue.

One of the most salient features of urban life, in the minds of many people today, is the relative prevalence of violence. Our tour down Germantown Avenue will focus on the role of violence in the social organization of the communities through which the avenue passes, and on how violence is revealed in the interactions of people up and down the street. The avenue, we will see, is a natural continuum characterized by a code of civility at one end and a code of conduct regulated by the threat of violence—the code of the street—at the other.[1] But the people living along this continuum make their own claims on civility and the streets as well.

We begin at the top of the hill that gives Chestnut Hill its name. Chestnut Hill is the first neighborhood within the city of Philadelphia as you come into town from the northwest. Often called the "suburb in the city," it is a predominantly residential community of mostly white, affluent, educated people, which is becoming increasingly racially and ethnically mixed. The houses are mostly large single buildings, surrounded by lawns and trees. The business and shopping district along Germantown Avenue draws shoppers from all over the city. At the very top of the hill is a large Borders Bookstore. Across the street is the regional rail train station, with the local library in close proximity. Moving southeast down the avenue, you pass a variety of mostly small, upscale businesses: gourmet food shops, a camera shop, an optician's, a sporting goods store, a bank, jewelry stores, clothing boutiques. Many of the buildings are old or built to look old and are made of fieldstone with slanted slate roofs, giving the area a quaint appearance. You see many different kinds of people—old and young, black and white, affluent, middle- and working-class, women (some of them black) pushing babies who are white. Couples stroll hand in hand. Everyone is polite and seems relaxed. When people pass one another on the sidewalk, they may make eye contact. People stand about nonchalantly on the sidewalk, sometimes with their backs to the street. You

---

[1] This is to be distinguished from Wolfgang and Ferracuti's (1967) position, which identified and delineated more explicitly a "subculture of violence." Wolfgang and Ferracuti postulated norms that undergirded or even defined the culture of the entire community, whereas the code of the street applies predominantly to public behavior and is normative for only the most alienated and socially isolated segment of the community.

do not get the feeling that there is any hostility or that people are on guard against being compromised or insulted or robbed. There is a pleasant ambience—an air of civility.

One of the things you see at this end of Germantown Avenue is that relations in public appear racially integrated, perhaps self-consciously so. There are integrated play groups among small children on the playgrounds. At the bank, there is relaxed interaction between a black teller and a white client. There are biracial friendship groups. At the Boston Market restaurant blacks and whites sit and eat together or simply share the restaurant. A black man drives by in a Range Rover; two well-dressed black women pull up in a black Lexus. In their clothing and cars, the black middle class choose styles and colors that stand out and are noticed as expensive: they are quite expressive in laying claim to middle-class status.

In the upscale stores here, there is not usually a great concern for security. During the day the plate-glass windows have appealing displays; some shops even have unguarded merchandise out on the sidewalk.

Once in a while, however, a violent incident does occur. There was a holdup at the bank in the middle of the day not long ago, ending in a shoot-out on the sidewalk. The perpetrators were black. Such incidents give the residents here the overly simplistic yet persistent view that blacks commit crime and white people do not. That does not mean that the white people here think that the black people they ordinarily see on the streets are bound to rob them: many of these people are too sophisticated to believe that all blacks are inclined to criminality. But the fact that black people robbed the bank does give a peculiar edge to race relations, and the racial reality of street crime speaks to the relations between blacks and whites. Because everybody knows that the simplistic view does exist, even middle-class blacks, as well as whites, have to work against that stereotype. Both groups know that the reality is that crime is likely to be perpetrated by young black males. While both blacks and whites behave as though they deny it, this background knowledge threatens the civility of the neighborhood. The cleavages of wealth, and the fact that black people are generally disenfranchised and white people are not, operate in the back of the minds of people here.

One can see this as a black male walking into the stores, especially the jewelry store. The sales personnel pay particular attention to people until they feel they have passed inspection, and black males almost always are given extra scrutiny. Most blacks in Chestnut Hill are middle-class or even wealthy, although some come into the neighborhood as day workers, and many are disturbed by the inability of some whites to make distinctions between middle- and lower-class blacks or between people who are out to commit crime and those who are not.

The knowledge that there are poor blacks further down the avenue also results in people "here" being on guard against people from "there." Security guards may follow young black males around stores, looking for the emblems and signs that they are from there and not from here. And at night the stores do have interior security devices, although they are outwardly decorative. These elements can, but most often do not, compromise civility between the races in Chestnut Hill; in fact, people generally "get along."

Down the hill, beyond the Boston Market, is Cresheim Valley Road, a neighborhood boundary. On the other side, we are in Mount Airy, a different social milieu. Here there are more black homeowners, interspersed among white ones, and there is more black street traffic on Germantown Avenue. Mount Airy is a much more integrated neighborhood than Chestnut Hill, and the black people who live here are mostly middle class. But Germantown Avenue in Mount Airy and the shops and stores along it are disproportionately used by blacks rather than whites and by poorer blacks rather than middle-class blacks. Whites and middle-class black adults tend to use the stores in Chestnut Hill, finding them more consistent with their tastes. As a result, the shops here are blacker, even though they may be middle-class.

A sign that we are in a different social milieu is that exterior bars begin to appear on the store windows and riot gates on the doors, at first on businesses such as the liquor store. Pizza parlors, karate shops, take-out stores that sell beer, and storefront organizations such as neighborhood health care centers appear—establishments that are not present in Chestnut Hill. There are discount stores of various sorts, black barbershops, and other businesses that cater to the black middle class but also to employed working-class and poorer blacks. Many of the black middle-class youths use the streets as a place to gather and talk with their friends, and they adopt the clothing styles of the poorer people further down the avenue. So people who are not familiar with social types sometimes cannot distinguish between who is middle class and who is not. This confusion appears to be a standing problem for store owners and managers, and may lead to a sense of defensiveness among middle-class people who do not want to be violated or robbed. But it is a confusion that the youth tend not to mind.

Continuing down the avenue, we pass the Mount Airy playground with its basketball court, which is always buzzing. Evenings and week-ends it is full of young black men playing pick-up games. There is a real social mix here, with kids from middle-class, working-class, and poor black families all coming together in this spot, creating a staging area. The urban uniform of sneakers and baggy jeans is much in evidence, which gives pause to other people, particularly whites (many of whom avoid the area). In many ways, however, the atmosphere is easy-going. The place is not crime-ridden or necessarily feared by most blacks, but there is a certain edge to it compared with similar but less racially complex settings further up the avenue. Here it is prudent to be wary—not everyone on the street here recognizes and respects the rule of law, that law that is encoded in the criminal statutes and enforced by the police.

Yet next to the playground is a branch of the Free Library, one of the best in the city, which caters mainly to literate people of Mount Airy, both black and white. Indeed, the social and racial mix of the community is sometimes more visible in the library than on the street itself.

There are many beautiful old buildings in Mount Airy. But the piano repair shops, sandwich stores, and plumbing-supply companies tend to have exterior bars and riot gates, which militates against the notion of civility as the dominant theme of the place. A competing notion crystallizes, and that is the prevalence of crime, the perpetrators of which are more often concerned not with legality but with feasibility. Ten years ago there were fewer bars on the windows and the buildings were better maintained. Today more relatively poor people are occupying the public space. There are still whites among the store-keepers and managers of various establishments, but whites have been displaced in the outdoor public spaces by poorer blacks. Moreover, the further down the avenue we go, the less well maintained the buildings are. Even when they are painted, for example, the painting tends to be done haphazardly, without great regard for architectural detail.

In this section, a billboard warns that those who commit insurance fraud go to jail. (No such signs appear in Chestnut Hill.) There is graffiti—or signs that it has recently been removed. More dilapidated buildings appear, looking as though they receive no maintenance. Yet among them there are historic buildings, some of which are cared for for just that reason. One of them is the house where the Battle of Germantown was fought during the Revolutionary War. Another was a stop on the underground railroad.

As Mount Airy gives way to Germantown, check-cashing agencies and beeper stores appear, as well as more small take-out stores selling beer, cheese steaks, and other snack food. More of the windows are boarded up, and riot gates and exterior bars become the norm, evoking in the user of the street a certain wariness.

Germantown appears to be a more solidly black working-class neighborhood. Whites, including middle-class whites, do live here, but they either tend to avoid the business district or the stores simply do not attract them. On Germantown Avenue, discount stores of all sorts appear—supermarkets, furniture stores, and clothing stores. Of the people you pass, many more are part of the street element. Here people watch their backs, and more care is given to one's presentation of self. It is not that you are worried every moment that somebody might violate you, but people are more aware of others who are sharing the space with them, some of whom may be looking for an easy target to rob or just intimidate.

Germantown High School, once a model of racially integrated high-quality education, is now almost all black, a shadow of its former academic self. Resources have declined and many of the students are now impoverished and associated with the street element, and most of those who are not still have a need to show themselves as being capable of dealing with the street. In fact, the hallways of the school are in some ways an extension of the streets. Across the street from the high school is a store selling beer. Continuing down the avenue, we pass blocks of small businesses: taverns, Chinese take-out places, barbershops and hair salons, laundromats, storefront churches, pawnshops. Groups of young people loiter on street corners. We also begin to see boarded-up buildings, some of them obviously quite grand at one time, and empty lots. A charred McDonald's sign rises above a weed-covered lot. A police car is parked at the corner, its occupants keeping a watchful eye on the street activity. After a time, they begin to drive slowly down the street.

Just before Chelten Avenue, a major artery that intersects Germantown Avenue, is Vernon Park. The park has a caretaker who is trying to keep it maintained despite the carelessness and even vandalism of the people who like to gather there. A mural has been painted on the side of an adjacent building. Flowers have been planted. On warm days, couples "making time" sit about on the benches, on the steps of statues, and on the hoods of cars parked along the park's edge. But even during the day you can see men drinking alcohol out of paper sacks, and at night the park is a dangerous place where drug dealing and other shadowy business is conducted. This is what I call a major "staging area," because the activity that occurs here sets the stage for other activity, which may either be played out on the spot, in front of an audience of people who have congregated here, or in less conspicuous locations. An altercation in Vernon Park may be settled with a fight, with or without gunplay, down a side street. People come here to see and be seen, to "profile" and "represent," presenting the image of themselves by which they would like to be known—who they are and how they stand in relation to whom. The streets are buzzing with activity, legal and illegal. In fact, a certain flagrant disregard for the law is visible. We see a teenage boy walk by with an open bottle of beer in his hand, taking a swig when he wants to.

A young man in his twenties crosses the street after taking care of some sort of business with another young man, gets into his brand-new black BMW Sidekick, and sidles up next to his girlfriend who has been waiting there for him. He is dressed in a crisp white T-shirt with Hilfiger emblazoned across the back, black satin shorts with bright red stripes on the sides, and expensive white sneakers. He makes a striking figure as he slides into his vehicle, and others take note. He moves with aplomb, well aware that he is where he wants to be and, for that moment at least, where some others want to be as well. His presentation of self announces that he can take care of himself should someone choose to tangle with him.

Here in Germantown, especially in some pockets, there is less respect for the code of civility, and that fact necessitates a whole way of moving, of acting, of getting up and down the streets, which suggests that violence is just below the surface. The people of Germantown are overwhelmingly decent and committed to civility, yet there is something about the avenue, especially at night, that attracts the street element. When that element is present in numbers, there is a sense that you are on your own, that what protects you from being violated is your own body, your own ability to behave the right way, to look as though you can handle yourself, and even to be able to defend yourself. While it is not always necessary to throw down the gauntlet, so to speak, and be ready to punch someone out, it is important, as people here say, to "know what time it is." It is this form of regulation of social interaction in public that I call the "code of the street" in contrast to the "code of civility," based on trust and the rule of law, that strongly prevails up the avenue. You are not always tested, but you have to be ready for the test if you are. Mr. Don Moses, an old head of the black community, described the code this way: "Keep your eyes and ears open at all times. Walk two steps forward and look back. Watch your back. Prepare yourself verbally and physically. Even if you have a cane, carry something. The older people do carry something, guns in sheaths. They can't physically fight no more so they carry a gun." People here feel they must watch their backs, because everything happens here. And if the police are called, they may not arrive in time. People get killed here, they get stabbed, but they also relax and have a good time. In general, there is an edge to public life that you do not find in Chestnut Hill.

Chelten Avenue is lined with discount stores and fast-food restaurants. Yet just around the corner and two blocks down is a middle-class residential area. Most people here are black, but there are representatives of the wider society here, as well, including the police, the welfare office, the fast-food and clothing store chains. On Tuesday mornings, food-stamp lines snake around Greene Street at Chelten. There are also little people running small, sometimes fly-by-night businesses. Hustlers and small-time money men canvas the food stamp line with wads of cash—ready to buy discounted food stamps. It is this lack of resources that encourages a dog-eat-dog mentality that is concentrated at Chelten Avenue. Yet there is a great deal of other activity too. Especially during the summer, there is sometimes a carnival atmosphere. And the fact that the general area is diverse both racially and socially works to offset the feeling of social isolation that the poor black residents of Germantown have.

Occasionally, residents of Chestnut Hill drive this far down Germantown Avenue, and seeing what this neighborhood looks like has an impact on their consciousness. But they do not see below the surface. Mainly, they take in the noise and the seeming disorder, the poverty, and the incivility and when reading about urban violence they associate it with places like this, when in fact this neighborhood may not be as violent as they assume. To be sure, welfare mothers, prostitutes, and drug dealers are in evidence, but they coexist with—and are in fact outnumbered by—working people in legitimate jobs who are trying to avoid trouble.

As you move on past Chelten Avenue, you pass through quieter stretches colored by the residential nature of the surrounding streets, alternating with concentrated business strips. Many of the businesses are skin, hair, and nail salons. A common aspiration of the poorer girls in these neighborhoods is to go to beauty school and become cosmetologists.

We pass by the old town square of Germantown, which is surrounded by old, "historically certified" houses. Such houses appear sporadically for a long way down the avenue. Unfortunately, some are badly in need of maintenance. Just beyond the square is Germantown Friends School, a private school founded 150 years ago on what was then the outskirts of town but is now surrounded by the city.

Further down Germantown Avenue, thrift shops and discount stores predominate. Most are equipped with window bars and riot gates. Both the bars and the residents' understanding proclaim that this is a tough place. Some people can be counted on to behave according to the laws of force, not those of civility. Many people have to be forced to behave in a law-abiding way. The code has violence, or the possibility of violence, to back it up, and the bars on the windows signify the same thing—a lack of trust, a feeling that without the bars the establishment would be vulnerable. The code of the street has emerged.

The further we go down the avenue, the more boarded-up buildings there are, and more and more empty lots. In fact, certain areas give the impression of no-man's-lands, with empty overgrown or dirt lots, a few isolated buildings here and there, few cars on the street, and almost no people on the sidewalks. We pass billboards advertising "forties" (forty-ounce malt liquor) and other kinds of liquor. Churches are a prominent feature of the cityscape as a whole. Along this part of Germantown Avenue some of them are very large and well known, with a rich history, and are architecturally like those in Chestnut Hill and Mount Airy, but others are storefront churches that sometimes come and go with the founding pastor.

People move up and down the street. Even in the middle of the morning, groups of young men can be seen standing on corners, eyeing the street traffic. Yet the morning is the safest time of day. As evening approaches, the possibility of violence increases, and after nightfall the rule of the code of the street is being enforced all along the lower section of the avenue. Under that rule, the toughest, the biggest, the boldest prevail. We pass a school at recess. Kids are crowding into a makeshift store where someone is barbecuing hot dogs and ribs. Even at play, they hone their physical skills, punching each other lightly but seriously, sizing each other up. This sort of play-fighting, playing within the code, is commonplace.

Continuing, we pass collision shops—former gas stations surrounded by many cars in various states of disrepair—music stores, and nightclubs. We arrive at Broad Street, Philadelphia's major north-south artery, where Germantown Avenue also intersects Erie Avenue, forming a large triangle that is one of the centers of the ghetto of North Philadelphia. It is a staging area that is racially diverse, drawing all kinds of people from adjacent areas that are extremely poor. In Germantown there are a fair number of working people. In North Philly there is extensive concentrated poverty. North Philly is in the depths of the inner city—the so-called hyperghetto—and people here are more isolated from others who are unlike themselves in terms of both class and race (Massey and Denton 1993).

Just beyond Broad Street is a business strip with the same sort of establishments we saw further up the avenue—clothing stores, sneaker stores, furniture stores, electronics stores. Many offer layaway plans. In addition, there are businesses that cater mostly to the criminal class, such as pawnshops and beeper stores. Pawnshops are in a sense banks for thieves; they are places where stolen goods can be traded for cash, few questions asked. Check-cashing exchanges, which continue to be a common sight, also ask few questions, but they charge exorbitant fees for cashing a check. As in Chestnut Hill, merchandise is displayed on the sidewalk, but here it is under the watchful eye of unsmiling security guards. The noise level here is also much louder. Cars drive by with their stereo systems blaring. A young man wearing headphones saunters down the street. On the adjacent streets, open-air drug deals occur, prostitutes ply their trade, and boys shoot craps, while small children play in trash-strewn abandoned lots. This is the face of persistent urban poverty.

This is another staging area. People profile and represent here, standing around, "looking things over," concerned with who is where, but also aware of others "checking them out." Here, phrases like "watch your back," or as friends reassure their friends, "I got your back," takes on meaning, for some people are looking for opportunities to violate others, or simply to get away with something. A man opens his car door despite approaching traffic, seeming to dare someone to hit him. Further down the block a woman simply stops her car in the middle of the street, waiting for her husband or boyfriend to emerge from a barbershop. She waits for about ten minutes, holding up traffic. No one complains, no one honks his horn; they simply go around her, for they know that to complain is to risk an altercation, or at least heated words. They prefer not to incur this woman's wrath, which could escalate to warfare. In Chestnut Hill, where civility and "limited" warfare are generally the orders of the day, people might call others on such behavior, but here the general level of violence can keep irritation in check. In this way, the code of the street provides social organization and actually lessens the probability of random violence. When the woman's man arrives, he simply steps around to the passenger side and, without showing any concern for others, gets into the car. The pair drive off, apparently believing it to be their right to do what they just did.

At Tioga Street and Temple University Hospital, whose emergency room sees gunshot and stabbing victims just about every night, the code of the street is much in evidence. In the morning and early afternoon, the surrounding neighborhood is peaceful enough, but in the evening the danger level rises. Tensions spill over, drug deals go bad, fights materialize seemingly out of nowhere, and the emergency room becomes a hub of activity. Sometimes the victim bypasses the hospital: by the time he is found, there is no place to take him but the morgue. Nearby there is a liquor store and a place selling cold beer. People buy liquor there and drink it on the street, adding to the volatility of the street scene.

More and more gaps in the rows of houses appear, where buildings have burned down, been torn down, or simply collapsed. Others are shells, their windows and large parts of their walls gone, leaving beams exposed. Still others are boarded up, perhaps eventually to collapse, perhaps to be rebuilt. Indeed, there are signs of regeneration among those of destruction. Here and there a house is well-maintained, even freshly painted. Some of the exposed outer walls of standing structures have colorful, upbeat murals painted on them, often with religious themes. We pass a large building, a car repair shop, gaily decorated with graffiti art. Further down we pass a hotel that rents rooms by the hour.

There continue to be signs of the avenue's past life—large churches built by European immigrants at the turn of the century, an old cemetery, an occasional historic building. The many open areas—empty lots, little overgrown parks—underline the winding character of this old highway as it cuts through the grid pattern of streets formally laid out well after this became an established thoroughfare.

We drive through another business district with the usual stores catering to the very poor. Two policemen pass by on foot patrol. This is another staging area. The concentration of people drawn by the businesses increases the chance of violence breaking out. A lot of people are out, not just women and children but a conspicuous number of young men as well, even though it is still morning. Practically all of them are black, with just an occasional Asian and even rarer white face among them.

We enter an area where there seem to be more empty lots and houses you can see right through than solidly standing buildings. Some of the lots are a heap of rubble. Others are overgrown with weeds or littered with abandoned cars. This is a spot where the idea of a war zone comes to mind. Indeed, gunshot marks are visible on some of the buildings. The black ghetto here gives way to the Hispanic ghetto. The faces are different but the behavior is similar. Yet in the midst of this desolation there is a newly built gated community in the Spanish style. Just beyond it, we reach Norris Street; at this intersection three of the four corners are large empty lots. But we also pass an open area that has been transformed into a community garden. Now, in late spring, vegetables in the early stages of growth are visible.

We are now just north of Philadelphia's center city area. This used to be a bustling commercial area, with factories producing everything from beer to lace and huge warehouses in which the goods were stored before being shipped out either by rail, traces of which are still visible, or through a nearby port on the Delaware River. Here and there some of these behemoths are still standing, although one by one they are falling victim to arson.

And so we reach the other end of Germantown Avenue, in the midst of a leveled area about a block from the river and overshadowed by the elevated interstate highway that now allows motorists to drive over North Philadelphia rather than through it, thereby ignoring its street life, its inhabitants, and its problems.

II. The Code of the Street

Of all the problems besetting the poor inner-city black community, none is more pressing than that of interpersonal violence and aggression. This phenomenon wreaks havoc daily on the lives of community residents and increasingly spills over into downtown and residential middle-class areas. Muggings, burglaries, carjackings, and drug-related shootings, all of which may leave their victims or innocent bystanders dead, are now common enough to concern all urban and many suburban residents. The inclination to violence springs from the circumstances of life among the ghetto poor—the lack of jobs that pay a living wage, the stigma of race, the fallout from rampant drug use and drug trafficking, and the resulting alienation and lack of hope for the future.

Simply living in such an environment places young people at special risk of falling victim to aggressive behavior. Although there are often forces in the community that can counteract the negative influences—by far the most powerful is a strong, loving, "decent" (as inner-city residents put it) family committed to middle-class values—the despair is pervasive enough to have spawned an oppositional culture, that of "the streets," whose norms are often consciously opposed to those of mainstream society. These two orientations—decent and street—socially organize the community, and their coexistence has important consequences for residents, particularly for children growing up in the inner city. Above all, this environment means that even youngsters whose home lives reflect mainstream values—and most of the homes in the community do—must be able to handle themselves in a street-oriented environment.

The code of the street, evolved by the street culture, amounts to a set of rules governing interpersonal public behavior, particularly violence. The rules prescribe both proper comportment and the proper way to respond if challenged. They regulate the use of violence and so supply a rationale that allows those who are inclined to aggression to precipitate violent encounters in an approved way. The rules have been established and are enforced mainly by those who are street, but on the streets the distinction between street and decent is often irrelevant; everybody knows that if the rules are violated, there are penalties. Knowledge of the code is thus largely defensive, and it is literally necessary for operating in public. Therefore, though families with a decency orientation are usually opposed to the values of the code, they often reluctantly encourage their children to be familiar with it to enable them to negotiate the inner-city environment.

At the heart of the code is the issue of respect—loosely defined as being treated "right" or being granted one's "props" (or proper due) or the deference one deserves. However, in the deprived and trouble-some public environment of the inner city, as people increasingly feel buffeted by forces beyond their control, what one deserves in the way of respect becomes ever more problematic and uncertain. This situa-tion in turn further opens the issue of respect to sometimes intense interpersonal negotiations, at times resulting in physical fights. In the street culture, especially among young people, respect is viewed as al-most an external entity, one that is hard-won but easily lost, and so must constantly be guarded. The rules of the code in fact provide a framework for negotiating respect. With the right amount, individuals can avoid being bothered in public. This security is important, for if they are bothered, not only may they be in physical danger, but they will have been disgraced or "dissed" (disrespected). Many of the forms dissing can take may seem petty to middle-class people (maintaining eye contact for too long, for example), but to those invested in the street code, these actions become serious indications of the other per-son's intentions. Consequently, such people become very sensitive to signals of advances or slights, which could well serve as a warning of imminent physical attack or confrontation.

The hard reality of the world of the streets can be traced to the pro-found sense of alienation from mainstream society and its institutions felt by many poor inner-city black people, particularly the young. The code of the street is actually a cultural adaptation to a profound lack of faith in the police and the judicial system, and in others who would champion one's personal security. The police, for instance, are most often viewed as representing the dominant white society and as not caring enough to protect inner-city residents. When called, they may not even respond, which is one reason many residents feel they must be prepared to take extraordinary measures to defend themselves and their loved ones against those who are inclined toward aggression. Lack of police accountability has in fact been incorporated into the lo-cal status system: the person who is believed capable of "taking care of himself" is accorded a certain deference and regard, which translates into a sense of physical and psychological control. The code of the street emerges where the influence of the police ends and where per-sonal responsibility for one's safety is felt to begin. Exacerbated by the proliferation of drugs and easy access to guns, this volatile situation results in the ability of the street minority (or those who effectively "go for bad") to dominate their neighborhood's public spaces.

III. Campaigning for Respect

"Respect," as we have noted, is a key word in the code of the street. It is also a form of human capital, especially valuable when access to some of the forms of human capital of the wider community are not available. It is fought for, held, and challenged as much as "honor" was fought for, held, and challenged in the age of chivalry. Much of the code of the street has to do with achieving and holding respect. And children learn the rules early.

A. The Shuffling Process

Children from even the most decent homes must come to terms with the various and sundry influences of the streets, including that of their more street oriented peers. Indeed, as children grow up and their parents' control wanes, they go through a social shuffling process that can undermine, or at least test, much of the socialization they have received at home. In other words, the street serves as a mediating influence under which children may come to reconsider and rearrange their personal orientations. This is a time of status passage, when social identity can become very uncertain. It is a tricky time because a child can go either way—decent or street. For children from decent homes, the immediate and present reality of the street situation can overcome the compunctions against tough behavior that their parents taught them, so that the lessons of the home may be quickly put aside as children learn to deal with their social environment. The children are confronted with a local hierarchy based on toughness and the premium placed on being a good fighter. As a means of survival, one learns the importance of a reputation for being willing and able to fight, or even to go for bad. To build such a reputation is to gain respect among peers, and a physically talented child who starts down this track may find him- or herself increasingly committed to an orientation that can lead to trouble. Of course, a talented child from a decent or a street family may discover ways of gaining respect without unduly resorting to aggressive and violent responses—becoming a rapper or athlete, or, occasionally, a good student. The important point here is that the kind of home a child comes from is influential but not always determinative of the way he or she will ultimately turn out. The neighborhood and surrounding environmental influences—and how the child adapts to this environment—are key.

Typically, by the age of ten, children from both decent and street families in inner-city poor neighborhoods are mingling on the neighborhood streets and figuring out their identities. Here they try out roles and scripts in a process that challenges their talents and prior socialization and may involve more than a little luck, good or bad. In this volatile environment, they learn to watch their backs and to anticipate and negotiate those situations that might lead to trouble with others. The outcome of these cumulative interactions on the streets ultimately determines every child's life chances.

Here lies the real meaning of so many fights and altercations, behind the ostensible, usually seemingly petty, precipitating causes, including the competitions over girlfriends and boyfriends and the "he say, she say" conflicts of personal attribution. Adolescents are insecure and are trying to establish their identities. Children from the middle and upper classes, however, usually have more ways to express themselves as worthwhile and so have more avenues to explore. The negotiations they engage in among themselves may also include aggression, but they tend to be more verbal in a way not available to those of more limited resources, such as showing off with things and connections. In poor inner-city neighborhoods, physicality is a fairly common way of asserting oneself. It is also unambiguous. If you punch someone out, if you succeed in keeping someone from walking down your block, "you did it." It is a fait accompli and the evidence that you prevailed is there for all to see.

During this campaign for respect, through these various conflicts, the connection between being respected and the need for being in physical control of at least a portion of the environment become internalized, and the germ of the code of the street emerges. As children mature, they obtain an increasingly more sophisticated understanding of the code, and it becomes part of their working conception of the world, so that, by the time they reach adulthood, it has come to define the social order. In time, the rules of physical engagement and their personal implications become crystallized. Children learn the conditions under which violence is appropriate, and they also learn how the code defines their relationship to their peers. They thus come to appreciate the give-and-take of life in public—the process of negotiation. From all this they gain, in the words of the street, valued "street knowledge." And, to a degree, they learn to resolve disputes mainly through physical contests that settle—at least for the time being—who is the toughest, and who will take what from whom in what circumstances. In effect, they learn the social order of their local peer groups, an order that is always open to change, which is one of the reasons the youths take such a strong interest in the fight.

The ethic of violence is in part a class phenomenon. Lower-class people seem more inclined to resort to physical fighting to settle arguments than middle- or upper-middle-class people. And members of the lower classes more often find themselves in disputes that lead to violence. Because they are more often alienated from the agents and agencies of social control, such as the police and the courts, they more easily resort to settling disputes on their own. And, as indicated above, the parents, in turn, tend to socialize their children into this reality.

This reality of inner-city life is largely absorbed on the streets. At an early age, often even before they start school and without much in the way of adult supervision, children from street families gravitate to the streets, where they must be ready to "hang," to socialize with peers. Children from these generally permissive homes have a great deal of latitude and are allowed to "rip and run" up and down the streets. They often come home from school, put their books down, and go right back out the door. On school nights many eight- and nine-year-olds remain out until nine or ten o'clock (teenagers may come in whenever they want to). On the streets, they play in groups that often become the source of their primary social bonds.

In the street, through their play, children pour their individual life experiences into a common knowledge-pool mix, negating, affirming, confirming, and elaborating on what they have observed in the home and matching their skills against those of others out in the street. And they learn to fight; in particular, they learn the social meaning of fighting. In these circumstances, even small children test one another, pushing and shoving others, and are ready to hit other children over circumstances not to their liking. In turn, they are readily hit by other children, and the child who is toughest prevails. Thus the violent resolution of disputes—the hitting and cursing—gains social reinforcement. The child in effect is more completely initiated into a world that provides a strong rationale for physically campaigning for self-respect.

In a critical sense, violent behavior is determined by situations, thus giving importance to the various ways individuals define and interpret such situations, which become so many public trials. The individual builds patterns as outcomes are repeated over time. Behaviors, violent or civil, that work for a young person and are reinforced by peers will likely be repeated, particularly as the child begins to build a "name," or a reputation for toughness.

Moreover, younger children refine their understanding of the code by observing the disputes of older children, which are often resolved through cursing and abusive talk, and sometimes through outright aggression or violence. They are also alert and attentive witnesses to the verbal and physical fights of adults, after which they compare notes among themselves and share their own interpretations of the event. Almost always the victor is the person who physically won the altercation, and this person often enjoys the esteem and respect of onlookers. These experiences reinforce the lessons many children have learned at home: might makes right; toughness is a virtue, humility is not. The social meaning of fighting becomes clarified as they come to appreciate the real consequences of winning and losing. The child's understanding of the code becomes more refined but also an increasingly important part of his or her working conception of the world.

The street adults with whom children come in contact at home and on the street—including mothers, fathers, brothers, sisters, boyfriends, girlfriends, cousins, neighbors, and friends—help shape and reinforce this understanding by verbalizing the messages they are getting through public experience: "Watch your back." "Protect yourself." "Don't punk out." "Respect yourself." "If someone disses you, you got to straighten them out." Many parents actually impose sanctions if a child is not sufficiently aggressive. For example, if a child loses a fight and comes home upset, the parent might respond, "Don't you come in here crying somebody beat you up; you better get back out there and whup his ass. If you don't whup his ass, I'll whup yo' ass when you come home." Thus, the child gains reinforcement for being tough and showing nerve.

While fighting, some children cry as though they are doing something they are ambivalent about. The fight may be against their wishes, yet they may feel constrained to fight or face the consequences—not just from peers but also from caretakers or parents, who may administer another beating if they back down. Appearing capable of taking care of oneself as a form of self-defense is a dominant theme among both street and decent adults, who worry about the safety of their children. But taking care of oneself does not have to involve physical fighting; at times, it can involve getting "out of stuff" by outwitting adversaries, a tactic often employed by decent inner-city parents. The following incident related by Marge, a hard-working decent woman and the mother of Curtis, and three other children, is relevant:

> My son that's bad now—his name is Curtis. And he was going to Linden Junior High School, and he was in the eighth grade. And my son Terry was in the same grade. Terry's a year younger, but Curtis had gotten put back in the second grade. They had never had a fight.
>
> So he called me at work one day and told me that somebody was bothering him, and he was afraid. He was thirteen or fourteen at the time. He said he was also afraid to tell the teacher because if he told the teacher, they were gonna pick on him more. And he didn't have any men in his life at the time—my husband was not his father so that was another issue. So I said to him, "What are you gonna do? Are you gonna leave school?" He said he was afraid to leave school because if he left school, they would still pick on him. So I said to him, "Curtis, I'll tell you what you do. I'm gonna get off work early. What I want you to do, I want you to talk as bad as you can talk and don't act afraid. They don't know me. None of your friends in your classroom know me." I said, "I want you to come out and talk as bad as you can talk, but don't hit anybody. And then walk away." I said, "If a fight breaks out, then I'll come and break it up." And that's what he did and they left him alone. Isn't that something? See, he had to show nerve, it's very important for boys. It's easier for girls. The boys in the neighborhood—if you don't do some of the things they do, or even with the clothes, if you don't have nice things—at that time it was Jordache jeans and Sergio—if you don't have some of those things, people will pick on you and that type of thing.

Many decent parents encourage their children to stand up to those who might be aggressive toward them, but they also encourage their children to avoid the trouble of the streets. Given their superior resources and often their connections to the wider society, including schools, churches, and other institutions, the decent parents have the ability to see themselves beyond the immediate neighborhood; they tend to have more ways "to be somebody" than the typical street person. The difference in outlook has to do mainly with a difference in social class, particularly their sense of maintaining a class position while residing in the local inner-city environment. Hence, they tend to be in a position to encourage their children to avoid conflict by talk or by turning and walking away, and they sometimes do. But, as indicated above, this is not always possible, and as a last resort such children are taught to stand their ground.

Thus there is at times a convergence in their child-rearing practices of those labeled decent and street, although the rationales behind them may differ. In the stereotypical street home, disorder is everywhere, mothers curse at their children, stepfathers and boyfriends come and go, perhaps physically abusing the child as they pass through. Through observing the behavior of street adults in these circumstances, even small children gain lessons about the street and survival in their world. The following field note graphically illustrates both the efficacy of these informal lessons and the early age at which they are learned.

Casey is four years old and attends a local nursery school. He lives with his mom and stepfather. Casey's family is considered in the neighborhood to be a street family. At home, his mother will curse at him and, at times, will beat him for misbehavior. At times, his stepfather will spank him as well. Casey has attracted the attention of the staff of the nursery school because of his behavior. When Casey wants something, he will curse and hit other children. He now has the reputation of "bad" around the center. He regularly refers to members of the staff as "bitches" and "motherfuckers." For instance, he will say to his teacher, "Cathy, you bitch" or "What that bitch want?" At times this seems funny coming from the mouth of a four-year-old, but it reflects on Casey's home situation. Around the center, he knows that such behavior is disapproved of because of the way the teachers and others react to it, though he may get reinforcement for it because of its humorous character. Once when his teacher upset him, Casey slapped her and called her a "bitch."

On hearing of this incident, the bus driver refused to take Casey home, or even let him on his bus. The next day, when Casey saw the bus driver again, he said, "Norman, you left me. Why'd you leave me? You a trip, man." Members of the staff fear that Casey has a bad influence on other children at the center, for he curses at them "like a sailor," though they "don't know what he's talking about." In these ways, Casey acts somewhat grown up, or "mannish," in the words of the bus driver, who sometimes glares at him, wanting to treat him as another man, since "he seems to act that way." Staff members at the center have found they can control Casey by threatening to report his behavior to his stepfather, to which he replies, "Oh, please don't tell him. I'll be good. Please don't tell him." It seems that Casey fears this man and telling him might mean a beating.

Local decent blacks say Casey's home life is that of the typical street family, which is rife with cursing, yelling, and the physical abuse of children. Many of these parents do not want Casey to be playmate for their own children. They think he would be a bad influence, particularly encouraging them toward assuming a street identity. Children "like this one" worry them generally. They feel that certain neighborhoods breed such children, and that decent children are at some risk when placed in an environment with too many such kids.

In the minds of many decent parents, children from street families, because of their generalized ignorance and lack of opportunities, are considered at great risk of eventually getting into serious trouble.

B. Self-Image Based on "Juice"

By the time they are teenagers, most young people have internalized the code of the street, or at least learned to comport themselves in accordance with its rules. As indicated above, the code revolves around the presentation of self. Its basic requirement is the display of a certain predisposition to violence. A person's public bearing must send the unmistakable if sometimes subtle message that one is capable of violence and mayhem when the situation requires it, that one can take care of oneself. The nature of this communication can include both verbal and bodily expression—all geared mainly to deterring aggression. Physical appearance, including clothes, jewelry, and grooming, also plays an important part in how a person is viewed; respect requires the right look.

Even so, there are no guarantees against challenges, because there are always people around looking for a fight to increase their share of respect—or "juice," as it is sometimes called on the street. Moreover, if a person is assaulted, it is important in the eyes of his "running buddies" as well as his opponent for him to avenge himself. Otherwise he risks being "tried" (challenged) or "rolled on" (physically assaulted) by any number of others. Indeed, if he is not careful, he could lose the respect of his running buddies. This is an especially important consideration, for without running buddies or "homies," who can be depended on to "watch your back" in a "jam," the person is vulnerable to being rolled on by still others. Part of what protects a person in this environment is the number of people—and what their status is—who can be counted on to avenge his honor if he is "rolled on" in an "un-

fair" fight. Some of the most well-protected people in the environment
are members not only of "tough" street corner groups, but also of families and extended families of cousins, uncles, fathers, and brothers who
are known to be imbued with the code of the street. Their family
members, especially when the family's reputation is secure, "can go
anywhere, and won't nobody bother them. You just don't mess with
the Hardys!" The Hardy family consists of six streetwise brothers, two
of whom are in prison for murder, while the others are established hustlers in the community and two belong to a local gang. Generally, to
maintain his honor the young man must show that he himself, as an
individual, is not someone to be "messed with" or "dissed." To show
this, he may "act crazy"—that is, have the reputation for "going for
his piece [gun] quickly." But in general a person must "keep himself
straight" by managing his position of respect among others, including
his running buddies; fundamentally, this involves managing his self-
image, which is shaped by what he thinks others are thinking of him
in relation to his peers.

Objects play an important and complicated role in establishing self-
image. Jackets, sneakers, gold jewelry, and even expensive firearms reflect not just taste, which tends to be tightly regulated among adolescents of all social classes, but also a willingness to possess things that
may require defending. A boy wearing a fashionable, expensive jacket,
for example, is vulnerable to attack by another who covets the jacket
and either cannot afford to buy one or wants the added satisfaction of
depriving someone else of his. However, if a boy forgoes the desirable
jacket and wears one that is not hip, he runs the risk being teased or
even assaulted as an unworthy person. A youth with a decency orientation describes the situation:

Here go another thing. If you outside, right, and your mom's on
welfare and she on crack, the persons you trying to be with dress
[in] like purple sweatpants and white sneaks, but it's all decent,
right, and you got on some bummy jeans and a pair of dull sneaks,
they won't—some of the people out there selling drugs won't let
you hang with them unless you dress like [in] purple sweatpants
and decent sneaks everyday. . . .

They tease 'em. First they'll tease 'em and then they'll try to say
they stink, like they smell like pig or something like that, and then
they'll be like, "Get out of here. Get out. We don't want you near
us. You stink. You dirty." All that stuff. And I don't think that's

right. If he's young, it ain't his fault or her fault that she dressin'
like that. It's her mother and her dad's fault.

To be allowed to hang with certain prestigious crowds, a boy must
wear a different set of expensive clothes every day. Not to do so might
make him appear socially deficient. So he comes to covet such items—
especially when he sees easy prey wearing them. The youth continues:

> You can even get hurt off your own clothes: like, say, I'm walkin'
> down the street and somebody try to take my hat from me and I
> won't let 'em take it and they got a gun. You can get killed over one
> little simple hat. Or if I got a gold ring and a gold necklace on and
> they see me one dark night on a dark street, and they stick me up and
> I won't let 'em, and they shoot me. I'm dead and they hid me. I'm
> dead and won't nobody ever know [who did it].

In acquiring valued things, therefore, a person shores up his or her
identity—but since it is an identity based on having something, it is
highly precarious. This very precariousness gives a heightened sense of
urgency to staying even with peers, with whom the person is actually
competing. Young men and women who are able to command respect
through their presentation of self—by allowing their possessions and
body language to speak for them—may not have to campaign for regard but may, rather, gain it by the force of their manner. Those who
are unable to command respect in this way must actively campaign for
it.

One way of campaigning for status is by taking the possessions of
others. Seemingly ordinary objects can become trophies with symbolic
value far beyond their monetary worth. Possessing the trophy can sym-
bolize the ability to violate somebody—to "get in his face," to dis
him—and thus to enhance one's own worth by stealing someone else's.
The trophy does not have to be something material. It can be another
person's sense of honor, snatched away with a derogatory remark. It
can be the outcome of a fight. It can be meeting a certain standard,
such as a girl's getting herself recognized as the most beautiful. Material things, however, fit easily into the pattern: sneakers, a pistol, somebody else's girlfriend, all can become a trophy. A person who can take
something from another and then flaunt it gains regard by being the
owner, or the controller, of that thing. But this display of ownership

can then provoke a challenge from other people. On inner-city streets this game of who controls what is constantly being played, and the trophy—extrinsic or intrinsic, tangible or intangible—identifies the current winner.

In this often violent give-and-take, raising oneself up largely depends on putting someone else down. There is a general sense in the deprived inner-city ghetto community that very little respect is to be had, so everyone competes for what is available, and there is also much jealousy and envy. The resulting craving for respect makes some people "touchy" giving them thin skins and short fuses. Shows of deference by others are soothing and contribute to a sense of security, comfort, self-confidence, and self-respect. Unanswered transgressions diminish these feelings and are believed to encourage further transgressions. So constant vigilance is required against even appearing as if transgressions will be tolerated. Among young people, whose sense of self-esteem is particularly vulnerable, there is special concern with being disrespected. Many inner-city young men in particular crave respect to such a degree that they will risk their lives to attain and maintain it.

As indicated above, the issue of respect is thus closely tied to whether a person has an inclination to be violent, even as a victim. In the wider society, people, or local people with a decent orientation, may not feel required to retaliate physically after an attack, though they are aware that they have been degraded or taken advantage of. They may feel a great need to defend themselves during an attack, or to behave in a way that deters aggression, but they are much more likely than street people to feel that they can walk away from a possible altercation with their self-esteem intact. Some people may even have the strength of character to flee without thinking that their self-respect will be diminished.

In impoverished inner-city black communities, however, particularly among young males and perhaps increasingly among young females, such flight would be extremely difficult. To run away would likely leave one's self-esteem in tatters. Therefore people often feel constrained not only to stand up and at least attempt to resist during an assault but also to "pay back"—to seek revenge—after a successful assault on their person. Revenge may include going to get a weapon or even getting relatives and friends involved. Their very identity, their self-respect and honor are often intricately tied up with the way they perform on the streets during and after such encounters.

IV. Adapting to the Code

Every young person in deprived inner-city black neighborhoods must learn to live with the code of the street. The street kids must prove their manhood and achieve their identity under the intricate rules of the code. The decent kids must learn to coexist with it.

A. Manhood and Nerve

On the neighborhood streets, many of the concerns about identity have come to be expressed in the concept of "manhood." Manhood in the inner city means taking the prerogatives of men with respect to strangers, other men, and women. It implies physicality and a certain ruthlessness. Regard and respect are associated with this concept: if others have little regard for a person's manhood, his very life and those of his loved ones could be in jeopardy. There is an existential link between manhood and self-esteem, so that it has become hard to say which is primary. For many inner-city youths, manhood and respect are two sides of the same coin; physical and psychological well-being are inseparable, and both require a sense of control, of being in charge.

The operating assumption is that a man, especially a real man, knows what other men know—the code of the street. The code is seen as having a certain justice, since it is considered that everyone has the opportunity to know it and can be held responsible for being familiar with it. If the victim of a mugging, for example, does not know the code and so responds "wrong," the perpetrator may feel justified in killing him and may feel and show no remorse. He may think, "Too bad, but it's his fault. He should have known better."

A person venturing outside must adopt the code to prevent others from messing with him, and it is easy for people to think they are being tried or tested by others even when this is not the case. For something extremely valuable is at stake in every interaction, and people are encouraged to rise to the occasion, particularly with strangers. For people who are unfamiliar with the code—generally people who live outside the inner city—this concern with respect in the most ordinary interactions can be frightening and incomprehensible. But for those who are invested in the code, the clear object of their demeanor is to discourage strangers from even thinking about testing their manhood. The sense of power that attends the ability to deter others can be alluring even to those who know the code without being heavily invested in it—the decent inner-city youths. Thus a boy who has been leading a basically decent life can, in trying circumstances, suddenly resort to deadly force.

Central to the issue of manhood is the widespread belief that one of the most effective ways of gaining respect is to manifest nerve. Nerve is shown by taking another person's possessions, messing with someone's woman, throwing the first punch, or pulling a trigger. Its proper display helps check others who would violate one's person and helps build a reputation that works to prevent future challenges. But since such a show of nerve is a forceful expression of disrespect toward the person on the receiving end, the victim may be greatly offended and seek to retaliate with equal or greater force. The knowledge that a display of nerve can easily provoke a life-threatening response is part of the concept.

True nerve expresses a lack of fear of dying. Many feel that it is acceptable to risk dying over issues of respect. In fact, among the hardcore street, the clear risk of violent death may be preferable to being dissed. Conveying the attitude of being able to take somebody else's life if the situation demands it gives one a real sense of power on the streets. Many youths, both decent and street, try to achieve this appearance for both its practical defense value and the positive way it makes them feel about themselves. The difference between them is that the decent youth can code-switch: in other settings—with teachers, say, or at his part-time job—he can be polite and deferential. The seriously street-oriented youth has made the concept of manhood part of his very identity and has difficulty manipulating it.

B. Black Adolescent Identity in the Inner City

The reader may again ask what the source of the power of the code is. Why does it dominate the inner-city community? Why is it so central to young people's lives? Part of the answer lies in how these adolescents are trying to shape identities for themselves, and the roles of the elements that might be expected to influence this process.

Any discussion of black adolescent identity must consider the wide variations among black youths and the diversity in the youth culture. Differences of religion, class backgrounds, and orientations operate in the same school, church, mosque, or neighborhood. The picture is further complicated by the social isolation of the black community as a whole, reducing young people's ability to identify with the mainstream or their hope to become part of the wider society.

Note that social isolation can and does exist even for people who appear to be close to the wider society and culture. Isolation must be seen to some degree as a state of mind, the feeling that there is something profoundly alien about the wider society that discourages identification with it. People so isolated can begin thinking of themselves as an "own" and develop orientations toward the mainstream that reflect their distance and alienation; they may develop a counter-ideology that holds that society in contempt. In the inner-city community today, this is exactly what has happened in certain settings.

Moreover, the young people have been given powerful messages that it is actually wrong to harbor hope of identification, to "think white." They use things and issues associated with the wider society, but make them their own by using them in their own ways and so neutralizing the white negatives associated with them. Many such young people, as this essay shows, have come to pride themselves on knowing and being able to enact the code of the street, even though in settings of civility they may code-switch to more civil behavior.

Part of the code of the street is to dress and act as a member of the oppositional culture that has developed in this way. Young people gain points for being mean or successfully going for bad, especially in public places like streets, school hallways, or multiplex movie theaters. People adorn themselves, displaying what they have, or "what's to them." The jewelry and the name-brand sneakers and clothing attest to the wearers' social worth, and those who do not wear the right things may be viciously excluded and ostracized.

In school and in the neighborhood, adolescents are very much concerned with developing a sense of who they are, what they are, and what they will be. They try on many different personas, roles, and scripts. Some work, others do not. How do the roles of decent and street play in their identity considerations, and what parts do others play? What stages do these young people go through? What is the career of their identity as it takes shape in these circumstances?

Observing relations in the school and talking with adolescents reveals that school authority is often an extremely important issue for young people, but very often the authority figures are viewed as alien and unreceptive. The teachers and administrators are concerned that their own authority be taken seriously, and claims to authority are always up for grabs, if not subject to out-and-out challenge.

A black authority figure, particularly a black male, enjoys a certain prestige. He tends to be taken more seriously and given the benefit of the doubt for having experienced what the young people have experienced. On the surface, at least, he is more easily seen as "one of us." Such a person may be on probation with the students, but the period of testing may be seen as his to lose, since the students tend to be favorably disposed toward him.

Typically, such figures are quite exacting with the students. They tend to be strict and rule oriented, understanding that it is better to be seen that way at first and then possibly loosen up later. In the students' parlance, they are considered "mean." They may not be well-liked, but they do tend to be respected among the students.

White authority figures tend to be on constant probation. The students are very much concerned to test whether they are racist; the verdict is usually that they are. Some teachers who know what they are up to have a ready campaign to win the trust and approval of their charges. But it is often a very tough fight, and sometimes complete trust never comes. This is frustrating to many teachers and often leads to premature burnout.

Young people of course do not go about developing their identities solely from privileges and rewards by teachers. But some of this surely goes on. More often than not, students find the institution and its staff utterly unreceptive, but there are situations in which the school and its staff are truly nurturing and supportive.

The decent children especially put stock in the ability to code-switch, adopting one set of behaviors when inside the building and another when outside on the streets. But at times the two roles become confused and propriety for both settings is seen as the same. When this confusion goes unchecked, it can make discipline in the school elusive, for the children who seem to get away with it encourage others to follow their lead, especially if to behave decently can be seen as acting white. There is great incentive for young people to buy into the oppositional culture even in school, because to do so means they can "be something" in a world that is controlled by themselves.

Teachers as agents of the wider system really have to bend over backward to make a place for these students, saying "I'm here for you," to an extent that may compromise their own hard-won authority or respect. But if the students feel that the teachers as part of the wider system are dissing them, they turn to the oppositional culture to shape their identities in a way that seems positive to them.

Black students "do it" (take on the oppositional role) so effectively that they are models for other disaffected students. They are the authentic alienated people. They do it because they are profoundly at odds with the white culture and can see themselves visibly as different. But white students mimic them because they are such good models.

C. The Dilemma of the Decent Kid

At a certain critical point in development, say ages five through eight, the child of a decent inner-city family ventures into the street, away from home, out of the view and immediate control of his family. Here children begin to develop an identity beyond the family, one that is helped along by the way they go about meeting the exigencies of the streets. They find their level, get cool with others, adjust to the situation as they swim about the environment "looking for themselves" and trying to "be real."

They often experience a certain tension between what they learn at home and what they find in the streets. The family often becomes mildly concerned about the kinds of children their child is playing with. At this stage the child's peer group becomes extremely important. Often the child must go with what groups are available. A child from a decent home can easily be sucked up by the streets. The child may learn to code-switch, presenting himself one way at home and another with peers.

Many children are left on their own for long periods of time. Others in the neighborhood may be encouraged to look out for them, including "big brothers," "cousins," and neighborhood friends of the family. But at the same time the children are out to try new things, to find themselves, and to grow into independence. The child encounters the street in the form of peers, cousins, and older children, and begins to absorb the experience.

To many residents, the negative aspects of the street are exemplified by groups of young men who physically defend their neighborhoods by molesting interlopers. These young men often come from homes ravaged by unemployment and family disorganization. On the streets they develop contacts and "family" ties with other youths like themselves. The groups they form are extremely attractive to other youths and not simply to those whose lives have been seriously compromised by poverty. They dominate the public spaces and any young person must deal with them. Even the decent young people must make their peace with them.

It must be understood that these decent young people's connection with the street is not simply a matter of coercion. Often they have strong aspirations for feelings of self-worth, and to achieve it they must do more than make peace with the street group, they must actually come to terms with the street. On the streets, they must get cool with the youth who dominate the public spaces. They must let others know how tough they are, how hard they are to roll on, how much mess they will take. The others want to know what will make such a person's jaws tight, what will get him mad. To find out they will challenge the person to fight or test his limits with insults to his family. Some of the most decent youths reach their limits rather quickly, thus allowing others to "see what's to him," or what he's made of. Often a fight ensues: as the young men say, "it's showtime."

So the streets, or at least the public spaces, are extremely important for young people, because these are places where they are involved in the process of forging their own local identities—identities that carry over into other critical areas of their lives, including school, church, employment, and future family life. This is an issue for all the children in the environment, both decent and street. Even if the child is one of the most decent persons in the neighborhood, at some point there comes a time when he must display his degree of commitment to the street.

Life under the code might be considered a kind of game played by rules that are partly specified but partly emergent. The young person is encouraged to be familiar with the rules of the game and even use them as a metaphor for life, or else feel left out, marginalized, and ultimately be rolled on. So the young person is inclined to enact his own particular role, to show his familiarity with the game, and more specifically his street knowledge, to gain points with others.

It is extremely important that the child learn to play well. This ability is strongly related to who his mentors and "homies" are and how much interest and support they show for the child. How "good" he is to some important degree corresponds to how "bad" his neighborhood is viewed to be. The tougher the neighborhood, the more prestige he has in the minds of others he encounters. This prestige often provides a challenge to interlopers.

Young people who display decency are generally not given much respect in public. Decency or a "nice" attitude is taken as a sign of weakness, inviting others to roll on or try the person. To be nice is to risk being taken as a sissy, as someone who cannot fight, as a weakling, as someone to be rolled on. And to roll on someone once is not enough; it is often done again and again to establish the pattern of dominance in the groups. Young people who are out to make a name for themselves are actively looking for chumps to roll on. A name once achieved must be sustained, and its owner must live up to his reputation or be challenged. Decent kids serve as so much cannon fodder for such individuals. A name is like a fire: it needs fuel to exist. The decent kids serve as fuel, to be rolled on in order to maintain a name that, when established, wards off danger from others.

With some number of campaigns to his credit, a person may feel self-confident enough to try someone who has already established himself. Defeating such a person may be the ultimate trophy for someone on a campaign for respect. But he is likely to try the decent youths first. Knowing this encourages decent youths to mimic those who are more committed to the streets. Showing this street side of themselves blurs the lines separating one from the other, particularly for outsiders like prospective employers, teachers, and police, and sometimes for the young people themselves.

Respect is sometimes especially necessary for decent kids, and they may be quite impressed by the exploits and actions of their "sho' nuff" street peers. Often such a child is respect-needy, since decent values and behavior are not generally held in high esteem. A member of the street group might bring such a person around to his group. For the decent acquaintance there is the added attraction of the possibility of social acceptance, of getting cool with people on this side of the play-ground or classroom. The connection is at best tenuous and there are many sanctions against getting with the street crowd, but he is attracted just the same.

Occasionally, the decent kid will taste the ways of the street group, and they will "get good" to him. The feelings of deference, the suggestions of real respect and friendship are often too attractive to let pass. There is often a serious promise of such a turn of events. The decent group gradually loses its hold on the kid, or at least for the moment appears to. With this taste of the new way fresh on his mind, he feels able to resolve problems of self-esteem by joining up.

For a fifteen-year-old boy, there is also the issue of becoming a man. He is encouraged to try out his new-found size and strength to see what they will gain him in the game of social esteem.

A youngster who is able to gain some support for his new way of relating to others in the group of tough guys may be inclined to test out his new strength on others. With the help of his acquaintances, he is able to see himself in a different light, not to mention that other people are now seeing him in a different light, too. He is inclined to try out his new ways not just on other street kids, but on decent kids he knows well. And closely noting the social reaction to his new, if provisional identity, he may be inspired and motivated to continue. In these circumstances, he may gain points for going for bad as he tries out and forges this new identity through bullying other decent kids.

Here he models himself after what he has observed among the street kids, notes how he puts fear in the hearts of decent kids, and may well be encouraged to continue. An old head who has closely watched the youngster over the years may intervene, but this is less likely to happen today than in years past, mainly because of the spreading economic and social distress of so many such communities. Allowed to continue, he refines his skills, gaining a taste of respect, and comes to crave more: it gets good to him. Slowly he develops a different attitude about himself. He changes from a person who code-switched to go for bad to one who increasingly does not seem to have to put up a front to assume a street posture in defense of himself and of what belongs to him.

This "coming of age" process has implications for relations with parents, teachers, coaches, and other meaningful adults in the child's life. If he used to do his homework, now he may be less attentive to it. He may have a problem obeying teachers. His grades begin to suffer. When his mom asks him to go to the store or to run some other errand, he has a word of resistance. He develops difficulty in doing what he's told. He increasingly gives authority figures back talk. Arguments erupt more easily. Slowly his stance changes from cooperative child to adversary.

The changes are clear to those looking on, people who once depended on the image they had of him as a nice and decent youngster. But those closest to him, particularly mothers, aunts, uncles, and adult neighbors who remember him growing up, may resist any other definition of the person they know and love, a young man who to them is the same person. They are often incredulous when they hear of something terrible the boy is accused of doing.

Once such a street-oriented person has established himself, or has made a name, there is some disincentive for code-switching, for he has much to lose by letting the wrong people see him do it. He is not inclined to "sell-out" to appease "white people or striving blacks." On the streets he has respect precisely because he has opposed that wider society, and to switch back is to undermine his name or reputation. Here the alienation so many young people feel has taken on a life of its own and become institutionalized. Those deeply involved in the code of the street sometimes find themselves proselytizing others to join them. (We seldom hear of decent kids saying to street kids, "Hey, why don't you come join us?!") A common entreaty is "Hey! When you gon' get legal?" (meaning when are you going to come and sell drugs with us).

I might add that for the serious street element there is no need for a put-on; rather, the street is in the person, consuming his being, so much so that the person has a limited behavioral repertoire. The decent kid who has come through this socialization process often has a wider array of styles from which to choose how to act, and certainly with which to gauge and understand the conduct of others. And with such street knowledge the young person may avoid being taken advantage of on the streets (not a small accomplishment). To be more appealing to those of the street, however, he must present himself in contradistinction with adult authority, and to some degree make his peace with the oppositional culture. This behavior is reinforced by the street group.

It is important to appreciate here that the code of the street and the street knowledge it implies are very important for survival on the inner-city streets. If the code did not exist, there would be even more disorganization in the community than there is, and violence and crime would likely be more frequent. The code is a kind of policing mechanism, encouraging people to treat others with a certain respect or face the consequences.

By a certain age a young person becomes proficient on the streets and accumulates a certain amount of capital. This kind and form of capital is not always useful or valued in the wider society, but it is capital nonetheless. It is recognized and valued on the streets, and to lack it is to be vulnerable.

The issue here, that of social belonging, raises other issues and questions. Would the decent kid resolve his dilemma differently if there were more decent kids present? If there were a critical mass of decent kids, could he get by with his decency—in deed as well as behavior—intact? But the decent kids do not form a critical mass. There may be overwhelming numbers of youths who in some settings—home, work, church, in the presence of significant adults about whose opinions they care—display a commitment to decency, but they cannot do so here. They are encouraged by the dominant youths here to switch codes and play by the rules of the street, or face sanctions at the hands of peers about whose opinions they also care.

And, as has been indicated, there is a practical reason for such a tack. To avoid being bothered, both decent and street youth must say through behavior, words, and gestures, "If you mess with me there will be a severe penalty—coming from me. And I'm man enough to make you pay." This message must be given loudly and clearly if the youth is to be left alone, and simply exhibiting a decent orientation often does not do so forcefully enough.

V. Conclusion

This essay has explored the conditions of life in the impoverished inner-city community, and the code of the street that has developed in response to those conditions. This essay includes a summary of the elements—economic, racial, and social—that have led to those conditions.

America's urban centers have experienced profound structural economic changes, as deindustrialization—the movement from manufacturing to service and "high tech"—and the growth of the global economy have created new economic conditions. Job opportunities increasingly go abroad to Singapore, Taiwan, India, and Mexico, and to nonmetropolitan America, to satellite cities like King of Prussia, Pennsylvania. Over the last fifteen years, for example, Philadelphia has lost 102,500 jobs, and manufacturing employment has declined by 53 percent. Large numbers of inner-city people, in particular, are not adjusting effectively to the new economic reality. Where previously low-wage jobs—especially unskilled and low-skill factory jobs—existed simultaneously with poverty and there was hope for the future, now jobs simply do not exist. These dislocations have made many inner-city people unable to earn a decent living.

It often appears to outsiders that the ghetto consists of poor black people who engage in morally reprehensible behavior. The condition of these communities, however, was produced not by moral turpitude but by economic forces that have undermined black, urban, working-class life. Although it is true that such behavior as persistent welfare dependency, teenage pregnancy, drug abuse, drug dealing, violence, and crime reinforces economic marginality, much of that behavior originated in frustration and the inability to adjust to economic dislocation. In other words, the social ills that the companies moving out of these neighborhoods today use to justify their exodus are the same ones that their corporate predecessors, by leaving, helped to create.

To place the blame solely on individuals in urban ghettos is seriously misguided. The focus of the problem should be on the socioeconomic structure, because it was structural change that caused the number of jobs to decline and joblessness to increase in so many of these communities. Moreover, the people there lack good education. They lack both job training and good job networks, connections with people who could help them get jobs. They need sympathetic people, such as potential employers, who are able to understand their predicament and are willing to give them a chance. Government, which should be assisting people to adjust to the changed economy, is instead cutting what little help it does provide. At the same time, white and even black middle-class people are moving away from these inner-city areas, thereby both exacerbating bad conditions and removing role models for those left behind. This in turn leads to a weakening of social and family structure so that children are increasingly not being socialized into mainstream values and behavior.

Segregation and racism play important parts as well. After the abolition of slavery, segregation was introduced through both formal and informal means to keep blacks apart and ineligible for the rights, obligations, and duties of full citizenship. The creation of a black underclass living in jobless ghettos—to use sociologist William Julius Wilson's phrase—can thus be traced to the interaction of segregation and the effects of the global economy.

The attitudes of the wider society are deeply implicated in the code of the street. Most people in inner-city communities are not totally invested in the code, but the significant minority of hard-core street youths who have to maintain the code in order to establish their reputations because they have—or feel they have—few other ways to assert themselves. For these young people the standards of the street code are the only game in town. The extent to which some children—particularly those who through their upbringing have become most alienated, and those lacking in strong and conventional social support—experience, feel, and internalize racist rejection and contempt from mainstream society may strongly encourage them to express contempt for the more conventional society in turn. In dealing with this contempt and rejection, some youngsters will consciously invest themselves and their considerable mental resources in what amounts to an oppositional culture to preserve themselves and their self-respect. Once they do, any respect they might be able to garner in the wider system pales in comparison with the respect available in the local system; thus they often lose interest in even attempting to negotiate the mainstream system.

At the same time, many less alienated young blacks have assumed a street demeanor as a way of expressing their blackness while in reality embracing a much more moderate way of life; they, too, want a nonviolent setting in which to live and raise a family. These decent people are trying hard to be part of the mainstream culture, but the racism, real and perceived, that they encounter helps to legitimate the oppositional culture. And so on occasion they adopt street behavior. In fact, depending on the demands of the situation, many people in the community slip back and forth between decent and street behavior.

A vicious cycle has been formed. The hopelessness and alienation many young inner-city black men and women feel, largely a result of endemic joblessness and persistent racism, fuels the violence they engage in. This violence serves to confirm the negative feelings many whites and some middle-class blacks harbor toward the ghetto poor, further legitimating the oppositional culture and the code of the street in the eyes of many poor blacks. Unless this cycle is broken, attitudes on both sides will become increasingly entrenched, and the violence, which claims victims black and white, poor and affluent, will only escalate.

SELECT BIBLIOGRAPHY

Anderson, Elijah. 1978. *A Place on the Corner.* Chicago: University of Chicago Press.

———. 1989. "Sex Codes and Family Life among Poor Inner-City Youths." In *The Ghetto Underclass: Social Science Perspectives,* edited by William Julius Wilson. Special edition of *The Annals of the American Academy of Political and Social Science* 501:59–78.

———. 1990. *Streetwise: Race, Class and Change in an Urban Community.* Chicago: University of Chicago Press.

———. 1991. "Neighborhood Effect on Teen Pregnancy." In *The Urban Underclass,* edited by Christopher Jencks and Paul Peterson. Washington, D.C.: Brookings Institution.

———. 1997. "Violence and the Inner City Street Code." In *Violence and Childhood in the Inner City,* edited by Joan McCord. New York: Cambridge University Press.

Becker, Howard. 1970. *Sociological Work*. Chicago: Aldine.

Block, Fred, with Richard A. Cloward, Barbara Ehrenreich, and Frances Fox Piven. 1987. *The Mean Season: The Attack on the Welfare State*. New York: Pantheon.

Cloward, Richard A., and Lloyd Ohlin. 1960. *Delinquency and Opportunity: A Theory of Delinquent Gangs*. Glencoe, Ill.: Free Press.

Coleman, James. 1988. "Social Capital in the Creation of Human Capital." *American Journal of Sociology* 94:S95–S120.

Drake, St. Clair, and Horace Cayton. 1962. *Black Metropolis*. New York: Harper & Row.

Glasner, Barney G., and Anselm L. Strauss. 1972. *Status Passage*. Chicago: Aldine.

Katz, Jack. 1988. *Seductions of Crime: Moral and Sensual Attractions in Doing Evil*. New York: Basic.

Katz, Michael B. 1989. *The Undeserving Poor: From the War on Poverty to the War on Welfare*. New York: Pantheon.

Kirschenman, Joleen, and Kathy Neckerman. 1991. "We'd Like to Hire Them, But . . ." In *The Urban Underclass*, edited by Christopher Jencks and Paul Peterson. Washington, D.C.: Brookings Institution.

Massey, Douglas S., and Nancy A. Denton. 1993. *American Apartheid: Segregation and the Making of the Underclass*. Cambridge, Mass.: Harvard University Press.

Merton, Robert. 1957. "Social Structure and Anomie." In his *Social Theory and Social Structure*. Glencoe, Ill.: Free Press.

Short, James F., Jr., and Fred L. Strodtbeck. 1965. *Group Processes and Gang Delinquency*. Chicago: University of Chicago Press.

Simmel, George. 1971. *George Simmel on Individuality and Social Reforms*, edited by Donald L. Levine. Chicago: University of Chicago Press.

Wacquant, Loïc J. D., and William Julius Wilson. "The Cost of Racial and Class Exclusion in the Inner City." In *The Ghetto Underclass: Social Science Perspectives*, edited by William Julius Wilson. Special edition of *The Annals of the American Academy of Political and Social Science* 501:8–25.

Wilson, William Julius. 1987. *The Truly Disadvantaged*. Chicago: University of Chicago Press.

———. 1989. "The Underclass: Issues, Perspectives and Public Policy." In *The Ghetto Underclass: Social Science Perspectives*, edited by William Julius Wilson. Special edition of *The Annals of the American Academy of Political and Social Science* 501:183–92.

Wolfgang, M. E., and F. Ferracuti. 1967. *The Subculture of Violence*. London: Tavistock.

Jeffrey Fagan and Deanna L. Wilkinson

Guns, Youth Violence, and Social Identity in Inner Cities

ABSTRACT

While youth violence has always been a critical part of delinquency, the modern epidemic is marked by high rates of gun violence. Adolescents in cities possess and carry guns on a large scale, guns are often at the scene of youth violence, and guns often are used. Guns play a central role in initiating, sustaining, and elevating the epidemic of youth violence. The demand for guns among youth was fueled by an "ecology of danger," comprising street gangs, expanding drug markets with high intrinsic levels of violence, high rates of adult violence and fatalities, and cultural styles of gun possession and carrying. Guns became symbols of respect, power, identity, and manhood to a generation of youth, in addition to having strategic value for survival. The relationship between guns and youth violence is complex. The effects of guns are mediated by structural factors that increase the youth demand for guns, the available supply, and culture and scripts which teach kids lethal ways to use guns.

Adolescent violence has been part of the urban landscape in this country since its origins. From the colonial period (Sante 1991), to the waves of immigration in the early nineteenth century, to the formation of ethnic street gangs in the 1890s (O'Kane 1992), to the rise in delinquency and violence rates in the 1950s, fighting has been an integral part of adolescence. Beginning in the 1970s, rates of nonlethal adoles-

Jeffrey Fagan is professor of public health and director of the Center for Violence Research and Prevention, Columbia University School of Public Health, and Deanna L. Wilkinson is visiting assistant professor of criminal justice, Temple University. Support for this work was provided by grants from the Harry Frank Guggenheim Foundation, Centers for Disease Control and Prevention, National Institute of Justice, and the National Science Foundation. The opinions are solely those of the authors. We are grateful to the special efforts of our interviewers in making this research possible.

cent violence began slowly to rise. However, rates of lethal adolescent violence, primarily gun homicides, rose sharply through the 1970s, declined in the mid-1980s, and reached new highs in the early 1990s, before declining again (Cook and Laub, in this volume).

Today, guns are a central part of the changing character of youth violence, from being a minor concern prior to the 1970s to being a major youth violence problem in the past decade (see Blumstein 1995; Zimring and Hawkins 1997). Although always present in the background of urban delinquency, youth gun violence has become more prevalent and more concentrated spatially and socially in the past two decades. Virtually all increases in homicide rates from 1985 to 1990 among people ten to thirty-four years of age were attributable to deaths among African American males; most of the increase was in firearm homicides, and these were overwhelmingly concentrated demographically and spatially among African American males in urban areas (Fingerhut, Ingram, and Feldman 1992*a*, 1992*b*). Guns now play a significant role in shaping the developmental trajectories and behaviors of many inner-city youths. Estimates of gun carrying in school range from 5 percent (Vaughn et al. 1996) to 15 percent (LH Research 1993), providing minimal estimates of the overall frequency of gun carrying among adolescents. Gun violence also has become fuel for political and social mobilizations in the past decade, adding to recurring critiques of the juvenile justice system and inspiring communities to undertake a wide range of preventive and punitive measures.

The sharp increase in youth gun violence in the past decade, and its concentrated and severe consequences, suggests that it is an epidemic with moral, social, and health consequences. The health impacts are obvious and straightforward. For over a decade, fatality rates from nonfirearm intentional injuries have declined across all age groups (Fagan, Zimring, and Kim 1998). But from 1985 to 1991, firearm fatalities increased 127 percent among males fifteen to nineteen years of age, while declining by 1 percent for males twenty-five to twenty-nine years of age and 13 percent for males thirty to thirty-four years of age (Fingerhut 1993). Since 1991, while firearm fatality rates were declining generally, they have declined far more slowly for adolescents and young adults.

The concentration of adolescent gun violence among nonwhites in inner cities reveals the social effects of this epidemic. The increase in adolescent deaths from firearm injuries is disproportionately concentrated among nonwhites, and especially among African American teenagers and young adults. National death registry data show that from 1988 to 1992, for example, among African American teenage males fifteen to nineteen years old, 60 percent of deaths resulted from a firearm injury, compared to 23 percent for white teenage males. Among females fifteen to nineteen years of age, 22 percent of African American female deaths resulted from firearm injury, compared to 10 percent of deaths among white females (Fingerhut, Ingram, and Feldman 1992*a*).

In this period, young African American males were 4.7 times more likely to die from firearm injuries than from natural causes (Fingerhut 1993). In addition, there were 30 percent more deaths among ten- to fourteen-year-old African American males from firearms than from motor vehicle injuries, the second leading cause of death in this group. For teenagers (fifteen to nineteen) and young adults (twenty to twenty-four), there were three times as many deaths from firearms as from motor vehicle injuries (Fingerhut, Ingram, and Feldman 1992*a*).

How this epidemic came about is the focus of this essay. We show how guns have become an important part of the discourse of social interactions in modern urban life, with symbolic meaning (power and control), social meaning (status and identity), and strategic importance. Getting and using a gun against another person has become a rite of passage into manhood or at least into a respectable social identity within this context. Expressions of shortened life expectancies reflect processes of anticipatory socialization based on the perceived likelihood of victimization from lethal violence. Conversely and perversely, carrying firearms seems to enhance feelings of safety and personal efficacy among teenagers (LH Research 1993; Sheley and Wright 1995). The result is a developmental "ecology of violence," in which beliefs about guns and the dangers of everyday life may be internalized in early childhood and shape cognitive frameworks for interpreting events and actions during adolescence. In turn, this context of danger, built in part around a dominating cognitive schema of violence and firearms, creates, shapes, and highly values scripts skewed toward violence and underscores the central role of guns in achieving the instrumental goals of aggressive actions or defensive violence in specific social contexts. The processes of contagion, however, are little understood and are an important part of a future research agenda on this problem.

Section I of this essay begins with a review of the history and social epidemiology of adolescent gun carrying, use, victimization, and fatalities. Delinquency research prior to the 1960s rarely mentioned guns. However, an abrupt change occurred in the 1970s, overlapping with structural changes in communities and neighborhoods and recurring drug epidemics. These changes reshaped both social controls and street networks that in the past regulated violent transactions. We briefly review these historical dynamics, including current epidemiological studies on the correlates of gun possession and gun violence.

In Section II, we assess contemporary theories and explanations of gun violence, leading to a framework that integrates motivations and explanations for gun violence. We use an event-based approach to understand the dynamics of adolescent gun violence. This approach does not deny the importance of the individual attributes that bring people to situations but recognizes that, once there, other processes shape the outcomes of these events. Instead, we view gun violence as "situated transactions," including rules that develop within specific contexts, the situations and contexts where weapons are used, the motivations for carrying and using weapons, and the personality "sets" of groups in which weapons are used. There are "rules" that govern how disputes are settled, when and where firearms are used, and the significance of firearms within a broader adolescent culture. Because violence generally is a highly contextualized event (Luckenbill and Doyle 1989; Fagan 1993a, 1993b; Tedeschi and Felson 1994), we focus on how specific contexts and situations shape decisions by adolescents to carry or use weapons.

In Section III we present a dynamic framework that contextualizes adolescent violence within individuals, situations, and neighborhoods and discusses how the presence of weapons creates additional contingencies that shape the outcomes of disputes and other transactions. Gun violence among adolescents requires several levels of analysis: the sources of weapons, the nature of everyday life that gives rise to conflicts that turn lethal, the "scripts" of adolescent life that lead to escalation (and the factors that underlie those scripts), the motivations for carrying/using weapons, and the role of weapons in the decision processes of adolescents when they engage in disputes or even predatory violence. The presence of firearms is not an outcome of other processes, but part of a dynamic and interactive social process in which the anticipation or reality of firearms alters the decisions leading to violence and the outcomes of violent events.

In Section IV, we analyze data from recent research on violence among adolescents to illustrate three dimensions of this framework:

how normative rules and regulatory processes within networks and neighborhoods shape decisions to engage in violence and shape the course of violent events, the motivations and sources of arousal that lead to disputes where violence is used strategically or defensively, and situational contexts that introduce additional contingencies that influence the occurrence and outcomes of violent and "near-violent" encounters. Specifically, we examine the "ecology of danger" in which violence and gun events unfold in two inner-city neighborhoods. Second, we explore the establishment and maintenance of social and situational identities among adolescent males. We also analyze the role of drugs and alcohol on violent events. In each of these sections, we examine the influence of guns on these dynamics.

Section V concludes with an agenda for research on the role of firearms in adolescent violence that focuses on the role of firearms in the socialization of adolescents in neighborhood contexts of danger, including both the development of social identity and "scripts" that are employed in situations of conflict and threat. Research on cognition and decision making that focus specifically on the roles of guns in childhood and adolescence can inform the design of prevention efforts.

I. Historical and Current Dimensions of Adolescent Gun Violence

Gun violence has been a recurring theme in the literature on youth violence, dating back to the colonial era. In the modern era, studies of adolescent violence show that teenage males, whether in schools, gangs, or correctional institutions, report "self-defense" as the most important reason for carrying guns (LH Research 1993; Sheley and Wright 1995). As Wright and Rossi (1986) note, "self-defense" has a number of different meanings, including defense against other youth in an increasingly hostile and unsafe environment as well as self-defense from law enforcement officials during the course of illegal activity. Fear is a recurring theme in juvenile gun acquisition, and the escalating adolescent "weapons" race can be traced in the literature to the 1970s. While gun homicides among adolescents increased rapidly following the onset of the crack crisis in the mid-1980s, it is unclear whether these homicides can be traced to business violence in the drug trade or to other situational and ecological forces during that time. In part, the infusion of guns and their diffusion to teenagers may have had broad impacts on fear (Kennedy, Piehl, and Braga 1996), motivating gun acquisition as a form of self-defense.

But, as we show later, there also were effects of the drug trade on developmental trajectories of teenage men and women whose socialization occurred in the wake of the increase in homicides, and the dominating effect of drug economies on social relations and social control. While traditional themes of toughness and identity continued to shape adolescent development in inner cities, these processes were also skewed by the diffusion of guns into the hands of adolescents who reached their teenage years in communities that increasingly were socially and economically isolated. The ways in which guns altered the processes of achieving masculine identities, in economic contexts with attenuated routes to adult roles, coupled with the perception of fear and hostile intent among their peers, contributed to a significant shift in the rules of fighting and the processual dynamics among adolescents.

A. Sources of Knowledge

Most studies of the recurring problems of adolescent violence have not focused on the use of firearms or even distinguished events where firearms are present. Much of what we know about teenagers and guns comes from two sources: ethnographic research on youth gangs and "near groups" and the homicide literature. But even among studies of adolescent homicide, homicide events involving guns account for fewer than two in three homicides and often were not distinguished analytically from nonfirearm homicides. Until the 1980s, firearms often were casual mentions in the depiction of the contexts of adolescent violence. Because the focus of this review is the person-context interaction where guns are present, we begin by reviewing the situations where guns were present in the unfolding of events of adolescent violence.

Remarkably, there has been very little research on gun carrying or gun use among adolescents; the few studies focusing on adolescent gun violence are limited in several ways. First, most studies fail to distinguish guns from other more commonly carried weapons, especially cutting instruments. With few exceptions (e.g., LH Research 1993; Sheley and Wright 1995), most studies have been broad surveys that gauge how often adolescents bring weapons to school and how their outlooks have been affected by the weapons that surround them.

Second, most studies do not distinguish carrying from using weapons, regardless of type (see, e.g., the analysis by DuRant et al. [1994] of the Youth Risk Behavior Survey).

Third, most of these studies suffer from selection biases by excluding dropouts and institutionalized youths with higher rates of violence and weapons use (Fagan, Piper, and Moore [1986] estimates the extent of the bias). The few studies that include incarcerated adolescents use self-selected or otherwise nonsystematic samples (see Sheley and Wright 1995).

Fourth, the low base rates of violence in most studies have led to artifactual and confusing results. For example, many studies confound violence generally (including physical and sexual assault or robbery) with violence involving guns or other weapons. These studies equate adolescents who are violent without weapons with adolescents who carry or use firearms. Other studies confound adolescent violence (gun or nongun) with poor developmental outcomes such as drug use, school dropout, or adolescent pregnancy (Elliott, Huizinga, and Menard 1989). However, there is no evidence that firearms use by adolescents is part of a generalized pattern of adolescent violence or a maladaptive developmental outcome.

Fifth, despite the distinction among strategies for weapons carrying or use among adolescents, there are no developmental or criminological theories that can adequately distinguish gun from nongun violence among adolescents. Current theories of adolescent violence generally do not offer strong predictions of violent behavior.

Sixth, some research has examined the various situations and contexts in which adolescent gun violence may occur, including gang conflicts (Bjerregaard and Lizotte 1995; Hagedorn, in this volume), drug markets (Fagan and Chin 1990; Bourgois 1995), or interpersonal disputes (E. Anderson, in this volume). These studies attribute shootings to the dynamics and contingencies in those contexts without addressing the self-selection of people into those events. Some recent efforts have analyzed firearm "events" as a function of transactional-processual dynamics, the characteristics of the individuals involved, and the person-weapon contingencies that either escalate or defuse these events (Wilkinson and Fagan 1996a, 1996b; Fagan and Wilkinson 1997). These efforts specifically look at gun use as part of the situational dynamics of violent events.

B. Guns and Delinquency

Despite the small body of empirical research, gun violence nevertheless has been a recurrent factor in youth violence in several ways. Sante (1991), for example, describes the sometimes deadly and oftentimes comical struggles between the early street gangs of New York City to control territory and assert their authority. Although not involved in theft, robbery, or the "unsavory professions of gambling or tavernkeeping," these gangs warred regularly over territory with weapons including stones, hobnail boots (good for kicking), and early versions of the blackjack. Guns were rarely mentioned until the era following the Draft Riots of 1863, when gangs fought with every weapon then available, including pistols, muskets, and (rarely) cannons (Sante 1991, p. 201). As smaller and more portable guns were developed, they became an important part of the milieu of gangs and street groups over following decades. Portrayals of gang members in the 1940s through the 1970s included descriptions of both common and outrageous guns: Navy flare guns, zip guns, sawed-off shotguns, revolvers, and a few automatic weapons (see, e.g., Keiser 1969). These have become more common now as design changes make them even smaller, lighter, and more easily concealed. Then as today, guns played a strategic role in settling conflicts and asserting dominance in matters of honor, territory, and business (Strodtbeck and Short 1968).

Second, "toughness" has always been regarded as central to adolescent masculine identity and a source of considerable status among adolescents in a wide range of adolescent subcultures, from streetcorner groups to gangs (Whyte 1943). Physical prowess, emotional detachment, and the willingness to resort to violence to resolve interpersonal conflict are hallmarks of adolescent masculinity (Rodriguez 1993; Anderson 1994; Gibbs and Merighi 1994; Oliver 1994). Toughness requires young males to move beyond symbolic representation to physical violence. Guns often are used to perpetuate and refine the aesthetic of "toughness" and to claim the identity of being among the toughest. Owning a gun can be a symbol of masculinity and carrying a gun a source of identity (Gibbs and Merighi 1994, pp. 78–79).

Third, guns often transform robbery into a lethal event. Among adolescents, however, robberies often are unplanned or hastily planned events, the result of the instantaneous confluence of motivation and opportunity (see, e.g., Cook 1980). Guns provide a tactical advantage in robberies, even beyond the advantage first created by the selection of time and circumstances that undermine the victim's expectations of safety. While guns may often be present during robberies, their use in the course of a robbery reflects other contingencies, or what Zimring and Zuehl (1986) called "recreational violence." There are predictable stages for the robbery event, and when responses fail to meet the robber's expectations, threatened violence may become actual to gain compliance or to get the event back on its planned course (Feeney 1986; Katz 1988). Force, including firing guns, often is not gratuitous in robberies, unless a robbery becomes a stage for acting out "toughness" or meanness. In that case, the presence of a firearm opens the way for a robbery to become a homicide (Cook 1980).

But adolescents are impaired decision makers, and their bad decisions may short-circuit the pathway from robbery to homicide. Adolescence is a developmental stage when abstract reasoning about the consequences of using guns and cognitive capacities to read social cues are incomplete (Kagan 1989; Gibbs and Merighi 1994; Steinberg and Cauffman 1996). During the course of a robbery, the teenager armed with a gun becomes an unstable actor in a scenario whose outcomes are dependent on an unpredictable set of interactions between the robber and his victim. It is when the initial definition of the situation strays from robbery to a threat, personal slight, or conflict (in the wake of resistance) that seemingly irrational violence occurs. When guns are present, the violence often results in death.

Fourth, interpersonal disputes are fertile ground for violence, and guns have become a tactical choice in settling scores (Polk 1994; Canada 1995). While some disputes reflect inevitable clashes in social settings that concentrate the ingredients for interpersonal conflicts, others are precipitated as a means to display "toughness" and gain status or to achieve the sensual rewards of domination (Katz 1988). Disputes may be real, perceived, or imagined. They may involve women or girlfriends, drug deals gone bad, verbal aggression ("playing the dozens") that spins out of control, verbal attacks on masculinity, economic jealousy, and a variety of assaults on "respect" (Campbell 1986; Anderson 1994; Oliver 1994; Wilkinson and Fagan 1996a). Because "disrespect" is linked to the possibility of physical danger, it often engenders a defensive aggressive reaction both to ward off threats and to recoup lost social standing among witnesses. When guns are thought to be present, these defensive reactions become preemptive: using guns is a means to avoid losing in a dispute where loss may mean injury or death. Thus what many decry as the abandonment of "fair fight" rules in favor of guns reflects the convergence of normative beliefs about who is carrying weapons, assessments of how likely they are to use them (very likely, unfortunately), and given contemporary firepower, knowledge of the (deadly) consequences of being shot first.

C. Firearms and Adolescent Violence: Historical Perspectives

Many of the correlates of violence and homicide in the postmodern United States were also present a century ago: rapid urbanization, population mobility, ethnic tensions, abuse of intoxicants, class conflicts, and the spread of cheap handguns (Lane 1979, 1989). Yet Gurr (1981) notes that for much of the nineteenth century, homicide rates were declining. With the advent of concealable handguns around 1850, homicide rates increased slightly but not enough to offset a long downward trend that had begun early in the nineteenth century (Gurr 1981). The declines were part of a 150-year historical trend where violence reached its ebb as the twentieth century began, the result of urbanization and modernization that offered new economic opportunities to both immigrants and in-migrants to the cities from rural areas. Thus social arrangements had changed in this era in ways that fostered social controls.

Nevertheless, youth crime was considered both distinct and serious enough in this era to give rise to the creation of juvenile courts throughout the United States (Schlossman 1977). However, the crimes that motivated these reforms rarely involved violence or guns. Guns (both automatic weapons and handguns) played a prominent role in the growth of organized crime groups beginning in the 1920s. Organized crime groups employed teenagers and street gangs in a variety of support roles, from running numbers to serving as lookouts for illegal gambling operations or liquor distribution points (Haller 1989). Bootlegging and gambling provided a career ladder for teenagers. Of seventy-two "important" bootleggers identified by law enforcement authorities in the 1920s, most were young men in the later teenage years or early twenties (Haller 1989, p. 148). Guns were a prominent part of the security system used to protect liquor shipments, and Haller quotes documents from bootleggers and smugglers that claimed there was more danger from "rum pirates" than from other bootleggers or the police. However, despite the involvement of adolescents in street gangs and emerging organized crime groups, there is little evidence that this led to the use of guns by teenagers.

Even in this era, when youth gangs were increasingly a part of the urban landscape, there was little mention of gun use by adolescents in homicides or robberies. Analyses of homicides in the United States from 1900 to the early 1960s (Zahn 1980), as well as local studies such as Bourdouris's (1970) analysis of homicides in Detroit from 1926 to 1968, do not mention adolescents. These studies portray homicides as the product of quarrels between family members, lovers, or two males in disputes. Murders during robberies also were rare. None of these studies examined adolescent rates separately from adult rates. Either there were no noticeable differences between adolescents and adults or the base rates among adolescents were so small that they were not worth mentioning.

Nor were there were many mentions of guns in studies of delinquency from the Chicago School beginning in the 1920s. Beginning with Thrasher (1927) and continuing for nearly forty years, violence among youth gangs primarily involved fighting. Fighting was integral to the group identification of gangs and a central part of group interaction. Behavioral norms developed around fighting, and fighting had several meanings in gang life (Cohen 1955; Miller 1958; Cloward and Ohlin 1960; Yablonsky 1962). While both common and makeshift weapons were used strategically in gang fights, guns were not mentioned as part of the everyday life of gang members or other delinquent youths.

Guns often were carried for show, with little intention to use them. In "The Cherubs Are Rumbling," Walter Bernstein (1968) describes life in a gang of about thirty-five Italian-American teenagers in the Park Slope neighborhood of Brooklyn. Eddie was the only one in the Cherubs to have a gun. His "zip gun" cost him three dollars. But salesmen of second-hand weapons periodically visited Eddie's neighborhood offering guns at varying prices. A "revolver" (presumably a .38) in good condition cost about $10, but handguns could be bought for considerably less if they were imperfect (p. 36). Guns, however, were used more often for impression management—that is, to convey to others that someone with a gun "means business" and is a person to be taken seriously. In Bernstein's account, guns were carried by only a very few members of the Cherubs and almost never used. People carrying guns or even threatening to use them could be easily dissuaded from shooting if face-saving alternatives were presented (p. 37).

By the 1960s, mentions of guns in the delinquency literature were more common, but still relatively infrequent. Although guns were part of the background of streetcorner life, there were distinct situations where they were used and rules governing their use. They had a symbolic meaning in addition to their instrumental value and generally represented a threshold of commitment to "street life." Guns were rarely used by adolescents outside these contexts. Several studies of "streetcorner" life casually mentioned the presence of guns and their use in settling interpersonal disputes (Liebow 1967; Suttles 1968; Hannerz 1969; Anderson 1978). Keiser's (1969) portrait of the Vice Lords also showed that firearms were not central to gang life but were used selectively and strategically in conflicts with other gangs and in gang "business." Among both gangs and "near groups," guns were valued as defensive weapons but sometimes also for offensive purposes.

Gun use was confined to specific situations and contingencies. Strodtbeck and Short (1968) discussed an incident of gun use involving Duke, an important figure in the leadership clique of the Rattlers. Duke brandished a weapon to break up a fight among gang members and then shot three gang members when the incident unfolded in a way that challenged Duke's authority. Strodtbeck and Short characterized Duke's action as a complex decision reflecting elements of cognitive mediation of the risks and rewards of alternate outcomes, a function of a utility-risk paradigm where choices are contingent on in situ evaluations of the risks and rewards of actions given specific contingencies. These decisions involved a "two-person game" (p. 280), the actor against the environment, where alternative courses of action became narrower as the risks increased. What motivated Duke in this incident was the threat to his leadership status. Guns were a last resort option because of the risks of arrest, primarily, but the risks of not using the gun to his status in the Rattlers in the neighborhood were quite high.[1] The threat of retaliatory gun use was not evident in this incident. Duke never considered the possibility that the other Rattlers had guns or were willing to use them. In fact, the weapon was passed to Duke because of his leadership status, and "[o]nce it was in his hands, it seems likely that Duke's perception of the norms of the group, along with the exigencies of the violence he faced, strongly determined that he use the gun. In this sense, his actions arose 'in the line of duty,' as part of the leadership role" (p. 279).

The account of Duke's shooting of the three people captures several dimensions of the ecological dynamics of weapons use among adolescents in that era. Guns were a minor part of street scenes of delinquent

---

[1] There was cultural value to Duke's actions, as well, that enhanced his status. Duke did not carry the weapon. In that incident, it was passed to him. The expectation of using guns was fairly high for specific types of conflicts. Beyond gangs and near groups, the fear of guns and community support for their use reflected what Strodtbeck and Short described as the widespread fear of sudden violence and the inability of police to stop it (1968, pp. 283–84). Guns were status conferring and a valuable asset in a context where disputes were common, where they tended to be settled by violence, and where demonstrations of "toughness" were appropriate.

youths and usually the province of the "toughest" youths or the leadership of delinquent groups. They were more often shown than used; their use was reserved for specific people. Gun use was contingent and episodic, and gun episodes primarily were defensive or status conferring. Motivations for carrying and using guns often revolved around status concerns, and only after alternate outcomes had narrowed were guns actually fired. Although the neighborhoods where Duke and Eddie lived were commonly viewed as "dangerous" places, the likelihood of young people carrying or using guns was quite low. This relatively low prevalence of gun possession was a factor in the decisions about whether and how guns were used, and about their use in very narrow circumstances.

Ethnographic studies in the 1970s confirm the abrupt increase in adolescent violence and gun homicides shown by Cook and Laub (in this volume). This literature is dominated by studies on gangs, and little is known about gun violence outside this particular context (see, e.g., Sullivan's [1989] study). Even with this caveat, there is a startling change in the frequency of gun violence among teenagers, especially gang members, reported in the literature beginning in the 1970s. During this time, gun violence became an important theme in street life among teenagers. For example, Moore (1978) describes how behavior patterns were accelerated by each successive generation of *klikas* (Chicano gangs or sets): "White Fence violated a gang code when they first used guns; by the mid-1970s, guns were normal, and a fair fight (one person on one person without weapons) was fairly unusual, although it was the norm of an earlier period. In the mid-1970s, violations of gang codes included firing into a household where there was a mother present" (p. 40).

In another ethnography of barrio life, Vigil (1988) quotes a young Cholo who describes how the tradition of fighting had changed over the past twenty-five years and how guns had become commonplace features in barrio life: "We were riding around and this dude . . . just came up to us and asked where we were from and we said Cucamonga. He just pulled out a gun and started firing. He shot up . . . my car with a .38" (p. 133).

Many of these gun assaults involved intergang conflicts. Gun violence was both strategic and preemptive, but also retaliatory. Reacting to the shooting described above, another young male described this shooting to Vigil: "We got together to talk about how we were going to plan it. . . . We had a .22 automatic rifle with 18 shots and one

4-10 shotgun with only two shots. . . . As soon as we made a left, a white '64 Chevy started chasing us. I still don't know who exactly fired the gun from the truck, I just kept going faster and I think about eleven or twelve shots were fired at the '64 Chevy" (1988, p. 135).

In addition to violence toward other gangs, Vigil describes incidents where gun violence was used to redress grievances against businesses and resolve personal disputes over women or drugs. The wide range of motivations and contexts in which guns were used suggests the incorporation of guns into the foreground of decision making regarding violence within gangs. Recent studies by Wilkinson and Fagan (1996a) suggest that the influence of guns on motivation and decision making, as well as behavioral norms, is as important in nongang social networks as was identified in these important gang studies.

Cook and Laub (in this volume) point out that the increase in violence among adolescents since the 1960s is greater for males than for females. Homicide victimization data confirm that gun homicides by female adolescents have remained stable from 1984 to 1994 (unpublished analysis by the authors). However, empirical research on girls' involvement in gun violence is quite limited and generally limited to the gang literature. Beginning in the 1970s, violence was quite common among both male and female gang members. However, Vigil's data show that gun violence within gangs was almost exclusively a male activity. For many years, women in gangs remained on the sidelines for most fights and other criminal activities. Women were seen as auxiliaries to men, carrying weapons (including guns) and otherwise assisting boys. However, Campbell's (1984) study of girls in New York City gangs shows that guns were a common feature of female gang life.

Other portrayals suggested that girls in gangs had become in recent years similar to males in their involvement in violence and use of guns (see, e.g., Taylor 1993). Neither of these stereotypes, of course, is accurate. Gun violence by girls, whether in gangs or not, remains relatively infrequent and, as a share of all gun violence, is declining.

D. *Characteristics and Risk Factors for Adolescent Gun Possession and Homicide*

Several recent studies have estimated the prevalence of gun ownership, gun carrying, and gun use among adolescents. They provide a wide range of prevalence estimates of these three behaviors, consistent with the range of their sampling and measurement strategies. We focus below on three studies that offer detailed data on gun behaviors and show how guns have become a central feature of the context of adolescent life.

1. *The LH Survey.* LH Research (1993) conducted a survey of 2,508 adolescents in ninety-six randomly selected elementary, middle, and senior high schools. The survey was a simple random sample of classrooms in public, private, non-Catholic, and Catholic schools. The self-administered anonymous questionnaires included questions on gun ownership, carrying firearms, using guns, injury, and perceptions of safety. The sample was divided among central city schools (30 percent), suburban schools (46 percent), and schools in small towns or rural communities (24 percent). The sample was predominantly white (70 percent), with 16 percent African American students, 15 percent Latino students, and 4 percent Asian or Native American students. Most students (87 percent) attended public schools, with small samples from private non-Catholic schools (8 percent) and Catholic schools (5 percent). The results showed that handguns were a significant part of the students' everyday lives and immediate social contexts. About one in seven (15 percent) reported carrying a handgun in the preceding thirty days, and 4 percent reported taking a handgun to school during the preceding year. Nine percent of the students reported shooting a gun at someone else, while 11 percent had been shot at by someone else during the past year. Thirty-nine percent of the youth reported that they personally knew someone who had been either killed or injured from gun fire. Twenty-two percent reported that carrying a handgun would make them feel safer if they were going to be in a physical fight. Over 50 percent of youth (59 percent) could get a handgun if they so desired, often within twenty-four hours (40 percent).

The presence of guns also affected their emotional well-being, including fear and shortened life expectancies. For example, 42 percent said they worry about "being wiped out from guns" before reaching adulthood. Not surprisingly, those who worry most and those who carry guns often are the same individuals. Guns also affected the routine activities of both gun-carrying and gun-avoiding students: 40 percent reported behavioral changes to cope with violence, including decisions on where they go, where they stop on the street, night time activities, what neighborhoods they walk in, and their choice of friends.

There are several important limitations of the study, however, and in the end it fails to address the disproportionate rates of gun fatalities among African American youths. The school-based sample underrepresents African American young males who are at the highest risk of mortality from guns and have the highest concentration of risk factors. Dropouts, frequent absentees, and institutionalized youths also are excluded, a source of bias since these groups have higher rates of both violence and the risk factors for violence (Fagan, Piper, and Moore 1986). The analyses of gun possession and carrying by subgroups (area, gender, or ethnicity) were limited and selective, and the general population sample would likely yield cells too small for reliable comparisons when such controls are introduced. Nevertheless, the LH study suggests the pervasive influence of guns on the everyday decisions of young people in schools.

2. *The Sheley and Wright Survey.* Some of the limitations in the LH survey were addressed in research by Sheley, Wright, and Smith (1993) and reanalyzed in Sheley and Wright (1995). They interviewed 835 male inmates in juvenile correctional institutions in three states, complemented by surveys of 758 male high school students from ten inner-city public schools in the largest cities in each state. Both student and inmate samples were voluntary, and nonincarcerated dropouts were not included. Most (84 percent) of the inmate sample reported that they had been threatened with a gun or shot at, and 83 percent owned a gun prior to incarceration. Over one in three inmates (38 percent) reported shooting a gun at someone. Over half owned three or more guns, and the age of first acquisition was fourteen years old. The preferred type of gun among respondents was a "well-made handgun" of large caliber (the 9 mm was the most popular).

Both the inmate and student samples described in more detail the ecology of guns within the social organization of their neighborhoods. They claimed that firearms were widely available at low cost in their neighborhoods. Distribution was informal, with guns bought and sold through family, friends, and street sources. Among incarcerated young males, 45 percent reported that they "had bought, sold, or traded 'lots' of guns." Stealing guns and using surrogate buyers in gun shops were common sources for obtaining guns. Motivation for owning and carrying guns was reported to be more for self-protection than for status. The drug business was a critical context for gun possession: 89 percent of inmate drug dealers and 75 percent of student dealers had carried guns. So too was gang membership: 68 percent of inmates and 22 percent of students were affiliated with a gang or quasi-gang, and 72 percent of inmates were involved in the instrumental use of guns.

Although the Sheley, Wright, and Smith (1993) study focused on inner cities, the voluntary samples raise concerns regarding selection bias and other measurement error. The study sampled disproportionately from states and cities with concentrations of gang activity, perhaps overstating the importance of gangs as a context for gun use. Like the LH survey, this study did not focus on events where guns were used, only on individuals and their patterns of gun possession and gun use.

3. *The Rochester Youth Development Study.* Two studies from the Rochester Youth Development Study reported on gun possession among adolescents using a prospective longitudinal design. Samples were 987 students interviewed at six-month intervals for nine waves beginning when they were in grades seven and eight in the 1987–88 school year. Data also were collected from police, school, and other agency records, as well as parent or caretaker interviews. Lizotte et al. (1994) and Bjerregard and Lizotte (1995) report on data from waves 9 and 10, when respondents were aged fourteen or fifteen. However, data are reported only for boys since "girls rarely own guns, whether for sport or protection" (Bjerregard and Lizotte 1995, p. 43).

About 8 percent of the boys reported carrying a gun "regularly," and 4 percent reported using a gun in the past year (either wave 8 or wave 9). One in three respondents said that one of their peers "owned" a gun for protection, 10 percent said their parent(s) owned a gun for sport, and 6 percent said their parent(s) owned a gun for protection. Although gun ownership is illegal for juveniles, the motives for having a gun in the home can be attributed to the youth: children who report "owning a gun for sport" are extending their parents' ownership motives to themselves, and not unreasonably (Lizotte et al. 1994, p. 64). These motives turn out to be important: rates of gun crimes are nearly nine times higher for youths who "own" guns for protection, compared with sport gun owners. Rates of "street crimes" such as robbery are nearly four times higher for "protection" owners compared with sport owners, and five times higher compared with nongun owners. Crime rates for nongun owners are consistently lower than for "sport" gun owners, whose rates in turn are lower than "protection" gun owners. Extending this analysis to gang members, Bjerregard and Lizotte (1995) show that rates of "protection" gun ownership are far higher for gang members, but "sport ownership" is more common among nongang members.

Peers have a substantial impact on "protection" gun ownership among adolescents, especially among gang members, providing an example of the type of contagion model suggested by Wright and Rossi

(1986). Moreover, "protection" gun ownership often precedes gang involvement, suggesting processes of social or self-selection that anticipate higher rates of delinquency once in the gang (Thornberry et al. 1993). And, gangs appear to recruit those youths who already are involved in "protection" gun ownership. However, it is unclear whether this contagion is borne by fear or by simple peer pressure. Whatever the motive, the results suggest that guns spread quickly within specific social networks by age fifteen, contributing to the perception of danger in adolescents' social worlds.

4. *Other Adolescent Studies.*   Other studies have examined the prevalence of gun or weapon possession, but with little specificity. Inciardi, Horowitz, and Pottieger (1993) interviewed 611 youths in inner-city neighborhoods in Miami as part of a study of crack cocaine and "street crime." They report that 295 (48 percent) carried guns in the year preceding the interview. However, they do not report the percentage that used them or in what contexts (drug deals, robbery, or homicide). The National Youth Survey is generally silent on weapons (see, e.g., Elliott, Huizinga, and Menard 1989). Based on 1,203 student surveys and interviews with dropouts in three cities with high gang concentrations, Fagan (1990) reported that 42.5 percent of gang males and 17.6 percent of nongang males carried weapons. The findings made no distinction between guns and other weapons (e.g., knives).

Huff's research on fifty gang youths and matched samples of fifty "at risk" nongang youths in Cleveland (Ohio) show rates of gun "ownership" comparable to the Miami study. Among gang members, 40.4 percent reported carrying guns to school, compared with 10 percent of the "at risk" youths. Similar rates of participation in drive-by shootings were reported by gang members, compared with only 2 percent for the nongang youths. Collective gun carrying rates (among peers) were also far higher for gang youths (80.4 percent of peers carried guns in school) compared with nongang youths (34.7 percent).

5. *Gender, Firearms, and Youth Violence.*   The growing presence and influence of firearms has had minimal influences on female adolescents. Historically, female offenders have not used weapons, but girls may carry weapons for males (Moore 1978, 1991; Valentine 1978; Quicker 1983; Vigil 1988). Homicide data also show the rare involvement of both gang and nongang females in lethal violence (Maxson, Gordon, and Klein 1985; Sommers and Baskin 1992; Spergel 1995). Spergel (1995) reports that only one of 345 gang homicide offenders in Chicago between 1978 and 1981 was female; only six of 204 gang

homicide victims were female. Between 1988 and 1990, two of 286 gang homicide offenders were females; three of 233 gang homicide victims in this period were females. Spergel concludes that "the youth gang problem in its violent character is essentially a male problem" (p. 58). Uniform Crime Report data show that from 1976 to 1991, male homicide rates (involving both firearm and other weapons) among seventeen-year-olds were 11.5 times greater than female rates (Snyder and Sickmund 1995). Female adolescents accounted for a lower percentage of homicides in 1991 (6.0 percent) than in 1976 (12.1 percent); the decline reflected stable numbers of female homicide perpetrators compared with sharply rising numbers of male offenders (Blumstein 1995; Snyder and Sickmund 1995).

Survey data also indicate low rates of gun or other weapon use by teenage girls. The Youth Risk Behavior Survey (U.S. Department of Health and Human Services 1993) reported that 8 percent of female high school students carried a (nonspecified) weapon to school in 1990. When firearms are referred to specifically, the rates drop to about 1 percent (Sadowski, Cairns, and Earp 1989; Callahan and Rivera 1992). Sheley, Wright, and Smith (1993) report that 9 percent of the female respondents reporting having owned a revolver at some time in their lives, 5 percent had owned an automatic or semiautomatic weapon, and fewer than 5 percent owned other types of firearms. Fewer than 3 percent carried weapons to school, and 8 percent carried them outside the home.

Finally, context is extremely important in determining comparative rates of weapons offenses by gender. For example, in a survey of 1,200 high school students and school dropouts from central city neighborhoods in three cities with lengthy gang histories, Fagan (1990) found that female gang members had significantly higher participation and offending rates for weapons offenses, including firearms, compared with nongang males or females. The Sheley, Wright, and Smith (1993) survey also reported strong links between gun possession and drug and gang involvement in both female and male respondents. The importance of context for both males and females is discussed in greater detail later on in this essay.

II. Explanations of Adolescent Gun Violence

Explanations for the increase in adolescent gun violence have emphasized a wide range of factors, generally at the macro-social or aggregate levels of explanation (Short 1997). In this section, we review these explanations, criticizing them for their lack of specificity on gun violence. We offer, as an alternative, a framework for explaining adolescent gun violence that draws on recent research on the social processes of violent interactions. This social interactionist approach emphasizes the situational factors and dynamic processes within violent events. A situational framework depicts gun violence among adolescents as a situated, contextualized event that reflects the convergence of normative processes and expectancies, contingencies within the event itself, including the presence of guns, and decisions by actors that reflect simultaneously the codes that regulate street behavior and the functions or rewards of the specific event.

We offer a framework in which adolescent gun violence reflects the convergence of factors and processes within violent and "near violent" events. It does not deny the importance of the individual attributes that bring people to situations, such as "disputatiousness" (Luckenbill and Doyle 1989), but recognizes that once people are there other processes shape the outcomes of these events. Events are analyzed as "situated transactions," including rules that develop within specific sociocultural contexts, the situations and contexts where weapons are used, the motivations for carrying and using weapons, and the personality "sets" of groups where weapons are used. There are "rules" that govern how disputes are settled, when and where firearms are used or avoided, and the significance of firearms within a broader adolescent culture. Thus research must examine both the symbolic and instrumental meanings of firearms in the lives of young males.

Accordingly, gun "events" are analyzed as "situated transactions," including rules that develop within specific contexts, the situations and contexts where weapons are used, the motivations for carrying and using weapons, and the personality "sets" of groups in which weapons are used. There are "rules" that govern how disputes are settled, when and where firearms are used, and the significance of firearms within a broader adolescent culture. Violence "scripts," developed in a neighborhood context that values toughness and displays of violence, are invoked to achieve the goals of the event. Scripts also may limit the behavioral and strategic options for resolving disputes, and the presence of firearms may influence which scripts are invoked. Because violence generally is a highly contextualized event, specific contexts such as drug transactions shape decisions by adolescents to carry or use weapons, and which scripts are developed and shaped through diffusion within closed social groups.

A. *Current Explanations of Gun Homicides Rates*

No specific theories have been advanced to explain the sharp increase in adolescent gun violence in the past decade. Instead, theory and research have focused more generally on the increase in homicides and have centered on three domains: social structural factors and the concentration of poverty, the emergence of new street level drug markets that drew youths into drug selling and its attendant violence, and cultural developments that increase the salience of violence and justify its uses to achieve dominance and status. In addition, several epidemiological studies focus on the availability of guns as contributing to increased gun homicides, net of other factors. While each of these explanations contributes to our understanding of the epidemic of youth violence, they have limitations especially with regard to the role of firearms.

1. *Structural Explanations.* Structural explanations of homicide have generally ignored adolescents and rarely separate gun homicides from other types of homicide (see the review by Sampson and Lauritsen [1994]). For example, Land, McCall, and Cohen (1990) suggest that the correlates of homicide are stable across time and social areas but do not examine differences between adolescent and adult homicide rates or between gun and nongun homicides. Sampson (1987) cited the effects of family dissolution on social controls leading to violence generally, but not on homicide. These studies consistently point toward the concentration of poverty, or what Land et al. call *resource deprivation,* as ecological correlates of elevated homicide rates (see also Williams and Flewelling 1988). These correlates also are sources of social control within neighborhoods, including the presence of adults to supervise adolescents. The question whether weakening of social controls has contributed to elevated rates of adolescent homicides remains untested based on data for the past decade.

2. *Expanding Drug Markets.* Explanations focusing on the secondary effects of expanding drug markets rely on indirect measures and unfalsifiable assumptions but provide no direct evidence of a causal link between adolescent drug arrests and adolescent involvement in homicides (see, e.g., Blumstein 1995). One reason to doubt a direct causal link is that the precise relationship between drugs and guns is uncertain. Guns have been characterized as necessary tools of the drug trade to protect the money, protect dealers from assaults and robberies, to settle disputes over money or drugs, for instrumental displays of violence, to secure territory, and to preempt incursions (Goldstein et al.

1989; Fagan and Chin 1990; Sommers and Baskin 1993). However, the extent to which homicides by adolescents involve drug business remains unknown (see Hagedorn 1998, in this volume). Goldstein et al. (1989) showed that drug-related homicides remained a stable proportion of all homicides after the onset of the crack crisis in New York City, even as homicides increased. But that study did not report changes in the age distribution of homicides. Blumstein (1995) shows that the age distribution does reflect higher rates for adolescents in the early 1990s but fails to show a relationship of adolescent homicides to the drug business.

There is reason to consider the drug business a source of increasing adolescent homicide. Hamid (1994) suggests that young males may be more vulnerable to gun use and victimization in drug markets than are their older counterparts. They may lack experience or other skills to show the toughness necessary to survive. But homicides by and of young males continued to rise or remained stable even as drug markets began to contract after 1990 (Reiss and Roth 1993). Qualitative studies suggest that violence among adolescents in recent years seems to be unrelated or tangential to drugs, involving material goods or personal slights (Canada 1995; Wilkinson and Fagan 1996a; Anderson 1997). While the increase in homicides may have at one time reflected the expansion of drug markets, homicides in the late 1990s (nearly a decade after the emergence of crack markets) may reflect the residual effects of those markets. That is, guns that entered street networks during the expansion of drug markets remained part of the street ecology even as the drug economy subsided (Hamid 1994).

Drug markets are but one type of social context, and drug sellers are but one type of social network. Violence often is mediated by these contexts and networks, particularly with respect to drugs and alcohol (Fagan 1993a, 1993b). Several studies have controlled for social network and context in explaining situational factors that might motivate higher rates of homicide and gun carrying among adolescents. For example, both Sheley and Wright (1995) and the Rochester studies (Thornberry et al. 1993; Lizotte et al. 1994; Bjerregard and Lizotte 1995) focus on gangs as a context where gun possession and violence rates are high. However, neither of these studies focuses closely on adolescent gun use.

3. *Normative Social Processes.*   Sociocultural explanations of youth violence have appeared regularly in the delinquency literature for several decades. Several focused on gang life. Cohen's (1955) study of

gang boys showed the status value of toughness and fighting within gangs. Subcultural theories also were evident in studies such as Miller (1958) and Yablonsky (1962). More recently, Anderson (1994, 1997, in this volume) suggested a set of mediating constructs that provide a dynamic framework that views violence as a regulatory process designed to reinforce behavioral codes regarding identity and self-help (also see Black 1983, 1993). While previous cultural explanations focused on beliefs regarding violence, Anderson's framework suggests a more general code of social identity and normative behaviors that establish rules of conduct and "respect." Violations of these rules mandate several reactions, including a violent response. While not focused on guns or homicide, it provides an explanatory framework for violence as self-defense and functional violence designed to establish and maintain identity. We revisit these ideas below as a potentially important means of explaining gun violence.

4. *Specificity of Explanations of Gun Violence.* None of these explanations adequately addresses gun violence among adolescents. First, few studies have focused on gun violence among adolescents and, instead, include a wide range of violent or antisocial behaviors. Second, although gun carrying and gun ownership rates are high, gun violence remains a rare event and prediction and explanation of low base rate behaviors is difficult. Third, a corollary problem is the focus on characteristics of violent individuals generally, rather than on distinguishing individuals who carry, own, or use weapons compared with other forms of violence. With the exception of the Rochester studies, we know little about whether adolescents involved in gun violence differ from those committing other types of violence. Moreover, we do not know whether their involvement in gun violence is attributable to individual differences versus circumstantial or contextual factors.

Another set of concerns relates to explanations that differentiate gun carrying from gun use. Gun carrying and possession rates far exceed gun use rates. The fourth limitation then, is that we do not account for decisions to engage in gun violence. Fifth, and relative to this, we do not know if carrying guns influences either motivations or restraints on gun violence. That is, current theories, focused on individual propensities, do not account for the influence of violence *means* on arousal (motivations) or control (restraint). The absence of *agency* and decision making from explanations of gun violence reflects the deterministic nature of many theories that are focused on individual characteristics. Prior work on homicides as situated transactions (Luckenbill 1977;

Polk 1994) examines processual dynamics, but not the contingencies and evaluations that contribute to decisions to use guns. Nor are these studies focused on adolescents. In fact, few explanations of violence generally examine decision-making processes (but see Felson and Tedeschi [1995], whose notion of goal-oriented violence begins to build a contingent, decision-based framework).

Finally, current explanations do not account for individual differences across time and place, as well as the spatial concentration of gun use in specific social and physical locales. In other words, explanations of gun violence need to account for contextual influences, or person-place interactions. "Place," in this context, is a vector with several dimensions: behavioral norms that are attached to specific situations, such as displays of weapons or aggressive words; the aggressive features of a locale, such as the density of guns or drug-dealing activity; the composition and responses of the people present; and the social control attributes of the place, including both formal and informal controls. The interaction of these factors produces an ecological or situational dynamic that is likely to influence individual choices and behavior, including either defensive or offensive actions, as well as strategic decisions based on access to guns or other weapons.

B. An Explanatory Framework for Adolescent Gun Violence

Violence research has increasingly adopted a situational or transactional approach to explain violent transactions, including the use of firearms (Cook 1976, 1980, 1983; Luckenbill 1977; Felson and Steadman 1983; Katz 1988; Luckenbill and Doyle 1989; Cornish 1993*a*, 1993*b*, 1994; Felson 1993; Sommers and Baskin 1993; Oliver 1994). Situational approaches view violent events as interactions involving the confluence of motivations, perceptions, technology (in this case, weapons), the social control attributes of the immediate setting, and the ascribed meaning and status attached to the violent act. One advantage of this view is that it addresses both the motivations that bring individuals to situations where firearms are used and also the transactions and decisions that comprise the event. Individuals may employ "scripts" as part of a strategy of "impression management" to gain status and dominance in potentially violent transactions (Cornish 1994). These perspectives make possible explanations that sort out the proximal effects of the presence of firearms and other situational elements from the distal influences of social psychological factors.[2] Situational approaches are dynamic "theories of action" (Cornish 1993a, 1994) that take into account both motivations and decision making within events.

This seems to be an especially important perspective for understanding the dynamics of adolescent weapon use. Explanations of firearms use among adolescents require several levels of analysis: the motivations for carrying/using weapons, the nature of everyday life that gives rise to conflicts that turn lethal, the "scripts" of adolescent life that lead to escalation (and the factors that underlie those scripts), and the role of weapons in the decision-making processes of adolescents when they engage in disputes or even predatory violence. The presence of firearms is not an outcome of other processes, but part of a dynamic and interactive social process in which the anticipation or reality of firearms alters the decisions leading to violence and the outcomes of violent events.

However, few studies have examined the specific role of firearms in violent events.[3] The LH Research (1993) survey suggests that the number of events in which guns are used is a small fraction of the number of events in which guns are present. Although several studies attribute violence to the dynamics and contingencies in contexts such as gang conflicts, drug markets, domestic disputes, or robberies (Cook 1976; Fagan 1993), few have addressed the dynamics or antecedents of firearm use in inner cities among adolescents or young males, especially the mechanisms that escalate gun possession to gun use. That is, research on adolescent firearm use has not yet analyzed the interactions of the characteristics of the individuals involved, the interpersonal transactions and interactions between the parties, or how the presence of guns affects the outcomes of these interactions. And no studies have focused on specific social or neighborhood contexts that also shape the outcomes of putative violent events. Such an approach seems necessary to explain the increase in firearm fatalities among

---

[2] Proximal effects are those that are situated close to the event itself, in a temporal sequence of causal factors. Distal effects, conversely, are those that occur at a greater temporal distance from the observed event.

[3] These studies often confound firearms with other weapons, and confound weapons use generally with other forms of violence (see, e.g., Elliott, Huizinga, and Menard 1989). Moreover, the low base rates of violence in these studies limits efforts to explain the use of firearms or other weapons. Violence in these studies is more often concentrated in inner cities, leading to a potential confounding of individual characteristics with social area effects (Sampson and Wilson 1995).

young African Americans and to locate the problem in the specific contexts in which these events occur.

Violence researchers have come to understand dispute-related violent events as a process of social interactions with identifiable rules and contingencies. Numerous studies have applied this framework with respect to violence focusing on the interactional dynamics of situated transactions (Luckenbill 1977; Felson 1982; Felson and Steadman 1983; Campbell 1986; Luckenbill and Doyle 1989; Oliver 1994). The processual nature of violent interpersonal transactions is both rule-oriented and normative (Cornish 1993*b*). It is through these processes and contingencies that individual characteristics such as "disputatiousness" are channeled into violent events. Violent behavior can be viewed as a method of communicating social meanings within contexts where such action is either expected or at least tolerated.

The presence of firearms presents a unique contingency that shapes decision-making patterns of individuals. The presence of firearms influences decisions both in social interactions with the potential for becoming disputes and also within disputes that have already begun (see Wilkinson and Fagan 1996*a*). The influence on decision making is compounded by the social contexts where firearm injuries are concentrated: inner-city neighborhoods characterized by extensive "resource deprivation" (Land, McCall, and Cohen 1990; Sampson and Wilson 1995). We specify two socialization processes that have converged in these areas to create a unique influence of firearms: the emergence of a "street code" that shapes perceptions of grievances and norms on their resolution (see, e.g., Anderson 1994, 1997); and an "ecology of danger" where social interactions are perceived as threatening or lethal, and where individuals are normatively seen as harboring hostile intent and the willingness to inflict harm. The latter is the outcome of three successive generations in inner cities who grew up in epochs of high rates of homicide and firearm injuries. These concepts form the dimensions of an analytic framework that is specific to adolescent gun violence.

1. *Arousal and Aggression.* First, an explanatory framework must account for the factors that channel arousal into aggression and violence. There are many sources of arousal in everyday inner-city life, including a wide range of annoyances, complications in institutional and domestic arrangements, noxious settings, and interpersonal conflicts (Anderson 1990; Canada 1995). But not all of them translate into anger

and aggression. Understanding gun violence requires that we can discern the processes that transform interpersonal conflicts into lethal aggression. One part of this process is the attachment of meaning to words, actions, and threats, and the processing of that information as threatening or malevolent (Dodge and Coie 1987; Coie and Dodge 1997).

2. *Decision Making.*   Second, gun violence involves a series of decisions, and an explanatory framework must include a decision-making framework. Decisions to carry guns, to bring oneself to a setting where guns are likely to be present, to pursue a dispute that may turn deadly, to show a gun or make a threat with it, and ultimately to use the gun or to avoid its use, are decisions that reflect the outcomes of arousal and anger, as well as strategic decision making. Consistent with the rational choice perspective, Felson and Tedeschi (1995) argue that a violent action involves a sequence of decisions and that an actor evaluates alternatives before carrying out a violent action. Four elements of decisions were outlined: the value of the outcome, the expectations of success in reaching goals, the value of the costs, and the expectations of the costs. Costs and third parties can be inhibitors of violence. The actor makes a choice to engage in violent behavior because it seems to be the best alternative available in the situation. But adolescents are poor decision makers, with limited capacity to weigh consequences (Steinberg and Cauffman 1996). They also may lack the cognitive capital to understand the range of potential consequences or to fashion strategies that may exempt them from gun violence.

3. *Social Identity and Other Functions of Violence.*   Third, the decision to engage in gun violence suggests that it serves specific social or psychological functions. Both Katz (1988) and Felson (1993) identified three main goals of aggressive actions: to compel and deter others, to achieve a favorable social identity, and to obtain justice. These functions, which provide the motivational component for violence, can be understood in the context of adolescent development (Fagan and Wilkinson 1997). Prior research helps us to understand the range of possible functions served by adolescent violence: social control (Black 1983), identity and reputation (Goffman 1983), material acquisition (Katz 1988), and domination and conquest (Katz 1988; Polk 1994). An explanatory framework for adolescent gun violence should include a recognition of gun violence as a strategic means, indeed a sure bet, to achieve these goals.

The development of identity is a central and perhaps overarching function of violence. Goffman (1959) claims that people give staged performances to different social audiences. Individual behavior is "scripted" to the extent that scripts are used to convey the kind of impression (or situational identity) an actor wanted others to perceive. He argues that different audiences may have different preconceptions of the actor and the actor may have varying degrees of experience projecting alternate impressions in new situations. The importance of status and reputation (impression *given off*) in this social context influences the scripts an individual may choose when confronted with a dispute on the streets. One could argue that based on whatever limited knowledge is available at the start of the event, an individual will choose a script which casts him or her in the best light.

Identity in turn serves critical functions: attaining social status and accruing "props" or respect, and warding off attacks from others seeking to improve their "reps" by conquering someone with a higher status. In a neighborhood with limited means to conventional success and an imbalance of deviant social roles, the formation of violent "identities" is enhanced by the various uses of guns: show, threat, and use.

4. *Processual Dynamics of Violent Events.*   Fourth, social interactionist perspectives on violence suggest a focus on describing factors that produce conflict and those that inhibit it. This approach focuses on three central issues for understanding violence: the escalation of disputes, the role of social identities, and the role of third parties. Felson describes the stages of violent incidents, as do Luckenbill and Doyle (1989), calling the sequence of events a social control process. Violence is a function of events that occur during the incident and therefore is not predetermined by the initial goals of the actors (Felson and Steadman 1983).

Luckenbill and Doyle (1989) argue that dispute-related violence is the product of three successive events: "naming," "claiming," and "aggressing." At the naming stage, the first actor identifies a negative outcome as an injury which the second actor has caused (assigning blame). At the claiming stage, the injured party expresses his grievance and demands reparation from the adversary. The final stage determines whether the interaction is transformed into a dispute. The third event is the rejection of a claim (in whole or in part) by the harmdoer. According to Luckenbill and Doyle, "disputatiousness" is defined as the likelihood of naming and claiming, and aggressiveness is defined as the willingness to preserve and use force to settle the dispute. They claim that violence is triggered by norms of the code of personal honor and that differential disputatiousness and aggressiveness would depend on the situation. This conceptualization closely resembles Goffman's "Character Contest" used by Luckenbill (1977) to examine violent transactions resulting in homicide.

This approach is concerned with the actor's point of view. It suggests a complex, contingent pathway from distal factors such as gaining access to guns, to the proximal factors that determine whether they are used. Within events, a series of decisions and contingencies mediates the outcomes of events. Violence in this setting is an interaction in which decisions and actions at one stage are contingent on what happened before and judgments about what is likely to happen next. Considerations of whether an opponent is armed, whether retaliation is likely, if there are police or other social control actors nearby, how bystanders will react, are all made in a compressed time frame and are interdependent. These interactions and transactions suggest a series of decisions, albeit decisions that may be rational but also constrained by circumstances, cognition, and available information.

Accordingly, an explanatory framework requires an understanding of the processual and contingent nature of these decisions, and the interaction of two or more actors to produce gun violence. The increased availability of guns, especially among adolescents, who are incomplete decision makers and potentially high risk takers, changes these processes in important ways that are not now fully understood. The stages of violent events may be altered by the presence, expectancies, and lethality of firearms in specific social contexts.

5. *Violence Scripts.* Fifth, contingent decision making by adolescents is not ad hoc for each event but reflects cumulative knowledge gained through participation in and observation of violent interactions. This involves socialization processes that begin prior to adolescence and are refined along the way through interaction and practice. They develop into "scripts" and provide a bounded set of choices to be invoked in situations in which conflict or aggression may bring guns into play. The script framework provides a useful way to understand the decision-making process, including calculation of risks, strategic decisions, and assessments of available choices.

Research on child and adolescent violence suggests several ways in which script theory can explain violent events: scripts are ways of organizing knowledge and behavioral choices (Abelson 1976); individuals learn behavioral repertoires for different situations (Schank and Abelson 1977; Abelson 1981; Huesmann 1988; Tedeschi and Felson 1994); these repertoires are stored in memory as scripts and are elicited when cues are sensed in the environment (Abelson 1981; Huesmann 1988; Dodge and Crick 1990; Tedeschi and Felson 1994); choice of scripts varies between individuals and some individuals will have limited choices (see Dodge and Crick 1990); individuals are more likely to repeat scripted behaviors when the previous experience was considered successful (Schank and Abelson 1977; Tedeschi and Felson 1994); and scripted behavior may become "automatic" without much thought or weighing of consequences (Abelson 1981; Tedeschi and Felson 1994).

The application of script theory to adolescent gun events as "situated transactions" may provide a level of understanding for a complex process that is not well understood. Adolescents are likely to look to the streets for lessons on the rules of gun fighting, learn from experience in conflict situations, and practice moves they have observed others performing in handling disputes on the street (Anderson 1994; Canada 1995). The processes of learning and diffusion of this sort of gun "knowledge" remain unstudied and unknown. But adolescents in conditions of economic deprivation may not develop as complete decision makers. There may be a number of social interactional, developmental, contextual, cultural, and socioeconomic factors which impinge on the decision-making processes of young males in violent conflicts.

6. *Street Codes, Expectancies, and Normative Behaviors.* Finally, the development of scripts, the processes of decision making, and the social definitions of conflict and other functions served by violence form in specific social contexts. These contexts shape normative definitions, imperatives or expected behaviors, costs and rewards of violence. Firearm violence represents an extreme of a continuum of violence in the dynamics of inner-city youths. Yet only a few studies have examined the current social worlds of young inner-city males in depth (see Sullivan 1989; Anderson 1990, 1994; Canada 1995; Wilkinson and Fagan 1996*a*, 1996*b*). Anderson's study of inner-city Philadelphia is perhaps the most detailed description of violence and inner-city life (Anderson 1994, 1997). According to Anderson the causes of inner-city violence are both social structurally and situationally determined: "The inclination to violence springs from the circumstances of life among the ghetto poor—the lack of jobs that pay a living wage, the stigma of race,

the fallout from rampant drug use and drug trafficking, and the resulting alienation and lack of hope for the future (1994, p. 81).

He proposes that there are two types of normative systems operating within the inner-city context: the "decent" (locked into middle-class values) families and the "street" (opposed to mainstream society) families. He argues that while the majority of inner-city residents are of the "decent" orientation, the street orientation has come to govern the normative system regarding human behavior in public spaces, especially among the young. Thus community norms on the street are regulated and enforced by the smaller minority who possess the street orientation.

Competition over limited resources, including social status, respect, and material goods, by physically aggressive and violent means is a central part of this system. Young children who spend time playing outside in the neighborhood are exposed to all types of interpersonal conflict, displays of physical domination, social approval for violent behavior, and limited definitions of respect. These messages are reinforced at home by adults and in school by peers. Anderson argues that children learn to fight through their play with others in the street. The code of the street largely determines the structural and procedural "scripts" children acquire for handling interpersonal conflicts and identity formation. Children who are of street orientation will invariably learn scripts that accord with the street code while "decent" youths may learn alternative scripts in addition to those in line with the code of the streets.

In this context, Anderson describes the necessity for adolescents, whether "decent" or "street," to understand and play out appropriate roles to accord with the code of the street while traveling through and interacting with others in public. Acquiring fighting skills is considered important as a means of survival in the inner city (also see Sullivan 1989, p. 113). The process of self-preservation through displays of toughness, nerve, or violent behavior is considered a necessary part of day-to-day life for inner-city adolescents, especially young males (also see Canada 1995).

Social identity and respect are the most important features of the street code. Within this context there are clear-cut rules for using violence to gain respect. The public nature of a person's image or status identity oftentimes requires open displays of "nerve," including attacks on others, getting revenge for previous situations with an opponent, protecting members of one's social group, and having the right "props." There is only a limited amount of respect available, and the process of acquiring respect is highly competitive. Projecting the right image is everything in this context, and backing up the projection with violent behavior is expected.

According to Anderson, the street code provides rules for how individuals are to communicate with one another, how respect is to be earned, how and when respect is to be granted to another, and what should happen when someone disrespects or "disses" you. Violence and other types of domination are tools in promoting one's self-image; in other words, conquering others is one way to achieve higher levels of status. Developmentally as children begin to approach adolescence there is strong need for social approval and status. These needs may be even stronger in an inner-city context where fewer opportunities for receiving positive status are available to young adolescents.

The street code is a determining factor for proving one's manhood and knowing how to act accordingly when confronted with a variety of challenging situations. Anderson notes that the stakes are very high in this context because manhood is dependent upon being fearless and untouchable. He argues that decent youth can situationally act tough and macho but also maintain a more mainstream identity in other settings by being courteous and respectful when appropriate (Anderson 1994, p. 92). The street code has a functional purpose for the decent youth, while it is a defining characteristic of the street-oriented youth. The street-oriented youth is most likely blocked from other types of behavior. Again, the street code is useful for understanding the processes by which individuals internalize violent scripts. Anderson offers two ideal types of normative orientations of inner-city youths, hinting at a model for understanding the variations that exist within inner-city culture.

Anderson is mostly silent on the issue of lethal violence by firearms and the code of the streets. He states that possessing a willingness to "pull the trigger" is an important part of an individual's quest for respect; however, he does not analyze the implications of gun use on the code of the streets. The ready availability of guns in the inner city has undoubtedly raised the stakes of the code of the streets even higher. It seems that "nerve," "toughness," and being a "punk" would take on new meanings within a climate regulated by lethally armed actors. The increased availability of guns in our inner cities has been documented beginning in the late eighties. Sullivan (1989) reported that there were more guns on the streets and that they were more frequently in the hands of younger offenders. Current research on gun violence presented below sheds new light on some of these important issues.

III. Dynamics of Adolescent Gun Violence: Examples from Three Domains

In this section, we use this framework to identify how the presence of guns among adolescents creates unique contingencies that shape the course of violent events, decisions within them, and their outcomes. We illustrate the social processes of gun violence among adolescent males in three areas: the development of norms and expectations for the use of lethal or gun violence, the role of guns in the development of "violent identities" and how this identity contributes to gun violence, and the impact of violent identities and guns on events involving drugs and alcohol. These illustrations come from analyses of data on violent events involving male adolescents in two inner-city neighborhoods in New York City (see Fagan and Wilkinson 1995; Wilkinson and Fagan 1996a; Wilkinson 1997a, 1997b). Interviews were conducted with 125 young men aged sixteen to twenty-four from the East New York and Mott Haven neighborhoods, areas with high concentrations of injury violence and homicide since 1990. Respondents were asked to provide background information on themselves, their family, their school, and their neighborhood in a narrative interview protocol. Respondents were then asked to reconstruct up to four events involving violent or near violent situations, including events where guns were present or absent. Interviews were tape recorded and transcribed, and text analysis programs were used to identify recurring themes and domains (for details about the methods, see Wilkinson, McClain, and Fagan [1996]; Wilkinson [1997b]).

A. Normative Processes: Gun Violence and an Ecology of Danger

First, we examine normative social processes that influence cultural norms, the effects of omnipresent guns on these norms, and expectancies about one's own and others' behaviors. As illustrated by Anderson (1994, 1997), street codes have evolved in socially and economically isolated areas. These codes establish what is important in social relations among teenagers, and the methods for redressing grievances and disputes arising from violations of the code. The street code determines not only what is important but also appropriate means for resolving grievances and disputes. It also places values on "toughness" and violent identities. In an ecology of "danger," where actors presume that guns are present, conflicts and disputes arising from street codes may be potentially deadly. These beliefs have shaped the methods for resolving conflicts and have been conflated with the means for self-preservation and maintaining identity.

1. *Dangerousness and Need for Guns.* Young men often characterized their neighborhood as a "war zone." The street is described as dangerous and unpredictable. Violence is expected and can erupt out of a variety of situations. Public behavior on the streets is regulated by a general knowledge that life could be taken away at any moment (by guns, primarily).

Interviewer (DT):[4] "How would you describe your neighborhood in terms of safety? Is it safe compared to other New York areas?"

Respondent (ENYN13): "It depends. Safe how? Your mother try to make it safe for you or does the community?"

(DT): "Generally."

(ENYN13): "Nope. Anything could happen. That's what—that's the thing that really gets people. Like, you come outside, you don't know if you comin back in. You know, that could be your last day walkin' or somethin', so I really can't say it's too safe, you know. It depends you—if you goin' to school, you in school, that when they try keep you safe there. But, once you outside . . ."

An almost daily exposure to injurious or lethal violence has had lasting effects on the young men in these areas. This stark reality shapes attitudes, perceptions, behavior, and social identity. One respondent had this to say about his South Bronx neighborhood:

Interviewer (JM): "Tell me a little bit about that. How was it up there? Your experiences up there [referring to a block in the neighborhood]?"

Respondent (SBN18): "Very rough. People stabbing you, shooting at you. You can't trust nobody there. You get cut and stuff like that. People always bothering you, you know. They don't fight one on one, just straight up jump you. There is all drugs. People making money on the drugs. Lot of fights. Sometimes, no heat, you gotta watch your back. It is not a safe place to be."

(JM): "Was it rough for you, you couldn't handle it?"

(SBN18): "It was rough, I could handle it."

---

[4] The initials in parentheses designate which interviewer conducted the interview. Code numbers were assigned to respondents to protect personal identities.

(JM): "What was hardest for you?"

(SBN18): "Everything."

Interviewer (JM): "How would you describe your neighborhood in terms of safety? You know what's safe out there to be out there?"

Respondent (SBN26): "Safe? If you ain't in your house, you ain't safe. And even when you in your house you know, something could happen."

(JM): "Like what?"

(SBN26): "Like you be you could be in the living room watching T.V. and next thing you know, 'bow' 'bow,' gunshots through the windows. They might not be for you, but, you know. Bullets, bullets have no, you know, no names."

Guns play a big part in feelings of personal safety within this context. Another subject explained why he felt young males in his neighborhood had guns:

Interviewer (DT): "So who's carrying the guns out there? Like what age?"

Respondent (G-67): "You got you got you got everybody carrying guns. You got the girls carrying guns, you got the shortys (young teens)."

(DT): "You don't know what reason they carrying guns?"

(G-67): "They just want to be down with everybody else you know. And the one thing is another thing is a lot a people dropping in the hood you know."

(DT): "Yeah."

(G-67): "People dropping, so everybody walking around they ain't safe, they don't trust nobody you know that's why they got another reason for for a lot a homicides. The reason about trust you know trust, don't nobody trust nobody. Everybody growing up, everybody trying to get that money, everybody try to knock each off. So everybody say just ah fuck it . . . , everybody just grab the ghat (gun), you know, just be walking around. So it just be a jungle out there."

2. *Guns Dominate Social Interactions.* Gun carrying in this group varied from daily carrying to carrying only when there was an ongoing "beef" or conflict with others. When a respondent knew he had a "beef" with someone, he tried to be prepared for the moment when this beef would heat up into gun violence. It was understood that using a gun to harm his opponent was the best way to handle the situation both in terms of what was expected on the street and what an individual had to do to maintain a "positive" (respected) identity. Most often,

respondents reported having a gun close by in case it would be needed during a spontaneous conflict or retaliatory situation. They described many instances where they had time to prepare for a potential attack by going inside their building to get their guns or by sending others to get them. Individuals actively involved in drug selling, for example, either carried a firearm or stashed it in the drug spot in case of possible robbery or territorial attack.

The ready availability of guns in the inner city has undoubtedly shaped and skewed street codes toward the expectation of lethal violence. It also sets the value of violent behaviors in the social currency of the neighborhood and, as in the past (e.g., Cohen 1955), is the principal source of social status. "Nerve," "toughness," and being a "punk" take on new meanings within a climate regulated by lethally armed actors. Openly displaying a "willingness" to take the life of another when the situation "calls for it" is part of this process.

The prevalence of guns, coupled with the rapid social diffusion of episodes of gun violence, helps shape these perceptions of danger. Respondents report that "most" young males (i.e., fourteen to thirty years old) can and do have guns in these inner-city neighborhoods. Guns are available on the street to just about anyone who has the means to purchase, share, borrow, or steal them. Even people with less powerful identities can get access to firearms through associates, family members, or local drug dealers.

Respondents reported that their own experiences with the world of guns began as early as eight and as late as sixteen and were central to their socialization. Having a powerful gun was and is valued both for intrinsic and extrinsic reasons. Guns may fulfill a variety of personal needs for adolescents, including power, status, protection, and recreation. These processes begin at a young age, often before adolescence, as boys are being socialized into gun use on the street. These younger gun users were described as ruthless, heartless, unpredictable actors who were attempting to make impressions on older, more powerful characters on the street.

The presence of guns also has shaped the rules of fighting among teenagers. Fair fights have been described repeatedly in tales of inner-city street corner life (see, e.g., Cohen 1955; Cloward and Ohlin 1960; Anderson 1978, 1990; Moore 1978). "Fair ones" are defined as physical fights involving two parties of nearly equivalent size and strength who would fight each other one-on-one using their fists (with no weapons or additional guys). Fair ones, according to our sample, are not now the dominant type of violent events for young men aged sixteen to twenty-four. Examples of fair fights here included altercations between friends or associates over seemingly trivial disputes, fights with family members, fights by younger boys (six to eleven years old) and sometimes older men (thirty-five years and up), fights inside jail or prison, and fights on the block by people who are known to each other.

However, most respondents explained that "fair ones" no longer dominate conflict resolution in the inner-city neighborhood street life, especially in face-offs with strangers, whose willingness to abide by time-honored values is unproven. Many situations that start out as fair fights typically involve some type of "gun play" as the "beef" escalates over time. Thus the potential for an attack to involve guns is nearly certain for the young men in our sample. Guns raise the stakes in a variety of ways, and in many instances, firearms trump all other logic.

3. *Guns Change Decisions within Violent Events.* Guns have symbolic as well as strategic meaning. Gibbs and Merighi (1994) suggest that guns are symbols of both masculinity and identity. Respondents in this study say that showing a gun (threatening someone) is a disrespect, a violation of one's social and physical space. Guns also change the calculus of a dispute, raising the stakes both in terms of status and strategy. Once a gun is introduced into a conflict situation, it is perceived as a life-or-death situation. Following this type of disrespect, the opponent is expected to retaliate by getting a gun and shooting the other person. In a gun face-off situation, the main strategic move reported was to take the first shot in anticipation of the opponent using his weapon first if given the opportunity.

Some respondents reported about gun events from both sides of an attack (events where they initiated an attack and events where others initiated attacks against them). From these descriptions we are able to piece together some of the contingencies which affect an actor's decision-making process when faced with a gun threat.

a. *Intensity of the Threat (Level of Arousal).* Pulling a gun automatically increases the intensity of the conflict and limits the number of choices available to all parties. Certain actions or words warrant a violent response; if guns are available, guns are used in reply to a transgression. Actors within this context know when and where pulling out and using a gun is socially acceptable. Those who do not follow the code are either eliminated or extremely stigmatized. If either actor displays a gun in a conflict situation, the event is described as going to the next level (the gun level).

b. Prior Relationship with/Knowledge of Opponent. Prior knowledge and situational impressions of the opponent are important for shaping decisions about future action. Actors use this information. Gun threats by individuals with "large identities" are taken very seriously. Idle threats are not welcome and may result in serious violence. The idea of "fronting" or faking a threat is a big mistake. Therefore, in the neighborhood individuals who have and are carrying guns must be willing to use them if the situation calls for it.

c. Perception of Risk and Cost. Guns play an important part in actors' decisions about the risk and cost of violent actions. One of the first and most important decisions is the extent to which one's identity would be improved or damaged by engaging or avoiding gun violence. The actor's original social identity factors heavily into how the stages of a gun event would unfold. Some respondents have more to gain or lose than others. Most "lost" or unsuccessful gun events are considered damaging to the image and reputation of the loser, especially if that response involves retreat. A "successful" gun event is described as identity-enhancing. Inflicting harm on others or gaining total compliance over others are valued outcomes which are publicly reinforced through verbal and nonverbal displays of respect commonly referred to as "props."

Retreat could also have positive ramifications for social identity if used strategically. In some situations, retreat is used as a strategic technique when a respondent is caught off-guard (without his gun or people). In certain situations, respondents describe using their communication skills to talk their way out of getting shot or employ some other neutralization strategy in order to buy some time to arm themselves and get their people for back up. Once the subjects are "on point," they frequently go looking for their opponent.

d. Peer Influences: Co-offending, Instigation, and Torch Taking. Gun use often involved multiple shooters on both sides of a conflict. Sixty-six percent of gun events involved cooffenders, compared with only 33 percent of nongun situations. Many of the gun events reflected ongoing "beefs" between groups or networks of young men, which oftentimes meant the shooting of numerous members of rival cliques over a single dispute. Often, the reason for the original dispute seemed minor; however, once gun play came into the situation future violence was motivated by revenge or getting justice. Avenging the shooting of one's close friends is considered honorable and necessary for future relations on the street. According to the code, the shooting of one of a young man's street family becomes personal, it becomes a disrespect, even though it may have little or nothing to do with the respondent. These uses of violence suggest a self-help dimension that illustrates Black's (1983) "quantity of law" dynamic.

e. *Perception of Event by Bystanders (The Status and Identity of Observers).* The influence of third parties in violent conflicts has been well documented in the literature (see, e.g., Felson and Steadman 1983; Oliver 1994; and Decker 1995). The importance of observers is most critical during the period of adolescence where young males are developing and testing their personal and social identities (Kinney 1993; Eder 1995). Verbal and nonverbal expressions by others, as well as the respondent's internalized "other," will have a strong impact on his decision-making process. These cues help the actor decide how best to respond and what actions to anticipate from others. Others may play a central role in shaping the actor's definition of the situation and the outcome of events. The actor is concerned about how each situation will make him look to others. The "audience" as amplifier of the social identity won through violence helps to perpetuate the street code.

f. *Absence of Social Controls.* Many of the "squashed" (avoided) events resulted from interventions (real or anticipated) by parties not directly involved in the violent situation such as police, school officials, or other clique members. Some violent situations were dissolved simply because the risks of legal (and nonlegal) sanctions were too great. Interrupted conflicts could dissolve temporarily or permanently depending on the street identity of the mediator, intensity of the issue sparking the situation, future opportunities to continue or respark an event, or resolution of the conflict through alternative means.

Overall, within these gun events the thought of dying is always present. However, this cost competes with other costs and returns from gun violence: achieving or maintaining social identity and status bounded in that situation or moment may hold more value than life itself. It appears that more thought is given to what others may think of the actor and the actor's attempt to match his behavior to his self-image (mythical or actual) than to the possibility of one's own death or serious injury. Losing respect can be damaging to one's personal safety, economic livelihood, and associations with peers (and sometimes family members). This is not simply bravado, since losing respect in one arena marks a person for future victimizations until he reestablishes his identity through a display of toughness or violence.

4. *Guns and Gun Use Equal Respect.* Respect is the social currency

by which one attains status and protection within the neighborhood. Guns play an important role in the quest for respect on the street. Most respondents sought a tough or untouchable self-image, an image with a very high social and strategic value. On the streets, guns enhance one's potential for being tough.

Interviewer (MP): "What makes somebody tough or a big man in your neighborhood?"

(G-56): "What make 'em tough?"

(MP): "Yeah."

(G-56): "When they got guns. When they got a whole lot of friends know the guys back. Of course, he gon say he the big man, nobody could touch him. He got props, he got juice."

Another respondent explained that "bust[ing] a gun" was a primary way of achieving respect, especially when there were few alternative models. He explained:

Interviewer (WW): "What makes someone tough or a big man in your 'hood?"

Respondent (ENYN16): "In the 'hood it's easy for anybody to be called a big man, because, you know, anybody could bust a gun, anybody could rob somebody. You know, it's like most niggers out here don't really got role models, so seeing somebody do that, automatically you gain respect, or they think that makes them a big man."

Gun use is equated with status and with a high level of respect. Involvement in gun violence is described in terms of developmental achievements. The example below shows how one respondent earned a "stripe" by committing a murder. For this respondent, being "trigger happy" gave him status but also brought him into many additional conflicts. Clearly, he viewed these features of his identity as positive and rewarding.

Respondent (G-61): "Yeah it might turn out tragic . . ."

Interviewer (RM): "So when you shot the guy you shot, when you shot him, or when you found out he was dead or something—how did that make you feel, did that give you, did that boost you up?"

(G-61): "It ain't hype me, it didn't make me feel like going out there and doing it again, it just made me feel like . . . ; I just gotta stripe, that's how that made me feel, I got a stripe."

(RM): "Did you get a reputation after that?"

(G-61): "Well, I kept a reputation but . . . ; 'cause I was into a lot of stuff . . . ; and thing I did came to where I was like one of the people, I was like one of the most people they would come and get when it was time for conflict, then anybody . . . ; that I really be around, when there beef, when it's beef time they know who to come get and outta those people, I was one of the top ones they would come and get . . . ; 'cause they always known me . . . ; for being trigger happy and . . ."

The next example shows how lethal violence is necessary for building one's reputation on the street. This respondent thought about reputation in terms of how many "bodies one has under his belt."

Interviewer (WW): "How 'bout image and reputation? Describe how that's important in the projects or your neighborhood."

Respondent (G-81): "Shooting somebody, right there that's image and reputation. How many bodies you got under your belt, if you don't got more than three bodies under your belt. . . . If you ain't never killed nobody, you ain't nothing. . . . That's how niggers look at it though but . . . if it's . . if it's your people . . . they know . . . they knew you'll bust your gun but they know you never kilt nobody they'll show you some respect. . . . But other than that they come out slick out they mouth . . . Like if you get into an argument wit one of them, 'Nigger you ain't never bust your gun man. I got more bodies than you. You ain't really doin nothin. You ain't never kilt nobody. I kilt more niggers than you ever kilt.' You know what I'm saying. That's, that's, that's proving it right there."

B. Implementing the Street Code: Establishing and Maintaining Identity through Lethal Violence

Social interaction in public spaces is structurally organized in small groups or interpersonal affiliations. These groups are very significant in formation of personal and social identities in childhood and adolescence. According to Goffman (1963), group formation shores up personal and social identity. Social identity has a stronger influence because "individuals have little control over situations and especially going outside of the expected role for their particular social identity" (Goffman 1963, p. 128). Many of the vital functions of adolescent social life operate through these groupings whether they are loosely or tightly connected (e.g., social learning and mentoring, play, nurturing, social support, and economic opportunity). Goffman argues that the "norms regarding social identity pertain to kinds of role repertoires or profiles we feel it permissible for any given individual to sustain" (p. 63). The process of categorizing others (from one's own frame of reference) shapes human experience.

Goffman describes two types of honoring or (dishonoring) identities: prestige and stigma (1963, p. 59). We applied this notion in this research to the social identities of adolescent males in the inner city. The issue seems to be who gets "prestige" and who gets "stigma" and how do "mixed interactions" play out within this context. Clearly, the code of the streets calls for prestige to be granted to those who are tough, who have gained respect by proving their toughness, and who reenact their appropriate role in public. Someone who cannot or does not fit into a prestigious identity may be instead stigmatized. The "mixed contacts" between young males who are attempting to transcend a "punk" or "herb" (weaker individual or frequent victim) identity with those who "hold their own" or the "killers" are the primary sources of breaking down the stigmatization. "The very anticipation of such contacts can of course lead normals and the stigmatized to arrange life so as to avoid them. Presumably this will have larger consequences for the stigmatized, since more arranging will usually be necessary on their part" (Goffman 1963, p. 12).

The process of self-preservation through displays of toughness, nerve, or violent behavior is considered a necessary part of day-to-day life for inner-city adolescents, especially young males (Canada 1995). Acquiring fighting skills (and perhaps more importantly shooting experience) is considered important as a means of survival in the inner city (Sullivan 1989, p. 113). Teenagers with dual identities (i.e., street and "decent") may situationally engage in violent behavior to maintain a certain status within the broader social culture of the public community. Projecting the "right image" may have consequences for personal safety, social acceptance, and self-esteem. Individuals who attempt to "fit into" the street world walk a very dangerous line.

1. *Guns and Violent Identities.* Within the isolated social world where street codes dominate, the threat of gun violence introduces new complexities for the development of social identity. Displays of toughness in the context of gun play may involve "crossing a line" that shifts one's view of oneself from "holding your own" to "wild or crazy" and may result in severe role conflict. Negotiating the street requires tests of character, knowledge of the rules of respect, and open displays of violence. The streetwise can spot a phony miles away. Young men who present themselves as tough had better be prepared to back their presentation up with action. Putting on a "front" can be extremely dangerous.

Interviewer (RM): "What about image or a reputation on the streets?"

Respondent (G-61): "Image? Well, a image is something, is a very, it's important on the streets . . . ; we just show how we come out and show themselves as somebody they not, then people, some people could look and see a fake person between a real person. A real person is the person that . . . ; I see is that don't take no shit, just do any thing that he wanna do or whatever or he gets down for whatever . . . ; A fake nigga is a nigga who talk about it but when its time to get down, he got excuses, he got to do this or come up with an excuse or all he do as politic about, talk about. They never really get in the mix . . . ; he just talk about it . . . ; it's just, you know, you gotta, you just like, you look at you people as your son, daughter, you got to look out for them, and they gotta do the same for you . . . ; That comes with my other thing, 'cause you gotta, if you gotta problem I'm there and if I got a problem you there . . . ; and another thing when, in the streets police is mostly hated . . . ; they are least involved with anything . . . ; they got, they familiar what's goes on, but people do not want them involved with them."

(RM): "Why?"

(G-61): "I don't know. They feel more safer without the police than with the police."

The next example, repeated by many respondents, explained how representations of the "decent" orientation, including doing well in school, staying out of trouble, going to college, or working a nine-to-five (legit) job were devalued on the street. Other respondents suggested that being "goody two shoes" somehow was a denial of one's black identity. As the illustration shows, "busting" a gun gains respect in the neighborhood while getting a degree does not.

Interviewer (WW): "Describe the importance of image and reputation on the street."

Respondent (ENYN16): "Everything goes by image and reputation, yo. Really there is no importance, I think. It's just a way of the street. You got to have respect out there. A nigger will quicker praise somebody for busting guns than praise somebody because they got a degree. You never hear somebody say, 'Oh, yeah, someone just graduated from high school and is in the second year of college, doing well.' But you'll hear somebody talk about, 'Yeah, I just saw ———, you know, push a nigger wig back.' And from there it comes, you know, like respect and all that where niggers will know you steal all that shit. You know, you get a reputation as a *man*."

The status and reputations earned through these means provide street-oriented youth with positive feelings of self-worth and "large" identities. The street code is a determining factor proving one's manhood and knowing how to act accordingly when confronted with a variety of challenging situations.

Reputation is something that young inner-city males take seriously and put effort into building as a matter of survival. A young man may take up someone else's beef in order to make an impression on others or build up his reputation. A reputation can be won via several routes which are connected by the threat or use of violent force. One respondent explained how it works.

Interviewer (RM): "How you get a rep, you know? You know how some brothers, sometimes brothers just go out there looking to get a rep. Be the man."

Respondent (G-42): "Those are called like new comers. . . . Like a person that moves into a new community he's like, he's like damn you know 'nigga's out here is cool and they real I got to show these nigga's I ain't no punk yo.' So when he hangs out with them, he see any of them about to get into a 'scrobble' (fight) he be like 'yo step back money I'll handle this for you yo' . . . ; he's only doing it for a rep cause it's not like that's your brother and you like 'Nah, yo you ain't going to fight my brother. For that you fight me."

(RM): "Yeah?"

(G-42): "Nigga's is just doing it to get a name. Doing [it] so people could look at him and be like 'oh word that nigga bust that nigga's ass yo word.' I don't know that's the way I look at it."

The socialization process into the way of the streets is quite clear according to our respondents. The pressure to "be part of the scene" or to "fit in" is very great. Indeed, calculation about life and death is part of this pressure. The choices are limited.

Interviewer (DT): "So umm, why is it important to have a reputation?"

Respondent (G-58): "Cause if you ain't got no rep . . . ; it's gonna be like this, if you ain't got no rep, everybody is gonna pick on you . . . ; they gonna be like 'oh that nigga pussy, he don't do nothing,' they gonna try to pick you as a herb, you coming up the block niggas be trying to bump you, look at you, ice grill you, look at you up and down, you like . . . ; like you nobody."

(DT): "Yeah."

(G-58): "So that when you gotta go all out, man, you know?"

(DT): "What you mean by "go all out"?"

(G-58): "You gotta go all out, you go 'lace' (shoot) 'em . . . have a fight with duke or whatever, pull out a gun and blast 'em . . . you gotta be, niggas ain't gonna fuck with you if you shoot a nigga . . . ; just lace 'em, and niggas will say 'yo that nigga don't play,' he lace something in a heartbeat."

Another respondent describes why he got a gun, how it made him feel to have it, and how having a gun boosted his reputation.

Interviewer (DT): "When did you get your first gun you know? At what age?"

Respondent (G-51): "What age? I got my first gun at age of I think was sixteen."

(DT): "Why why'd you get it?"

(G-51): "Cause I wanted to be bad."

(DT): "You wanted to be bad, huh?"

(G-51): "I wanted to be like I had a reputation to keep so maybe with a gun, would have boost it up a little bit more."

2. *Three Social Identities: A Continuum.*   Teenagers may situationally engage in violent behavior to form or maintain certain social identities within the broader social context of the neighborhood. Projecting the "right image" may have consequences for personal safety, social acceptance, and self-esteem among individuals. Within the isolated social world where respect and valued social standing is limited, the threat of gun violence introduces new complexities for the development of social identity. The social identities described include being "crazy/wild" (frequent unstable fighter/shooter), "holding your own" (functional fighter/shooter), and being a punk or herb (frequent victim struggling for survival).[5] Social identities become more salient through repeated performance. The social meanings attached to each performance determine when and how an actor will be known to others in the neighborhood context, and in turn, subsequent interactions will be defined. Thus an individual's social identity can both prevent violence from coming (he won't get picked on) and promote additional violence (other young men will attempt to knock him off his elevated status). The individual who performs poorly becomes known and labeled as being a "punk" or "herb." The person who has a "successful" perfor-

---

[5] The three types of social identities described in this essay were most prominent among our sample. Most of the interactions were defined in terms of avoiding being classified as a punk or herb. Respondents did describe other violence-related social identities including: "the avoider," "the nice guy," "the beef handler," "too cool" for violence, etc.

mance gains status and becomes known for "holding his own." The young man who gives an "extraordinary" performance is labeled as being "wild" or "crazy." These social identities may be temporary or permanent.

This section describes the characteristics of three ideal identity types. The majority of respondents would classify themselves as being someone who "holds his own" at the time of the interview. A small number would be described as fitting into the "crazy," "wild," or "killer" identity at the time of the interview. Few, if any, of the respondents would classify themselves as a punk or herb during the period of the interview. Looking back over their life histories however, most respondents, 78 percent of those queried (seventy-one of ninety-six respondents), reported experiencing one or more situations during childhood or adolescence of feeling like a punk or herb as direct result of violence perpetrated against them by older, more powerful males. All of the 125 respondents described the importance of using violence to gain social status and personal security.

a. Being Known as "Tough": Displays of Toughness. "Toughness" has been central to adolescent masculine identity in many social contexts of American life. Physical prowess, emotional attachment, and the willingness to resort to violence to resolve interpersonal conflicts are hallmarks of adolescent masculinity (Anderson 1994; Canada 1995). While these terms have been invoked recently to explain high rates of interpersonal violence among nonwhites in central cities, "toughness" has always been highly regarded and a source of considerable status among adolescents in a wide range of adolescent subcultures, from street corner groups to gangs (Whyte 1943; Goffman 1959, 1963, 1967; Wolfgang and Ferracuti 1982; Canada 1995). In some cases, displays of toughness are aesthetic: facial expression, symbols and clothing, physical posture and gestures, car styles, graffiti, and unique speech are all part of "street style" that may or may not be complemented by physical aggression. While changing over time with tastes, these efforts at "impression management" to convey a "deviant aesthetic" and "alien sensibility" have been evident across ethnicities and cultures (Katz 1988). Toughness requires young males to move beyond symbolic representation to physical violence. Firearms often are used to perpetuate and refine the aesthetic of "toughness" and to claim the identity of being among the toughest.

Respondents in this world believed quite strongly that "toughness"

and "being the man" were two central concepts that rang true univer-
sally, both within individuals and across events. The perpetuation of
the sense of self and the image in the minds of others also is an instrumental goal of much weapon use. There is a very low threshold for the
use of violence for these ends. Some subcultures or networks may also
reflect norms in which excessive violence, including weapons use, is
valued, gains social rewards, and gives great personal pleasure. For example, this is true in some gang contexts where "locura" (crazy) acts
of violence establish one's status in the gang (Vigil 1988). It is senseless
only in the fact that the violence is an end unto itself. The use of weapons, especially guns, has elevated the level of domination. Guns can be
used tactically to disable an opponent or to humiliate an opponent by
evoking fear (begging, tears, soiling his pants, etc.). Our data show that
guns are an important part of these social processes.

The use of weapons may reflect a total identity that is geared to
dominate if not humiliate adversaries. Some adversaries are created in
order to express this dominance. These young men seemed willing and
motivated to use violence to obtain anything they desired without
much remorse or forethought. For them, violence is viewed as justified
and necessary in the situation. Their identity is wrapped up in maintaining the image that they are the most violent or toughest head on
the street.

At the top of the identity hierarchy of the street is the "crazy,"
"wild," or "killer" social identity. Individuals who perform extraordinary acts of violence are frequently feared and granted a level of respect that others cannot easily attain. A small number of respondents
in our sample described themselves or others as being "wild," "crazy,"
or a "killer." Some took on this identity temporarily or situationally
while others described themselves as always that way. The performances are often socially defined as shocking or judged to be beyond
what was necessary to handle a situation. Once an individual gives an
extraordinary performance he may notice changes in the way others
relate to him. He may also start viewing himself differently. This status
brings with it a certain level of power and personal fulfillment that may
be reinforced by projecting this identity. Future violent performances
would enable him to maintain the image of the most violent or toughest on the street.

Respondent (SBN37): "I seen him [top man in the neighborhood],
one kid, everybody used to look up to, and he thought he was impossi-

ble, he thought nobody couldn't, he thought he was serious gangster. Couldn't be killed. . . . He was the big man, he used to walk up to spots and rob people."

Interviewer (RM): "What made him a big man?"

(SBN37): "I guess the way he presented his self. The way he went after people's spots, take their drugs, he didn't care. Like he was God or something, you know what I'm saying? He got shot maybe a couple of times and thought he couldn't die. So I guess that's what made him the big man or made him feel like he was the big man."

Respondent (ENYN15): "Well they get respect like that, they want respect. Now a days niggas bust their gun, they ain't got to be trying to shoot you, they just bust their gun at you, make them self look big, that's the only thing, that's how it go, then they get respect, everybody going to be thinking he's a killer, he know he ain't no killer, but everybody think he a killer, unless he [just] shine [front with] a gun."

Interviewer (JM): "So what you was saying when the beef was going down?"

Respondent (G-88): "Yo, when the beef, at that time kid yo, you mind blanks out. You just go crazy man. Especially me, I went crazy. I didn't give a fuck what was going to happen to me Bee. I just soon. . . . I just want to get the shit done you know I'm saying. To you it's all about respect. You gotta get your respect out here man. Gotta get your respect."

(JM): "True."

A person who has an identity as someone who is crazy, wild, or a killer gives off the impression that he has extreme heart, is untouchable, and does not care about what happens. He has the capability to use extreme violence and gets respect for dominating others. Others may want to associate with him to benefit from his high status on the street. The identity itself carries privileges, expectations, and obligations which may open the individual to additional opportunities for violence. The powerful identity may be forced downward by someone else's extraordinary performance.

b. Being Known as Holding Your Own. Many respondents described the process of "holding their own" in violent situations and how personal identities formed around displays of "doing what you got to do" are generally positive on the street. The majority of our respondents would be classified as "holding their own." Individuals who "hold their own" are respected on the street although they will eventually face challenges to their ability to do "what it takes" in heated situations and in all likelihood faced numerous challenges on the way up to that status (Strauss 1996, p. 90). A person who has an identity as someone who holds his own, gives off the impression that he has the capability to use extreme violence but does so only when necessary. This person will face a challenge directly and is respected for that position. This identity allows an individual to be considered an "insider" with the street world; however, this status can be unstable and may require acts of violence when faced with public attacks on identity. Several respondents describe their social identities as holding his own.

Respondent (ENYN20): "[Someone] who can just handle their own, who's not no trouble maker, but who finishes trouble when it comes."

Respondent (G-09): "It's a lot a popularity, you know. Your image that you hold is your reputation. You need that on the streets cause without that then anybody . . . and everybody can do what they want to you. If . . . if you let them. But the rep. that you have shall keep . . . you know if it's a good rep, it will keep these people away from you, keep 'em on your good side. I mean most people who know of you and know how you get down for yours, they know you don't play, that they won't mess with you, because they don't wanna get hurt, because of the reputation that you had. Maybe they don't wanna start because they know you cool, whatever."

Respondent (ENYN05): "Yeah, you will go through people trying to get to know you. This of course is a problem because it starts when you younger by getting that reputation you know you not trying to be a killer or a thug, but you just want people to know yo who you is don't fuck with me I won't fuck with you. So you got to break up a few heads you got to do what ever to get that reputation."

Respondent (ENYN16): "I was always one holding my own. I always had people's behind me. I was always a fighter."

Respondent (ENYN13): "Somebody who doesn't fight over B.S."

Interviewer (DT): "Yeah."

(ENYN13): "Somebody who think, you know, who wants to shoot a fair one, it will be just a fight and he could hold his ground, hold his own. But it gotta be over somethin' important. It gotta be either somethin' personal between that nigga—you know, everybody ain't gonna get along, but if you have a fight you might as well fight and get it over with. One lost—one lost, you know. They don't always go down like that. That's why I hate that, too."

As illustrated by the above examples, an individual who "holds his own" has used violence as a resource for obtaining that status. These young men face the same type of testing process as the punk or herb; however, it is expected that this class of men will handle their conflicts with violence and it will be effective. If violence was not effective, someone who is known to "hold his own" will be granted respect for putting up a good fight or taking a bullet "like a man." If this character is situationally "punked" or "herbed" by someone with a lower status, his identity could face a downward slide.

c. A Stigmatized Identity: Being a Punk or a "Herb."   At the bottom of the status hierarchy of the street is the punk or herb. Like, the school-based "nerd" or "dweeb," the "punk" or "herb" identity is assigned to those who do not fit into the deemed high status or tough identities (see Kinney 1993). In the inner city, those who cannot fight or prove their toughness may instead be stigmatized either temporarily or permanently. Other guys in the neighborhood will act upon that stigma. The process of punking or herbing someone, as respondents called it, closely resembled the process of "fool-making" described by Klapp (cited in Strauss 1996). Strauss writes:

> Orrin Klapp has suggested the different conditions that determine how a person can become a fool and remain one: Because fool-making is a collective imputation it is not necessary, however, that a person actually have the traits or perform the role of the fool. A person is a fool when he is socially defined. . . . What makes a fool role stick? Among the factors responsible for permanent characterization as a fool we may particularly note (1) repeated performances or obvious personal traits which continually suggest the role of a fool; (2) a striking, conclusive, or colorful single exhibition which convinces the public that the person is irremediably a fool; (3) a story or epithet so "good" that it is continually repeated and remembered, making up an imperishable legend; and (4) failure to contradict a fool role by roles or stories of a different category. [Klapp 1949, pp. 159–60, cited in Strauss 1996, pp. 80–81]

If someone has the punk or herb identity he is considered "fair game" for attacks and robberies. The attacks are motivated both by the need to restate the dominance hierarchy and as a sort of punishment for not living up to group norms. If a young man does not have a tough identity or at least have close associates or relatives who can protect him either by association or literally, he is a punk. Others in the setting degrade, dominate, and victimize those individuals who have punk or herb characteristics. The degradation typically involves a direct or implicit emasculation of the "weaker" males. Punks and herbs are also called "soft," "suckers," "wimps," "pussy," "bitch," "ass," and "chumps." Given the intensified acceptance of hegemonic masculinity in the inner-city context, these messages would have a strong negative impact on a punk or herb's self-image. Most young men assume that "outsiders" in the neighborhood (and relevant social network) are punks or herbs and the presumed punk or herb must prove otherwise. Several respondents offered definitions of the punk or herb identity.

Respondent (SBN49): "The definition for a punk or a herb, well around my hood, [it] is like somebody that don't want to fight and shit. Like somebody would go up to them and push them or whatever and they won't fight back. So you know everybody call him a punk. And the definition for a herb is like say somebody who is being nice, or somebody who is scared of somebody, and they tell him 'yo go do that or go do this.' And you know he is just, he listens to whatever they say. [The guys] is just sunning him, he's herbing um."

Respondent (ENYN36): "Psss. That's easy yo. A punk or a herb is somebody who, it's somebody . . . who let . . . some next person . . . make the nigga do things or . . . Make him do shit, make him feel like a sucker. Like if somebody walk up on you . . . and start talking and start mushing you in your face or putting his fingers in your face . . . and you ain't constantly doing nothing about it or he's constantly mother fucking disrespecting you on the real that's a herb. When you let that nigga get away with it you [are] a herb."

Respondent (ENYN24): "A person who can't defend himself or scared to defend himself."

Respondent (ENYN56): "Punk or a herb, getting played and not doing nothing about it, you know."

Respondent (ENYN20): "A herb is a bad ass nigga, someone who's bad and who snitches. You know, [he] gets into a altercation and they loose or something and [then] snitch. . . ."

Interviewer (RM): "Can you remember a time when you felt like a punk or a herb?"

Respondent (ENYN17): "Yeah, when I was little."

(RM): "Was it?"

(ENYN17): "I was in a public school."

(RM): "What happened?"

(ENYN17): (laughter) "There was these guys that I used to hang with."

(RM): "Yeah."

(ENYN17): "But they was doing a lot, they was starting fights and everything and, but I wasn't with that, but I still wanted to be with these dudes."

(RM): "Yeah."

(ENYN17): "So they calling me a herb and punk and you know what I'm saying?"

(RM): "Cause, cause you ain't wanted to get with that?"

(ENYN17): "Cause I ain't want to get with them, I wanted to be with them, but I couldn't do what they was doing, you know what I'm saying?"

(RM): "How old was you?"

(ENYN17): "I was like nine."

(RM): "So what, what happened after that, did you like stop hanging with them or?"

(ENYN17): "Well they dropped out of school and I kept it moving."

Punks and herbs take all sorts of abuse in our inner-city neighborhoods. They get used by more powerful street guys to test their nerve. A young male who "holds his own" may face threats from punks who are attempting to transcend into a high social identity. A gun is useful in transcending identity:

Interviewer (WW): "Have you ever felt you needed to do something violent to amp up your own reputation?"

Respondent (ENYN16): "When I was young, yeah, I thought, you know. Being that I lived in a private house and the projects was right across the street. You know, project kids automatically assume that shit was sweet on a private house, so, you know . . ."

(WW): "So what did you do?"

(ENYN16): "So I like, one incidents, my man, I got chased from the park. If I'm young, you know, I always had a little joint or my pops always a ghat so, you know, kids just came over with no problem because they figured that many niggers on the block and obviously if we living in the private houses we must be rich. But being that I had a burner [gun], you know, as soon as they came with the shit, they came with bats and sticks, I already had a gun so I squeezed it off at them. Actually, I didn't really squeeze it off at them. I just pulled it out to let them know, you know, that I wasn't afraid. You know, I pull it out to let them know that, you know, ain't nothing sweet over here, you know. And I wanted to squeeze after but, you know, back there and I still had some of my little teachings in me, so I didn't really do it. But I wanted to, just to let niggers know, you know, ain't nothing sweet over here. But they got the message by just seeing me pull out. They had sticks and bats and I had a gun."

(WW): "So did that help?"

(ENYN16): "Yeah, that helped. You know, no one really saw me as no punk or herb after that situation. You know, they'll bring the bull-shit to everybody else except me and my brother."

The dynamics of violent events reflect several interesting processes: achieving a highly valued social identity occurs through extreme displays of violence; achieving a "safe" social identity may also require the use of extreme forms of violence; the ready availability of guns clearly increases the stakes of how one achieves status; much behavior is motivated by avoiding being a punk or herb (sucker or weakling); identities can change from being a punk or herb into a more positive status such as "hold your own"; guns equalize the odds for some smaller young men through the process of "showing nerve"; and one can feel like a punk for a specific situation but not take on a punk identity. If the street orientation is dominant in public spaces and personal safety is attributed to adherence to the code as Anderson (1994) suggests, then those who do not conform will be victimized.

Impression management, reputation, and image are necessary to maintain an identity that assures daily survival (see Anderson 1994; Canada 1995; Sheley and Wright 1995). Impression management also seems to be an important aspect of negotiating the street world. The data presented below illustrate how this process unfolds. The data also suggest that guns play a significant role in forming and sustaining "positive" social identities within the neighborhoods.

3. *Identity Attacks: Dissing and Other Transgressions.* Social interaction is regulated through a strict adherence to a proscribed dominance hierarchy in which there are only a limited number of desirable identities to attain. Information and impression management are the most critical tools young men use to negotiate the street. There is competition for respect in the inner city, and the quantity of respect seems to establish one's place on a dominance hierarchy as well as one's social status. Knowledge of the "players" in the neighborhood is needed to determine what type of action is appropriate in a face-to-face encoun-

ter and how respect is to be apportioned. Displays of respect are expected by those who have higher levels of status on the street. Respect in this context may include stepping down from violence out of deference to the other person's status (almost respecting a loss before the battle). Displays of disrespect are also expected in situations where identity posturing is called for, for example, when confronted with someone who is being fake or fronting. However, shows of disrespect or "dissing" are often an intended or unintended attack on someone else's identity and must according to the "code of the street" be addressed aggressively. This negotiation or testing process is not very well understood. One respondent described how "testing" occurs.

Interviewer (DT): "So what usually happens when nigger gets like this with you in your face or somethin'?"

Respondent (ENYN13): "Oh, man, that's like testing your manhood. That's like anything you ever been taught since you was younger, what's gonna come out now."

(DT): "Yeah."

(ENYN13): "Should you wait now, do it now, or handle it? Do you try to talk? Usually that don't even work, cause nobody's talking to you, they either—the more and more you try to talk, the more and more they gonna disrespect you. That's how I feel."

(DT): "So, what happens if somebody, I mean disrespect somebody, what—what happens?"

(ENYN13): "They fight. I mean, they fight or they—or they threaten. They make threats to your mom, your—to mom, all types of threats, and you like—you can't let this dude come after your moms, you know."

(DT): "Yeah."

(ENYN13): "and they say, black-on-black crimes, this-on-this crime, but it really don't have nothin to do with it, it's between the individuals, because a lot of blacks will . . . don't even be fightin each other, they be teamed up, you know, they be tryin hype it up. There may be one—just two, three people and they—just buck wild over there. It didn't even be like that. And the more and more they hype it up, the more and more people read, damn, it's like? So, now they feels—that's how they see somebody doin that shit—he ain't fuckin with me. And it just keeps growin, keeps growin, almost nonsense."

(DT): "Yeah."

(ENYN13): "hate and that."

As shown above, violence is a central tool in gaining or losing respect. Thus an individual's reputation can both prevent violence from coming (he won't get picked on) and promote additional violence (other young men will attempt to knock him off his elevated status).

Interviewer (DT): "Can you describe to me the importance of a reputation?"

(ENYN13): "A reputation is important in a way, because a lotta times it keeps you from gettin into a real problem."

(DT): "Yeah."

(ENYN13): "Somebody don't know you or know who you are, what you about, they all gonna test you, all are gonna try to see what you about. It goes both ways, too. Maybe somebody think you cool and wanna know who you are. They wanna know if you blood or a bad guy, want to know if you good."

(DT): "Yeah."

(ENYN13): "Some people like drug people, you know."

As another respondent explained, having a strong reputation can protect young men from attacks or robberies by others.

Respondent (G-44): "Yeah. You make money, if you make money it's just gonna come."

Interviewer (RM): "If you make, then you get your props?"

(G-44): "You'll get your respect then everybody gonna want to be down with you instead of robbing you . . . instead of robbing you everybody think 'yo why should I rob him . . . he show, if he could show me something, he could show me how to make mine."

(RM): "True."

(G-44): "They, while they robbing him they going home getting a certain amount of money, but he making more, he making the money that he lost. And everybody want that, everybody want to make the money that they lost and not stress. I'm saying he stole like five Gs from us already. Don't stress it I'm making more money, I'm make it again next week."

(RM): "True. That's true."

Within the context of status and identity posturing, ordinary conflicts that occur over personal slights, looks, insults, or playful threats may turn to murder in a matter of minutes. One respondent describes such a scene below.

Interviewer (RM): "Did you ever shoot anyone?"

Respondent (G-61): "Yeah."

(RM): "When? Before you got shot or after?"

(G-61): "After, after I got shot. I shot somebody, we had this conflict, this kid, I don't know him but we was just sitting next, and he exchanged words with my friend, so he told, he came to the kid, the kid came to my friend and my friend told him to move . . . ; so my man was like 'move, what you mean move, man, the word is excuse me,' he was like 'no move' . . . ; some rude boy. So he was like, I heard them, so I turned around and said 'yo what the fuck is going on, yo,' the kid talking about 'what you gonna do,' so I said 'what you mean what I'm gonna do,' so I shot 'em."

(RM): "Where you shoot 'em?"

(G-61): "I don't know where I shot 'em at, I shot 'em up in the face."

(RM): "What you just shot 'em and left. So umm, you left?"

(G-61): "Yeah."

(RM): "So what happened you ain't hear what happened?"

(G-61): "I heard he was dead."

(RM): "Oh, you heard he was dead?"

(G-61): "Mm-hum."

(RM): "Oh, so umm, how that made you feel?"

(G-61): "Fine. But then again it made me feel like, after that I felt like I was still on my mission, I was like fuck that. He ain't mean nothing to me . . . ; he wasn't nobody to me so, he ain't mean nothing to me."

(RM): "Did you feel like your life was threatened like?"

(G-61): "I ask myself that question all the time, I be saying to myself 'damn, did I make the right decision? Was that the right decision or not . . .; And I haven't come up with an answer yet."

Interviewer (RM): "So what usually happens like when a guy insult you to your face, like what happens to that person?"

(ENYN15): "Beef is next. (laughter). Beef is next, straight up, beef is next. If it ain't beef, it's going to take like at least two days or threes days maybe, or if he thinking like yeah, he's going to call me pussy, that's the only thing he have on his mind is he is going to call me pussy, he think I'm a fagot, he going to feel like you got plague if you don't nothing, so he going to learn to do something regardless, that's how shit is now a days."

(RM): "That true."

(ENYN15): "Nigger being about play, like if I go over to somebody's face and be like you fag ass nigger and just walk away, he know that I bust my gun, he won't think twice, he going to be like, alright, I'm going to get this mother fucker, he trying to play me, you know what I'm saying? Cause if he don't do right, every time he smoke weed or whatever he do, he always going to have that on his mind, well why is he trying to play me, you're going to feel like you're a pussy, you're just going to keep thinking, so he going to learn to do something and make you, kick your chest."

Here a respondent describes the importance of getting dissed (disrespected).

Respondent (G-61): "Getting dissed?"

Interviewer (RM): "Is that deep or what?"

(G-61): "That's deep, according to the street that's really deep, 'cause if a nigga diss you, he feel you dissed everything, he just ran over you like a mop, just just walked over you like a mat. If somebody disrespect you everybody will, that's why there be a lot of killing in the neighborhoods today, niggas ain't trying to get disrespected."

(RM): "But why do words have to end in death?"

(G-61): "Just, it's not like it used to be, most of the time some people just talk it out, or fight it out."

(RM): "Yeah."

(G-61): "But now since there are so much guns, people ask 'why should I scuffle my knuckles out or bruise up my face when I can use some that will take care of the problem in less than five minutes?' most people just say fuck fighting."

(RM): "That's taking a life, man."

(G-61): "Most people don't look at it like that, they be like 'that's one less problem in life I got to worry about.'"

Respondents often talked about verbal attacks on one's mother and how that type of attack could not be tolerated. The consequences of this seemingly harmless insulting may turn deadly as one respondent described:

Interviewer (MP): "Why you fired, what was the situation?"

Respondent (G-56): "What was the situation?"

(MP): "Yeah."

(G-56): "Well somebody played themselves in trying, try to disrespect my moms, so I had to handle my business. May he rest in peace black."

C. Situational Contexts: Drugs and Gun Violence

Violent events related to drugs and alcohol provide a rich illustration of the multiple meanings of context. The relationship between intoxication and aggression is highly contingent, mediated by the set (composition of persons), setting (social context), and substances that are consumed. For example, drinking behavior and related consequences depend on the drinking context (Harford 1983; Fagan 1993*a;* Holyfield, Ducharme, and Martin 1995). The same individual, drinking or using drugs in similar patterns, is likely to behave differently in different social settings. This suggests that settings may channel the arousal effects of intoxicants into aggression, and specific drugs may moderate the arousal effects of specific contexts into varying behavior patterns (Fagan 1993*a,* 1993*b*). Despite agreement on the importance of context, there has been no consensus on which elements of context influence violent outcomes of drinking events. For example, one view of context emphasizes situational factors in the physical setting where drinking takes place, including the occasion for drinking or using drugs, the number and relationships of companions and strangers in the setting, and the regulatory processes or permissiveness of the situation (Burns 1980; Levinson 1983*a,* 1983*b*).

However, spatial and social control dimensions, such as the rules and mechanisms for distributing drugs or alcohol, are basic to other conceptions of context (Roncek and Maier 1991; Parker 1995). Specific contexts carry norms for violent behavior and intoxication that influence their interaction. Such norms may dictate which provocations merit a physical response (Felson 1993; Anderson 1994), the status accorded to violence (Schwendinger and Schwendinger 1985; Sullivan 1989), the types and quantities of alcohol to be consumed (Holyfield, Ducharme, and Martin 1995), and the social controls on drugs, alcohol, and violence in the immediate setting (Burns 1980; Buford 1991).

Research on alcohol use and aggression in laboratory studies suggests that provocations, threats, expectancies, availability of nonaggressive response options, and the presence of others are important aspects of the situation that determine whether an aggressive response occurs (Bushman and Cooper 1990; Graham, Schmidt, and Gillis 1995; White 1997). Accordingly, the immediate setting, the broader social and cultural environment supporting fighting, and beliefs about alcohol and other drugs (expected and experienced drinking outcomes) are important to the violence outcomes of events where adolescents gather together to get high (for greater detail, see Holyfield, Ducharme, and Martin 1995).

Drug selling also is a fertile context for violent events (Goldstein 1985, 1989; Fagan and Chin 1990; Fagan 1993*a;* Bourgois 1995; Sommers, Baskin, and Fagan, 1998). Disputes related to money or quality or quantity of drugs, robberies of money or drugs, disputes over selling locations, disciplinary concerns within drug-selling organizations, and other routine business conflicts are often settled using violence and, again, often with guns. There also appears to be a consistent spatial and social overlap between drug selling, drug and alcohol use, and gun homicides (Chaiken and Chaiken 1990). Accordingly, we queried the data on adolescent gun violence to determine the extent and nature of drug and alcohol as a context for violence.

Drinking, drug use, and drug selling were one of the most commonly identified settings for violent events. Clearly, drugs are in both the *background* and the *foreground* of gun violence in the South Bronx and East New York. Background signifies the social context or cultural landscape which influences and shapes perceptions and experiences of inner-city residents. Foreground refers to the immediate influence of drug and alcohol use effects on the processes and outcomes of violent events. Together, drugs and alcohol are a pervasive influence on the daily lives of young people, fueling events in several ways. Rampant drug use and drug selling dwarf other activities as social contexts for interactions, conflicts, and public stages for status attainment in the social world in these neighborhoods. These events in turn contribute to and form the codes and expectancies that regulate street behaviors and the ecology of "danger."

1. *Drugs and Alcohol in the Background of Violent Events.* Drug and alcohol use was cited as the most common type of social/recreational activity for young males. Respondents frequently reported being high or drunk on a very frequent, oftentimes daily, basis. Drug addiction was also widespread among respondents' family members, friends, and neighborhood associates. One respondent describes the relationship to drug selling in his South Bronx neighborhood. When asked if any of his friends sold drugs, he answered:

Respondent (SBN24): "All my fucking people I know in my building, my fucking neighborhood, they have done [it] in their life or they are still doing it [drug selling] right now."

Interviewer (JM): "How long have they been doing that for?"

(SBN24): "In my neighborhood, mostly, you know, [the] last six months. Then a new nigger comes in and he wants to take over your fucking spot."

(JM): "But is there anyone that ever lasted more than six months?"

(SBN24): "If I count the days, I don't know, but it's a short period of time."

(JM): "Is guns a part of that scene in your neighborhood?"

(SBN24): "Yes, it's part, you know what I am saying. When niggers try to front on you with the loot, and when niggers want to take over your fucking spot, or your property, they are going to pull out, so you got to be ready too."

(JM): "Do your friends drink or use drugs in your neighborhood?"

(SBN24): "That's the only thing to do, you know what I'm saying. I think it's part of depression. Niggers don't know what the fuck to do with their lives, so yeah, that's what we mostly do. We fucking drink and smoke."

(JM): "How often?"

(SBN24): "I would say fucking, it's like breakfast, lunch, and dinner, you know what I'm saying. Three course meal!" (Laughing).

The drug economy was described as the primary means of financial support for many of our respondents. Many are the second or third generation of drug dealers in their neighborhoods and were socialized into the drug trade by older family members. These respondents described being drawn into drug selling by the lure of "easy money" and having the means to acquire the "gear" (clothes, jewelry, sneakers, guns, and other accessories) needed for social acceptance and popularity on the street. They describe growing up seeing older guys getting "props" (rewards, respect) off the drug trade both in times of money and material possessions and interpersonal rewards.

Gun carrying and use are central features to the drug business. Access to guns is widespread and not simply limited to those involved in the drug trade. In our data, guns are still being used by drug dealers in the ways described by Goldstein (1985, 1989) over a decade ago. Recognition of the etiological relevance of drug trafficking to violence has resulted in more careful formulation of theories of the drug-violence relationship. There are several influences on violence that occurs in the context of street-level (seller-user) drug distribution. Violence may be used to enforce organizational discipline or resolve business disputes. Disputes over drugs and drug paraphernalia are commonplace among users and sellers. Territorial disputes are commonplace among drug sellers. Street-level sellers may skim profits from mid-level suppliers or crew bosses. In the absence of legal recourse for illegal activities, such disputes are likely to be settled either by economic reprisal or by violence. Violence in drug dealing can be viewed as an extension of behaviors that are associated with efficiency and success in legitimate businesses (Black 1983; Edelhertz, Cole, and Berk 1984).

The social milieu of drug selling/buying areas also is conducive to robbery of sellers and users for either cash or drugs. One respondent described the risks involved in maintaining a drug spot and how a gun is a necessary tool of the trade.

Interviewer (DT): "Why did you have the gun on you that day when you was with your father?"

Respondent (ENYN05): "Cause I'm saying You know what I'm saying we was hustling yo, when you out there in the street, You know what I'm saying, the stick up man could come. And I'm not going to let nobody stick up me and my pops. Cause if a stick up man come and you got over 5 thousand dollars worth of drugs on you, you got money, he going to kill you, You know what I'm saying, so I just had to protect me and my family yo."

Another respondent described a gun incident where he felt he was enforcing street justice by shooting a drug addict who robbed his friend's drug spot. He explains:

Interviewer (JM): "All right, what happened? Describe, you know, it."

Respondent (SBN16): "I go—I was turning in my block and shit and I see this nigga and shit. So, BOOM. I was pitching—pitching, doing my thing, this kid came on and shit, my man shit, he came out, and I like, yeah, do this real quick, cop this bundle for me real quick. So, this dude was holding it down while I was gonna be back 'cause I gotta go to the store. So, I like I'm goin' to the store and shit, this other nigger from the other spot went to my spot and took the shit. So, my man came back, he was addict, they robbed me—they robbed me, motherfucking nigger from the other spot. I went over there nicely and said that was my shit, where my shit at? It was like, I don't know. The guy went upstairs, [I] got five of my niggers be, So we was ready to set it, first nigger, the nigger that got robbed, my—my man that got robbed, he had a—a nine, he just blast that nigger right in the face, POW. And from there it was just on. It was shooting. Caught a nigger in the leg— I caught a nigger in the leg and in the chest and in the stomach— caught a nigger in the stomach."

(JM): "What kind of gun you have?"

(SBN16): "I had a nine, too."

(JM): "What started it? They . . ."

(SBN16): "They robbed my man."

The spurious relationship of drug use and violence suggests that drug selling will be concentrated in social areas with concentrations of the social structural features of violent crime and victimization. The reciprocal nature of the drug business and violence may influence the decision to participate in drug selling—individuals averse to violence may avoid street-level drug transactions, leaving only those willing to engage in violent behaviors as participants. Self-selection of violent individuals for participation in the drug business also may increase the likelihood of violence during drug transactions. For example, Fagan (1989) found that the drug selling–violence relationship among youth gangs was strongest for gangs most frequently involved in all types of violence.

A variety of drug-business-related gun events was described by our sample, including disputes over selling turf and customers, product price, quantity, and quality, shortages of drugs or money, retaliation for dishonest business practices, or protection from robberies during the course of drug selling. Some of the situations described included shootouts involving just two parties (both had firearms), two parties (only one had a firearm), multiple parties on one or both sides of the dispute (armed), multiple parties on one side but not the other (one side armed), drive-bys, sniper attacks from roof tops or other distant locations, and set ups. The worlds of drugs and guns are closely linked, although there is a considerable amount of gun use that has little or nothing to with the drug business. Below one respondent describes a gun event related to a business dispute over the crack spot.

Interviewer (DT): "How did it happen and what started it?"

Respondent (ENYN26): "Well what happened was this, on my block right the niggers crack spot. Now and let me tell ya, my man got killed and this is basically why—let me tell you how [he] got killed, but what led up to it was he had beef with the niggers from the crack spot and that's my man (we grew up together). And he fucked up the manager of the crack spot and he was like a monthly shit, he'll fuck him up and beat the shit out of him. So I guess the nigger from the crack spot was tired of getting his ass whooped so one day they pulled out on him. And he was telling him just kill me, you motherfucker, kill me. They didn't he shoot him. So, I—So he started, the day—thing is we could run to our roofs, and shoot at them from down you know like they won't know who the hell is shooting at them so my man did that, he went on his roof and he had a assault rifle M16 so he was pow, pow, pow, pow, letting loose from the top of the roof and niggers was scattering all over and they didn't know who did it, but I am sure they [the guys from the crack spot] knew it was him."

(ENYN26): "So then like about a week later, there is some new niggers at the crack spot some young nigger, mad young, he like sixteen years old and he was up there with two other cats. It was me, my brother and my man, rest in peace, you know what I'm saying. He— we were walking to the corner because we were going to go to weed- gate (Drug spot) and get some weed and all of a sudden the nigger stepped to him, then I yell what's up man, you know, you diss nigger and I ain't mentioning no names, but you diss nigger and they were like, and he was like yeah why, he was like yo—that shit is over son that nigger got to chill with shit you know whatever. You know like telling us either dead it or you are dead. So my man says like what, what, stupid son this is my fucking block man. Those niggers don't own shit, this is my block so that money (guy) pulled out, he pulled out a two-five on my man and it jammed. He aimed that shit at me, my brother and him, it jammed and you know it didn't want to shoot. So my man snuffed him boom and he ran back up into the crack spot 'cause it was house so he ran up in there and then I thought the man was going to get his tech [semi-automatic gun], 'cause I know he got a (tech), so he ran back to the house and came down with nothing. He stepped to him again, this time that kid bust open the door and came out with a nine and starting shooting pow, pow, pow and my man ran around a Van. He caught him at the other side of the Van and lit six shots into him man and he died in my arms that day son. The man died in my arms man and to this day man, niggers still be shooting at the niggers, but the niggers—because they fucked with some Morello's [phonetic] from my block and the Morello's [phonetic] are crazy, buck- wild, those niggers live like five or six them heads in the last three months. 5-0 [police] always rolling around so those niggers broke up. So his man dead right now. They don't even know who was shooting at them from like that. Those are my peeps [close friends]. The Morel- lo's are my peeps, because we all grew up together—each other."

2. *Drugs and Alcohol in the Foreground of Violent Events.* We identi- fied a range of dynamic processes that show the interactions of intoxi- cation effects, situational contexts, and individual propensities to con- tribute to violence or its avoidance. Some involve affective states following intoxication, others involve events that occur in drinking or drug use locations, and still others involve problems in drug businesses that spill over into other areas of social life. Throughout all these, guns are present as a strategic factor and also as a threshold criterion in deci- sion making about violence.

Drug and alcohol affects are evident in decision making, cognition, intensified emotional states, exaggerated affect, diminished capacity for self-regulation, deviance disavowal, and other cognitive processes. For example, respondents indicated that language when intoxicated was more provocative, and language often "amped up" otherwise minor disputes into violent encounters. Some said they tended to take by-standers' provocations to fight more seriously. More boastful language and exaggerated verbal displays of toughness and "nerve" were com-monplace during drinking events.

Interviewer (DT): "Do you know if he was high?"

Respondent (G-75): "Yeah he was drunk, high or drunk the niggar was fucked up man. I think that is why he thought he was superman for that night."

(DT): "Everybody drinking think they somebody."

(G-75): "That just goes to show that superman can't stop a bullet. Everybody got skin, this flesh under that is bone."

Interviewer (WW): "Do you know if the other guy had been drink-ing or using drugs before you guys started fighting?"

Respondent (G-02): "He looked pretty much out of it. So I guess yeah."

(WW): "Do you think the use of alcohol influenced the way he han-dled the situation between you and him?"

(G-02): "The way he spoke, yeah."

(WW): "How?"

(G-02): " 'Cause he just, you know, he said like a lot of dumb things that like, just really, like it heated up the moment more."

Interviewer (RM): "Do you feel, think that the situation was relating to you using, drinking?"

Respondent (G-78): "Yeah I think so yeah I know so matter of fact because if I wouldn't have been drinking I would have handled it in a more calm manner."

(RM): "It was more impulsive because of the drinking?"

(G-78): "I was very much more aggressive."

Interviewer (RM): "Umm, you ever have got into any beef or a fight while you was drunk?"

Respondent (G-17): "Yes I did."

(RM): "What you, what that was about?"

(G-17): "Well, about me having a big mouth."

(RM): "Oh, when you get drunk you start joking and shit. . . ."

(G-17): "When I'm drunk, when I'm drinking and smoking weed, talking shit to people, you know what I mean, you talk to people. . . ."

(RM): "What happened with that?"

(G-17): "Well, I was smoking weed one day, alright, my man, I was smoking weed one day, drinking, getting fucked up, we got into a little technical difficulties, you know, we had a fight, I got my ass wiped."

(RM): "What y'all fought over, some bullshit?"

(G-17): "Just bullshit, just talking, you know, talking out your ass, arguing back and forth, you know what I mean, so niggas said 'yo pipe that shit down, dead it,' nigga ain't pipe it down, I'm still talking out my mouth."

(RM): "Who said 'pipe it down, dead it,' somebody else?"

(G-17): "Yeah, one of my home boys, you know what I mean? Nigga said 'I ain't with that shit no more, you know,' and I'm still talking out my mouth, so you know, niggas told me it was a lesson to be learnt, so it happened it happened, you know, it happened to me like three times, you know, but you learn from that."

(RM): "All three times was anybody trying to calm the situation down?"

(G-17): "Yeah, but I wasn't trying to hear that."

(RM): "It wasn't working 'cause you up on the influence and shit."

(G-17): "I was in the influence of drinking and everything and like, 'fuck you, get the fuck outta here,' you know, 'let me do my thing, let me handle my business,' you know what I'm saying?"

Some people simply made bad decisions while high, leading to fights that might have been avoided in other circumstances.

Interviewer (RM): "Did you have any kind of strategy you were going to use to win this confrontation?"

Respondent (ENYN13): "Not at the moment no, I was tipsy, I was off focus."

These behaviors often increased the stakes in everyday interactions, transforming them from nonchallenging verbal interactions into the types of "character contests" whose resolution often involved violence. Alcohol exaggerated the sense of outrage over perceived transgressions of personal codes (respect, space, verbal challenges), resulting in violence to exert social control or retribution.

Respondents often indicated that drinking places themselves were especially prone to violent confrontations, often independent from the drinking patterns of the people present. Young men prepared for these potential dangers by carrying guns to parties or clubs in anticipation of violent events. In many cases the potential danger of drinking places increased the appeal for attending with groups of friends when one was prepared to defend himself. In other cases, the risk of injury at parties deterred future attention and participation. One person, describing an event where he was hurt, said that:

Interviewer (RM): "You ever been shot?"

Respondent (G-17): "Nope, I been grazed."

(RM): "You been grazed, where?"

(G-17): "My back."

(RM): "Why, was they shooting at you deliberately?"

(G-17): "Nah it was a mistake. It was. . . ."

(RM): "What happened, tell me about that."

(G-17): "It was, it was, it was a whole bunch of things, it wasn't meant towards me, it was meant for somebody else, and I was just sitting on the corner drinking beer and it just happen. I was in the wrong place at the wrong time. But I thank God that it didn't hit me, you know what I mean?"

(RM): "Yeah."

A wide range of drug effects was reported. Some "chilled" when smoking marijuana, others sought out victims to dominate or exploit, and a few reported becoming paranoid and avoiding any type of human interaction. But paranoia also contributed for some to hostile attributions that created an air of danger and threat, leading to defensive or preemptive violence.

Interviewer (CL): "I noticed you were drunk when all of this happened."

Respondent (G-05): "I wasn't really, I wasn't not really drunk I was just like 'nice.' "

(CL): "But the drug, did the liquor have anything to do with your actions?"

(G-05): "Nah, you crazy?"

(CL): "Huh, if you weren't drinking you wouldn't react the same way?"

(G-05): "It's worst, I feel I'm worst when I'm not drinking, not that, like when I smoke weed I turn soft, you know what I'm saying, like when I smoke weed, I get nice and shit I, I, you know what I'm saying, shit be having me nervous and shit, yeah."

(CL): "Paranoid?"

(G-05): "Yeah, that paranoid and shit."

(CL): "And you don't really wanna get into it?"

(G-05): "Nah, when I smoke weed, nah, sometimes I get paranoid, I don't like smoking weed."

Interviewer (RM): "Thinking back, why do you think you did what you did?"

Respondent (G-78): "In that instant, cause I was drinking and my state of thinking was altered to a more how would you say 'machismo.' When I had to prove that I guess at that moment feeling the way I was feeling buzzed up like that."

(RM): "You felt dissed . . . ?"

(G-78): "I felt disrespected and you gotta prove yourself."

Still others noted the human guidedness[6] of drinking behaviors, where drinking often was an intended behavior that created the emotional and affective conditions in which violence was likely. Consider the two opposite descriptions of marijuana effects:

Interviewer (WW): "Had you been drinking or doing drugs before that fight? Were you high?"

Respondent (G- 32): "Smoke some weed."

(WW): "So you was high?"

(G-32): "Yeah I was kind of fucked up."

(WW): "Do you think alcohol or drugs influenced you the way you handle the situation?"

(G-32): "Nah. Marijuana keeps you fucking . . ., it keeps you down, it keeps you more or less in a mellow state. Alcohol will take you to that level you wanna fucking hurt someone. I wanted to chill and watch a basketball game. I didn't want to go out there and fight on no hot fucking summer day."

Interviewer (DT): "So do you think sometimes when you were high that shit amps you up more?"

Respondent (G-60): "Sometimes I think it depends on the smoke too, like some smoke."

(DT): "You be finding out you going to that store. Smoking the trees over there. I don't fuck around with weed personally, I used to fuck around. Like you said sometimes you do shit for fun, I do shit for fun, I smoke weed and go fuck somebody up for fun. That is why I don't even fuck around with that shit, that is why I leave that shit alone, I drink my little beer here and there, little 40 here and there but I don't get so drunk I hate throwing up son."

(G-60): "I hate that shit."

---

[6] Human guidedness refers to the internalization of justifications or expectancies for one's behavior after consuming alcohol or getting high. Aggressive behavior is blamed on the substance use as a "guiding force" leading to such behavior. It is a complex social-psychological process (see Pernanen 1991).

Several respondents reported that their decision making within violent events was compromised. Some felt invincible and instigated fights that they lost. Some made disproportionately aggressive responses that became instigations for fights, responses that in retrospect seemed unnecessary and stupid. Still others said they were "too fuzzy" to make good decisions about whether or how to fight.

While cognitive impairment was evident for some, others noted that their decisions while drinking reflected complex strategic judgments about the chess game that often precedes the decision to fight or withdraw. The decision to "squash" or to "dead" a fight involved complex perceptions and decisions as well as verbal skills. One respondent told how he and his friends decided to withdraw from a potential fight at a party after deciding that they could not win, that their opponents outnumbered them, and that even if a temporary peace could be negotiated, it would be fragile and short-lived. But their withdrawal required that they offer "accounts" that permitted both sides to maintain share "props" while not appearing to be weak. This required both mental and verbal agility, skills that had to be summoned despite a long night of drinking.

Intoxication also appears to have indirect influences on violence or may even be an outcome of violence. Some respondents described violent events while intoxicated where drinking or drug use was unrelated to violence. Still others disavowed responsibility for their violence, blaming it entirely on being high. Others got high after violent events as a form of self-medication.

Interviewer (MP): "You was high that day? Drunk, high, weed?"
Respondent (G-63): "No I wasn't high. I wasn't drunk."
(MP): "What about after that? After the fight?"
(G-63): "After the fight, when I got back around my way, I told my friends about it and we planned to go back."
(MP): "Y'all got high and started laughing after that?"
(G-63): "No we didn't. We got high, but we wasn't laughing."
(MP): "What kinda drug did y'all use to get high?"
(G-63): "Marijuana."
(MP): "And that's it?"
(G-63): "That's it."

Finally, one respondent told us how the complications from the drug business spill over into other social interactions, or themselves become challenges to codes involving family and respect, code violations that mandate a violent response. Consider the following story that weaves together these themes.

Respondent (G-42): "And then like my cousin right I had a cousin. He was black too, and he was skinny you know he was a good kid and he was young. Then he started smoking, he got caught up in the game he started smoking. And you know the rest of his friends was looking down on him they was like 'yo what's wrong with you,' you know what I'm saying you supposed to be chilling with us, look at us we chilling, we fat what. You over here smoked out (from crack) why go there. They use to dis him and all that. They use to look out for him and all that, pay him, 'yo here go to the store for me yo here, here' look out for him. They always took care of him and all that but he never de-graded himself where he was robbing people, snatching anybodies chain, robbing peoples moms of something like that. He never went low like that but he just liked to smoke he liked to get high. And umm. He was chilling with this other crack head that was the bad. He was the opposite of him. He would always be sticking nigga's moms up, sticken, he stick anybody up. Catch a little nigga for his work, take him, take his money take whatever. And he use to always rob this one guy constantly. And them two since they stood together you know a lot. And they like to get together because the nigga, he would rob mad people and he would have mad work and he would come and be 'yo what's up don come get high with me?' 'Alright, alright Fuck it yo.' So they kind of stood together and the other person saw that. He was like 'yo damn I want that nigga but I guess I'm gonna have to use him to get to him.' So they kind of made a set up one day. He tried to set him up in the building. You know what I'm saying? And my cousin he didn't know what time it was. He was like yo what's up come get high with me 'alright.' He was supposed to bring the other nigga, that's where they went wrong. Cause he told my cousin he was like yo 'come get high go tell Markie come' and the other guy Markie he was like 'Nah. Nah. I'm not trying to hear that yo you know what saying' so he tried to stay away from that. He was like Nah. He felt funny he was like 'Nah. I going with that I'm always sticking you up and you trying to light me up now' (support his habit). Nah. I aint fucking with you. So he got one. He got my cousin into the building and for one reason or another there was somebody waiting in the staircase with a 'shoty' (shotgun) but it was supposed to be for the other guy and it was a case of mistaken identity, and they shot my cousin in the face 'boom.' "

Interviewer (RM): "He killed him?"

(G-42): "Killed him."

(RM): "Pssst."

(G-42): "And that kind of, it didn't happen to me, it happen, it was my birthday that day. The last time I saw him was right there on the corner before I went upstairs. I had a little joint, I was puffing it and boom and he you know whenever I had 'blunts' I always smoked with him to you know what I'm saying? You know what I'm saying get high off of this leave that other shit alone that stuff ain't good for you."

(RM): "Yeah."

(G-42): So I was smoking my joint with him and before I went upstairs I gave it to him. I was like yo I'm out see you tomorrow and he was like 'ah-ight.' Usually sometimes and I was kind of close to him. In the mornings he use to come to my house, I use to cook a fat breakfast for both of us he use to always eat with me and we use to just kick it, chill, bugging watching TV and everything. Then it happen like three in the morning that night and I had went upstairs about twelve. That was the last time I ever saw him."

IV. Understanding the Epidemic of Youth Violence

The crisis of youth gun violence reflects broader trends in youth violence but also significant changes in material conditions and social controls in the communities where gun violence is most common. Understanding youth gun violence requires that we also understand the dynamic contexts of these neighborhoods, the influence of these social processes on socialization, social control, and behavior, and the role of guns in shaping norms and behaviors. Youth gun violence is central to the ecological background of many neighborhoods and also to the developmental landscape that shapes behavioral expectancies and scripts.

A. Guns as Cues of Danger

The development of an ecology of danger reflects the confluence and interaction of several sources of contagion. First is the contagion of fear. Weapons serve as an environmental cue that in turn may increase aggressiveness (Slaby and Roedell 1982). Adolescents presume that their counterparts are armed and, if not, could easily become armed. They also assume that other adolescents are willing to use guns, often at a low threshold of provocation.

Second is the contagion of gun behaviors themselves. The use of guns has instrumental value that is communicated through urban "myths" and also through the incorporation of gun violence into the social discourse of everyday life among preadolescents and adolescents. Guns are widely available and frequently displayed. They are salient symbols of power and status, and strategic means of gaining status, domination, or material goods.

Third is the contagion of violent identities, and the eclipsing or devaluation of other identities in increasingly socially isolated neighborhoods. These identities reinforce the dominance hierarchy built on "toughness" and violence, and its salience devalues other identities. Those unwilling to adopt at least some dimensions of this identity are vulnerable to physical attack. Accordingly, violent identities are not simply affective styles and social choices, but strategic necessities to navigate through everyday dangers. The complexities of developing positive social and personal identities among inner-city minority males is both structurally and situationally determined. Our data and previous research suggests that for inner-city males, prestige is granted to those who are tough, who have gained respect by proving their toughness, and who reenact their appropriate role in public. Majors and Billson (1992) explain the structural difficulties young African American males encounter in identity development. They state: "Masculine attainment refers to the persistent quest for gender identity among all American males. Being a male means to be responsible and a good provider for self and family. For black males, this is not a straightforward achievement. Outlets for achieving masculine pride and identity, especially in political, economic, and educational systems, are more fully available to white males than to black males. . . . The black male's path toward manhood is lined with pitfalls of racism and discrimination, negative self-image, guilt, shame, and fear" (Majors and Billson 1992, p. 31).

One important development is a breakdown in the age grading of behaviors, where traditional segmentation of younger adolescents from older ones, and behavioral transitions from one developmental stage to the next, are short-circuited by the strategic presence of weapons.

The street environment provides the "classroom" for violent "schooling" and learning about manhood. Elsewhere we present a conceptual model for understanding the relationship between age and violence in this context (see Wilkinson 1997b). Mixed age interactions play an important role in this process. Older adolescents and young adults provide modeling influences as well as more direct effects. We found that they exert downward pressure on others their own age and younger through identity challenges which, in part, shape the social identities for both parties. At younger ages, boys are pushing upward for status by challenging boys a few years older.

The social meanings of violent events reach a broader audience than those immediately present in a situation. Each violent event or potentially violent interaction provides a lesson for the participants, firsthand observers, vicarious observers, and others influenced by the communication of stories about the situation which may follow. Children learn from both personal experience and observing others using violence to "make" their social identity or "break" someone else's identity on the street. In addition, we have attempted to illustrate what happens when an identity challenge occurs for both primary actors in the situation. We describe three different types of performance that may be given in a violent event: poor, successful, and extraordinary performance. Again, guns define what constitutes each class of violent performance uniquely compared to a nongun performance (see Wilkinson 1997*b*).

Gun use may involve "crossing a line" or giving what we call an extraordinary performance that shifts one's view of oneself from a "punk" or even "cool/holding your own" to "crazy" or "wild." Guns were used by many as a resource for improving performance. We hypothesize that the abundance of guns in these neighborhoods have increased the severity for violent performances. For the majority of our sample, guns became relevant for conflict resolution around the age of fourteen.

B. The Complexities of Adolescent Identity Development

The maintenance and reinforcement of violent identities is made possible by an effective sociocultural dynamic that sets forth a code that includes both behaviors and the means of resolving violations of the code. The illustrations in this chapter show the strong influence of street code, similar to the codes identified by Anderson (1994, in this volume), over the behaviors of young children, adolescents, and young adults. Children growing up in this environment learn these codes, or behavioral-affective systems, by navigating their way through interpersonal situations which oftentimes involve violence encounters.

Delinquency research in earlier eras showed how conventional and deviant behaviors often lived side by side within groups and also within individuals (Cohen 1955; Cloward and Ohlin 1960). One effect of "danger" as a dominant ecological marker is the difficulty that adolescents face in maintaining that duality of behavior and of orientation. The street code has a functional purpose for attaining status and avoiding danger, even for adolescents who harbor conventional attitudes and goals. Negotiating safety within this context is extremely difficult, especially when much of the social activity available to young men who have left school and are "hanging out" on the inner-city street corner involves expressing dominance over others. But the opportunities for dual identities are narrow. The social isolation of areas of concentrated poverty has given rise to oppositional cultures that devalue conventional success and even interpret conventional success as a sign of weakness. For adolescents who may want to have one foot in the conventional world and the other on the street, this balancing act has become not only difficult but also dangerous. The effects are a hardening of street codes and an eclipsing of other avenues for social status and respect.

C. Research and Intervention on Adolescent Gun Violence

These perspectives suggest specific directions for research and interventions. The development of scripts, the contingencies within scripts that lead to violence, the diffusion and contagion of lethal violence, and the role of violence in both scripts themselves and the contingencies that evoke them, should be specific foci of prevention and intervention efforts. Because gun events are different from other violent events (Fagan and Wilkinson 1997; Wilkinson 1997*a*, 1997*b*), these efforts should focus on guns.

Focusing on the role of guns within scripts assumes that guns may alter scripts in several ways. For example, guns may change the contingencies and reactions to provocations or threats, and change strategic thinking about the intentions and actions of the other person in the dispute. The presence of guns in social interactions may also produce "moral" judgments that justify aggressive, proactive actions. Accordingly, the development of interventions should be specific to the contexts and contingencies of *gun* events, rather than simply interpersonal conflicts or disputes.

For example, decisions involving firearms often are effected under conditions of angry arousal (i.e., "hot cognitions") and intensified emotional states. In many cases, firearms introduce complexity in decision making introduced by the actions of third parties or the long-standing nature of disputes that erupt periodically over many months. In other cases, firearms simply trump all other logic.

Preventive interventions should address the growing reality of fire-arms in the ecological contexts of development and the internalization of firearms in the development of behavioral norms. Firearms present a level of danger—or strategic uncertainty—that is unequaled in events involving other weapons or in "fair fights." In other words, guns trump other decision logics in the course of a dispute. These attributes of conflict, including the presence of guns and their effects on cognition and decision making, should inform the design of preventive efforts and interventions. Contingencies in a variety of contexts should be included: schools, parties, street corner life, the workplace, and in dating situations.

Prevention and interventions should be specific to developmental stages. At early developmental stages, preventive efforts must recognize that for many youngsters with high exposure to lethal violence, the anticipation of lethal violence influences the formation of attitudes favorable to violence and scripts that explicitly incorporate lethal violence. At later developmental stages, the incorporation of strategic violence via firearms in the presentation of self can alter the course of disputes and narrow options for nonviolent behavioral choices or behavioral choices that do not include firearms or other lethal weapons.

Prevention and intervention efforts should be built on a foundation of research that also specifically addresses gun violence. This research should address several concerns. First, comparison of gun and nongun events within persons can illustrate how guns shape decision making. Second, sampling plans should generate data across both social networks and neighborhoods. If diffusion and contagion are central to the dynamics of gun violence, then research should address how these processes link across networks of adolescents and also how neighborhood contexts shape interactions within and across social networks where much violence unfolds.

The important role of age-grading also suggests longitudinal designs with both younger and older cohorts. If identity is a central focus of these dynamics, research with younger children is necessary to assess how behavioral progressions are tied to personality development and situational avoidance techniques. The interactions of adolescents across age cohorts also is an important point of diffusion of behavioral norms and identity development. The development of scripts at specific age junctures also is important.

Other methods also can help understand processes of contagion and diffusion of "violent identities" and behavioral norms surrounding the use of guns. For example, capture-recapture designs may inform us about the extent to which violence transgresses social networks, neighborhood boundaries, and age strata.

Finally, the development of prevention efforts should be based on "hot cognitions" that better typify the types of situations in which guns are used. Research on the avoidance of violence, even in the face of weapons and other strong cues and motivations, should be central to prevention theory.

D. Conclusion

While youth violence has always been with us, the modern version of it seems distinctly different: the epidemic of adolescent violence is more lethal, in large part due to the rise of gun violence by adolescents. In this essay, we provide perspective and data on the role of guns in shaping the current epidemic of youth violence. At the descriptive level, the answer is clear: Adolescents in cities are possessing and carrying guns on a large scale, guns often are at the scene of youth violence, and guns often are being used. This is historically unique in the United States, with significant impacts on an entire generation of adolescents. The impacts are most seriously felt among African American youths in the nation's inner cities.

It is logical and important to ask whether an exogenous increase in gun availability fueled the increase in youth violence. If this were true, then, regardless of its initial role in causing the epidemic, reducing the availability of guns to kids would in turn reduce the levels and seriousness of youth violence. However, we know little about changes in gun availability to adolescents; estimating supply-side effects is difficult. Ethnographic reports show a steadily increasing possession of guns by youths, but little insight into how guns were obtained.

Instead, we consider competing hypotheses that see a less central (but not insignificant) role of guns in initiating, sustaining, or elevating the epidemic of youth violence. These include the idea that the demand for guns among youth was driven up by the development of an "ecology of danger," with behavioral norms that reinforce if not call for violence, and in which popular styles of gun possession and carrying fuel beliefs that violence will be lethal. These shifts in demand, occurring in the context of widespread availability of weapons, led to increased possession, carrying, and use. Concurrently, guns became symbols of respect, power, and manhood in an emerging youth culture that sustained a continuing demand and supply side of weapons, reciprocally increasing the overall level of gun possession and the desire to use them.

This essay offers a framework to explain how the supply and demand for guns has had an impact on the overall level and seriousness of youth violence, presenting evidence both from existing literature and from original sources to help understand the complex relationship between guns and youth violence. Guns play an important role in the recent epidemic of lethal youth violence. However, the relationship is a complex one in which the effects of guns are mediated by structural factors that increase the youth demand for guns, the available supply, and culture and scripts which teach kids lethal ways to use guns. These effects appear to be large enough to justify intensive efforts to reduce availability, possession, and use of guns by American adolescents.

REFERENCES

Abelson, Robert P. 1976. "Script Processing in Attitude Formation and Decision-Making." In *Cognition and Social Behavior*, edited by J. S. Carroll and J. W. Payne. Hillsdale, N.J.: Erlbaum.
———. 1981. "Psychological Status of the Script Concept." *American Psychologist* 36(7):715–29.
Anderson, Elijah. 1978. *A Place on the Corner*. Chicago: University of Chicago Press.
———. 1990. *Streetwise*. Chicago: University of Chicago Press.
———. 1994. "The Code of the Streets." *Atlantic Monthly* (May), pp. 81–94.
———. 1997. "Violence and the Inner City Code of the Street." In *Violence and the Inner City*, edited by Joan McCord. New York: Cambridge University Press.
———. In this volume. "The Social Ecology of Youth Violence."
Bernstein, Walter. 1968. "The Cherubs Are Rumbling." In *Gang Delinquency and Delinquent Subcultures*, edited by James F. Short, Jr. New York: Harper & Row.
Bjerregaard, B., and Alan Lizotte. 1995. "Gun Ownership and Gang Membership." *Journal of Criminal Law and Criminology* 86(1):37–58.
Black, D. 1983. "Crime as Social Control." *American Sociological Review* 48:34–45.
———. 1993. *The Social Structure of Right and Wrong*. Orlando, Fla.: Academic Press.
Blumstein, Alfred. 1995. "Youth Violence, Guns, and the Illicit-Drug Industry." *Journal of Criminal Law and Criminology* 86(1):10–36.
Bourdouris, James. 1970. "Trends in Homicide: Detroit, 1926–1968." Ph.D. dissertation, Wayne State University.

Bourgois, Philippe. 1995. *In Search of Respect: Selling Crack in El Barrio.* New York: Cambridge University Press.

Buford, Bill. 1991. *Among the Thugs: The Experience, and the Seduction of, Crowd Violence.* New York: Norton.

Burns, Thomas F. 1980. "Getting Rowdy with the Boys." *Journal of Drug Issues* 10:273–86.

Bushman, B. J., and H. M. Cooper. 1990. "Effects of Alcohol on Human Aggression: An Integrative Research Review." *Psychological Bulletin* 107:341–54.

Callahan, C. M., and F. P. Rivera. 1992. "Urban High School Youth and Handguns." *Journal of the American Medical Association* 267:3039–42.

Campbell, Anne. 1984. *The Girls in the Gang.* New York: Blackwell.

———. 1986. "The Streets and Violence." In *Violent Transactions: The Limits of Personality*, edited by A. Campbell and J. Gibbs. New York: Blackwell.

Canada, Geoffrey. 1995. *Fist, Knife, Stick, Gun.* Boston: Beacon.

Chaiken, J., and M. Chaiken. 1990. "Drugs and Predatory Crime." In *Drugs and Crime*, edited by Michael Tonry and James Q. Wilson. Vol. 13 of *Crime and Justice: A Review of Research*, edited by Michael Tonry and Norval Morris. Chicago: University of Chicago Press.

Cloward, Richard A., and Lloyd E. Ohlin. 1960. *Delinquency and Opportunity.* Glencoe, Ill.: Free Press.

Cohen, Albert. 1955. *Delinquent Boys.* New York: Free Press.

Coie, J. D., and K. A. Dodge. 1997. "Aggression and Antisocial Behavior." In *Handbook of Child Psychology*, vol. 3, *Social, Emotional and Personality Development*, edited by Nancy Eisenberg. New York: Wiley.

Cook, Philip J. 1976. "A Strategic Choice Analysis of Robbery." In *Sample Surveys of the Victims of Crime*, edited by W. Skogan. Cambridge, Mass.: Ballinger.

———. 1980. "Reducing Injury and Death Rates in Robbery." *Policy Analysis* 6(1)21–45.

———. 1983. "The Influence of Gun Availability on Violent Crime Patterns." In *Crime and Justice: An Annual Review of Research*, vol. 4, edited by M. Tonry and N. Morris. Chicago: University of Chicago Press.

Cook, Philip J., and John H. Laub. In this volume. "The Unprecedented Epidemic in Youth Violence."

Cornish, Derek. 1993*a*. "Crimes as Scripts." Paper presented at the second annual seminar on Environmental Criminology and Crime Analysis, University of Miami, Coral Gables, Fla., May 26–28.

———. 1993*b*. "Theories of Action in Criminology: Learning Theory and Rational Choice Approaches." In *Routine Activity and Rational Choice Advances in Criminological Theory*, vol. 5, edited by Ronald V. Clarke and Marcus Felson. New Brunswick, N.J.: Transaction Press.

———. 1994. "The Procedural Analysis of Offending." In *Crime Prevention Studies*, edited by R. V. Clarke. Monsey, N.Y.: Criminal Justice Press.

Decker, Scott H. 1995. "Reconstructing Homicide Events: The Role of Witnesses in Fatal Encounters." *Journal of Criminal Justice* 23(5):439–50.

Dodge, Kenneth A., and John D. Coie. 1987. "Social-Information Processing

Factors in Reactive and Proactive Aggression in Children's Peer Groups." *Journal of Personality and Social Psychology* 53:1146–58.

Dodge, Kenneth A., and N. R. Crick. 1990. "Social Information Processing Bases of Aggressive Behavior in Children." *Personality and Social Psychology Bulletin* 16(1):8–22.

DuRant, R. H., C. Cadenhead, R. A. Pendergrast, G. Slavens, and C. W. Linder. 1994. "Factors Associated with the Use of Violence among Urban Black Adolescents." *American Journal of Public Health* 84(4):612–17.

Edelhertz, Herbert, Roland J. Cole, and Bonnie Berk. 1984. *The Containment of Organized Crime.* Lexington, Mass.: Lexington Books.

Eder, Donna. 1995. *School Talk: Gender and Adolescent Culture.* New Brunswick, N.J.: Rutgers University Press.

Elliott, Delbert S., David Huizinga, and Scott Menard. 1989. *Multiple Problem Youth: Delinquency, Drugs, and Mental Health.* New York: Springer-Verlag.

Fagan, Jeffrey. 1989. "The Social Organization of Drug Use and Drug Dealing among Urban Gangs." *Criminology* 27(4):633–69.

———. 1990. "Social Processes of Delinquency and Drug Use among Urban Gangs." In *Gangs in America,* edited by C. Ronald Huff. Newbury Park, Calif.: Sage.

———. 1993a. "Set and Setting Revisited: Influences of Alcohol and Illicit Drugs on the Social Context of Violent Events." In *Alcohol and Interpersonal Violence: Fostering Multidisciplinary Perspectives,* edited by S. E. Martin. NIAAA Research Monograph no. 24. Rockville, Md.: National Institute of Alcohol Abuse and Alcoholism.

———. 1993b. "Interactions among Drugs, Alcohol, and Violence." *Health Affairs* 12(4):65–77.

Fagan, Jeffrey, and Ko-lin Chin. 1990. "Violence as Regulation and Social Control in the Distribution of Crack." In *Drugs and Violence,* edited by Mario de la Rosa, Bernard Gropper, and Elizabeth Lambert. NIDA Research Monograph no. 103. Rockville, Md.: U.S. Public Health Administration, National Institute of Drug Abuse.

Fagan, Jeffrey, Elizabeth Piper, and Melinda Moore. 1986. "Violent Delinquents and Urban Youths." *Criminology* 24(4):439–71.

Fagan, Jeffrey, and Deanna L. Wilkinson. 1995. *Situational Contexts of Gun Use Events among Young Males in the Inner City.* Grant SBR-9515327. Arlington, Va.: National Science Foundation, Law and Social Science Program.

———. 1997. "Firearms and Youth Violence." In *Handbook of Antisocial Behavior,* edited by D. Stoff, J. Belinger, and J. Maser. New York: Wiley.

Fagan, J., F. E. Zimring, and J. Kim. 1998. "Declining Homicide in New York City: A Tale of Two Trends." *Journal of Criminal Law and Criminology* (forthcoming).

Feeney, Floyd. 1986. "Decision Making in Robberies." In *The Reasoning Criminal,* edited by Ronald V. Clarke and Derek Cornish. New York: Springer-Verlag.

Felson, Richard B. 1982. "Impression Management and the Escalation of Aggression and Violence." *Social Psychology Quarterly* 45(2):245–54.

———. 1993. "Predatory and Dispute-Related Violence: A Social Interactionist Approach." In *Routine Activity and Rational Choice: Advances in Criminological Theory*, vol. 5, edited by Ronald V. Clarke and Marcus Felson. New Brunswick, N.J.: Transaction Press.

Felson, Richard B., and Henry J. Steadman. 1983. "Situational Factors in Disputes Leading to Criminal Violence." *Criminology* 21(1):59–74.

Felson, Richard, and James T. Tedeschi. 1995. "A Social Interactionist Approach to Violence: Cross-Cultural Applications." In *Interpersonal Violent Behaviors: Social and Cultural Aspects*, edited by R. Barry Ruback and Neil A. Weiner. New York: Springer.

Fingerhut, Lois A. 1993. "Firearm Mortality among Children, Youth and Young Adults 1–34 years of Age, Trends and Current Status: United States, 1985–1990." *Advance Data from Vital and Health Statistics, no. 231*. Hyattsville, Md.: National Center for Health Statistics.

Fingerhut, Lois A., D. D. Ingram, and J. J. Feldman. 1992*a*. "Firearm and Non-firearm Homicide among Persons 15 through 19 Years of Age: Differences by Level of Urbanization, United States, 1979 through 1989." *Journal of the American Medical Association* 267(22):3048–53.

———. 1992*b*. "Firearm Homicide among Black Teenage Males in Metropolitan Counties: Comparison of Death Rates in Two Periods, 1983 through 1985 and 1987 through 1989." *Journal of the American Medical Association* 267(22):3054–58.

Gibbs, Jewelle Taylor, and Joseph R. Merighi. 1994. "Young Black Males: Marginality, Masculinity, and Criminality." In *Men, Masculinities, and Crime: Just Boys Doing Business?* edited by Tim Newburn and Elizabeth Stanko. London: Routledge.

Goffman, Erving. 1959. *The Presentation of Self in Everyday Life*. Garden City, N.Y.: Doubleday.

———. 1963. *Stigma*. Englewood Cliffs, N.J.: Prentice Hall. ·

———. 1967. *Interaction Ritual*. New York: Doubleday.

———. 1983. "The Interaction Order." *American Sociological Review* 48:1–17.

Goldstein, P. J. 1985. "The Drugs-Violence Nexus: A Tri-partite Conceptual Framework." *Journal of Drug Issues* 15:493–506.

———. 1989. "Drugs and Violent Crime." In *Pathways to Violent Crime*, edited by N. A. Weiner and M. E. Wolfgang. Newbury Park, Calif.: Sage.

Goldstein, Paul J., Henry H. Brownstein, Patrick Ryan, and Patricia A. Belluci. 1989. "Crack and Homicide in New York City, 1989: A Conceptually-Based Event Analysis." *Contemporary Drug Problems* 16(4):651–87.

Graham, K., G. Schmidt, and K. Gillis. 1995. "Circumstances When Drinking Leads to Aggression: An Overview of Research Findings." Paper presented at the International Conference on Social and Health Effects of Drinking Patterns, Toronto.

Gurr, Ted Robert. 1981. "Historical Trends in Violent Crime: A Critical Review of the Evidence." In *Crime and Justice: An Annual Review of Research*, vol. 3, edited by Michael Tonry and Norval Morris. Chicago: University of Chicago Press.

Hagedorn, John M. In this volume. "Gang Violence in the Postindustrial Era."

Haller, Mark H. 1989. "Bootlegging: The Business and Politics of Violence." In *Violence in America, Part I,* edited by Ted Robert Gurr. Thousand Oaks, Calif.: Sage.

Hamid, Ansley. 1994. *Beaming Up.* New York: Guilford.

Hannerz, Ulf. 1969. *Soulside: Inquiries into Ghetto Culture and Community.* New York: Columbia University Press.

Harford, T. 1983. "A Contextual Analysis of Drinking Contexts." *International Journal of the Addictions* 8:825–34.

Holyfield, L., L. J. Ducharme, and J. K. Martin. 1995. "Drinking Contexts, Alcohol Beliefs, and Patterns of Alcohol Consumption: Evidence for a Comprehensive Model of Problem Drinking." *Journal of Drug Issues* 25:783–98.

Huesmann, L. Rowell. 1988. "An Information Processing Model for the Development of Aggression." *Aggressive Behavior* 14(1):13–24.

Inciardi, James A., Ruth Horowitz, and Ann E. Pottieger. 1993. *Street Kids, Street Drugs, Street Crime.* Belmont, Calif.: Wadsworth.

Kagan, Jerome. 1989. *Unstable Ideas: Temperament, Cognition, and Self.* Cambridge, Mass.: Harvard University Press.

Katz, Jack. 1988. *Seductions of Crime: Moral and Sensual Attractions of Doing Evil.* New York: Basic.

Keiser, R. Lincoln. 1969. *The Vice Lords: Warriors of the Streets.* New York: Holt, Rinehart, & Winston.

Kennedy, David, Anne Piehl, and Anthony Braga. 1996. "Youth Violence in Boston: Gun Markets, Serious Youth Offenders and a Use-Reduction Strategy." *Law and Contemporary Problems* 59(1): 147–96.

Kinney, David A. 1993. "From 'Nerds' to 'Normals': Adolescent Identity Recovery within a Changing School Social System." *Sociology of Education* 66:21–40.

LH Research. 1993. *A Survey of Experiences, Perceptions, and Apprehensions about Guns among Young People in America.* Cambridge, Mass.: Harvard University, School of Public Health.

Land, Kenneth, Patricia McCall, and Lawrence Cohen. 1990. "Structural Covariates of Homicide Rates." *American Journal of Sociology* 95(4):922–63.

Lane, Roger. 1979. *Violent Death in the City: Suicide, Accident and Murder in Nineteenth-Century Philadelphia.* Cambridge, Mass.: Harvard University Press.

———. 1989. "On the Social Meaning of Homicide Trends in America." In *Violence in America, Part I,* edited by Ted Robert Gurr. Thousand Oaks, Calif.: Sage.

Levinson, D. 1983*a*. "Social Setting, Cultural Factors, and Alcohol-Related Aggression." In *Alcohol, Drug Abuse, and Aggression,* edited by E. Gottheil, K. A. Druley, T. E. Skoloda, and H. M. Waxman. Springfield, Ill.: Charles C. Thomas.

———. 1983*b*. "Alcohol Use and Aggression in American Subcultures." In *Alcohol and Disinhibition: Nature and Meaning of the Link,* edited by R. Room and G. Collins. Research Monograph no. 12. Rockville, M.D.: U.S. Public Health Service, National Institute on Alcohol Abuse and Alcoholism.

Liebow, Eliot. 1967. *Talley's Corner: A Study of Negro Streetcorner Men.* Boston: Little, Brown.

Lizotte, Allan J., James M. Tesoriero, Terence Thornberry, and Marvin D. Krohn. 1994. "Patterns of Adolescent Firearms Ownership and Use." *Justice Quarterly* 11(1):51–73.

Luckenbill, David F. 1977. "Homicide as a Situated Transaction." *Social Problems* 25:176–86.

Luckenbill, David F., and Daniel P. Doyle. 1989. "Structural Position and Violence: Developing a Cultural Explanation." *Criminology* 27(3):419–36.

Majors, R., and J. M. Billson. 1992. *Cool Pose: The Dilemmas of Black Manhood in America.* New York: Simon & Schuster.

Maxson, Cheryl L., Margo A. Gordon, and Malcolm W. Klein. 1985. "Differences between Gang and Nongang Homicides." *Criminology* 23(2):209–22.

Miller, Walter B. 1958. "Lower Class Culture as a Generating Milieu of Gang Delinquency." *Journal of Social Issues* 14(1):5–19.

Moore, Joan W. 1978. *Homeboys.* Philadelphia: Temple University Press.

———. 1991. *Goin' Down to the Barrio: Homeboys and Homegirls in Change.* Philadelphia: Temple University Press.

O'Kane, James. 1992. *The Crooked Ladder: Gangsters, Ethnicity, and the American Dream.* New Brunswick, N.J.: Transaction.

Oliver, William. 1994. *The Violent Social World of Black Men.* New York: Lexington Books.

Parker, Robert Nash. 1995. *Alcohol and Homicide: A Deadly Combination of Two American Traditions.* Albany, N.Y.: SUNY Press.

Pernanen, Kai. 1991. *Alcohol in Human Violence.* New York: Guilford Press.

Polk, Kenneth. 1994. *When Men Kill: Scenarios of Masculine Violence.* New York: Cambridge University Press.

Quicker, John. 1983. *Homegirls: Characterizing Chicana Gangs.* San Pedro, Calif.: International Universities Press.

Reiss, Albert J., Jr., and Jeffrey A. Roth, eds. 1993. *Understanding and Preventing Violence.* Washington, D.C.: National Academy Press.

Rodriguez, Luis. 1993. *Always Running: Gang Days in L.A.* New York: Touchstone.

Roncek, Dennis, and Patricia A. Maier. 1991. "Bars, Blocks, and Crimes Revisited: Linking the Theory of Routine Activities to the Empiricism of Hot Spots." *Criminology* 29:725–54.

Sadowski, L., R. Cairns, and J. Earp. 1989. "Firearms Ownership among Nonurban Adolescents." *American Journal of Disease of Children* 1434: 1410–13.

Sampson, Robert J. 1987. "Urban Black Violence: The Effect of Male Joblessness and Family Disruption." *American Journal of Sociology* 93(2):348–82.

Sampson, Robert J., and Janet Lauritsen. 1994. "Individual and Community Factors in Violent Offending and Victimization." In *Understanding and Preventing Violence,* vol. 3, edited by Albert J. Reiss, Jr. and Jeffrey A. Roth. Washington, D.C.: National Academy Press.

Sampson, Robert J., and William J. Wilson. 1995. "Race, Crime and Urban

Inequality." In *Crime and Inequality*, edited by J. Hagan and R. Peterson. Stanford, Calif.: Stanford University Press.

Sante, Luc. 1991. *Low Life: Lures and Snares of Old New York*. Farrar, Giroux & Straus.

Schank, Richard, and Robert Abelson. 1977. *Scripts, Plans, Goals and Understanding*. Hillsdale, N.J.: Erlbaum.

Schlossman, Stephen. 1977. *Love and the American Delinquent: The Theory and Practice of "Progressive" Juvenile Justice*. Chicago: University of Chicago Press.

Schwendinger, Herman, and Julia Schwendinger. 1985. *Adolescent Subcultures and Delinquency*. New York: Free Press.

Sheley, Joseph, and James Wright. 1995. *In the Line of Fire: Youth, Guns, and Violence in Urban America*. New York: Aldine de Gruyter.

Sheley, Joseph, James Wright, and M. Duane Smith. 1993. "Firearms, Violence and Inner-City Youth: A Report of Research Findings." Final report. Washington, D.C.: U.S. Department of Justice, National Institute of Justice.

Short, James F., Jr. 1997. *Poverty, Ethnicity, and Violent Crime*. Boulder, Colo.: Westview.

Slaby, R. G., and W. C. Roedell. 1982. "Development and Regulation of Aggression in Young Children." In *Psychological Development in the Elementary Years*, edited by J. Worrell. New York: Academic Press.

Snyder, H. N., and M. Sickmund. 1995. *Juvenile Offenders and Victims: A National Report*. Monograph. Washington, D.C.: U.S. Department of Justice, Office of Juvenile Justice and Delinquency Prevention.

Sommers, Ira D., and Deborah Baskin. 1992. "Sex, Race, Age, and Violent Offending." *Violence and Victims* 7(3):191–215.

———. 1993. "The Situational Context of Violent Female Offending." *Journal of Research in Crime and Delinquency* 30(2):136–62.

Sommers, I., D. Baskin, and J. Fagan. 1998. *Workin' Hard for the Money: The Social and Economic Lives of Women Drug Dealers*. New Brunswick, N.J.: Rutgers University Press (forthcoming).

Spergel, Irving A. 1995. *The Youth Gang Problem: A Community Approach*. New York: Oxford University Press.

Steinberg, L., and E. Cauffman. 1996. "Maturity of Judgment in Adolescence: Psychosocial Factors in Adolescent Decision Making." *Law and Human Behavior* 20:249–72.

Strauss, A. L. 1996. *Mirrors and Masks: The Search for Identity*, 2d ed. New Brunswick, N.J.: Transaction.

Strodtbeck, Fred L., and James F. Short, Jr. 1968. "Aleatory Risks versus Short-Run Hedonism in Explanation of Gang Action." In *Gang Delinquency and Delinquent Subcultures*, edited by James F. Short, Jr. New York: Harper & Row.

Sullivan, Mercer L. 1989. *Getting Paid: Youth Crime and Culture in the Inner City*. Ithaca, N.Y.: Cornell University Press.

Suttles, Gerald D. 1968. *The Social Order of the Slum*. Chicago: University of Chicago Press.

Taylor, Carl S. 1993. *Women, Girls, Gangs, and Crime.* East Lansing: Michigan State University Press.

Tedeschi, James T., and Richard B. Felson. 1994. *Violence, Aggression, and Coercive Actions.* Washington, D.C.: American Psychological Association.

Thornberry, T. M., D. Krohn, A. J. Lizotte, and D. Chard-Wierschem. 1993. "The Role of Juvenile Gangs in Facilitating Delinquent Behavior." *Journal of Research in Crime and Delinquency* 30(1):55–87.

Thrasher, Frederick M. 1927. *The Gang: A Study of 1,313 Gangs in Chicago.* Chicago: University of Chicago Press.

U.S. Department of Health and Human Services. 1993. "Youth Risk Behavior Survey." *Journal of the U.S. Public Health Service* 108:60–66.

Valentine, Bettylou. 1978. *Hustling and Other Hard Work: Life Style in the Ghetto.* New York: Free Press.

Vaughn, Roger D., Heather J. Walter, Bruce Armstrong, Lorraine Tiezzi, Pamela D. Waterman, and James F. McCarthy. 1996. "Carrying and Using Weapons: A Survey of Urban Minority Junior High School Students." *American Journal of Public Health* 86:568–72.

Vigil, James Diego, 1988. *Barrio Gangs.* Austin: University of Texas Press.

White, H. R. 1997. "Alcohol, Illicit Drugs, and Violence." In *Handbook of Antisocial Behavior,* edited by D. Stoff, J. Brieling, and J. D. Maser. New York: Wiley.

Whyte, William F. 1943. *Street Corner Society.* Chicago: University of Chicago Press.

Wilkinson, Deanna L. 1997a. "Decision Making in Violent Events among Adolescent Males: A Comparison of Gun and Non-gun Events." Paper presented at the forty-ninth annual American Society of Criminology meeting, San Diego, California, November.

———. 1997b. "Male Adolescent Social Identity in the Inner-City 'War Zone.'" Paper presented at the American Sociological Association annual meeting, Toronto, August.

Wilkinson, Deanna L., and Jeffrey Fagan. 1996a. "The Role of Firearms in Violence 'Scripts': The Dynamics of Gun Events among Adolescent Males." *Law and Contemporary Problems* 59(Winter):55–90.

———. 1996b. "Guns and the Code of the Streets." Paper presented at the forty-eighth annual American Society of Criminology meeting, Chicago, November.

Wilkinson, Deanna L., Richard McClain, and Jeffrey Fagan. 1996. "Using Peer Interviewers to Enhance Data Collection Efforts in a Study of Gun Use among Young Males in the Inner City: Tales from the Field." Paper presented at the Academy of Criminal Justice Sciences annual meeting Las Vegas, March 15.

Williams, K. R., and R. Flewelling. 1988. "The Social Production of Criminal Homicide: A Comparative Study of Disaggregated Rates in American Cities." *American Sociological Review* 53:421–31.

Wolfgang, Marvin, and Franco Ferracuti. 1982. *The Subculture of Violence: Toward an Integrated Theory in Criminology,* 2d ed. Beverly Hills, Calif.: Sage.

Wright, James D., and Peter H. Rossi. 1986. *Armed and Considered Dangerous: A Survey of Felons and Their Firearms.* New York: Aldine.

Yablonsky, Lewis. 1962. *The Violent Gang.* New York: Macmillian.

Zahn, Margaret. 1980. "Homicide in the Twentieth Century United States." In *History and Crime: Implications for Criminal Justice Policy,* edited by James Inciardi and Charles Faupel. Beverly Hills, Calif.: Sage.

Zimring, F., and G. Hawkins. 1997. *Crime Is Not the Problem: Lethal Violence in America.* New York: Oxford University Press.

Zimring, Franklin E., and James Zuehl. 1986. "Victim Injury and Death in Urban Robbery: A Chicago Study." *Journal of Legal Issues* 15:1–40.

Barry C. Feld

Juvenile and Criminal Justice Systems' Responses to Youth Violence

ABSTRACT

Within the past decade, nearly every state has amended its juvenile code in response to perceived increases in serious, persistent, and violent youth crime. These changes diminish the jurisdiction of juvenile courts as judicial decisions and statutory changes transfer more youths from juvenile courts to criminal courts so that young offenders can be sentenced as adults. Amendments to juvenile sentencing laws increase the punitiveness of sanctions available to juvenile court judges. Other strategies attempt to "blend," or merge, juvenile and criminal court jurisdiction and sentencing authority over violent young offenders. These "get tough" policies affect the numbers and types of youths confined in adult and juvenile correctional facilities and pose fundamental problems for administrators in both systems; accelerate procedural, jurisprudential, and substantive convergence between the juvenile and criminal justice systems; and erode the rationale for a separate juvenile court.

Public frustration with crime, fear of the recent rise in youth violence, and the racial characteristics of violent young offenders fuel the desire to "get tough" and provide political impetus to prosecute larger numbers of youths as adults. These initiatives simplify the transfer of young offenders to criminal courts and expose many waived youths to mandatory minimum sentences as adults, or require juvenile court judges to impose determinate or mandatory minimum sentences on youths who remain in the juvenile system. Both approaches deemphasize rehabilitation and individualized consideration of the offender, stress personal and justice system accountability and punishment, and base waiver and

Barry C. Feld is Centennial Professor of Law at the University of Minnesota Law School.

sentencing decisions on the seriousness of the present offense and prior record. Sentencing young offenders as adults increases the number of chronological juveniles confined in adult prisons and poses substantial challenges for adult correctional officials. Juvenile institutional administrators confront similar challenges as judges confine more serious young delinquents for longer periods of time.

Every jurisdiction uses one or more statutory devices to prosecute some juveniles as adults. The principal devices include judicial waiver, legislative offense exclusion, and prosecutors' choices among concurrent jurisdictions; these allocate to different branches of government the decision whether to prosecute a youth as a criminal or a delinquent. Each reflects different ways of asking and answering similar questions: who are the serious offenders, by what criteria should the state identify them, which branch of government can best make these decisions, and how should the juvenile or adult systems respond to them?

The "simple" question whether a young offender should be handled as a juvenile or an adult poses difficult theoretical and practical dilemmas. For example, judicial waiver legislation that requires a judge to decide whether a youth is amenable to treatment or poses a threat to the public presupposes that juvenile courts can rehabilitate at least some youths, that judges possess diagnostic tools that enable them to classify for treatment, and that judges can predict offenders' future dangerousness. At another level, recent changes in waiver legislation provide an indicator of the jurisprudential shift in emphasis from rehabilitation to retribution, as exclusion statutes increasingly emphasize characteristics of the offense rather than the offender. Jurisdictional waiver policies that define the boundary of adulthood also implicate the relationship between juvenile and criminal court sentencing practices. Finally, criminal prosecution of younger offenders implicates fundamental cultural assumptions about juveniles' criminal responsibility because waiver allows juries and judges to impose the death penalty on at least some youths convicted as criminals.

This essay draws on judicial opinions, statutory amendments, evaluation research, and criminological writings to analyze changes in sentencing policy responses to chronic and violent young offenders in both the criminal and juvenile justice systems. It examines recent revisions of waiver laws and juvenile court sentencing laws that reveal the changing jurisprudence of juvenile courts, empirical research on the relative efficacy of alternative waiver strategies as mechanisms to control violent and chronic young offenders, and available evidence on the consequences for youths convicted and sentenced in criminal or in juvenile court. Finally, it examines "blended jurisdiction," a relatively new sentencing option that attempts to bridge the gap between juvenile treatment and adult punishment and to provide graduated and escalating sanctions for serious younger offenders.

Policy toward youthful offenders is balanced precariously between America's century-old experiment with the paternalistic, individualizing, and rehabilitation-premised juvenile court and a modern movement to punish youthful offenders as if they were adults. Proponents of special procedures for young offenders continue to argue that "kids are different" and less blameworthy than adults, that protection and enhancement of troubled children's life chances should remain a major youth policy goal, and that modern sentencing policies for adults are too harsh and ham-fisted to apply to young people.

Some critics argue that juvenile courts and correctional agencies provide young offenders the worst of two systems—fewer procedural protections than adults receive in exchange for punitive treatment programs that demonstrate little evidence of effectiveness. Other critics insist that serious youth violence is as seriously damaging as serious adult violence and that concern for public protection requires use of harsh punishments that juvenile courts cannot impose.

Current policy innovations—reducing the maximum age of juvenile court jurisdiction, removing some crimes from the juvenile court regardless of the offender's age, and making transfers from juvenile to adult courts easier—are premised on retention of the current two-systems approach. This raises a series of perplexing policy issues: perpetuation of two information systems that often prevents adult court judges from learning about prior juvenile offenses; arbitrary and idiosyncratic patterns of discretionary decisions by judges and prosecutors that produce wide inconsistencies in waiver and retention decisions; anomalous punishment patterns in which violent offenders transferred to adult courts receive much harsher sentences than comparable violent offenders who were not transferred, while transferred property offenders often receive less severe sentences than if sentenced in the juvenile court; stark racial disparities in sentencing in the juvenile system that are exacerbated by new transfer policies; and failure of criminal courts to take account of the diminished responsibility and immaturity of many juvenile offenders convicted as adults.

There is a better way, which combines reconceptualized divisions of function between social welfare and justice system agencies with the creation of a single, integrated criminal justice system that gives youthful offenders the same procedural protections afforded adults while providing systematic reductions of sentence (a "youthful offender discount") to take account of young people's lesser responsibility and maturity (Feld 1998). This essay, after documenting the failures of both the traditional and the current transitional approaches, explains what an integrated approach would look like and why it makes sense.

Section I provides a brief overview of the juvenile court, the recent increase in youth violence, and the political impetus it provides for policies that "crack down" on youth crime. Section II analyzes changes in juvenile court jurisdiction and the processes by which states transfer some youths from juvenile to criminal courts. This section also examines the sentences that criminal court judges impose on transferred youths, the use of juvenile delinquency records to enhance the sentences of young adult offenders, and the correctional housing and programming provided for these younger offenders. Section III analyzes changes in juvenile court sentencing laws, their implications for conditions of confinement, and the availability and efficacy of treatment programs for serious young offenders. Section IV analyzes the emergence of blended jurisdiction. Section V concludes that the various changes in both systems erode the foundations for a separate juvenile court and proposes a sentencing policy framework that provides a graduated system of criminal sentencing consistent with the developmental continuum by formally recognizing youthfulness as a mitigating factor.

I. Juvenile Courts, Youth Violence, and Get Tough Policies

Nineteenth-century changes in cultural conceptions of children and in strategies of social control led to the creation of the juvenile court. The juvenile court movement attempted to remove children from the adult justice and corrections systems and to provide them with individualized treatment. The Progressives envisioned juvenile court professionals using indeterminate procedures and substituting a scientific and preventative approach for the criminal law's punitive policies. By separating children from adults and providing a rehabilitative alternative to punishment, juvenile courts rejected both the criminal law's jurisprudence and its procedural safeguards such as juries and lawyers. Under the guise of *parens patriae*, the juvenile court emphasized treatment, supervision, and control rather than punishment. The juvenile court's "rehabilitative ideal" envisioned a specialized judge trained in social science and child development whose empathic qualities and insight would enable him or her to make individualized therapeutic dispositions in the "best interests" of the child (Platt 1977; Ryerson 1978; Rothman 1980). Reformers pursued benevolent goals, individualized their solicitude, and maximized discretion to provide flexibility in diagnosis and treatment of the "whole child." They regarded a child's crimes primarily as a symptom of his or her "real needs," and consequently the nature of the offense affected neither the degree nor the duration of intervention. Rather, juvenile court judges imposed indeterminate and nonproportional sentences that potentially continued for the duration of minority.

Progressives situated the juvenile court on a number of cultural and criminological fault lines and institutionalized several binary conceptions for the respective juvenile and criminal justice systems: either child or adult, either determinism or free will, either treatment or punishment, either procedural informality or formality, either discretion or the rule of law. Serious youth crime challenges these dichotomous constructs. Many recent juvenile code revisions represent efforts to modify the Progressives' bifurcations between these competing conceptions of children and crime control.

The Supreme Court in *In re Gault*, 387 U.S. 1 (1967), began to transform the juvenile court into a very different institution than the Progressives contemplated. In *Gault*, the Supreme Court engrafted some formal procedures at trial onto the juvenile court's individualized treatment sentencing regime and fostered a procedural and substantive convergence with adult criminal courts (Feld 1993*a*). *Gault*'s emphasis on procedural formality shifted the focus of delinquency proceedings from a child's best interests to proof of legal guilt in adversary proceedings, highlighted the connection between a youth's crime and subsequent sanctions, and ironically may have legitimated more punitive dispositions for young offenders. In *McKeiver v. Pennsylvania*, 403 U.S. 528 (1971), however, the Court denied to juveniles the constitutional right to jury trials in delinquency proceedings. *McKeiver* relied on the contrasts between juvenile courts' treatment rationale and criminal courts' punitive purposes to justify the procedural differences between the two systems. Several recent reforms provide some juveniles with a statutory right to a jury in order to expand juvenile courts' punitive options.

It is a criminological truism that young people commit a disproportionate amount of crime and that their arrest rates for the most serious crimes peak in mid- to late adolescence and then gradually decline (Blumstein 1995). Although violent crimes constitute a smaller component of the overall serious crime index and juveniles constitute a small proportion of all arrests for violence, the arrest rates of juveniles for violence and, especially, homicide surged dramatically beginning in the mid-1980s (see Cook and Laub, in this volume). Not only did the juvenile violence and homicide rates increase at a faster pace than those of adults, but the average age of juvenile arrestees decreased (Blumstein and Cork 1996).

The recent increase in juvenile homicide rates accompanied the proliferation of handguns among youths. Blumstein (1995; Blumstein and Cork 1996) attributes the changing patterns of age-specific homicide rates among adolescents to the availability of guns in conjunction with the crack cocaine drug industry that emerged in the mid-1980s. Blumstein (1995) hypothesizes that the drug distribution industry attracts youths, especially urban, African American males who lack alternative economic opportunities; that youths in the drug industry take more risks than would adults; and that they arm themselves for self-protection and to resolve disputes. Although guns constitute a "tool of the trade" in the drug industry, their diffusion into the broader youth population for self-defense and status accounts for many of the "excess homicides" among urban black males recorded in the late 1980s and early 1990s (Reiss and Roth 1993; Blumstein 1995).

The increases in youth violence and homicide, especially among African American males in the late 1980s, constitutes the proximate cause of recent legislative strategies to "get tough" and "crack down" on youth crime. This served to accelerate punitive policy trends already at work to criminalize juvenile justice (Feld 1984). Even prior to the late 1980s, a discernible trend was evident to transfer more youths to criminal court and to base waiver decisions on the seriousness of the offense rather than the characteristics of the offender (Feld 1987). There was a similar legislative trend to impose determinate or mandatory minimum sentences in juvenile courts based on the seriousness of the offense rather than the real needs of the offender (Feld 1988b). Although the rate and scope of statutory changes have accelerated dramatically within the past decade, these developments represent continuations of the prior convergence of juvenile and criminal courts' sentencing policies. Significantly, because of the substantial differences in violent offense arrest rates by race, policies that increase sanctions for youth violence inevitably have a disproportionate effect on young black males.

II. Changes in Waiver Legislation and Sentencing of Transferred Youths

Transfer of juvenile offenders for adult prosecution provides the nexus between the more deterministic and rehabilitative premises of the juvenile court and the free will and punishment assumptions of the adult criminal justice system. Although juvenile courts theoretically attempt to rehabilitate young offenders, a small but significant proportion of miscreant youths resist their efforts. These are typically older delinquents nearing the maximum jurisdictional age and often recidivists who have not responded to prior intervention and for whom successful treatment may not be feasible during the time remaining to the juvenile court (Podkopacz and Feld 1995, 1996; U.S. General Accounting Office 1995). Politicians and the public perceive these youths as mature and sophisticated offenders. Moreover, these career offenders may account for a disproportionate amount of all juvenile crime and violence. Highly visible, serious, and violent offenses evoke community outrage or fear that politicians believe only punitive adult sanctions can mollify. Mechanisms to prosecute some juveniles as adults provide a safety valve that permits the expiatory sacrifice of some youths, quiets political and public clamor, and enables legislators to avoid otherwise irresistible pressures to lower the maximum age of juvenile court jurisdiction (Feld 1978).

A. Jurisdictional Policy Changes

In response to the resurgence of youth crime in the late 1980s, politicians, juvenile justice personnel, and criminologists debated extensively the relative merits of different strategies to prosecute some serious young offenders in criminal courts (Feld 1987, 1995; Fagan and Deschenes 1990). Jurisdictional waiver represents a type of sentencing decision. Juvenile courts traditionally assigned primary importance to rehabilitation and attempted to individualize treatment. Criminal courts accorded greater significance to the seriousness of the offense committed and attempted to proportion punishment accordingly. All of the theoretical differences between juvenile and criminal courts' sentencing philosophies become visible in transfer proceedings and in legislative policy debates. Transfer laws simultaneously attempt to resolve both fundamental crime control issues and the ambivalence embedded in our cultural construction of youth. The jurisprudential conflicts reflect current sentencing policy debates: the tensions between rehabilitation and incapacitation or retribution, between decisions based on characteristics of the offender or the seriousness of the offense, between discretion and rules, and between indeterminacy and determinacy. Waiver laws attempt to reconcile the contradictory impulses engendered when the child is a criminal and the criminal is a child. What processes best enable us to choose between competing conceptions of youths as responsible and culpable offenders and as immature and salvageable children? In the early stages of a criminal career and prospectively, what criteria best differentiate between adolescent-only offenders and life-course persistent offenders?

Although the technical and administrative details of states' transfer legislation vary considerably, judicial waiver, legislative offense exclusion, and prosecutorial choice of forum represent the three generic approaches (Feld 1987; Fritsch and Hemmens 1995; Snyder and Sickmund 1995; U.S. General Accounting Office 1995). They represent different ways to identify which serious young offenders to try as adults, emphasize a different balance of sentencing policy values, rely on different organizational actors or administrative processes, and elicit different information to determine whether to try and sentence particular young offenders as adults or as children.

Judicial waiver represents the most common transfer strategy. A juvenile court judge may waive jurisdiction on a discretionary basis after conducting a hearing to determine whether a youth is amenable to treatment or poses a threat to the public. These assessments reflect the traditional individualized sentencing discretion characteristic of juvenile courts (Feld 1987).

Legislative offense exclusion frequently supplements judicial waiver provisions. This approach emphasizes the seriousness of the offense and reflects the retributive values of the criminal law (Feld 1987; Snyder and Sickmund 1995). Because legislatures create juvenile courts, they can define their jurisdiction and exclude youths from juvenile court on the basis of their age and the seriousness of their offenses. A number of states, for example, exclude youths sixteen or older and charged with murder from juvenile court jurisdiction (Sanborn 1996). Legislative line drawing that sets the maximum age of juvenile court jurisdiction at fifteen or sixteen, below the general eighteen-year-old age of majority, results in the adult criminal prosecution of the largest numbers of chronological juveniles (U.S. General Accounting Office 1995). This type of line drawing resulted in the criminal prosecution of 176,000 youths below age eighteen in 1991 (Snyder and Sickmund 1995). Two states, Wisconsin and New Hampshire, recently lowered their age of juvenile court jurisdiction from seventeen to sixteen and criminalized large numbers of youth on a wholesale, rather than a retail, basis.

Prosecutorial waiver, the third method, is used in about a dozen states to remove some young offenders from the juvenile justice system. With this strategy, juvenile and criminal courts share concurrent jurisdiction over certain ages and offenses, typically older youths and serious crimes, and prosecutors may, for example, exercise their discretion to select juvenile or adult processing for youths sixteen or older and charged with murder (McCarthy 1994; Snyder and Sickmund 1995). To the extent that a prosecutor's decision to charge a case in criminal courts divests the juvenile court of jurisdiction, prosecutorial waiver constitutes a form of offense-based decision making, like legislative offense exclusion (Thomas and Bilchik 1985).

Analyzing waiver as a sentencing decision addresses two interrelated policy issues: the bases for sentencing and waiver practices within juvenile courts and the relationship between juvenile and criminal court sentencing practices. The first implicates individualized sentencing decisions and the tension between discretion and the rule of law. The second implicates the contradictory criteria used by juvenile and criminal court judges when sentencing offenders. Formulating rational and consistent social control responses to serious and chronic young offenders requires coordinated justice system responses to youths who make the transition between the two systems. I emphasize serious and chronic young offenders because waiver policies affect two, somewhat different, albeit overlapping, populations of juveniles—violent offenders and persistent offenders. Criminal courts respond differently to violent youths and to chronic offenders currently charged with property crimes when prosecutors try these youths as adults (Podkopacz and Feld 1995, 1996).

It is unfortunate that neither arbitrary age-and-offense lines nor idiosyncratic judicial prosecutorial waiver decisions have any criminological relevance other than their legal consequences. Waiver statutes increasingly use offense criteria in a vain effort to constrain judicial sentencing discretion and to improve the fit between waiver decisions and criminal court sentencing practices. Ultimately, however, they fail because they embody the binary dichotomies—either treatment or punishment, either child or adult, either offender or offense—that purportedly distinguish juvenile from criminal courts.

1. *Judicial Waiver and Individualized Sentencing Decisions.*   From the juvenile court's inception, judges could deny some young offenders its protective jurisdiction and transfer them to adult courts (Rothman 1980). Judicial waiver reflects juvenile courts' traditional individualized approach to decide whether a youth should be treated as a juvenile or punished as an adult (Zimring 1981*a*, 1991). In *Kent v. United States*, 383 U.S. 541 (1966), the United States Supreme Court formalized the waiver process and held that juvenile courts must provide youths with some procedural protections (Feld 1978). In *Breed v. Jones*, 421 U.S. 519 (1975), the Court applied the double jeopardy clause of the Fifth Amendment to delinquency convictions and required states to decide whether to try and sentence a youth as a juvenile or as an adult before proceeding to trial on the merits of the charge.

Kent and *Breed* provide the formal procedural framework within which judges make waiver sentencing decisions. But the substantive bases of waiver decisions pose the principal difficulty. Until recent amendments, most states' waiver statutes allowed judges to transfer jurisdiction on the basis of their discretionary assessment of subjective clinical factors, such as a youth's amenability to treatment. The Court in *Kent*, 383 U.S. at 566–67 (1966), appended to its opinion a list of substantive criteria that juvenile court judges might consider. Legislatures specify amenability criteria with varying degrees of precision and frequently adopt the general and contradictory list of *Kent* factors. Although some states limit judicial waiver to felony offenses and establish a minimum age for adult prosecutions, typically sixteen, fifteen, or fourteen, others provide neither offense nor minimum age restrictions (Feld 1987; Snyder and Sickmund 1995).

In practice, judges appear to assess "amenability" and "dangerousness" by focusing on three sets of variables. The first consists of a youth's age and the length of time remaining within juvenile court jurisdiction. Juvenile court judges waive older youths more readily than younger offenders (Fagan and Deschenes 1990; Podkopacz and Feld 1995, 1996; U.S. General Accounting Office 1995). A youth's age in relation to the juvenile court's maximum dispositional jurisdiction limits the court's sanctioning powers and provides the impetus to waive or exclude some older juveniles if the seriousness of the offense deserves a longer sentence than those available in juvenile court. Judges in states where juvenile court dispositions can continue until age twenty-one waive youths at about half the rate as judges in states where juvenile court jurisdiction ends at ages eighteen or nineteen (Snyder and Hutzler 1981; Vereb and Hutzler 1981; Nimick, Szymanski, and Snyder 1986).

A second constellation of amenability factors includes the youth's treatment prognosis as reflected in clinical evaluations and prior correctional interventions. Once a juvenile exhausts the available correctional resources, transfer becomes increasingly more likely (Podkopacz and Feld 1995, 1996).

Finally, judges assess dangerousness and the threats youths pose to others based on the present offense and prior record. Dangerousness variables include the seriousness of the offense, whether the youth used a weapon, and the length of the prior record (Fagan and Deschenes 1990; Podkopacz and Feld 1995, 1996; Howell 1996). Balancing these factors entails a trade-off between offense seriousness and offender persistence.

Asking a judge to decide a youth's amenability to treatment or dangerousness implicates many of the most fundamental issues of juvenile jurisprudence (Feld 1978). Legislation mandating an amenability or dangerousness inquiry assumes that effective treatment programs exist for at least some serious or chronic young offenders, presupposes that classification systems exist with which to differentiate among youths' treatment potentials or dangerousness, and presumes that clinicians or judges possess valid and reliable diagnostic tools with which to determine the appropriate disposition for a particular youth. Evaluation research challenges the legislative presuppositions, raising questions whether interventions systematically reduce recidivism among chronic or violent young offenders or whether judges or clinicians possess diagnostic tools with which to identify those who will or will not respond to treatment (Feld 1978, 1983, 1987; Sechrest 1987; Lab and Whitehead 1988, 1990). Statutes that authorize judges to waive jurisdiction if a youth poses a threat to the public require judges to predict future dangerousness even though clinicians and jurists lack the technical capacity reliably to predict low base-rate serious criminal behavior (Monahan 1981; Morris and Miller 1985; Fagan and Guggenheim 1996).

Judicial waiver criteria framed in terms of amenability to treatment or dangerousness give judges broad, standardless discretion. Lists of substantive factors such as those appended in *Kent* do not provide adequate guidance (Twentieth Century Fund 1978; Zimring 1981*a*).

Rather, catalogues of contradictory factors reinforce judges' discretion and allow them selectively to emphasize one element or another to justify any decision. Zimring (1981*a*) describes judicial waiver laws as the juvenile equivalent of the standardless capital punishment statutes condemned by the Supreme Court in *Furman v. Georgia*, 408 U.S. 238 (1972). Waiver also exposes some transferred juveniles to the possibility of capital punishment.

The subjective nature of waiver decisions, the absence of effective guidelines to structure outcomes, and the lack of objective indicators or scientific tools with which to classify youths allows judges to make unequal and disparate rulings without any effective procedural or appellate checks. Empirical analyses provide compelling evidence that judges apply waiver statutes in an arbitrary, capricious, and discriminatory manner (Hamparian et al. 1982; Fagan and Deschenes 1990; Feld 1990). States' waiver rates for similar types of offenders vary extensively (Hamparian et al. 1982; U.S. General Accounting Office 1995). Even within a single jurisdiction, judges do not administer, interpret, or apply waiver statutes consistently from county to county or court to court (Hamparian et al. 1982; Feld 1987, 1990). Research in several states reports a contextual pattern of "justice by geography" in which where youths lived, rather than what they did, determined their juvenile or adult status (Hamparian et al. 1982; Heuser 1985; Feld 1990, 1995). In some states, for example, rural judges waive jurisdiction over youths more readily than urban judges (Hamparian et al. 1982; Feld 1990; Lemmon, Sontheimer, and Saylor 1991; Poulos and Orchowsky 1994). Even within a single urban county, judges in the same court decide cases of similarly situated offenders differently (Podkopacz and Feld 1995, 1996). These differences influence both the characteristics of youths waived and the sentences they receive.

A youth's race also may affect waiver decisions (Eigen 1981*a*, 1981*b*; Hamparian et al. 1982; Fagan, Forst, and Vivona 1987). In analyses in four states in which the U.S. General Accounting Office (1995) could control for the effects of race on judicial waiver decisions, it found that judges transferred black youths charged with violent, property, or drug offenses more readily than comparable white offenders. Differences in judicial philosophies, the location of a waiver hearing, a youth's race, or organizational politics may explain as much about transfer decisions as do a youth's offense or personal characteristics.

2. *Legislative Exclusion and Prosecutors' Choices.* Legislative waiver provides the primary conceptual alternative to judicial waiver and ex-

cludes from juvenile court jurisdiction youths of certain ages charged with specified offenses or with particular prior records (Feld 1987). Concurrent-jurisdiction laws grant prosecutors the power to choose the forum without justifying that decision in a judicial hearing (McCarthy 1994). Youths have no constitutional right to a juvenile court. Legislatures create them by statute and define their jurisdiction, powers, and purposes. What they create, they also may modify or take away. States freely set juvenile courts' maximum age jurisdiction at seventeen, sixteen, or fifteen years old as a matter of state policy and without constitutional infirmity. If they define juvenile court jurisdiction to include only those persons below a jurisdictional age and whom prosecutors charge with a nonexcluded offense, then, by statutory definition, all other persons are adults.

Critics of offense exclusion question whether legislators can exclude offenses and remove discretion without making the process excessively rigid and overinclusive (Zimring 1981a, 1991). In a get tough climate, politicians experience considerable difficulty resisting their own impulses to adopt expansive lists of excluded "crimes de jour." Once a legislature adopts an excluded-offense or presumptive waiver statute, the list of offenses often lengthens quickly and results in far more youths being tried as adults than would occur under a more flexible, discretionary system. California amended its' presumptive waiver offense criteria seven times between 1977 and 1993 and increased the initial list of eleven serious violent crimes to twenty-three, including drug crimes, carjacking, and escape from a correctional facility (Feld 1995). Critics of prosecutorial waiver strategies contend that locally elected prosecutors often succumb to the same get tough pressures that influence legislators. Prosecutors often lack the experience or maturity that judges possess, exercise their discretion just as subjectively and idiosyncratically as do judges, and introduce additional geographic variability (Bishop, Frazier, and Henretta 1989; Bishop and Frazier 1991).

In short, excluded-offense and prosecutor-choice waiver legislation may suffer from the rigidity, inflexibility, and overinclusiveness characteristic of mandatory sentencing statutes (Tonry 1995, 1996). In practice, offense exclusion transfers discretion from judges to prosecutors who determine delinquent or criminal status by manipulating their charging decisions. States that use a concurrent-jurisdiction prosecutor-choice strategy simply make the allocation of power and sentencing authority explicit. While a rule-of-law approach can improve on unstructured judicial discretion, offense exclusion and prosecutor-choice laws do not provide either a jurisprudentially satisfactory or politically practical solution.

3. *Toward an Integrated Sentencing System.* Judicial waiver, offense exclusion, and prosecutor-choice laws determine the ultimate disposition of serious young offenders. States base the distinctions between treatment as a juvenile and punishment as an adult on waiver decisions or legislative lines that have no criminological significance other than their legal consequences. These jurisprudential antinomies may frustrate attempts to rationalize social control of serious and persistent young offenders. By adopting these policies, legislatures create false dichotomies and fail to acknowledge that young people mature constantly and criminal careers develop over time. Adolescence comprises a developmental continuum; young people do not graduate from irresponsible childhood one day to responsible adulthood the next, except as a matter of law.

Moreover, the strong correlation between age and criminal activity makes the current jurisdictional bifurcation especially problematic. The rates of many kinds of criminality peak in mid- to late adolescence, exactly at the juncture between the juvenile and criminal justice systems (Blumstein et al. 1986; Farrington, in this volume). Criminal careers research indicates that young offenders do not specialize in particular types of crime, that serious crime occurs within an essentially random pattern of persistent delinquent behavior, and that a small number of chronic delinquents commits many of the offenses and most of the violent crimes perpetrated by juveniles (Blumstein et al. 1986). Serious offenders are persistent offenders who simply add violent crimes to their diverse repertoire of active law-breaking. Although we cannot accurately or reliably predict future violence on the basis of an initial offense, a prior record of offending provides the best indicator of similar behavior in the future.

Waiver statutes and youth sentencing policies unsystematically attempt to differentiate between adolescent-only offenders and life-course persistent offenders. For virtually all purposes, most of the significant differences in seriousness of delinquency are between adolescent-only offenders, those juveniles with one or two delinquencies, and chronic offenders, those with five or more justice system involvements (Wolfgang, Figlio, and Sellin 1972; Farrington, in this volume). Age of onset of delinquency provides an important indicator of career criminality (Farrington 1986). Youths who begin delinquent careers early and become chronic offenders as juveniles appear more likely to continue to engage in serious and violent offending into adulthood (Blumstein, Farrington, and Moitra 1985). While most adolescent-only offenders desist after one or two contacts with the justice system, the probabilities of subsequent criminality for chronic offenders remain high and persist into adulthood (Blumstein et al. 1986). The small subset of chronic offenders account for most of the total delinquencies and even more of the violent offenses and homicides of their cohorts (Petersilia 1980; Blumstein et al. 1986; Tracy, Wolfgang, and Figlio 1990). Moreover, as they age, chronic offenders account for an increasingly larger proportion of the total and violent crimes committed by their cohort.

A rational sentencing policy requires integrated and coordinated penal responses to young career offenders on both sides of the current juvenile-adult line, especially when they make the transition between the two systems. Despite the research on criminal careers, however, juvenile and criminal courts' sentencing policies often may work at cross-purposes and frustrate rather than harmonize responses as serious young offenders move between the two systems (Greenwood 1986; Feld 1995). Until the recent amendments of waiver laws, criminal courts typically imposed longer sentences on older offenders because of their cumulative adult prior records even though their current rate of criminal activity was on the wane and sentenced more leniently chronic younger offenders whose rate of criminal activity was increasing or at its peak.

The lenient responses to many young career offenders when they make the transition to criminal courts occur because the criteria for removal from juvenile court and sentencing practices in adult criminal court lack congruence. A number of studies, primarily in jurisdictions that use judicial waiver, examine the sentences that criminal courts impose on transferred juveniles and consistently report a "punishment gap" (Greenwood, Petersilia, and Zimring 1980; Hamparian et al. 1982; Greenwood 1986; Feld 1995; Podkopacz and Feld 1996). The "lack of fit" between waiver decisions and criminal court sentences allowed many chronic and active young criminal offenders to fall between the cracks of the two systems.

Judicial waiver decisions actually involve two somewhat different but overlapping populations of young offenders, older chronic property offenders and violent youths. Criminal courts respond differently to these two types of offender clusters because of the differences in the nature of their present offense. In earlier times, prosecutors filed waiver motions against less than 2 percent of all delinquents (Nimick, Szymanski, and Snyder 1986). Even though the number of waiver motions increased by 68 percent between 1988 and 1992, they still constituted less than 2 percent of all delinquency petitions. Although prosecutors sought waiver for a larger proportion of youths charged with crimes against the person (2.4 percent) than with property offenses (1.3 percent), because of their numerical predominance, the largest number and proportion of waived juveniles were property offenders (5,200 and 45 percent of all waivers) rather than person offenders (4,000 and 34 percent of all waivers; Snyder and Sickmund 1995). About a decade ago, juvenile court judges transferred only about one-third (34.3 percent) of youths for offenses against the person and waived the largest proportion of juveniles for property crimes such as burglary (40.3 percent; Nimick, Szymanski, and Snyder 1986). Despite the recent rise in violent youth crime, juvenile court judges continued to transfer the largest plurality of youths for property offenses (45 percent) rather than for violent crimes against the person (34 percent; Snyder and Sickmund 1995). Only in 1993, for the first time, did the proportion of waived violent offenders (42 percent) exceed that of property offenders (38 percent; Snyder, Sickmund, and Poe-Yamagata 1996).

The nature of the offenses for which juvenile courts transferred juveniles and their relative youthfulness affected their first criminal court sentences. Although analyses of dispositions of youths tried as adults in several jurisdictions report substantial variation in sentencing practices, a policy of leniency often prevails. Several earlier studies reported that urban criminal courts incarcerated younger offenders at a lower rate than they did older offenders, youthful violent offenders received lighter sentences than did older violent offenders, and for about a two-year period after becoming adults, youths benefitted from informal lenient sentencing policies in adult courts (Twentieth Century Fund 1978; Greenwood, Abrahamse, and Zimring 1984). More recent research reports that juvenile court judges judicially waived primarily older chronic offenders charged with a property felony like burglary rather than with a violent crime (Snyder and Sickmund 1995), and criminal courts subsequently fined or placed on probation most juveniles judicially transferred (Hamparian et al. 1982; Gillespie and Norman 1984; Heuser 1985; Feld 1995). Moreover, criminal court judges imprisoned these transferred youths at lower rates than they did adults convicted of comparable offenses, and many incarcerated juveniles received sentences of one year or less, often shorter than the sentences juvenile court judges could impose on "deep-end" delinquents (Hamparian et al. 1982; Heuser 1985; Bortner 1986). Podkopacz and Feld (1995, 1996) compared the sentences received by youths tried as adults and those retained in juvenile court in an urban county and found that the juvenile court judges sentenced delinquent property offenders for terms longer than those ordered by their criminal court counterparts.

Other factors also contribute to the justice systems' failure to sentence persistent young offenders consistently when they make the transition to criminal court. Qualitative differences between juveniles' and adults' offenses and youths' group participation may contribute to the anomalous breach in social control. Juveniles' crimes may differ qualitatively from those committed by adults even within serious offense categories. Younger offenders may be less likely to be armed with guns, to inflict as much injury, or to steal as much property as adults charged with comparable offenses, and these age-related differences may affect the eventual sentences criminal courts impose (Greenwood, Petersilia, and Zimring 1980; McDermott and Hindelang 1981; Greenwood 1986). In a similar manner, juveniles commit their crimes in groups to a much greater extent than do adult offenders, and criminal court judges typically sentence accessories more leniently than principals (Zimring 1981*b*; Greenwood 1986). Because police arrest juveniles as multiple perpetrators of a single crime more frequently than adults, arrest statistics tend to overstate youths' contribution to the overall amount of violent crime. Juvenile robberies involve two or more actors about twice as often as do adult robberies (Greenwood, Petersilia, and Zimring 1980). About half of all juveniles arrested for homicide were involved in crimes with more than one criminal actor (Snyder, Sickmund, and Poe-Yamagata 1996). Thus qualitative differences in youths' offenses or their degree of participation may affect their eventual sentences.

4. *Recent Changes in Waiver Statutes.* State legislatures in the past two decades have extensively modified their transfer laws. Legislatures use offense criteria as a form of sentencing guidelines to limit judicial discretion, to guide prosecutorial charging decisions, or to exclude automatically certain youths from juvenile court jurisdiction (Feld 1987; Snyder and Sickmund 1995; Torbet et al. 1996). These amendments use offense criteria to integrate juvenile transfer and adult sentencing practices and reduce the punishment gap. Waiver statutes that focus on offense seriousness and criminal history, whether committed as a juvenile or an adult, rather than amorphous clinical considerations bet-

ter enable adult courts to respond more consistently to chronic and violent young offenders and to maximize social control of young career offenders. One cannot overemphasize either the amount and scope of legislative activity or the rapidity with which these changes spread (Snyder and Sickmund 1995; U.S. General Accounting Office 1995). Since 1992, forty-eight of the fifty-one states and the District of Columbia have amended provisions of their juvenile codes, sentencing statutes, and transfer laws to target youths who commit chronic, serious, or violent crimes (Torbet et al. 1996). The overarching legislative theme is a shift from the principle of individualized justice to the principle of offense, from rehabilitation to retribution (Feld 1987, 1988*b*).

a. Judicial Waiver. Although judicial waiver remains the predominant method of transfer, about three dozen states recently have amended waiver statutes to reduce their inconsistent application, to lessen intrajurisdiction disparities, and to improve the fit between waiver decisions and criminal sentencing practices (Fristch and Hemmens 1995; Snyder and Sickmund 1995). Lawmakers use offense criteria as a type of sentencing guideline to control judicial discretion, to focus on serious offenders, and to increase the numbers of youths waived. Reflecting these statutory changes, the numbers of youths judicially waived in the United States each year increased by 68 percent between 1988 and 1992, from about 7,000 cases to about 11,700 (Snyder and Sickmund 1995). During this same period, the numbers of youths judicially transferred for violent crimes increased 100 percent, from about 2,000 to 4,000 cases. In 1993, judges transferred about 11,800 juveniles, of whom 5,000 were charged with violent crimes (Snyder, Sickmund, and Poe-Yamagata 1996).

By focusing on serious crimes, often in combination with prior records, these amendments restrict judicial discretion and increase the probabilities that criminal courts will impose significant sentences following waiver. These amendments use offense criteria to limit judicial waiver only to certain serious offenses, to identify certain offenses alone or in combination with prior record for special procedural handling, or to prescribe the dispositional consequences that follow from proof of serious offenses or prior records. Some states use offense criteria to make transfer hearings mandatory for certain categories of offenses or to create a presumption for transfer and to shift to the youth the burden of proof to demonstrate why the juvenile court should retain jurisdiction (Feld 1987, 1995). Other states have enacted "once waived, always waived" provisions so that criminal courts decide

all subsequent cases involving transferred chronological juveniles (Torbet et al. 1996). About twenty states have lowered from sixteen to fourteen or even twelve the age at which judges may transfer youths
charged with serious offenses to criminal courts (Fritsch and Hemmens
1995; Torbet et al. 1996). Recent changes also shift the jurisprudential
focus of waiver hearings from the offender to the offense. States have
rejected amenability to treatment as the waiver criteria in favor of
"public safety," defined on the basis of the present offense, prior record, and the youth's culpability (Feld 1995).

b. *Offense Exclusion.*   Nearly two-thirds of the states now exclude
some serious offenses from juvenile court jurisdiction (Snyder and
Sickmund 1995; U.S. General Accounting Office 1995). These exclusion statutes typically supplement judicial waiver statutes. While some
states exclude only youths charged with capital crimes, murder, or offenses punishable by life imprisonment, others exclude longer lists of
offenses or youths charged with repeat offenses (Feld 1987; Snyder and
Sickmund 1995). Because most excluded-offense legislation targets serious violent offenses—murder, rape, kidnapping, or armed robbery—
youths identified by such provisions face the prospects of substantial
sentences if convicted as adults. Since 1992, nearly half the states have
expanded the lists of excluded offenses, lowered the ages of eligibility
for exclusion from sixteen to fourteen or thirteen years of age, or
granted prosecutors authority to direct file more cases in criminal
court (Fritsch and Hemmens 1995; U.S. General Accounting Office
1995; Torbet et al. 1996). As a result, increasing numbers of young
offenders charged with very serious crimes find themselves automatically in criminal court. However, as legislators expand lists of excluded
offenses to encompass less serious crimes or lesser included offenses
and lower the ages at which prosecutors may charge youths as adults,
they also reduce the certainty that criminal court judges will impose
significant adult sentences. Moreover, legislation in several excluded-
offense jurisdictions allows criminal court judges to "transfer back"
some youths for disposition in juvenile court (Snyder and Sickmund
1995). Because chronological juveniles charged with excluded offenses
begin as "automatic adults," we have virtually no data on the numbers
of youths in criminal courts below the general jurisdictional age, the
subsequent sentences they receive, or the numbers or dispositions of
those youths transferred back to juvenile courts (Snyder and Sickmund
1995; U.S. General Accounting Office 1995).

Under concurrent-jurisdiction statutes, legislatures also grant prosecutors more authority to charge youths directly in criminal courts. Again, the number of states that authorize this waiver strategy has more than doubled within the past decade (Feld 1987; Fritsch and Hemmens 1995; Snyder and Sickmund 1995). A few states employ charging guidelines based on the *Kent* criteria or other offense factors to structure prosecutorial direct-file decisions, although most leave the decision to individual prosecutors. As with excluded-offense legislation, we lack extensive data on the numbers of youths against whom prosecutors directly filed in criminal court. However, the U.S. General Accounting office (1995) estimates that prosecutors in some jurisdictions may charge as many as 10 percent of chronological juveniles in adult court. Indeed, by some calculations, prosecutors in Florida alone may direct file as many juveniles into criminal courts in that state as judges waive judicially nationwide (Bishop, Frazier, and Henretta 1989; Bishop and Frazier 1991; U.S. General Accounting Office 1995).

   c. Criminal Court Careers of Targeted Juvenile Offenders.   Judicial waiver statutes that use offense criteria explicitly to target serious violent offenders and laws that grant prosecutors discretion to choose the forum or that exclude violent offenses from juvenile court jurisdiction increase the likelihood that young offenders will receive significant sentences as adults. Recall that until the recent spate of statutory amendments, prosecutors typically charged most judicially waived juveniles with property offenses, not violent crimes, and that criminal courts neither imprisoned most of these adult first offenders nor imposed sentences longer than those available in juvenile courts. The limited research on the adult sentences received by violent youths produces mixed results (Snyder and Sickmund 1995).

   Restricting waiver to serious offenses and specifying special procedures apparently increases the likelihood that juvenile courts will waive and that criminal courts will impose significant adult sentences. Several studies examine the sentences that waived or excluded youths receive when tried as adults in jurisdictions that target them as serious offenders and found that their probabilities of significant adult sanctions increased. In 1976, California amended its judicial waiver statute, created a presumption that juvenile courts should waive youths charged with certain serious crimes, and shifted the burden of proof to the juvenile defendant (Cal. Welf. and   Inst. Code § 707[b] [1976]; Feld 1981*a*). Initial evaluations indicated that the changes increased the number of youths tried, convicted, and sentenced as adults after being charged with one of the enumerated offenses (Teilmann and Klein n.d.). Criminal court judges in Los Angeles did not sentence juveniles tried as adults more leniently than they did other offenders, the gravity or violence of the crime rather than the age or record of the offender determined the sentence for more serious crimes, and the prior juvenile record influenced the severity of the first adult sentence for marginal crimes like burglary (Greenwood, Petersilia, and Zimring 1980). A study in a northern California county reported that prosecutors filed waiver motions for four presumptive-transfer violent offenses for every one property offense, and judges waived about half the youths. Youths transferred and convicted as adults for crimes against the person received substantially greater punishment based solely on the seriousness of the present offense than did youths retained in juvenile court or transferred as chronic property offenders (Barnes and Franz 1989). As a result of the legislative changes, in 1990 and 1991 California juvenile courts waived the vast majority of youths (85.1 percent) to adult courts for violent offenses (U.S. General Accounting Office 1995).

A number of studies have analyzed prosecutorial waiver practices in Florida. The majority of youths whom prosecutors direct filed in Dade County (Miami), Florida, consisted of older males with multiple felony charges, primarily property crimes (55 percent burglary), and prior delinquency convictions, and criminal courts sentenced approximately two-thirds of them to substantial terms of imprisonment (Thomas and Bilchik 1985). Bishop, Frazier, and Henretta (1989) and Bishop and Frazier (1991) examined a broader sample of Florida direct-file cases and reported that between 1979 and 1987 the percentage of youths transferred increased from 1.29 percent to 7.35 percent of all delinquency petitions, and the proportion of transfers directly filed by prosecutors increased from 48 percent to 88 percent of all waivers. They found that prosecutors charged a majority (55 percent) of direct-file youths with property felonies and less than one-third of youths with crimes against the person. Moreover, as legislative amendments expanded prosecutors' authority to direct file, the proportion of violent offenders transferred actually declined from 30 percent in 1981 to 20 percent in 1984 (Bishop, Frazier, and Henretta 1989). Prosecutors apparently transferred many youths simply because they neared the age jurisdictional limits of juvenile courts. Frazier (1991) compared the characteristics of youths against whom prosecutors direct filed with those retained and confined in the deep end of the juvenile system and found that the latter youths appeared to be more serious offenders than the transferred youths in terms of their present offense, amount and quality of prior records, and prior correctional dispositions. Bishop et al. (1996) compared the postconviction recidivism of youths whom prosecutors direct filed in 1987 for noncapital or life offenses with a matched sample of retained juveniles and found that, by all measures, the youths whom prosecutors tried as adults did worse—they committed additional and more serious offenses more quickly than did those youths retained in juvenile jurisdiction.

The transfer decision has profound consequences for waived violent youths even though the decision itself lacks any apparent or consistent rationale. A study of the dispositions received by waived and retained youths in four urban sites whom prosecutors charged with a violent offense and who had a prior felony conviction reported that criminal courts incarcerated over 90 percent and imposed sentences five times longer than those given to youths with similar offense characteristics but who remained in juvenile court (Rudman et al. 1986). However, analysts could not identify the factors that juvenile court judges used initially to distinguish between the juveniles whom they waived or retained within this sample of violent youths (Fagan and Deschenes 1990).

A natural quasi-experiment compared young robbery and burglary offenders in New York, whose excluded offenses placed them in criminal court, with a similar sample of fifteen- and sixteen-year-old youths in matched counties in New Jersey whose age and offenses placed them in juvenile courts (Fagan 1995, 1996). The New York criminal courts convicted and incarcerated a somewhat larger proportion of youths, but both justice systems imposed sentences of comparable length. Although burglary offenders in both jurisdictions recidivated at about the same rate, adult robbery offenders in New York reoffended more quickly and at a higher rate than did the juveniles in New Jersey. Criminalizing adolescent crimes provides only symbolic benefits but allows youths to acquire criminal records earlier and thereby receive more severe sentences for subsequent adult offenses (Fagan 1995).

Several studies consistently indicate that criminal courts imprison more often and impose longer sentences on violent youths tried as adults than do juvenile courts. Although violent offenders constituted a small subset of all juveniles judicially waived in Oregon, criminal courts incarcerated 75 percent of the violent juveniles and imposed prison sentences in excess of six years (Heuser 1985). In Hennepin County (Minneapolis), Minnesota, criminal courts convicted and incarcerated transferred youths at higher rates than juvenile courts did the retained juveniles (Podkopacz and Feld 1995, 1996). Although juvenile courts imposed longer sentences on young property offenders than did criminal courts, the latter sentenced the violent young adults to terms about five times longer than those received by violent juveniles sentenced as delinquents (Podkopacz and Feld 1996). In Arizona, criminal court judges incarcerated only 43 percent of all transferred juveniles but imprisoned youths convicted of violent crimes almost three times as often as they did youths convicted of other types of offenses (McNulty 1996).

   d. *Persistent and Violent Young Offenders.*   Waiver laws, in all their guises, appear to confront two somewhat different but overlapping populations of offenders—persistent and violent youths. One group consists of chronic offenders currently charged with property crimes, but whose extensive delinquency histories, prior correctional exposures, and advancing age in relation to juvenile courts' maximum jurisdiction render them eligible for adult prosecution (Podkopacz and Feld 1995; U.S. General Accounting Office 1995). A second group consists of violent offenders. While some violent youths also are chronic offenders, others have less extensive prior records or exposure to juvenile court correctional treatment. Judges appear more likely to waive violent offenders at younger ages than to waive property offenders (Podkopacz and Feld 1995; McNulty 1996). For example, while 71.9 percent of all youths whom Arizona juvenile court judges waived were seventeen years of age, prosecutors charged three-quarters (75 percent) of the youths transferred at age fourteen with violent crimes but only 43.7 percent of the oldest waived juveniles (McNulty 1996).

   Because of differences in rates and types of offending by race, laws that target violent offenses for presumptive judicial waiver or for automatic exclusion indirectly have the effect of identifying larger proportions of black juveniles than white youths and exposing them to more severe adult penal consequences. As the number of judicially waived cases increased from 1988 onward and the proportion of violent offenses among waived cases increased, the percentage of black juveniles judicially waived to criminal court increased from 43 percent to 50 percent of all transferred youths. Although juvenile court judges waived an equal proportion of black and white youths (49 percent) in 1989, by 1993 the proportion of waived white youths decreased to 45 percent while black youths made up 52 percent of all waived juveniles (Snyder, Sickmund, and Poe-Yamagata 1996).

   The inconsistencies in criminal court sentencing practices—shorter adult sentences for waived property offenders than for those tried as juveniles and dramatically longer sentences for violent youths tried as adults—reflect jurisdictional bifurcation and the interplay between the differing characteristics of these two types of waived youths. How should both justice systems strike the balance between persistence and seriousness or respond when a youth who commits a serious crime manifestly is a child?

B. Criminal Court Processing and Sentencing of Waived and Excluded Juveniles

The recent changes in waiver laws increase the number of chronological juveniles charged, tried, detained, and sentenced in criminal courts. It is unfortunate that many states amended their waiver statutes without analyzing their systemic effect on various components of the juvenile or criminal justice systems (Torbet et al. 1996). An influx of serious young offenders in criminal courts may impose greater demands on prosecutorial and judicial resources without corresponding increases in criminal justice personnel. In many states, waived juveniles' pretrial detention status remains ambiguous and may result in lengthy confinement pending an appeal by the youth or by a prosecutor if a judge denies a waiver motion (Torbet et al. 1996). During site visits to evaluate conditions of confinement, researchers found "a growing percentage of the detainees were juveniles waiting transfers. These juveniles were often detained for many months, straining the capacity of the [detention] centers, which were designed for short-term confinement, to provide effective programming" (Parent et al. 1997, p. 3). In a similar manner, as criminal courts impose more severe sentences on young offenders, prison populations may increase without any corresponding increases in bed space or age-appropriate programs.

Despite legislative efforts to transfer more youths to criminal courts, surprisingly few analysts compare the rates of conviction or sentences of waived or excluded youths with those of retained juveniles or similar adult defendants. The few studies of waived juveniles' conviction rates in criminal courts suggest that criminal courts convict them at higher rates than do juvenile courts and perhaps more readily than they do other adult defendants (U.S. General Accounting Office 1995). Of course, these findings may reflect prior prosecutorial and judicial screening decisions and the sample selection bias of youths waived to criminal court. Fagan (1995, 1996) reports that criminal courts convicted youths charged with robbery at a significantly higher rate than did juvenile courts. Podkopacz and Feld (1995, 1996) reported higher rates of conviction and some type of incarceration for waived youths in criminal courts than for those retained in juvenile courts. The U.S. General Accounting Office (1995) analyzed conviction rates of waived youths in seven states and found that, although conviction rates varied from state to state and by type of offense, criminal courts convicted waived juveniles at about the same rates as other young adult offenders.

Adult criminal courts sentence waived young offenders primarily on the basis of the seriousness of their present offense. The emphasis on the present offense reflects ordinary criminal sentencing practices as well as the failure to include juvenile convictions systematically in young adults' criminal histories. As a result, criminal courts often sentence violent and persistent young offenders significantly differently. The former may receive substantial sentences of imprisonment, including life without parole or the death penalty. As noted above, many studies report that waived violent youths receive sentences four or more times longer than do their retained juvenile counterparts. Moreover, violent youths often receive these disparate consequences simply because judges or prosecutors idiosyncratically or legislators arbitrarily decided to try them as adults rather than as juveniles. Persistent offenders, by contrast, often receive more lenient sentences as adult first offenders than do their retained juvenile counterparts. Young property offenders sentenced in criminal court benefit from the comparative leniency accorded to property offenders generally, to younger offenders specifically, and to those without substantial adult prior criminal histories. As a result, chronic property offenders sentenced as juveniles often receive longer sentences than youths whom judges waived because they were not amenable to treatment or posed a threat to the community.

1. *Use of Juvenile Records to Enhance Youths' Criminal Sentences.* Juvenile and adult criminal courts' failure to maintain centralized repositories of offenders' prior records of arrests and convictions or to integrate them across both justice systems may frustrate sentencing of persistent career offenders when they make the transition between the two systems. Although extensive juvenile criminality provides the most reliable indicator of the onset of a criminal career, the failure to combine criminal histories across both systems creates a disjunction that "serious offenders can exploit to escape the control and punishment their chronic or violent offenses properly deserve" (Farrington, Ohlin,

and Wilson 1986, p. 126). Criminal courts often lack access to the juvenile component of offenders' criminal histories because of the confidentiality of juvenile court records, the functional and physical separation of juvenile and criminal court staff who must collate and combine these records, sheer bureaucratic ineptitude, and the difficulty of maintaining an integrated system to track offenders and compile complete criminal histories across both systems (Petersilia 1980; Greenwood 1986). The juvenile court practice of sealing or purging records to avoid stigmatizing offenders impedes the use of juvenile court records to identify young career offenders and to enhance their subsequent sentences.

Despite the traditional confidentiality of and restricted access to juvenile courts records, states increasingly use prior juvenile convictions to enhance adult sentences (Miller 1995; Torbet et al. 1996). Several states' sentencing guidelines and the United States Sentencing Commission's guidelines include some juvenile prior convictions in an adult defendant's criminal history score (Feld 1995; *U.S. Sentencing Guidelines Manual* § 4A1.2 [1995]). Under California's three-strikes sentencing law, a juvenile adjudication can constitute a prior felony conviction for purposes of sentence enhancements (Cal. Penal Code § 667[d][3] [1994]). A survey of state statutes reports that about half of the states systematically consider juvenile records in setting adult sentences (Miller 1995). Sentencing judges often assert the importance of access to defendants' prior records of juvenile convictions (e.g., *United States v. Davis*, 48 F.3d 277, 280 [7th Cir. 1995]).

Some states include the juvenile record as a discretionary factor to consider when available while others formally include some component of a juvenile record in calculating a youth's criminal history score (Miller 1995). Most states' sentencing guidelines weight juvenile prior offenses less heavily than comparable adult convictions and include, for example, only juvenile felonies committed after age sixteen (Feld 1981*a*, 1995). However, a few states do not distinguish qualitatively between juvenile and adult prior convictions and include both equally in an offender's criminal history score (e.g., Kan. Stat. Ann. § 21-4170[a] [1995]).

States' expanded uses of juveniles' prior records to integrate the justice systems' responses to career offenders and to enhance the sentences of young adult offenders raise sometimes troubling issues in light of the quality of procedural justice by which juvenile courts obtain those original convictions. Juvenile courts in some states may adjudicate as many as half of all youths delinquent without the assistance of counsel (Feld 1988*a*, 1989, 1993*b*), and most states deny juveniles access to a jury trial (Feld 1984, 1995). The Supreme Court denied juveniles a constitutional right to a jury trial in juvenile courts because delinquents supposedly received treatment rather than punishment (*McKeiver*, 403 U.S. 528 [1971]; Feld 1995). States use those delinquency convictions obtained with less stringent procedures to *treat* youths as juveniles in order subsequently to *punish* them more severely as adults (*United States v. Williams*, 891 F.2d 212 [9th Cir. 1989]). The courts reason that the subsequent use for enhancement of a conviction valid at the time it was obtained does not violate due process (*United States v. Johnson*, 28 F.3d 151 [D.C. Cir. 1994]). However, it does seem contradictory to provide youths with less procedural justice in the name of rehabilitation and then to use those convictions to sentence them more severely as adults. Although rational sentencing policy supports systematic use of juvenile records of convictions, justice and fairness require adult criminal procedural safeguards to assure the quality and legitimacy of their use.

The increased use of juvenile court records to enhance criminal sentences reflects a more widespread erosion of confidentiality in juvenile court proceedings. Recent juvenile code amendments increase public access to juvenile court proceedings, expand centralized repositories of juveniles' fingerprints and arrest records, and broaden the dissemination of information about juvenile delinquency adjudications (Torbet et al. 1996). Between 1992 and 1995, ten states expanded public access to delinquency proceedings; now nearly half of all states permit or require public access to juvenile proceedings involving youths charged with violent, serious, or repeat offenses (Torbet et al. 1996). About half the states maintain a central repository to hold juvenile arrest and disposition records (Miller 1995). Forty-six states and the District of Columbia allow police to fingerprint juveniles for at least some types of offenses (Miller 1995; Torbet et al. 1996). States increasingly authorize information sharing among juvenile courts, law enforcement, schools, and youth-serving agencies to coordinate services and social control (Torbet et al. 1996).

2. *Proportionality and Capital Punishment.* Waiver of youths to criminal courts for sentencing as adults implicates legal and cultural understandings of juveniles' criminal responsibility. For example, waiver legislation that excludes capital offenses from juvenile court jurisdiction exposes some youths to the possibility of execution for of-

fenses they committed as juveniles (Streib 1987). Imposing sentences of life without parole on waived youths for crimes they committed at thirteen or fourteen years of age and executing them for crimes they committed at sixteen or seventeen years of age challenges the social construction of adolescence and the idea that juveniles are less criminally responsible than adults.

Questions about young people's criminal responsibility arise in the broader contexts of differing views about culpability and deserved punishments, tensions between retributive and utilitarian sentencing policies, and ambiguities concerning the social and legal construction of childhood. Laws that expose children to mandatory life terms or to the death penalty constitute a political and cultural judgment that young people may be just as blameworthy and culpable as their somewhat older counterparts (Van den Haag 1975).

a. The Death Penalty. Both historically and at present, some states have executed people for crimes committed while they were children (Streib 1987). States have executed nearly three hundred people for crimes committed as chronological juveniles, and courts currently impose about 2 percent of death penalties on minors (Streib 1987). Since the reinitiation of capital punishment in 1973 after *Furman v. Georgia*, 408 U.S. 238 (1972), states have executed nine offenders for crimes they committed as juveniles, six since 1990 (Streib 1995). During this period, judges have pronounced death sentences on 140 offenders for crimes committed as juveniles, or 2.6 percent of all capital sentences (Streib 1995).

The Supreme Court considered the culpability of young offenders on several occasions in the 1980s in the context of death penalty litigation. In *Thompson v. Oklahoma*, 486 U.S. 815 (1988), the Court pondered whether a state violated the Eighth Amendment prohibition on cruel and unusual punishments by executing an offender for a heinous murder he committed when he was fifteen years old. A plurality of the Court overturned the capital sentence and concluded that "a young person is not capable of acting with the degree of culpability [as an adult] that can justify the ultimate penalty" (*Thompson*, 486 U.S. at 823 [1988]). The following year in *Stanford v. Kentucky*, 492 U.S. 361 (1989), a different plurality upheld the death penalty for murders committed by juveniles sixteen or seventeen years of age at the time of their offense. Of the thirty-eight states that authorize the death penalty, twenty-one states allow the execution of offenders for crimes committed at age sixteen, and an additional four permit their execution for crimes committed at age seventeen (Streib 1987, 1995; Snyder and Sickmund 1995). Thus *Stanford* left to state legislatures the task of formulating a death penalty sentencing policy for older juveniles.

b. Proportionality and Youthfulness. The Supreme Court gives even greater constitutional deference to states' sentencing policy decisions outside of the context of capital punishment, upholds mandatory life sentences even for drug crimes, and eschews proportionality analyses (*Harmelin v. Michigan*, 111 S. Ct. 2680 [1991]). The Court's deference to states' criminal policy judgments grants state legislatures virtually unreviewable authority to prescribe penalties for crimes. The Court's rejection of proportionality as a constitutional limit on states' criminal sentences has special significance for juveniles tried as adults. Sound bites of contemporary politics—"adult crime, adult time" or "old enough to do the crime, old enough to do the time"—convey current youth sentencing policy. Many of the most serious crimes for which criminal courts convict youths carry substantial sentences, mandatory minima, or even life without parole. Exclusion statutes without minimum age restrictions expose even very young offenders to such harsh penalties. Although section 5H.1 of the federal sentencing guidelines explicitly rejects youthfulness as a justification to mitigate sentences outside of the guidelines range, several state laws recognize youthfulness as a mitigating factor. These statutes typically enumerate mitigating factors that include some recognition of youthfulness.[1] Under such aggravating-mitigating sentencing laws, trial court judges regularly consider youthfulness both de jure and de facto; appellate courts remand them for resentencing if they do not (e.g., *State v. Strunk*, 846 P.2d 1297 [Utah 1993]). However, states that recognize youthfulness as a mitigating factor simply treat it as one element to weigh with other factors when sentencing (*State v. Adams*, 864 S.W.2d 31 [Tenn. 1993]).

In most jurisdictions, whether a trial judge treats youthfulness as a mitigating factor rests within his or her sound discretion, and failure to exercise leniency does not constitute reversible error or an abuse of discretion. Appellate courts regularly affirm mandatory sentences of life without parole for thirteen-year-old juveniles convicted as adults and reject any special consideration of the youth's age (e.g., *State v. Massey*, 803 P.2d 340 [1990]; *State v. Furman*, 858 P.2d 1092 [1993]).

---

[1] Typical mitigating factors include "the defendant's age, immaturity, or limited mental capacity" (N.C. Gen. Stat. § 15A-1340.16[e][4]), "the defendant was too young to appreciate the consequences of the offense" (Fla. Stat. § 921.0016[4][k]), or simply "the youth of the offender at the time of the offense" (La. Stat. § 905.5[f]).

In a singular exception, the Nevada Supreme Court ruled that a mandatory term of life without parole imposed on a fourteen-year-old convicted of murder constituted cruel and unusual punishment under the state constitution (*Naovarath v. State*, 779 P2d 944 [Nev. Sup. Ct. 1989]). Because the waiver statute excluded murder from juvenile court jurisdiction without any minimum age restriction (Nev. Rev. Stat. § 62.040 [1979]), the Nevada court held that there must be some very young age at which a criminal sentence of life without parole would constitute a cruel and unusual punishment (*Naovarath*, 779 P.2d 944 [1989]). The court concluded that even for the most serious crimes, a sentence of life without parole constituted a disproportionately cruel and unusual penalty because of "the undeniably lesser culpability of children for their bad actions, their capacity for growth and society's special obligation to children" (*Naovarath*, 779 P.2d at 948 [1989]). Although the Nevada court affirmed proportionality analyses and juveniles' reduced culpability, it provided virtually no practical protections or limitation on the legislature's power to prescribe severe penalties for youths. By a three to two vote, the court held only that, in order to pass state constitutional muster, a youth must receive a parole hearing at some time in the distant future.

3. *Correctional Consequences of Sentencing Youths as Adults.* As a result of recent changes in waiver laws, criminal courts sentence increasing numbers of youths to adult correctional facilities. It is unfortunate that we lack reliable data on the number of incarcerated juveniles because most states do not classify young inmates on the basis of the process that brought them to prison. Many youths who committed their crimes as chronological juveniles may be adults by the time courts have waived, convicted, and sentenced them to prison. Because of the recency of many changes in waiver statutes, correctional administrators have not yet fully experienced the population or programming implications of these policy changes.

A 1991 survey of state correctional administrators reported that convicts seventeen years old or younger constituted less than 1 percent of 712,000 prisoners but did not distinguish between waived or excluded youths and those in states in which juvenile court jurisdiction ended at fifteen or sixteen years of age (U.S. General Accounting Office 1995). Another recent survey reported that offenders younger than eighteen years of age constituted about 2 percent of new court commitments to prisons in thirty-five states and the Federal Bureau of Prisons and that about three-quarters of those youths were seventeen at the time of their confinement (Snyder and Sickmund 1995). In 1993, criminal courts sentenced about 5,200 youths seventeen years old or younger to adult prisons (Parent et al. 1997).

Recall that criminal courts sentenced juveniles waived for property and for violent crimes differently as adults and that recent waiver legislative amendments increasingly target violent youths. As a result, among persons sentenced to prison, a substantially larger proportion of younger offenders are committed for violent crimes than is true for adult prison commitments. For example, for violent crimes of youths under age eighteen sentenced to prison, 50 percent had been convicted of violent crimes, compared with 29 percent of adults admitted to prison. The percentages of youths committed to prison who had been convicted of serious violent crimes exceeded the proportions for sentenced adults for murder (7 percent vs. 3 percent), robbery (22 percent vs. 10 percent), and assault (13 percent vs. 8 percent). Moreover, because of the disparities in rates of violent offending by race, criminal courts sentenced a majority of black youths (54 percent) to prison for violent offenses and a majority of white youths (57 percent) for property crimes. Because of the differences in lengths of sentences imposed for violent and property offenses, racial disparities in prison inmate populations will grow over time.

The infusion of juvenile offenders poses a challenge to corrections officials to develop more programming and age-appropriate conditions of confinement for young or more vulnerable inmates (Torbet et al. 1996). Adult correctional administrators anticipate "increased pressure on an already burdened state corrections system" (LIS 1995, p. 2). Half the agencies responding to a recent survey expect increases of 10 percent or more, and a quarter expected increases of more than 50 percent in their inmate population under age eighteen over the next five years (LIS 1995).

Subject to variations in state laws and available facilities, correctional options for handling juveniles include straight adult incarceration with minimal differentiation between juveniles and adults other than routine classification of inmates by age, offense, size, or vulnerability; graduated incarceration in which youths begin their sentences in a juvenile or separate adult facility and then serve the remainder of their sentence in the adult facility; or age-segregated incarceration either in separate facilities within the prison or in separate youth facilities for younger adults (LIS 1995; Torbet et al. 1996). Recent analyses of correctional policies reported that nearly all states confine juveniles sentenced as adults in adult correctional facilities either with younger adult offenders or in the general population if the juvenile is of a certain age, for example, sixteen (Torbet et al. 1996). "In 1994, thirty-six states dispersed young inmates in housing with adult inmates (half as a general practice and half only in certain circumstances). Nine states housed young inmates with those ages eighteen to twenty-one but not with older inmates. Only six states never housed young inmates with people eighteen and older; they either have transferred young inmates to their state juvenile training schools until they reached the age of majority or have housed them in segregated living units within an adult prison" (Parent et al. 1997, p. 5). Prison officials generally regarded juveniles convicted in criminal courts as adults and employed the same policies, programs, and conditions of confinement for waived youths as for other adult inmates (U.S. General Accounting Office 1995). A few states house younger criminal offenders in facilities separate from adults. A one-day count on June 30, 1994, reported approximately 250 inmates ages thirteen to fifteen and 3,100 ages sixteen to seventeen housed in separate adult correctional facilities (Torbet et al. 1996).

The influx of younger offenders poses management, programming, and control challenges for correctional administrators. Young peoples' dietary and exercise needs differ from those of older inmates (Parent et al. 1997). Younger inmates may engage in more institutional misconduct, and management techniques appropriate for adults may be less effective when applied to juveniles. Evaluations of the prison adjustment of serious or violent youthful offenders are mixed. A few states report that young offenders pose special management problems or commit more disciplinary infractions than do older inmates while other states report few differences (LIS 1995). One systematic study of the prison adjustment of young offenders in Texas compared a sample of waived youths convicted of violent crimes committed before the age of seventeen with a matched sample of incarcerated inmates ages seventeen to twenty-one at the time of their offenses (McShane and Williams 1989). The waived violent youths adapted less well, experienced more difficulty adjusting to institutional life, accumulated more extensive disciplinary histories, earned less good time, and received higher custody classifications (McShane and Williams 1989).

III. Sentencing in the Juvenile Justice System

The jurisprudential and policy shifts that altered waiver policies also affect the sentences that juvenile court judges impose on serious delinquents (Feld 1988*b*; Torbet et al. 1996). Some changes represent symbolic responses, like relabelling "dispositional" hearings as "sentencing" hearings (Idaho Stat. § 20-520 [1995]) or renaming a "department of youth treatment and rehabilitation" as a "department of juvenile corrections" (Ariz. Code § 8-241 [1995]). It is ironic that *Gault*'s extension of procedural rights legitimated the imposition of more severe sanctions by providing delinquents with a veneer of due process.

For the Supreme Court in *McKeiver*, the differences between juvenile treatment and criminal punishment provided the primary rationale to deny jury trials in delinquency proceedings and to maintain a juvenile court separate from the adult system (Gardner 1982; Feld 1988*b*). Although most people readily understand that punishment involves involuntary and coerced loss of personal liberty or autonomy because a person committed a crime (Hart 1968), those elementary features eluded the Supreme Court in *McKeiver*. Rather, the indeterminate and nonproportional length of juvenile dispositions and the "eschewing [of] blameworthiness and punishment for evil choices" satisfied the Court that "there remained differences of substance between criminal and juvenile courts" (*McKeiver*, 403 U.S. at 551–52).

Perhaps the Court's failure to distinguish between treatment and punishment stemmed from its own constitutional uncertainty about the conceptual differences between the two. Maybe it refrained from systematically analyzing the differences because it realized that, practically, none might exist for youths charged with crimes. Perhaps, more charitably, the Court possessed less information about juvenile justice reality than we do today. The President's Commission on Law Enforcement and Administration of Justice (1967*a*, 1967*b*) had only begun to reveal the bankruptcy of juvenile courts' treatment ideology when the landmark juvenile court decisions were made.

This section analyzes juvenile sentencing laws and policy, judicial administration, and correctional practices. Statutes and practices that base a youth's sentence on past conduct—present offense or prior record—typically impose determinate and proportional, or mandatory minimum, sanctions for purposes of retribution or deterrence. Statutes and practices that sentence offenders to improve their future welfare—diagnoses or predictions about the effects of intervention on a person's future conduct—typically impose indeterminate and nonproportional dispositions for purposes of rehabilitation or incapacitation. Many states have recently enacted determinate and mandatory minimum statutes to regulate judicial sentencing discretion, to enhance the cer-

tainty and predictability of juvenile sanctions, and to displace rehabilitative, indeterminate sentences with more punitive ones (Feld 1988*b*).
In practice, a youth's present offense and prior record dominate juvenile court sentencing decisions. Evaluations of juvenile court sentencing practices, treatment effectiveness, and conditions of confinement
reveal increasingly punitive juvenile court and corrections systems.
These various indicators strongly suggest that despite juvenile courts'
persisting rehabilitative rhetoric, the reality of *treating* juveniles closely
resembles *punishing* adult criminals. This jurisprudential and administrative convergence erodes *McKeiver*'s constitutional rationale and the
justifications for a separate criminal system for young offenders.

A. Punishment and Treatment

Most states' juvenile court statutes contain a purposes clause or pre-
amble that articulates the underlying rationale of the legislation to aid
courts in interpreting the statutes (Walkover 1984; Feld 1988*b*). The
traditional purpose of juvenile courts was benevolent: "to secure for
each minor . . . such care and guidance, preferably in his own home,
as will serve the moral, emotional, mental, and physical welfare of the
minor and the best interests of the community" (Ill. Ann. Stat. chap.
37, paras. 701–2 [Smith-Hurd 1972]) and to remove "the taint of
criminality and the penal consequences of criminal behavior, by substituting therefore an individual program of counseling, supervision,
treatment, and rehabilitation" (N.H. Rev. Stat. Ann. § 169-B:1 II
[1979]). In the decades since *Gault* and *McKeiver*, however, more than
one-quarter of the states have revised their juvenile codes' statement
of legislative purpose, deemphasized rehabilitation and the child's best
interest, and asserted the importance of public safety, punishment, and
accountability in the juvenile justice system (Feld 1988*b*).[2] Some courts
recognize that these changes signal basic changes in philosophical direction and acknowledge that "punishment" constitutes an acceptable
purpose of juvenile courts' dispositions. In *State v. Lawley*, the Washington Supreme Court reasoned in Orwellian fashion that "sometimes
punishment is treatment" and upheld the legislature's conclusion that

---

[2] States' redefined juvenile code purposes include objectives such as "the protection
and safety of the public" (Cal. Welf. & Inst. Code § 202 [West Supp. 1988]), "the application of sanctions which are consistent with the seriousness of the offense" (Fla. Stat.
Ann. § 39.001[2][a] [West Supp. 1988]), to "render appropriate punishment to offenders" (Haw. Rev. Stat. § 571-1 [1985]), and to "promote public safety [and] hold juvenile
offenders accountable for such juvenile's behavior" (Kan. Stat. § 38-1601 [1997]).

"accountability for criminal behavior, the prior criminal activity and punishment commensurate with age, crime, and criminal history does as much to rehabilitate, correct, and direct an errant youth as does the prior philosophy of focusing upon the particular characteristics of the individual juvenile" (91 Wash. 2d at 656–57, 591 P.2d at 773 [1979]). In a similar manner, the Nevada Supreme Court endorsed punishment as an appropriate function of juvenile courts. "By formally recognizing the legitimacy of punitive and deterrent sanctions for criminal offenses juvenile courts will be properly and somewhat belatedly expressing society's firm disapproval of juvenile crime and will be clearly issuing a threat of punishment for criminal acts to the juvenile population" (*In re Seven Minors*, 99 Nev. at 432, 664 P.2d at 950 [1983]).

1. *Juvenile Court Sentencing Statutes and Dispositional Practices.* Originally, juvenile courts fashioned indeterminate and nonproportional sentences to meet the child's real needs (Mack 1909; Rothman 1980). In principle, a youth's offense constituted only a diagnostic symptom, and treatment personnel released the offender once they determined that rehabilitation had occurred. By contrast, when courts punish offenders, they typically impose determinate or mandatory sentences based on the gravity of the past offense. Contrasting indeterminate, nonproportional, and offender-oriented dispositions with determinate, proportional, and offense-based sentences provides another indicator of juvenile courts' increasing reliance on punishment as a response to delinquency.

a. Indeterminate and Determinate Sentences. Most states' juvenile codes authorized courts to impose indeterminate sentences because penal therapists cannot predict in advance the course or duration of treatment necessary to attain success (Mack 1909; Ryerson 1978; Rothman 1980). While some statutes instruct judges to consider the "least restrictive alternative," most allow the court to confine a delinquent within a range for a period of years or until the offender reaches the age of majority or some other statutory limit (Feld 1988*b*). Traditionally, juvenile court judges exercised virtually unrestricted discretion to dismiss, place on probation, remove from home, or institutionalize a youth.

In many states, once a judge sentences a youth to the state's juvenile correctional agency, the judge loses authority over the youth, and the correctional authority or parole board determines when to release the juvenile (Krisberg and Austin 1993). Indeterminate sentencing statutes typically provide for an unspecified period of confinement and a wide range between the minimum and maximum terms available. Corrections officials base their release decisions, in part, on youths' behavior during confinement and progress toward rehabilitative goals rather than on formal standards or the committing offense (Coates, Forst, and Fisher 1985).

By contrast, when judges sentence juveniles under a determinate or presumptive sentencing framework, they typically impose proportional sanctions within a relatively narrow dispositional range based on the seriousness of the offense, offense history, and age. In several states, courts impose mandatory minimum sentences based on the offense for which they convicted the youth. In other states, correctional administrators determine youths' presumptive length of institutional stay or eligibility for parole shortly after their commitment based on formal standards that prescribe terms proportional to the seriousness of the offense or prior record (Coates, Forst, and Fisher 1985).

Currently, nearly half of the states use some type of determinate or mandatory minimum offense-based sentencing provisions to regulate aspects of juvenile dispositions, institutional commitment, or release (Sheffer 1995; Torbet et al. 1996). As with legislative changes in waiver statutes, amendments to juvenile court sentencing statutes allocate to the judicial, legislative, and executive branches the power to make institutional commitment and release decisions (Guarino-Ghezzi and Loughran 1996). Determinate sentencing provisions restrict judicial sentencing discretion, mandatory minimum statutes reflect legislative sentencing decisions, and correctional or parole release guidelines enable the executive branch to determine lengths of confinement. And, as with waiver, these provisions use offense criteria to rationalize sentencing decisions, to increase the penal bite of juvenile court sanctions, and to enable legislators symbolically to demonstrate their "toughness" regardless of the effect on juvenile crime rates (Altschuler 1994). It is difficult to attribute the various statutory responses exclusively to youth violence, but rather to the political "felt need" to punish serious and persistent offenders.

b. Determinate Sentences in Juvenile Courts.   In 1977, the state of Washington departed dramatically from traditional rehabilitative dispositions, revised its juvenile code to emphasize "just deserts," and became the first state to enact a determinate sentencing statute for delinquents (Schneider and Schram 1983; Castellano 1986). The Washington law used presumptive sentencing guidelines to achieve offender and system accountability and based youths' sentences on the seriousness and persistence of their offending rather than their real needs. The Washington guidelines created three categories of offenders—serious, middle, and minor—and imposed presumptive, determinate, and proportional sentences based on a juvenile's age, present offense, and prior record (Fisher, Fraser, and Forst 1985). The statute provided standard dispositional ranges that include both upper and lower limits, specified aggravating and mitigating factors for sentencing within the range, and allowed a judge to depart from the standard range only when imposing the presumptive sentence would result in a manifest injustice. The guidelines prohibited confinement of a first or minor offender and provided that serious offenders serve sentences ranging from 125 weeks to three years. The Washington code revisions significantly increased the proportionality of sentences and produced a stronger relationship between the seriousness of youths' offenses and their lengths of institutional stay than prevailed under the previous, indeterminate regime (Schneider and Schram 1983; Fisher, Fraser, and Forst 1985). Despite greater equality and uniformity in sentencing, social structural and geographic variations continued to produce higher rates of referral and confinement for minority youths than for white delinquents (Bridges et al. 1995).

Other jurisdictions also employ offense-based sentencing principles in juvenile courts. In New Jersey, juvenile court judges consider offense, criminal history, and statutory aggravating and mitigating factors to sentence juveniles (New Jersey Juvenile Delinquency Disposition Commission 1986; N.J. Stat. Ann. §§ 2A:4A-43[a], 4A-44[a], 4A-44[d] [West 1993]). Recently, Oklahoma adopted a serious and habitual juvenile offender law that targets violent youths and those persistent offenders with three separate felony adjudications and creates a mechanism to develop determinate sentencing guidelines (Okla. Stat. Ann. tit. 10 § 7303.5.3 [West. 1995]). In 1994, the Arizona legislature mandated the Arizona Supreme Court to promulgate dispositional guidelines that focused on the seriousness of a youth's present offense and prior record in order to regularize judges' institutional commitment decisions (McNulty and Russell 1995). In 1996, Texas adopted "progressive sanctions guidelines" to "ensure . . . uniform and consistent consequences and punishments that correspond to the seriousness of each offender's current offense, prior delinquent history . . . [and] balance public protection and rehabilitation while holding juvenile offenders accountable" (Tex. Fam. Code Ann. § 59.001 [Vernon Supp. 1996]). The Texas guidelines assign a youth to one of seven sanction levels based on the seriousness of the offense and attach dispositional consequences to each severity level. For some proponents of a more traditional rehabilitative juvenile court, concepts like "progressive sanctions" or "graduated sanctions" represent an effort to enlist punitive principles like determinacy and proportionality in the service of treatment goals (Wilson and Howell 1995). Combining "risk assessment" with "needs assessment" permits immediate, intermediate, and increasing intervention based on seriousness and persistence (Krisberg et al. 1995).

c. Legislative Sentencing Decisions—Mandatory Minimum Terms of Confinement. Nearly half (twenty-two) of the states use some type of offense-based guidelines to regulate judicial sentencing discretion. These statutes typically include age and offense criteria to define serious or persistent offenders and prescribe their sentences (Sheffer 1995). Juvenile codes in a number of states allow or require judges to impose mandatory minimum sentences for certain serious crimes or designated felonies (Feld 1988*b*; Sheffer 1995). Under some laws, judges retain discretion whether or not to impose the mandated sanctions, whereas others require a judge to commit a youth convicted of a defined offense for the mandatory minimum period (Feld 1988*b*; Torbet et al. 1996). In Delaware, for example, judges "shall" sentence any youth convicted of any second felony within one year to a minimum term of six months confinement (Del. Code. tit. 10 § 1009).

While states' nomenclatures differ, these mandatory minimum sentencing laws typically apply to "violent and repeat offenders," "mandatory sentence offenders," "aggravated juvenile offenders," "habitual offenders," "serious juvenile offenders," or "designated felons" (e.g., Ala. Code § 12-15-71.1 [1990]; Colo. Rev. Stat. § 19-1-103 [1993]; Feld 1988*b*). The statutory criteria target those violent and persistent juvenile offenders over whom juvenile courts do not waive jurisdiction either because of their youthfulness or lesser culpability. Youths charged with violent crimes like murder, rape, robbery, aggravated assault or those who have prior felony convictions constitute the primary legislative concerns. Recent amendments add to these lists of serious offenders youths charged with crimes involving firearms or who commit violent or drug crimes on school grounds (e.g., Ark. Stat. § 9-27-330[c] [1989]). And, as with changes in waiver laws, the rate of legislative change accelerates. "Since 1992, fifteen states and the District of Columbia have added or modified statutes that provide for a mandatory minimum period of incarceration of juveniles committing certain violent or other serious crimes" (Torbet et al. 1996, p. 14).

Most of these mandatory minimum sentencing statutes target youths similar to or only somewhat less serious or younger than those considered eligible for waiver or exclusion to criminal court. In the event that juvenile courts retain jurisdiction over serious young offenders, legislators use mandatory minimum sentences to assure that judges and corrections officials confine these youths for significant terms. For youths convicted of these serious offenses, the statutes prescribe mandatory minimum terms of confinement that range from twelve to eighteen months, to age twenty-one, or to the adult limit for the same offense (Feld 1988b). For example, in Georgia, juvenile court judges may sentence a youth convicted of a designated felony to the Department of Youth Services for a term of five years with a minimum period of confinement of twelve months or eighteen months, depending on the offense, in a "youth development center" (Ga. Code § 15-11-37[2] [1994]). In 1990, Alabama enacted a serious juvenile offender law that provided mandatory minimum sentences—"shall be committed"—for youths convicted of a Class A felony or felonies involving physical injury or the use of a firearm (Ala. Code § 12-15-71.1[a] and [b] [1990]). In 1993, Louisiana enacted a mandatory sentencing statute that targeted youths convicted of violent felonies, for example, rape, kidnapping, and armed robbery, and provided that the juvenile "court *shall commit* the child . . . [to] *a secure detention facility* until the child attains the age of twenty-one years *without benefit* of parole, probation, suspension of imposition or execution of sentence" (emphasis added; La. Children's Code art. 897.1 [1993]). Regardless of the statutory details, mandatory minimum sentences based on youths' serious or persistent offending preclude individualized consideration of their real needs. Moreover, mandating extended minimum terms of confinement for serious offenders increases the average length of stay, increases institutional populations, and exacerbates overcrowding (Krisberg and Austin 1993).

d. Executive Sentencing Decisions—Correctional or Parole Release Guidelines. A number of states' departments of corrections have adopted administrative security classification and release guidelines that use offense criteria to specify proportional or mandatory minimum terms of institutional confinement (Forst, Friedman, and Coates 1985; Feld 1988b). These guidelines constitute still another form of offense-based sentencing. Unlike presumptive or mandatory sentencing statutes that attempt to regulate judicial sentencing discretion, administrative or parole guidelines affect only those youths whom judges commit to state correctional agencies. Except when constrained by presumptive or mandatory minimum sentencing statutes, judges in most states retain discretion over the "in-out" decision whether to commit a youth.

The Arizona legislature required its department of corrections to adopt length of confinement guidelines; the agency created five categories based on the seriousness of the commitment offense and specified mandatory minimum terms that range in length from three to eighteen months to govern juvenile release decisions (Arizona Department of Corrections 1986; Ariz. Rev. Stat. Ann. § 8-241 [1987]). Minnesota's department of corrections adopted determinate length of stay guidelines based on the present offense and other risk factors, such as the prior record and probation or parole status (Minnesota Department of Corrections 1980; Feld 1995). Georgia's Division of Youth Services employs a "uniform juvenile classification system" that classifies committed delinquents into one of five categories of "public risk" with corresponding correctional consequences primarily based on the seriousness of the present offense (Forst, Friedman, and Coates 1985). The California Youthful Offender Parole Board decides the release eligibility of juveniles committed to the Youth Authority on the basis of a seven category scale of offense seriousness (Forst and Blomquist 1991). Other states use similar offense-based classification systems to determine institutional lengths of stay and security levels of committed youths (Guarino-Ghezzi and Loughran 1996). All of these de jure sentencing provisions—determinate as well as mandatory minimum laws and correctional as well as parole release guidelines—share the common feature of offense-based dispositions. They represent different strategies to relate the duration and intensity of a youth's sentence to the seriousness of the offense and prior record.

2. *Empirical Evaluations of Juvenile Court Sentencing: Principle of Offense and Racial Disparities.* Several actors in the juvenile justice process—police, intake social workers, detention personnel, prosecutors, and judges—make dispositional decisions; their decisions cumulate and affect the judgments that others make subsequently (McCarthy and Smith 1986; Bishop and Frazier 1988). Juveniles' prior records reflect the discretionary decisions that people in the justice process make over time, and previous dispositions affect later sentences (Hen-

retta, Frazier, and Bishop 1986). Despite recent changes in sentencing laws, juvenile court judges exercise greater sentencing discretion than do criminal court judges because juvenile courts' *parens patriae* ideology still presumes a need to look beyond the offense to the child's best interests.

Within this flexible dispositional process, minority youths are disproportionately overrepresented at every stage of the juvenile justice process (Krisberg et al. 1987; Pope and Feyerherm 1990*a*, 1990*b*). An analytic review of the juvenile court sentencing research literature concluded that "there are race effects in operation within the juvenile justice system, both direct and indirect in nature" (Pope and Feyerherm 1992, p. 41). Studies consistently report racial disparities in case processing after controls for offense variables, that inequalities occur at various stages of the process in different jurisdictions, and that discriminatory decisions amplify minority overrepresentation as youths proceed through the system (e.g., Bishop and Frazier 1996).

The discretion inherent in a *parens patriae* system raises concerns that the cumulative effect of individualized decisions contributes to the substantial overrepresentation of minority youths (McCarthy and Smith 1986; Fagan, Slaughter, and Hartstone 1987; Krisberg et al. 1987; Kempf-Leonard, Pope, and Feyerherm 1995). What methodologists call sample selection bias others might view as racial discrimination. Quite apart from overt discrimination, juvenile justice personnel may view black youths as more threatening or more likely to recidivate than white youths and process them differently (Sampson and Laub 1993; Singer 1996). More benignly, if juvenile courts sentence youths on the basis of social circumstances that indirectly mirror socioeconomic status or race, then minority youths may receive more severe dispositions than white youths because of their personal characteristics or real needs.

Minority overrepresentation may also reflect racial group differences in involvement in criminal activity. If court personnel and judges base their screening decisions and youths' sentences on the seriousness of juveniles' offenses and criminal history, then minority overrepresentation may result from real differences in the incidence and prevalence of offending by race (Wolfgang, Figlio, and Sellin 1972; Hindelang 1978). Or, the structural context of juvenile justice decision making may redound to the detriment of minority juveniles. For example, urban courts tend to be more formal and to sentence all juveniles more severely (Kempf, Decker, and Bin 1990; Feld 1991, 1993*b*). Urban courts also have greater access to detention facilities, and youths held in pretrial detention typically receive more severe sentences than do those who remain at liberty (Feld 1993*b*; Bishop and Frazier 1996). A larger proportion of minority youths reside in urban settings, and police disproportionately arrest and detain them for violent and drug crimes (Snyder and Sickmund 1995). Thus crime patterns, urbanism, "underclass threat," and race may interact to produce minority over-representation in detention and institutions (Sampson and Laub 1993).

a. The Principle of the Offense. Despite sometimes discrepant findings, two general conclusions emerge clearly from the research evaluating juvenile court sentencing practices. First, the "principle of offense"—present offense and prior record—accounts for virtually all of the variance in juvenile court sentences that can be explained. Every methodologically rigorous study of juvenile court sentencing practices reports that judges focus primarily on the seriousness of the present offense and prior record when they impose sentences; these legal and offense variables typically explain about 25–30 percent of the variance in sentencing (Clarke and Koch 1980; McCarthy and Smith 1986; Fagan, Slaughter, and Hartstone 1987; Bishop and Frazier 1996). In short, juvenile court judges attend to the same primary sentencing factors as do criminal court judges. Second, after controlling for legal and offense variables, the individualized justice of juvenile courts produces racial disparities in the sentencing of minority offenders (McCarthy and Smith 1986; Krisberg et al. 1987; Bishop and Frazier 1996). Other than the principle of offense—present offense, prior record, previous disposition—and age, gender, and detention status, youths' race appears as a significant factor in most multivariate sentencing studies (Pope and Feyerherm 1992; Bishop and Frazier 1996).

While youths' chronic or serious offending may indicate greater treatment needs, courts necessarily respond to their criminal behavior regardless of their ability to change it. Practical administrative and bureaucratic considerations induce juvenile court judges to give primacy to offense factors when they sentence juveniles. Organizational desire to avoid public exposure, unfavorable political and media attention, and "fear of scandal" constrain judges to impose more restrictive sentences on more serious offenders (Matza 1964; Cicourel 1968; Emerson 1969). Moreover, present offense and prior record provide efficient organizational tools with which to classify youths on the basis of the risk they pose to the public and of the scandal to the court and provide a court with a means to rationalize, defend, and legitimate its decisions.

b. Racial Disparities. The second consistent finding from juvenile court sentencing research is that, after controlling for the present offense and prior record, individualized sentencing discretion is often synonymous with racial discrimination (McCarthy and Smith 1986; Fagan, Slaughter, and Hartstone 1987; Krisberg et al. 1987; Pope and Feyerherm 1990*a*, 1990*b*, 1992). In 1988, Congress amended the Juvenile Justice and Delinquency Prevention Act to require states receiving federal funds to assure equitable treatment on the basis, inter alia, of race and to assess the sources of minority overrepresentation in juvenile detention facilities and institutions (42 U.S.C. § 5633[a][16] [1993 Supp.]). In response to this mandate, a number of states examined and found racial disparities in their juvenile justice systems (e.g., Bishop and Frazier 1988, 1996; Pope and Feyerherm 1992; Krisberg and Austin 1993; Bridges et al. 1995; Kempf-Leonard, Pope, and Feyerherm 1995). A summary of these evaluation studies reported that, after controlling for legal variables, forty-one of forty-two states found minority youths overrepresented in secure detention facilities, and all thirteen of thirteen states that analyzed other phases of juvenile justice decision making found evidence of minority overrepresentation (Pope 1994).

Discretionary decisions at various stages of the justice process amplify racial disparities as minority youths proceed through the system and result in more severe dispositions than for comparable white youths. The research emphasizes the importance of analyzing juvenile justice decision making as a multistage process rather than focusing solely on the final dispositional decision. For example, dramatic increases in referral rates of minority youths to juvenile courts in seventeen states result in corresponding increases in detention and institutional placement (McGarrell 1993). Juvenile courts detain black youths at higher rates than they do white youths charged with similar offenses, and detained youths typically receive more severe sentences (Bortner and Reed 1985; Frazier and Cochran 1986; Feld 1989, 1993*b*; Krisberg and Austin 1993). A national study of incarceration trends reported confinement rates for minority youths three to four times greater than those of similarly situated white juveniles and that judges sentenced proportionally more minority youths to public secure facilities and committed more white youths to private facilities (Krisberg et al. 1987). By 1991, juvenile courts confined less than one-third (31 percent) of non-Hispanic white juveniles in public long-term facilities; minority youths made up more than two-thirds (69 percent) of confined youths (Snyder and Sickmund 1995). Juvenile courts committed black juveniles at a rate nearly five times higher than that for white youths, and blacks made up half (49 percent) of all youths in institutions (Snyder and Sickmund 1995).

Juvenile courts, as extensions of criminal courts, give primacy to offense factors when they sentence youths. To the extent that *parens patriae* ideology legitimates individualization and differential processing, it also exposes "disadvantaged" youths to the prospects of more extensive state intervention. Of course, if states provided exclusively benign and effective treatment services to youths, then this might mute some of the concerns about racial disparities.

B. Conditions of Confinement and Evaluations of Effectiveness

Examining juvenile correctional facilities and evaluating their effectiveness provides another indicator of the shift from treatment to punishment in juvenile justice. Juvenile courts intervene extensively in the lives of many young offenders. Juvenile court judges removed from their homes more than one-quarter (28 percent) of youths petitioned and adjudicated delinquent and placed them in group homes, privately operated facilities, ranches, camps, "boot camps," or training schools (Snyder and Sickmund 1995). Courts and correctional administrators confined about three-quarters of youths placed in public long-term facilities in training schools (Snyder and Sickmund 1995). Between 1979 and 1989, the rate of juvenile confinement increased 45 percent, and the absolute numbers of youths in confinement increased 30 percent, despite an 11 percent decline in the number of eligible youth in the population during the decade (Altschuler 1994). Another study reported that the rate of confinement of juveniles increased from 241 per 100,000 juveniles in 1975 to 353 per 100,000 in 1987, and the number of children confined in public facilities increased by 19 percent (National Research Council 1993). Reflecting the racial disparities in juvenile court sentencing practices, minority youths now constitute the majority of all offenders confined in training schools (Snyder and Sickmund 1995).

The Supreme Court in *Gault* correctly perceived incarceration as a severe penalty, a substantial deprivation of autonomy, and a continual reminder of one's delinquent status, all of which constitute elements of punishment (387 U.S. at 26–27). The contradictions between the rhetoric of rehabilitation and the reality of institutional conditions of confinement motivated the *Gault* Court to grant juveniles some procedural safeguards. Punitive delinquency institutions have characterized the juvenile justice system from its inception. Historical analyses of the early training schools under the aegis of Progressivism described institutions that failed to rehabilitate and scarcely differed from their adult penal counterparts (Schlossman 1977; Rothman 1980).

1. *Conditions of Confinement.* Evaluations of juvenile correctional facilities in the decades following *Gault* reveal a continuing gap between the rhetoric of rehabilitation and its punitive reality (Bartollas, Miller, and Dinitz 1976; Wooden 1976; Feld 1977; Lerner 1986). Research in Massachusetts described violent and punitive facilities in which staff physically punished inmates and frequently failed to prevent inmates' physical abuse and homosexual rape by other inmates (Feld 1977, 1981*b*). A study in Ohio revealed a similarly violent and oppressive institutional environment for treating young delinquents (Bartollas, Miller, and Dinitz 1976). A study of the Texas juvenile correctional system found extensive staff and inmate violence, degrading make-work tasks, beating and hazing of "fresh fish" by other boys and by staff, "picking" for hours at a time with heavy picks, and "grass pulling" by hand for six hours per day (Guggenheim 1978). Although the California Youth Authority (CYA) aspired to realize the juvenile court's rehabilitative ideal (Krisberg and Austin 1993), by the 1980s youths committed to CYA institutions clearly experienced punishment rather than treatment in overcrowded and dangerous youth prisons (Lerner 1986; Forst and Blomquist 1991). An evaluation of the Louisiana training schools described institutions populated predominantly by black juveniles whom guards regularly physically abused, kept in isolation for long periods of time, restrained with handcuffs, and confined in punitive facilities surrounded by high chain-link fences topped with coiled razor wire (Human Rights Watch 1995).

A study sponsored by the Office of Juvenile Justice and Delinquency Prevention (OJJDP), *Conditions of Confinement: Juvenile Detention and Corrections Facilities,* used nationally recognized professional standards to assess the quality of 984 juvenile detention centers and training schools that housed more than two-thirds (69 percent) of all the confined delinquents in the nation (Parent et al. 1994). It reported endemic institutional overcrowding. In 1991, almost half (44 percent) of all long-term public institutions operated above their design capacity, as did more than three-quarters (79 percent) of the largest facilities, those that housed more than 350 inmates (Snyder and Sickmund 1995). Nearly two-thirds (62 percent) of all delinquent inmates resided in overcrowded facilities operating well above their design capacity. As states sentenced more youths to juvenile institutions, they increased their prison-like character, relied more extensively on fences and walls to maintain perimeter security, and used surveillance equipment to provide internal security (Snyder and Sickmund 1995). The OJJDP evaluation classified nearly half (46 percent) the training schools as medium or maximum security facilities with perimeter fences, locked internal security, or both (Parent et al. 1994).

Coinciding with these post-*Gault* evaluation studies, lawsuits challenged conditions of confinement in juvenile correctional facilities and alleged that they denied inmates' their Fourteenth Amendment due process right to treatment or violated the Eighth Amendment's prohibition on cruel and unusual punishment (Feld 1978, 1988*b*). When a state incarcerates a person for purpose of treatment or rehabilitation, due process requires that conditions of confinement bear some reasonable relationship to the purpose for which the state commits the individual (*Youngberg v. Romeo*, 457 U.S. 307 [1982]). These right to treatment, cruel and unusual punishment, and conditions of confinement cases provide an impartial judicial view of the reality of juvenile corrections. Judicial opinions and investigative reports from around the country report routine staff beatings of inmates, the use of drugs for social control purposes, extensive reliance on solitary confinement, and a virtual absence of meaningful rehabilitative programs.[3]

Despite extensive judicial findings of deplorable conditions of confinement, juvenile correctional facilities probably remain less harsh or abusive than most adult prisons. Interviews with violent juvenile offenders in training schools and comparable waived youths in adult correctional facilities indicate that the juveniles rated their training school treatment, programs, services, and institutional personnel more posi-

[3] Illustrative recent cases highlight the continuing severity of the problem. In D.B. v. Tewksbury, 545 F. Supp. 896 (D.C. Ore. 1982), the court found that the conditions of juvenile pretrial detainees who were incarcerated in an adult jail were deliberately punitive and worse than those experienced by adult convicts. Reports of abusive practices in the press and in other opinions describe youths shackled spread-eagled to their bed frames, locked in isolation for "mouthing off" or swearing, and restrained with handcuffs, leather straps, or leg irons (Krisberg et al. 1986; Alexander S. v. Boyd, 876 F. Supp. 773 [D.S.C. 1995]). Nearly two-thirds (65 percent) of all juveniles confined in training schools reside in facilities subject to a court order or consent decree governing conditions of confinement or decrying the adequacy of their treatment programs (Parent et al. 1994). It is unfortunate that these cases are not atypical, as the list of judicial opinions documenting institutional abuses demonstrates (Krisberg et al. 1986; Alexander S. v. Boyd, 876 F. Supp. 773 [D.S.C. 1995]; Feld 1995). In a review of additional, unreported cases litigating conditions of confinement around the country, Krisberg et al. (1986, p. 32) conclude that there is "growing evidence that harsh conditions of confinement continue to plague juvenile detention centers and training schools."

tively than did the youths in prisons (Forst, Fagan, and Vivona 1989). Even large training schools do not typically house as many inmates locked in individual cells as do adult maximum security prisons. Moreover, youths incarcerated in the juvenile correctional system may exhibit lower recidivism rates than comparable waived youths incarcerated in adult prisons. Fagan (1995, 1996) compared recidivism rates of fifteen- and sixteen-year-old robbery and burglary offenders processed as adult offenders in two southeastern counties in New York with comparable youths processed as juveniles in two contiguous counties in northern New Jersey. Fagan found that the New York adult robbery offenders had higher rates and frequency of reoffending than did those processed in New Jersey as juveniles, although the outcomes for the burglary offenders did not differ between the two systems. Bishop et al. (1996) compared juveniles whom prosecutors waived to criminal court in Florida with a matched set of equivalent cases retained in the juvenile justice system and found that the transferred youths reoffended more often, more quickly, and more seriously than did those youths confined in the juvenile correctional system. Despite these apparent comparative advantages, however, juvenile correctional institutions certainly do not provide such benign and therapeutic facilities as to justify depriving those confined in them adequate procedural safeguards. Rehabilitative euphemisms, such as "provid[ing] a structured treatment environment," should not disguise their punitive reality (Office of Juvenile Justice and Delinquency Prevention 1993, p. 21).

While incarcerating youths in the general population in adult facilities holds little appeal, the well-documented prevalence of staff violence, inmate aggression, and homosexual rape in juvenile prisons provides scant consolation (Bartollas, Miller, and Dinitz 1976; Feld 1977, 1981b). Evaluations of juvenile institutions consistently attribute violent inmate subcultures to staff security arrangements. Authoritarian efforts to impose control and maintain internal security tend to alienate inmates from staff and increase levels of covert inmate violence within the subculture (Bartollas, Miller, and Dinitz 1976; Feld 1977; Lerner 1986). As states confine more youths in overcrowded facilities, staff security policies to manage larger groups of youths aggravate the violent character of the inmate subculture. Thus organizational imperatives may frustrate even well-intended corrections personnel.

The recent changes in juvenile court sentencing legislation exacerbate the deleterious side effects associated with institutional overcrowding (Krisberg et al. 1986). Youths confined under get tough sentencing laws to long terms often make up the most serious and chronic delinquent population. Yet the institutions that house them often suffer from overcrowding, limited physical mobility, and inadequate program resources. Overcrowding also contributes to higher rates of inmate violence and suicide (Parent et al. 1994). These juvenile correctional "warehouses" exhibit most of the negative features of adult prisons and function as little more than youth prisons in which inmates "do time" (Greenwood and Zimring 1985). The large custodial institutions enable politicians to demonstrate their toughness, provide the public with a false sense of security, afford employment for correctional personnel, and minimize the demands placed on custodial staff to maintain institutional order but do little to improve the life chances of troubled youths (Greenwood and Zimring 1985; Bernard 1992).

Evaluation research indicates that incarcerating young offenders in large, congregate juvenile institutions does not effectively rehabilitate and may affirmatively harm them (Bartollas, Miller, and Dinitz 1976; Feld 1977; Andrews et al. 1990; Office of Juvenile Justice and Delinquency Prevention 1993). By contrast, experiments with supervision and treatment in the community suggest that many confined youths do not require institutional restraints (Coates, Miller, and Ohlin 1978). The Massachusetts experiment and some other research suggests that small, community-based, intensive supervision programs may reduce or postpone some delinquents' likelihood or rate of reoffending (Greenwood and Zimring 1985; Steele, Austin, and Krisberg 1989; Office of Juvenile Justice and Delinquency Prevention 1993). Promising programs provide a continuum of services from early secure care in small, nondebilitating settings with a maximum of fifteen to twenty residents, individualized treatment, accountability, and case management, followed by community reintegration with extensive aftercare supervision and intervention (Fagan 1990; Krisberg and Austin 1993; Altschuler 1994). A few states' juvenile sentencing laws attempt to integrate punishment with treatment for serious and habitual offenders by combining a period of confinement with a period of aftercare that uses multiagency case-management techniques to facilitate a youth's reentry into the community (e.g., Cal. Welf. & Inst. Code § 501[a] [West 1995]).

Despite the manifest failures of large institutions to rehabilitate young offenders or reduce recidivism, the apparent success in Massachusetts with closing training schools (Coates, Miller, and Ohlin 1978; Guarino-Ghezzi and Loughran 1996), the relative superiority or cost-effectiveness of small, community-based facilities over congregate facilities as humane living environments, and the feasibility of dealing with many youths in their communities rather than in confinement (Fagan 1990; Krisberg and Austin 1993; Altschuler 1994), the correctional pendulum currently swings toward incarcerating more delinquents for longer periods in institutions. We possess considerable evaluation research and knowledge about the types of correctional environments conducive to adolescent growth and development. And a century of experience with training schools and youth prisons demonstrates that they constitute the one extensively evaluated and clearly ineffective method to treat delinquents (Office of Juvenile Justice and Delinquency Prevention 1993).

2. *Treatment Effectiveness.* Progressive reformers expressed considerable optimism that delinquents' youthfulness and greater malleability would enable them to respond more readily to treatment. By contrast, a comprehensive assessment of rehabilitation research conducted by the National Academy of Sciences questioned both the efficacy of juvenile justice interventions and the assumption that youths manifest greater treatment responsiveness (Sechrest, White, and Brown 1979). "The current research literature provides no basis for positive recommendations about techniques to rehabilitate criminal offenders. The literature does afford occasional hints of intervention that may have promise, but to recommend widespread implementation of those measures would be irresponsible. Many of them would probably be wasteful, and some would do more harm than good in the long run" (Sechrest, White, and Brown 1979, p. 102).

Evaluations of juvenile institutional programs provide little evidence that they effectively treat youths or reduce their recidivism rates (Lab and Whitehead 1988; Whitehead and Lab 1989). Evaluations of training schools, the most common form of institutional treatment for the largest numbers of serious and chronic delinquents, report consistently negative findings. Most state training schools "fail to reform . . . [and] make no appreciable reductions in the very high recidivism rates, on the order to 70 to 80 percent, that are expected for chronic offenders" (Greenwood and Zimring 1985, p. 40). An analysis in Minnesota of recidivism rates of youths released from state correctional and private facilities in 1985 and 1991 found that between 53 percent and 77 percent continued their criminal careers into adulthood (Feld 1995; Minnesota Legislative Auditor 1995). Analyses of recidivism among 926 males released from Washington state's residential facilities in 1982 reported that over half (58.8 percent) reoffended within one year and more than two-thirds (67.9 percent) reoffended within two years (Steiger and Dizon 1991). A study of 527 males released from ten residential facilities in Pennsylvania in 1984 reported that police rearrested more than half (57 percent) and courts recommitted to residential facilities or prisons about one-quarter (23 percent) within two years (Goodstein and Sontheimer 1987).

Despite these generally negative results, evaluation researchers continue the quest for the elusive rehabilitative grail. One methodological strategy to identify "what works" entails metaanalyses, or studies of studies. By coding each evaluation study on a number of variables (e.g., characteristics of the research design, subjects studied, type of treatment applied, and outcome measures) and combining and reanalyzing the studies, metaanalyses attempt to separate treatment effects from differences due to uncontrolled characteristics of the subjects or other limitations of research design (Logan and Gaes 1993). One metaanalysis of juvenile correctional treatment evaluations appearing in the professional literature between 1975 and 1984 and meeting certain criteria of methodological rigor concluded that "the results are far from encouraging for rehabilitation proponents" (Lab and Whitehead 1988, p. 77).

Proponents of treatment reject Martinson's (1974) suggestion that "nothing works" and offer literature reviews, metaanalyses, or program descriptions that report that some interventions may produce positive effects on selected clients under certain conditions (Greenwood and Zimring 1985; Gendreau and Ross 1987; Fagan 1990). Metaanalyses of evaluation studies of delinquents in residential treatment concluded that some programs produce positive results (Garrett 1985; Andrews et al. 1990; Izzo and Ross 1990; Roberts and Camasso 1991; Lipsey 1992). It is typical for positive treatment effects to occur in small, experimental programs that provide an intensive and integrated response to the multiplicity of problems—educational deficits, family dysfunction, inadequate social and vocational skills, and poverty—that delinquent youths present. In general, positive treatment effects occur only under optimal conditions, such as high treatment integrity in an established program with services provided by non–criminal justice personnel (Lipsey 1996).

Research on the elements of effective correctional programs suggest some promising directions either to provide more humane short-term correctional experiences or to improve youths' long-term life chances.

Some model intervention programs may work for some offenders under appropriate conditions. However, most states do not elect to provide these programs or services to delinquents generally. Rather, they continue to confine most incarcerated juveniles in euphemistically sanitized, youth prisons. If either consistently favorable outcomes or universal access remain far from certain, it seems difficult to justify confining most youths with fewer procedural safeguards than those provided to adults.

IV. Blended Jurisdiction: Groping toward an Integrated Sentencing Framework

Although states' adoption of determinate and mandatory juvenile sentencing laws reflect the influence of just deserts jurisprudence and punitive politics, delinquency sentences invariably differ from criminal sentences because juvenile courts' maximum age jurisdiction limits their potential duration. Because juvenile courts lose authority over offenders when they attain the age of majority or some other statutory termination date, they cannot achieve proportionality when sentencing either older chronic juveniles or those youths convicted of very serious offenses. The jurisdictional limits heighten public and political perceptions that juvenile courts inadequately punish or control some youths and provide impetus either to increase juvenile courts' sanctioning powers further or to transfer more youths to criminal courts.

Statutes that increase juvenile courts' punitive capacity or give criminal courts a juvenile sentencing option represent another offense-based sentencing strategy to respond to violent and persistent young offenders. These blended jurisdiction laws attempt to meld the sentencing authority of juvenile with criminal courts, to provide longer sentences for serious crimes than otherwise would be available to the juvenile court, or to increase the rehabilitative sentencing options available to criminal courts (Feld 1995; Torbet et al. 1996). These blended sentences provide juvenile courts with the option to punish as well as to treat and criminal courts with therapeutic alternatives to imprisonment for youths of certain ages charged with serious or repeated offenses. Several variants of youthful offender, blended, or extended jurisdiction sentences exist. The nature of the sanctions depend on whether the prosecutors try the youth initially in juvenile or in criminal court.

A. Convicted in Criminal Court and Sentenced as Youthful Offender

For decades, states and the federal government have used a "youthful offender" status to preserve therapeutic sentencing options in criminal courts following the trial of young offenders as adults. A "youthful offender" status constitutes an intermediate category of chronological juveniles sentenced as adults as well as young adult offenders, typically sixteen to twenty-one years of age at the time of sentencing. Youthful offender laws separate this group by age, either in separate facilities or in age-segregated sections within adult facilities; limit the maximum penalty that criminal courts may impose to a period shorter than that authorized for adults; and provide for some relief from disabilities of conviction following successful completion of the sentence. Under the Federal Youth Corrections Act, subsequently repealed with the adoption of the federal sentencing guidelines, federal judges had discretion to commit convicted offenders between the ages of sixteen and twenty-two to special facilities as youth offenders if they determined that the youth would benefit from treatment (18 U.S.C. §§ 5005–5026 [1976]). The California Youth Authority Act provides criminal court judges with the option of sentencing young adults and waived youths convicted as adults to the CYA for housing and programs, rather than to prison, and the CYA's jurisdiction continues until age twenty-five (Cal. Welf. & Inst. Code § 1731.5 [West 1995]). Because Florida prosecutors direct file many chronological juveniles in criminal court (Bishop, Frazier, and Henretta 1989; Bishop and Frazier 1991), the state's Youthful Offender Act provides criminal court judges with an alternative to sentencing them all as adults (Fla. Stat. § 958 [1995]). On the basis of a presentence investigation report and statutory *Kent*-like criteria, a criminal court judge may sentence a youth either as a youthful offender or to prison. In New York, criminal court jurisdiction begins at age sixteen, but youths as young as thirteen years of age charged with murder or youths fourteen or fifteen years old charged with other violent crimes may be prosecuted as juvenile offenders (JO). Criminal courts may give youths sixteen to nineteen years old a youthful offender (YO) status. Youths sentenced as JOs or YOs may receive a closed hearing, sealed record, or shorter sentence in a separate facility operated by the Division for Youth rather than a straight sentence to the Department of Corrections (Singer 1996). Criminal sentencing laws in several other states also give judges the option to sentence youths convicted as adults to some type of youthful status rather than an adult prison commitment (Torbet et al. 1996).

B. Convicted in Juvenile Court but Sentence Increased

A second variant of blended sentencing begins with a youth's trial in juvenile court and then authorizes the judge to impose enhanced sentences beyond those used for ordinary delinquents (Feld 1995; Torbet et al. 1996). New Mexico, Minnesota, and Texas provide three different versions of these enhanced sanctions for youths whom judges have not transferred to criminal court for prosecution as adults.

In 1993, New Mexico created a three-tier classification of "delinquent offender," "youthful offender," and "serious youthful offender" (N.M. Stat. Ann. § 32A-2-3[C], [H], [I] [Michie 1993]; Mays and Gregware 1996). The prosecutor selects which category to charge a young offender based on age and offense. A youth sixteen or seventeen years of age and charged with first degree murder constitutes a "serious youthful offender," and the court must sentence the youth as an adult. "Youthful offenders" consist of juveniles fifteen to eighteen years of age charged with legislatively designated aggravated or violent crimes, such as second degree murder, assault, rape, or robbery, or youths charged with any felony who have three prior felony adjudications within the previous two-year period. All delinquents and youthful offenders in New Mexico enjoy a statutory right to a jury trial in juvenile court, and the same judge would preside over a case whether it was tried as a juvenile or criminal proceeding (Mays and Gregware 1996). Following conviction as a youthful offender, the juvenile court judge conducts a quasi-waiver sentencing hearing to decide whether to sentence the juvenile as an adult or as a youthful offender. Depending on the judge's assessment of a youth's amenability to treatment or rehabilitation (N.M. Stat. Ann. § 32A-2-20[B][1] [1993]), the court may impose either an adult criminal sentence or a juvenile disposition with jurisdiction extended until age twenty-one (N.M. Stat. Ann. § 32A-2-20 [1993]). Essentially, New Mexico tries youths in juvenile court with adult criminal procedural safeguards and then, after a finding of guilt, allows the judge either to impose an extended juvenile sentence or to sentence the youth as an adult.

In 1995, Minnesota created an intermediate category for serious young offenders called extended jurisdiction juvenile (EJJ) prosecutions (Feld 1995; Minn. Stat. Ann. § 260.126 [1995]). The statutes restrict eligibility for EJJ prosecutions to youths sixteen years of age or older and charged with presumptive commitment to prison offenses like murder, rape, aggravated robbery, and assault; to youths whom judges decline to waive to criminal courts and sentence instead as EJJs; and to younger juveniles whom judges determine in an EJJ hearing meet offense-based public safety criteria (Feld 1995). Juvenile courts try these EJJ youths in juvenile courts but provide them with all of the adult criminal procedural safeguards, including the right to a jury trial.

The right to a trial by jury constitutes an essential component of this quasi-adult status because the judge imposes both a juvenile delinquency disposition and an adult criminal sentence, the execution of which is stayed, pending compliance with the juvenile sentence (Feld 1995; Minn. Stat. Ann. § 260.126 [1995]). Juvenile court dispositional jurisdiction continues until age twenty-one for EJJ youths rather than terminating at age nineteen as it does for ordinary delinquents. If the EJJ youth violates the conditions of the juvenile sentence, then the court may revoke the probation and execute the adult criminal sentence (Feld 1995). Trying youths in juvenile courts with adult criminal procedural safeguards preserves access to juvenile correctional resources, provides longer periods of correctional supervision and control, and retains the possibility of adult incarceration if youths fail on probation or reoffend. Several other states have emulated this blended sentencing strategy (Torbet et al. 1996).

In 1987, Texas adopted a determinate sentencing law for juveniles convicted of certain violent crimes or as habitual offenders to provide an alternative to sentencing them either as ordinary delinquents or waiving them for adult prosecution (Dawson 1988, 1990; Tex. Fam. Code Ann. §§ 53.045, 54.04[d][3] [Vernon Supp. 1988]; Fritsch, Hemmens, and Caeti 1996). To invoke the determinate sentencing law, the prosecutor may submit a petition to a grand jury and allege one of the enumerated violent or habitual crimes. If the indicted youth is convicted, "the court or jury may sentence the child to commitment to the Texas Youth Commission with a possible transfer to the institutional division or the pardons and paroles division of the Texas Department of Criminal Justice for a term of not more than" forty years for a capital or first degree felony, twenty years for a second degree felony, or ten years for a third degree felony (Tex. Fam. Code Ann. § 54.04[d][3] [Vernon Supp. 1995]). Juveniles receive the same procedural rights as do adult criminal defendants including the right to a jury trial. Juveniles begin their determinate sentences in juvenile facilities, and at age eighteen, a court conducts a sentencing review hearing, using *Kent*-like statutory criteria, to decide whether to retain them within the juvenile correctional system for the duration of their minority, until age twenty-one, or to complete their determinate sentence in the adult correction system (Tex. Fam. Code Ann. § 54.11[k] [Vernon 1995]). The Texas law greatly increases the power of juvenile courts to impose substantial sentences on youths below fifteen years of age, the minimum age to transfer juveniles to criminal courts, as well as on older juveniles, and gives prosecutors a powerful plea bargaining tool and alternative to adult prosecution (Dawson 1988, 1990; Fritsch, Hemmens, and Caeti 1996). In 1995, the Texas legislature increased from the original list of six to thirteen the number of offenses for which youths could receive determinate sentences and increased the maximum length of determinate sentences from thirty to forty years (Tex. Fam. Code Ann. §§ 53.045, 54.04[d][3] [Vernon 1995]). Determinately sentenced youths served actual terms considerably longer than those of youths sentenced as ordinary delinquents (Fritch, Hemmens, and Caeti 1996). A few other states, for example, Colorado and Massachusetts, have enacted provisions like Texas's that enable a juvenile court judge to impose a sentence on a youth convicted of a serious crime that extends beyond the maximum age of the juvenile court dispositional jurisdiction with completion of the sentence in adult correctional facilities (Torbet et al. 1996).

Although the New Mexico, Minnesota, and Texas statutes differ in many details, the blended jurisdiction strategy shares several common features. Because they provide these intermediate offenders with adult criminal procedural safeguards, they can acknowledge the reality of juvenile punishment. Once a state gives a juvenile the right to a jury trial and other criminal procedural safeguards, then it retains the option to punish without apology and thereby gains greater flexibility to treat a youth as well. These various enhanced sentencing strategies recognize that age jurisdictional limits of juvenile courts create binary forced choices, either juvenile or adult, either treatment or punishment. By trying a juvenile with criminal procedural rights, these states preserve the option to extend jurisdiction for a period of several years or more beyond that available for ordinary delinquents. Finally, these statutes recognize the futility of trying to rationalize social control in two separate systems. These blended provisions embody the procedural and substantive convergence between juvenile and criminal courts, provide a conceptual alternative to binary waiver statutes, and recognize that adolescence constitutes a developmental continuum that requires an increasing array of graduated sanctions.

V. Toward an Integrated Justice System

Juvenile courts initially depicted young offenders as not criminally responsible and proposed to treat them. By contrast, lawmakers now view even very young people as just as criminally responsible as adults and propose to punish them as adults. Neither formulation adequately addresses adolescent developmental continuities, the progression of criminal careers, or gradations of criminal responsibility.

Several sentencing policy dilemmas, contradictions, and discontinuities result from maintaining separate criminal justice systems for juveniles and adults. Justice system bifurcation produces a lack of integrated criminal career record keeping, arbitrary or inflexible waiver processes, sentencing disparities based on the system that convicts a youth rather than the nature of the offense, a lack of proportionality in both systems, and failure to recognize youthfulness as a mitigating factor in sentencing. Waiver strategies represent legal attempts to reconcile the irreconcilable. Judicial waiver laws allow judges to decide which children are criminals but do not define adequately the criteria by which to make that determination. Judicial discretion results in disparate decisions for similarly situated offenders, a lack of fit between judicial waiver and criminal court sentencing practices, and a punishment gap. Prosecutorial waiver suffers from all of the vagaries of individualized discretion and without even the redeeming virtues of formal criteria, written reasons, an evidentiary record, or appellate review. Legislative offense exclusion suffers from rigidity, overinclusiveness, and politicians' demagogic tendency to get tough.

Legislatures and courts transfer youths to criminal court so that they may receive longer sentences as adults than they could in the juvenile system. However, chronic property offenders constitute the bulk of juveniles judicially waived in most states; they may receive shorter sentences as adults than as property offenders retained in juvenile court. By contrast, youths convicted of violent offenses in criminal courts may receive substantially longer sentences than their juvenile counterparts, although they still may benefit from an informal policy of leniency vis-a-vis adult violent offenders. For juveniles and youths tried as adults and convicted of comparable crimes, both types of disparities raise issues of sentencing policy fairness and justice. Some youths experience dramatically different sanctions than do other, similarly situated offenders simply because of the disjunction between two separate criminal justice systems. Because jurisdictional bifurcation occurs around the peak of youths' criminal careers, it may undermine the ability of the criminal justice system to respond adequately either to persistent or violent offenders. Without an integrated criminal record system, chronic offenders may "slip through the cracks" and receive inappropriately lenient sentences as "first-time" adults.

The simultaneous shift from treatment to punishment in juvenile courts further erodes many sentencing policy differences between the two systems and the rationale for a separate criminal justice system for youths. The various blended sentencing statutes reflect a convergence between the juvenile and criminal justice systems, an effort further to blur the edges and tighten the seams between the two. But juvenile courts must provide youths with all adult criminal procedural safeguards in order fairly explicitly to punish, to enhance sanctions, or to preserve adult sentencing options. Thus efforts to enhance juvenile courts' sanctions further reduce their procedural differences with criminal courts.

Once youths make the transition to criminal court, current sentencing laws typically treat them as if they possess the same degree of criminal responsibility as any other adult offender. The Eighth Amendment's prohibition of cruel and unusual punishments bars only the execution of youths fifteen years of age or younger at the time of their offense and provides no additional proportionality requirements. Although state legislatures have the task of formulating a youth sentencing policy, once states prosecute youths as adults, most adult sentencing statutes reject juvenile courts' deterministic premises that youths' crimes are "not their fault" and ignore differences between adolescents' and adults' criminal responsibility or culpability.

The existence of juvenile courts and resistance to their abolition reflect a cultural consensus that young people somehow differ from adults and should receive more lenient sentences. Shorter sentences for younger offenders enable them to survive the mistakes of adolescence with their life chances intact (Zimring 1982). But, shorter sentences for young people do not require a separate juvenile court simply to determine their guilt. Explicit recognition of youthfulness as a mitigating factor in sentencing would enable criminal courts to dispense appropriately shorter sentences for younger offenders on the basis of their reduced culpability.

Assessments of culpability are normative and evaluative and represent legal, moral, and social judgments. While younger offenders may be less criminally responsible than more mature violators, they do not differ as inherently or fundamentally as the legal dichotomy between juvenile and criminal courts suggest. The distinction between infant and adult that provides the jurisprudential premise for the juvenile court ignores the reality that adolescent development is a continuum. In contrast to get tough policies that endorse a youth-blind justice system and treat fourteen-year-olds as the moral equivalents of adults, we can devise a youth sentencing policy more responsive to the adolescent and criminal career developmental continuum and still protect public safety.

Shorter sentences for reduced responsibility provides a more modest rationale to sanction young people differently than adults than did the rehabilitative claims advanced by Progressive child savers. In this context, an assessment of responsibility represents a global judgment about the degree of youths' deserved punishment, rather than a technical legal judgment about whether the youth possessed the requisite mens rea or mental state defined in the criminal statute (Morse 1984, 1985). Adolescents characteristically may exercise poorer judgment than do adults, but the social costs of their criminal choices affect both their victims and themselves (Cauffman and Steinberg 1995). While the justice system can do nothing to alleviate the harm already done to their victims, legal policies can reduce the long-term harm that adolescents cause to themselves (Scott 1992). Protecting young people from the full penal consequences of the criminal law reflects a policy to preserve their life chances for the future when they presumably will learn to make more responsible choices. Even though young offenders possess sufficient culpability to hold them accountable, their choices remain less blameworthy than those of adults.

Criminal courts in some jurisdictions already consider youthfulness in the context of aggravating and mitigating factors and may impose shorter sentences on a discretionary basis. However, states that recognize youthfulness as a mitigating factor simply treat it as one element to be weighed with many other aggravating and mitigating factors in determining what sentence to impose. A preferable sentencing policy would provide youths with categorical fractional reductions of adult sentences. Attempting to individualize adolescent culpability assessments carries all of the risks of discretionary subjectivity inherent in amenability determinations with no greater likelihood of success. Rather, because youthfulness constitutes a universal form of diminished responsibility, sentencing regimes should treat it categorically as a mitigating factor without regard to nuances of individual developmental differences. Recognizing youthfulness as a mitigating sentencing factor represents a social, moral, and criminal legal policy judgment, not a clinical or psychiatric one about culpability.

This categorical approach might take the form of an explicit "youth discount" at sentencing. A fourteen-year-old offender would receive, for example, 25 percent of the adult penalty; a sixteen-year-old defendant, 50 percent; and an eighteen-year-old, the adult penalty, as is presently the case. The "deeper discounts" for younger offenders correspond to the developmental continuum of responsibility (Scott 1992). A youth discount based on diminished responsibility functions as a sliding scale. Just as we regard adolescents as less criminally responsible than adults, fourteen-year-old youths should enjoy a greater mitigation than seventeen-year-olds.

Several policy groups implicitly endorsed the concept of a youth discount or sliding scale of criminal responsibility for younger offenders. The Juvenile Justice Standards (American Bar Association 1980, p. 35) emphasized the relationship between age and sanctions. "The age of the juvenile is also relevant to the determination of the seriousness of his or her behavior. In most cases, the older the juvenile, the greater is his or her responsibility for breaking the law." The Twentieth Century Fund Task Force on Sentencing Policy toward Young Offenders (1978, pp. 6–7) also concluded that most young offenders, by age thirteen or fourteen, should be held accountable, at least to some degree, for their criminal harms and "the older the adolescent, the greater the degree of responsibility the law should presume." The sentencing principles of frugality or parsimony of punishment (Morris 1974) and the least restrictive alternative also provide rationale for a youth discount.

Discounted sentences that preserve young offenders' life chances require that the maximum sentences that youths receive remain considerably below those imposed on adults. "The principle of diminished responsibility makes life imprisonment and death penalties inappropriate," for example, even in cases of intentional murder by juveniles (Twentieth Century Fund 1978, p. 17). Several serious juvenile offender or designated felony statutes provide examples of sentence lengths for young offenders that are considerably shorter than the sentences their adult counterparts receive and some policy guidance about the degree of discount.

The specific discount value—the amount of fractional reduction—reflects several empirical and normative considerations. It requires a judgment about adolescent development. To what extent do specific physical and psychological characteristics of youth—depreciation of future consequences, risk taking, peer influences, lack of self-control, hormonal changes, and the like—induce them to engage in behavior that reasonable adults would avoid simply because they are young (Steinberg and Cauffman 1996)? How much developmental difference does sentencing policy require for what degree of moral and legal mitigation? To what extent will severe, unmitigated adult penalties permanently and irrevocably alter youths' life chances (Zimring 1982)?

Explicit fractional reductions of youths' sentences can only occur under realistic, humane, and determinate adult sentencing regimes (Tonry 1987, 1995; Frase 1991). One can only know the value of a discounted sentence in a criminal sentencing system in which we know in advance the standard, or "going rate," for adults. In many jurisdictions, implementing a youth discount would require significant modification of the current criminal sentencing statutes used for adults, including presumptive sentencing guidelines with strong upper limits on punishment severity, elimination of all mandatory minimum sentences, and some judicial flexibility to mitigate penalties (Tonry 1995). In short, the adult sentencing system must reflect elements of equality, equity, desert, and proportionality (von Hirsch 1976). Efforts to apply a youth discount within the flawed indeterminate sentencing structures that prevail in many jurisdictions will simply reproduce all of the existing inequities and inconsistencies.

Youthful development is highly variable, and chronological age provides a crude and imprecise indicator of criminal maturity. However, a categorical youth discount that uses age as a conclusive proxy for reduced culpability and a shorter sentence remains preferable to an individualized inquiry into each young offender's criminal responsibility. Developmental psychology does not possess reliable indicators of moral development that equate readily with criminal responsibility or accountability. Thus for administrative and functional convenience, age alone remains the most useful criterion on which to allocate mitigation. Once we find young actors criminally responsible, it hardly seems worth the administrative burden and diversion of resources to try to precisely tailor sanctions on the basis of clinical testimony. Moreover, a policy of mitigation for youthful offenders avoids the undesirable forced choice between either inflicting undeservedly harsh punishments on less culpable actors or "doing nothing" about the manifestly guilty (Bernard 1992). Mitigation avoids the historical pressures on judges and juries to nullify and acquit the "somewhat guilty." A formal commitment to mitigation provides a buffer against political pressure to increase penalties every time a young offender subsequently commits a serious offense.

A number of advantages follow from trying all offenders in an integrated criminal justice system. A graduated age-culpability sentencing system avoids the binary "either/or" inconsistency and injustice that occurs currently depending on whether a state tries and sentences a particular youth as a juvenile or adult. Depending on which forum tries a youth, the same offender's sentence can differ by orders of magnitude, if not by life and death. Because of the differences in consequences, waiver hearings consume a disproportionate amount of judicial time and resources ultimately to no point. Youths are not irresponsible children one day and responsible adults the next, except as a matter of law. Sentencing policy requires a graduated social control system that responds consistently to the developmental continuum. Trying youths in one integrated court eliminates the need for transfer hearings, avoids the inconsistencies produced by offense exclusions or prosecutorial direct files, obviates any punishment gap, and assures comparable sentences for similarly situated offenders. A single criminal justice system allows for an integrated criminal history record-keeping system to identify and enhance the sentences of chronic career offenders. Because states confine juveniles because they commit crimes, incarceration constitutes punishment and requires criminal procedural safeguards that juvenile courts simply do not provide. Eliminating a separate juvenile court does not require incarcerating youths in adult jails and prisons. Existing training schools and institutions provide the option of separate age-segregated dispositional facilities. And evaluation research provides some support for a juvenile rather than adult correctional placements of younger offenders (Fagan 1995, 1996; Bishop et al. 1996; Guarino-Ghezzi and Loughran 1996).

One of the principal virtues of the insanity defense, Goldstein (1967) argues in his seminal work, is that it dramatically affirms the idea of individual responsibility. The idea of personal responsibility and holding people accountable for their behavior provides an important counterweight to a popular culture that endorses the idea that everyone is a victim, that all behavior is determined and no one is responsible, and that therefore wrongdoers cannot be blamed (Packer 1968). The rehabilitative ideal of the juvenile court elevated determinism over free will and characterized delinquent offenders as victims rather than perpetrators. Progressives attempted to design the therapeutic juvenile court to resemble more closely a preventive, forward-looking civil commitment process than a criminal court. While the paternalistic stance of the traditional juvenile courts rests on the humane desire to protect young people from the adverse consequences of bad decisions, protectionism simultaneously disables young people from the opportunity to learn to make choices and to bear responsibility for their consequences. By denying youths' responsibility, juvenile justice ideology reduces offenders' obligation to learn and exercise self-control and erodes their need to change.

The pendulum now has swung to the opposite extreme. State juvenile and criminal justice policies currently emphasize accountability, responsibility, and punishment virtually to the exclusion of individual considerations. Especially in criminal courts, states' sentencing policies treat young offenders as if they were adults, make the same blameworthy choices, and possess the same level of culpability as adult offenders. Get tough politicians adopt youth-blind public policies that disregard the entire social construct of childhood (Ainsworth 1991, 1995).

By contrast, an integrated criminal court that formally recognizes youthfulness as a mitigating factor at sentencing avoids these polar extremes and binary dichotomies and permits a nuanced response to youth crime. A youth discount recognizes the greater competence of young people, but simultaneously incorporates an appropriately protective element into criminal justice policy. Because a criminal conviction represents an official condemnation, the idea of blame reinforces for the public and provides for the defendant the incentive to develop individual responsibility. But a criminal law that disproportionately punishes according to the culpability of the offender undermines its own legitimacy.

REFERENCES

Ainsworth, Janet E. 1991. "Re-imagining Childhood and Re-constructing the Legal Order: The Case for Abolishing the Juvenile Court." *North Carolina Law Review* 69:1083–1133.

———. 1995. "Youth Justice in a Unified Court: Response to Critics of Juvenile Court Abolition." *Boston College Law Review* 36:927–51.

Altschuler, David M. 1994. "Tough and Smart Juvenile Incarceration: Reintegrating Punishment, Deterrence, and Rehabilitation." *St. Louis University Public Law Review* 14:217–44.

American Bar Association and Institute of Judicial Administration. 1980. *Juvenile Justice Standards Relating to Dispositions.* Cambridge, Mass.: Ballinger.

Andrews, D. A., Ivan Zinger, Robert D. Hoge, James Bonta, Paul Gendreau, and Francis T. Cullen. 1990. "Does Correctional Treatment Work? A

Clinically Relevant and Psychologically Informed Meta-analysis." *Criminology* 28:369–404.

Arizona Department of Corrections. 1986. *Length of Confinement Guidelines for Juveniles.* Tucson: Arizona Department of Corrections.

Barnes, Carole Wolff, and Randal S. Franz. 1989. "Questionably Adult: Determinants and Effects of the Juvenile Waiver Decision." *Justice Quarterly* 6:117–35.

Bartollas, Clemens, Stuart J. Miller, and Simon Dinitz. 1976. *Juvenile Victimization: The Institutional Paradox.* New York: Wiley.

Bernard, Thomas J. 1992. *The Cycle of Juvenile Justice.* New York: Oxford University Press.

Bishop, Donna M., and Charles S. Frazier. 1988. "The Influence of Race in Juvenile Justice Processing." *Journal of Research in Crime and Delinquency* 25:242–63.

———. 1991. "Transfer of Juveniles to Criminal Court: A Case Study and Analysis of Prosecutorial Waiver." *Notre Dame Journal of Law, Ethics and Public Policy* 5:281–302.

———. 1996. "Race Effects in Juvenile Justice Decision-Making: Findings of a Statewide Analysis." *Journal of Criminal Law and Criminology* 86:392–413.

Bishop, Donna M., Charles E. Frazier, and John Henretta. 1989. "Prosecutorial Waiver: Case Study of a Questionable Reform." *Crime and Delinquency* 35:179–201.

Bishop, Donna M., Charles E. Frazier, Lonn Lanza-Kaduce, and Lawrence Winner. 1996. "The Transfer of Juveniles to Criminal Court: Does It Make a Difference?" *Crime and Delinquency* 42:171–91.

Blumstein, Alfred. 1995. "Youth Violence, Guns, and the Illicit-Drug Industry." *Journal of Criminal Law and Criminology* 86:10–36.

Blumstein, Alfred, Jacqueline Cohen, Jeffrey A. Roth, and Christy A. Visher, eds. 1986. *Criminal Careers and "Career Criminals."* Washington, D.C.: National Academy Press.

Blumstein, Alfred, and Daniel Cork. 1996. "Linking Gun Availability to Youth Gun Violence." *Law and Contemporary Problems* 59:5–24.

Blumstein, Alfred, David P. Farrington, and Soumyo Moitra. 1985. "Delinquency Careers: Innocents, Desisters, and Persisters." In *Crime and Justice: An Annual Review of Research*, vol. 6, edited by Michael Tonry and Norval Morris. Chicago: University of Chicago Press.

Bortner, M. A. 1986. "Traditional Rhetoric, Organizational Realities: Remand of Juveniles to Adult Court." *Crime and Delinquency* 32:53–73.

Bortner, M. A., and W. L. Reed. 1985. "The Preeminence of Process: An Example of Refocused Justice Research." *Social Science Quarterly* 66:413–25.

Bridges, George S., Darlene J. Conley, Rodney L. Engen, and Townsand Price-Spratlen. 1995. "Racial Disparities in the Confinement of Juveniles: Effects of Crime and Community Social Structure on Punishment." In *Minorities in Juvenile Justice*, edited by K. Kempf-Leonard, C. Pope, and W. Feyerherm. Thousand Oaks, Calif.: Sage.

Castellano, Thomas C. 1986. "The Justice Model in the Juvenile Justice System: Washington State's Experience." *Law and Policy* 8:397–418.

Cauffman, Elizabeth, and Laurence Steinberg. 1995. "The Cognitive and Affective Influences on Adolescent Decision-Making." *Temple Law Review* 68:1763–89.

Cicourel, Aaron V. 1968. *The Social Organization of Juvenile Justice*. New York: Wiley.

Clarke, Stevens H., and Gary G. Koch. 1980. "Juvenile Court: Therapy or Crime Control, and Do Lawyers Make a Difference?" *Law and Society Review* 14:263–308.

Coates, Robert, Martin Forst, and Bruce Fisher. 1985. *Institutional Commitment and Release Decision-Making for Juvenile Delinquents: An Assessment of Determinate and Indeterminate Approaches—a Cross-State Analysis*. San Francisco: URSA Institute.

Coates, Robert, Alden Miller, and Lloyd Ohlin. 1978. *Diversity in a Youth Correctional System*. Cambridge, Mass.: Ballinger.

Cook, Philip J., and John H. Laub. In this volume. "The Unprecedented Epidemic in Youth Violence."

Dawson, Robert O. 1988. "The Third Justice System: The New Juvenile Criminal System of Determinate Sentencing for the Youthful Violent Offender in Texas." *St. Mary's Law Journal* 19:943–1016.

———. 1990. "The Violent Juvenile Offender: An Empirical Study of Juvenile Determinate Sentencing Proceedings as an Alternative to Criminal Prosecution." *Texas Tech Law Review* 21:1897–1939.

Eigen, Joel. 1981*a*. "The Determinants and Impact of Jurisdictional Transfer in Philadelphia." In *Readings in Public Policy*, edited by John Hall, Donna Hamparian, John Pettibone, and Joe White. Columbus, Ohio: Academy for Contemporary Problems.

———. 1981*b*. "Punishing Youth Homicide Offenders in Philadelphia." *Journal of Criminal Law and Criminology* 72:1072–93.

Emerson, Robert M. 1969. *Judging Delinquents: Context and Process in Juvenile Court*. Chicago: Aldine.

Fagan, Jeffrey. 1990. "Social and Legal Policy Dimensions of Violent Juvenile Crime." *Criminal Justice and Behavior* 17:93–133.

———. 1995. "Separating the Men from the Boys: The Comparative Advantage of Juvenile versus Criminal Court Sanctions on Recidivism among Adolescent Felony Offenders." In *A Sourcebook of Serious, Violent, and Chronic Juvenile Offenders*, edited by James C. Howell, Barry Krisberg, J. David Hawkins, and John J. Wilson. Thousand Oaks, Calif.: Sage.

———. 1996. "The Comparative Advantage of Juvenile versus Criminal Court Sanctions on Recidivism among Adolescent Felony Offenders." *Law and Policy* 18:77–114.

Fagan, Jeffrey, and Elizabeth Piper Deschenes. 1990. "Determinants of Judicial Waiver Decisions for Violent Juvenile Offenders." *Journal of Criminal Law and Criminology* 81:314–47.

Fagan, Jeffrey, Martin Forst, and Scott Vivona. 1987. "Racial Determinants of the Judicial Transfer Decision: Prosecuting Violent Youth in Criminal Court." *Crime and Delinquency* 33:259–86.

Fagan, Jeffrey, and Martin Guggenheim. 1996. "Preventive Detention and the

Judicial Prediction of Dangerousness for Juveniles: A Natural Experiment." *Journal of Criminal Law and Criminology* 86:415–48.

Fagan, Jeffrey, Ellen Slaughter, and Eliot Hartstone. 1987. "Blind Justice? The Impact of Race on the Juvenile Justice Process." *Crime and Delinquency* 33:224–58.

Farrington, David P. 1986. "Age and Crime." In *Crime and Justice: An Annual Review of Research*, vol. 7, edited by Michael Tonry and Norval Morris. Chicago: University of Chicago Press.

———. In this volume. "Predictors, Causes, and Correlates of Youth Violence."

Farrington, David P., Lloyd E. Ohlin, and James Q. Wilson. 1986. *Understanding and Controlling Crime: Toward a New Research Strategy*. New York: Springer Verlag.

Feld, Barry C. 1977. *Neutralizing Inmate Violence: Juvenile Offenders in Institutions*. Cambridge, Mass.: Ballinger.

———. 1978. "Reference of Juvenile Offenders for Adult Prosecution: The Legislative Alternative to Asking Unanswerable Questions." *Minnesota Law Review* 62:515–618.

———. 1981*a*. "Juvenile Court Legislative Reform and the Serious Young Offender: Dismantling the 'Rehabilitative Ideal.'" *Minnesota Law Review* 69:141–242.

———. 1981*b*. "A Comparative Analysis of Organizational Structure and Inmate Subcultures in Institutions for Juvenile Offenders." *Crime and Delinquency* 27:336–63.

———. 1983. "Delinquent Careers and Criminal Policy: Just Deserts and the Waiver Decision." *Criminology* 21:195–212.

———. 1984. "Criminalizing Juvenile Justice: Rules of Procedure for Juvenile Court." *Minnesota Law Review* 69:141–276.

———. 1987. "Juvenile Court Meets the Principle of Offense: Legislative Changes in Juvenile Waiver Statutes." *Journal of Criminal Law and Criminology* 78:471–533.

———. 1988*a*. "*In re Gault* Revisited: A Cross-State Comparison of the Right to Counsel in Juvenile Court." *Crime and Delinquency* 34:393–424.

———. 1988*b*. "Juvenile Court Meets the Principle of Offense: Punishment, Treatment, and the Difference It Makes." *Boston University Law Review* 68:821–915.

———. 1989. "The Right to Counsel in Juvenile Court: An Empirical Study of When Lawyers Appear and the Difference They Make." *Journal of Criminal Law and Criminology* 79:1185–1346.

———. 1990. "Bad Law Makes Hard Cases: Reflections on Teen-Aged Axe-Murderers, Judicial Activism, and Legislative Default." *Journal of Law and Inequality* 8:1–101.

———. 1991. "Justice by Geography: Urban, Suburban, and Rural Variations in Juvenile Justice Administration." *Journal of Criminal Law and Criminology* 82:156–210.

———. 1993*a*. "Criminalizing the American Juvenile Court." In *Crime and Justice: A Review of Research*, vol. 17, edited by Michael Tonry. Chicago: University of Chicago Press.

———. 1993b. *Justice for Children: The Right to Counsel and the Juvenile Court.* Boston: Northeastern University Press.

———. 1995. "Violent Youth and Public Policy: A Case Study of Juvenile Justice Law Reform." *Minnesota Law Review* 79:965–1128.

———. 1998. *Bad Kids: The Transformation of the Juvenile Court.* New York: Oxford University Press (forthcoming).

Fisher, Bruce, Mark Fraser, and Martin Forst. 1985. *Institutional Commitment and Release Decision-Making for Juvenile Delinquents: An Assessment of Determinate and Indeterminate Approaches, Washington State—a Case Study.* San Francisco: URSA Institute.

Forst, Martin, and Martha-Elin Blomquist. 1991. "Cracking Down on Juveniles: The Changing Ideology of Youth Corrections." *Notre Dame Journal of Law, Ethics and Public Policy* 5:323–75.

Forst, Martin, Jeffrey Fagan, and T. Scott Vivona. 1989. "Youth in Prisons and Training Schools: Perceptions and Consequences of the Treatment-Custody Dichotomy." *Juvenile and Family Court Journal* 40:1–14.

Forst, Martin, Elizabeth Friedman, and Robert Coates. 1985. *Institutional Commitment and Release Decision-Making for Juvenile Delinquents: An Assessment of Determinate and Indeterminate Approaches, Georgia—a Case Study.* San Francisco: URSA Institute.

Frase, Richard. 1991. "Sentencing Reform in Minnesota: Ten Years After." *Minnesota Law Review* 75:727–54.

Frazier, Charles E. 1991. *Deep-End Juvenile Justice Placements or Transfer to Adult Court by Direct File?* Tallahassee: Florida Legislature, Commission on Juvenile Justice.

Frazier, C. E., and J. K. Cochran. 1986. "Detention of Juveniles: Its Effects on Subsequent Juvenile Court Processing Decisions." *Youth and Society* 17:286–305.

Fritsch, Eric, and Craig Hemmens. 1995. "Juvenile Waiver in the United States, 1979–1995: A Comparison and Analysis of State Waiver Statutes." *Juvenile and Family Court Judges Journal* 46:17–35.

Fritsch, Eric, Craig Hemmens, and Tory J. Caeti. 1996. "Violent Youth in Juvenile and Adult Court: An Assessment of Sentencing Strategies in Texas." *Law and Policy* 18:115–36.

Gardner, Martin. 1982. "Punishment and Juvenile Justice: A Conceptual Framework for Assessing Constitutional Rights of Youthful Offenders." *Vanderbilt Law Review* 35:791–847.

Garrett, Carol J. 1985. "Effects of Residential Treatment on Adjudicated Delinquents: A Meta-analysis." *Journal of Research in Crime and Delinquency* 22:287–308.

Gendreau, Paul, and Bob Ross. 1987. "Revivification of Rehabilitation: Evidence from the 1980s." *Justice Quarterly* 4:349–407.

Gillespie, L. Kay, and Michael D. Norman. 1984. "Does Certification Mean Prison: Some Preliminary Findings from Utah." *Juvenile and Family Court Journal* 35:23–34.

Goldstein, Abraham S. 1967. *The Insanity Defense.* New Haven, Conn.: Yale University Press.

Goodstein, Lynn, and Henry Sontheimer. 1987. *A Study of the Impact of 10 Pennsylvania Residential Placements on Juvenile Recidivism.* Shippensburg, Pa.: Center for Juvenile Justice Training and Research.

Greenwood, Peter. 1986. "Differences in Criminal Behavior and Court Responses among Juvenile and Young Adult Defendants." In *Crime and Justice: An Annual Review of Research,* vol. 7, edited by Michael Tonry and Norval Morris. Chicago: University of Chicago Press.

Greenwood, Peter, Allan Abrahamse, and Franklin Zimring. 1984. *Factors Affecting Sentence Severity for Young Adult Offenders.* Santa Monica, Calif.: RAND.

Greenwood, Peter, Joan Petersilia, and Franklin Zimring. 1980. *Age, Crime, and Sanctions: The Transition from Juvenile to Adult Court.* Santa Monica, Calif.: RAND.

Greenwood, Peter, and Franklin Zimring. 1985. *One More Chance: The Pursuit of Promising Intervention Strategies for Chronic Juvenile Offenders.* Santa Monica, Calif.: RAND.

Guarino-Ghezzi, Susan, and Edward J. Loughran. 1996. *Balancing Juvenile Justice.* New Brunswick, N.J.: Transaction.

Guggenheim, Martin. 1978. "A Call to Abolish the Juvenile Justice System." *Children's Rights Reporter* 2:7–19.

Hamparian, Donna, Linda Estep, Susan Muntean, Ramon Priestino, Robert Swisher, Paul Wallace, and Joseph White. 1982. *Youth in Adult Courts: Between Two Worlds.* Washington, D.C.: Office of Juvenile Justice and Delinquency Prevention.

Hart, H. L. A. 1968. *Punishment and Responsibility.* New York: Oxford University Press.

Henretta, John, Charles Frazier, and Donna Bishop. 1986. "The Effects of Prior Case Outcomes on Juvenile Justice Decision-Making." *Social Forces* 65:554–62.

Heuser, James Paul. 1985. *Juveniles Arrested for Serious Felony Crimes in Oregon and "Remanded" to Adult Criminal Courts: A Statistical Study.* Salem: Oregon Department of Justice Crime Analysis Center.

Hindelang, Michael. 1978. "Race and Involvement in Common Law Personal Crimes." *American Sociological Review* 43:93–109.

Howell, James C. 1996. "The Transfer of Juvenile Offenders to the Criminal Justice System: State of the Art." *Law and Policy* 18:17–60.

Human Rights Watch. 1995. *Children in Confinement in Louisiana.* New York: Human Rights Watch.

Izzo, Rhena L., and Robert R. Ross. 1990. "Meta-analysis of Rehabilitation Programs for Juvenile Delinquents." *Criminal Justice and Behavior* 17:134–42.

Kempf, Kimberly L., Scott H. Decker, and Robert L. Bin. 1990. *An Analysis of Apparent Disparities in the Handling of Black Youth within Missouri's Juvenile Justice Systems.* St. Louis: University of Missouri, Department of Administration of Justice.

Kempf-Leonard, Kimberly, Carl Pope, and William Feyerherm. 1995. *Minorities in Juvenile Justice.* Thousand Oaks, Calif.: Sage.

Krisberg, Barry, and James Austin. 1993. *Reinventing Juvenile Justice.* Thousand Oaks, Calif.: Sage.

Krisberg, Barry, Elliot Currie, David Onek, and Richard G. Wiebush. 1995. "Graduation Sanctions for Serious, Violent, and Chronic Juvenile Offenders." In *A Sourcebook: Serious, Violent, and Chronic Juvenile Offenders,* edited by James C. Howell, Barry Krisberg, J. David Hawkins, and John J. Wilson. Thousand Oaks, Calif.: Sage.

Krisberg, Barry, Ira Schwartz, Gideon Fishman, Zvi Eisikovits, Edna Guttman, and Karen Joe. 1987. "The Incarceration of Minority Youth." *Crime and Delinquency* 33:173–205.

Krisberg, Barry, Ira Schwartz, Paul Lisky, and James Austin. 1986. "The Watershed of Juvenile Justice Reform." *Crime and Delinquency* 32:5–38.

Lab, Steven P., and John T. Whitehead. 1988. "An Analysis of Juvenile Correctional Treatment." *Crime and Delinquency* 34:60–83.

———. 1990. "From 'Nothing Works' to 'the Appropriate Works': The Latest Stop on the Search for the Secular Grail." *Criminology* 28:405–17.

Lemmon, John H., Henry Sontheimer, and Keith A. Saylor. 1991. *A Study of Pennsylvania Juveniles Transferred to Criminal Court in 1986.* Harrisburg: Pennsylvania Juvenile Court Judges' Commission.

Lerner, Steven. 1986. *Bodily Harm.* Bolinas, Calif.: Common Knowledge Press.

Lipsey, Mark W. 1992. "Juvenile Delinquent Treatment: A Meta-analytic Inquiry into the Variability of Effects." In *Meta Analysis for Explanation: A Casebook,* edited by Thomas D. Cook. New York: Russell Sage.

———. 1996. "Effective Intervention for Serious Juvenile Offenders: A Synthesis of Research." Unpublished manuscript. Nashville: Vanderbilt University.

LIS, Inc. 1995. *Offenders under Age 18 in State Adult Correctional Systems: A National Picture.* Longmont, Colo.: National Institute of Corrections.

Logan, Charles H., and Gerald G. Gaes. 1993. "Meta Analysis and the Rehabilitation of Punishment." *Justice Quarterly* 10:245–63.

Mack, Julian W. 1909. "The Juvenile Court." *Harvard Law Review* 23:104–22.

Martinson, Robert. 1974. "What Works? Questions and Answers about Prison Reform." *Public Interest* 35:22–54.

Matza, David. 1964. *Delinquency and Drift.* New York: Wiley.

Mays, G. Larry, and Peter R. Gregware. 1996. "The Children's Code Reform Movement in New Mexico: The Politics of Expediency." *Law and Policy* 18:179–93.

McCarthy, Belinda, and Brent L. Smith. 1986. "The Conceptualization of Discrimination in the Juvenile Justice Process: The Impact of Administrative Factors and Screening Decisions on Juvenile Court Dispositions." *Criminology* 24:41–64.

McCarthy, Francis Barry. 1994. "The Serious Offender and Juvenile Court Reform: The Case for Prosecutorial Waiver of Juvenile Court Jurisdiction." *St. Louis University Law Journal* 389:629–71.

McDermott, M. J., and Michael J. Hindelang. 1981. *Juvenile Criminal Behavior in the United States: Its Trends and Patterns.* Washington, D.C.: U.S. Government Printing Office.

McGarrell, Edmund F. 1993. "Trends in Racial Disproportionality in Juvenile Court Processing: 1985–1989." *Crime and Delinquency* 39:29–48.

McNulty, Elizabeth W. 1996. "The Transfer of Juvenile Offenders to Adult Court: Panacea or Problem?" *Law and Policy* 18:61–76.

McNulty, Elizabeth W., and J. Neil Russell. 1995. *Juvenile Commitment Guidelines Departure Research Project.* Phoenix: Arizona Supreme Court.

McShane, Marilyn D., and Frank P. Williams III. 1989. "The Prison Adjustment of Juvenile Offenders." *Crime and Delinquency* 35:254–69.

Miller, Neal. 1995. *State Laws on Prosecutors' and Judges' Use of Juvenile Records.* Washington, D.C.: National Institute of Justice.

Minnesota Department of Corrections. 1980. *Juvenile Release Guidelines.* St. Paul: Minnesota Department of Corrections.

Minnesota Legislative Auditor. 1995. *Residential Facilities for Juvenile Offenders.* St. Paul, Minn.: Office of Legislative Auditor.

Monahan, John. 1981. *Predicting Violent Behavior: An Assessment of Clinical Techniques.* Beverly Hills, Calif.: Sage.

Morris, Norval. 1974. *The Future of Imprisonment.* Chicago: University of Chicago Press.

Morris, Norval, and Marc Miller. 1985. "Predictions of Dangerousness." In *Crime and Justice: An Annual Review of Research,* vol. 6, edited by Michael Tonry and Norval Morris. Chicago: University of Chicago Press.

Morse, Steven. 1984. "Undiminished Confusion in Diminished Capacity." *Journal of Criminal Law and Criminology* 75:1–55.

———. 1985. "Excusing the Crazy: The Insanity Defense Reconsidered." *Southern California Law Review* 58:779–836.

National Research Council. 1993. *Losing Generations: Adolescents in High-Risk Settings.* Washington, D.C.: National Academy Press.

New Jersey Juvenile Delinquency Disposition Commission. 1986. *The Impact of the New Jersey Code of Juvenile Justice: First Annual Report.* Trenton, NJ: Juvenile Delinquency Disposition Commission.

Nimick, Ellen, Linda Szymanski, and Howard Snyder. 1986. *Juvenile Court Waiver: A Study of Juvenile Court Cases Transferred to Criminal Court.* Pittsburgh, Penn.: National Center for Juvenile Justice.

Office of Juvenile Justice and Delinquency Prevention. 1993. *Comprehensive Strategy for Serious, Violent, and Chronic Juvenile Offenders.* Washington, D.C.: U.S. Government Printing Office.

Packer, Herbert L. 1968. *The Limits of the Criminal Sanction.* Stanford, Calif.: Stanford University Press.

Parent, Dale G., Terence Dunworth, Douglas McDonald, and William Rhodes. 1997. *Key Legislative Issues in Criminal Justice: Transferring Serious Juvenile Offenders to Adult Courts.* Washington, D.C.: U.S. Department of Justice, National Institute of Justice.

Parent, Dale G., Valierie Lieter, Stephen Kennedy, Lisa Livens, Daniel Wentworth, and Sarah Wilcox. 1994. *Conditions of Confinement: Juvenile Detention and Corrections Facilities*. Washington, D.C.: Office of Juvenile Justice and Delinquency Prevention.

Petersilia, Joan. 1980. "Criminal Career Research: A Review of Recent Evidence." In *Crime and Justice: An Annual Review of Research*, vol. 2, edited by Norval Morris and Michael Tonry. Chicago: University of Chicago Press.

Platt, Anthony. 1977. *The Child Savers: The Invention of Delinquency*. 2d ed. Chicago: University of Chicago Press.

Podkopacz, Marcy Rasmussen, and Barry C. Feld. 1995. "Judicial Waiver Policy and Practice: Persistence, Seriousness and Race." *Law and Inequality Journal* 14:73–178.

———. 1996. "The End of the Line: An Empirical Study of Judicial Waiver." *Journal of Criminal Law and Criminology* 86:449–92.

Pope, Carl E. 1994. "Racial Disparities in Juvenile Justice System." *Overcrowded Times* 5(6):1, 5–7.

Pope, Carl E., and William H. Feyerherm. 1990*a*. "Minority Status and Juvenile Justice Processing: An Assessment of the Research Literature (Part I)." *Criminal Justice Abstracts* 22:327–35.

———. 1990*b*. "Minority Status and Juvenile Justice Processing: An Assessment of the Research Literature (Part II)." *Criminal Justice Abstracts* 22:527–42.

———. 1992. *Minorities and the Juvenile Justice System*. Washington, D.C.: Office of Juvenile Justice and Delinquency Prevention.

Poulos, Tammy Meredith, and Stan Orchowsky. 1994. "Serious Juvenile Offenders: Predicting the Probability of Transfer to Criminal Court." *Crime and Delinquency* 40:3–17.

President's Commission on Law Enforcement and Administration of Justice. 1967*a*. *The Challenge of Crime in a Free Society*. Washington, D.C.: U.S. Government Printing Office.

———. 1967*b*. *Task Force Report: Juvenile Delinquency and Youth Crime*. Washington, D.C.: U.S. Government Printing Office.

Reiss, Albert J., Jr., and Jeffrey A. Roth, eds. 1993. *Understanding and Preventing Violence*. Washington, D.C.: National Academy Press.

Roberts, Albert R., and Michael J. Camasso. 1991. "The Effects of Juvenile Offender Treatment Programs on Recidivism: A Meta-analysis of 46 Studies." *Notre Dame Journal of Law, Ethics and Public Policy* 5:421–42.

Rothman, David J. 1980. *Conscience and Convenience: The Asylum and Its Alternative in Progressive America*. Boston: Little, Brown.

Rudman, Cary, Eliot Hartstone, Jeffrey Fagan, and Melinda Moore. 1986. "Violent Youth in Adult Court: Process and Punishment." *Crime and Delinquency* 36:75–96.

Ryerson, Ellen. 1978. *The Best-Laid Plans: America's Juvenile Court Experiment*. New York: Hill & Wang.

Sampson, Robert J., and John H. Laub. 1993. "Structural Variations in Juvenile Court Processing: Inequality, the Underclass, and Social Control." *Law and Society Review* 27: 285–311.

Sanborn, Joseph B., Jr. 1996. "Policies Regarding the Prosecution of Juvenile

Murderers: Which System and Who Should Decide?" *Law and Policy* 18:151–78.

Schlossman, Steven. 1977. *Love and the American Delinquent: The Theory and Practice of "Progressive" Juvenile Justice.* Chicago: University of Chicago Press.

Schneider, Anne L., and Donna Schram. 1983. *A Justice Philosophy for the Juvenile Court.* Seattle: Urban Policy Research.

Scott, Elizabeth S. 1992. "Judgment and Reasoning in Adolescent Decisionmaking." *Villanova Law Review* 37:1607–69.

Sechrest, Lee B. 1987. "Classification for Treatment." In *Prediction and Classification: Criminal Justice Decision Making,* edited by Don M. Gottfredson and Michael Tonry. Volume 9 of *Crime and Justice: A Review of Research,* edited by Michael Tonry and Norval Morris. Chicago: University of Chicago Press.

Sechrest, Lee B., Susan O. White, and Elizabeth D. Brown, eds. 1979. *The Rehabilitation of Criminal Offenders.* Washington, D.C.: National Academy of Sciences.

Sheffer, Julianne P. 1995. "Serious and Habitual Juvenile Offender Statutes: Reconciling Punishment and Rehabilitation within the Juvenile Justice System." *Vanderbilt Law Review* 48:479–512.

Singer, Simon I. 1996. *Recriminalizing Delinquency: Violent Juvenile Crime and Juvenile Justice Reform.* New York: Cambridge University Press.

Snyder, Howard N., and John L. Hutzler. 1981. *The Serious Juvenile Offender: The Scope of the Problem and the Response of Juvenile Courts.* Pittsburgh, Pa.: National Center for Juvenile Justice.

Snyder, Howard N., and Melissa Sickmund. 1995. *Juvenile Offenders and Victims: A National Report.* Washington, D.C.: Office of Juvenile Justice and Delinquency Prevention.

Snyder, Howard N., Melissa Sickmund, and Eileen Poe-Yamagata. 1996. *Juvenile Offenders and Victims: 1996 Update on Violence.* Washington, D.C.: Office of Juvenile Justice and Delinquency Prevention, National Center for Juvenile Justice.

Steele, Patricia A., James Austin, and Barry Krisberg. 1989. *Unlocking Juvenile Corrections: Evaluating the Massachusetts Department of Youth Services.* San Francisco: National Council on Crime and Delinquency.

Steiger, John C., and Cary Dizon. 1991. *Rehabilitation, Release, and Reoffending: A Report on the Criminal Careers of the Division of Juvenile Rehabilitation "Class of 1982."* Olympia, Wash.: Department of Social and Health Services.

Steinberg, Laurence, and Elizabeth Cauffman. 1996. "Maturity of Judgment in Adolescence: Psychosocial Factors in Adolescent Decision Making." *Law and Human Behavior* 20:249–72.

Streib, Victor L. 1987. *Death Penalty for Juveniles.* Bloomington and Indianapolis: Indiana University Press.

———. 1995. *The Juvenile Death Penalty Today: Present Death Row Inmates under Juvenile Death Sentences and Death Sentences and Executions for Juvenile Crimes.* Cleveland: Cleveland-Marshall College of Law.

Teilmann, Katherine S., and Malcolm Klein. n.d. *Summary of Interim Findings of the Assessment of the Impact of California's 1977 Juvenile Justice Legislation.* Los Angeles: University of Southern California, Social Science Research Institute.

Thomas, Charles W., and Shay Bilchik. 1985. "Prosecuting Juveniles in Criminal Courts: A Legal and Empirical Analysis." *Journal of Criminal Law and Criminology* 76:439–79.

Tonry, Michael. 1987. "Prediction and Classification: Legal and Ethical Issues." In *Prediction and Classification: Criminal Justice Decision Making,* edited by Don M. Gottfredson and Michael Tonry. Volume 9 of *Crime and Justice: A Review of Research,* edited by Michael Tonry and Norval Morris. Chicago: University of Chicago Press.

———. 1995. *Malign Neglect: Race, Crime, and Punishment in America.* New York: Oxford University Press.

———. 1996. *Sentencing Matters.* New York: Oxford University Press.

Torbet, Patricia, Richard Gable, Hunter Hurst IV, Imogene Montgomery, Linda Szymanski, and Douglas Thomas. 1996. *State Responses to Serious and Violent Juvenile Crime: Research Report.* Washington, D.C.: Office of Juvenile Justice and Delinquency Prevention, National Center for Juvenile Justice.

Tracy, Paul E., Marvin E. Wolfgang, and Robert M. Figlio. 1990. *Delinquency Careers in Two Birth Cohorts.* New York: Plenum.

Twentieth Century Fund Task Force on Sentencing Policy toward Young Offenders. 1978. *Confronting Youth Crime.* New York: Holmes & Meier.

U.S. General Accounting Office. 1995. *Juvenile Justice: Juveniles Processed in Criminal Court and Case Dispositions.* Washington, D.C.: U.S. General Accounting Office.

Van den Haag, Ernest. 1975. *Punishing Criminals: Concerning a Very Old and Painful Question.* New York: Basic.

Vereb, Thomas S., and John L. Hutzler. 1981. *Juveniles as Criminals: 1981 Statutes Analysis.* Pittsburgh: National Center for Juvenile Justice.

von Hirsch, Andrew. 1976. *Doing Justice.* New York: Hill & Wang.

Walkover, Andrew. 1984. "The Infancy Defense in the New Juvenile Court." *University of California Los Angeles Law Review* 31:503–62.

Whitehead, John T., and Steven P. Lab. 1989. "A Meta-analysis of Juvenile Correctional Treatment." *Journal of Research in Crime and Delinquency* 26:276–95.

Wilson, John J., and James C. Howell. 1995. "Comprehensive Strategy for Serious, Violent, and Chronic Juvenile Offenders." In *A Sourcebook: Serious, Violent, and Chronic Juvenile Offenders,* edited by James C. Howell, Barry Krisberg, J. David Hawkins, and John J. Wilson. Thousand Oaks, Calif.: Sage.

Wolfgang, Marvin, Robert Figlio, and Thorsten Sellin. 1972. *Delinquency in a Birth Cohort.* Chicago: University of Chicago Press.

Wooden, Kenneth. 1976. *Weeping in the Playtime of Others: America's Incarcerated Children.* New York: McGraw-Hill.

Zimring, Frank. 1981*a*. "Notes toward a Jurisprudence of Waiver." In *Readings in Public Policy,* edited by John C. Hall, Donna Martin Hamparian, John

M. Pettibone, and Joseph L. White. Columbus, Ohio: Academy for Contemporary Problems.

———. 1981*b*. "Kids, Groups and Crime: Some Implications of a Well-Known Secret." *Journal of Criminal Law and Criminology* 72:867–902.

———. 1982. *The Changing Legal World of Adolescence*. New York: Free Press.

———. 1991. "The Treatment of Hard Cases in American Juvenile Justice: In Defense of Discretionary Waiver." *Notre Dame Journal of Law, Ethics and Public Policy* 5:267–80.

James C. Howell and J. David Hawkins

Prevention of Youth Violence

ABSTRACT

Research on the epidemiology of violence has identified two groups of offenders: life-course-persistent offenders and adolescent-limited offenders. Violence prevention programs should seek either to prevent the emergence of violent behavior in childhood or to prevent the spread of violence in adolescence. Research has identified predictors of both patterns of behavior. Prevention programs should explicitly seek to address these risk and protective factors. A variety of intervention programs have reduced risk for violence and enhanced protection against violent behavior. Comprehensive community-wide strategies for the prevention of violence hold particular promise.

Current violence prevention approaches seek to reduce or eliminate factors that predict a greater probability of violence in adolescence and young adulthood and strengthen factors that mediate or moderate exposure to risk. Not all of the known risk factors for violence and delinquency can be changed. Yet knowledge of the factors that increase risk for violence can help define populations that should receive preventive interventions to enhance protection in the face of risk exposure. Research has identified protective processes that mediate or moderate effects of risk exposure, promote resilience in children, and prevent health and behavior problems. Current preventive interventions seek to enhance protection in communities, families, schools, and individuals by using tested strategies that reduce risk and enhance protection.

James C. Howell is adjunct researcher at the National Youth Gang Center in Tallahassee, Florida. J. David Hawkins is director of the Social Development Research Group and professor in the School of Social Work at the University of Washington, Seattle.

In Section I, following Moffitt (1993), we distinguish two groups of young people who commit violent acts, and who may require different preventive interventions. The first group includes those who begin with oppositional behaviors and aggressive acts in childhood and persist into more violent behaviors through adolescence and into adulthood. The second group engages in violent acts only during adolescence. We contend that violence prevention efforts can be more effective if interventions are designed specifically to reduce risk and enhance protection in these two groups.

Predictors of violence in both groups are reviewed in Section II, as are protective factors that have been found to mediate or moderate the effects of exposure to risk. In Section III we review how violence spreads in adolescence, among adolescence-limited offenders. The spread of violence in three social contexts—peer groups, schools, and youth gangs—is discussed. Section IV reviews the foundations of prevention science using the concepts of risk- and protective-focused prevention. Section V reviews effective interventions that reduce known risk factors and enhance protective factors in childhood and adolescence. These are presented in relation to the two groups of offenders discussed earlier. We review interventions developmentally, from the prenatal period to age twelve. Next, we review interventions that hold potential for preventing violence in peer groups, in schools, and in youth gangs.

In Section VI we discuss the prospects for community-wide violence prevention at the current stage of knowledge. We discuss the Communities that Care strategy that uses epidemiologic assessments of risk and protection to guide the selection and implementation of tested violence prevention interventions matched to each community's profile of risk and protection. The strategy uses community activation and strategic planning methods to engage community residents, organizations, and government agencies in planning, selecting, and implementing tested interventions for preventing violence. Section VII is a brief conclusion.

I. Life-Course-Persistent and Adolescence-Limited Offenders

Two distinct groups of offenders have been identified: "life-course-persistent offenders" and "adolescence-limited offenders" (Moffitt 1993). Their profiles are substantially different.

A. Life-Course-Persistent Offenders

Moffitt (1993, p. 679) describes the offense history of life-course persisters. In childhood they engage in troublesome behaviors, including a variety of self-destructive behaviors (e.g., drug abuse), and they demonstrate a lack of ability to concentrate. They exhibit changing manifestations of antisocial behavior across the life course as age and circumstances alter opportunities for antisocial involvement. They engage in biting and hitting at age four, shoplifting and truancy at age ten, selling drugs and stealing cars at age sixteen, robbery and rape at age twenty-two, and fraud and child abuse at age thirty.

Past age forty, the co-occurring problems of life-course-persistent offenders include drug and alcohol addiction; unsatisfactory employment; unpaid debts; normlessness; drunk driving; violent assault; multiple and unstable relationships; spouse battery; abandoned, neglected, or abused children; and psychiatric illnesses (Robins 1966; Sampson and Laub 1990; Moffitt 1993, p. 679; see also Farrington and West 1990, 1993).

Four criteria distinguish life-course-persistent offenders: an early onset of offending (Moffitt 1991, 1993), active offending during adolescence, persistence in crime in adulthood, and escalation of offense seriousness (Tracy and Kempf-Leonard 1996; Loeber and Hay 1997; Loeber, Keenan, and Zhang 1997). Approximately 13 percent of the boys in the Dunedin, New Zealand, sample were life-course-persistent offenders (Moffitt et al. 1996).

B. Adolescence-Limited Offenders

Adolescence-limited offenders do not have a childhood history of antisocial behavior (Moffitt 1993, p. 686). They engage in antisocial behavior only during adolescence. As teenagers, their behavior may vary with the situation. They may shoplift while with a group of friends, but obey school and family rules. They "are likely to engage in antisocial behavior in situations where such responses seem profitable to them, but they are also able to abandon antisocial behavior when prosocial styles are more rewarding" (p. 686).

Moffitt observed the spread of delinquency as the adolescent-limited group joined the life-course persisters in early adolescence (Moffitt 1991, 1993; see also Moffitt, Lynam, and Silva 1994). The mean number of self-reported offenses by boys doubled from age thirteen to age fifteen, then tripled between ages fifteen and eighteen. The adolescent-limited group—those whose offending did not exceed normative levels by age eleven—represented 31 percent of the Dunedin sample (Moffitt et al. 1996).

A large majority of offenders, including some who commit serious violent acts, confine their offenses to the adolescent period. Three-fourths of the National Youth Survey adolescents who began serious violent offending after age eleven confined their careers to adolescence (Elliott 1994a). Only one-fourth of the adolescent-onset group continued their offending into adulthood.

Three criteria distinguish adolescence-limited offenders: onset of offending after age eleven to thirteen (Hamparian et al. 1978; Moffitt 1991, 1993; Elliott 1994a), desistance from crime by age eighteen (Moffitt 1991, 1993; Tracy and Kempf-Leonard 1996), and a lack of progression in offense seriousness (Loeber, Keenan, and Zhang 1997).

C. Other Empirical Evidence of Life-Course-Persistent and Adolescent-Limited Offending

A number of studies have distinguished between chronic and non-chronic offenders, but these studies are not always relevant for distinguishing life-course-persistent from adolescent-limited offenders because offenders who commit multiple offenses only during their adolescent years are identified as chronic offenders (Wolfgang, Figlio, and Sellin 1972; Hamparian et al. 1978; Shannon 1988; Farrington and West 1993).

Although the nomenclature differs, other studies have identified these two groups of offenders (Patterson, DeBaryshe, and Ramsey 1989; Denno 1990; Nagin and Paternoster 1991; Nagin and Farrington 1992a, 1992b; Nagin and Land 1993; Patterson and Yoerger 1993; Sampson and Laub 1993; Simons et al. 1994; Nagin, Farrington, and Moffitt 1995; Bartusch et al. 1997; Dean, Brame, and Piquero 1997).[1]

---

[1] Not all studies are in agreement with respect to particular characteristics of the two groups and the strength of explanatory models (see Nagin and Land 1993; Nagin, Farrington, and Moffitt 1995; Dean et al. 1997; Paternoster and Brame 1997). Other subgroups of offenders have been identified: one, for whom onset begins in adolescence with continued offending into adulthood (Nagin, Farrington, and Moffitt 1995); another, for whom onset begins in adulthood (Tracy and Kempf-Leonard 1996). There also is disagreement regarding the extent to which life-course-persistent offenders are empirically distinct from adolescence-limited offenders (see Loeber and Hay 1997). As Loeber and Hay note, most studies of the two groups use official records, which miss a great deal of offending (Elliott 1995). Few studies have followed the same participants into adulthood, to see if the adolescence-limited offenders indeed desist (cf. Nagin, Farrington, and Moffitt 1995). Finally, most of the research identifying the two groups is based on studies of males. Females usually have a later onset of delinquency than males,

Both life-course-persistent offenders and adolescent-limited offenders were identifiable in the Hamparian et al. (1978) study of birth cohorts of offenders arrested for violent offenses (murder, rape, robbery, and sexual imposition) in Columbus, Ohio. The first group of high-rate violent offenders was first arrested between ages six and twelve. A second group was first arrested at ages thirteen to fifteen. The early-onset group (ages six to twelve) evidenced a significantly higher mean number of violent arrests in adolescence. Further, 66 percent of those arrested before age twelve were arrested as adults, compared with 56 percent of those first arrested after age twelve (Hamparian et al. 1984). Other studies have produced similar patterns with respect to persistence in adolescence and adulthood (cf. Farrington 1986; Shannon 1988; Farrington and West 1993; Tracy and Kempf-Leonard 1996, pp. 37–46).

Among those who self-reported committing their first violent offense at age nine or younger in the Causes and Correlates of Delinquency studies of the Office of Juvenile Justice and Delinquency Protection, 39 percent in Rochester, New York, 41 percent in Pittsburgh, and 62 percent in Denver eventually became chronic violent adolescent offenders (Thornberry, Huizinga, and Loeber 1995).

Tracy and Kempf-Leonard (1996) also found evidence of the two groups in their age twenty-six follow-up of all Philadelphia youth born in 1958. Using police contacts, court referrals, and juvenile correctional commitment data, almost 8 percent of the entire cohort were life-course-persistent offenders; that is, they were arrested for delinquent acts in adolescence and criminal acts in adulthood (p. 81). The adolescence-limited group was about twice as large: almost 16 percent had an official record of delinquency, but were not arrested in adulthood. From another perspective, about one-third of the delinquents became adult criminals; two-thirds limited their offending to the adolescent period (p. 106).

Tracy and Kempf-Leonard (1996) found that several offending patterns were predictive of life-course-persistent offending: early onset, frequency of offending, offense specialization, offense seriousness, an offense escalation.[2]

---

and peak at a younger age, but a proportion of these late-onset females become life-course-persistent offenders (Elliott 1994a).

[2] The findings reported below generally held for females as well as for males, but were much more pronounced among males. Hence, our discussion of Tracy and Kempf-Leonard's findings centers on males.

D. Characteristics of the Two Groups

Moffitt (1990, 1991, 1993) suggested that life-course-persistent offenders are predisposed to chronic deviance throughout their lives by cumulative interactions between family adversity and individual neuropsychological impairments. Moffitt identified several sources of these deficits, including maternal drug abuse, poor prenatal nutrition, prenatal or postnatal exposure to toxic agents such as lead, and heritable variation. She suggested that neuropsychological impairments disrupt normal development and increase vulnerability to the criminogenic features of disadvantaged social environments. Early childhood deficits are manifested in such behaviors as attention deficit disorder, impulsivity, hyperactivity, and learning disorders. Life-course-persistent offenders are substantially more likely than adolescence-limited offenders to be violent, to display antisocial personalities, and to leave school early (Moffitt et al. 1996).

A key characteristic of life-course-persistent offenders is continuity in aggressive behavior. "The stability of aggressive behavior patterns throughout the life course is one of the most consistently documented patterns found in longitudinal research" (Laub and Lauritsen 1993, p. 239). Individuals who are aggressive in childhood are more likely than others to engage in violence in adolescence and adulthood (see Laub and Lauritsen 1993, 1994; Moffitt 1993; and Tracy and Kempf-Leonard 1996 for reviews of other studies).

Moffitt (1993) suggests that much adolescence-limited delinquent behavior involves mimicking life-course-persistent adolescents (see Warr 1996). These youths may also acquire aggressive behavior patterns through victimization by others (Olweus 1978). They may experience other problem behaviors that increase the likelihood of violent offending. Huizinga and Jakob-Chien (1998) found that the likelihood of violent offending was more than doubled when victimization experiences were combined with school failure and mental health problems in adolescence.

II. Risk Factors for Life-Course-Persistent and Adolescence-Limited Violence

To the extent that life-course-persistent offenders and adolescent-limited offenders are separable types of offenders, each responsible for a significant amount of violent behavior, it is worthwhile to consider how both types of offending could be prevented. Recent reviews have synthesized knowledge regarding the predictors of violent behavior

(Lipsey and Derzon 1998; Hawkins, Herrenkohl, et al. 1998; Farrington, in this volume). These reviews, and the studies they summarize, have focused on predicting violent offending in adolescence and young adulthood, but they have not consistently focused on identifying predictors of life-course-persistent as opposed to adolescence-limited offending. Given the difference in prevalence of these two types of offending in the population, it is plausible that different factors contribute to these types of offending. For example, factors that contribute to early oppositional and aggressive behavior may predict life-course-persistent behavior, but not adolescent-limited offending. Conversely, adolescent norms favorable to violent behavior may increase the incidence or spread of violence across adolescents in the population, but might not affect the rate or frequency of violent behavior during adolescence among life-course-persistent offenders. More work is needed to distinguish risk factors for life-course-persistent offending from risk factors for adolescence-limited offending. To the extent that different factors produce these different patterns of violent behavior, different prevention strategies are likely to be needed to reduce each type.

A. Risk Factors for Life-Course-Persistent Offending

Moffitt (1993) hypothesized that neuropsychological impairments and poor social environments interacted to produce an early onset of offending. Life-course-persistent offending is characterized by an early onset of oppositional and aggressive behavior in childhood (Robins 1978; Farrington 1991; Institute of Medicine 1994). A difficult temperament during the first four years of life, including frequent temper tantrums and displays of frustration and aggression toward adults and peers, predict later aggression (Loeber and Hay 1997).

Early predictors of childhood oppositional and defiant behaviors have been identified. These include prenatal and perinatal difficulties (including preterm delivery, low birth weight, and anoxia) (Brewer et al. 1995), though the associations between pregnancy and delivery complications and violence in adolescence are relatively weak (Lipsey and Derzon 1998). There is some evidence that prenatal trauma and pregnancy complications predict later violence only among children reared in unstable home environments (Reiss and Roth 1993), suggesting the interaction hypothesized by Moffitt. Research should continue to seek to differentiate the strength of prenatal and perinatal difficulties in predicting life-course-persistent violence as opposed to adolescent-limited violence in different family contexts.

Minor physical abnormalities and brain damage (e.g., from infectious disease, traumatic head injury, or pre/postnatal exposure to toxins such as heavy metals, alcohol, tobacco, or cocaine) may also increase risk for life-course-persistent offending, including violent behavior and substance abuse (Denno 1990; Raine, Brennan, and Mednick 1994; Brewer et al. 1995), though Lipsey and Derzon (1998) did not find strong associations between medical/physical predictors and violence at ages fifteen to twenty-five. It is plausible that some conditions, such as brain damage, impair reasoning and impulse control, and may lead to increases in violence across the life course. Again, more research is needed to identify the contribution of physiological conditions to risk for life-course-persistent offending.

Consistent with Moffitt's hypotheses regarding the contribution of neuropsychological disorders to early offending, social cognitive difficulties have been found to contribute to aggressive behavior. Some aggressive children consistently misunderstand others' intentions, perhaps misinterpreting prosocial overtures as aggressive, resulting in conflict between these children, their mothers, and their peers, and in rejection by peers in childhood (Dodge, Murphy, and Buchsbaum 1984; Dodge, Bates, and Pettit 1990; Dodge 1991). Rejection is often accompanied by anger. Impairments in cognitive processes and in the ability to regulate anger may contribute to life-course-persistent violence (Loeber and Hay 1997). Similarly, early attention problems and hyperactivity (e.g., attention-deficit hyperactivity disorder, ADHD) also appear to predict persistent aggressive behavior and offending (Loeber and Hay 1997).

Moffitt (1993) argues that cognitive deficits also contribute to problems in learning, reading, speech, writing, and memory among antisocial children (see also Loeber and Hay 1997). It is clear that poor academic performance is related to early onset of antisocial behavior (Maguin and Loeber 1996). Academic failure from the elementary grades is predictive of increased risk for later violent behavior (Hawkins, Farrington, and Catalano 1998). Thus early academic difficulties may also increase risk for life-course-persistent offending.

Both Moffitt and Patterson have suggested that the individual characteristics of developing children interact with characteristics of the immediate social environment to increase risk for early offending. Poor family management practices, including parents' failure to set clear expectations for children's behavior, failure to supervise and monitor children, and excessively severe, harsh, or inconsistent punishment have been found to increase risk for early aggressive behavior and offending (Yoshikawa 1994, 1995). Child-rearing practices such as poor supervision, poor communication, parent-child conflict, and frequent physical punishment predict physical aggression, including fighting by boys aged seven to eight (Loeber and Hay 1997; Loeber, Keenan, and Zhang 1997).

Parental criminality (Farrington 1989; Lipsey and Derzon 1998) and family violence, including parent-child conflict, spouse abuse, and childhood maltreatment (Institute of Medicine 1994; Thornberry 1994; Yoshikawa 1994, 1995; Smith and Thornberry 1995; Loeber and Hay 1997) also are characteristics of the family environment that may contribute to life-course-persistent violence. More research is needed to understand the extent to which these factors contribute differentially to life-course-persistent as opposed to adolescent-limited offending.

Moffitt (1993) argued that both neuropsychological impairments and family environmental risks are exacerbated by poverty and by living in disorganized, economically disadvantaged neighborhoods. In this way, neighborhood disorganization and economic deprivation increase risk for life-course-persistent offending (Sampson 1983, 1985, 1987; Curry and Spergel 1988; Bursik and Grasmick 1993; Fagan and Wilkinson, in this volume; Hagedorn, in this volume).

Farrington (in this volume) found that family dependence on welfare significantly increased the odds of later violent behavior in both Pittsburgh and London data sets. Violent delinquency is more prevalent in inner-city areas characterized by poverty (Elliott, Huizinga, and Menard 1989). Lipsey and Derzon's (1998) meta-analysis found poverty to be a risk factor for violent behavior at ages fifteen to twenty-five, whether measured in childhood or in adolescence.

There is evidence that neighborhoods contribute to the early initiation of violent behavior itself. Loeber and Wikstrom (1993) found that the worse the quality of the neighborhood, the greater the likelihood that ten- to twelve-year-old boys progressed from aggression to physical fighting or violence. "Early onset of juvenile aggression and violence occurred mostly in the worst neighborhoods, but with age, juvenile aggression and violence also becomes evident in more advantaged neighborhoods" (Loeber and Hay 1997, p. 398). Disorganized and impoverished neighborhoods may contribute both to the development of life-course-persistent violence and to the spread of violence during adolescence (see Shannon 1988, 1991).

B. *Risk Factors for Adolescence-Limited Offending*

In a meta-analysis of longitudinal studies, Lipsey and Derzon (1998) identified five categories of risk factors measured at ages twelve to fifteen that predicted violence between ages fifteen and twenty-five. These were prior antisocial behavior (delinquency, aggression, and physical violence), poor parent-child relations, poor school attitudes/ performance, antisocial peers, and individual psychological conditions. Neither drug use nor antisocial parents were strong predictors of violence during adolescence.

Poor parent/child relations was found to be the strongest family predictor of adolescent violence in Lipsey and Derzon's analysis. It consisted of three separable dimensions: poor family management practices, low degree of involvement and interaction of parent with child, and low bonding to family. Poor family management practices at ages fourteen and sixteen predict self-reported violence at age eighteen (Herrenkohl et al. 1998). A lack of parental interaction and involvement in children's lives during adolescence also contributes to the spread of violence during adolescence (Hawkins, Herrenkohl, et al. 1998). The relationship between family bonding and violence may be moderated by the degree to which other family members themselves engage in violent behavior (Hawkins, Herrenkohl, et al. 1998).

Poor academic performance from ages twelve to fifteen also appears to contribute to adolescent delinquency. In their meta-analysis, Maguin and Loeber (1996) found that poor academic performance is related not only to prevalence but also to escalation in the frequency and seriousness of offending in adolescence. Lipsey and Derzon (1998) found that poor "school attitudes/performance" as indicated by dropping out of school, low interest in education, low level of education, low school achievement, poor quality school, and truancy measured at ages twelve to fifteen was among the stronger predictors of later violent behavior they assessed. Similar findings have been reported in a more recent analysis (Herrenkohl et al. 1998).

Several aspects of school participation are important predictors of violence. High truancy rates in adolescence and leaving school prior to the age of fifteen predict later teenage violence (Hawkins, Herrenkohl, et al. 1998). Youths who change schools often are also more violent later in adolescence (Herrenkohl et al. 1998). Finally, boys who attended schools with high delinquency rates at age eleven reported slightly, but not significantly, more violent behavior than other youths suggesting the role school social contexts play in the spread of adolescence (Farrington 1989).

III. The Spread of Violence in Adolescence

The growth in adolescent violence in the early 1990s (see Cook and Laub, in this volume) appears to reflect a spread in adolescence-limited offending rather than an increase in the prevalence of life-course-persistent offenders in the population. Elliott (1994*b*, p. 1) estimates that over the past decade "there has been a relatively small increase (8–10 percent) in the proportion of adolescents involved in some type of serious violent offending," but that the frequency of offending is about the same.

This trend is also observed in Snyder's (1998) analysis of the juvenile court careers of all persons born between 1962 and 1977 who were referred to the Maricopa County (Arizona) juvenile court for a delinquent offense before their eighteenth birthday. His study classified this population by the year its members turned eighteen years of age, that is, the sixteen "graduating classes" from 1980 through 1995. Snyder found a small increase (from about 15 percent to about 18 percent) in the proportion of chronic offenders in the juvenile justice graduating classes of the 1990s compared to the classes of the 1980s. However, the nature of the individual chronic career remained about the same. They were not more active, more serious, or more violent than chronic offenders in the graduating classes of the 1980s.

Compared to the 1980s, a somewhat greater proportion of youths in the 1990s were charged with a violent offense (10 percent versus 8 percent). But Snyder found that the average number of violent-offense referrals in the careers of youth with a violent-offense referral remained constant over the sixteen graduating classes, averaging 1.2 violent referrals per career. Thus it appears that the increase in adolescent violence over the past ten to fifteen years is accounted for by the spread of violence in adolescence, that is, by an increase in the number of adolescence-limited offenders, not by an increase in the number of life-course-persistent offenders. How does violence spread among adolescents?

Loftin (1986) emphasizes the contagious characteristic of violence: it is clustered in space, escalates over time, and also escalates from person to person. Violence spreads in social contexts where adolescents interact: in peer groups, at school, and in youth gangs.

Peer group interaction is a factor contributing to the spread of violence in adolescence. Lipsey and Derzon's (1998) meta-analysis showed antisocial peers from ages twelve to fifteen to be the strongest of the measured predictors of later violent behavior. In contrast, Lipsey and Derzon found that having antisocial peers at ages six to twelve did not predict later violent behavior. Delinquent peers are not important in the etiology of life-course-persistent offending, but they contribute to the spread of delinquency and violence in adolescence. Warr (1996) reports that "instigators," who tend to be older offenders with longer offense histories, play a key role in the spread of adolescent offending. "Joiners" (less-experienced offenders, characteristic of adolescence-limited offenders) appear to be linked to instigators by friendship bonds. Some offenders shift frequently between these two roles as they move from group to group. These "mixed" offenders constitute about half of all offenders. Pure joiners represent about a third of all offenders, and nearly half of them commit several offenses.

The school setting is a key social context in which adolescent violence spreads (see D. Anderson, in this volume). Garofalo, Siegel, and Laub (1987) show that a large proportion of school-related victimizations stem from peer interactions occurring in the course of routine daily activities that escalate. Much violence that occurs at school is instigated in classrooms, hallways, on school buses, and in areas not closely supervised by teachers and other school staff, such as in gyms, locker rooms, and on playgrounds (Lockwood 1997). The largest percentage of incidents in Lockwood's study involved pushing, grabbing, shoving, kicking, biting, and hitting. Many of these incidents are unprovoked; others relate to possessions, backbiting, insults, verbal teasing, and rough physical play. The culmination of these incidents in violence is supported by normative expectations (Lockwood 1997).

Youth gangs are another context in which adolescent violence spreads (see Hagedorn, in this volume). An eleven-city survey of eighth graders found that 9 percent were then members of a gang, and 17 percent said they had belonged to a gang at some point in their lives (Esbensen and Osgood 1997). Surveys indicate that up to 30 percent of adolescents in some urban inner-city areas join gangs at some point (Howell 1998). In the past twenty-five years, the numbers of reported youth gang problem cities and of gang members have increased nearly seven times, while the estimated number of youth gangs has increased over ten times (Miller 1992; Moore 1997; National Youth Gang Center 1997). Youth gangs may contribute to an increase in violence in school contexts. The percentage of students reporting fighting gangs in their school increased from 15 percent in 1989 (Bastian and Taylor 1991) to 35 percent in 1993 (National Center for Education Statistics 1994). Students who reported gangs and weapons in school were about twice as likely to report having been victims of a violent crime (physical attack, robbery, or bullying).

Studies show that the influence of the gang on levels of violent offending is greater than the influence of other delinquent peers (Huizinga 1997; Thornberry 1998; Battin et al. 1998). Moreover, while in gangs, youths commit offenses at higher rates than before joining or after leaving (Esbensen and Huizinga 1993; Thornberry et al. 1993; Hill et al. 1996). While in gangs, adolescents commit serious and violent offenses at a rate several times higher than do nongang adolescents (Esbensen and Huizinga 1993; Thornberry et al. 1993; Hill et al. 1996).

Many youth gangs are governed by norms supporting the expressive use of violence to settle disputes (Short and Strodtbeck 1965; Horowitz 1983). These norms favorable to violence help to explain the contribution of youth gangs to adolescent-limited violent offending. Decker (1996) explains how the threat of attack by another group ignites the gang through contagion, which, in turn, increases cohesion, and produces violence. Most gang violence, he argues, is retaliatory, a response to violence—real or perceived—against the gang, often leading to retaliation and revenge, creating a feedback loop (Decker and Van Winkle 1996). Thus youth gangs represent a key context in which adolescent violence spreads, supported by normative expectations.

IV. Risk and Protective-Focused Prevention
To prevent youth violence, both the predictors of life-course-persistent offending and the factors that contribute to the spread of violence in adolescence should be addressed. In this section, we discuss risk- and protective-focused prevention to provide a framework for our review of effective violence prevention programs.

Risk- and protective-focused prevention was pioneered by public health research that demonstrated that such conditions as cardiovascular disease and traffic-related injuries can be prevented (Institute of Medicine 1994). The aim of risk-focused prevention is to interrupt the causal processes that lead to a problem (Catalano and Hawkins 1996). Risk factors are conditions in the individual or environment that predict an increased likelihood of developing a problem such as violent behavior. Protective factors are conditions in the individual or environment that mediate or moderate the effects of risk factors or increase resistance to them, and thus inhibit the development of problems even in the face of risk exposure. Risk and protective factors predict increased or decreased probability of developing problem behaviors. However, just as actuarial tables, used, for example, by life insurance companies to establish individual premiums, do not predict an individual's life experience, the presence of risk factors does not guarantee that an individual will develop or avoid delinquent and violent behavior problems.

Risk- and protective-focused approaches to the prevention of delinquency and violence seek to reduce or eliminate factors that predict a greater probability of developing these problems during adolescence and young adulthood and strengthen factors that mediate or moderate exposure to risk. Not all of the known risk factors for violence and delinquency can be changed. Yet knowledge of these risk factors can help define populations that should receive preventive interventions that enhance protection in the face of risk exposure. To illustrate, a family history of heart disease is a risk factor for cardiovascular disease. Although this risk factor cannot be changed, protective measures including a low-fat diet, regular exercise, and routine medical checkups can reduce the likelihood of cardiovascular disease in individuals characterized by this risk factor.

Hawkins and his colleagues identify three classes of protective factors: factors inherent in the individual; factors related to the development of social bonding; and healthy beliefs and clear standards for behavior (Hawkins, Catalano, and Associates 1992). Individual characteristics that appear to be protective against violent behavior include female gender, high intelligence, a positive social orientation, and a resilient temperament (Hawkins, Catalano, and Associates 1992). Social bonding includes warm, supportive, affective relationships or attachments with family members or other adults (Garmezy 1985). It also includes the development of commitment to the lines of action valued by a social institution such as family, school, or a religious organization. Healthy beliefs and clear standards include family and community norms opposed to crime and violence and supportive of educational success and healthy development.

Risk and protective factors stabilize as predictors of delinquency and violence at different points in human development. If risk and protective factors are addressed at, or slightly before, the developmental point when they begin to predict later delinquency and violence, it is more likely that risk reduction efforts will be effective.

V. Prevention of Life-Course-Persistent and
Adolescence-Limited Offending

Approaches that have shown promise for preventing life-course-persistent and adolescent-limited violent offending are discussed in this section. To be included, evaluations needed to satisfy six criteria (modified from Institute of Medicine 1994, pp. 217–22):

First, the program addressed known risk and protective factors for violence. While some investigators did not present a program described in terms of the risk factors it addressed, if it could be reasonably assumed that the program addressed an identified risk or protective factor for delinquency and violence, then the program was judged to have met this criterion.

Second, the demographic, social, and risk characteristics of the population served by the program were specified.

Third, the preventive intervention itself was adequately described, including the goals and content of the intervention, personnel delivering the program, and methods of service delivery.

Fourth, the evaluation used a quasi experimental or experimental research design in testing program effects. Uncontrolled, pre-experimental pretest/post-test designs suffer from too many threats to internal validity to allow reasonable interpretation of results, and such studies were not included here.

Fifth, the evaluation provided evidence that the intervention was delivered according to plan.

Sixth, quantitative evidence was presented regarding program outcomes on delinquency, violence, and/or associated risk and protective factors. Unless otherwise noted, in the evaluations reviewed here, the investigators controlled for preprogram differences between experimental and control/comparison groups in assessing program outcomes.

We suggest that two classes of interventions are needed: interventions that address developmental predictors of life-course-persistent offending, and interventions that counter the spread of violence in adolescence in three main contexts: schools, delinquent peer groups, and delinquent youth gangs.

A. Preventing Life-Course-Persistent Offending

Intervention with life-course persisters must occur early, before unconventional behavioral patterns are established. The strongest risk factor in childhood is a history of antisocial behavior (Lipsey and Derzon 1998), but other early risk factors have been linked to early onset. As we noted above, these include prenatal and perinatal difficulties, poor family management practices, family violence during the infant and childhood years, parental problem behaviors, and early academic problems. Moreover, children who live in economically deprived areas and disorganized neighborhoods in urban low-income communities are at risk for early onset. Programs designed to prevent early onset of life-course offending should address these risk factors in neighborhoods, families, and children themselves to prevent or reduce early aggressive behavior in multiple domains (Loeber and Hay 1997).

The reforms necessary to eliminate neighborhood-level conditions that contribute both to early onset and life-course-persistent violence are beyond the scope of this essay (see Fagan and Wilkinson, in this volume). Current programs include community reconstruction (Eisenhower Foundation 1990), Empowerment Zones (revitalization of communities through economic and social services), and Enterprise Communities (promoting physical and human development). Empowerment Zones and Enterprise Communities are large-scale programs supported through the federal Department of Housing and Urban Development (see Office of Juvenile Justice and Delinquency Prevention 1995) that aim to reconstruct selected inner-city areas.

Interventions that address specific risk factors for life-course-persistent offending are reviewed next.

1. *Prenatal and Infancy.*   Routine prenatal and perinatal medical care decreases the incidence of perinatal difficulties and minor physical abnormalities (Institute of Medicine 1994). Interventions should follow the broad definition of prenatal care recommended by the U.S. Public Health Service Expert Panel on the Content of Prenatal Care (1989) and include education for the mother regarding the physiological and emotional changes of pregnancy, fetal growth and development, and psychosocial preparation for childbirth. Furthermore, home visitation by health professionals during pregnancy, which includes intensive health education for the mother, improves high-risk mothers' (e.g., smokers, teens) health-related behaviors and reduces the rates of preterm deliveries and low birthweight babies (Olds and Kitzman 1993). Health education can decrease the pregnant mother's use of alcohol and other drugs, which helps to prevent brain damage in the infant.

The Prenatal/Early Infancy Project (Olds et al. 1986) targeted a geographical area with high rates of poverty and child abuse in the semirural Appalachian region of New York State. A subsample of mothers were unmarried and from the lowest socioeconomic group, and nearly half were teenagers. One group received only prenatal home visitation. A second group received home visitation by a nurse during pregnancy and until the child was two years old. In their work with families, nurse home visitors followed a comprehensive program plan focused on the mother's personal health, environmental health, quality of caregiving for the infant and toddler, and the mother's own personal development (such as preventing unintended subsequent pregnancies and finding work). The nurse home visitors also were expected to involve family members and friends in the program and to help families use other needed community health and human services.

A fifteen-year follow-up (Olds et al. 1997) showed that home visitation through infancy significantly reduced child abuse and neglect. In contrast to women in the comparison group, women who were visited by nurses during pregnancy and infancy were identified as perpetrators of child abuse and neglect in significantly fewer verified reports (a mean of .29 versus .54 reports). Among women who were unmarried and from households of low socioeconomic status at initial enrollment, nurse-visited women also had significantly fewer subsequent births (a mean of 1.1 versus 1.6 subsequent births in the control group), sixty versus ninety months' receiving Aid to Families with Dependent Children, significantly lower rates of impairment due to use of alcohol and other drugs, and fewer arrests, measured both by New York State records and by self-reports.

Another implementation and evaluation of the Prenatal/Early Infancy Project was carried out in Memphis, Tennessee, with primarily African American women with at least two sociodemographic risk characteristics (unmarried, less than twelve years of education, unemployed). The evaluation was conducted two years after the birth of the child. In contrast to counterparts assigned to the comparison condition, fewer women visited by nurses during pregnancy had pregnancy-induced hypertension. During the first two years after delivery, women visited by nurses during pregnancy and the first two years of the child's life had fewer health care encounters for children in which injuries or ingestions were detected, days that children were hospitalized with injuries or ingestions, and second pregnancies (Kitzman et al. 1997). These results indicate that nurse home visitation through pregnancy and infancy can reduce risks for violent offending in children.

2. *Age Two to Age Six.* Three types of interventions in this developmental substage address risk and protective factors for violence and substance abuse: immunizations, home/family-based interventions, and educational preschool. In practice, several types of interventions are typically combined into one multicomponent program.

All children, regardless of individual circumstance, should be immunized against such infectious diseases as poliomyelitis, diphtheria, pertussis, tetanus, measles, mumps, rubella, meningitis, and hepatitis B. Protection against many of these diseases helps to reduce risk for associated brain damage, a risk factor for later crime, violence, and substance abuse (Institute of Medicine 1994).

As in infancy, effective home and family-focused interventions during this developmental period usually involve a professional or trained paraprofessional service provider visiting the family at home. Home visitors can act as advocates for the family, help family members obtain needed social services, and encourage the mother to pursue her educational and occupational plans (Olds and Kitzman 1993). Provision of instrumental support to mothers, such as child care, offsets some of the hardships caused by economic deprivation. Transportation to health clinics and early education centers is another example of instrumental support which can be helpful. A toy and/or book-lending library, which is intended to aid in children's cognitive development, also may be offered in conjunction with home visitation services or an early education program (Olds and Kitzman 1993). Home visitors' provision of social support to mothers helps engage parents in an intervention and can reinforce parents' learning and behavior changes. By becoming a friend of the family who cares and listens, the home visitor is in a good position to educate and influence family members in positive ways.

Parent training can also serve to reduce the risks of poor family management practices and a child's early aggressive behaviors and conduct problems (Hawkins, Catalano, and Associates 1992; Olds and Kitzman 1993). Parent training typically entails instructing parents on how to set clear expectations for behavior, monitor children's behavior, reinforce positive behavior, provide consequences for inappropriate behavior, develop and use effective communication skills, and nurture children.

Programs designed to enhance parent-child interaction that promote a child's bonding to family (Hawkins, Catalano, and Miller 1992; Olds and Kitzman 1993) involve structured activities, such as a parent and child playing games together, that may be monitored by a home visitor. Parent-Child Interaction Training is a parenting intervention that effectively reduced risk factors, including poor family management practices and early antisocial behavior (Strayhorn and Weidman 1991). The program focused on low-income parents who had complained that their preschool children (ages two to five) exhibited at least one behavioral or emotional problem. Most parents were unmarried and experiencing depressive symptoms. Parents were taught parenting skills, including behavioral management, and trained to play constructively with their preschool child. A randomized trial showed that at a one-year follow-up, program children improved significantly more than controls in terms of teacher-rated attention-deficit hyperactivity, and aggressive and anxious behavior. Parent training interventions can also be successfully implemented individually through videotaped instruction (Webster-Stratton 1984, 1992), parent groups, and home visitors.

Early childhood education is another effective intervention approach during this period. Preschool programs that emphasize language development (including teacher-directed, student-centered, and student-initiated programs) advance children's cognitive and social development (Yoshikawa 1994).

Yoshikawa (1995) reviewed evaluations of forty parent training and childhood education programs, and found four programs that demonstrated positive long-term effects on serious, violent, and chronic delinquency. All of them focused on improving individual capacity (cognitive ability) and family functioning through a combination of early childhood education and family support services. The programs offered both home visits (parent training) and center-based educational child care or preschool (aimed at improving cognitive skills). They are the High/Scope Perry Preschool Project (Schweinhart, Barnes, and Weikart 1993), the Syracuse University Family Development Research Program (Lally, Mangione, and Honig 1988), the Yale Child Welfare Project (Seitz and Apfel 1994), and the Houston Parent Child Development Center (Johnson and Walker 1987). All four programs served urban, low-income families.

The High/Scope and Syracuse programs have been shown to be effective in reducing severe and chronic delinquency in long-term follow-ups. High/Scope Perry Preschool was designed to prevent delinquency by targeting preschoolers. The follow-up of High/Scope study groups at age twenty-seven showed that significantly fewer program group members than no-program group members were frequent offenders; that is, arrested five or more times in their lifetimes (7 percent vs. 35 percent), or as adults (7 percent vs. 31 percent) (Schweinhart et al. 1993). The program group also had noticeably fewer juvenile arrests and significantly fewer arrests for drug manufacturing or drug distribution offenses (7 percent vs. 25 percent). The Syracuse program also produced a decrease in the total number, severity, and chronicity of later involvement in officially recorded offenses (Lally, Mangione, and Honig 1988). Yoshikawa (1995) concluded the combination of early education for the child and family support produced the strongest long-term effects on antisocial behavior and delinquency. He attributes their success to their effects on multiple risks for chronic delinquency.

Yoshikawa (1995, p. 70) issued a cautionary note concerning these programs. Because they were carried out in the 1970s, "numerous demographic, social and economic changes have occurred since then which might affect the outcomes of early intervention." For example, the higher rate of employment among women might reduce the attractiveness of frequent home visiting. Yoshikawa suggests that "family-focused interventions alone, without broader efforts to attack these neighborhood-level causal factors, may not have their intended impact" (p. 70). Nevertheless, "as one element in a comprehensive plan to address poverty, drugs, guns, and other environmental causes of crime, early education and family support programs may lessen the current devastating impact of chronic delinquency on America's children and families" (Yoshikawa 1995, p. 71). In sum, community-based prevention and early childhood programs should be combined in a comprehensive approach.

3. *Ages Six to Twelve.* Early antisocial behavior in this age range includes delinquency and substance use, physical and verbal aggression, and other problem behaviors (e.g., temper tantrums). This is an opportune time for curbing aggressive behaviors and ensuring that youngsters experience early academic success. From a protective standpoint, this is the time to ensure that these children become bonded to school and other positive social influences.

a) Parent Training. One means of reducing the onset of delinquent and violent childhood behavior is through reducing abuse and neglect (Smith and Thornberry 1995). Parent training using Multisystemic Therapy (MST; see Henggeler 1997) has been successfully applied to abusive and neglectful parents of elementary school-aged children. Brunk, Henggeler, and Whelan (1987) randomly assigned abusive and neglectful families either to MST or traditional behavioral parent training. At post-test, parents who received either treatment showed reductions in emotional distress, overall stress, and severity of identified problems. However, analyses of sequential observational measures showed that MST was more effective than parent training at restructuring parent-child relations in those behavior patterns that differentiate maltreating parents from nonproblem parents. In the postprogram period, MST parents controlled their child's behavior more effectively, maltreated children exhibited less passive noncompliance, and neglecting parents became more responsive to their child's behavior.

Two multicomponent interventions involving parent training during the elementary school years have demonstrated significant preventive effects on delinquency and violence. The first was a two-year intervention directed at disruptive kindergarten boys from white, French-speaking families of low socioeconomic background in Montreal (Tremblay et al. 1991, 1992). The two primary program components were home-based parent training and school-based social skills training for the boys. The parent training included a reading program and emphasized monitoring children's behavior, positive reinforcement for prosocial behavior, effective and nonabusive punishment, family crisis management, and generalization skills. The social skills training was conducted within groups including both disruptive and prosocial boys. Skills training sessions focused on initiating social interaction, improving interpersonal skills, making verbal requests, following rules, handling anger, and mastering "look and listen" techniques for regaining self-control. The researchers used a true experimental design.

Experimental boys' teacher-rated fighting behavior decreased significantly relative to observational and control boys at the three-year follow-up when boys were age twelve. Experimental boys, in comparison to observational and control boys, were also significantly less likely at the three-year follow-up to be held back a school grade or placed in special classes, schools, or institutions. By age twelve, experimental boys were 50 percent less likely to have serious school adjustment problems and significantly less likely to have initiated delinquent behaviors, including trespassing and theft, than observational and control boys.

Kazdin, Siegel, and Bass (1992) conducted a true experimental evaluation of a similar program. They found that for boys and girls aged seven to thirteen who were exhibiting antisocial behavior, a combination of parent training and problem-solving skills training significantly reduced self-reported and parent-rated aggressive, antisocial, and delinquent behavior at one-year follow-up compared with parent-training or problem-solving skills training alone. This study indicates that parent- and child-training interventions are more effective when combined.

b) Behavior Management. A second major strategy for reducing behavior problems during the elementary period (ages six to twelve) is the use of behavior management methods in school classrooms and on playgrounds. Two examples follow. Kellam and Rebok (1992) and Kellam et al. (1994) evaluated the impacts of a behavioral classroom management technique called the "Good Behavior Game." Program teachers measured students' levels of aggression and disruption during a baseline period and then assigned students to one of three heterogeneous teams that included equally aggressive/disruptive children. When the Good Behavior Game was in progress, teachers assigned check marks on the chalkboard to a team when a student in that team engaged in a disruptive behavior. At the end of a particular game period, teams with less than five check marks earned a reward. During the beginning of the program, game periods were announced and tangible rewards such as stickers were immediately distributed to team members. As the program progressed, the teacher began the game unannounced and provided less tangible rewards, like participation in a rewarding activity such as extra recess or class privileges that were delayed until the end of the day or week. Teams that "won" (by having less than five check marks) the most times during the week received a special reward on Friday. The two-year program was tested beginning with first-grade students in public schools in eastern Baltimore. The participating urban public schools recruited children from low- and middle-income residential areas and included neighborhoods varying in ethnic diversity.

The researchers used a true experimental design to evaluate program effects. Within each of five urban areas, schools were assigned to receive the Good Behavior Game, a mastery learning instructional intervention, or no intervention (the control group). Within each Good Behavior Game experimental school, teachers and entering students were randomly assigned to intervention or control classrooms. During the first weeks of the program, the Good Behavior Game was played for three ten-minute periods a week. The duration of game periods gradually increased in subsequent weeks to a maximum of three hours.

After one year of the program, experimental students were rated as significantly less aggressive and shy by teachers and peers in comparison to control students. The largest program effects after one year were found for the most aggressive children. There were no overall program effects on sixth-grade teacher-rated aggression when first-grade teacher-rated aggression was controlled. However, experimental boys rated as highly aggressive in first grade were rated as significantly less aggressive in the sixth grade than boys in the control and mastery learning conditions who were rated as highly aggressive in the first grade, controlling for the level of first-grade aggression.

Murphy, Hutchison, and Bailey (1983) evaluated a playground program at an elementary school in Tallahassee, Florida. Children gathered on the school playground beginning an hour before school started. Prior to the program, school staff regarded students' disruptive and aggressive behavior on the playground as a problem during this morning period. The program consisted of organized games (jump rope and running races) for kindergarten to second-grade children on the playground in the forty minutes before school started. Three aides supervised these activities and used a time-out procedure for students who committed particularly unruly behaviors. For time-out, the disruptive student was required to sit quietly on a bench for two minutes. Twelve days of baseline observations of student playground behavior (during which teacher aides monitored unorganized activities as usual) were followed by observations during seven days of the experimental program. The next four days were the second baseline observation period, which were followed by six more days of the experimental program. Seven observers stationed on the perimeter of the playground observed students' behavior in different thirds of the play area in the twenty minutes before the beginning of school.

The children participated vigorously in the organized games, although they were still free to play on their own. The mean number of disruptive incidents per observation period during the experimental periods was 53 percent less than during the baseline periods. While situation specific reductions in aggressive behavior on the playground were observed, program effects on student behavior in other settings were not investigated.

c) Promoting School Functioning. Promoting academic adjustment and school achievement is another effective approach to reducing risks (for antisocial behavior) from ages six to twelve. Three comprehensive approaches for addressing multiple risks and enhancing achievement and protection during the elementary school period have been evaluated and found to be effective: the Success for All program, the Fast Track program, and the Seattle Social Development Project (SSDP).

Slavin and his colleagues developed and evaluated the Success for All program (Slavin et al. 1990, 1994, 1995). This program, for preschool and K–3 students, is based on two essential principles: prevention and immediate, intensive intervention. The first principle is to prevent learning problems by providing children with the best available classroom programs and by engaging parents in support of their children's success. When learning problems do appear, corrective interventions, including one-to-one tutoring, are employed immediately to help students who are having difficulty keeping up with their reading groups before their problems become significant. Students are assessed every eight weeks to determine whether they are making adequate progress in reading. Regrouping allows all children continually to progress at a challenging rate.

The Success for All curriculum emphasizes the development and use of language and provides a mix of academic readiness and music, art, and movement activities. The program also provides a family support team consisting of social workers, parent liaisons, counselors, and other school workers who provide parenting education and assist parents in support of their children's school success. Family support staff also provide family assistance when there are indications that students are not working up to their full potential because of problems at home. For example, assistance is provided when students are not receiving adequate sleep or nutrition, need glasses, are not attending school regularly, or are exhibiting serious behavior problems. Referrals to appropriate community service agencies are facilitated, when appropriate.

Evaluation of the initial Success for All program in Baltimore found that participating students scored significantly higher than control students on a variety of academic achievement tests (Slavin et al. 1990). The strongest effects were seen at the third-grade level. The Success for All program has been expanded in Baltimore schools and across the country. As of April 1994, the program was being implemented in a total of eighty-five schools in thirty-seven school districts in nineteen states (Slavin et al. 1994). Every Success for All school is matched with a control school that is similar in poverty level (percentage of students qualifying for free lunch), historical achievement level, ethnicity of the student body, and other factors. Students within treatment and control schools are matched using achievement test scores, as in the original study. Slavin et al. (1994) report significant positive effects in evaluations of Success for All programs in Philadelphia; Charleston, South Carolina; Fort Wayne, Indiana; and Montgomery, Alabama. Success for All has been found to be successful in increasing reading achievement among very disadvantaged students. Only one evaluation has failed to show positive effects in comparison with control students.

Fast Track is a comprehensive, multisite intervention designed to prevent serious and chronic antisocial behavior among children selected at school entry because of their conduct problems in kindergarten and at home (Conduct Problems Prevention Research Group 1996). The program targets kindergarten children with early conduct problems from low-income, high-crime communities that place stressors and negative influences on children and families. Other risk factors addressed by the program include peers with behavior problems and families characterized by marital conflict and instability. The Fast Track program seeks long-term prevention of children's antisocial behavior by immediate enhancement of competencies among the children, their parents, and teachers.

The first of six Fast Track components is a teacher-led classroom curriculum called PATHS (Providing Alternative THinking Strategies; Greenberg and Kusche 1993), which is directed toward emotional and relationship development, problem solving, and self-control. In addition, the following five programs were administered to the intervention participants: parent training groups designed to promote the development of positive family-school relationships and to teach parents behavior management skills, particularly in the use of praise, time-out, and self-restraint; home visits for the purpose of fostering parents' problem-solving skills, self-efficacy, and life-management; child social-skill training groups (called Friendship Groups) in which a target child and a prosocial peer partner left the classroom for intensive instruction; child tutoring in reading; and child friendship enhancement in the classroom (called Peer Pairing). The universal intervention continued each year through the fifth grade for each of the original designated intervention schools. Parent and child training groups met biweekly during the second grade and then shifted to a monthly schedule for all succeeding years of the project. Home visiting, academic tutoring, and child case management activities followed a criterion-based schedule.

Evaluation of the program by the Conduct Problems Prevention Group (1996) has produced first-year results. Preliminary outcomes indicate strong and consistent evidence of better social skills and more positive peer relations as a result of the intervention and some, although only partial, indication of fewer conduct problems. Intervention children also developed better basic reading skills and better social and emotional coping skills than the control children. Intervention parents demonstrated more positive involvement in their children's schools and more effective discipline strategies, as well as more positive relations with their children. The research team suggests that if these positive findings are maintained over the life course of these children, the guiding developmental theory leads them to expect that the intervention children will demonstrate fewer conduct problems in adolescence than control children. Indeed, the classrooms that received the PATHS curriculum were rated by teachers as having significantly fewer behavior problems than matched control classrooms, and the intervention classrooms had significantly lower mean scores for peer aggression.

The SSDP is a multicomponent intervention designed to prevent delinquency and other problem behaviors. It provided parent training, a social competence curriculum for students, and a package of classroom management and instruction methods in the elementary grades (Hawkins, Catalano, and Associates 1992; O'Donnell et al. 1995).

Teachers of the elementary grades were trained to use three methods of instruction: cooperative learning, proactive classroom management, and interactive teaching. Structured cooperative learning groups were used in experimental classrooms from grades two through six. Proactive classroom management consists of establishing expectations for classroom behavior; using methods of maintaining classroom order that minimize interruptions to instruction and learning; and giving frequent, specific, and contingent praise and encouragement for student effort and progress. Interactive teaching involves clear specification of learning objectives, continuous monitoring of students, and remediation, requiring students to master specific learning objectives before proceeding to more advanced work.

Child skill development is the second SSDP intervention. First-grade teachers of the full treatment group received instruction in the use of a cognitive and social skills training curriculum, Interpersonal Cognitive Problem Solving (Shure and Spivack 1980a, 1980b), which teaches communication, decision making, negotiation, and conflict resolution skills to children so that they can think through and enact alternative solutions to problems with peers. This intervention developed children's skills for classroom involvement so that they could participate in cooperative learning groups and other social activities without resorting to aggressive or other problem behaviors. When students in both intervention conditions were in the sixth grade, they also received training in skills to recognize and resist influences to engage in criminal behavior, drug use, and other problem behaviors.

Parent training is the third SSDP intervention. Parent training classes appropriate to the developmental level of the children were offered on a voluntary basis to parents or adult caretakers of children in the full intervention condition. Child behavior management skills were offered to parents, teaching them how to observe and pinpoint desirable and undesirable behavior in their children, teach expectations for behavior, and provide positive reinforcement for desired behavior and moderate punishment for undesired behavior in a consistent and contingent fashion. Academic support skills were also provided for parents. Finally, skills to reduce risks for drug use initiation were offered to parents when children were in grades five and six.

The SSDP was implemented with a multiethnic urban sample. A full intervention group received the intervention package from grade one through grade six. A late intervention group received the intervention package in grades five and six, and a control group received no special intervention.

By the end of grade two, boys in full intervention classrooms were rated as significantly less aggressive than boys in control classrooms (Hawkins, Von Cleve, and Catalano 1991). By the beginning of grade five, full intervention students were significantly less likely to have initiated delinquent behavior and alcohol use than controls (Hawkins, Catalano, and Associates 1992). By the end of grade six, intervention boys from low-income families had significantly greater academic achievement, better teacher-rated behavior, and lower rates of delinquency initiation than did control boys from low-income families (O'Donnell et al. 1995). A six-year follow-up at age eighteen found significantly higher achievement and lower rates of lifetime violent delinquent behavior among children exposed to the full intervention compared with controls (Hawkins, Catalano, et al. 1998).

These intervention studies indicate that risks for violence can be reduced during the elementary grades by combined interventions with parents, teachers, and children themselves, focused on promoting academic success, cognitive-emotional development, and behavioral self-regulation.

B. Preventing the Spread of Violence in Adolescence

In this subsection, we review specific interventions for preventing the spread of violence in adolescence. These are of three types: school-based programs, programs targeting delinquent peer groups, and programs targeting youth gangs.

1. *School-Based Interventions.*   School-based interventions are needed to prevent the spread of violence in adolescence (see D. Anderson, in this volume). Hawkins, Farrington, and Catalano (1998) suggest four protective strategies to prevent violence in the secondary school context: promoting school bonding and achievement, promoting nonviolent norms, teaching young people skills for living according to nonviolent norms, and eliminating use of weapons/firearms. We have already discussed interventions that promote academic achievement during the elementary grades. We review here examples of interventions that seek to promote achievement in secondary grades, promote nonviolent norms, and teach skills for living according to nonviolent norms (see also Hawkins, Farrington, and Catalano 1998). Means of preventing and reducing firearm use are discussed in the youth gangs section.

Project PATHE (Positive Action Through Holistic Education) was a comprehensive school organization intervention for secondary schools. PATHE's six main components were: (1) teams composed of teachers, other school staff, students, parents, and community members, which designed, planned, and implemented school improvement programs with the assistance of two full-time project staff; (2) curriculum and discipline policy review and revision, including student participation in the development of school and classroom rules and ongoing in-service training for teachers in instructional and classroom management practices; (3) schoolwide academic innovations, including study skills programs and cooperative learning techniques; (4) schoolwide climate innovations, including expanded extracurricular activities, peer counseling, and a school pride campaign intended to improve the overall image of the school; (5) career-oriented innovations, including a job-seeking skills program and a career exploration program; and (6) special academic and counseling services for low-achieving and disruptive students.

The evaluation (D. C. Gottfredson 1986) showed that the intervention was well-implemented, efficiently managed, and regarded positively by teachers. Because the author did not directly compare the experimental and comparison schools, it is difficult to ascertain the effects of the schoolwide intervention. However, the low-achieving and disruptive students in intervention schools who received special academic and counseling services scored significantly higher on standardized tests of basic academic skills and were significantly less likely to report drug involvement or repeat a grade than were control group students. Students who received these services were significantly more likely to graduate than were seniors in the corresponding control group. However, there were no significant differences between students who received special services and their controls on delinquency, court contacts, or other educational or behavioral measures.

The School Transition Environment Project (STEP) provided a "school within a school" to facilitate the transition to high school. Students entering the ninth grade were assigned to units of sixty-five to 100 students. Homeroom and academic classes were composed only of students in the same unit, and classrooms for the same unit were located in close proximity to each other. Academic subject teachers also served as homeroom teachers and as the main administrative and counseling link between the teachers, their parents, and the rest of the school. Homeroom teachers contacted parents before the school year and also held brief check-in sessions with homeroom students once a month.

The intervention increased bonding to school (Felner et al. 1993). Experimental students had significantly more positive perceptions of school, teachers, and other school personnel than did comparison students at the end of the year-long intervention. Moreover, intervention students showed significantly smaller decreases in academic performance and attendance during the transition between junior and senior high school. Intervention students also had a significantly lower school dropout rate (24 percent) than did comparison students (43 percent).

Promotion of norms antithetical to violence has been attempted primarily through conflict resolution and violence prevention curricula (see Brewer et al. 1995 for a comprehensive review; see also Hawkins, Farrington, and Catalano 1998). Programs operating conflict resolution curricula and peer mediation in tandem have shown positive effects on attitudes toward conflict and violence (Jenkins and Smith 1987; Benenson 1988). However, only one study with an adequate design has indicated a decrease in aggressive behavior associated with peer mediation (Tolson, McDonald, and Moriarty 1992). Students referred to the assistant deans for interpersonal conflicts in this program were randomly assigned to either peer mediation or the control condition of traditional discipline (e.g., warnings, demerits, suspensions). The program was implemented in a predominantly middle-class, ethnically diverse, suburban high school that had a dropout rate of less than 2 percent. Peer mediation participants were significantly less likely to be referred again in two and one-half months to the assistant dean for interpersonal conflicts than were students receiving traditional discipline.

The best evidence regarding the effectiveness of a violence prevention curriculum in the classroom comes from an evaluation of the Second Step curriculum in the elementary grades. The Second Step violence prevention curriculum uses thirty specific lessons to teach skills related to anger management, impulse control, and empathy. It is designed to increase prosocial behavior through increasing children's competence in peer interactions and friendships, and in interpersonal conflict resolution skills to help them avoid and resolve interpersonal conflicts. Versions of the curriculum are specifically tailored to students in preschool/kindergarten, grades one to three, grades four and five, and grades six to eight. Trained teachers implement the curriculum.

A randomized controlled trial evaluation of the program (Grossman et al. 1997) was conducted in twelve schools (49 classrooms, 790 students) in which the curriculum was implemented in grades one to three. The curriculum led to modest reductions in levels of observed aggressive behavior and increases in neutral and prosocial behavior in school among second and third graders. An overall decrease in physical aggression was observed in the playground and cafeteria areas of schools immediately after the curriculum was taught. Most of these effects persisted for six months. Relative to comparison students, experimental students improved significantly in their empathy, interpersonal problem-solving, anger management, and behavioral social skills as measured by interview responses to hypothetical social conflict situations.

The Positive Adolescents Choices Training (PACT) program was developed specifically for African American middle school or junior high students. It uses a cognitive-behavioral group training curriculum to reduce violent behaviors and also to reduce victimization risks. Trained doctoral-level facilitators led group instruction and practice in six social skills (giving positive feedback, giving negative feedback, accepting negative feedback, resisting peer pressure, problem solving, and negotiation). Skills were introduced with videotaped vignettes featuring African American teen role models in ethnically relevant social contexts. Students' practice role-playing sessions also were videotaped and reviewed. Students attended two fifty-minute training sessions per week for a semester. A randomized controlled trial of the program (Hammond and Yung 1993) found in a third-year follow-up that treatment group youth were less likely than control youth (18 percent versus 49 percent) to be referred to juvenile court, and project youth were also less likely to be charged with violent offenses.

A successful school antibullying program was conducted in Bergen, Norway, by Olweus (1991). It consisted of four program components: (1) a booklet for school personnel was distributed to all Norwegian comprehensive schools (grades one to nine) that described bully/victim problems, provided suggestions about what teachers and the school could do to counteract and prevent such problems, and dispelled myths about the nature and causes of bullying; (2) an information packet with information about bullying and advice was distributed to all families in Norway with school-age children; (3) a video cassette that depicted episodes from the daily lives of two early adolescent bullying victims was made available for purchase or rental at a subsidized price; and (4) a brief anonymous questionnaire about bullying problems was administered to students in all comprehensive schools, the results of which were used to inform school and family interventions.

The program was evaluated using before-and-after measures of bullying and victimization of children at each age. For example, the self-reported prevalence of bullies and victims among thirteen-year-olds before the program was compared with the prevalence of bullies and victims among (different) thirteen-year-olds twenty months after the program. Generally, the prevalence of victims decreased substantially (Olweus 1991). A similar program was implemented in 1992 in Sheffield, England, schools by Smith and Sharp (1994). The core program involved establishing a "whole-school" antibullying policy, increasing awareness of bullying, and clearly defining roles and responsibilities of teachers and students so that everyone knew what bullying was and what they should do about it. Optional interventions were also made available. Evaluation proved the program to be successful in reducing bullying among young children, but had relatively small effects on older children. Farrington (1993) provides a comprehensive overview of bullying interventions.

2. *Preventing the Spread of Violence among Delinquent Peer Groups.* Efforts to prevent the formation and negative influence of delinquent peer groups historically have not produced encouraging results (Brewer et al. 1995). G. D. Gottfredson (1987) reviewed evaluations of peer counseling approaches, variously referred to as guided group interaction, positive peer culture, peer culture development, and peer group counseling. Peer counseling in elementary and secondary

schools did not have desired effects on delinquency or associated risk factors, including association with delinquent/violent peers (G. D. Gottfredson 1987).

Jones and Offord (1989) evaluated the effects of an after-school recreation program that targeted low-income children ages five to fifteen residing in a public housing project in Ottawa, Ontario. Program staff actively recruited all children in the housing development to participate in structured after-school courses for improving skills in sports, music, dance, scouting, and other nonsport areas. After children reached a certain skill level, they were encouraged to participate in ongoing leagues or other competitive activities in the surrounding community.

The thirty-two-month-long program was evaluated with a nonequivalent comparison group design. The experimental housing project was matched with another public housing project that had only minimal city-provided recreational services. The number of arrests for juveniles residing in the experimental complex during the program declined significantly from the two years before the intervention relative to the number of juvenile arrests for youths residing in the comparison project over the same time period (there was a 75 percent decrease in the experimental project but a 67 percent increase in the comparison project). In addition, the number of security reports due to juveniles at the experimental complex declined significantly after the intervention began, in comparison to the comparison complex. Sixteen months after the program had ended, these positive changes had diminished significantly. The reductions in antisocial behavior in the experimental complex did not carry over to home and school. Parent and teacher-rated social behavior of experimental complex youths did not change significantly over the course of the intervention.

From these results, it seems likely that observed program effects were due to the program providing prosocial opportunities for youths in the after-school hours where these opportunities had not previously existed. Providing these opportunities appears to have reduced youths' involvement in delinquent behavior in the community. Using a similar design, Schinke, Cole, and Orlandi (1991) evaluated boys and girls clubs in fifteen housing projects in a representative sample of American cities. Although they caution that their positive results are not definitive (because of a lack of comparability between club sites and control sites, and small samples), the boys and girls clubs appeared to be associated with an overall reduction in substance abuse, drug trafficking, and other drug-related criminal activity in the housing projects where they were located.

After-school recreation programs that aggressively recruit youths and maintain high participation rates may be a promising intervention for preventing delinquency and violence, but should be evaluated further with research designs employing random assignment to study groups. This same observation can be made of mentoring programs, with the proviso that studies to date suggest that mentoring needs to be tied to behavioral contingencies for effectiveness (Brewer et al. 1995). In addition, a thirteen-site youth violence prevention program funded by the Centers for Disease Control bears watching (see Powell and Hawkins 1996). Several of these hold potential for preventing the spread of violence in adolescence.

3. *Preventing Youth Gang Violence.* We noted above the disproportionate contribution of youth gang members to the total volume of youth violence and the elevated rate of violent offending among youth gangs (see also E. Anderson, in this volume; Hagedorn, in this volume). We suggest three strategies for preventing gang contributions to the spread of violence among adolescents: preventing adolescents from joining gangs, preventing gang-related violence, and preventing gun violence.

We are aware of only two well-evaluated programs designed specifically to prevent adolescents from joining youth gangs. The two components of a Chicago program were a gang prevention curriculum and after-school recreational activities. The curriculum included twelve classroom sessions conducted over twelve weeks that focused on background information on gangs, gang violence, and substance abuse in gangs, gang recruitment and methods of resisting recruitment, consequences of gang membership, and values clarification. Most sessions were led by project staff, but some were led by a prosecuting attorney and by ethnic minority guest speakers who held various occupations. The curriculum was taught to eighth-grade students in Chicago middle schools located in lower- and lower-middle-class areas with high gang activity. After the curriculum ended, youths considered to be at high risk for joining a gang were invited to participate in after-school recreational activities including organized sports clinics, competition with youths both in their own and other neighborhoods, job skills/training workshops, educational assistance programs, and social activities. Results showed that experimental youths were less likely to become gang members than comparison youths, but the difference was only marginally statistically significant (Thompson and Jason 1988). This evaluation was limited by a short-term follow-up period and a relatively small sample size.

A newer curriculum designed to discourage elementary and second- ary students from joining gangs, called the Gang Resistance and Edu- cation Training (GREAT), is being evaluated and shows promise (Es- bensen and Osgood 1997). The GREAT program is a school-based intervention in which uniformed law enforcement officers teach a nine-week curriculum to middle school students (seventh graders). These weekly sessions consist of nine lessons: an introduction ac- quainting students with the GREAT program and the presenting offi- cer; crime/victims and your rights—in which students learn about crimes, their victims, and their impact on the school and neighbor- hood; cultural sensitivity/prejudice—teaching students how cultural differences affect their school and neighborhood; and conflict resolu- tion (two lessons)—students learn how to create an atmosphere of understanding that would enable all parties to better address interper- sonal problems and work together on solutions; meeting basic needs— teaching students how to satisfy their basic social needs without joining a gang; drugs/neighborhoods—students learn how drugs affect their school and neighborhood; responsibility—students learn about the di- verse responsibilities of people in their school and neighborhood; and goal setting—teaching students the need for personal goal setting and how to establish short- and long-term goals.

A preliminary study compared students who completed the GREAT program with others who either had not participated or had enrolled but failed to finish, in forty-two schools in eleven cities. Data were gathered on one occasion only, a year after students had completed the program, in the eighth grade. Respondents were divided into two groups: those who completed it and those who did not. Students who completed GREAT reported lower levels of gang affiliation and self- reported delinquency, including drug use, minor offending, property crimes, and crimes against persons. Compared with the comparison group, the treatment group reported more positive attitudes toward the police, more negative attitudes about gangs, having more friends involved in prosocial behavior, higher levels of perceived guilt at com- mitting deviant acts, more commitment to school, higher levels of at- tachment to both mothers and fathers, more communication with par- ents about their activities, fewer friends involved in delinquent activity, less likelihood of acting compulsively, lower likelihood of engaging in risky behavior, and lower levels of perceived blockages to academic success.

The nonequivalent comparison group design used in the study requires that these results be viewed with caution. Significant differences existed between the two groups on background characteristics, and noncompletion of the program may reflect a preexisting tendency toward antisocial behavior.

These preliminary evaluations of gang prevention curricula are encouraging. Both of the reviewed curricula give participants skills for avoiding gangs and interpersonal conflicts. An after-school component may be an important program element. As Wiebe's time-of-day analysis of gang crimes in Orange County, California, showed, immediately after school dismissal is the peak time of day for gang offenses during the school year (cited in Sickmund, Snyder, and Poe-Yamagata 1997, p. 26).

Preventing gang violence in chronic gang cities may well be more difficult than preventing adolescents from joining gangs. A comprehensive gang violence prevention, intervention, and suppression program has been implemented in the Little Village area of Chicago (Spergel and Grossman 1997). Called the Gang Violence Reduction Program, it consists of two coordinated strategies: targeted control of violent or potentially hard-core violent-youth gang offenders, in the form of increased probation department and police supervision and suppression, and provision of a wide range of social services and opportunities for targeted youth, to encourage their transition to conventional legitimate behaviors through education, jobs, job training, family support, and brief counseling. Managed by the Neighborhood Relations Unit of the Chicago Police Department, the project is staffed by tactical police officers, probation officers, community youth workers from the target neighborhood, and workers in Neighbors against Gang Violence, a new community organization comprised of local public and private representatives. The program incorporates a comprehensive set of strategies: suppression, social intervention, opportunities provision, and community mobilization, which are employed together.

Evaluation results after four years of operation are positive (Spergel and Grossman 1997; see also Thornberry and Burch 1997, p. 3). Positive results include a lower level of serious gang violence among the targeted gangs than among comparable gangs in the area. There is also noted improvement in residents' perceptions of gang crime and police effectiveness in dealing with it. In addition, there were fewer arrests for serious gang crimes (especially aggravated batteries and aggravated assaults) by members of targeted gangs as compared with control youth from the same gangs and members of other gangs in Little Village.

Boston's comprehensive enforcement, intervention, and prevention program incorporates a variety of individual programs—both old and new—in a three-pronged strategy to prevent and reduce youth violence, including gang homicide and other violent crimes (see U.S. Department of Justice 1996 for more detailed information on these and other program elements). Enforcement-oriented programs are the cornerstone of Boston's comprehensive approach.

One key Boston enforcement-oriented program is the police department's Youth Violence Strike Force (YVSF). It is a multiagency coordinated task force of forty-five full-time Boston police officers and fifteen officers from outside agencies. Membership includes the Massachusetts State Police Bureau of Alcohol, Tobacco, and Firearms (BATF); Massachusetts Corrections, Probation, Parole, and Division of Youth Service (juvenile corrections) officers; and other agencies as appropriate. In addition to strategies detailed below, the YVSF uses Racketeering Influenced Criminal Organizations statutes and criminal and civil forfeiture laws to help secure the safety of the community.

The second key Boston enforcement-oriented program is Operation Nightlite. It is a cooperative effort between YVSF and the Massachusetts Department of Probation. Police officers and probation officers, working in teams, make nightly visits to the homes of youth on probation to ensure that they are complying with terms and conditions of their probation. In addition to providing intensive scrutiny and securing parental involvement, the teams foster communication with the Boston School Department to reduce truancy and increase school performance. City "streetworkers" (gang prevention and mediation specialists) also work in tandem with police and probation, helping resolve conflicts and linking youngsters who want help with needed services. Operation Nightlite and police operations are aided by a comprehensive computer database and geographical mapping, which help target tough enforcement efforts against gang leaders. Positive interventions are also offered to those who are at risk of becoming hard-core gang members.

Operation Cease Fire is another part of Boston's antigang strategy (see Kennedy, Piehl, and Braga 1996). An explicit communication campaign, begun with an orientation for community groups, is often carried out face-to-face with gang members, delivering the message that gang violence has provoked authorities' "zero tolerance" approach, and only an end to gang violence will stop suppression activities. The long sentences that offenders receive are publicized in the neighborhoods. Gang mediation specialists are deployed to gang "hot spots," which are generally already known through mapping that shows the overlap of gangs, intergang conflicts, and gun-related crime. Heightened surveillance for shootings, assaults, and other selected incidents triggers deployment of interagency crisis interventions teams. After this "calming" operation, patrol officers intensively monitor the "hot spot" for violent retaliations between street groups in conflict with one another.

The Boston Gun Project is the fourth program enforcement-oriented element (U.S. Department of Justice 1996). This gang-suppression approach targets violence and gun use rather than the gangs themselves (Kennedy, Piehl, and Braga 1996). It is based on an analysis of Boston's youth violence problem, resulting in the determination that it is gang centered, defined broadly, and neighborhood based. That is, certain neighborhoods contain high violence rates and tend to be gang locations. These neighborhoods and the young persons who are gang members are targeted.

Simultaneously, the Boston Gun Project aims to interrupt the self-sustaining cycle of fear, weapon use, and violence that has driven youth violence in the city, by reducing use of guns in a "coerced use-reduction" strategy, and by reducing access to firearms (Kennedy, Piehl, and Braga 1996). The latter strategy, using gun-tracing capabilities of the Boston Police Department and the BATF, entails disrupting the illicit gun market. The rationale supporting the supply-reduction strategy is that disruption of the illicit market will interrupt the dynamics of fear-driven gun acquisition and use, thus reducing gang violence in Boston. Using federal firearm laws, the project "makes the market much less hospitable by strategically removing the most dangerous gang and drug offenders from the streets, and stemming the flow of firearms into Massachusetts" (p. 5). In addition, felons and those who put guns into the hands of juveniles and older gang members are severely punished.

A wide variety of intervention- and prevention-oriented partnerships and programs, both old and new, contribute to Boston's citywide strategy (see U.S. Department of Justice 1996 for detailed information). Evaluation results are not yet available, although a reduction in juvenile homicides of some 80 percent from 1990 to 1995 in the city has been reported (U.S. Department of Justice 1996). Other official data indicate lower juvenile arrest rates for aggravated assault and battery with a firearm (1993–95), and fewer violent crimes in public schools from 1995 to 1996 (U.S. Department of Justice 1996).

The Boston project, in effect, implements two gun-control measures previously identified as promising interventions: restrictions on the sale, purchase, and transfer of guns; and regulations on the place and manner of carrying firearms (Brewer et al. 1995). Other gun-control strategies appear to be promising. These include restricting access to guns by dangerous people (Cook and Leitzel 1996); supply-reduction (Koper and Reuter 1996); provision of bounties for information leading to confiscation of an illegal gun (Blumstein and Cork 1996); use of metal detectors in schools (Kamin 1996); police seizures of illegally carried guns in "hot spot" areas (Sherman, Shaw, and Rogan 1995); obtaining parental permission for warrantless searches (Rosenfeld and Decker 1996); and undercover purchases of firearms from adolescents, control of the supply channels, creation of ammunition scarcity, bilateral buy-back agreements, and nonuse treaties with financial compliance incentives (Zimring 1996).

VI. A Strategy for Community-Wide Youth Violence Prevention

The Annie E. Casey Foundation launched the New Futures Initiative in 1987 (Center for the Study of Social Policy 1995). Ten mid-sized cities, all of which had high poverty levels, high dropout rates, and large minority populations, were awarded $5–$12.5 million over five years to improve the life chances of disadvantaged youths in their communities. Each was to restructure and realign existing institutions to be more responsive to the needs of at-risk youths and their families to accomplish four objectives: reduce the school dropout rate, improve students' academic performance, prevent teen pregnancies and births, and increase the number of college entrants. These were to be accomplished through the formation of new local governance bodies, called collaboratives, made up of representatives of local agencies, parents, community representatives, government officials, business representatives, and elected officials. New policies and practices for meeting the needs of at-risk youth would be devised, while requiring accountability for positive outcomes.

The results of an evaluation of the program by the Center for the Study of Social Policy (1995) were disappointing. None of the sites achieved the objectives of the program. "For the most part, the collaboratives were largely unable to define a comprehensive action plan that cut across multiple organizations. Instead, they reverted to what they knew best: funding discrete interventions" (p. xiii). The evaluators concluded that "our collective rhetoric about cross-system change is far ahead of any operational knowledge about how to get there from here" (p. xiii).

There is an important lesson to be learned from the results of this effort. To be effective, a change strategy must be grounded in research on the problems to be addressed. Communities are likely to have different profiles of risk and protection. The greatest effects will likely result from interventions that address those factors that put children in a particular community at most danger of developing criminal or violent behavior. Prevention programs should address the highest priority risk factors to which people in a community are exposed. Each community should assess its unique profile of risk and protection as a foundation for selecting and designing preventive interventions that address the factors most in need of attention in that community. Efforts to change communities to reduce risk and enhance protection need to be guided by analyses of both the most noxious risk factors and the existing strengths of the community. This will help move communities away from funding discrete, piecemeal programs that do not address the specific factors contributing to violence in that community.

The overall effectiveness of a community's prevention efforts will be determined by the framework and processes used to decide on the preventive interventions to be included, by the specific preventive interventions used, and by the methods used to implement these interventions (Catalano et al. 1998). Preventive interventions should organize community leaders and grassroots residents to take ownership of the efforts to change the profile of risk and protection in the community. Without this ownership it is difficult for even the most potent intervention to be applied with sufficient vigor to change a neighborhood.

Interventions must be able to reach and communicate effectively with the population they seek to serve. Combining knowledge of effective risk- and protection-focused prevention programs with local ownership of prevention initiatives should result in the best outcomes.

Sustained efforts are required to change and shape behavior patterns. "Quick fixes" are unlikely to have enduring effects in preventing violence. Preventive interventions require a service delivery system that is unified in its vision of risk- and protection-focused prevention and employs personnel trained for specific intervention tasks to be successful.

Those who control social, health, legal, and educational resources in a community as well as service providers and citizens should be guided by a shared understanding of the risk- and protection-focused approach to prevention, if well-focused, well-coordinated, and comprehensive risk reduction efforts are to be implemented. Beyond this, service providers, whether professionals or paraprofessionals, must be given thorough training in the preventive methods they are expected to implement. All staff require regular in-service training, supportive supervision, and sufficient compensation in order to provide quality services, engage families and children in the intervention, and alleviate job stress. Special prevention-oriented training and technical assistance may be needed in order to facilitate these changes in a community's service delivery system.

Expectations about the magnitude of intervention effects should be realistic. Individual interventions, or those focused on only one domain or developmental stage, should not be considered a "silver bullet" to serve all prevention needs. Larger reductions in violence are more likely if preventive efforts include a combination of programs targeted to reduce salient risks and enhance protection across developmental stages and in multiple domains.

Finally, for maximum and sustained impact, violence prevention needs to be linked with early intervention and graduated sanctions components in a comprehensive strategy (Wilson and Howell 1993; Howell 1995). Comprehensive approaches to delinquency prevention and intervention require collaborative efforts between prevention agencies, the juvenile justice system, and other service provision systems, including mental health, health, child welfare, and education. If prevention programs are effective in reducing the number of youths who reach the juvenile justice system, the resources devoted to costly correctional services and sanctions can be reallocated to prevention services.

Recent advances in prevention science and health epidemiology are providing tools communities can use to plan and implement strategic, outcome-focused plans for reducing the prevalence of antisocial behavior among adolescents and young adults. The Communities that Care (CTC) strategy (Hawkins, Catalano, and Associates 1992) is an example of a comprehensive system for planning and implementing risk- and protection-focused prevention at the community level. It consists of three phases. In the first phase, key community leaders, serving as an oversight body, are trained in risk- and protection-focused prevention. They appoint a community prevention board that, in the second phase, conducts a community risk and resource assessment, gathers archival and survey data on indicators of the risk and protective factors for adolescent behavior problems in the community, and, based on these results, the board prioritizes risk factors for preventive action. To complete phase two, the board designs its prevention strategy to address targeted risk factors and enhance protective factors, selecting preventive interventions from a menu of programs and strategies that have shown positive results in experimental and quasi experimental studies.

Using task forces composed of community members with a stake in the outcome to insure implementation of each component, the board implements and evaluates the prevention strategy in the third phase. Baseline risk and protective factor data serve as the benchmark against which to judge community progress in risk reduction and protective factor growth in subsequent years. This strategic process activates both community leaders and grassroots sectors of the community to take ownership of the prevention planning process.

The Dauphin County, Pennsylvania, CTC's project is an example of the use of CTC's risk and protective framework to guide the selection of preventive interventions (U.S. General Accounting Office 1996). Four sets of risk factors were determined to be significant and of highest priority as a result of the community risk and resource assessment: low neighborhood attachment and community disorganization; extreme economic and social deprivation; family management problems; and early and persistent antisocial behavior. The project set three goals: economic empowerment—to encourage healthy beliefs by youth regarding their economic futures; family support—to strengthen internal management capacities of families with young children; and mobilization against violence—to create a nonviolent culture among and around youth and their families.

Economic development initiatives included fostering successful neighborhood-based family/community-owned businesses and cooperatives to complement ongoing job training and business development projects. Economic development and training components targeted youth as potential employees, promoted neighborhood economic growth through business development training, and provided technical assistance to small business owners and potential owners.

Two new family centers were established to develop family support networks, sponsor collaborative education workshops, and provide in-home parent education visits. Ineffective family management was addressed through development of skills, confidence, support networks, and capacities of at-risk families to enable them to manage more effectively their day-to-day lives. These efforts were seen as helping to create protective factors for youth by stabilizing their home lives, helping parents to promote healthy beliefs and clear standards, and establishing bonds with prosocial others (parents, prosocial peers, and adults) that reinforce healthy behavioral norms.

The mobilization against youth violence component was designed to counteract the risk of early and persistent antisocial behavior, particularly the spread of violent behavior such as fighting among elementary school children. It aimed to prevent juvenile violence through educational activities that teach and reinforce nonviolent means of social interaction and conflict resolution. The project also included an intensive, year-round, violence prevention campaign that sponsored conflict resolution seminars and organized recreational and social family nights at youth centers.

Communities That Care was initially field-tested in the states of Washington and Oregon, then implemented more broadly under funding from states, local communities, and the federal Office of Juvenile Justice and Delinquency Prevention (see Catalano et al. [1998] for results). Altogether, CTC is being implemented in about three hundred communities in the United States.

Although CTC has not been rigorously evaluated using a randomized controlled trial, an early version of it was field-tested in Washington State, which demonstrated that key community leaders could be successfully engaged in creating community boards, and that these boards could effectively use the risk-reduction and protective-factor-enhancement approach to prevention. Four years later, thirty-one of thirty-six boards were still active (see Catalano et al. 1998). By comparison, in a similar project in Washington State using a different community risk-reduction strategy, only thirteen of fifty-six community teams remained active after one year.

VII. Conclusion

Youth violence can be prevented. Efforts will be more effective if preventive interventions target two important groups of offenders—life-course-persistent offenders and adolescent-limited offenders—because different interventions are required for these groups at different developmental stages.

Several early intervention programs have demonstrated positive long-term effects on serious, violent, and chronic delinquency. These have focused largely on urban, low-income families that produce a disproportionate share of life-course-persistent offenders. The effective programs in early childhood focused on improving individual capacity (cognitive ability) and family functioning through a combination of early childhood education and family support services. The most effective programs offered both home visits (parent training) and center-based educational child care or preschool (aimed at improving cognitive skills).

School-based prevention programs for children ages six to twelve have also been found to be effective in preventing adolescent problem behaviors, including violence. Multiple component programs involving teachers and parents, as well as children themselves, have shown positive effects. Results of research show that the organization and management of schools can be improved so that they are more effective in educating children and reducing disruption, delinquency, and violence in the school setting.

With respect to the goal of preventing the spread of violence in adolescence, we concentrate on three contexts: delinquent peer groups, the school setting, and youth gangs. We think that efforts to prevent violence among both life-course-persistent offenders and adolescent-limited offenders will be enhanced by use of a risk- and protection-focused approach that engages and empowers communities to use prevention science to guide their prevention work.

REFERENCES

Anderson, D. In this volume. "Curriculum, Culture, and Community: The Challenge of School Violence."
Anderson, E. In this volume. "The Social Ecology of Youth Violence."
Bartusch, D. R. J., D. R. Lynam, T. E. Moffitt, and P. A. Silva. 1997. "Is Age Important? Testing a General versus a Developmental Theory of Antisocial Behavior." *Criminology* 35:13–48.
Bastian, L. D., and B. M. Taylor. 1991. *School Crime: A National Crime Victimization Report*. Washington, D.C.: U.S. Department of Justice, Bureau of Justice Statistics.

Battin, S. R., K. G. Hill, R. D. Abbott, R. F. Catalano, and J. D. Hawkins. 1998. "The Contribution of Gang Membership to Delinquency beyond Delinquent Friends." *Criminology* 36:93–115.

Benenson, W. 1988. "Assessing the Effectiveness of a Peer Based Conflict Management Program in Elementary Schools." Ph.D. dissertation, University of Idaho, College of Education.

Blumstein, A., and D. Cork. 1996. "Linking Gun Availability to Gun Violence." *Law and Contemporary Problems* (special issue) 59(Winter):5–24.

Brewer, D. D., J. D. Hawkins, R. F. Catalano, and H. J. Neckerman. 1995. "Preventing Serious, Violent, and Chronic Offending: A Review of Evaluations of Selected Strategies in Childhood, Adolescence, and the Community." In *Sourcebook on Serious, Violent, and Chronic Juvenile Offenders*, edited by J. C. Howell, B. Krisberg, J. D. Hawkins, and J. Wilson. Thousand Oaks, Calif.: Sage.

Brunk, M., S. W. Henggeler, and J. P. Whelan. 1987. "A Comparison of Multisystemic Therapy and Parent Training in the Brief Treatment of Child Abuse and Neglect." *Journal of Consulting and Clinical Psychology* 63:569–78.

Bursik, R. J., and H. G. Grasmick. 1993. *Neighborhoods and Crime: The Dimension of Effective Community Control.* New York: Lexington Books.

Catalano, R. F., M. W. Arthur, J. D. Hawkins, L. Berglund, and J. J. Olson. 1998. *Comprehensive Community and School-Based Interventions to Prevent Antisocial Behavior.* In *Serious and Violent Juvenile Offenders: Risk Factors and Successful Interventions*, edited by R. Loeber and D. P. Farrington. Thousand Oaks, Calif.: Sage.

Catalano, R. F., and J. D. Hawkins. 1996. "The Social Development Model: A Theory of Antisocial Behavior." In *Delinquency and Crime: Current Theories*, edited by J. D. Hawkins. New York: Cambridge University.

Center for the Study of Social Policy. 1995. *Building New Futures for At-Risk Youth: Findings from a Five-Year, Multi-site Evaluation.* Washington, D.C.: Center for the Study of Social Policy.

Conduct Problems Prevention Research Group. 1996. "An Initial Evaluation of the Fast Track Program." Paper presented at the fifth annual conference on Prevention Research, National Institute of Mental Health, Washington, D.C.

Cook, P. J., and J. H. Laub. In this volume. "The Unprecedented Epidemic in Youth Violence."

Cook, P. J., and J. A. Leitzel. 1996. " 'Perversity, Futility, Jeopardy': The Dynamics of Gun Events among Adolescent Males." *Law and Contemporary Problems* (special issue) 59(Winter):55–90.

Curry, G. D., and I. A. Spergel. 1988. "Gang Homicide, Delinquency, and Community." *Criminology* 26:381–405.

Dean, C. W., R. Brame, and A. R. Piquero. 1997. "Criminal Propensities, Discrete Groups of Offenders, and Persistence in Crime." *Criminology* 34:547–74.

Decker, S. H. 1996. "Collective and Normative Features of Gang Violence." *Justice Quarterly* 13:243–64.

Decker, S. H., and B. Van Winkle. 1996. *Life in the Gang: Family, Friends, and Violence*. New York: Cambridge University Press.

Denno, D. 1990. *Biology and Violence*. Cambridge: Cambridge University Press.

Dodge, K. A. 1991. "The Structure and Function of Reactive and Protective Aggression." In *The Development and Treatment of Childhood Aggression*, edited by D. J. Pepler and K. H. Rubin. Hillsdale, N.J.: Erlbaum.

Dodge, K. A., J. E. Bates, and G. S. Pettit. 1990. "Mechanisms in the Cycle of Violence." *Science* 250:1678–83.

Dodge, K. A., R. R. Murphy, and K. Buchsbaum. 1984. "The Assessment of Intention-Cue Detection Skills in Children: Implications for Developmental Psychopathology." *Child Development* 55:163–73.

Eisenhower Foundation. 1990. *Youth Investment and Community Reconstruction: Street Lessons on Drugs and Crime for the Nineties*. Washington, D.C.: Eisenhower Foundation.

Elliott, D. S. 1994*a*. "Serious Violent Offenders: Onset, Developmental Course, and Termination." American Society of Criminology 1993 Presidential Address. *Criminology* 32:1–21.

———. 1994*b*. *Youth Violence: An Overview*. Boulder, Colo.: Center for the Study and Prevention of Violence.

———. 1995. "Lies, Damn Lies, and Arrest Statistics." Paper presented at the forty-seventh annual meeting of the American Society of Criminology, Boston, November.

Elliott, D. S., D. Huizinga, and S. Menard. 1989. *Multiple Problem Youth: Delinquency, Substance Use and Mental Health Problems*. New York: Springer-Verlag.

Esbensen, F., and D. Huizinga. 1993. "Gangs, Drugs, and Delinquency in a Survey of Urban Youth." *Criminology* 31:565–89.

Esbensen, F., and D. W. Osgood. 1997. *National Evaluation of G.R.E.A.T.* Research in Brief. Washington, D.C.: U.S. Department of Justice, National Institute of Justice.

Fagan, Jeffrey, and Deanna L. Wilkinson. In this volume. "Guns, Youth Violence, and Social Identity in Inner Cities."

Farrington, D. P. 1986. "Age and Crime." In *Crime and Justice: An Annual Review of Research*, vol. 7, edited by M. Tonry and N. Morris. Chicago: University of Chicago Press.

———. 1989. "Later Adult Life Outcomes of Offenders and Non-offenders." In *Children at Risk: Assessment, Longitudinal Research, and Intervention*, edited by M. Brambring, F. Losel, and H. Skowronek. Berlin: De Gruyter.

———. 1991. "Childhood Aggression and Adult Violence: Early Precursors and Later Life Outcomes." In *The Development and Treatment of Childhood Aggression*, edited by D. J. Pelper and K. H. Rubin. Hillsdale, N.J.: Erlbaum.

———. 1993. "Understanding and Preventing Bullying." In *Crime and Justice: An Annual Review of Research*, vol. 17, edited by M. Tonry. Chicago: University of Chicago press.

———. In this volume. "Predictors, Causes, and Correlates of Youth Violence."

Farrington, D. P., and J. D. Hawkins. 1991. "Predicting Participation, Early

Onset, and Later Persistence in Officially Recorded Offending." *Criminal Behavior and Mental Health* 1:1–33.

Farrington, D. P., and D. J. West. 1990. "The Cambridge Study in Delinquent Development: A Long-Term Follow-up of 411 London Males." In *Criminality: Personality, Behavior and Life History*, edited by H. Kerner and G. Kaiser. Berlin: Springer-Verlag.

———. 1993. "Criminal, Penal, and Life Histories of Chronic Offenders: Risk and Protective Factors and Early Identification." *Criminal Behavior and Mental Health* 3:492–523.

Felner, R. D., S. Bran, A. M. Adan, P. F. Mulhall, N. Flowers, B. Sartain, and D. L. DuBois. 1993. "Restructuring the Ecology of the School as an Approach to Prevention during School Transitions: Longitudinal Follow-ups and Extensions of the School Transition Environment Project (STEP)." *Prevention in Human Services* 10:103–36.

Garmezy, N. 1985. "Stress-Resistant Children: The Search for Protective Factors." In *Recent Research in Developmental Psychopathology*, edited by J. E. Stevenson, *Journal of Child Psychology and Psychiatry* (book supplement) 4:213–33.

Garofalo, J., L. Siegel, and J. Laub. 1987. "School-Related Victimizations among Adolescents: An Analysis of National Crime Survey (NCS) Narratives." *Journal of Quantitative Criminology* 3:321–38.

Gottfredson, D. C. 1986. "An Empirical Test of School-Based Environmental and Individual Interventions to Reduce the Risk of Delinquent Behavior." *Criminology* 24:705–31.

Gottfredson, G. D. 1987. "Peer Group Interventions to Reduce the Risk of Delinquent Behavior: A Selective Review and a New Evaluation." *Criminology* 25:671–714.

Greenberg, M. T., and C. A. Kusche. 1993. *Promoting Social and Emotional Development in Deaf Children: The PATHS Project.* Seattle: University of Washington Press.

Grossman, D. C., H. J. Neckerman, T. D. Koepsell, K. Asher, P. Y. Liu, K. N. Beland, K. Frey, and F. P. Rivara. 1997. "A Randomized Controlled Trial of a Violence Prevention Curriculum among Elementary School Children." *Journal of the American Medical Association* 277:1605–11.

Hagedorn, John M. In this volume. "Gang Violence in the Postindustrial Era."

Hammond, W. R., and B. R. Yung. 1993. "Evaluation and Activity Report: Positive Adolescent Choices Training." Unpublished grant report. Washington, D.C.: U.S. Maternal and Child Health Bureau.

Hamparian, D. M., J. M. Davis, J. M. Jacobson, and R. T. McGraw. 1984. *The Young Criminal Years of the Violent Few.* Cleveland, Ohio: Federation for Community Planning.

Hamparian, D. M., R. Schuster, S. Dinitz, and J. P. Conrad. 1978. *The Violent Few: A Study of Dangerous Juvenile Offenders.* Lexington, Mass.: D.C. Heath.

Hawkins, J. D., R. F. Catalano, and Associates. 1992. *Communities That Care: Action for Drug Abuse Prevention.* San Francisco: Jossey-Bass.

Hawkins, J. D., R. F. Catalano, R. Kosterman, R. D. Abbott, and K. G. Hill.

1998. *Promoting Academic Success and Preventing Adolescent Health Risk Behaviors: Six-Year Follow-up of the Seattle Social Development Project.* Seattle: University of Washington, School of Social Work.

Hawkins, J. D., R. F. Catalano, and J. Y. Miller. 1992. "Risk and Protective Factors for Alcohol and Other Drugs Problems in Adolescence and Early Adulthood: Implications for Substance Abuse Prevention." *Psychological Bulletin* 112:64–105.

Hawkins, J. D., D. P. Farrington, and R. F. Catalano. 1998. "Reducing Violence through the Schools." In *Schools and Violence*, edited by D. S. Elliott, K. Williams, and B. Hamburg. New York: Cambridge University Press.

Hawkins, J. D., T. Herrenkohl, D. P. Farrington, D. Brewer, and R. F. Catalano. 1998. "A Review of Predictors of Youth Violence." In *Serious and Violent Juvenile Offenders: Risk Factors and Successful Interventions*, edited by R. Loeber and D. P. Farrington. Thousand Oaks, Calif.: Sage.

Hawkins, J. D., E. Von Cleve, and R. F. Catalano. 1991. "Reducing Early Childhood Aggression: Results of a Primary Prevention Program." *Journal of the American Academy of Child and Adolescent Psychiatry* 30:208–17.

Henggeler, S. W. 1997. *Treating Serious Anti-social Behavior in Youth: The MST Approach.* Juvenile Justice Bulletin. Washington, D.C.: U.S. Department of Justice, Office of Juvenile Justice and Delinquency Prevention.

Herrenkohl, T., E. Maguin, K. Hill, J. D. Hawkins, R. Abbott, and R. F. Catalano. 1998. *Childhood and Adolescent Predictors of Youth Violence.* Seattle: University of Washington, Seattle Social Development Project.

Hill, K. G., J. D. Hawkins, R. F. Catalano, R. Kosterman, R. Abbott, and T. Edwards. 1996. "The Longitudinal Dynamics of Gang Membership and Problem Behavior: A Replication and Extension of the Denver and Rochester Gang Studies in Seattle." Paper presented at the forty-eighth annual meeting of the American Society of Criminology, Chicago, November.

Horowitz, R. 1983. *Honor and the American Dream: Culture and Identity in a Chicano Community.* New Brunswick, N.J.: Rutgers University.

Howell, J. C., ed. 1995. *Guide for Implementing the Comprehensive Strategy for Serious, Violent, and Chronic Juvenile Offenders.* Washington, D.C.: U.S. Department of Justice, Office of Juvenile Justice and Delinquency Prevention.

Howell, J. C. 1998. *Youth Gangs: An Overview.* Research Bulletin. Youth Gang Series. Washington, D.C.: U.S. Department of Justice, Office of Juvenile Justice and Delinquency Prevention.

Huizinga, D. 1997. "The Volume of Crime by Gang and Nongang Members." Paper presented at the forty-ninth annual meeting of the American Society of Criminology, San Diego, California, November.

Huizinga, D., and C. Jakob-Chien. 1998. "The Contemporaneous Co-occurrence of Serious and Violent Offending and Other Problem Behaviors." In *Serious and Violent Juvenile Offenders: Risk Factors and Successful Interventions*, edited by R. Loeber and D. P. Farrington. Thousand Oaks, Calif.: Sage.

Institute of Medicine. 1994. *Reducing Risks for Mental Disorders: Frontiers for Preventive Intervention Research.* Washington, D.C.: National Academy Press.

Jenkins, J., and M. Smith. 1987. *Mediation in the Schools: 1986–1987 Program Evaluation.* Albuquerque: New Mexico Center for Dispute Resolution.

Johnson, D. L., and T. Walker. 1987. "Primary Prevention of Behavior Problems in Mexican American Children." *American Journal of Community Psychology* 15:375–85.

Jones, M. B., and D. R. Offord. 1989. "Reduction of Antisocial Behavior in Poor Children by Nonschool Skill-Development." *Journal of Child Psychology and Psychiatry and Allied Disciplines* 30:737–50.

Kamin, S. 1996. "Law and Technology: The Case for a Smart Gun Detector." *Law and Contemporary Problems* (special issue) 9(Winter):221–62.

Kazdin, A. E., T. C. Siegel, and D. Bass. 1992. "Cognitive Problem-Solving Skills Training and Parent Management Training in the Treatment of Antisocial Behavior in Children." *Journal of Consulting and Clinical Psychology* 60:733–47.

Kellam, S. G., and G. W. Rebok. 1992. "Building Developmental and Etiological Theory through Epidemiologically-Based Preventive Intervention Trials." In *Preventing Antisocial Behavior: Interventions from Birth through Adolescence,* edited by J. McCord and R. E. Tremblay. New York: Guilford.

Kellam, S. G., G. W. Rebok, N. Ialongo, and L. S. Mayer. 1994. "The Course and Malleability of Aggressive Behavior from Early First Grade into Middle School: Results of a Developmental Epidemiologically-Based Prevention Trial." *Journal of Child Psychology and Psychiatry* 35:259–81.

Kennedy, D. M., A. M. Piehl, and A. A. Braga. 1996. "Youth Violence in Boston: Gun Markets, Serious Youth Offenders, and a Use-Reduction Strategy." *Law and Contemporary Problems* 197:147–96.

Kitzman, H., D. L. Olds, C. R. Henderson, C. Hanks, R. Cole, R. Tatelbaum, K. McConnochie, K. Sidora, D. W. Luckey, D. Shaver, K. Engelhardt, D. James, and K. Barnard. 1997. "Effect of Prenatal and Infancy Home Visitation by Nurses on Pregnancy Outcomes, Childhood Injuries, and Repeated Childbearing: A Randomized Controlled Trial." *Journal of the American Medical Association* 278(August 27):644–52.

Koper, C. S., and P. Reuter. 1996. "Suppressing Illegal Gun Markets: Lessons from Drug Enforcement." *Law and Contemporary Problems* (special issue) 9(Winter):119–46.

Lally, J. R., P. L. Mangione, and A. S. Honig. 1988. "The Syracuse University Family Development Research Project: Long-Range Impact of an Early Intervention with Low-Income Children and Their Families." In *Annual Advances in Applied Developmental Psychology,* edited by D. R. Powell, 3:79–104. Norwood, N.J.: Ablex.

Laub, J. H., and J. L. Lauritsen. 1993. "Violent Criminal Behavior over the Life Course: A Review of the Longitudinal and Comparative Research." *Violence and Victims* 8:235–52.

———. 1994. "The Precursors of Criminal Offending across the Life Course." *Federal Probation* 58:51–57.

Lipsey, M. W., and J. H. Derzon. 1998. "Predictors of Serious Delinquency in Adolescence and Early Adulthood: A Synthesis of Longitudinal Research." In *Serious and Violent Juvenile Offenders: Risk Factors and Successful*

Interventions, edited by R. Loeber and D. P. Farrington. Thousand Oaks, Calif.: Sage.

Lockwood, D. 1997. *Violence among Middle School and High School Students: Analysis and Implications for Prevention*. Research in Brief. Washington, D.C.: U.S. Department of Justice, National Institute of Justice.

Loeber, R., and D. F. Hay. 1997. "Key Issues in the Development of Aggression and Violence from Childhood to Early Adulthood." *Annual Review of Psychology* 48:371–410.

Loeber, R., K. Keenan, and Q. Zhang. 1997. "Boys' Experimentation and Persistence in Developmental Pathways toward Serious Delinquency." *Journal of Child and Family Studies* 6:321–57.

Loeber, R., and P. H. Wikstrom. 1993. "Individual Pathways to Crime in Different Types of Neighborhood." In *Integrating Individual and Ecological Aspects of Crime*, edited by D. P. Farrington, R. J. Sampson, and P. H. Wikstrom. Stockholm: National Council for Crime Prevention.

Loftin, C. 1986. "Assaultive Violence as a Contagious Social Process." *Bulletin of the New York Academy of Medicine* 62:550–55.

Maguin, E., and R. Loeber. 1996. "Academic Performance and Delinquency." In *Crime and Justice: An Annual Review of Research*, vol. 20, edited by M. Tonry. Chicago: University of Chicago Press.

Miller, W. B. 1992. *Crime by Youth Gangs and Groups in the United States*. Washington, D.C.: U.S. Department of Justice, Office of Juvenile Justice and Delinquency Prevention. (Originally published 1982.)

Moffitt, T. E. 1990. "Juvenile Delinquency and Attention Deficit Disorder: Boys' Developmental Trajectories from Age 3 to Age 15." *Child Development* 61:893–910.

———. 1991. "Juvenile Delinquency: Seed of a Career in Violent Crime, Just Sowing Wild Oats—or Both?" Paper presented at the Science and Public Policy Seminars of the Federation of Behavioral, Psychological, and Cognitive Sciences, Washington, D.C., September.

———. 1993. "Adolescence-Limited and Life-Course-Persistent Antisocial Behavior: A Developmental Taxonomy." *Psychological Review* 100:674–701.

Moffitt, T. E., A. Caspi, N. Dickson, P. Silva, and W. Stanton. 1996. "Childhood-Onset versus Adolescent-Onset Antisocial Conduct Problems in Males: Natural History from Ages 3 to 18 Years." *Development and Psychopathology* 8:399–424.

Moffitt, T. E., D. Lynam, and P. Silva. 1994. "Neuropsychological Tests Predicting Persistent Male Delinquency." *Criminology* 32:277–300.

Moore, J. P. 1997. *Highlights of the 1995 National Youth Gang Survey*. Fact Sheet no. 63. Washington, D.C.: U.S. Department of Justice, Office of Juvenile Justice and Delinquency Prevention.

Murphy, H. A., J. M. Hutchison, and J. S. Bailey. 1983. "Behavioral School Psychology Goes Outdoors: The Effect of Organized Games on Playground Aggression." *Journal of Applied Behavior Analysis* 16:29–35.

Nagin, D. S., and D. P. Farrington. 1992a. "The Stability of Criminal Potential from Childhood to Adulthood." *Criminology* 30:235–60.

————. 1992*b*. "The Onset and Persistence of Offending." *Criminology* 30:501–23.

Nagin, D. S., D. P. Farrington, and T. E. Moffitt. 1995. "Life-Course Trajectories of Different Types of Offenders." *Criminology* 33:111–39.

Nagin, D. S., and K. C. Land. 1993. "Age, Criminal Careers, and Population Heterogeneity: Specification and Estimation of a Nonparametric, Mixed Poisson Model." *Criminology* 31:327–62.

Nagin, D. S., and R. Paternoster. 1991. "On the Relationship of Past to Future Delinquency." *Criminology* 29:163–89.

National Center for Education Statistics. 1994. *Student Victimization at School.* Statistics in Brief. Washington, D.C.: U.S. Department of Education.

National Youth Gang Center. 1997. *1995 National Youth Gang Survey.* Washington, D.C.: U.S. Department of Justice, Office of Juvenile Justice and Delinquency Prevention.

O'Donnell, J. A., J. D. Hawkins, R. F. Catalano, R. D. Abbott, and L. E. Day. 1995. "Preventing School Failure, Drug Use, and Delinquency among Low-Income Children: Long-Term Prevention in Elementary Schools." *American Journal of Orthopsychiatry* 65:87–100.

Office of Juvenile Justice and Delinquency Prevention. 1995. *Matrix of Community-Based Initiatives.* Washington, D.C.: U.S. Department of Justice, Office of Juvenile Justice and Delinquency Prevention.

Olds, D. L., J. Eckenrode, C. R. Henderson, H. Kitzman, J. Powers, R. Cole, K. Sidora, P. Morris, L. M. Pettit, and D. W. Luckey. 1997. "Long-Term Effects of Home Visitation on Maternal Life Course and Child Abuse and Neglect: Fifteen-Year Follow-up of a Randomized Trial." *Journal of the American Medical Association* 278 (August 27):637–43.

Olds, D. L., C. R. Henderson, Jr., R. Chamberlin, and R. Tatelbaum. 1986. "Preventing Child Abuse and Neglect: A Randomized Trial of Nurse Home Visitation." *Pediatrics* 78:65–78.

Olds, D. L., and H. Kitzman. 1993. "Review of Research on Home Visiting for Pregnant Women and Parents of Young Children." *Future of Children* 3:53–92.

Olweus, D. 1978. *Aggression in the Schools.* New York: Wiley.

————. 1991. "Bully/Victim Problems among Schoolchildren: Basic Facts and Effects of a School-Based Intervention Programme." In *The Development and Treatment of Childhood Aggression,* edited by D. J. Pepler and K. H. Rubin. Hillsdale, N.J.: Erlbaum.

Paternoster, R., and R. Brame. 1997. "Multiple Routes to Delinquency? A Test of Developmental and General Theories of Crime." *Criminology* 35:49–84.

Patterson, G. R., B. D. DeBaryshe, and E. Ramsey. 1989. "A Developmental Perspective on Antisocial Behavior." *American Psychologist* 44:329–25.

Patterson, G. R., and K. Yoerger. 1993. "Developmental Models for Delinquent Behavior." In *Mental Disorder and Crime,* edited by S. Hodgins. Newbury Park, Calif.: Sage.

Powell, K. E., and D. F. Hawkins, eds. 1996. "Youth Violence Prevention: Descriptions and Baseline Data from Thirteen Evaluation Projects." *Ameri-*

can Journal of Preventive Medicine, supplement to vol. 12 (September/ October).

Raine, A., P. Brennan, and S. Mednick. 1994. "Birth Complications Combined with Early Maternal Rejection at Age One Year Predispose to Violent Crime at Age Eighteen Years." *Archives of General Psychiatry* 51:984–88.

Reiss, A. J., and J. A. Roth. 1993. *Understanding and Preventing Violence.* Report of the Panel on the Understanding and Control of Violent Behavior, National Academy of Sciences. Washington, D.C.: National Academy.

Robins, L. N. 1966. *Deviant Children Grown Up: A Sociological and Psychiatric Study of Sociopathic Personality.* Baltimore: Williams & Wilkins.

———. 1978. "Sturdy Childhood Predictors of Adult Outcomes: Replications from Longitudinal Studies." In *Stress and Mental Disorder,* edited by J. M. Barrett, R. M. Rose, and G. L. Klerman. New York: Raven.

Rosenfeld, R., and S. H. Decker. 1996. "Consent to Search and Seize: Evaluating an Innovative Youth Firearm Suppression Program." *Law and Contemporary Problems* (special issue) 9(Winter):197–220.

Sampson, R. J. 1983. "Structural Density and Criminal Victimization." *Criminology* 21:276–93.

———. 1985. "Neighborhood and Crime: The Structural Determinants of Personal Victimization." *Journal of Research in Crime and Delinquency* 22:7–40.

———. 1987. "Urban Black Violence: The Effect of Male Joblessness and Family Disruption." *American Journal of Sociology* 93:348–82.

Sampson, R. J., and J. H. Laub. 1990. "Crime and Deviance over the Life Course: The Salience of Adult Social Bonds." *American Sociological Review* 55:609–27.

———. 1993. *Crime in the Making: Pathways and Turning Points through Life.* Cambridge, Mass.: Harvard University Press.

Schinke, S. P., K. C. Cole, and M. A. Orlandi. 1991. *The Effects of Boys and Girls Clubs on Drug Abuse and Related Problems in Public Housing Projects.* New York: Columbia University, School of Social Work.

Schweinhart, L. J., H. V. Barnes, and D. P. Weikart. 1993. *Significant Benefits.* Ypsilanti, Mich.: High/Scope.

Seitz, V., and N. Apfel. 1994. "Parent-Focused Intervention: Diffusion Effects on Siblings." *Child Development* 65:667–83.

Shannon, L. W. 1988. *Criminal Career Continuity: Its Social Context.* New York: Human Sciences Press.

———. 1991. *Changing Patterns of Delinquency and Crime: A Longitudinal Study in Racine.* Boulder, Colo.: Westview.

Sherman, L. W., J. W. Shaw, and D. P. Rogan. 1995. *The Kansas City Gun Experiment.* Research in Brief. Washington, D.C.: U.S. Department of Justice, National Institute of Justice.

Short, J. F., Jr., and F. L. Strodtbeck. 1965. *Group Process and Gang Delinquency.* Chicago: University of Chicago Press.

Shure, M. B., and G. Spivack. 1980a. "Interpersonal Problem Solving as a Mediator of Behavioral Adjustment in Preschool and Kindergarten Children." *Journal of Applied Developmental Psychology* 1:29–44.

———. 1980*b*. "Interpersonal Cognitive Problem Solving." In *Fourteen Ounces of Prevention: A Casebook for Practitioners*, edited by R. H. Price, E. L. Cowen, R. P. Lorion, and J. Ramos-McKay. Washington, D.C.: American Psychological Association.

Sickmund, M., H. N. Snyder, and E. Poe-Yamagata. 1997. *Juvenile Offenders and Victims: 1997 Update on Violence*. Washington, D.C.: U.S. Department of Justice, Office of Juvenile Justice and Delinquency Prevention.

Simons, R. L., C. Wu, R. D. Conger, and F. O. Lorenz. 1994. "Two Routes to Delinquency: Differences between Early and Late Starters in the Impact of Parenting and Deviant Peers." *Criminology* 32:247–75.

Slavin, R. E., N. A. Madden, L. J. Dolan, B. A. Wasik, S. M. Ross, and L. J. Smith. 1994. " 'Whenever and Wherever We Choose': The Replication of Success for All." *Phi Delta Kappan* (April): 639–47.

Slavin, R. E., N. A. Madden, L. J. Dolan, B. A. Wasik, S. M. Ross, L. J. Smith, and M. Dianda. 1995. "Success for All: A Summary of Research." Paper presented at the annual meeting of the American Educational Research Association, San Francisco.

Slavin, R. E., N. A. Madden, N. L. Karweit, B. J. Livermon, and L. Dolan. 1990. "Success for All: First-Year Outcomes of a Comprehensive Plan for Reforming Urban Education." *American Educational Research Journal* 27:255–78.

Smith, C., and T. P. Thornberry. 1995. "The Relationship between Childhood Maltreatment and Adolescent Involvement in Delinquency." *Criminology* 33:451–77.

Smith, P. K., and S. Sharp. 1994. *School Bullying*. London: Routledge.

Snyder, H. N. 1998. "Serious, Violent, and Chronic Juvenile Offenders: An Assessment of the Extent of and Trends in Officially-Recognized Serious Criminal Behavior in a Delinquent Population." In *Serious and Violent Juvenile Offenders: Risk Factors and Sucessful Interventions*, edited by R. Loeber and D. P. Farrington. Thousand Oaks, Calif.: Sage.

Spergel, I. A., and S. F. Grossman. 1997. "The Little Village Project: A Community Approach to the Gang Problem." *Social Work* 42:456–70.

Strayhorn, J. M., and C. S. Weidman. 1991. "Follow-up One Year after Parent-Child Interaction Training: Effects on Behavior of Preschool Children." *Journal of American Academy of Child and Adolescent Psychiatry* 30:138–43.

Thompson, D. W., and L. A. Jason. 1988. "Street Gangs and Preventive Interventions." *Criminal Justice and Behavior* 15:323–33.

Thornberry, T. P. 1994. *Violent Families and Youth Violence*. Fact Sheet no. 21. Washington, D.C.: U.S. Department of Justice, Office of Juvenile Justice and Delinquency Prevention.

———. 1998. "Membership in Youth Gangs and Involvement in Serious and Violent Offending." In *Serious and Violent Juvenile Offenders: Risk Factors and Successful Interventions*, edited by R. Loeber and D. P. Farrington. Thousand Oaks, Calif.: Sage.

Thornberry, T. P., and J. H. Burch. 1997. *Gang Members and Delinquent Behavior*. Juvenile Justice Bulletin. Washington, D.C.: U.S. Department of Justice, Office of Juvenile Justice and Delinquency Prevention.

Thornberry, T. P., D. Huizinga, and R. Loeber. 1995. "The Prevention of

Serious Delinquency and Violence: Implications from the Program of Research on the Causes and Correlates of Delinquency." In *A Sourcebook: Serious, Violent, and Chronic Juvenile Offenders*, edited by J. C. Howell, B. Krisberg, D. Hawkins, and J. J. Wilson. Thousand Oaks, Calif.: Sage.

Thornberry, T. P., M. D. Krohn, A. J. Lizotte, and D. Chard-Wierschem. 1993. "The Role of Juvenile Gangs in Facilitating Delinquent Behavior." *Journal of Research in Crime and Delinquency* 30:55–87.

Tolson, E. R., S. McDonald, and A. R. Moriarty. 1992. "Peer Mediation among High School Students: A Test of Effectiveness." *Social Work in Education* 14:86–93.

Tracy, P. E., and K. Kempf-Leonard. 1996. *Continuity and Discontinuity in Criminal Careers.* New York: Plenum.

Tremblay, R. E., J. McCord, H. Boileau, P. Charlebois, C. Gagnon, M. Le Blanc, and S. Larivee. 1991. "Can Disruptive Boys Be Helped to Become Competent?" *Psychiatry* 54:148–61.

Tremblay, R. E., F. Vitaro, L. Bertrand, M. Le Blanc, H. Beauchesne, H. Boileau, and L. David. 1992. "Parent and Child Training to Prevent Early Onset of Delinquency: The Montreal Longitudinal-Experimental Study." In *Preventing Antisocial Behavior: Interventions from Birth through Adolescence*, edited by J. McCord and R. E. Tremblay. New York: Guilford.

U.S. Department of Justice. 1996. "Youth Violence: A Community-Based Response." Washington, D.C.: U.S. Department of Justice. (pamphlet).

U.S. General Accounting Office. 1996. *Status of Delinquency Prevention Program and Description of Local Projects.* Washington, D.C.: U.S. General Accounting Office.

U.S. Public Health Service Expert Panel on the Content of Prenatal Care. 1989. *Caring for Our Future: The Content of Pre-natal Care.* Washington, D.C.: U.S. Department of Health and Human Services.

Warr, M. 1996. "Organization and Instigation in Delinquent Groups." *Criminology* 34:11–37.

Webster-Stratton, C. 1984. "Randomized Trial of Two Parent Training Programs for Families with Conduct-Disordered Children." *Journal of Consulting and Clinical Psychology* 52:666–78.

———. 1992. "Individually Administered Videotape Modeling Parent Training: Who Benefits?" *Cognitive Therapy and Research* 16:31–35.

Wilson, J. J., and J. C. Howell. 1993. *A Comprehensive Strategy for Serious, Violent and Chronic Juvenile Offenders.* Washington, D.C.: U.S. Department of Justice, Office of Juvenile Justice and Delinquency Prevention.

Wolfgang, M. E., R. M. Figlio, and T. Sellin. 1972. *Delinquency in a Birth Cohort.* Chicago: University of Chicago Press.

Yoshikawa, H. 1994. "Prevention as Cumulative Protection: Effects of Early Family Support and Education on Chronic Delinquency and Its Risks." *Psychological Bulletin* 115:1–27.

———. 1995. "Long-Term Effects of Early Childhood Programs on Social Outcomes and Delinquency." *Future of Children* 5:51–75.

Zimring, F. E. 1996. "Kids, Guns, and Homicide: Policy Notes on an Age-Specific Epidemic." *Law and Contemporary Problems* (special issue) 59:25–38.

David C. Anderson

Curriculum, Culture, and Community: The Challenge of School Violence

ABSTRACT

It is possible to imagine a school designed and managed effectively for safety as well as education. Public schools, once considered a response to urban violence and disorder, now are widely believed to be hostage to them. Although broad national studies do not demonstrate a dramatic increase in school violence since the 1970s, serious violence and disorder are real for some students in some schools. Factors associated with risk are poverty, inner-city residence, enrollment in junior high school, and living in a family and community where violence is common. Physical security measures like metal detectors are only a partial solution. Curricular responses include classes in conflict resolution, self-esteem, multicultural sensitivity, and other subjects. Administrative responses include alternative schools, staff development, and efforts to alter the school culture. Community-outreach programs include principal-led committees of school, neighborhood, and city officials; joint projects with local police; and aggressive efforts to bring social services to students' families. Evaluation findings remain mixed but suggest that altering a school's internal culture can do much to reduce violence even for schools in violent communities.

In the beginning, America's public schools were supposed to be the cure for violence and social disorder. Under the leadership of the nineteenth-century education reformer Horace Mann, a Massachusetts Senate committee declared in 1846 that, while a poorly educated child might turn to delinquency, one "placed under the care of judicious men, taught to labor, be furnished with a good moral and intellectual

David C. Anderson is the author of several volumes, including *Crimes of Justice: Improving the Police, the Courts, the Prisons; Crime and the Politics of Hysteria: How the Willie Horton Story Changed American Justice;* and *Sensible Justice: Alternatives to Prison.*

education . . . would, in nine cases out of 10, perhaps, become a good and useful citizen" (Menacker 1995, p. 4).

An 1881 report to the National Education Association called public high schools "the most potential agency . . . to root up vice [and] to lessen crime." "Later on," Julius Menacker writes, "the public school extended its social role by providing playgrounds, after-school programs, summer school, and even the kindergarten, for the express goal of inhibiting juvenile delinquency" (Menacker 1995, p. 4).

As America's growing cities confronted waves of immigration and rising crime, authorities continued to view public schools as islands of order and moral strength in a sea of social chaos. "As crime increased in the cities," Menacker observes, "the response was to apply the 'accepted solution' in heavier doses, leading to the development of summer schools as a means of preventing youthful idleness that stimulated criminal activity" (Menacker 1995, p. 5).

The belief in schools as the antidote to delinquency persisted into the 1960s, when President Lyndon Johnson's Commission on Law Enforcement and Administration of Justice observed that the school, "unlike the family, is a public instrument for training young people. . . . It is the principal public institution for development of a basic commitment by young people to the goals and values of our society" (Menacker 1995, p. 5).

By then, however, growing awareness of schools' evident failure to meet public expectations had engendered a new debate. Liberals argued that schools were too authoritarian and repressive, while conservatives called for a new focus on academic skills, competition, and tough discipline.

In 1978, concern about safety led to a congressional commission and a study, "Violent Schools—Safe Schools: The Safe School Study Report to Congress," prepared by the National Institute of Education (1978). The study found that about 13 percent of junior and senior high school students were victims of crimes like larceny, assault, and robbery in an average month during the school year and that schools were the sites of about a third of all assaults and robberies suffered by urban teenagers. It also found 3 million students who said they avoided locations in school buildings for fear of attack and 5 million who said they were always afraid while at school. These apparently shocking figures prompted more public discussion.

Events of the eighties and nineties made matters worse. Crack cocaine turned into a marketing bonanza for drug dealers, and the drug dealing created new demand for guns (Blumstein 1995, pp. 6–7). Teenagers who once carried knives and clubs switched to firearms, vastly increasing the lethal potential of adolescent confrontations over clothing, jewelry, sexual jealousy, or insults.

Schools also began to see their own versions of the "lone-gunman massacres," the most famous being a 1988 incident in Stockton, California, in which a deranged man fired an assault rifle at children playing in a school yard, killing five and injuring twenty-nine. In other cases, students brought guns to school and fired them at classmates and teachers (Larson 1995).

News coverage of youth and school violence ended the denial of earlier years. Drugs, guns, and gangs had created issues that Horace Mann and the later nineteenth-century reformers could never have imagined. By 1989, awareness of the problem had developed to the point that the president and the nation's governors, meeting at an education summit, acknowledged it in a set of national education goals to be reached by the year 2000. Goal 6 calls for schools to be free of drugs and violence and able to offer a safe, disciplined learning environment (U.S. Department of Education 1993). But educators and other public officials remained divided or confused about how to pursue such a goal, for they faced big obstacles.

Family breakdown in urban neighborhoods had reduced the number of involved parents who were traditional, and essential, allies in the enforcement of discipline and academic performance. The Supreme Court in rulings like *Tinker v. Des Moines School District* (1969) and *Goss v. Lopez* (1975) had guaranteed students' rights to free speech and due process before suspension or expulsion. Teachers backed by powerful unions complained, with reason, that their duty to maintain control of classrooms should not include having to deal with students armed with knives and guns or linked to violent gangs. In the 1990s, especially in big urban school systems, it seemed harder than ever for schools to guarantee students basic freedom from fear.

To what extent are concerns about school safety based in reality? Though the landmark Safe School Study documented levels of violence that the public considered shocking, subsequent surveys found that it remained relatively stable through the 1980s and 1990s. Measured nationally, much of the problem involves disorder—verbal assaults, scuffles, and petty thefts—rather than serious crime. At the same time, school officials suggest that, while serious violence is not increasing in quantity, it is growing qualitatively worse, especially as students carry guns. Problems of violence are greatest in large urban public schools serving communities afflicted by poverty, drugs, crime, and other social pathologies. Schools in these communities are also those least equipped to fight back.

What responses might work? Though schools continue to rely heavily on traditional discipline and sanctions like suspension and expulsion, research confirms plausible areas for innovation. Though additions to school curricula designed to confront drug abuse and violence appear to be largely ineffective when based on standard lectures and discussions, those that emphasize cognitive-behavioral training methods show real promise. Research also documents the value of administrative steps that establish special programs for troublesome students, clarify school rules, and generally transform a school culture of disorder to one of control. The most ambitious and creative responses mobilize both the school and its surrounding community to identify specific safety problems and develop practical ways to address them.

This essay has five sections. The first summarizes findings of a series of large-scale surveys of school violence, the second draws on those and other data sources to describe the correlates of school violence, and the third presents data showing that the seriousness of school violence—especially as embodied in gun use and possession—is getting worse even though the volume of school violence appears to be stable. Section IV examines research and practical experience with a wide range of curricula, administrative, and community-outreach preventative programs. Section V summarizes major conclusions from the earlier sections and sets out a proposal for comprehensive antiviolence programs in school.

I. Patterns and Trends

Since the 1978 Safe School Study, researchers have attempted national assessments of school violence in at least six more surveys. Table 1 summarizes the studies' key features. While all of them document a preoccupying level of crime in and around schools, they do not indicate a dramatic overall increase since 1976, and the results provide thin support for the idea of rampant violence in public schools across the country.

The Safe School Study was based on victimization questionnaires administered to 31,373 students and 23,895 teachers in more than 600 junior and senior high schools. The schools were selected from a statistically representative "probability sample" of 5,578 schools. The survey, conducted by the National Institute of Education, found that 12.8 percent of junior and senior high school students and about 13 percent of teachers were victimized in a given month.

While those figures seemed alarming, the overwhelming majority of both students (11 percent) and teachers (12 percent) suffered theft; only 1.3 percent of students and .5 percent of teachers were assaulted, and another .5 percent of both teachers and students were robbed. About 80 percent of thefts were valued at less than $10 for both groups. The typical student loss involved "small amounts of money, sweaters, books, notebooks, and other property commonly found in lockers" (National Institute of Education 1978, p. 3). Only 4 percent of the student assaults resulted in injuries serious enough to require medical treatment. As for student robberies, the report noted that "most of them are not robberies in the usual sense of the term . . . but instances of petty extortion—shakedowns—which for some student victims become an almost routine part of the school day" (p. 60).

For a School Crime Supplement to the National Crime Survey in 1989, interviewers questioned more than 10,000 youngsters between the ages of twelve and nineteen who had attended school during the previous six months. They were said to represent an estimated total of 21.6 million junior and senior high school students in the United States that year (Bastian and Taylor 1991).

The questions focused on personal crimes of violence and theft committed in school buildings or on school property. Overall, 9 percent of students surveyed reported being victimized at school over a six-month period; 7 percent were victims of property crimes while 2 percent were victims of violence. The violent crimes were "largely composed" of simple assaults—attacks without weapons that cause minor injuries—though there were also some aggravated assaults, robberies, and rapes. The survey did not give more precise figures for kinds of crimes. Since the household survey is believed to undercount mobile, minority, and inner-city populations, it may also undercount school violence occurring among them (Bastian and Taylor 1991, p. 1).

In 1991, the U.S. Department of Education's National Center for Education Statistics (NCES) asked a national sample of 1,350 public school teachers to report on victimizations by students during their whole teaching careers and during recent time periods. The largest number complained of verbal abuse. Fifty-one percent reported such incidents during their whole careers; 16 percent said students had threatened them with injury; and 7 percent said they had suffered

TABLE 1
National Assessments of School Violence, 1978–96

Study	Source	Sample	Subject	Findings
Violent Schools—Safe Schools: The Safe School Study Report to the Congress (1978)	National Institute of Education (1978)	31,373 students, 23,895 teachers selected from statistically representative probability sample of 5,578 schools.	Victimization survey about theft, assault, and robbery.	11 percent of students reported theft; 1.3 percent assault, .5 percent robbery. 11 percent of teachers reported theft; .5 percent assault, .5 percent robbery
School Crime: A National Crime Victimization Survey Report (1991)	Bastian and Taylor (1991)	More than 10,000 teenagers representative of all teenagers in American schools.	Victimization survey about personal crimes of violence and theft on school property over a six-month period.	9 percent reported being victimized; 7 percent property crimes, 2 percent violent crimes.
Teacher Survey on Safe, Disciplined, and Drug-Free Schools (1991)	Mansfield, Alexander, and Farris (1991)	1,350 public school teachers.	Survey of victimizations during teaching careers and shorter time periods.	During careers: threats of injury, 16 percent; physical attacks, 7 percent. During 12 months: threats of injury, 8 percent; physical attacks, 2 percent.

Student Victimization at School (1995)	Nolin, Davies, and Chandler (1995)	Representative national sample of 6,504 students in grades six through twelve.	Asked about personal knowledge of bullying, personal attacks and robbery over course of a school year.	Bullying, 8 percent; physical attack, 4 percent; robbery, 1 percent.
Violence in America's Public Schools (1993); Violence in America's Public Schools: The Family Perspective (1994)	Metropolitan Life Insurance Company (1993, 1994)	Representative national samples of 1,180 third to twelfth graders, teachers, parents, and police.	Victimization surveys about violence in and around schools.	23 percent of students and 11 percent of teachers victimized. Of students, 44 percent in an "angry confrontation" within the past month; 24 percent in a physical fight.
Monitoring the Future (1983–95)	Maguire and Pastore (1996)	Nationally representative sample of 15,000 to 17,000 seniors at 130 public and private high schools.	Victimization survey about theft, property damage, injury, and threats.	From 1983 to 1995, only theft of property worth more than $50 increased substantially, from 16.3 percent to 23.9 percent.

physical attacks. Nineteen percent reported verbal abuse within the previous four weeks, while 8 percent said they had been threatened with injury during the previous twelve months, and 2 percent said they had been attacked physically in the same period. The report noted, however, that physical attacks included kicks or punches from kindergartners along with more serious assaults by teenagers (Mansfield, Alexander, and Farris 1991, p. 13, table 1).

In 1993, The National Household Education Survey, sponsored by the National Center for Education Statistics, conducted telephone interviews with a representative national sample of 6,504 students in grades 6–12 and with 10,117 of their parents. The respondents for questions about school violence were identified through a "screener" administered to households called at random for the more general education survey. The researchers attempted to correct for the 8 percent of students who do not live in homes with phones.

Students were asked about personal knowledge of three kinds of incidents—bullying (repeated threats of harm), physical attacks, and robberies—that occurred either at school or on the way to or from school (Chandler, Nolin, and Zill 1993; Chandler, Nolin, and Davies 1995; Nolin, Davies, and Chandler 1995). Twelve percent reported being victims of such activity since the beginning of the 1992–93 school year; 25 percent said they worried about it; 56 percent said they had witnessed it, and 71 percent said they had heard about it. But again, the most common kind of incident bulking up the overall figures was verbal threat. Eight percent of the students had experienced it personally and 56 percent had knowledge of it. As for physical attack (which apparently included everything from a minor scuffle to aggravated assault), 4 percent had suffered it, while 43 percent had knowledge of it; for robbery, the figures were 1 percent and 12 percent (Nolin, Davies, and Chandler 1995, pp. 2–3).

In 1993 and 1994, the Metropolitan Life Insurance Company hired the Louis Harris polling organization to do two surveys on violence in public schools as part of an annual series devoted to American public education. For the 1993 survey, the researchers interviewed 1,000 teachers of third to twelfth graders, 1,180 third- to twelfth-grade students, and 100 officials of police departments. These were said to be nationally representative samples; the police were from urban, suburban, and rural departments selected in proportion to numbers of urban, suburban, and rural households. For the 1994 survey, Harris interviewed a representative sample of 1,000 parents whose children were in third to twelfth grades (Metropolitan Life Insurance Co. 1993, 1994).

These were the only surveys that appear to document high levels of serious violence. Twenty-three percent of students and 11 percent of teachers said they had been victims of violence in and around school (Metropolitan Life Insurance Co. 1993). When students were asked if they had been involved in an "angry scene or confrontation with people your age" in the past month, 44 percent said yes, and 24 percent said they had been involved in a physical fight. Twenty-six percent of students said they were "very worried" or "somewhat worried" about their safety going to and from school (Metropolitan Life Insurance Co. 1994).

Asked about types of school violence, the largest group of students (38 percent) cited stealing (not a violent crime) as a "major problem" in school, while 34 percent complained of verbal insults and 23 percent cited threats. But 33 percent considered "pushing, shoving, grabbing, or slapping" a major problem, and 27 percent were equally troubled by "kicking, biting, or hitting someone with a fist." A worrisome 20 percent said threatening someone with a knife or gun was a major problem in school, and 19 percent cited use of knives or firing of guns (Metropolitan Life Insurance Co. 1993).

Whether the Metropolitan Life studies indicate an increase over levels of school violence documented in earlier research is not clear, given differences in the studies. The most reliable measure of long-term trends might be found in the questions about victimization at school that the Institute for Social Research at the University of Michigan includes in the national surveys of high school seniors it conducts each year for its "Monitoring the Future" project. Each spring, the project interviews between 15,000 and 17,000 seniors at 130 public and private high schools selected to represent a cross section of students throughout the United States. The seniors are asked about six kinds of victimization: theft, deliberate property damage, injury with a weapon, threat with a weapon, injury without a weapon, and threat without a weapon. Between 1983 and 1995, only thefts of property worth more than $50 increased substantially; 23.9 percent of those surveyed reported such victimization in 1995, compared with 16.3 percent in 1983. Vandalism and threats with and without weapons also increased, but by less than 1 percent each (Maguire and Pastore 1996, p. 253).

II. Correlates of School Violence

While the big national studies fail to document a dramatic increase in school violence since the mid 1970s, they are no excuse for complacency, for safety problems affect some schools and some students more acutely than others. These, not surprisingly, are often schools surrounded by unsafe communities, a finding pointed out in a major reanalysis of the Safe School Study data by Denise Gottfredson and Gary Gottfredson. They found neighborhood social conditions to be an important predictor of disorder within schools, along with school size and resources, organization of instruction, and school climate and discipline (Gottfredson and Gottfredson 1985). Subsequent research examined different aspects of serious school crime problems, including how they relate to geographic location, poverty, grade level, and other factors.

The 1990–91 NCES study found consistent differences in levels of school disorder according to the school's location, its enrollment size, and the number of students from poor families (as indicated by the percentage receiving free or reduced-priced lunches). Levels of disorder were greater for schools located in cities, those with large enrollments, and where more than 41 percent of the students received lunch subsidies.

For example, the percentage of teachers who reported being threatened with physical injury in the past twelve months was 15 percent in city schools, but only 4 percent in rural schools. For schools enrolling more than 300 students, the figure was 9 percent, compared with 4 percent for smaller schools. And in schools where more than 41 percent of students got lunch subsidies, the figure was 13 percent, compared with only 3 percent for schools with fewer subsidized students (Mansfield, Alexander, and Farris 1991, p. 13).

A 1993 survey by the National School Boards Association found that student fighting occurred in 71 percent of schools overall, but it was a problem for schools in 93 percent of urban districts, 81 percent of suburban districts, and only 69 percent of rural districts. And while 13 percent of all schools reported shootings and knifings, the figure was 39 percent for urban districts. Gang-related violence was a problem for 60 percent of urban districts, though the overall figure was 24 percent (National School Boards Association 1993, p. 4).

A 1995 study reveals more starkly the violence problems facing schools in certain urban neighborhoods. The study, conducted by Joseph F. Sheley, Zina T. McGee, and James D. Wright, examined weapon-related victimization of students in inner-city high schools (Sheley, McGee, and Wright 1995). It was based on a broader survey, conducted in 1991, that probed gun acquisition and possession by students as well as inmates of nearby juvenile correctional institutions in California, New Jersey, Louisiana, and Illinois (Sheley and Wright 1993). The researchers found that 20 percent of the students had been either shot at (12 percent) or stabbed (8 percent) in school or on the way to or from school in the preceding few years. Another 13 percent had been injured with another type of weapon. The figures were more than twice as high for male students as for females. Fully 47 percent of the males had been shot at (20 percent), stabbed (10 percent), or injured with another weapon (17 percent). For females the figures were 6 percent, 7 percent, and 10 percent for a total of 23 percent (Sheley, McGee, and Wright 1995, table 1).

The second NCES study of student victimization in 1993 found sizable differences in students' experiences according to their ages and whether they were enrolled in public or private schools. Only 8 percent of senior high school students said they were personally victimized, compared with 17 percent of middle or junior high school students. And more than 70 percent of public school students (the study broke them down between those assigned to public schools and those attending ones they had chosen) reported knowledge of victimizations occurring in the three categories (bullying, physical attack, robbery); for private school students, the figure was only 45 percent (Nolin, Davies, and Chandler 1995, p. 3).

Twelve percent of students in the assigned public schools said they were victims of bullying, physical attack, or robbery, compared with 7 percent for those in private school. In both the assigned and chosen public schools, 4 percent of students reported physical attacks, compared with only 1 percent of students in private schools (Nolin, Davies, and Chandler 1995, pp. 3–4).

The 1989 School Crime Supplement to the National Crime Victimization Survey found similar, if less pronounced, differences. While 9 percent of all students reported being victims of either violent or property crimes, the figures were 10 percent and 11 percent for thirteen- and fourteen-year-olds, compared with 8 percent for seventeen-year-olds and 5 percent for eighteen-year-olds.

The survey also found that private school students suffered crime at a rate of 7 percent and that more students in central city schools (10 percent) reported being victimized than did those in suburban schools

(9 percent) or rural schools (8 percent) (Bastian and Taylor 1991, pp. 1–2, table 1, table 2).

A subsequent analysis of the School Crime Supplement results, published by Ringwalt et al. (1992), offered a profile of students who find reason to fear dangerous conditions in and around schools.

Their study focused on levels of personal victimization and "avoidance behaviors"—steps students said they took to keep themselves out of harm's way either in school or in transit to and from school, and it confirmed that perceptions of rampant school violence nationwide are exaggerated.

During the six months before the study, only one student in eighty reported staying home at least once for fear of being attacked at school, and only one in forty said they avoided school rest rooms, the site considered most dangerous in school. While one student in fifty said they had been violently victimized at school, this was less than the one in forty-three who had been victimized elsewhere.

"These findings clearly indicate that violent school crime and the fear of school crime cannot be said to have reached epidemic proportions across the country," the study's authors observe. "That is not to say that violent crime is not a very real concern to that minority of youth who have suffered its effects either because they are victims of violence or because they do not consider the school building or yard to be a safe place for them. Furthermore, schools in certain cities may have a very high incidence of crime, thereby affecting a large number of youth in a concentrated area" (Ringwalt et al. 1992, p. 34).

Regression analysis suggested eight factors that elevate a students' risk of school violence: poverty, inner-city residence, enrollment in public (rather than private) school, being a middle school student, being a victim of personal violence at school or elsewhere, being a victim of personal larceny at school, having family members who are victims of violence, and being fearful of attack at school or in transit to or from school (Ringwalt et al. 1992, p. 35).

III. The Changing Character of School Violence

There is broad agreement among educators that the nature of school violence has changed for the worse in recent years, an aspect of the issue not always revealed in the compilation of incident statistics. The National School Boards Association survey asked districts if student violence had increased in the past five years. Eighty-two percent said that it had either "increased significantly" (35 percent) or "increased somewhat" (47 percent), but many apparently felt the increase was more qualitative than quantitative. "There is no change in the number of our violent incidents, but the degree of violence has increased," one respondent observed (National School Boards Association 1993, pp. 3–4).

Research confirms a substantial level of weapon possession by students at school. Thirteen percent of students answering the Metropolitan Life survey admitted bringing weapons to class (Metropolitan Life Insurance Co. 1993). When Kelly J. Asmussen administered a survey to 859 tenth, eleventh, and twelfth graders in public high schools in a medium-sized Midwestern city, 15.6 percent said they carried a weapon to school during the 1991–92 school year (Asmussen 1992, p. 29). Statistics compiled by California school officials showed that over a four-year period that ended in 1989, incidents of weapons possession increased despite a slight overall decrease in school crime (Moles 1991, p. 5).

In a disquieting number of cases, the weapons in students' hands are guns. A 1987 study of 11,000 eighth- and tenth-grade students in twenty states found that 3 percent of the males reported bringing a handgun to school during the year before the survey (Sheley, McGee, and Wright 1995, p. 1). A 1990 federal study of 11,631 students chosen as a nationally representative sample found 4 percent reporting that they had carried a gun at least once in the thirty days prior to the survey (Sheley, McGee, and Wright 1995, p. 1). In addition to finding that 13 percent of school districts had experienced shootings or knifings in the 1992–93 school year, the National School Boards Association study found that 9 percent had experienced drive-by shootings, a crime relatively unknown a decade earlier. For urban school districts, the drive-by shooting figure was 23 percent (National School Boards Association 1993, p. 5).

Narrower studies of students in single cities or a few cities found similar or higher percentages of gun carriers. Asmussen's study of students in the unnamed Midwestern city found 2.9 percent admitting they carried guns to school (Asmussen 1992, p. 29). In Baltimore in 1987, almost half of the male students surveyed said they had carried a gun to school at least once (Sheley, McGee, and Wright 1995, p. 1). In Seattle, a 1990 study of eleventh graders found 6 percent of male students who had carried a gun to school at some time in the past (Callahan and Rivara 1992, p. 3038).

In 1993, Sheley and Wright published an initial report on the 1991 survey of juvenile offenders and students in California, New Jersey, Louisiana, and Illinois. The 758 male students were from ten inner-city public high schools in large cities near the correctional facilities surveyed.

Twenty-two percent of the students reported owning some kind of gun at the time of the survey; 12 percent said they carried a gun "all" or "most of the time," while another 23 percent said they carried one "now and then." Three percent said they carried a gun to school all or most of the time, and another 6 percent said they did so now and then, for a total of 9 percent carrying guns to school (Sheley and Wright 1993, p. 5).

The researchers considered the self-reporting credible: "In one school, surveyors observed a student taking a gun from his jacket to examine it before responding to a questionnaire item about caliber," they write (Sheley and Wright 1993, p. 2). They also were satisfied with results of statistical validity tests. At the same time, they cautioned against any effort to generalize their findings to other schools. The study was intended to examine behaviors related to gun acquisition and possession, and the schools were chosen from troubled inner-city neighborhoods in order to maximize the number of gun-involved students available for study.

Even so, reports of gun violence in schools nationwide further bolster the concern. In 1991, the Center to Prevent Handgun Violence published a report based on a compilation of more than 2,500 newspaper articles about gun incidents in schools since 1986. The study found that seventy-one people—sixty-five students and six school employees—had been killed by gunfire in schools during the five-year period. In addition, 201 suffered serious gunshot wounds, and 242 were held hostage at gun point. The shootings and hostage takings took place in thirty-five states and the District of Columbia (Lane 1991).

The carrying of guns and other weapons in schools appears to be overwhelmingly male behavior. Though the 1990 federal study found that 4 percent of all students had carried guns to school, the figure for black males was 21 percent (Sheley, McGee, and Wright 1995, p. 1). The Metropolitan Life studies, which did not break down weapons by type, found that the 13 percent of all students who said they brought weapons to school consisted of 22 percent of the males and only 4 percent of the females (Metropolitan Life Insurance Co. 1993). Asmussen found, similarly, that one-fourth of male students carried weapons to school compared with 6.6 percent of female students (Asmussen 1992,

p. 29). In the Seattle study, 11.4 percent of males reported owning a handgun, compared with only 1.5 percent of females (Callahan and Rivara 1992, p. 3040, table 3).

Weapons carrying may also be more common among younger high school students. Asmussen found that tenth graders accounted for almost half of all students bringing weapons to school; 19 percent of students in that grade carried weapons, compared with 14 percent for eleventh graders and 12 percent for twelfth graders (Asmussen 1992, p. 29).

Asked why they carried weapons to school, students in the different studies cited self-esteem and self-protection. Sixty-six percent of students told the Metropolitan Life researchers that students bring weapons to school to impress friends and be accepted by peers; 56 percent said weapons help them feel more powerful and important. Smaller numbers said they need weapons to protect themselves going to and from school (49 percent) and in school (36 percent) (Metropolitan Life Insurance Co. 1993).

Asmussen expressed some puzzlement over the reasons for weapons carrying given by students he surveyed. Though 9 percent said they carried a weapon for self-protection, 70 percent of the weapon carriers also said they had not been threatened with a weapon at school. Students in his smaller Midwestern city appeared to be responding to a perception of danger more than any reality. The higher level of weapons possession among tenth graders, he suggests, results from their fears as incoming students.

"In speaking confidentially with students in this survey," Asmussen writes, "many expressed that they 'had heard how bad it was going to be on the high school level,' so they 'brought their protection' with them 'just in case.'" Some students said violence was worse in junior high schools than in senior high schools. "This may indicate that the fear of violence may carry over from previous school experiences and then slowly decrease as students progress through high school" (Asmussen 1992, p. 30).

In their 1993 paper, Sheley and Wright reported how students responded when asked to give "very important" reasons for obtaining a gun. "Protection" and "enemies had guns" topped the lists of reasons, which were recorded according to types of guns acquired. Seventy percent of students with handguns cited protection, while 28 percent cited enemies. For students with military assault weapons, the figures were 75 percent and 42 percent; for those with rifles or shotguns, the figures were 59 percent and 29 percent. Sizable numbers had guns in order "to get someone": 13 percent of handgun owners, 25 percent of those with assault weapons, and 20 percent of those with rifles or shotguns. Only 10 percent of handgun owners said they wanted the gun "to impress people"; for those with assault weapons and rifles or shotguns, the figures were 9 percent and 7 percent (Sheley and Wright 1993, p. 8, table 4).

Sheley, McGee, and Wright's 1995 study related victimization in school or on the way to and from school to dangerous aspects of the students' general environment (friends and family members who carried guns, awareness of weapons in school, and the violence level in the school) as well as students' high-risk behavior (criminal activity, weapons carrying, drug involvement, gang membership). A multivariate analysis confirmed that "the dangerous environment outside of school is related to violent victimization, but the dangerous environment inside of school is less obviously related" (Sheley, McGee, and Wright 1995, p. 10).

"Perhaps the most striking of the present findings is the apparent level of danger that characterized so many students' social environments," the researchers state. Forty percent of students said that male relatives carried guns, a third had friends who did so, and 25 percent found guns easy to obtain (Sheley, McGee, and Wright 1995, p. 10).

"Judging from the present findings," Sheley, McGee, and Wright conclude,

> it appears that schools do not generate weapon-related violence as much as they represent the location (exactly or approximately) where violence spawned outside the institution is enacted. That is, inner-city youths do not assume new personae upon passing through school gates. Most weapon-related violence in schools is imported and occurs because the social worlds of some students encourage the use of weapons (students see males in their families carrying guns, for example), because some pupils engage in potentially violent behaviors (criminal activity, for example), or because simply carrying weapons promotes more injurious outcomes of standard juvenile disputes. (Sheley, McGee, and Wright 1995, p. 11)

Perhaps the most extreme examples of school violence and its effects on schools and students are documented anecdotally in research compiled by John Devine, an anthropologist, and his students at New York University's School of Education. Since 1986, Devine has directed a program that sends graduate students into New York City public high schools to tutor "at-risk" adolescents. The graduate students keep weekly journals that have become the field notes for an ongoing ethnographic study of life in the high schools serving the city's poorest and most violent communities. Here are two typical excerpts:

> Yesterday a student was apprehended with an Uzi submachine gun and several rounds of ammunition in the students' cafeteria. He was trying to hide the weapon in his girlfriend's knapsack when the security guard arrived. He said he was going to "waste" two students who had insulted him the previous day. Word of this incident spread quickly throughout the teachers' cafeteria today.

> Last week a student shot a rubber band at a girl in the cafeteria. The boy and the girl's boyfriend came to blows over it. Both swore revenge and then met yesterday on the fourth floor hallway, the scene of many such showdowns, between classes. The first student pulled a knife. The other brandished a .38 caliber gun and shot the first boy in the back as he tried to flee. . . . The dean who had made his way to the center of the fray handed [a security guard] the knife after he took it from the boy who had been shot . . . at this writing the bullet is still lodged in the boy's lower back as the operation to remove it is considered too dangerous to perform. The boy who did the shooting was placed in jail. (Devine 1995, pp. 174–75)

The level of violence so intimidates teachers and administrators, Devine writes, that they have abandoned much of their authority for an unhealthy level of denial. They "are forced into a position that inhibits their involvement with the youth culture (either through direct confrontations or friendly encounters), restricts their role to narrow cognitive interactions only, and encourages them deliberately not to see even the most flagrant violations or aggressive and destructive behaviors" (Devine 1995, p. 179). The school system's decision to turn more and more responsibility for discipline over to a force of school safety officers reinforces the reduction in the teacher's role and influence:

> This total abandonment of the in loco parentis role by the teachers is the first social fact noted by the incoming ninth

graders. . . . The school is perceived by them as a space totally lacking structure, one to which they must quickly adapt if they are to survive in an environment in which teachers attempt not to see disruptive student behaviors . . . and in which security guards and hall deans react only to the most outrageous activities. . . . The youth culture, for its part, interprets this unwillingness to confront unacceptable behaviors as reflecting a society totally without boundaries, one that is fearful of challenging adolescents. (Devine 1995, pp. 176, 178)

IV. Prevention of School Violence

Much national research on schools' responses to violence remains at the stage of compilation and description. It depicts school districts mostly adhering to traditional discipline and "hard" security measures. Even so, a considerable amount of innovation has begun, and research is beginning to sort out approaches that show promise as they attempt to alter school cultures, reinforce rules, and mobilize whole communities.

The National School Boards Association's 1993 study identified 750 programs operating in its affiliated school districts; they fell into 30 generic categories. The districts reported a variety of hard security measures to deter violence: 50 percent searched students' lockers for contraband, 44 percent closed their campuses at lunch hour, 36 percent deployed school security officers and conducted regular searches of students, 32 percent required students to carry photo identification, and 24 percent had even brought in drug-sniffing dogs. Smaller numbers had installed phones in classrooms (22 percent), used metal detectors (15 percent), or watched for misconduct with closed circuit television (11 percent) (National School Boards Association 1993, p. 7).

Such measures have some effect. For example, when the Dayton, Ohio, public school system installed metal detectors after a surge of expulsions for weapons carrying, such expulsions dropped from 200 in 1991–92 to 120 the following year. Suspensions for those years declined 5 percent, from 3,483 to 3,311 (U.S. General Accounting Office 1995, p. 28). New York City began scanning students with handheld metal detectors in 1988 and saw serious incidents in participating schools decline by 58 percent in three years, compared with a decline of 43 percent at other schools (New York City Board of Education 1991).

But most school administrators are well aware that control measures, however necessary, are a limited response at best. John Devine even argues that by symbolizing the collapse of deans' and teachers' traditional authority security guards and elaborate security technology do as much or more to encourage violence as to control it (Devine 1995, p. 187).

The most common curricular approaches identified by the National School Boards Association were classes in conflict resolution, mediation training, or peer mediation (61 percent). The districts also cited mentoring programs (43 percent), law-related education and multicultural sensitivity training (both 39 percent), support groups (36 percent), and classes in coping with adolescent problems (27 percent).

Administrative responses identified by the study include imposition of sanctions like expulsion and suspension, changes in school board policy, staff-development measures, and dress codes. Sanctions were the most common response; 78 percent of all school districts cited them. For urban schools, the figures for individual sanctions exceeded 85 percent. A sizable 66 percent also established alternative programs or schools for disruptive students.

Community-outreach measures included collaboration with other agencies (73 percent of districts), better communication with parents of troublesome students (42 percent), classes in parenting skills for students' parents (38 percent), establishment of gun-free school zones (31 percent), and recruiting parents to patrol schools on a voluntary basis (13 percent) (National School Boards Association 1993, p. 7).

Some studies of curriculum, administration, and community outreach at the local level deserve closer scrutiny.

A. Curriculum

In 1995, the U.S. General Accounting Office included three programs, with preliminary evaluative data, in a report on "Promising Initiatives for Addressing School Violence" (U.S. General Accounting Office 1995).

1. *Positive Adolescents Choices Training Program (PACT) at the Roth Middle School in Dayton, Ohio.* Doctoral-level psychology students from Wright State University work with students referred by teachers because of behavioral problems, violent victimization, or deficiencies in social skills. They meet twice weekly during school hours for a total of thirty-eight sessions. The curriculum includes social skills ("giving negative feedback, receiving negative feedback, and negotiation"), anger management and control, and discussions of the nature of vio-

lence. Students who excel in role-playing exercises and other activities earn "success dollars" that may be exchanged for tapes, candy, T-shirts, jewelry, and games.

An evaluation of the program in 1992–93 compared PACT students with a control group and found that students with PACT training behaved less aggressively in school, had fewer juvenile court charges, and lower per-person rates of offending (U.S. General Accounting Office 1995, pp. 28–30).

2. *Resolving Conflict Creatively Program in New York City Public Schools.* The program offers conflict resolution and multicultural education in 180 schools, involving 70,000 students and 3,000 teachers. Classes focus on "active listening," assertiveness, expressing feelings, perspective-taking, cooperation, negotiation, and interrupting bias. The program works intensively with teachers, administrators, and parents and trains students to mediate their own disputes.

An evaluation of the program in 1988–89 surveyed teachers, students, and school staff and found that students had learned the concepts of conflict resolution and could apply them. Seventy-one percent of the teachers said the program had reduced physical violence, and 67 percent said it had reduced verbal abuse (U.S. General Accounting Office 1995, pp. 32–34).

3. *Alternatives to Gang Membership (ATGM) in the Paramount, California, Unified School District.* The program offers second, fifth, and seventh graders instruction in resisting peer pressure and the dangers of drug abuse. Guest speakers focus on self-esteem, "consequences of the criminal lifestyle," the importance of education, and career choices. Parents are encouraged to attend neighborhood meetings where they learn about gangs and are offered help in keeping children from joining. The classes and the parent meetings may lead ATGM staff members to meet one-on-one to offer counseling and support for families when students face pressure to join gangs.

Follow-up studies found that few students who had participated in the program had become gang members as teenagers (U.S. General Accounting Office 1995, pp. 36–38).

In 1997, Denise C. Gottfredson reviewed 149 studies of school-based violence prevention for a section of a broader report to Congress on crime prevention. The idea was to identify approaches credibly validated by social science. She found huge areas of the crime and drug-abuse curriculum for which research turned out to be weak or unforgivingly negative. The survey suggested, for example, that "instructional programs focusing on information dissemination, fear arousal, moral appeal, and affective education are ineffective for reducing substance abuse" (Gottfredson 1997, p. 5-56). That includes the enormous D.A.R.E. (Drug Abuse Resistance Education) program that now assigns police officers to lecture 25 million students in 70 percent of the school districts in America. Research showed only minor positive effects of instructional programs like the fifteen-session Community Violence Prevention Program in Washington, D.C., and the nineweek Gang Resistance Education and Training program taught by Phoenix police officers in city schools (p. 5-39).

Gottfredson's survey also determined that community service and recreational activities (like midnight basketball) by themselves had little effect on delinquent behavior; nor did counseling programs, especially those based on peer groups. In effect, researchers found, peer counseling was likely to increase delinquency, apparently because bringing troubled youngsters together for rap sessions in school tended to reinforce their bad behavior rather than motivate them for good.

At the same time, Gottfredson found reason for optimism in studies documenting the value of "comprehensive instructional programs that focus on a range of social competency skills (e.g., developing self-control, stress-management, responsible decision-making, social problem-solving, and communication skills) and that are delivered over a long period of time" (Gottfredson 1997, p. 5-55). "The more extensive the reliance on cognitive-behavioral training methods such as feedback, reinforcement, and behavioral rehearsal . . . rather than the traditional lecture and discussion," she writes, "the more effective the program" (p. 5-42).

She points to two examples: a "social competence promotion" program enrolled middle school students for sixteen sessions of "impulse control and stress-management skills; thinking skills for identifying problem situations and associated feelings; establishing positive prosocial goals; and generating alternative solutions to social problems, anticipating the likely consequences of different actions, choosing the best course of action, and successfully enacting the solution." Teachers credited the program with reducing misconduct and improving students' academic motivation and problem solving skills. These positive effects continued in a second year as the classes were continued (Gottfredson 1997, pp. 5-36, 5-37).

The sixty-lesson Promoting Alternative Thinking Strategies

(PATH) program for elementary school children included role-playing exercises and "modeling by teachers and peers" as well as instruction and discussion. The lessons were divided into units on self-control, emotions, and problem solving, all focused on the "Control Signals Poster." The poster, displayed in every classroom, used the image of a traffic light: "a red light to signal 'Stop—Calm Down,' a yellow light for 'Go Slow—Think,' a green light to signal 'Go—Try My Plan,' and at the bottom, the words 'Evaluate—How Did My Plan Work?'" A study of the program involving 286 elementary school students in the state of Washington found "immediate positive effects" on their behavior (Gottfredson 1997, pp. 5-37, 5-38).

B. Administration

School managers respond to safety concerns with alternative schools and programs, special staff training, and efforts to beef up traditional discipline to alter the school's culture. The National School Boards Association survey documented the popularity of alternative schools, despite the ambitiousness of such programs (if done well) and their capacity to provoke controversy (National School Boards Association 1993, pp. 7, 13–18). Critics of the schools assert that they may become more youth prisons than schools or, in other circumstances, nonrigorous diploma mills for problem students. And where they occupy free-standing space, the idea of concentrating delinquent students in one place may incite furious neighborhood reactions.

Even so, officials like Leo Klagholz, New Jersey's commissioner of education, argue that alternative schools are the best way out for school systems confronted with the drawbacks of simply expelling disruptive students: with nothing better to do, expelled students cause new trouble for the wider community, and all but the most severely violent and troubled remain legally entitled to public education, a right the courts protect in a growing body of case law.

A "Safe School Initiative" in New Jersey called for establishment of alternative programs at the district level either in existing schools or at off-campus sites. It also envisioned a statewide network of county schools for the most troublesome cases, with tuition support from the districts sending students to them. The proposed policy called for immediate removal to an alternative school of students possessing firearms on school property or who threaten students or school staff with other dangerous weapons. It also required that students released from correctional facilities spend at least a year in an alternative program (Klagholz 1995, p. 6).

While acknowledging that "alternative education strategies can help address the underlying social causes of students' violent or severely/chronically disruptive behavior," Klagholz frankly stated that "the primary purpose of the strategies is to meet students' educational needs in an alternative environment so that they can be removed from the regular environment more readily" (Klagholz 1995, p. 5).

The winter 1995 issue of *School Safety*, a magazine published by the National Center for School Safety, compiled descriptions of five apparently successful alternative programs.

1. Beuchel Metropolitan High School in Louisville, Kentucky, offers "educational intensive care" to 100 middle school students and 200 high school students. The program combines strict discipline with a low student-teacher ratio and an array of positive rewards for good behavior (field trips in exchange for perfect attendance, free soft drinks for the "student of the week"). Put together with other troublemakers, Beuchel students no longer see much advantage in disruptive behavior, and they have a chance at leadership in school activities denied to them in mainstream schools (Daeschner 1995).

2. Houston's Independent School District places disruptive or emotionally disturbed students at the Terrell Alternative Middle School and the Harper Alternative School. Both programs feature low student-teacher ratios and strong support staffs that focus on diagnosing students' problems and developing responses to them. Harper offers a special program for students facing expulsion because of weapons violations (Paige 1995).

3. John H. Martyn High School in Jefferson, Louisiana, helps "behavior-disordered adolescents" with a program based on "behavior management." Students earn up to ten points per period for good behavior and academic achievement. Steady achievement earns elevation through six "levels," finally earning return to a mainstream school. Students also enter into behavior contracts with their parents and the principal. The curriculum includes extensive social skills and vocational training (Caudle 1995).

4. Raymond Telles Academy in El Paso, Texas, enrolls 250 students facing expulsion from mainstream schools for gang activity, drugs, fighting, truancy, and other offenses. Students earn points for appearance, attendance, behavior, and grades, progressing through four levels before return to a regular school. No one graduates from the academy;

instead, its students use it as a place to "get their act together" in order to graduate from a mainstream school (Hart 1995).

5. Fairfax County (Virginia) Public Schools send teachers into county agencies dealing with juvenile offenders, mental patients, and substance abusers. The programs may enroll as few as eight and as many as eighty students. The idea is to prevent arrest or other troubles from interrupting a students' education. Teachers are available to students as they move from juvenile detention centers to short-term treatment programs and then to long-term placements with agencies that serve their needs. The teachers work with the students' base schools to make sure their academic progress stays on track. The program also emphasizes social skills and study habits, appropriate dress and language, promptness, class participation, and completion of homework (Recasner and Turk 1995).

There is some evidence to vindicate promoters of alternative schools. Denise Gottfredson, in her 1997 review of school violence research, refers to her husband Gary Gottfredson's 1987 examination of alternative schools, which concluded that "they are far too variable in nature, student composition, structure, and purpose to warrant any blanket statement about their effectiveness" (Gottfredson 1997, p. 5-28). He evaluated one program, "based on the theory that intense personal involvement of the educators with the youth would reduce delinquency through increased bonding," and found "remarkable improvements in several risk factors for delinquency." Examination of another program, based on rigorous discipline and behavior modification, found "significantly more delinquent behavior than the comparison students" (Gottfredson 1997, p. 5-28).

Denise Gottfredson also looked at studies of two programs that group high-risk students together for special classes, School Transitional Environment Program (STEP) and Student Training Through Urban Strategies (STATUS). The STEP program, for students entering high school, kept small groups of students together for homeroom and academic classes and redefined the role of homeroom teacher to include guidance counseling. While one study of the program found positive effects, they could not be replicated in another. Researchers found that STATUS, which combined the school-within-the-school concept with innovative teaching methods, "reduced delinquency and drug use . . . and changed in the desired direction several risk and protective factors related to delinquency" (Gottfredson 1997, p. 5-26).

Overall, Gottfredson concludes, "programs which group high-risk students to create smaller, more tightly knit units for instruction show promise for reducing delinquency, drug use, and dropout." She cautioned, however that "these programs are risky," given other research documenting the backfire of programs putting troubled students together for peer counseling (Gottfredson 1997, p. 5-26).

Structural remedies like alternative schools address only part of the problem since they deal only with students who have caused enough trouble to risk expulsion. Educators also recognize the need for greater sophistication on the part of teachers and other school staff to deal with potential violence. Charlotte Reed and David Strahan (1995), for example, argue the case for "gentle discipline" as more effective than "get-tough" responses to school violence.

Echoing John Devine, they assert that the central issue for students in many schools is that they fear for their safety and do not believe that teachers, administrators, counselors, and security guards can protect them. Citing research that probed reasons students resort to violence, the authors point out that "students choose violent behaviors in an attempt to establish control over situations" (Reed and Strahan 1995, p. 3). "In addition to all the other exposures to violence [in inner-city neighborhoods], schools are now a dominant source of violence in the lives of many children. Students are attending schools where classmates settle their differences by whatever means necessary, anything from a push or a slap to a fatal stab or gunshot. Students do not feel safe in schools anymore" (p. 2).

Administrators who respond only with more rigid, authoritarian policies and stricter sanctions fail to acknowledge the broad, systemic nature of the problem, the authors assert. "Although clear policies and explicit procedures may be necessary, getting tough may limit the type of proactive planning necessary to reduce violence" (Reed and Strahan 1995, p. 1).

They outline a set of principles on which to base staff behavior toward students: respect, "intentionality" (helping empower students to make responsible choices and share control), optimism (about the capacity of every student to learn), and trust. By basing a code of conduct on such ideas, they say, "we can counteract violence by developing a gentle stance towards violent students and tough situations" (Reed and Strahan 1995, p. 10).

Peter Martin Commanday, writing in *School Safety*, supports that idea with more practical advice. A consultant who trains teachers to cope with violent situations, Commanday asserts that "the trouble with trouble is that the emotions of individuals involved often cloud their judgment and their ability to effectively communicate." He counsels teachers not to take students' verbal abuse personally and to remember that "to a disrupter, saving face will always be more important than adhering to any school rule" (Commanday 1992, p. 15).

He offers techniques for "mental self-defense":

> A female teacher had just started up the stairs to her classroom on the third floor, when she saw Jason sitting on the steps.
> "Hi, Jason."
> Silence.
> "Jason, it's time to go to your homeroom class."
> Jason jumped to his feet, glared at her and screamed: "Get the f—— out of my face. Who do you think you are, b——. Don't tell me what to do; you're not my mother!"

Commanday recommends against responding with the angry lecture or outburst the student expects, suggesting instead that the teacher throw him off balance and defuse the situation with a mild "Jason, what's up?" (Commanday 1992, p. 15).

Should a teacher be confronted by a student with a knife, he cautions against demanding " 'John, give me the knife.' He may indeed do that—'give it to you.' Do not make such a dangerous suggestion."

Instead, he counsels a more limited response that allows the combatant to retain some sense of control: " 'John, please move that knife just a bit to the left. It makes me nervous. See, I won't move, just a bit to the left. Thanks.' Once this is done, follow with: 'What's up?' " (Commanday 1992, p. 17).

Other educators acknowledge the need for staff development by encouraging the recruitment of teachers with urban youth leadership skills. Tracy A. Taylor describes, for example, the U.S. Department of Defense "Troops to Teachers" program funded in 1994 to provide $5,000 stipends to former members of the armed forces who agree to become licensed as teachers within two years after leaving the military and then to work as teachers for at least five years. The program also included financial grants to schools experiencing a shortage of teachers as an incentive to hire military veterans.

While the program served a number of agendas, particularly the government's desire to ease the pain of military downsizing, Taylor pointed out the implications for schools disrupted by violence. In addition to military education in mathematics, science, or foreign languages, "former service personnel have managerial and organizational skills to oversee classrooms and maintain discipline. A substantial proportion of military personnel is from minority groups that are underrepresented in the teaching profession. . . . In training new recruits for combat, service personnel already have experience instructing and mentoring young people" (Taylor 1994).

The staff development issue reflects a larger one: the need to address violence by altering a school's everyday climate. A school's inability to protect students and teachers from violence creates a daily atmosphere of anxiety that quickly translates into an ongoing culture of demoralization. So long as it remains unaddressed, the students' supposedly primary obligations to pay attention, learn, and behave necessarily become secondary to safety and survival. Teachers who feel at risk share in the demoralization, while administrators who insist on enforcing ineffective rules look either hypocritical or hopelessly out of touch. The sense of impotence in the face of crisis infects the school's all-important relationships with parents and the surrounding community.

Statistics offer little reason to think the cultural issue is being addressed rigorously on a widespread scale. The National School Boards Association survey found that sanctions like suspension and expulsion are by far the most popular answer to violence in school districts nationwide. Yet administrators of troubled schools also freely acknowledge that they are an inadequate response. One participant in the survey, referring to out of school suspension, observed that "allowing a kid to sleep late, watch television, and spend a day unsupervised is hardly a punishment for most students." Another stated bluntly that "suspensions do not work. Students don't care whether they are suspended or not" (National School Boards Association 1993, p. 8).

Denise Gottfredson found a number of studies that examined school culture, including efforts to emphasize norms for behavior and rules and attempts to build a school's capacity to control its own destiny. These are carried out by teams of school staff and students, sometimes joined by parents and neighbors, who meet to decide on ways to improve the school. Her review of the research led her to conclude that "the way schools are run predicts the level of disorder they experience. Schools in which the administration and faculty communicate and work together to plan for change and solve problems have higher teacher morale and less disorder. . . . Schools in which students notice clear school rules, reward structures, and unambiguous sanctions also experience less disorder. . . . Schools in which students feel as though they belong and that people in the school care about them also experience less disorder" (Gottfredson 1997, p. 5-14).

She refers to studies of a method known as "program development evaluation" used in the early 1980s to help troubled schools by putting researchers together with school staff to develop systematic plans for improvement. Plans typically included "efforts to increase clarity of rules and consistency of rule enforcement and activities to increase students' success experiences and feelings of belonging" (Gottfredson 1997, p. 5-15). Evaluations of the approach in a group of seven schools found a number of positive effects, including reduced delinquent behavior (Gottfredson p. 5-16).

Other research examined a 1993 "intervention to empower students to improve safety in schools" by organizing government and history students for problem solving. The students followed the four-step method—identify problems, analyze possible solutions, formulate and implement a strategy, evaluate the outcomes—that is common to problem-oriented policing. Researchers "found that students in the treatment school reported significantly less fighting and less teacher victimization and were less fearful about being in certain places in the school at the end of the two-year period compared with their baseline." This effect was not seen in a comparison school (Gottfredson 1997, p. 5-17).

Gottfredson also notes an effort in Norway in the early 1990s to reduce bullying by adolescents in schools, behavior that adults tended to ignore. School officials set out to "alter environmental norms regarding bullying" by "redefining the behavior as wrong" in forty-two schools in the city of Bergen. They came up with a strategy that involved "establishing clear class rules against bullying; contingent responses (praise and sanctions); regular class meetings to clarify norms against bullying; improved supervision of the playground; and teacher involvement in the development of a positive school climate." The program reduced bullying by 50 percent (Gottfredson 1997, p. 5-19).

Continuing concern about school cultures and school safety produced two studies in 1996, in Toledo, Ohio, and Philadelphia that examined the relationship of school discipline and management to school violence.

A study of forty-four public and Catholic schools in Lucas County (Toledo), Ohio, by Lab and Clark (1996) examined a number of school safety issues, focusing on whether a "humanistic" approach to discipline and control had a greater effect on victimization in schools than did a more traditional coercive approach.

The researchers surveyed 11,085 students, 1,045 teachers, and 43 principals in junior and senior high schools. Nearly 40 percent of students said they had been victims of theft in the previous six months; the figures were 13 percent for assault and 12 percent for robbery. Seventh and eighth graders were victimized at higher rates than senior high school students. Many of the crimes were serious: nearly 53 percent of robberies and 37 percent of thefts involved losses of more than ten dollars; 33 percent of the assaults produced injuries requiring medical attention (Lab and Clark 1996, p. 44, tables 4.1a, 4.1b, 4.1c).

The study measured students' perceptions of their school environments. While more than half considered their schools "very safe" or "safe," a sizable 16 percent rated them "unsafe" or "very unsafe" (Lab and Clark 1996, p. 54, table 4.9a). More than 11 percent said they feared being attacked while at school "sometimes" or "most of the time" (p. 56, table 4.10a). Nine percent said they had stayed home from school because they feared assault, while 8.1 percent said fear caused them to avoid rest rooms and 7.7 said it caused them to forgo extracurricular activities (p. 58, tables 4.11a, 4.11c).

Nor had Toledo schools escaped the epidemic of weapons. Overall, 24 percent of students said they carried a weapon to school for protection; 15.8 percent carried knives, while 8.4 percent carried guns (Lab and Clark 1996, p. 60, tables 4.12a, 4.12b).

The researchers identified coercive or custodial measures that included teacher monitoring of student activities; student codes of conduct; rules controlling movements of visitors and students out of class; security measures like guards, locks, and alarms; and rates of suspension and expulsion. They also recorded teachers' and students' perceptions of punishments for different types of misbehavior (disrespect, fighting, drinking, cutting classes, disruption, and possessing a weapon).

Then they identified measures of "humanistic" discipline: consultation with and involvement of students in setting punishments; students' and teachers' assessments of punishments' fairness; outreach to parents on school safety issues, and the existence of a student court.

Bivariate and multivariate analyses of the victimization figures showed that all of the discipline measures were related to reduced victimization in school and that the "humanistic" policies appeared to be more effective than coercive ones: "Humanistic measures of control are more highly related to lower in-school victimization. Not only are these variables consistently associated with lower victimization levels, student humanism is the only variable that is related to each type of victimization. . . . The consistency of the results and the strength of humanistic measures in both the bivariate and multivariate analyses suggest that a more normative approach to discipline and control is a fruitful direction in which schools should move" (Lab and Clark 1996, pp. 101–2).

In addition, the researchers analyzed the relationship of in-school victimization to environmental factors in surrounding communities gleaned from census data, police records, and "windshield" surveys—visual assessments of neighborhood conditions from the street.

Interestingly, bivariate analysis of these data and the school victimization figures failed to show much relationship between the level of violence in a school and the nature of the surrounding community. The only detectable relationship was between theft and the economic level of the neighborhood—schools in poorer communities had more theft. But the associations were only marginally significant.

"These results," the authors comment, "fail to support the oft heard claims that in-school problems are caused by the local environment and, therefore, beyond the control of the school" (Lab and Clark 1996, p. 75).

The Philadelphia study added support for the ideas that schools should not be so quick to surrender to negative community influences and that efforts to alter a school's climate are worth pursuing. The study by Welsh, Jenkins, and Greene (1996) sought to examine the climate of Philadelphia schools in the context of an ongoing effort to develop school-based management citywide. It began with a "macro-level" study of all 255 schools in the Philadelphia school district. The researchers probed relationships among school safety, school size, and resources and the social and demographic aspects of neighborhoods where students live. A second "intermediate-level" study explored the relationships of school organization and climate to school violence by interviewing and surveying principals of forty-two middle schools and administering an "effective school battery survey" to students, teachers, and administrators in eleven of the same schools. A final "micro-level" survey took a closer look at structure and safety issues in three schools.

The macro-level study compiled data on household income, household size, single parenthood, household stability, race, and crime for all communities sending students to Philadelphia schools. But it pursued bivariate and multivariate analysis of relationships between such data and school safety only for middle schools.

The researchers found a notable lack of direct correlation between school safety and conditions in students' home communities. Instead, it found that school size, in terms of enrollment, was a significant predictor of suspensions for serious misconduct and rates of school incidents reported to police. The study also found a relationship between attendance, academic achievement, and neighborhood stability. Schools with high rates of attendance had low rates of disorder and violence. "Thus, a students' neighborhood environment does contribute to disorder, but in an indirect manner" (Welsh, Jenkins, and Greene 1996, pp. 72–73).

Even so, the researchers concluded, "the best overall predictors of school disorder in Philadelphia's middle schools are measures which are primarily related to internal school factors of school size and achievement levels of students and not to community and crime. . . . School disorder is essentially a function of the internal school environment and not of the community itself" (Welsh, Jenkins, and Greene 1996, p. 70).

The researchers found that many of the middle schools had implemented the two central features of school-based management: a structure for involving all parts of the school community (administrators, students, teachers, parents) in school decision making and a regular system for communicating policies and soliciting feedback (Welsh, Jenkins, and Greene 1996, p. 79). The analysis showed that "school safety was positively associated with school-based management. . . . It would appear that the basic principles of [school-based management], when used constructively, are conducive to shaping an environment where students feel safer" (p. 95).

The study's most striking finding arose from the analysis of school climate according to thirteen subscales measuring students' feelings about peer association, educational expectations, social integration, clarity of school rules, self-confidence, and other matters. The analysis showed that liking for the school and involvement in school activities were not related to student feelings of safety. The strongest predictors were the students' feelings of integration with the school ("greater alienation strongly predicts lower safety," the researchers found) and individual self-confidence. However, feelings of safety were negatively related to a students' willingness to conform (Welsh, Jenkins, and

Greene 1996, pp. 97–98). "Those who feel safest are not necessarily 'good' kids who follow the rules, but those who perceive they are able to cope with a dangerous environment," the researchers conclude. "This is a disturbing finding, for it suggests that schools have left many students to fend for themselves" (p. 103).

C. Community Outreach

In concept, the idea of mobilizing students' families, the surrounding neighborhood, and other public agencies to address safety problems promises obvious benefits, yet achieving them in practice turns out to be a complex and frustrating task. Assessments of recent experiments in three cities (New York, Philadelphia, and St. Louis) suggest the possibilities and the difficulties.

The New York attempt followed the recommendation of a panel that examined school safety issues in the city and in 1993 completed a lengthy report on them for the chancellor of the city's huge public school system (Travis, Lynch, and Schall 1993). The city had not neglected safety issues in its schools. It had expanded its force of school safety officers to 3,000, making it one of the nation's larger law enforcement agencies. In addition to patrolling school halls and grounds in traditional police fashion, the school safety officers used handheld metal detectors and X-ray machines to scan students for weapons at forty-one schools one day per week. The system also developed photo-identification cards that included a magnetic strip encoding identifying information that would call up data about the students' attendance history and disciplinary status. And it introduced a number of conflict-resolution and mediation programs to school curriculums.

Even so, the panel recommended a new approach: strategic planning and problem solving coordinated by the school principal but reaching out to include police, social agencies, and people from the surrounding neighborhood. "The Panel envisions a planning process that occurs around a large table," the report stated, "large enough to include students, teachers, parents, guidance counselors, probation officers, police personnel, local business leaders, youth service providers, and clergy" (Travis, Lynch, and Schall 1993, p. 38).

A local nonprofit group with a track record in neighborhood organizing supplied facilitators for a pilot program to test the concept. The facilitators' plan was to identify "stakeholders" and convene small "focus groups" for discussions of safety problems specific to the schools and to recommend participants for larger working committees.

The working committees then would craft specific plans and implement them.

No formal evaluation of the project exists, but the results are recorded in a final report issued by the Citizens Committee for New York City (1995) and in the observations of a journalist hired to prepare an informal assessment (Anderson 1995).

According to these documents, the schools and their communities never completed the process envisioned by the facilitators. In only one school did the principal wind up chairing a working group. The principal of another, having seen her school singled out for negative media coverage because of its apparently high rate of violent incidents, viewed the project with suspicion and gave only reluctant support. In the third, the working group never got fully organized, and the principal found it more effective to act on his own.

The project also suffered greatly from so mundane an issue as scheduling. "The logistics of collaborative problem solving turned out to be far more daunting for stakeholders in a school than for those in a neighborhood," the journalist observer writes.

> A task apparently as straightforward as the scheduling of meetings turned out to be a continuing source of frustration. Teachers and school administrators already bearing heavy workloads found it hard to find time for lengthy meetings of the collaborative team and its working groups. In addition, while they were available at the school during the day, they dispersed to distant communities at night. Parents, merchants, and leaders of community organizations, however, were more available for meetings in the evening. Students were available at school during the day, but attending meetings meant excusing them from classes. Teachers and administrators were reluctant to excuse them from too many classes in any case, and at certain times, like exam weeks, they simply could not be excused. (Anderson 1995, pp. 16–17)

As a result, the composition of the working groups changed substantially from meeting to meeting.

The central issue of student participation confronted school officials with special problems. Gathered around the table in a group that included the principal, deans, teachers, and police officers, students often seemed intimidated and unwilling to speak their minds. "These, furthermore, were the 'good' students, selected by school administrators

for their positive academic records and sense of school citizenship. Yet
. . . a genuinely collaborative process to control student misbehavior
would also have to include some of the students who misbehaved; addressing other safety issues ought to include school truants and dropouts." But some school officials understandably resisted that idea; to
include such students in the group would appear to reward bad conduct (Anderson 1995, pp. 17–18).

By the end of the first year, with funding due to expire in another
three months, the facilitators abandoned the formal collaborative planning process and continued the effort simply by sitting down regularly
with the various stakeholders to discuss safety issues.

In the end, the project's leaders could point to a number of concrete
results. One school persuaded the well-respected teacher of a leadership class to organize her students in projects related to school safety.
School administrators also upgraded metal detectors and X-ray machines and convened two days of training for school safety officers on
issues specific to the school. They worked with police to assign special
narcotics units to the area around the school and even to send youth-
ful-looking police cadets in plainclothes into local stores to watch for
illegal sales of alcohol to students.

The principal of another school, after consultation with police and
other agencies, secured a nearby city park that had become a hangout
for drug dealers and other troublemakers who preyed on students. At
the third school, the principal deployed a special force equipped with
walkie-talkies to secure a dangerous locker room and persuaded police
to help mount a crackdown on truants hanging around outside the
school while school staff accosted "hallwalkers" causing trouble inside
it. Both measures apparently reduced theft and violence.

It remains far from clear whether such things might have happened
without the collaborative process. In the end, however, principals of
the schools felt that it had helped. The journalist observer writes,

> All three of the school principals involved said that the process
> enabled them to develop better working relationships with the
> New York Police Department and the Division of School Safety.
> . . . If nothing else, police attendance at the school safety meetings
> impressed the police with the fact that the principal took safety
> issues seriously, that an outside group was involved in facilitating
> the process, and that the process could bring in many other parts
> of the community. This surely made police commanders far

more willing to grant the school's requests for help than if the principal had made them without the support of the wider group. . . . "A process has developed to make action possible" [said a principal quoted in the report]. "The finger pointing has stopped" (Anderson 1995, pp. 35–36).

A Philadelphia project, subjected to much more formal scrutiny, offered less reason for optimism. The Center for Public Policy at Temple University worked with the Philadelphia Police Department, the Philadelphia Housing Authority Police, the Temple University Department of Security and Protection, and four public middle schools to develop a "safe corridor" for students attending one of the schools. This was considered an exercise in problem-oriented policing as well as community-based school safety.

To assess the schools' safety problems, the project staff convened focus groups of up to ten participants at each school. The groups included students, teachers, parents, school security officers, and police. School administrators were purposely excluded for fear their presence might intimidate others and inhibit honest discussion.

Students at the schools filled out questionnaires asking about how they came to and went from school, their perceptions of danger along the way, their experiences of victimization, and ways they coped with their fear. About 20 percent said they had been victimized during the current school year (Stokes et al. 1996, p. 46).

Computer software used the students' responses along with their home addresses to generate maps pinpointing unsafe locations along students' routes to and from school. The map for the Wanamaker School showed addresses concentrated in two distinct clusters and concentrations of unsafe activity in four distinct areas. This made it easier to design a safe corridor for Wanamaker students than for those at the other schools, whose maps showed greater dispersion of addresses and dangerous activity. The police decided to design and patrol a safe corridor for Wanamaker and monitor the results, using the other three schools as controls for the research.

The focus groups and the survey yielded other notable insights into school violence. Despite the apparently pervasive fear of crime, nearly 70 percent of students said they never worried about being attacked, while 5.6 percent said they often felt such fear (Stokes et al. 1996, p. 35, table 3). Those who walked to and from school alone did not appear to be victimized any more than those who walked in groups

(p. 39, table 7). Students who were fearful or victimized identified the objects of their fear as other students rather than as older criminals who prey on students (p. 41, table 10). Twelve percent of students admitted bringing weapons to school; a higher percentage of those who had been victimized felt the need for weapons (p. 39, table 8). And while the largest plurality (45.8 percent) said they were most likely to be attacked in school (p. 42, table 11), when victims were asked what time of day they were attacked, the largest plurality (47 percent) said it happened on the way home from school (p. 43, table 12).

"While certain students feel threatened during school and may well be the object of ridicule or harassment while inside the school, the actual attack may be happening after school hours away from adult supervision," the researchers speculate. "In all likelihood, the school is often the environment where tension originates and, later, spills out on to the streets" (Stokes et al. 1996, p. 43).

Based on the maps of addresses and unsafe areas, the project staff designated a zone ten blocks long and three blocks wide as a safe corridor for students attending Wanamaker Middle School. For a six-week period in the spring of 1995, the corridor was patrolled from 8 A.M. to 9 A.M. and from 2:30 P.M. to 4:00 P.M. For the morning shift, the three police agencies (city, housing, and Temple University) contributed three patrol cars, two officers on bicycles, and one on foot. Two more housing officers on bikes and a fourth car joined the patrol for the afternoon, the time when trouble seemed more likely as students poured out of school en masse.

The officers were informed of routes children took to and from school, but effective patrol sometimes proved frustrating because "students frequently took routes that cut through abandoned lots, backyards, and courtyards. Ironically, . . . many students identified such areas as 'unsafe' places, yet, . . . it seemed that many students continued to use these more risky routes" (Stokes et al. 1996, p. 30).

The results proved disappointing. A follow-up survey of students after six weeks found a slight increase in the percentage of Wanamaker students victimized during the safe corridor period (20.2 percent, compared with 19.4 percent). The percentage victimized in the control schools declined from 21.2 percent to 15.2 percent. Figures for perceived risk moved in similar ways. After the six-week experiment, the percentage of Wanamaker students saying they felt they would be picked on one or more times rose slightly from 32.4 percent to 33.4 percent, while the figure for the control schools declined from 30.4 percent to 28.4 percent (Stokes et al. 1996, p. 46). The researchers compared 31 different variables between Wanamaker and the control schools and between the first and second surveys in search of the cause for an increase in victimization at the test school. They speculated that changes in the number of students walking to and from school and the number staying late after school might be related to rates of victimization. But they could find no differences between the test and control schools (p. 47).

The researchers considered the project successful to the extent that it demonstrated the potential for law enforcement agencies, schools, and a university to work together on defining a problem, developing a strategy, carrying it out, and evaluating the results. The project also yielded valuable insights and lessons for future research and policy planning.

Specifically, the researchers pointed to the finding that students are likely to be victimized on or near school grounds, after school, because of tensions developing during the school day. They noted that programs offering support for students who had been victims could result in a decrease in the number of weapons brought to schools since the victims seemed more likely to carry weapons than nonvictims.

As for the ineffectiveness of the strategy itself, the researchers observed that "violence directed at students, because it is often from other students, may be more insidious—and less amenable to a 'safe corridor' crime amelioration strategy—than we had anticipated. . . . The relative ineffectiveness of the safe corridor project in the test school may suggest that other factors are at play in the dynamics of student victimization and that investigations into the climate of schools and how community and socio-economic variables affect victimization and reporting patterns may prove beneficial" (Stokes et al. 1996, p. 51).

The state of Missouri pursued a more ambitious program that began at the Walbridge Elementary School in St. Louis in 1989. With support from the Danforth Foundation, the state's departments of Health, Mental Health, Social Services, and Elementary and Secondary Education mobilized to provide intensive health and social services to students and their families in Walnut Park, a poor neighborhood of North St. Louis. The idea was to use the school as a base for addressing family and neighborhood problems. The project was managed by a board consisting of parents, school staff, community leaders, and representatives from the participating state agencies, the St. Louis Public Schools, and the Danforth Foundation.

The group developed a menu of ten programs that included academic tutoring, substance abuse case management, "day-treatment" counseling for disruptive students, training for parents, antidrug education, health monitoring, African-American culture, and after-school care for children of working parents. The school also provided "Families First," which sent in-home workers for twenty hours per week to help families at risk of losing children gain "concrete skills." An antidrug task force composed of parents began aggressively picketing crack houses and organizing residents of the area for neighborhood watch activities.

The project, known as Caring Communities, received much favorable publicity, especially as the police began to credit the weekly antidrug picketing and demonstrations for closing down crack houses. By 1995, twenty-two had closed down, greatly improving the neighborhood's safety and general morale. The project's evident successes prompted Missouri's legislature in 1995 to fund sixty new Caring Communities sites across the state (Cohen 1995).

While a formal evaluation reinforced the favorable impressions in some ways, it provided only partial confirmation that the program was having the effect social service planners had envisioned. Researchers interviewed fifty-two randomly selected parents of Walbridge students and fifty parents from a nearby elementary school serving families from the same neighborhood but without the Caring Communities programs. They asked teachers at Walbridge and the comparison school to fill out questionnaires and interviewed the local police precinct captain. They examined records of the State Department of Social Services and local juvenile justice agencies along with academic records of students at Walbridge and the comparison school.

The researchers found that both parents and teachers of Walbridge students had a more positive view of the school than did parents and teachers of students at the comparison school. "Most parents at Walbridge believe they take an active part in school decisionmaking," the researchers write. "Walbridge parents see school as a source of help for the problems of their children as well as a source of help for their own problems and needs." The teachers agreed that at Walbridge they could get more help for students and their families and that Walbridge parents are more involved in the school than those at the comparison school (Philliber Research Associates 1994, p. 38). Based on their interview with the police captain, the researchers concluded that the police view Caring Communities "as a potent force for crime reduction" (Philliber Research Associates 1994, p. 39).

A review of academic records produced a mixed result. The researchers divided the Walbridge children into two groups: those who received the most intensive Caring Community services, which included Families First, case management, and day treatment; and others who received the other schoolwide services. The students who were subject to the most intensive services over the evaluation periods improved reading scores by 26 percent, on average, compared with an improvement of 11 percent for students at the comparison school (Philliber Research Associates 1994, p. 35, fig. 25). The figures for work-habits grades were 27 percent and 12 percent (p. 34, fig. 23); for social-emotional growth grades, 26 percent and 15 percent (p. 34, fig. 24); for math grades, 27 percent and 4 percent (p. 36, fig. 26).

These favorable results were undercut by another, however. For all but math, grades of Walbridge students who received the less intensive schoolwide Caring Community services declined during the same time periods. Overall, intensively served Walbridge students improved their grades by 23 percent; the comparison school students increased theirs by 10 percent, while grades of less intensively served Walbridge students fell by 1 percent (Philliber Research Associates 1994, p. 36, fig. 27). Figures for the children whose grades improved showed a similar pattern: 69.6 percent of intensively served students showed improved grades, compared with 48.4 percent at the comparison school and 38.9 percent of less intensively served students at Walbridge (p. 37, fig. 28). While the researchers call the disparity "inexplicable," it may suggest that focus on the families needing intensive services led to neglect of the others in the Caring Community program.

The most disappointing figures, however, resulted from the examination of social service and juvenile justice agency records. They showed virtually no difference in levels of child abuse and neglect cases or juvenile court cases for families whose children attended the two schools. The researchers speculate that Walbridge may have had a higher rate of social service and juvenile justice referrals before the project began or that the intensive focus on Walbridge families caused more reporting of cases that would have been ignored before; in other words, the number of reports may have increased even as the actual amount of child abuse and other offending went down.

But the bottom line remains unsatisfying for a program that had shown so much promise. "These are disappointing results," the researchers conclude, "and these indicators will have to be tracked over a longer period of time" (Philliber Research Associates 1994, p. 30).

V. Future Prospects

This survey of recent school safety research reveals no dramatic surprises, unless one finds it surprising that the national trendlines remain much flatter than is suggested by media hype. Instead it confirms the predictable: schools with the most serious safety problems serve communities troubled by broader neighborhood and family breakdown aggravated by drugs, guns, and gangs. The afflicted schools attract the special attention of a wider public because they are schools. Once upon a time, communities looked to them as places of safety, order, and wholesome activity that could serve as powerful agents of crime prevention, giving young people moral guidance and basic preparation for law abiding life. Laws requiring school attendance reflect the seriousness of that tradition, even as they lend special urgency to youth crime occurring in and around schools: a government that forces parents to turn over custody of their children for part of each day incurs an obligation to keep them safe while they are in its care.

Government's continuing failure to meet that obligation in some schools violates a fundamental part of the social contract. It sends messages that compound the hopelessness of parents and other members of already demoralized communities. More important, however, it forces children and adolescents to develop their own strategies for coping with fear on a daily basis; all too often the results are deep alienation and cynicism. These are the starkest and most disturbing of the findings detailed above.

Reed and Strahan observe that, "in addition to all the other exposures to violence, schools are now a dominant source of violence in the lives of many children" (Reed and Strahan 1995, p. 2) and that "students choose violent behaviors in an attempt to establish control over situations" (p. 3). The Philadelphia researchers discovered a negative relationship between feelings of safety and a students' willingness to conform and that "those who feel safest are not necessarily 'good' kids who follow the rules, but those who perceive they are able to cope with a dangerous environment" (Welsh, Jenkins, and Greene 1996, p. 103). Asmussen found gun-toting junior high school students acting out of naive anxiety more than swaggering bravado. "In speaking confidentially with students . . . many expressed that they 'had heard how bad it was going to be on the high school level,' so they 'brought their protection' with them 'just in case' " (Asmussen 1992, p. 30). Devine finds incoming students who perceive school "as a space totally lacking structure, one to which they must quickly adapt if they are to survive." (Devine 1995, p. 176).

Fear breeds alienation, alienation leads to more violence, which then increases fear. The cycle strikes some observers as so daunting that they reach for radical answers. Jackson Toby, who has studied school safety issues since the 1970s, argues that the most effective response should be the end of laws requiring high school attendance. He points to the problem of "internal dropouts"—students who come to school but are uninterested in learning—who "turn school into a recreation center" (Toby 1995, p. 162). The only way to achieve stability and security is to allow them to drop out so that teachers can be guaranteed a "critical mass of willing students" (p. 161). "A voluntary high school program," he declares, "is the best alternative to shooting ourselves in the foot by keeping internal dropouts in school" (p. 163).

It is an appealingly simple idea, promising safer schools without any need for new investment of public funds. Yet it leaves many educators and parents with a queasy feeling, not unlike that inspired by proposals to reduce crime by legalizing drugs. This is because, beyond any practical issues (Toby insists that legalizing truancy would not cause an increase in crime), such a step represents an abandonment of the historic commitment to universal public education, the final repudiation of Horace Mann's belief in "good moral and intellectual education" for all. Adolescents, by definition, lack mature judgment. Allowing fourteen-year-olds so large a measure of responsibility for their own futures is not likely to produce many happy endings.

As important, if research vindicates pessimism, it also suggests reason for enough hope to make radical responses seem premature. The commonsense assumption that school violence simply reflects the violence of surrounding communities deserves a close look. To be sure, Sheley, McGee, and Wright, echoing earlier findings of Gottfredson and Gottfredson, remarked on "the apparent level of danger that characterized so many students' social environments. . . . It appears that schools do not generate weapon related violence as much as they represent the location (exactly or approximately) where violence spawned outside the institution is enacted" (Sheley, McGee, and Wright 1995, p. 11). But the studies of safety and school administration in Toledo and Philadelphia found surprisingly little direct relationship between violence inside schools and violence in communities that supplied schools with students.

The studies are not necessarily in conflict. Schools serving students from communities where weapons and violence are common are likely to see more of weapons and violence than do schools serving other students. While this creates a special problem, it hardly means weapons and violence are beyond the control of the school. Control depends instead on the school's internal climate, which remains a function of resources, staffing, and creative management. Denise Gottfredson's review of 149 school studies leads her to conclude that schools can develop their capacity to innovate and change, given commitment and resources. While this is obviously easier for a school located in a good neighborhood, the possibilities should not be dismissed for those located in bad ones. The violent schools in violent communities may demonstrate more official neglect than inevitable fate.

While the school safety research does not identify any magic bullets, it does offer a rich menu of possibilities. At best they might reduce violence; at worst they could alter the climate of a school in ways that allow for improved morale and better education even if numbers of violent incidents do not decline.

For now, the problem is not that nothing works but that too little has been tried. Gottfredson wound up advising Congress that the low level of federal funding for school-based crime prevention activity, when compared with the $1.4 billion spent on police and $617 million for prison construction, "represents a lost opportunity for preventing crime" (Gottfredson 1997, p. 5-62).

The National School Boards Association survey, meanwhile, found that while many schools report more innovative and proactive strategies, the most popular response to school violence by far remains the traditional—and largely ineffective—"individual sanctions," sending students to disciplinary classes for in-school suspension, sending them home for out-of-school suspension, or expelling them from school altogether. While many different schools in many different places experiment with physical security, curriculum, administrative measures, and community outreach, few if any attempt to implement them all at the same time.

Imagine a school designed for the security that allows teachers to teach and students to learn. It begins with planning at the city and district level. Research confirms that schools of unwieldy size and coping with overcrowding suffer chronic disorder more than those with student bodies small enough to manage. Overall population and student-teacher ratios may be the most basic factors controlling the level of violence in schools.

Given a guaranteed limit on population, planners might then move on to physical design: a building free of dangerous stairwells, catacomb locker rooms, and other space that invites trouble; metal detectors and magnetic identification card readers built into its entrance lobby to keep intruders and contraband out without hopelessly delaying the start of school each day or sending a panicked message about the administration's lack of moral authority; sophisticated communications that allow teachers, hall monitors, and security staff to keep track of all activity in the school and to report trouble or summon help on a moment's notice.

The curriculum makes room for full education in safety and citizenship. All students attend classes that examine the challenge of finding productive, prideful lives without drugs, gangs, or guns. Other classes help them deal with their own anger and that of others in their community. Some are recruited for an ongoing corps of peacemakers and mediators of conflicts likely to escalate into violence in and out of school. The school treats citizenship as an important topic for ongoing study and discussion, giving academic credit and recognition to students who understand its principles and practice them.

The school's administrators make safety as important an issue for management as education. They recruit and train staff to deal with violence rather than deny it or resent it. They establish alternative programs for disruptive, truant, chronically unmotivated, or drug-abusing students. In general, they recognize the supreme importance of social integration to the school's safety and morale, fostering an atmosphere of inclusiveness, open communication, and shared decision making on safety and other important issues with students, staff, and parents.

The school establishes an ongoing relationship with the broader community it serves. The principal organizes a committee composed of administrators, teachers, students, parents, neighborhood business and civic leaders, and local police. It also includes representatives of social agencies involved in youth work, health, and substance-abuse prevention and treatment. The committee meets regularly to analyze specific sources of trouble for school and neighborhood, mobilizing resources to address them.

It is more than likely such a school, constructed and organized for safety as well as education, would show reduced levels of violence if compared with other schools in a formal evaluation. Even if it did not, however, by institutionalizing ample communication and full participation of students, teachers, parents, and the community, it might at least sustain morale at a level that permits education to proceed.

The impediments to creating such schools are, of course, hardly unfamiliar. Most schools are housed in buildings that predate modern issues of violence and are not about to be moved into new ones. Modern security and communications hardware do not come cheap. Neither does new curriculum or staff development, which may also raise issues for teachers' unions. Career administrators trained in a different era may show little enthusiasm for humanistic discipline and inclusive management. And community outreach may lead the school into potentially nasty thickets of local politics.

But the stakes are high. For schools seriously troubled by violence, the status quo is not acceptable. Defeatist proposals like repeal of laws mandating high school attendance raise huge practical and moral issues. If government would continue to honor the vision of Horace Mann, the way is apparent. The will remains to be seen.

REFERENCES

Anderson, David C. 1995. "Final Report to the Citizens Committee for New York City." New York: Citizens Committee for New York City.

Asmussen, Kelly J. 1992. "Weapon Possession in Public High Schools." *School Safety* (Fall), pp. 28–30.

Bastian, Lisa D., and Bruce M. Taylor. 1991. *School Crime: A National Crime Victimization Survey Report.* Washington, D.C.: U.S. Department of Justice, Bureau of Justice Statistics.

Blumstein, Alfred. 1995. "Violence by Young People: Why the Deadly Nexus?" *National Institute of Justice Journal*, no. 229 (August), pp. 2–9.

Callahan, Charles M., and Frederick P. Rivara. 1992. "Urban High School Youth and Handguns." *Journal of the American Medical Association* 267(22):3038–42.

Caudle, Melissa C. 1995. "The Martyn System Facilitates Positive Changes." *School Safety* (Winter), p. 8.

Chandler, Kathryn, Mary Jo Nolin, and Elizabeth Davies. 1995. *Student Strategies to Avoid Harm at School.* Washington, D.C.: National Center for Education Statistics.

Chandler, Kathryn, Mary Jo Nolin, and Nicholas Zill. 1993. *Parent and Stu-*

dent Perceptions of the Learning Environment at School. Washington, D.C.: National Center for Education Statistics.

Citizens Committee for New York City. 1995. *Final Report for the Pilot School Safety Project.* New York: Citizens Committee for New York City.

Cohen, Deborah. 1995. "A Lesson in Caring." *Education Week* 14:41–53.

Commanday, Peter Martin. 1992. "The Trouble with Trouble." *School Safety* (Fall), pp. 15–17.

Daeschner, Stephen. "Helping Students to Succeed at Beuchel Metropolitan." *School Safety* (Winter), p. 7.

Devine, John. 1995. "Can Metal Detectors Replace the Panopticon?" *Cultural Anthropology* 10(2):171–95.

Gottfredson, Denise. 1997. "School-Based Crime Prevention." In *Preventing Crime: What Works, What Doesn't, What's Promising,* edited by Lawrence W. Sherman, Denise Gottfredson, Doris MacKenzie, John Eck, Peter Reuter, and Shawn Bushway. Washington, D.C.: U.S. Department of Justice, Office of Justice Programs.

Gottfredson, G. D. 1987. "Peer Group Intervention to Reduce the Risk of Delinquent Behavior: A Selective Review and a New Evaluation." *Criminology* 25:671–714.

Gottfredson, G. D., and D. C. Gottfredson. 1985. *Victimization in Schools.* New York: Plenum.

Hart, Charles F., Jr. 1995. "Students Get Act Together at Raymond Telles Academy." *School Safety* (Winter), p. 9.

Klagholz, Leo. 1995. "A Safe School Environment for All." *School Safety* (Winter), pp. 4–6.

Lab, Steven P., and Richard D. Clark. 1996. *Discipline, Control and School Crime: Identifying Effective Intervention Strategies.* Final report to the National Institute of Justice, under grant no. 93-IJ-CX-0034. Washington, D.C.: U.S. Department of Justice, National Institute of Justice.

Lane, June R. 1991. "Schools Caught in the Crossfire." *School Safety* (Spring), p. 31.

Larson, Erik. 1995. *Lethal Passage: The Story of a Gun.* New York: Vintage.

Maguire, Kathleen, and Ann L. Pastore, eds. 1996. *Sourcebook of Criminal Justice Statistics, 1995.* Washington, D.C: U.S. Department of Justice, Bureau of Justice Statistics.

Mansfield, Wendy, Debbie Alexander, and Elizabeth Farris. 1991. *Teacher Survey on Safe, Disciplined, and Drug-Free Schools.* Washington, D.C.: National Center for Education Statistics.

Menacker, Julius. 1995. "Public Schools and Urban Youth Disorder." *School Safety* (Spring), pp. 4–9.

Metropolitan Life Insurance Co. 1993. *Violence in America's Public Schools.* New York: Metropolitan Life Insurance Company.

———. 1994. *Violence in America's Public Schools: The Family Perspective.* New York: Metropolitan Life Insurance Company.

Moles, Oliver C. 1991. "Student Misconduct and Intervention." *School Safety* (Winter), pp. 4–7.

National Institute of Education. 1978. *Violent Schools—Safe Schools: The Safe*

School Study Report to the Congress. Vol. 1. Washington, D.C.: U.S. Department of Health, Education and Welfare.

National School Boards Association. 1993. *Violence in the Schools: How America's School Boards Are Safeguarding Our Children.* Alexandria, Va.: National School Boards Association.

New York City Board of Education. 1991. "Fernandez Moves to Bolster School Safety." Press release. New York: New York City Board of Education, Division of Public Affairs.

Nolin, Mary Jo, Elizabeth Davies, and Kathryn Chandler. 1995. *Student Victimization at School.* Washington, D.C.: National Center for Education Statistics.

Paige, Rod. 1995. "Houston Alternative Schools: 'A Positive Trend.'" *School Safety* (Winter), p. 8.

Philliber Research Associates. 1994. *An Evaluation of the Caring Communities Program at Walbridge Elementary School.* Accord, N.Y.: Philliber Research Associates.

Recasner, Ann, and Ann Turk. 1995. "Educational Intensive Care." *School Safety* (Winter), pp. 7–10.

Reed, Charlotte, and David B. Strahan. 1995. "Gentle Discipline in Violent Times." *Journal for a Just and Caring Education* 1:320–32.

Ringwalt, Chris, Pamela Messerschmidt, Laura Graham, and Jim Collins. 1992. *Youth's Victimization and Experiences, Fear of Attack or Harm, and School Avoidance Behaviors.* Final report to the National Institute of Justice, under grant no. 91-BJ-CX-0002. Washington, D.C.: U.S. Department of Justice, National Institute of Justice.

Sheley, Joseph F., Zina T. McGee, and James D. Wright. 1995. *Weapon-Related Victimization in Selected Inner-City High School Samples.* Final summary report to the National Institute of Justice. Washington, D.C.: U.S. Department of Justice, National Institute of Justice.

Sheley, Joseph F., and James D. Wright. 1993. *Gun Acquisition and Possession in Selected Juvenile Samples.* Washington, D.C.: U.S. Department of Justice, National Institute of Justice.

Stokes, Robert, Neil Donahue, Dawn Caron, and Jack R. Greene. 1996. *Safe Travel to and from School: A Problem-Oriented Policing Approach.* Research supported under award no. 94-IJ-CX-K015 from the National Institute of Justice. Philadelphia: Temple University Center for Public Policy.

Taylor, Tracy A. 1994. "New to the Ranks: Moving from the Military into Teaching." *ERIC Digest* (electonic download). Washington, D.C.: ERIC Clearinghouse on Teaching and Teacher Education.

Toby, Jackson. 1995. "The Schools." In *Crime*, edited by James Q. Wilson and Joan Petersilia. San Francisco: ICS Press.

Travis, Jeremy, Gerald W. Lynch, and Ellen Schall. 1993. *Rethinking School Safety: The Report of the Chancellor's Advisory Panel on School Safety.* New York: New York City Board of Education.

U.S. Department of Education. 1993. *Reaching the Goals: Goal 6, Safe, Disciplined and Drug-Free Schools.* Washington, D.C.: United States Department of Education, Office of Educational Research and Improvement.

U.S. General Accounting Office. 1995. *School Safety: Promising Initiatives for Addressing School Violence.* Report to the Ranking Minority Member, Subcommittee on Children and Families, Committee on Labor and Human Resources, U.S. Senate. Washington, D.C.: U.S. General Accounting Office.

Welsh, Wayne N., Patricia H. Jenkins, and Jack R. Greene, with Dawn Caron, Eric Hoffman, Ellen Kurtz, Donna Perone, and Robert Stokes. 1996. *Building a Culture and Climate of Safety in Public Schools in Philadelphia: School-Based Management and Violence Reduction.* Final report to the National Institute of Justice, under award no. 93-IJ-CX-0038. Washington, D.C.: U.S. Department of Justice, National Institute of Justice.

John M. Hagedorn

Gang Violence in the Postindustrial Era

ABSTRACT

Economic restructuring may have as many implications for today's gangs as the industrial revolution did for yesterday's. In recent decades, there have been increases in the number of male gangs, and probably of female gangs, in cities and towns of all sizes, and there have been large increases in gang violence. Many gangs operate as well-armed economic units inside a vastly expanded informal economy. Gang membership now extends for many males into their adult years. More violence-prone prison gangs may be claiming a new role in the outside community, complicating an already dangerous situation. Finally, the contrast between media images of the rich and famous and limited real-life opportunities may have encouraged many poor young men to abandon conventional norms and sell drugs instead. When combined with the abundance of handguns and the need to regulate the illegal drug business, the emphasis on profits may be changing the way young adult gang members define their gangs and the nature of postindustrial gang violence.

> *Q:* "Our last study was done in 1986. What has happened to the gang these last five years? What's changed the most?"
>
> *A1:* "It's more business now, it's more money. Money is more the reason people get into gangs now."
>
> *A2:* "I come from three generations of gangs. . . . We're in a new generation now. Back then . . . everything was like fistfights. . . . It's gotten worse, it's like shoot-outs all the time. . . . It's scary walking down the street and knowing that you're on the opposition's turf. Nowa-

John M. Hagedorn is assistant professor of criminal justice at the University of Illinois at Chicago.

days you're afraid to get shot at. You know, before, you
didn't even worry about that!" (Transcript, intervention with two male Milwaukee gang members, 1991)

The gang problem in the United States has roots that can be traced
back to the urban slums of the early nineteenth century (see Spergel
1990; Fagan 1996). Gangs have always been popularly conceived of as
the wild, law-violating kids of immigrants or lower-class ethnic groups.
Katz (1988) captured this when he called gang members "aliens,"
strangers in our familiar land. Gangs, for many people, are simply *un-
American*, not welcome in an America "the way it oughta be."

While these notions have endured through the years, there have
been some notable changes in how Americans think about gangs and
the violence they produce. Prior to the 1970s, gang violence was usually seen by the public as some version of *West Side Story* (1961) male
ethnic youths fighting with fists and knives over turf, respect, or ro-
mance. Gang members were typically envisioned as "foreigners,"
southern European or Latin American immigrants with hot-blooded,
violent ways.

By the 1990s, the movies *Scarface* (1983), *Colors* (1988), and *New Jack
City* (1991) had popularized a different image: cold-blooded minority
gangsters shooting it out in drive-bys or disputes over drugs. The dark
foreigner was replaced by the dark African American or Latino. To the
established image of violent gang rivalries was added a lethal mix of
drugs, guns, and easy money.

Such sensationalized media images are often overdrawn and promoted by the needs of journalists, law enforcement agencies, and ambitious politicians (see Klein 1995). But might the popular media's notion that "gangs have changed" contain a kernel of truth? Perhaps
gang violence in an era of deindustrialization is not the same as gang
violence in an era of industrialization. The formation of ethnic, fighting gangs was one by-product of the industrial revolution in urban
America. Likewise, might some violence produced by contemporary
gangs reflect the equally sweeping consequences of global economic
restructuring?

Before I advance into the argument, I have to face the troublesome
issue of defining a "gang." Young children and teenagers form peer
groups every day. But where the peer group ends and the gang begins
is where the controversy heats up.

The debate on the definition of gang is long and rancorous, and I do not intend to repeat it here.[1] Rather, one place to start is to adapt from Thrasher (1963) the notion that "ganging" is a normal peer activity of adolescents within a continuum of behaviors from conventional to wild. For many scholars (e.g., Klein 1971; Spergel 1990), criminal acts are intrinsic behaviors of those peer groups called "gangs," while for others (e.g., Short 1997) they are not. Most social scientists agree, however, that gangs over time have formed as peer groups of mainly male youth on the wild side of the continuum. And social scientists seem to agree that these young males—and also females—organize, to a varying degree, some of their rowdy, delinquent, and criminal activities.

For example, Moore (1998) has said that "gangs are unsupervised peer groups who are socialized by the streets rather than by conventional institutions. They define themselves as a gang or 'set' or some such term, and have the capacity to reproduce themselves, usually within a neighborhood." This definition omits criminality as a defining characteristic since changing levels of violence and criminality are what Moore seeks to explain. Other social scientists might include criminal behavior in this definition, and that would not change the substance of the matter. Social science perspectives differ from those of law enforcement in social science's more dynamic focus on the processes of young people adapting, as they grow up, to various economic and social conditions. Law enforcement agencies, mainly concerned with apprehending criminals, more statically define gangs as intentional and cohesive criminal associations (e.g., Chicago Crime Commission 1995). In my view, Moore's definition captures the essence of earlier industrial-era gangs while being broad enough to describe gangs today.

Social scientists have disagreed on the relative weight to place on individual, family, group process, cultural, and structural factors in understanding gang participation and violence. These issues have been reflected recently in the broader sociological debate on the underclass (Wilson 1987, 1996). How much do structural variables, such as social isolation, explain the apparent increases in gang activity and violence? If gangs are basically a reflection of individual characteristics or the product of distinct subcultural values, we might observe quantitative increases in some behaviors but stability in the age-old form of the gang. However, if gangs organize not only out of youthful wildness but

[1] For reviews of this long debate in gang research, see Spergel (1990), Bursik and Grasmick (1993), and Ball and Curry (1995). For a helpful analysis, see Moore's (1991, pp. 39–41) application of Fine's concept of "normal deviance" to gangs.

also in response to more immediate economic and institutional forces, the effect of economic restructuring may have led to significant changes in the form of some gangs and the nature of their violence.

There is little doubt that the numbers of gangs and gang members have substantially increased over the last two decades. Most social scientists agree there are many more male gangs today than ever before, and that they can be found in cities, towns of all sizes, and even rural areas. There may also be more female gangs, but there is less evidence of the scope of a female gang problem. Male gang violence appears to have increased alongside national increases in violence (see Cook and Laub, in this volume). Much gang violence, most scholars concur, is still boys or men acting like "tough guys," picking a fight with other boys or men, who are also acting like tough guys. Such struggles for reputation, status, or "turf" probably describe most of today's, as well as yesterday's, gang violence. While there are differences of view among researchers, the weight of the evidence supports the notion that the spread of guns and unsettled cocaine markets are also related to increases in gang violence.

This increased violence, however, may also be associated with some significant qualitative changes in modern gangs. Most social scientists today agree with Thrasher (1963) that "no two gangs are alike" and that many gangs still look like the delinquent adolescent peer groups of the industrial era. However, economic restructuring may have altered the characteristics of a growing assortment of new postindustrial gangs. For example, many gangs now operate as well-armed economic units inside a vastly expanded informal economy, replacing factory work for young males with jobs selling drugs. Gang membership now extends for many males into their adult years. The old turf or neighborhood, which was once a place to protect, has for some gangs become little more than a market. The vastly increased number of gang members who have gone to prison, and returned, find few legitimate opportunities and may be more likely to look to their gangs for illicit employment. More violence-prone prison gangs may be claiming a new role in the outside community, complicating an already dangerous situation.

Cultural and structural factors may have influenced changes in many gangs. In recent decades, most Americans have reduced associations with neighbors and replaced them with TV and the mass media (Putnam 1995). The ever-present contrast between media images of the rich and famous and limited real-life chances has been one factor that has encouraged many poor young men to "make their money" by "any means necessary" (Messner and Rosenfeld 1994). When combined with the abundance of handguns (Blumstein 1995*b*) and the need to regulate the illegal drug business (Black 1983; Fagan and Chin 1990), this one-sided emphasis on profits may be changing the ways gang members define their gangs.

This essay reviews an extensive literature on industrial and postindustrial gang violence. The classic studies in the industrial era include ethnographic fieldwork such as Whyte (1943), Thrasher (1963), Yablonsky (1966), and Miller (1973), and theoretical analyses such as Cohen (1955), Miller (1958), and Cloward and Ohlin (1960). The literature is especially indebted to Short and Strodtbeck's (1965) test of various gang theories in empirical research in Chicago. For the two decades after the 1960s, Moore (1978), Horowitz (1983), and Campbell (1984) were among the few serious studies of gangs (see Horowitz and Bookin-Weiner 1983). Then at the end of the 1980s and the early 1990s, gang research experienced a resurgence. New field research studies were initiated, beginning with my work in Milwaukee (Hagedorn 1988), Vigil's work in Los Angeles (1988), and Taylor's work in Detroit (1989), and the most extensive survey research of gangs in history led by Maxson and Klein (1990, 1996; see also Klein 1995) and Spergel and Curry (1995; see also Spergel 1990, 1995). Interest in female gangs also rose with Taylor's (1993) Detroit studies, Moore's (1991) continuing Los Angeles work, our own Milwaukee studies (Moore and Hagedorn 1996), and Joe and Chesney-Lind's (1995) Hawaiian work, among others (see Campbell 1990). This essay reviews these vast literatures and uses data from my fifteen years of research on gangs in Milwaukee as a case study of the changes taking place across the country in gangs and gang violence.

The essay begins with a brief overview of gangs and gang violence in the industrial era. Section II examines empirical data on the extent of the postindustrial gang problem, increases in gang violence, diffusion of gangs to small cities and towns, and probable increases in the number of female gangs. It also looks at continuities between industrial-era and postindustrial-era gangs. Section III examines five factors that may have influenced the changes in modern gang violence: the adoption of economic functions by some urban gangs, the use of violence to regulate illicit commerce, the proliferation of firearms, the effect of prison on neighborhood gangs, and the effect of mainstream cultural values of money and success on gang youth with limited opportunities. The essay concludes with comments on implications of the nature of postindustrial gangs for public policy.

I. Gangs in the Industrial Era

What do we know about industrial-era gangs and gang violence? It is important to note that while there are a number of classic sociological studies of male gangs in a few big cities from the 1920s through the 1960s, few reliable data are available on the number of gangs in different cities at different times, the number of gang crimes, or even the number of gang-related homicides. Law enforcement officials simply did not keep consistent data on gang-related crimes. Miller (1975, 1990) has long argued that the lack of a centralized database on gangs is one reason why the media can so easily manipulate the gang problem (see esp. Spergel 1990).

With so little systematic knowledge about gangs in the past, what generalizations can be drawn? The most important one is that American gangs and their violence were basically the product of the problems of young people acculturating to life in poor urban communities. The classic gang was a rebellious, working-class, teenage male peer group.

A. The Nature of Gangs in the Industrial Era

Thrasher (1963, p. 21) began his description of gangs by describing "gangland," or "natural areas" inhabited by immigrants attempting to work their way out of poverty and become Americanized (Thrasher 1963, pp. 130, 154). Many different kinds of gangs formed in response to the massive economic and social upheavals accompanying industrialization and immigration. Polish youth in Chicago and Mexican boys in Los Angeles experienced in different ways the familial and social strains of acculturating to America (Vigil and Yun 1996).

Male gangs were closely tied to specific neighborhoods and to the invasion of those areas by new immigrant groups (Thrasher 1963, p. 93; see also Moore 1978). As men worked in the factory and women struggled to make ends meet or to care for large families, unsupervised preteen play groups developed into teenage gangs. Male gangs developed cohesion through conflict with each other and with ineffective social institutions, such as schools and police. Girls were more likely to stay in the home than to hang out, and so it seemed that fewer formed gangs. As gang boys matured, they got jobs, got married, and settled down, with only a few going on to a life of crime (Thrasher, 1963, p. 287; see also Whyte 1943; and, for females, Brown 1977).

Two decades later, Cohen (1955) defined the delinquent subculture or gang as a solution to the problem of adjustment for working-class "corner boys"; the heart of the delinquent gang problem was working-class boys' "reaction formation" to their inability to attain "status" in a middle-class world. In a similar way, Cloward and Ohlin (1960) argued that different kinds of gangs resulted from lower-class males' various sub-cultural responses when denied legitimate means to attaining success. Female problems of adjustment, strain theorists Cloward and Ohlin (1960) and Cohen (1955) believed, did not typically lead to collective, subcultural responses (see Cloward and Piven 1979 and Morris 1964).

In the industrial era, "success" for working- and lower-class boys meant being able to "mature out" of the gang: get a decent job, get married, and move into a better neighborhood. The gang was a product of the lack of controls over youthful play, but it was also a kind of anticipatory rebellion by boys against a dreary future life as men in the factory (Willis 1981; Sanchez-Jankowski 1991) and by girls against a dreary future life as housewives (Campbell 1984). Gangs were shaped by both the class structure and the varying means of access by ethnic groups to industrial jobs. Industrial-era gangs were an adolescent by-product of the difficulties experienced by immigrant and migrant groups in realizing the American Dream.

B. Gang Violence in the Industrial Era

Since few reliable statistics exist on industrial-era gang violence, there is no good way to compare the prevalence or incidence of gang violence between cities or over time. All we can reliably conclude is that there was less lethal gang violence before the 1970s than today. However, considerable data and theorizing are available about the *nature* of industrial-era gang violence. Gang violence in the industrial era was seen as an inevitable product of group processes within male gangs in poor communities and a characteristic response of boys in poor neighborhoods lacking social controls.

In Thrasher's (1963, p. 116) classic Chicago School view, the gang "is a conflict group. It develops through strife and thrives on warfare." Gangs were groups "integrated by conflict" (Thrasher 1963, p. 46). Two basic ingredients for violence were male adolescent peer groups and neighborhoods. Gang violence fundamentally was the result of neighborhood peer groups fighting over turf, defending their neighborhood play areas in ways that mimicked war and romantic tales of feudal rivalries. Violence was exciting and helped to consolidate the group.

Violence, for Thrasher, had little to do with the family or certain kinds of troubled kids. He argued that "any condition in family life that promotes neglect and repression of its boy member" (Thrasher 1963, p. 339) led to boys joining gangs. But violence was largely a group affair, entered into after the boy had joined.

Violence by girls was not discussed. For Thrasher, girls were "more supervised" than males and had less chance to fight. Those who did were "tomboys," girls who rejected the female role and were treated like guys. For Thrasher, "ganging" was a male thing, but anticipating Adler (1975), he thought women might become more violent, just like men, if given the opportunity: "Since the occupations of men, formerly closed to women, have been opened to them, what is implausible about their entering the time-honored profession of the highwayman? They may do it for thrills, they may do it because hard pressed to make a living, they may do it simply as a matter of course; but at least it is more wholesome than becoming a prostitute" (Thrasher 1963, p. 168).

Short and Strodtbeck (1965, 1970) tested Cohen's, Miller's, and Cloward and Ohlin's theories by interviewing groups of African American and white Chicago gang members. One of their most valuable contributions to the literature was their extension of Thrasher's classic view of male gang violence with their notion of violence as "status threat." Taking issue with the popular notion that gang violence is the product of kids who come from emotionally disturbed families, Short and Strodtbeck examined the functions of violence for group cohesion. Gang leaders, they found, used violence against "out-groups" as a way to maintain their leadership and the solidarity of the gang (Short and Strodtbeck 1965, p. 198). Contrasting their perspective to more universalistic and structuralist perspectives, Short and Strodtbeck (1965, p. 249) argued that "striving for status within the group rather than class mobility . . . explains continued participation in incidents of group action." In other words, most gang violence was "aleatory," acts that contributed toward maintaining the status of gang members within the group (Short and Strodtbeck 1965, p. 264).

Miller (1969) provided a remarkable empirical description of day-to-day violence by industrial-era gangs. His research assistants charted all the violent acts of members of five gangs over a ten-month period in the 1960s and their court-charged offenses over twelve years. Miller (1969, p. 696) concluded that "violence appeared neither as a dominant preoccupation of city gangs nor as a dominant form of criminal activity." Miller found that violence increased as a teenager approached eighteen years of age and almost completely disappeared by age twenty-two (Miller 1969, pp. 698–99). Contrary to popular stereotypes of the time, whites in the fictitiously named "Midcity" were twice as likely to engage in violence as African Americans (Miller 1969, p. 697). In stark contrast to today, Miller reported that no one was killed because of gang fighting in the ten-month period of his study, and there were no reports of even a single firearm being used (Miller 1969, p. 701).

Miller also found that only about a third of all violence by gang members consisted of "gang-bangs," or gang-versus-gang wars. Gang violence was typically more talk than action: fourteen of fifteen recorded plans for gang wars were averted by talk or mediation. Finally, Miller argued that most gang violence was not violence for its own sake, as the media of the time claimed. Rather, gang violence, like the violence of great nations, was engaged in to defend the "honor of males; to secure and defend the reputation of their local area and the honor of their women" (Miller 1969, p. 707). For Miller, gang violence was fundamentally a lower-class male cultural response to threats to honor and prestige.

Miller was critical of Yablonsky (1966), who lent academic support to media portrayals of irrational acts of violence by gangs. Rather than seeing violence as a lower-class male cultural response, Yablonsky found 1950s gang violence to be outbursts from emotionally troubled, "sociopathic" youth: "The gang is a convenient and malleable structure quickly adaptable to the needs of emotionally disturbed youths who are unable to fulfill the demands required for participation in more normal groups" (Yablonsky 1966, p. 2).

Yablonsky argued that fifties gang violence had changed from Thrasher's day. Unlike Thrasher's gangs, which were "friendship organizations," gangs of the fifties were more malicious, and their members were "sociopaths." Yablonksy agreed with the group-process perspective in that he saw much sociopathic violence as reflecting the leaders' needs for control. But for Yablonsky, gang sociopaths had little empathy and presumably lacked adult role models. New York gangs of the fifties "are in action hysterical, moblike cliques, that kill and maim for no logical purpose" (Yablonsky 1966, p. 3).

The industrial era was also a pre-TV era, a time before television occupied more time for juveniles than did school, hanging out with friends, or interacting with parents (Slaby and Roedell 1982). Yablonsky, however, borrowing from Merton, pointed out that TV westerns in the fifties influenced sociopathic behavior by justifying violence, and not just violence by the "bad guy." "The 'good guy,' sheriff or lawman, is as sociopathic and enjoys his violence as much as the . . . outlaw" (Yablonsky 1966, p. 210).

Yablonsky argued that the sociopathic nature of gang members derived from a more disorganized "slum" community. In tones that sound much like William Julius Wilson's descriptions (1987, 1996) of underclass communities twenty years later, Yablonsky argued that the "stable slum" had been replaced in some areas by the "disorganized slum" (Yablonsky 1966, p. 167). It was in these communities that social controls broke down, sociopaths were raised by ineffective parents, and violence occurred at high rates.

Yablonsky's views closely paralleled Cloward and Ohlin's. They argued that gang violence was the product of the lack of both legitimate and illegitimate opportunities. In poor neighborhoods where there were few jobs, and without adult criminal enterprises, a "conflict subculture" formed among the neighborhood youth (see also Spergel 1964, pp. 93–123). These youth were not sociopathic but rebellious, wild kids from the neighborhood. Having no legitimate or illegitimate futures to look forward to, male gang members fought. "We suggest that many lower-class male adolescents experience desperation born of the certainty that their position in the economic structure is relatively fixed and immutable—a desperation made all the more poignant by their exposure to a cultural ideology in which failure to orient oneself upward is regarded as a moral defect and failure to become mobile as proof of it" (Cloward and Ohlin 1960, p. 107).

Criminal subcultures, for Cloward and Ohlin, were made up of male adults who recruited youths for criminal moneymaking ventures and who had interest in keeping youthful violence under control (Cloward and Ohlin 1960, pp. 166–71). Conflict subcultures developed in those slum areas, like African American housing projects, characterized by transience, instability, and other signs of social disorganization. Most important, such unorganized areas did not develop stable adult criminal operations, like the Italian Mafia. The violent behavior of gang members lacked not only formal social controls by schools and police but also informal controls by adult criminals (Cloward and Ohlin 1960, p. 172).

Adult women with child-care responsibilities have always played stabilizing roles for families and have been unlikely to be involved in criminal organizations (Stack 1974). Morris (1964) argued that women's goals are more relationship-centered and that they have more legitimate means to meet these goals than do lower-class males, whose goals are more success-oriented. Women also have less access than males to illegitimate means. Cloward and Ohlin, however, do not discuss female gang participation.

C. Continuity and Change

There is continuity and change in modern gangs (Short 1990, 1996, 1997; Spergel 1990). The gang has always been a variable form: Thrasher's dictum that "no two gangs are just alike" (1963, p. 36) remains valid today. Gangs in East Los Angeles (Moore 1991) look considerably different from gangs in Chicago (Spergel 1995) or St. Louis (Decker and Van Winkle 1996) or from Asian gangs in San Francisco (Joe 1992). Gangs still vary by ethnicity, gender, and age and by region, city size, and neighborhood. Gangs still begin as groups of youngsters who grow up together and get in trouble together (e.g., Hagedorn 1988). The juvenile gang still promotes delinquency in various ways, including petty crime, alcohol and drug use, and periodic violence. Studies in both the industrial and the postindustrial eras have found that no more than 10 percent of youth in most poor neighborhoods ever join gangs (Short 1997; but see Kobrin 1951). Gangs still experience changes over time in activities, structure, and extent of violence (see esp. Moore 1978, 1991; Short 1996). What we know about a gang at one time may become dated just a few months or even weeks later. Kids' lives are like that.

Gangs have been largely, but not wholly, tied up with the experience of ethnic groups trying to make it in America. The vast majority of today's gangs are African American, Latino, or Asian, just as gangs in the past were largely composed of European immigrants (Miller 1975; Curry, Ball, and Decker 1996). Ethnicity still strongly influences gang forms and behavior (Vigil and Yun 1996).

In many cities, gangs still occupy the same neighborhoods where gangs have always formed—only the ethnicity of the gangs has changed (Shaw and McKay 1942; Wilson and Sampson 1995). The social disorganization perspective finds powerful support when one looks at how gangs continue to form in the same poor urban areas. Lack of formal controls and family difficulties are still prime correlates of gang membership.

Postindustrial male gangs, like their industrial-era predecessors, are composed of young people in certain neighborhoods who come from a variety of troubled family backgrounds. There is little support in the gang literature for the notion that economic restructuring has led to the formation of gangs made up, as Yablonsky (1997) or Fleisher (1995) have claimed, of sociopaths. Ethnic gangs, including Native American gangs in Minneapolis and Samoan gangs in Las Vegas (Spergel 1990), continue to organize in ways consistent with ethnic and local cultural traditions.

The gang is still primarily a male phenomenon. But there appear to be more female gangs and more kinds of female gangs than ever before. Caution must be exercised here, however, since we do not know whether there are more female gangs or whether it is simply that more attention is being paid to them. Still, there is a strong consensus that there are fewer female than male gangs and that girl gangs have always been less violent than boy gangs (see Campbell 1993). For the male gang, aggression is still strongly tied to notions of masculinity, lack of controls, and status within the group.

Finally, the gang is still the focus of demonization and scapegoating. "Moral panics" and media scare stories about wild, dangerous youth have been a staple of American journalism for the last hundred years. These "moral panics" have always been closely tied to racial antagonisms (see Zatz 1987; Huff 1989; Jackson 1993).

II. Postindustrial Gangs and Gang Violence

There are important quantitative differences between industrial- and postindustrial-era gangs. Before considering possible qualitative changes, I examine evidence for the increase in the numbers and violence of male gangs, their expansion to small cities and towns, and probable increases in female gangs.

A. The Extent of America's Contemporary Gang Problem

One important change in modern gangs is that there are more of them. In the last decade, social scientists have undertaken numerous field studies in many different locales, documenting a wide variety of gangs in all sizes of cities. Efforts have been made to collect survey data estimating the numbers of gangs and the amount of gang crime. One study of city characteristics concluded that decline in manufacturing employment was significantly correlated with urban crime rates and gangs, suggesting links between gang patterns and economic restructuring (Jackson 1995).

What emerges is a picture of increasing and more violent gang activity almost everywhere: in large cities, small cities, and towns; among African Americans, Asians, Latinos, whites, and Native Americans; and among both women and men. Gang members appear to be being recruited at younger ages and to be leaving gangs at older ages (e.g., Klein 1995; Curry, Ball, and Decker 1996).

Estimates of the numbers of gangs, gang members, and gang crimes, however, are just that: estimates, mainly by law enforcement agencies. Much of what is labeled "gang violence" consists of fights between individuals that have little or nothing to do with the gang. Overall rises in homicide rates mask variations by neighborhood and even within gangs (Moore 1993). Curry, Ball, and Decker (1996) point out that the sources of error in law enforcement estimates include jurisdictional differences in definitions of gangs and gang crime, uneven keeping of data within jurisdictions, and the political nature of the gang problem. For example, in some jurisdictions, it is not politically acceptable to admit the existence of gangs (see Hagedorn 1988; Huff 1989; Klein 1995). As Miller (1975, p. 3) pointed out in discussing the limitations of his own surveys, "official" data on gangs "are frequently presented in such a way as to best serve the organizational interests of the particular agency rather than the interests of accuracy" (also see Klein 1971, pp. 15–19).

In the seventies, Miller found that 201 cities had gangs and that this number had increased to 468 cities by the 1980s (Miller 1975, 1982; see also Maxson 1996). Miller estimated there were 52,000 gang members in fifteen major cities in the 1970s, 43,000, or 80 percent, in New York, Chicago, and Los Angeles alone. He concluded that gangs were predominately a phenomenon of the largest cities (Miller 1982).

Curry, Ball, and Decker (1996, p. 35) capture what are probably large increases in gang activity across the United States since Miller's earlier surveys. Their survey (see table 1) found almost 300 cities with 16,000 gangs with more than half a million members. Curry (1995) elsewhere estimates that only about 5 percent of all gang members in the United States are female, or about 25,000 total active female gang members. Others (e.g., Moore 1991; Esbensen and Huizinga 1993) es-

TABLE 1

"Reasonable" Estimates of the National Gang Problem, 1993

Jurisdiction Size	No. of Gangs	No. of Members	No. of Crimes
Cities:			
Over 200,000	4,722	246,431	51,155
150,000–200,000	788	19,478	46,616
25,000–150,000	8,964	122,508	89,232
Less than 25,000	251	31,498	3,156
Selected counties	1,918	135,266	390,172
National total	16,643	555,181	580,331

SOURCE.—Taken from the National Institute of Justice 1994 Extended Survey. Adapted from Curry, Ball, and Decker (1996), p. 31.

NOTE.—The number of "gang crimes" in this table is included although estimates of gang crimes vary by the nature of the official definition, police coding practices, political and organizational interests of police and reporting agencies, among other factors. Even more so than estimates of gangs and gang members, estimates for the number of "gang crimes" are highly unreliable. These estimates of one crime per gang member, Klein (personal communication, 1997) argues, represent a substantial undercount.

timate that up to a third or half of all gang members in some cities are female.

While the number of gangs in some cities has fallen and some cities report the disappearance of gangs (Spergel 1990), the consensus is that nation-wide the number of male and female gangs is increasing, that gangs are forming in cities of all sizes, and that gangs are becoming more violent (see Moore 1997).

B. Violence and the Postindustrial Gang

Most researchers agree that gang violence has substantially increased. Miller found that gangs in the 1960s were becoming more mobile and using weapons more than ever before (also see Bloch and Niederhoffer 1958, pp. 183–85). Miller's chilling conclusion *in 1975* was that "the amount of lethal violence currently directed by youth gangs in major cities . . . is without precedent."

While there does not appear to be much disagreement over whether gang-related violence has increased, there are differences between law enforcement jurisdictions in how to define "gang-related" crime. Maxson and Klein have shown that if homicides with a "gang-related motive" are counted, there are only about half as many homicides than if homicides with "any" gang participation are counted. Thus homicide

TABLE 2

Cities with the Highest Levels of Gang Homicides, 1991

Cities	No. of Gang Homicides	City Population (1990)	No. of Gang Members	Date of Gang Emergence
Los Angeles	371	3,485,398	55,927	1922
Chicago	129	2,783,726	28,500	1920
Long Beach, Calif.	53	429,433	11,200	1970
Inglewood, Calif.	44	109,602	6,500	1961
Commerce, Calif.	40	12,135	9,000	1925
Cleveland	37	505,616	1,900	1987
San Bernardino, Calif.	37	164,146	1,550	1988
Kansas City, Mo.	35	435,146	420	1988
Compton, Calif.	30	90,454	3,000	1970
Fresno, Calif.	30	354,202	1,750	1988
Milwaukee	30	628,088	5,000	1976
Oakland, Calif.	30	372,242	2,500	1966

SOURCE.—Adapted from Maxson (1998).

NOTE.—The Commerce, Calif., gang member totals are unusually high since they represent gang members living in nearby areas.

rates in Chicago, where law enforcement counts only homicides for which the motive is to kill a rival gang member over gang-related issues, are not directly comparable to rates in Los Angeles, where any homicide in which a gang member participated counts as "gang related" (Maxson and Klein 1990, 1996).

But no matter how they are counted, gang homicides are increasing. In Chicago, gang-related homicides jumped five-fold from 1987 to 1994 (Block et al. 1996), and in Los Angeles they doubled (Maxson, 1998). It is hard to disagree with the assertion that the increases were "unprecedented " (Block et al. 1996). But increases in gang homicides were not evenly distributed across cities. Short (1997) reports that 44 percent of all homicides in Los Angeles and 32 percent of all Chicago homicides in 1994 were gang-related, but New York, for example, is absent from the list of cities with a significant number of gang homicides (see table 2). In surveys reported by Klein (1995), 60 percent, or 453, of the responding officials from 752 cities who reported a gang problem said there were no gang-related homicides, and more than 80 percent reported fewer than ten.

While researchers agree that gang violence has increased, there is much less agreement on why. Gang homicides, Klein's (1995) work instructs, typically differ from nongang homicides by taking place in the street, not at a residence; being more likely to be committed by un-identified assailants; being more likely to injure bystanders; and usually by involving cars and guns. But what about drugs? Is there a gang/drug nexus that can help explain recent increases in gang violence?

Blumstein (1993, 1995*b*) has argued that the rise of the cocaine trade in the mid to late 1980s, and a corresponding availability on the street of firearms, are linked with the rise in juvenile homicides. With the introduction of cocaine into drug markets, guns were needed for self-protection, and an "arms race" ensued. Once on the street, guns be-came an ongoing threat and increased the risk of violence. Fagan (1996) concurs, although he adds that gang drug-related violence may also be the result of the drug trade recruiting more individuals with a proclivity to violence (see also Fagan and Chin 1990). In the past, simi-lar, though smaller, increases in homicide rates have been attributed by researchers to narcotics activities (see Cook 1983, p. 71).

Some gang researchers, however, have questioned what appears to be commonsense connections among gangs, drugs, and violence. How-ell (1996, p. 26), for example, in a comprehensive review of the litera-ture, concludes that "there is little support for Blumstein's notion" of the link between cocaine sales and gang violence. Howell relies heavily on Chicago studies by Block and Block (1991, 1992, 1995). Using of-ficial data, these Chicago researchers found that drug-related motives accounted for only 3 percent of gang-related homicides in Chicago be-tween 1987 and 1990. Gang homicides, they found, were almost en-tirely related to assaultive behavior, gang rivalries, or reactions to sta-tus threats (1995, pp. 8–9). Violence varied over time, with different types of violence associated with different types of neighborhoods. But the Blocks found little evidence of drug involvement in gang homi-cides.

Klein (1995) also has strongly argued that the drug and gang worlds are related but often separate. In several studies of California police data, Klein and his associates concluded that the gang/drug/violence connection is "overstated" (Klein, Maxson, and Cunningham 1991; see also Fagan 1989). In an update of earlier findings, Maxson and Klein (1996, p. 18) say that "these findings do not support a strong connec-tion between gang drug sales and violence."

However, studies disputing the gang/drug/violence nexus may not be as conclusive as they appear. One of the main threads of Klein's argument (1995) has been that law enforcement officials have falsely claimed that street gangs dominated the drug trade, but he and his colleagues admit that gangs are deeply involved with drugs (e.g., Maxson 1995). What Maxson and Klein (1996) found is that, depending on how one defines "gang-related," in South Central Los Angeles, between 29 percent and 41 percent of all gang-related homicides had some drug involvement. This is a considerable percentage of homicides by gang members of all ages. Since older gang members are more likely to be in the drug economy, the percentage of violence related to drugs is probably even higher among older gang members.

The Blocks's conclusion that few Chicago gang homicides are drug-motivated relies on how "gang-motivated" and "drug-motivated" are distinguished. For example, two pages after a comprehensive report on gang violence in which Block et al. (1996, p. 18) claim that only forty-three of all Chicago gang homicides over thirty years were drug-motivated, they discuss a war over drug markets between the Black Gangsters and Disciples that claimed forty-five lives over seven years and another, more violent, episode in which the Black P. Stones attempted to claim new drug markets and sixty-one members died over just a few years. No matter how gang violence is technically defined, drug-related violence appears to be playing a large and perhaps predominant role in some modern gang rivalries.

There is other empirical support for a gang/drug/violence relationship. W. B. Sanders (1994, p. 52) argues from police data in San Diego that a reduction in gang violence directed toward non–gang members reflects reduced gang involvement in robbery as gang rock cocaine sales increased. Waldorf and Lauderback (1993) report that 21.4 percent of gang drug sellers they interviewed had been knifed, shot at, or beaten "because of drugs."

Our Milwaukee field data (Hagedorn, forthcoming) is consistent with Maxson and Klein, Sanders, and Waldorf. Using Goldstein's (1985) typology, we questioned ninety male gang members about the last three fights they had participated in, the last three times they were shot at, and the last three people they personally saw killed. These data are presented in table 3. Forty percent of all incidents of lethal violence witnessed by gang members were drug-related, and those who used drugs heavily were significantly more likely to have been shot at many times.

Police data like those Block and Block use suffer from several weaknesses. The Chicago definition of "gang-related" means that a Chicago homicide must be motivated by a gang dispute, which, by definition, minimizes and at times excludes a drug connection (see Maxson

TABLE 3

Percent of Gang Members Responding to Questions about Gang
Drug-Related Violence in Milwaukee

Type of Incident In Which Gang Member Was Involved	Occurred While Stealing to Get Drugs	Happened after the Drugs Were All Gone	Related to a Dope Deal Gone Bad
Last three fights gang member was in (N = 129)	4.70	12.00	6.00
	(11)	(28)	(6)
Last three times gang member was shot at (N = 115)	5.80	13.30	11.20
	(10)	(22)	(19)
Last three persons gang member has seen killed (N = 77)	19.60	18.80	23.20
	(19)	(13)	(23)

SOURCE.—Hagedorn (1998).
NOTE.—Subsample sizes are in parentheses.

and Klein 1990, 1996). It is unclear how beat police would code drug involvement in gang disputes—this is a problem at the micro level of how police code data. There may be reasons that some police in different cities might decide to label some homicides "gang-related" rather than "drug-related." Ryan et al. (1990) have shown how police have underestimated the drug connection in New York City homicides.

In our Milwaukee research, we found that gang members have reasons not to admit drug ties and might attribute violence to gang rivalries to police as a way to divert attention from their own participation in drug selling. Given other close observers' reports about the transformation of gang wars into drug wars in Chicago (Perkins 1987; Venkatesh 1996, 1997), Block and Blocks's estimates that only 3 percent of all gang homicides are drug-related based on police data are probably too low.

Rose, Maggiore, and Hanalon (1995), in a detailed study of Milwaukee homicides, concur with Blumstein's (1993) findings of a drug-homicide linkage. They found that while the number of white victims stayed the same between 1980 and 1990, African American victimization tripled. They also argue that the characteristics of homicide are changing among African Americans. By 1990, the number of stranger homicides surpassed the more traditional family- and friend-related homicides. Rose, Maggiore, and Hanalon attribute the increase in in-

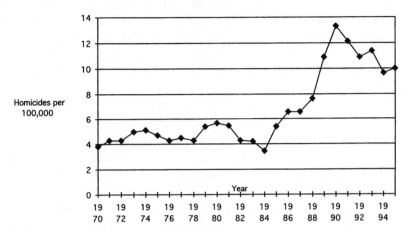

Homicides in Milwaukee

Homicides per
100,000

F[IG]. 1.—Homicides in Milwaukee, 1970–94. Source: Federal Bureau of Investigation (various years, 1971–95).

strumental "stranger" homicides in part to gangs and drugs. Males aged fifteen to twenty-four in Milwaukee have supplanted twenty-five to thirty-four-year-olds as the age group with the highest risk of becoming a homicide victim.

Other official data from Milwaukee show large increases in homicide rates of young African Americans in the late 1980s. These increases did *not* coincide with an upsurge in gang activity, which exploded in Milwaukee in the early 1980s. Instead, sharp increases in homicides coincided with a drop in the price of cocaine and a drug war in 1989 and 1990 between rival gangs for control of neighborhood drug markets (Hagedorn 1994*b*) (see fig. 1).

Rates of violence in aggregate do not appear to be rising across the country, and, seen from a colder, statistical perspective, the raw numbers of homicides are not very large. Miller (1996, p. 33) points out that only 1 percent of all "violent crimes" require a hospital stay and that homicides make up only .003 percent of all violent crimes (for more, see Donziger 1996). Even for gangs, homicides are a small percentage of gang arrests—only 1.5 percent in Chicago (Block et al. 1996). However, while homicide and victimization rates may have been relatively stable in recent years, the last ten years have seen major changes in the racial and age makeup of those participating in homicides and in the character of the homicide event itself. As Tonry (1995,

p. 68) points out, aggregate data often mask changes in specific locales. For example, in Milwaukee, homicide rates for African American males are twenty times higher than the Milwaukee Standard Metropolitan Statistical Area rate of eight per 100,000. Male gang violence is increasing, much of it appears to be related to the drug trade, and most of it takes place in poor neighborhoods of some, but not all, cities.

C. More Small Cities and Towns Have Gangs

The gang problem today is quite different than when Miller (1975) found that the vast majority of all gang members were from three cities. The *Economist* of May 25, 1996, carried an article about the spread of gangs to small U.S. towns and rural areas. An accompanying picture showed a barn in a rural area covered with gang graffiti. Klein (1995, p. 90) documents this change. He reports that gangs have been confirmed in more than 800 cities and towns, including 91 towns with populations of under 10,000. Many of these local gangs have adopted the names of gangs from Los Angeles and Chicago. This has led law enforcement and the media to conclude that there has been a kind of gang colonialism in which big-city gangs spread out to smaller cities in search of new markets for drugs.

This thesis receives some academic support. Skolnick, Blumenthal, and Correl (1993) conclude, on the basis of interviews with a few dozen prisoners and law enforcement officials, that California gang members frequently travel to set up new drug markets. They reject simplistic "Mafia" stereotypes of gangs that have evolved into sophisticated organized crime groups and "franchise" their operations (e.g., Knox et al. 1996). They also reject the "symbolic association" view of gang members migrating to new cities and setting up new gangs named after their old Los Angeles or Chicago gang because of the "panache" of the name. Rather, for Skolnick, Blumenthal, and Correl, horizontally organized gangs like those in southern California provide gang members with resources and facilitate individual initiatives that promote gang migration in order to establish lucrative new drug markets.

While this is plausible, Skolnick's (1990) typology of horizontally organized southern California gangs versus vertically organized northern California gangs has been dismissed by some California field researchers as inaccurate (Waldorf 1993; Waldorf and Lauderback 1993), and he has been criticized for generalizing from a questionable sample (Klein 1995; Hagedorn 1996).

Maxson, Woods, and Klein (1995) conducted surveys of law enforcement and other officials in cities across the country to determine the nature and extent of the problem of gang migration. Their findings were quite different from Skolnick's. They found that the major reason for gang migration was the movement of families seeking a better life. In other words, as economic restructuring makes good jobs in large cities scarcer and life harder, people move. Families with youngsters in gangs often try to find a better, gang-free environment for their kids. My Milwaukee research (Hagedorn 1988) described in detail how young people formed homegrown gangs that took Chicago names. While drug dealers certainly move between cities—Klein's study (1995) reports that about a third of all gang members do so for drug-related reasons—Klein's overall conclusion is that the spread of gangs is more strongly related to the economic difficulties of families.

However, both the spread of gangs and the popularity of gang names such as the Crips, Bloods, Vice Lords, Latin Kings, and Black Gangster Disciples cannot be explained in terms only of the movement of families or drug markets. A process of cultural diffusion is also taking place that has strongly influenced gang development across the United States. Short (1996) points out that the popularization of youth culture by the media glamorizes youth-oriented consumer products and seduces less affluent youth. The model for teenage rebellion today is a glamorized image of the big-city gang, and the big-city drug-dealing gang at that. Music videos, VCRs, and cable TV provide youth more exposure to diverse fashions, language, music, and styles of living than ever before. Klein (1995) points to the international ramifications of this phenomenon, especially when movies are America's leading export (Thurow 1997).

In the 1950s, Marlon Brando and the movie *The Wild One* (1954) helped stylize the rebellion of white youth in cities of all sizes, giving their acting-out a role model, a style of clothes, and a way to talk. Similarly, movies such as *Scarface* (1983), *Colors* (1988), and *New Jack City* (1991), and the popularity of "gangsta rap" have helped shape the form, dress, and speech of teenage rebellion in cities and towns across the United States (Klein 1995). This contemporary cultural barrage must have been more effective in spreading notions about gang culture to young people than have personal contact with the few thousand gang members who migrated to a few hundred cities across the United States.

However, just as migrating gang members are not the prime "cause" of small-town gang emergence, neither is cultural diffusion. Problems within particular communities must be examined to explain why youth rebel and become alienated (Klein 1995). Given the greater availability of jobs in exurbia, small-town gangs are less likely to become institutionalized than their big-city counterparts. For one thing, many alienated youths move to bigger cities as they become adults and do not stay around to develop age-integrated small-town gang structures. No studies have found that small-town gang members remain involved with their gangs as adults. Maintaining a drug sales-ring is difficult in small towns, where everyone knows everyone else, including the neighborhood Officer Friendly. While small-town youth gangs are likely sporadically to deal drugs, as do their big-city counterparts, it is unlikely they will be as consistently violent or as persistent.

The central problem of gang migration appears to be the alienation of local youth, combined with the displacement of the families of gang members by economic restructuring and cultural diffusion.

D. More Female Gangs

Curry, Ball, and Decker (1996) give a low estimate that less than 5 percent (about 25,000) of all gang members are female. Their data are based on estimates by police, who often pay little attention to female gangs. While there are no reliable national estimates, researchers in some cities consistently have found that female gangs make up between a third and half of all gang members (e.g., Moore 1991; Bjerregaard and Smith 1995). Police estimates may systematically underestimate the number of female gangs.

Recent studies have documented a wide variety of female gangs (Moore 1991; Taylor 1993; Joe and Chesney-Lind 1995; Hagedorn and Devitt, forthcoming), giving credence to Klein's observation: "Another thing to note about the girl gangs, just as with the boys, is that they came in a wide variety of sizes, structures, age ranges, and levels of criminal involvement. The best generalization is not that they had a particular character but that they showed considerable variation on just about all dimensions of interest" (1995, pp. 65–66).

However, almost all available data on female gangs in the industrial era come from male researchers or from studies in which the female gangs were seen as auxiliaries of male gangs. This may have been true, but it also may have been an artifact of male bias, as Campbell (1990) suggested. Taylor (1993), for example, argued that, in Detroit, gang women were becoming more independent, while Moore (1991) suggested the opposite for some cliques of girls in East Los Angeles gangs. At the very least, gang researchers should reconsider their practice of defining female gangs solely, following Miller (1975; see also Spergel 1990), by whether or not they are male gang auxiliaries. Adolescent girl gangs vary by ethnicity, structure, type of criminal activities, drug use, and age, as well as type of relationship to a male gang (Brotherton 1996; Hagedorn and Devitt, forthcoming). But while there is no way to know for certain whether the numbers or kinds of female gangs have increased, has the female gang changed since the industrial era?

There are two different views: the "liberation hypothesis" and the "social-injury hypothesis" (Curry 1995). For supporters of the liberation hypothesis, the changing gender roles that accompany woman's entrance into the labor market have made women more like men (Adler 1975) and more likely to form gangs, commit crime, and act independently. Taylor (1993, p. 48) writes emphatically about women involved with the sales of drugs, claiming "the gang generally does not differentiate between the sexes." Women become liberated by doing whatever a man can do, including selling drugs (see also Lauderback, Hansen, and Waldorf 1992; Fagan 1993).

Supporters of the social-injury hypothesis claim the opposite effect of economic and social changes on gangs (Joe and Chesney-Lind 1995). For them, the modern gang harms women more than it does men. Moore and Mata (1981) and Moore (1991) have shown how East Los Angeles Mexican American gang girls come from more troubled families than do gang boys and are stigmatized more in later life. The reasons for female gang involvement may differ from those for males. Female drug use and gang involvement may also have more lasting consequences (Moore and Devitt 1989). Some, but not all, gang women are sexually victimized by male gang members (Hagedorn and Devitt, forthcoming).

The twilight days of the industrial era saw the entrance of women into the workforce in large numbers. However, the beginning of the postindustrial era saw job opportunities for poor women that were insufficient to support a family, particularly as women increasingly became the sole support for their children. With cutbacks in welfare and declining prospects for themselves and their families, more women than ever before turned to drug use (Maher and Curtis 1991) and were exploited in the crack economy (Fagan 1993; Bourgois 1995). The misogynist nature of most street-level drug selling may be one factor limiting women's involvement in the drug economy (Hagedorn 1998*a*, Moore and Hagedorn, forthcoming).

Few studies have looked at what happens to gang girls as they leave adolescence; that has been a special focus of our Milwaukee work (Hagedorn and Devitt, forthcoming; Moore and Hagedorn 1996). More than 98 percent of 176 women who were the founding members of six Milwaukee female gangs had left the gangs by the end of their teens, as opposed to less than 25 percent of the men in male gangs. The reasons that women left the gangs varied: most said they grew out of the gang, others that their parents left the gang neighborhood, ending their gang membership. One other reason stuck out. Two-thirds of the women became teen mothers and more than 90 percent were mothers before their mid-twenties. In all cases these gang women felt themselves mainly responsible for the children. While much has changed for women, their child-rearing responsibilities have not. Fathers may risk imprisonment by drug selling, but most mothers feel much more constrained and limit both their gang membership and participation in risky illegal ventures (Hagedorn 1998*a*).

One other factor seems to have stayed the same through the decades: women are less violent than men. There is a considerable literature on "difference" feminism (e.g., Gilligan 1982; Johnson 1988; Lorber 1994) that argues that male and female conceptions of gender roles have qualitative differences that are not easily changed by economics. Violence by women does not appear to be increasing significantly (Steffensmeier and Steffensmeier 1980; Nagel and Hagan 1983; Chesney-Lind and Sheldon 1992), though one Chicago study found that gang violence against gang women had increased in the previous decade (Block et al. 1996).

Ann Campbell (1993) argues that women use violence more expressively than men, who are more instrumental about the use of violence to attain various ends, including the control of women (see also Morash 1986). In our Milwaukee study, most female gang members "loved to fight" and many claimed they fought as teenagers even more than did gang boys. But gang girls fought differently than the boys. For one thing, they possessed significantly fewer weapons and seldom used guns in battle. Forty percent never used weapons in a fight, and 80 percent used weapons no more than once. The adult gang women were exposed to significantly less gunfire over the course of their lives

TABLE 4

Lifetime Exposure To Violence, by Gender of Gang Members

	Total Number of Times Gang Member Was Shot At	Mean per Gang Member	Total Number of People Gang Member Has Seen Killed	Mean per Gang Member
Male gang members (N = 68)	617	9.1	143	2.1
Female gang members (N = 68)	23	.33	21	.31

Source.—Hagedorn (1998).
Note.—Median Age of gang members: 28.

than similarly aged gang men and had personally witnessed many fewer homicides (see table 4).

Postindustrial gangs appear to differ from their industrial-era counterparts quantitatively: there are more male gangs, these male gangs are more violent, gangs are in more cities of different sizes than ever before, and there are probably more female gangs. Why have these significant changes occurred?

III. Possible Explanations for Changes in Gangs and Gang Violence

Some findings about the extent of drug involvement in gang violence are not in dispute. For example, it is clear that homicides in African American communities across the country jumped at the same time that large numbers of young males, including gang members, began selling cocaine and establishing new drug markets. This participation of jobless males in a violent drug economy occurred while America restructured well-paying jobs away from the central city (Kasarda 1985; Wilson 1987; Hagedorn 1994b). Was this a coincidence or a spurious correlation? I believe five factors help explain the changes in the nature and prevalence of gang-related violence in the postindustrial era.

A. The Informal Economy

The most important factor influencing increases in violence is changes in the functions of gangs. The "disappearance of work" (Wilson 1996) has as a corollary an increase in the importance of informal work in poor communities (Castells and Portes 1989). The belief that economic prosperity would eventually allow African Americans, Latinos, and other minorities to leave the ghettoes behind proved invalid (Bernard 1970). For many young minority males, "getting paid" (Sullivan 1989) or "making your money" now means informal or illegal work, especially the potentially lucrative and dangerous sale of drugs. The story of male gang involvement with drug sales at the end of the 1980s has been repeated in studies in Detroit (Taylor 1989), San Francisco (Waldorf 1993), Chicago (Padilla 1992; Venkatesh 1996, 1997), New York (Fagan 1989), Los Angeles (Vigil 1988), and St. Louis (Decker and Van Winkle 1996).

The economic functions of gangs were becoming apparent in our first Milwaukee interviews (Hagedorn 1988). "Gangs are all about survival now," one twenty-year-old male gang leader told me. This statement contains two salient points.

First, "survival" meant that this gang was all about "hustling," trying to make money any way they could, rather than mainly fighting. Most of the young men we interviewed in 1986 were unemployed and trying to figure out how to survive, on their own or with the help of their friends. Only a few had sold or used cocaine. By 1991, three-quarters of the 236 founding members of fourteen male Milwaukee gangs were reported as having been involved with the sale of cocaine (Hagedorn 1998a). This male African American gang member summarized the experience of most Milwaukee gang members as they left their teenage years: "I got out of high school and I didn't have a diploma, wasn't no jobs, wasn't no source of income, no nothing. That's basically the easy way for a black young man to be—selling some dope—you can get yourself some money real quick, you really don't have nothing to worry about, nothing but the feds. You know everybody in your neighborhood. Yeah, that's pretty safe just as long as you don't start smoking it yourself."

Second, it should be emphasized that this was a young adult speaking, not a teenager. Urban gang members today remain in the gang longer than before (Moore 1991; Curry, Ball, and Decker 1996). The thesis of *People and Folks* (Hagedorn 1988) was that economic restructuring had altered the maturing-out cycle for male gang members. Rather than getting a job, getting married, and settling down, the lack of formal work kept young adults hanging out on street corners trying to figure out, individually or collectively, how to make a buck.

TABLE 5

"Dope House" Survey in Milwaukee, 1993

Neighborhood	Blocks Surveyed	Number of Drug Houses	All Places Where Cocaine Was Sold	Percent of Drug Selling Places Run by Gangs
Hustletown	30	16	23	61
Posse Park	36	15	19	74
La Parcela	50	30	43	49
Totals	116	61	85	58

SOURCE.—Hagedorn (1998).

While some gang members have always dealt drugs, the extent of gang drug sales far exceeds the penny-ante dealing of the past. Block et al. (1996) report that more than 50 percent of all arrests of African American gang members in Chicago over the seven years previous to their study had been on drug charges, confirming a strong gang/drug nexus.

In 1993 in Milwaukee, we carefully surveyed three neighborhoods where local gangs had developed and found that a drug-dealing locale could be located on every other block (see table 5). While most drug dealing in cities is not by gang members, drug dealing is dominated by the gangs in neighborhoods with long-standing youth gangs like those we studied. We estimated that each of our Milwaukee drug-selling locales employed an average of about seven persons. This meant that the cocaine economy in these three neighborhoods over the course of a year employed at least 600 people, most of them young male gang members, earning over $17 million dollars annually. The drug economy exerts a powerful economic effect on these job-poor communities. In the early 1990s in Milwaukee, drug selling employed more young African American males than did any other sector of the economy (Hagedorn 1998a; for a comparison with the numbers game in the industrial era, see Drake and Cayton [1970]).

How much money do gang members make selling drugs? Studies of drug dealing generally find that, as in most businesses, only a very few people ever get rich. MacCoun and Reuter (1992) found that the typical Washington, D.C., small dealer made about $300 per month, and the typical big dealer $3,700 monthly, with an average of about $1,300 of drug income per month. These figures are very close to our findings in Milwaukee (Hagedorn 1994*b*) when we charted the licit and illicit employment history of ninety male gang members over three years.

While those who sold drugs averaged about $2,400 per month, they made less than $700 in legitimate jobs. However, even though they could earn four times as much by dealing, most of these young adult gang drug dealers worked more months in low-wage legitimate jobs than they did selling drugs. The reach of conventional morality, the desire to settle down with a family, and fear of violence and prison proved, over the long haul, more powerful for most gang members than did the prospect of fast money.

A minority of gang members—we called them "new jacks"—had given up any hope of settling down and became recklessly committed to the drug economy, at least for a time. But for most gang members, the age-crime curve held, and adult gang members looked for steady "legit" jobs by the end of their twenties. Participation in the postindustrial gang has been extended from the juvenile to the young adult years, but it sharply tails off by the time most gang members turn thirty.

If gangs now perform economic functions, how organized are they? Has the street gang become a new form of organized crime? Spergel (1990, p. 197) claims that the gang structure "dissolves under the impact of drug use and selling." Gang rivalries, Spergel found, are not functional for drug sales and other criminal enterprises. In the same vein, Klein (1995) distinguishes between street gangs and drug gangs, in order to dispel simplistic associations between gangs and drugs. Klein reiterates that not all gangs sell drugs and that most people who sell drugs are not in gangs. There are undoubtedly drug gangs whose members are adults with no previous adolescent ties.

However, in today's jobless conditions for disadvantaged minority males, some researchers have found that "drug gangs" are routinely formed by young adults who transform their adolescent gang ties into various kinds of economic partnerships. For example, Taylor charts the development of Detroit gangs from "scavenger" gangs to "corporate" gangs (1989). Padilla (1992) studied one gang that transformed itself into a drug-selling unit. But are these gangs "organized crime"?

That is what some law enforcement agencies believe (Chicago Crime Commission 1995), but on the basis of sparse and unreliable research evidence (e.g., Knox et al. 1996). While some gangs have undoubtedly developed structures that enable them to sell drugs more effectively, it might be prudent to look at the business literature to investigate what kind of organization is best suited for selling a product like illegal drugs. One strand of organizational theory, contingency theory (e.g., Lawrence and Lorsch 1969), predicts that a highly volatile and unpredictable business like drug sales would tend to be decentralized and responsive to fluctuating customer demand and an uncertain business climate. Tightly centralized bureaucratic structures, like a police department or the army, may not be effective in selling drugs, especially in an unpredictable and rapidly changing local market (Hagedorn 1994*a*).

Most researchers (e.g., Moore 1991; Waldorf 1993; Decker and Van Winkle 1996) find that most gang drug sales tend to be individual enterprises, with loosely coupled links to central distribution organizations, consistent with contingency theory (see also Weick 1976). Our Milwaukee research found that gang drug-selling organizations varied with the type of market, among other factors. Where markets attracted whites and more affluent customers, organization tended to be more structured. When customers were poor and mainly from the local neighborhoods, gang organization disintegrated, replaced by individual "dog-eat-dog" competition. There is still more media speculation than research on the structure of drug selling by gangs in big cities, like the Black Gangster Disciples, Crips, Bloods, or Latin Kings.

But to be skeptical of a centralized gang drug conspiracy or to discover that drugs make few people rich does not contradict the emergence of sustained economic functions for some gangs. These economic functions, while dangerous, have nonetheless been attractive for many uneducated young male gang members, trying to figure out how to survive in a postindustrial world.

Gang-related economic activity has also redefined what young kids expect the gang to do for them.[2] Young adult gang members, trying to make their money, not only use juveniles in illegal ventures but are ever-present role models in age-integrated gangs, reminiscent of Cloward and Ohlin's (1960) criminal subcultures. They transmit a body of knowledge about gangs and drug dealing from one generation to the next (Shaw and McKay 1942). The lesson that the gang "is all about survival now" is not lost on today's youths, with unpredictable future consequences (see esp. Moore 1991).

The widespread involvement of some, but not all gangs, in drug

[2] For female gang members, these added functions of the gang have less meaning, as most gang girls adopt the traditional role of mother rather than a life of hustling (Moore and Hagedorn 1996; Hagedorn and Devitt, forthcoming).

dealing means an increase in possible sources of violence. But does that necessarily mean that the incidence of gang violence will increase?

B. *Violence as Regulation of the Drug Economy*

Violence as regulation of the drug business is, in part, a function of the nature of illicit markets. Product purity, customer safeguards, unfair business practices, and monopolies are not regulated by public agencies (Reinarman and Levine 1990). Drug selling is a private matter between participants, with enforcement of contracts a matter of raw private power. Violence in the drug business can be conceptualized as social control and self-help in an area of commerce that the state has decided not to regulate as it does other business (Black 1983). The drug game has been described by the New York City Police Department as "capitalism gone mad" (Fagan and Chin 1990).

This lack of state involvement with a multibillion dollar business has severe consequences. Most studies agree with Goldstein (1985) that only a small portion of lethal drug-related violence is "economic-compulsive" (stealing to pay for drugs) or "psychopharmacological" (caused by drug reactions). Our Milwaukee gang members reported that some violent reactions to crack cocaine were caused by lack of experience with the drug, and psychopharmacological reactions may have become more under control over time, helping explain more recent reductions in homicide rates.

Lethal drug violence, however, is mainly "systemic," which means it is tied to the unregulated nature of the drug sales transaction. Some studies suggest that more structured cocaine-selling operations tend to be more likely to use violence to control and intimidate rivals, employees, and customers (Taylor 1989; Fagan and Chin 1990). Hamid and Curtis (1996) describe a New York enforcer who went around the neighborhood with a baseball bat inscribed with the names of his intended victims. Once they had been beaten, their names were scratched out. Violence is also a handy way to intimidate addicts, who will sometimes threaten to go to the police unless a dealer provides more or cheaper dope. Employees can also be kept in line by the fear of violence (Williams 1989; Bourgois 1995).

Systemic drug violence, however, is not a constant but a variable. Violence as regulation should increase when markets are unstable and various actors are fighting for control and decrease when the market stabilizes. Our Milwaukee research illustrates how a sharp increase in violence was a characteristic of the early years of establishing cocaine markets between gangs.

In the beginning days of the expansion of cocaine markets, sales in Milwaukee's African American communities were largely controlled by individual dealers and neighborhood gangs. But in the late 1980s, the new markets were disturbed by a lethal drug war. The "Citywide Drug Gang" attempted to dominate drug markets throughout the community. They used violence and terror to set up drug operations everywhere. One leader described it this way: "Any neighborhood was ours. [We] just move in that neighborhood and let everybody know we here."

Violence swept the city as police and rival gangs alike traded fire with the Citywide Drug Gang. Unlike New York, where monopolistic drug organizations setting up "drug supermarkets" succeeded in dominating local markets (Hamid and Curtis 1996), in Milwaukee the Citywide Drug Gang failed; its leaders were imprisoned or killed. The consequence of Milwaukee's gang drug wars was that Milwaukee's cocaine markets were left fragmented, neighborhood-based, and not controlled by any one force and homicide rates did not significantly decline.

Fagan and Chin (1990) argue that much of the increase in violence due to drug dealing is spurious since the drug economy recruits people who already have a proclivity for violence. Such people are indispensable to a smooth-running illicit operation, and their incapacitation by incarceration helps explain variations in homicide rates. Guns are ever present in drug houses, and a substantial gun market exists to keep drug dealers armed. Our interviews show that a customer could always barter for drugs by bringing in guns. Slaby and Roedell (1982, p. 37) argue that the presence of weapons in an environment is a "cue" that acts to incite aggressiveness. This "cue" can result from contact with other armed drug dealers, armed customers, or police.

Law enforcement policies also may influence rates of violence. While incarceration removes violent individuals from the streets, it typically leaves the volume of drug trafficking untouched. Clear (1996) has attributed this to "replacement effects." Arrest and incarceration of a gang member creates an opening in "sales," and new gang members who might otherwise not have sold drugs replace him. In this way, Clear argues, policies of increased incarceration may have the unintended effect of recruiting more people into drug dealing and into related acts of violence. Aggressive police strategies, like those of New York's TNT or gang squads in Milwaukee or elsewhere, are hated by gang members and residents alike for their brutality and corruption, and they increase alienation (Hamid and Curtis 1996). When such tactics help stabilize drug markets, they may reduce violence. However, when they destabilize local markets, by removing a drug dealer and opening up his territory to others, they may increase violence.

In Cloward and Ohlin's (1960) typology, age integration of gangs acted to restrain violence since reckless juvenile violence was "bad for business." Control of more reckless juveniles by adults may indeed tend to stabilize drug markets over time and reduce violence. The uneven trend toward stabilization of drug markets may account for recent declines in the rates of violence in some cities (Goldstein and Hagedorn 1997). Where cocaine markets are dominated by a feared central player, as in some areas of New York, or "cooled out" by agreements to keep the peace between gangs, as in some Milwaukee and Chicago neighborhoods, drug markets may stabilize and violence may be reduced. Gang drug sellers may also reduce violence in response to community norms (Venkatesh 1997; Hagedorn 1998a).

Overall, however, the age integration of postindustrial gangs, combined with a profusion of firearms, and the involvement by so many different gangs and other dealers in the drug economy, has likely normalized the use of instrumental violence in gang drug selling.

C. Guns, Status Threats, and Masculinity

The third factor is interactions among guns, status threats, and masculinity. In 1975 Miller was concerned about an increase in gun-related violence (see also Cook 1983). Since the 1970s, firearms have greatly proliferated. While in 1968 there were about 80 million guns in the United States, by 1978 there were about 120 million, and by 1990 there were 200 million guns (Reiss and Roth 1993) including 50 million handguns (Prothrow-Stith with Weisman 1991). One in every three firearms is used at some time in the commission of a crime. The United States has more federally licensed guns shops than public high schools. Since 1990, 60,000 people have been killed by handguns, more than the number of Americans killed in the Vietnam War (B. Sanders 1994; see also Cook and Laub, in this volume).

Prevalence of firearms alone does not by itself correlate to violence. Switzerland has a homicide rate only about one-tenth of the U.S. rate, even though it requires all its adult citizens to own firearms. Messner and Rosenfeld (1994) point out that the U.S. nonfirearm homicide rate is higher than the overall homicide rate of every other industrialized country. They argue that high levels of American homicide are related to a culture that promotes means over ends and sets goals of money and success before people who have no legitimate means to obtain them.

Have gangs shared in this proliferation of firearms? From Miller's 1975 study to Sheley and Wright's (1995) research with students, most surveys have demonstrated that gang members are more likely to possess handguns and to use them than are non–gang members. The consequences are well demonstrated by Decker and Van Winkle (1996). Out of 101 gang members they interviewed, eleven were dead a few years later. While this may reflect sample selectivity, it is nonetheless a chilling finding. Our research in Milwaukee found that 6 percent of 234 gang members had died by their late twenties, nearly all by homicide (Hagedorn 1998a).

Our Milwaukee research has also confirmed the gun/gang link. In 1985–86 interviews, I was most surprised by answers to the question "What kind of gun do you possess?" The first respondent I interviewed said a ".22." I began to go on to the next question and he interrupted and said, "And a sawed off and a .38." I was ready to dismiss this answer as teen bragging, but I got similar responses from my next several interviews. Most of the teenage Milwaukee gang members I interviewed in the mid-1980s had access to multiple firearms. In 1991 follow-up interviews, male gang members reported access to even more firearms, most citing the need for self-protection in selling drugs.

The large number of guns in the hands of gang members increases lethal violence not only in connection with the drug economy. Both industrial era and postindustrial gangs engage in much expressive violence. Today, as in the past, gang members fight for honor, prestige, ambition, fear, frustration, and status (Sanchez-Jankowski 1991). Violence is also firmly rooted in volatile situations, such as routine and random confrontations between rival gangs (W. B. Sanders 1994; Decker and Van Winkle 1996).

Having a handgun, or potentially having one, changes the situation, sometimes transforming a harmless fistfight into a homicide. Most firearms, Sheley and Wright (1995, p. 262) confirm, are fired with no intention to kill. Block and Block (1995) call these kinds of events "sibling offenses" since they begin as nonlethal fights and escalate into homicides. Gang violence, they argue, often follows this kind of escalating pattern of hostile events, ending in lethal shootings. The presence of a gun in a violent incident has been shown to increase the probability of serious harm and death (Cook 1983).

Consider again the scenarios of industrial-era teenage–gang violence described by Miller. Gang wars were typically averted by talk. Gang members were more likely to blow off steam and look for a way out of situations while preserving their honor and status. But the potential possession of a handgun by the enemy changes this equation (Blumstein 1993; Hamid and Curtis 1996). Our respondents in Milwaukee repeated the point again and again that today on the streets one has to assume the other guy has a gun. This leads to situations, especially in certain locations (Kennedy and Baron 1997), which might have been defused in the past, that quickly and unintendedly turn deadly.

Lethal violence is primarily a problem of young men. Our Milwaukee data suggest that the nature of violence for men and for women differs. While gang women told us they fought as teenagers mainly for turf, honor, and the thrill of fighting, they did not see violence as power or domination (Campbell 1993; Hagedorn and Devitt, forthcoming). But for men, violence means power and power today means guns. Ro (1996, p. 7), in a series of essays on rap music, points out that for men on the street, gangsta rap "equated guns with masculinity."

Gang men define their masculinity in different ways. Ethnographic data suggests that how they define their masculinity influences the extent and nature of their violence. Horowitz (1983) looked at differences in how gang members construct their "reps" to avoid or provoke violence, in a manner consistent with Short and Strodtbeck's (1965) discussion of "aleatory" gang violence. My research typed gang "masculinities" (see Messerschmidt 1986, 1993; Connell 1995) into "tough guys," "reluctant warriors," and "new jacks" (Hagedorn, forthcoming) and looked at variations in the use of violence in various situations, particularly against women (Hagedorn 1998c).

What these and other empirical studies (e.g., Majors and Billson 1992) demonstrate is that not all gang men construct their masculinity in the same way and that not all constructions of masculinity lead to violence in all circumstances. But what all types of male gang violence appear to have in common, both today and yesterday, are aggressive notions of masculinity. When aggressive notions of masculinity are combined with a jobless life hanging out on a corner or in a bar, alco-

hol or drug use, the dangers of selling drugs, and possession of firearms, increased violence is a predictable consequence.

D. Prison Contributes toward Institutionalizing Gangs

A fourth change influencing rates of violence is the expanded influence of prison. Since the end of the 1960s, America has been waging
a war on crime and, more recently, on drugs. The result has been a
fivefold increase in the federal and state prison population over the
past twenty years while crime rates have not declined but risen by a
quarter. The end of this century finds the United States in a new Jack-
sonian era, with states cutting social benefits while building more and
more prisons. The United States now has more people incarcerated
per 100,000 population than any other industrialized country in the
world (Mauer and Huling 1995).

This increased reliance on incarceration may be a result of economic
restructuring. What does a country do with a surplus population of
"social dynamite" or "social junk" (Spitzer 1975) who are superfluous
to a new education-based economy (see Thurow 1997)? Drug dealers,
gang members, immigrants, and welfare recipients may be the most
recent "folk devils" in U.S. domestic policy (Cohen 1972).

Gang suppression strategies and simplistic notions that America's
gang problem can be jailed away have been sharply criticized by many
criminologists (e.g., Klein 1995; Spergel 1995). Still, these social scientists have had little apparent effect on our nation's bipartisan policy of
incarceration. With the war on drugs continuing, and with increased
gang involvement in the drug economy, more and more gang members
are likely to spend more time behind bars.

There have been several unintended effects of this strategy for
gangs. First, there has been a vast increase in the number of prison
gangs (Camp and Camp 1985), though there is little social science research on male prison gangs. There do not appear to be many female
prison gangs. Male prison gangs have become a principal form of inmate organization in many prisons and prison gang members are more
likely to be more violent than nongang inmates (Ralph et al. 1996).
The ranks of prison gangs have grown as they recruit non–gang members and as more gang members are incarcerated. Gangs have also
come to dominate underground drug markets in prisons, increasing
both corruption and violence.

Second, the poor communities that typically spawn gangs are disproportionately affected by increases in incarceration (Moore 1996). For example in New York, 80 percent of all Riker's Island inmates came from seven (admittedly large) communities in the city (Fulbright 1996). More studies need to detail the extent to which released convicts return to a comparatively few neighborhoods. The concentration of gang members who have been to prison and, once released, confront more limited licit economic opportunities may indicate further troubles for these already beleaguered neighborhoods.

Our Milwaukee research indicates that those men and women who return to the old neighborhood as adults are especially likely to return to drug use and sales. By their midtwenties, three-quarters of all Milwaukee male gang members and nearly half of all female gang members had been incarcerated for some period of time. Those who had spent time in prison were more likely to be heavy drug users and less likely to be working a legitimate job (Hagedorn 1998*a*).

Third, prison gang members, back on the streets, may remain in their prison gang, in opposition to their prior neighborhood gang, prompting more violence. While many inmates return to old peer relationships, there has been evidence for some time that prison gangs and their leaders may spread their influence back on the streets (e.g., Jacobs 1974). The fact that prison gang experience places more status on violence (Moore 1978) and that drug markets are now plentiful within prisons (Ralph et al. 1996) causes turbulence and a shake-up in the inmate culture (Hunt et al. 1993). In some cities, released members of prison gangs, rather than street gangs, have been seen as dominating community drug markets (Moore 1996; Valdez, personal communication, 1996).

Finally, long prison sentences for minority drug offenses have fanned racial antagonisms. In Milwaukee, 80 percent of those sent to prison for dealing crack cocaine possessed less than five grams, or the weight of a nickel. Those doing time are overwhelmingly small-time dealers selling to survive, not drug suppliers (Mauer and Huling 1995). And 80 percent of those sent to prison for cocaine offenses are members of minority groups, even though National Institute of Drug Abuse surveys show that 80 percent of cocaine users are white. This builds and increases long-standing racial hostilities while reducing, for some groups, the stigma of prison (Clear 1996). For deterrence to be effective, Nagin (1998) points out, prison needs to be stigmatizing (see also Braithwaite 1989). Prison may not have a stigmatizing effect in communities where a majority of men have served time.

The effects of prisons on gangs are just beginning to be felt. It is an important area for further research, for males and females. What we can reliably say is that extensive prison experiences of male gang members are likely to increase the influence of gangs in prison and correspondingly increase the influence of some prison gangs on poor neighborhoods. This likely will contribute to the demise of those neighborhoods by concentrating large numbers of discouraged ex-con job seekers in them. At the same time, prison is unlikely to reduce gang drug selling and may help institutionalize more violent, drug dealing, postindustrial gangs.

E. The Mass Media, American Culture, and Anomie

Finally, increases in gang violence may be related to cultural factors. As legal work disappeared in central cities, the promise of fast money from the dope game was an almost irresistible lure for disadvantaged gang members. As poor young men, gang members had dollar signs in their eyes. Consider these 1991 exchanges with Latino and African American Milwaukee gang members:

> Q: "Why did you start selling dope?"
> A: "Shit, fast money man. Don't you want a big car too? Don't you want cash? Don't you want a house on Lake Drive?" (Latino gang member)
> A: "Why? For the money. For the profits, you know, make money, have everything that I can get—'cause the more I got the more I want, know what I'm saying?" (African American gang member)

In America, wanting more material goods is not a deviant goal but the product of heavy advertising in a consumer culture (Nightengale 1993; see also Leach 1993). For gang members and other poor youth, the pursuit of money and success by innovative, illegal means is a close fit with both Durkheim's (1951) and Merton's (1938) concepts of anomie (see Hagedorn 1998b). If the pursuit of money is an essential characteristic of the American Dream, the modal answer to the question "Why did you start selling dope?" was something like this: "My main reason was for the money. I'm in love with the money" (Transcript of interview with male African American Milwaukee gang member, 1991).

Many studies have investigated the links among violence, gangs, criminality, "social isolation," and other structural variables (Wilson

1987, 1996). However, fewer studies have examined the effects of mainstream cultural values on gang members and other poor youth. Gang members grow up in homes like most others in their neighborhood. The TV set is always on, showcasing media stars like Michael Jordan shilling for expensive Nike shoes. Young gang members' daily lives are not only often spent learning from an unemployed older brother but also spent being constantly tantalized by television's showcasing the lives of the rich and famous and seeing movie stars flaunt their flashy jewelry and fashionable clothes. Television, movies, and popular songs portray women as little more than sexual objects. One message from the mass media comes across loud and clear: the best thing in life is to have plenty of money and foxy women. Reflecting these values, the group N.W.A. rapped: "Life ain't nothin' but bitches and money" and rapper Snoop Doggy Dogg told his listeners to "keep your mind on your money and your money on your mind."

There is a vast literature on the effects of TV on violence, with the opponents in the debate finding strong causal effects (e.g., Eron 1982; Friedrich-Cofer and Huston 1986; Huesmann and Eron 1986) or only mild effects (Freedman 1986). The broader point, however, is that violence is learned not only from "role models" on the street corner or in the home, as in classical differential association theory (Sutherland 1934), but also from the media. According to a cross-national investigation of the effect of television, 81 percent of all U.S. TV shows contained violence, at an average of 5.2 violent acts per hour—a far greater rate and extent than in any other country (Huesmann and Eron 1986, p. 46). The typical teenager watches twenty-one hours per week of TV and spends five minutes alone with his or her father and twenty minutes alone with his or her mother. The economist Lester Thurow (1997, p. 82) sums it up bleakly: "Human culture and human values are for the first time being shaped by a profit-maximizing electronic media."

Television dehumanizes "enemies" for young children in cartoon programming and paints a world of good and evil, with American capitalism representing the good and foreigners representing evil (Hesse and Mack 1991). In the early 1980s, women made up only one in three of the 300 or so regular characters people saw each week: forty-one of those 300 were law enforcement officers and twenty-three were criminals (Gerbner 1985). Prothrow-Stith with Weissman (1991, p. 37) pointed out that the creators of heavy metal and rap music are the first generation of people "nurtured on television's steady diet of fictional and nonfictional mayhem." This steady diet apparently influences aggressiveness of both young boys and girls, and for boys, at least, this effect appears to be as stable as IQ scores into adulthood (Olweus 1979; Slaby and Roedell 1982; but see Sampson and Laub 1993).

Television may also have played a role in the alienation of Americans from civic life. Time spent watching TV has replaced various forms of civic engagement. Putnam, in a critical review, found that television may be the most significant variable in decreasing civic participation of all Americans. He pointed out: "The weight of the available evidence confirms that Americans are significantly less engaged with their communities than was true a generation ago" (Putnam 1995, p. 666).

The mass media also fill homes with images of the rich and famous. Nightengale has pointed out that media images of money and success increase the strain on poor youth and their need to develop "compensatory status symbols" such as Nike shoes, gold jewelry, and fancy clothes. He argues: "Changes in the nature of childhood, the economic well-being of American families, and the technology of mass communication helped increase the inclusion of inner-city residents in a culture of abundance and consumption in the early post–World War II era—just as the urban industrial job market was about to begin its historic disappearing act" (Nightengale 1993, p. 138).

In other words, the main cultural influences on poor youths growing up in jobless poor communities are the result not of social isolation but, rather, of immersion in an unobtainable culture of affluence. Messner and Rosenthal apply this cultural analysis to the extent of instrumental violence in the United States. They argue that normlessness, or anomie, is an inevitable consequence for some of the false promises of the American Dream. Today, the gun is the way to get money or anything one desires "by any means necessary." "High rates of gun-related violence, in particular, result in part from a cultural ethos that encourages the rapid deployment of technically efficient methods to solve interpersonal problems" (Messner and Rosenfeld 1994, p. 4).

Our Milwaukee research has come to the same conclusion and applied it to variations within gangs. While most Milwaukee gang members who sold drugs had violent histories, most of their violence was expressive, that is, fights over women, disputes with friends, or chance encounters with rival gang members where manhood or status were challenged. These "homeboys" also believed drug selling was wrong but necessary for survival, and they held strong conventional aspirations. A minority of gang members—"new jacks"—had given up any hope of settling down and recklessly committed themselves to the drug economy, at least for a time.

Contrast the attitudes of homeboys and new jacks toward the dope game. First, this twenty-five year old black homeboy typifies what most adult gang members, who have been selling drugs for several years, want from life:

> *Q:* "Looking back over the past five years, what major changes have taken place in your life—things that made a difference about where you are now?"
> *A:* "I don't know, maybe maturity. . . . I don't give a fuck about getting rich or nothing, but I want a comfortable life, a decent woman, a family to come home to. I mean, everybody needs somebody to care for. This [selling dope] ain't where it's at."

For most of the adult gang members we interviewed, violence was a part of life but something to be avoided, just as Miller (1969) described it long ago. In our terms they changed from being "tough guys" as teenagers to becoming "reluctant warriors" as young adults (Hagedorn, forthcoming). Even in drug selling, homeboys discussed how they would give extra cocaine to customers claiming to be shorted, rather than get into a potentially violent situation. The new jacks, however, saw violence differently, as this exchange with a black, new jack gang member shows:

> *Q:* How much power does selling drugs give you?
> *A:* Oh it's given me a lot of power. You know, it's just a sensation of you can do anything you want. When you got money in your pocket, you can do anything you want. You can go out there and slap these bitches. You can go out here and shoot this nigger, you just get a power, you just think you are God because you have so much money you think you can do whatever you want to do and everybody knowed what you about. . . . They will not mess with you, they will respect you, they'll like you, because you make your money."

Sixty years ago, Merton saw the same process at work with Al Capone: "Within this context, Capone represents the triumph of amoral intelligence over morally prescribed 'failure,' when the channels of vertical mobility are closed or narrowed in a society that places a high premium on economic affluence and social ascent for all its members" (Merton 1938, pp. 679–80).

My data found strong statistically significant relationships between "new jack" attitudes and instrumental violence (Hagedorn, 1998*b*). In other words, those gang members who used violence regularly in the dope game or took part in drive-by shootings were more likely to be characterized by overemphasis on the goal of making money and a deterioration of the belief in legitimate means to get it. In Merton's (1938) terms, this is "acute anomie."

Most of the Milwaukee gang members we studied learned aggression as children, perhaps through a combination of punitive parenting practices and imitation of media images, became active in fighting gangs, and participated in mainly expressive violence as adults. Instrumental violence in our sample, however, is more related to the development of anomic attitudes among those who had given up on conventional means to adhere to a heavily advertised and promoted ethic of making money as the definition of success.

IV. The Nature of the Postindustrial Gang and Implications for Policy

> A science of society . . . should rather cause us to see things in a different way from the ordinary man, for the purposes of any science is to make discoveries, and all such discoveries more or less upset accepted opinions (Durkheim 1982, p. 31).

Thrasher (1963) is still right: no two gangs are alike. Many of the gangs that inhabit poor communities in American cities are similar to the wild peer groups of the industrial era. Gangs are still made up of an endless variety of peer groups that are socialized to the streets rather than to conventional institutions. Gang violence still is mainly boys and young men getting into fights with other young men over male honor, turf, and status within the group (West and Zimmerman 1987). The presence of guns adds lethal volatility.

But something else is happening, to which social scientists need to pay attention. The large increases in the number of gangs, their diffusion to small cities, and the explosion in rates of violence are quantitative increases that may divert us from looking at more qualitative changes in gangs. The evidence is convincing that many male gangs in many cities are institutionalizing, becoming a permanent fixture in certain neighborhoods (see Moore 1991). Economic restructuring has resulted in many of those gangs, in many cities, developing economic functions within an expanding and violent informal economy. The drug economy has changed the relationship of those gangs to their neighborhoods, increasing violence and making social peace captive to the stability of drug and other illicit markets.

While female gangs are less violent than male gangs, we do not yet have data on how the ending of public assistance as an entitlement will influence poor women, including female gang members. Long prison sentences for drug offenses do not appear to be abating, despite state expenditures on corrections that are increasing much more rapidly than expenditures on higher education. The effects of prison on the nature of gangs and how those gangs affect their home communities needs to be carefully observed.

Economic restructuring may have as many implications for the gangs of today as the industrial revolution did for gangs of yesterday. There may be a kernel of truth in media sensationalism: gang violence may be quite different today than in the past. The form of the male gang seems to have been responsive to economic and institutional changes. Many gang members also appear to be influenced more by stable elements of mainstream American culture than by deviant subcultural values. These issues of change need more careful study (Levine and Rosich 1996).

The gang problem demands both economic and cultural responses that go far beyond any probable agendas of contemporary mainstream politics. I foresee no quick solutions. However, a few points warrant emphasis as interim responses that can minimize violence, while working toward overall solutions.

First, social scientists can help politicians, community groups, and law enforcement officials define the problem of violence more precisely. One major problem of public policy is the tendency to favor crisis management of problems without adequately understanding what the problems are (Cohen, March, and Olsen 1972). As Block and Block (1995) point out, social scientists can help in defining kinds of violence in such a way that solutions can be tailored to the real nature of the problem. Thus, if violence in a neighborhood is mostly gang related, and not drug related, early warning indicators by police, neighborhood groups, and outreach workers need to be acted on to prevent violence from escalating. Similarly, homicides at specific drug-selling sites can be curtailed temporarily by police tactics, which will cause the drug selling to move. This may only help one neighborhood at the expense of another, but it brings short-term relief. There is an important role for social scientists in working with neighborhood groups and law enforcement in helping more dispassionately to define the nature of the problem in order to help fashion appropriate immediate responses.

While social science skills can help community groups and law enforcement, it is important that gang members and ex–gang members are included in intervention and prevention efforts. Antagonisms toward police are long-standing, and repression is a poor answer for joblessness and racism. Since the time of Shaw and McKay (1942), ex-gang members have played important roles in reaching out to delinquent youth (Glaser 1976) and bringing communities together (for a contrary view, see Miller [1962] and Klein [1971]).

As Venkatesh (1996, 1997) and others have shown, drug sellers are often hated for the violence they bring but sometimes tolerated for their economic benefits. A sensible policy, and one that takes into account new economic realities, would seek to isolate and reserve incarceration for those who commit violence while attempting to assist, with job training and drug treatment, those gang members who are mainly trying to settle down (Bursik and Grasmick 1993). The goal of such a policy would be to unite the vast majority of a community, including most who participate in the informal economy. Such efforts have been successful in Cali, Columbia (Moore 1998), and I see no reason that such a policy could not bring increased unity and safety to poor American neighborhoods (see also Fremon 1995).

To do this implies a truce in the drug war. Distinctions need to be made between those who import large quantities of drugs onto the streets (or corruptly allow it to happen) and street-level hustlers, like Milwaukee's homeboys, who are mainly struggling to survive. In Wisconsin, 80 percent of those who go to prison for cocaine violations possess less than five grams of cocaine. There is some evidence that "drug-only" offenders have lower nondrug felony rates than other felons (Nagin 1998). Targeting big-time dealers and violent criminals for long terms of incarceration and channeling the small fry, "drug-only" offenders, into treatment and job training may moderate the long-term effects of prison on poor minority neighborhoods.

Still the problem of guns remains. In *People and Folks* (1998a) I was skeptical of the usefulness of gun-control legislation since nearly all guns possessed by gang members were obtained from the streets, not legally. Thus gun registration and other laws prohibiting felons from possessing guns are likely to have little effect. Passing gun-control laws is like putting a finger in the dike as the ocean flows in: brave, but not very useful when fifty million handguns are in private hands with one-in-three used at some time in a crime.

This may be an area where short-term proposals might have had an effect twenty years ago but will have no effect today. Perhaps such policies as total prohibition of handguns in any setting outside a shooting range should be considered. Hunters seldom use handguns, and police would have less need for them if no one else had them. With fewer handguns, escalation of assaults into homicides because someone has, or might have, a gun could be sharply curtailed. The new Labour government in Great Britain is moving toward such a policy. With the overwhelming presence of handguns on the streets, half-step measures are likely to fail.

Conflict mediation programs, like those advocated by Prothrow-Stith with Weissman (1991), can also help young males define masculinity in ways that do not emphasize violence. Young boys can be taught to measure success by something other than the size of a man's billfold. No analysis of the causes of violence should ever slur over the often neglected, but highly significant and consistent, finding that men are more violent than women.

The solution to the gang problem given in 1988 by one of our gang respondents, "give 'em all jobs," is still valid today. No violence reduction effort will be successful without a jobs program that gives hope to men and women in poor communities (Wilson 1996). The effects of economic restructuring on our most vulnerable populations must be softened. While the full-time jobs of the industrial era may be gone forever, policies that lend money to aid small local businesses and create jobs in the redevelopment of poor communities need to be supported. Along with more jobs, we need to advocate a more humane family policy. Current welfare "reform" may spark more, not less, participation by women in the illegal economy.

Stated simply, gang violence will not be permanently reduced unless the United States develops a more equitable jobs and family policy in this postindustrial era. While more sweeping federal change is needed, reforms on the local and state level in welfare and educational bureaucracies can ameliorate inhumane conditions and help make poor communities more safe and more livable (Hagedorn 1991, 1995).

Finally, we need cultural as well as economic solutions to the problem of gang violence. This review of gang research implies that both liberal and conservative agendas are one-sided. More jobs and fewer prisons are needed, as is an adjustment of the cultural messages that promote materialism and celebrate monetary success. We need an emphasis on responsibility—both corporate and individual—to the community, rather than the promotion of unrestrained individualism. In the final analysis, the problem of postindustrial gang violence is a crisis not only of economics but also of values.

Making good public policy demands that social scientists throw off "the yoke of those empirical categories that long habit often make tyrannical" (Durkheim 1982, p. 73) and develop new empirical categories and more robust explanations. Research on gangs today needs to be concerned with what is different or emerging, not just with those characteristics of gangs that have stayed the same. For gang research to show the way for change in public policy may require a rethinking of old paradigms.

REFERENCES

Adler, Freda. 1975. *Sisters in Crime*. New York: McGraw-Hill.
Ball, Richard A., and G. David Curry. 1995. "The Logic of Definition in Criminology: Purposes and Methods for Defining 'Gangs.' " *Criminology* 33:225–46.
Bernard, Jesse. 1970. *The Sociology of Community*. Glenview, Ill.: Scott, Foresman.
Bjerregaard, Beth, and Carolyn Smith. 1995. "Gender Differences in Gang Participation, Delinquency, and Substance Use." In *The Modern Gang Reader*, edited by Malcolm W. Klein, Cheryl L. Maxson, and Jody Miller. Los Angeles: Roxbury.
Black, Donald. 1983. "Crime as Social Control." *American Sociological Review* 48:34–45.
Bloch, H. A., and Arthur Niederhoffer. 1958. *The Gang: A Study in Adolescent Behavior*. New York: Philosophical Library.
Block, Carolyn Rebecca, and Richard Block. 1991. "Beginning with Wolfgang: An Agenda for Homicide Research." *Journal of Crime and Justice* 14:31–70.

———. 1995. "Street Gang Crime in Chicago." In *The Modern Gang Reader*, edited by Malcolm W. Klein, Cheryl L. Maxson, and Jody Miller. Los Angeles: Roxbury.

Block, Carolyn Rebecca, Antigone Christakos, Ayad Jacob, and Roger Przybylski. 1996. "Street Gangs and Crime." Research Bulletin. Chicago: Illinois Criminal Justice Information Authority.

Block, Richard, and Carolyn Rebecca Block. 1992. "Homicide Syndromes and Vulnerability: Violence in the Chicago Community over 25 years." *Studies on Crime and Crime Prevention* 1:61–87.

Blumstein, Alfred. 1993. "Making Rationality Relevant." *Criminology* 31:1–16.

———. 1995a. "Violence by Young People: Why the Deadly Nexus?" *National Institute of Justice Journal* 229:1–9.

———. 1995b. "Youth Violence, Guns, and the Illicit-Drug Industry." *Journal of Criminal Law and Criminology* 86:10–36.

Bourgois, Philippe. 1995. *In Search of Respect: Selling Crack in El Barrio*. Cambridge: Cambridge University Press.

Braithwaite, John. 1989. *Crime, Shame, and Reintegration*. New York: Cambridge University Press.

Brotherton, David C. 1996. " 'Smartness,' 'Toughness,' and 'Autonomy': Drug Use in the Context of Gang Female Delinquency." *Journal of Drug Issues* 26:261–77.

Brown, Waln. 1977. "Black Female Gang Members in Philadelphia." *International Journal of Offender Therapy and Comparative Criminology* 21:221–28.

Bursik, Robert J., Jr., and Harold G. Grasmick. 1993. *Neighborhoods and Crime: The Dimensions of Effective Community Control*. New York: Lexington Books.

Camp, George, and Camille Graham Camp. 1985. *Prison Gangs: Their Extent, Nature, and Impact on Prisons*. Washington, D.C.: U.S. Department of Justice.

Campbell, Ann. 1984. *The Girls in the Gang*. Oxford: Blackwell.

———. 1990. "Female Participation in Gangs." In *Gangs In America*, edited by C. Ronald Huff. Newbury Park, Calif.: Sage.

———. 1993. *Men, Women, and Aggression*. New York: Basic.

Castells, Manuel, and Alejandro Portes. 1989. "World Underneath: The Origins, Dynamics, and Effects of the Informal Economy. In *The Informal Economy: Studies in Advanced and Less Advanced Countries*, edited by Alejandro Portes, Manuel Castells, and Laura A. Benton. Baltimore: Johns Hopkins University Press.

Chesney-Lind, Meda, and Randall G. Sheldon. 1992. *Girls, Delinquency, and Juvenile Justice*. Pacific Grove, Calif.: Brooks/Cole.

Chicago Crime Commission. 1995. *Gangs: Public Enemy Number One*. Chicago: Chicago Crime Commission.

Clear, Todd R. 1996. "Backfire: When Incarceration Increases Crime." In *The Unintended Consequences of Incarceration*, edited by Karen Fulbright. New York: Vera Institute of Justice.

Cloward, Richard, and Lloyd Ohlin. 1960. *Delinquency and Opportunity*. Glencoe, Ill.: Free Press.

Cloward, Richard A., and Frances Fox Piven. 1979. "Hidden Protest: The Channeling of Female Innovation and Resistance." *Signs* 4:651–69.

Cohen, Albert. 1955. *Delinquent Boys.* Glencoe, Ill.: Free Press.

Cohen, Michael D., James G. March, and Johan P. Olsen. 1972. "A Garbage Can Model of Organizational Choice." *Administrative Science Quarterly* 17:1–25.

Cohen, Stanley. 1972. *Moral Panics and Folk Devils.* London: MacGibbon & Kee.

Connell, Robert W. 1995. *Masculinities.* Berkeley and Los Angeles: University of California Press.

Cook, Philip J. 1983. "The Influence of Gun Availability on Violent Crime Patterns." In *Crime and Justice: An Annual Review of Research,* vol. 4, edited by Michael Tonry and Norval Morris. Chicago: University of Chicago Press.

Cook, Philip J., and John H. Laub. In this volume. "The Unprecedented Epidemic in Youth Violence."

Curry, G. David. 1995. "Responding to Female Gang Involvement." Paper presented at the forty-seventh annual meeting of the American Society of Criminology, Boston, November.

Curry, G. David, Richard A. Ball, and Scott H. Decker. 1996. "Estimating the National Scope of Gang Crime from Law Enforcement Data." In *Gangs in America,* 2d ed., edited by C. Ronald Huff. Thousand Oaks, Calif.: Sage.

Decker, Scott, and Barrik Van Winkle. 1996. *Life in the Gang: Family, Friends, and Violence.* New York: Cambridge.

Donziger, Stephen A. 1996. *The Real War on Crime: The Report of the National Criminal Justice Commission.* New York: Harper Perennial.

Drake, St. Clair, and Horace R. Cayton. 1970. *Black Metropolis.* New York: Harcourt, Brace, & World.

Durkheim, Emile. 1951. *Suicide: A Study in Sociology.* New York: Free Press.

———. 1982. *The Rules of Sociological Method and Selected Texts on Sociology and Its Method.* New York: Free Press.

Eron, Leonard D. 1982. "Parent-Child Interaction, Television Violence, and Aggression of Children." *American Psychologist* 37:197–211.

Esbensen, Finn A., and David Huizinga. 1993. "Gangs, Drugs, and Delinquency in a Survey of Urban Youth." *Criminology* 31:565–87.

Fagan, Jeffrey. 1989. "The Social Organization of Drug Use and Drug Dealing Among Urban Gangs." *Criminology* 27:633–67.

———. 1994. "Women and Drugs Revisited: Female Participation in the Cocaine Economy." *Journal of Drug Issues* 24(2):179–226.

———. 1996. "Gangs, Drugs, and Neighborhood Change." In *Gangs in America,* 2d ed., edited by C. Ronald Huff. Thousand Oaks, Calif.: Sage.

Fagan, Jeffrey, and Ko-lin Chin. 1990. "Violence as Regulation and Social Control in the Distribution of Crack." Research Monograph. In *Drugs and Violence: Causes, Correlates, and Consequences,* edited by Mario De La Rosa, Elizabeth Y. Lambert, and Bernard Gropper. Washington, D.C.: National Institute of Drug Abuse Research.

Federal Bureau of Investigation. Various years, 1971–95. *Crime in the United*

States, Uniform Crime Reports. Washington, D.C.: U.S. Government Printing Office.

Fleisher, Mark S. 1995. *Beggars and Thieves: Lives of Urban Street Criminals.* Madison: University of Wisconsin Press.

Freedman, Jonathan L. 1986. "Television Violence and Aggression: The Debate Continues." *Psychological Bulletin* 100:372–78.

Fremon, Celeste. 1995. *Father Greg and the Homeboys: The Extraordinary Journey of Father Greg and His Work with the Latino Gangs of East L.A.* New York: Hyperion.

Friedrich-Cofer, Lynette, and Aletha Huston. 1986. "Television Violence and Aggression: The Debate Continues." *Psychological Bulletin* 100:364–71.

Fulbright, Karen. 1996. "Introduction." In *The Unintended Consequences of Incarceration*, edited by Karen Fulbright. New York: Vera Institute of Justice.

Gerbner, George. 1985. "Children's Television: A National Disgrace." *Pediatric Annals* 14:822–27.

Gilligan, Carol. 1982. *In A Different Voice: Psychological Theory and Women's Development.* Cambridge, Mass.: Harvard University Press.

Glaser, Daniel. 1976. "Marginal Workers: Some Antecedents and Implications of an Idea from Shaw and McKay." In *Delinquency, Crime, and Society*, edited by James F. Short, Jr. Chicago: University of Chicago Press.

Goldstein, Paul J. 1985. "The Drugs/Violence Nexus: A Tripartite Conceptual Framework." *Journal of Drug Issues* 39(Fall):143–74.

Goldstein, Paul J., and John M. Hagedorn. 1997. "The Decline of Drug-Related Violence: A Case Study in Self Regulation and Social Learning." Paper presented at the forty-ninth annual meeting of the American Society of Criminology, San Diego, November.

Hagedorn, John M. 1988. *People and Folks: Gangs, Crime, and the Underclass in a Rustbelt City.* Chicago: Lakeview Press.

———. 1991. "Gangs, Neighborhoods, and Public Policy." *Social Problems* 38:529–42.

———. 1994a. "Neighborhoods, Markets, and Gang Drug Organization." *Journal of Research in Crime and Delinquency* 31:264–94.

———. 1994b. "Homeboys, Dope Fiends, Legits, and New Jacks: Adult Gang Members, Drugs, and Work." *Criminology* 32:197–219.

———. 1995. *Forsaking Our Children: Bureaucracy and Reform in the Child Welfare System.* Chicago: Lakeview Press.

———. 1996. "The Emperor's New Clothes: Theory and Method in Gang Research." *New Inquiry for a Creative Sociology* 24(2):111–22.

———. 1998a. *People and Folks: Gangs, Crime, and the Underclass in a Rustbelt City.* 2d ed. Chicago: Lakeview Press.

———. 1998b. "Homeboys, New Jacks, and Anomie." *Journal of African American Men* 3:7–28.

———. 1998c. " 'Frat Boys, Bossmen, Studs, and Gentlemen': A Typology of Gang Masculinities." In *Masculinities and Violence*, edited by Lee Bowker. Beverly Hills, Calif.: Sage.

———. Forthcoming. "As American as Apple Pie: A Case Study of Postindustrial Gang Violence." In *Cultural Perspectives on Youth, Radicalism, and Violence*, edited by Meredith Watts. Stamford, Conn.: JAI Press.

Hagedorn, John M., and Mary L. Devitt. Forthcoming. "Fighting Female: The Social Construction of the Female Gang." In *Female Gangs in America: Essays on Girls, Gangs, and Gender*, edited by Meda Chesney-Lind and John M. Hagedorn. Chicago: Lakeview Press.

Hamid, Ansley, and Richard Curtis. 1996. "State-Sponsored Violence in New York City and Indigenous Attempts to Contain It: The Mediating Role of the Third Crown (Sgt. at Arms) of the Latin Kings." Paper presented at the annual meeting of the American Sociological Association, New York, August.

Hesse, Petra, and John E. Mack. 1991. "The World Is a Dangerous Place." In *The Psychology of War and Peace*, edited by Robert Rieber. New York: Plenum.

Horowitz, Ruth. 1983. *Honor and the American Dream*. New Brunswick, N.J.: Rutgers University Press.

Horowitz, Ruth, and Hedy Bookin-Weiner. 1983. "The End of the Youth Gang." *Criminology* 21:585–600.

Howell, James C. 1996. *Youth Gangs, Homicides, Drugs and Guns*. Tallahassee, Fla.: National Youth Gang Center.

Huesmann, L. Rowell, and Leonard D. Eron. 1986. "The Development of Aggression in Children of Different Cultures: Psychological Processes and Exposure to Violence." In *Television and the Aggressive Child: A Cross-National Comparison*, edited by L. Rowell Huesmann and Leonard D. Eron. Hillsdale, N.J.: Erlbaum.

Huff, C. Ronald. 1989. "Youth Gangs and Public Policy." *Crime and Delinquency* 35:524–37.

Hunt, Geoffrey, Stephanie Riegel, Tomas Morales, and Dan Waldorf. 1993. "Changes in Prison Culture: Prison Gangs and the Case of the 'Pepsi Generation.'" *Social Problems* 40:398–409.

Jackson, Pamela Irving. 1995. "Crime, Youth Gangs, and Urban Transition: The Social Dislocations of Postindustrial Economic Development." In *The Modern Gang Reader*, edited by Malcolm W. Klein, Cheryl L. Maxson, and Jody Miller. Los Angeles: Roxbury.

Jackson, Patrick, with Cary Rudman. 1993. "Moral Panic and the Response to Gangs in California." In *Gangs: The Origins and Impact of Contemporary Youth Gangs in the United States*, edited by Scott Cummings and Daniel J. Monti. Albany: State University of New York.

Jacobs, James. 1974. "Street Gangs behind Bars." *Social Problems* 21:395–408.

Joe, Karen. 1992. "The Social Organization of Asian Gangs, the Chinese Mafia, and Organized Crime on the West Coast." Paper presented at the forty-fourth annual meeting of the American Society of Criminology, New Orleans, November.

Joe, Karen, and Meda Chesney-Lind. 1995. "Just Every Mother's Angel." *Gender and Society* 9:408–31.

Johnson, Miriam M. 1988. *Strong Mothers, Weak Wives*. Berkeley and Los Angeles: University of California.

Kasarda, J. D. 1985. "Urban Change and Minority Opportunities." In *The New Urban Reality*, edited by P. E. Peterson. Washington, D.C.: Brookings Institute.

Katz, Jack. 1988. *Seductions of Crime*. New York: Basic.

Kennedy, Leslie W., and Stephen W. Baron. 1997. "Routine Activities and a Subculture of Violence: A Study of Violence on the Street." In *Gangs and Gang Behavior*, edited by G. Larry Mays. Chicago: Nelson-Hall.

Klein, Malcolm W. 1971. *Street Gangs and Street Workers*. Engelwood Cliffs, N.J.: Prentice Hall.

———. 1995. *The American Street Gang: Its Nature, Prevalence, and Control*. New York: Oxford University Press.

Klein, Malcolm W., Cheryl L. Maxson, and Lea C. Cunningham. 1991. " 'Crack,' Street Gangs, and Violence." *Criminology* 29:623–50.

Knox, George W., James G. Houston, Edward D. Tromanhauser, Thomas F. McCurrie, and John L. Laskey. 1996. "Addressing and Testing the Gang Migration Issue: A Summary of Recent Findings." In *Gangs: A Criminal Justice Approach*, edited by J. Mitchell Miller and Jeffrey P. Rush. Cincinnati: Anderson.

Kobrin, Solomon. 1951. "The Conflict of Values in Delinquency Areas." *American Sociological Review* 16:653–61.

Lauderback, David, Joy Hansen, and Dan Waldorf. 1992. "Sisters Are Doin' It for Themselves: A Black Female Gang in San Francisco." *Gang Journal* 1:57–70.

Lawrence, P. R., and J. W. Lorsch. 1969. *Organization and Environment: Managing Differentiation and Integration*. Homewood, Ill.: Irwin.

Leach, William. 1993. *Land of Desire: Merchants, Power, and the Rise of a New American Culture*. New York: Random House.

Levine, Felice J., and Katherine J. Rosich. 1996. *Social Causes of Violence: Crafting a Science Agenda*. Washington, D.C.: American Sociological Association.

Lorber, Judith. 1994. *Paradoxes of Gender*. New Haven, Conn.: Yale University Press.

MacCoun, Robert, and Peter Reuter. 1992. "Are the Wages of Sin $30 an Hour? Economic Aspects of Street-Level Drug Dealing." *Crime and Delinquency* 38:477–91.

Maher, Lisa, and Richard Curtis. 1991. "Women on the Edge of Crime: Crack Cocaine and the Changing Contexts of Street Level Sex Work in New York City." In Joint Meetings of the Law and Society Association and Research Committee on the Sociology of Law of the International Sociological Association, June, Amsterdam.

Majors, Richard, and Janet Mancini Billson. 1992. *Cool Pose: The Dilemmas of Black Manhood in America*. New York: Simon & Schuster.

Mauer, Marc, and Tracy Huling. 1995. *Young Black Americans and the Criminal Justice System: Five Years Later*. Washington, D.C.: Sentencing Project.

Maxson, Cheryl L. 1995. *Street Gangs and Drug Sales in Two Suburban Cities*. Research in Brief. Washington, D.C.: U.S. Department of Justice, National Institute of Justice.

———. 1996. *Street Gang Members on the Move: The Role of Migration in the*

Proliferation of Street Gangs in the U.S. Los Angeles: University of Southern California, Social Science Research Institute, Center for the Study of Crime and Social Control.

———. 1998. "Gang Homicide." In *Issues in the Study and Prevention of Homicide*, edited by M. Dwayne Smith and Margaret A. Zahn. Thousand Oaks, Calif.: Sage.

Maxson, Cheryl L., and Malcolm W. Klein. 1990. "Street Gang Violence: Twice as Great or Half as Great?" In *Gangs in America*, edited by C. Ronald Huff. Newbury Park, Calif.: Sage.

———. 1996. "Defining Gang Homicide: An Updated Look at Member and Motive Approaches." In *Gangs in America*, 2d ed., edited by C. Ronald Huff. Thousand Oaks, Calif.: Sage.

Maxson, Cheryl L., Kristi J. Woods, and Malcolm W. Klein. 1995. *Street Gang Migration in the United States.* Los Angeles: University of Southern California, Center for the Study of Crime and Social Control.

Merton, Robert K. 1938. "Social Structure and Anomie." *American Sociological Review* 3:672–82.

Messerschimdt, James W. 1986. *Capitalism, Patriarchy, and Crime.* Totowa, N.J.: Rowman & Littlefield.

———. 1993. *Masculinities and Crime: Critique and Reconceptualization of Theory.* Totowa, N.J.: Rowman & Littlefield.

Messner, Steven F., and Richard Rosenfeld. 1994. *Crime and the American Dream.* Belmont, Calif.: Wadsworth.

Miller, Jerome G. 1996. *Search and Destroy: African American Males in the Criminal Justice System.* New York: Cambridge University Press.

Miller, Walter. 1958. "Lower Class Culture as a Generating Milieu of Gang Delinquency." *Journal of Social Issues* 14:5–19.

———. 1962. "The Impact of a 'Total-Community' Delinquency Control Project." *Social Problems* 10:168–91.

———. 1969. "Violent Crime in City Gangs." In *Delinquency, Crime, and Social Process*, edited by Donald R. Cressey and David Ward. New York: Harper & Row.

———. 1973. "The Molls." *Society* 11(1):32–35.

———. 1975. *Violence by Youth Gangs and Youth Groups as a Crime Problem in Major American Cities.* Washington, D.C.: U.S. Department of Justice.

———. 1982. "Crime by Youth Gangs and Groups in Major American Cities." Washington, D.C.: U.S. Department of Justice, National Institute of Juvenile Justice and Delinquency Prevention.

———. 1990. "Why the United States Has Failed to Solve Its Youth Gang Problem." In *Gangs in America*, edited by C. Ronald Huff. Newbury Park, Calif.: Sage.

Moore, Joan W. 1978. *Homeboys: Gangs, Drugs, and Prison in the Barrios of Los Angeles.* Philadelphia: Temple University Press.

———. 1991. *Going Down to the Barrio: Homeboys and Homegirls in Change.* Philadelphia: Temple University Press.

———. 1993. "Gangs, Drugs, and Violence." In *Gangs*, edited by Scott Cummings and Daniel J. Monti. Albany: State University of New York.

————. 1996. "Bearing the Burden: How Incarceration Policies Weaken Inner-City Communities." In *The Unintended Consequences of Incarceration*, edited by Karen Fulbright. New York: Vera Institute of Justice.

————. 1998. "Overcoming American Ethnocentrism about Street Gangs." In *Cross Cultural Perspectives on Youth, Radicalism, and Violence*, edited by Meredith Watts. New York: JAI.

Moore, Joan, and Mary Devitt. 1989. "The Paradox of Deviance in Addicted Mexican American Mothers." *Gender and Society* 3:53–70.

Moore, Joan W., and John M. Hagedorn. 1996. "What Happens to Girls in the Gang?" In *Gangs In America*, 2d ed., edited by C. Ronald Huff. Beverly Hills, Calif.: Sage.

————. Forthcoming. "Female Gangs." NIJ Research in Brief. Washington, D.C.: National Institute of Justice.

Moore, Joan W., and Alberto Mata. 1981. "Women and Heroin in Chicano Communities." Los Angeles: Chicano Pinto Research Project.

Moore, Michael. 1997. *National Youth Gang Survey*. Washington, D.C.: U.S. Department of Justice, National Institute of Justice.

Morash, Merry. 1986. "Gender, Peer Group Experiences, and Seriousness of Delinquency." *Journal of Research in Crime and Delinquency* 23(1):43–59.

Morris, Ruth R. 1964. "Female Delinquency and Relational Problems." *Social Forces* 43:82–89.

Nagel, Ilene H., and John Hagan. 1983. "Gender and Crime: Offense Patterns and Criminal Court Sanctions." In *Crime and Justice: An Annual Review of Research*, vol. 4, edited by Michael Tonry and Norval Morris. Chicago: University of Chicago Press.

Nagin, Daniel S. 1998. "Criminal Deterrence Research at the Outset of the Twenty-First Century." In *Crime and Justice: A Review of Research*, vol. 23, edited by Michael Tonry. Chicago: University of Chicago Press.

Nightengale, Carl Husemoller. 1993. *On the Edge: A History of Poor Black Children and Their American Dreams*. New York: Basic.

Olweus, D. 1979. "Stability of Aggressive Reaction Patterns in Males: A Review." *Psychological Bulletin* 86:852–75.

Padilla, Felix. 1992. *The Gang as an American Enterprise*. New Brunswick, N.J.: Rutgers University Press.

Perkins, Useni Eugene. 1987. *Explosion of Chicago's Black Street Gangs*. Chicago: Third World Press.

Prothrow-Stith, Deborah, with Michaele Weissman. 1991. *Deadly Consequences: How Violence is Destroying Our Teenage Population and a Plan to Begin Solving the Problem*. New York: Harper Collins.

Putnam, Robert D. 1995. "Tuning In, Tuning Out: The Strange Disappearance of Social Capital in America." *Political Science and Politics* 28:664–83.

Ralph, Paige, Robert J. Hunter, James W. Marquart, Steven J. Cuvelier, and Dorothy Merianos. 1996. "Exploring the Differences between Gang and Non-gang Prisoners." In *Gangs in America*, 2d ed., edited by C. Ronald Huff. Thousand Oaks, Calif.: Sage.

Reinarman, Craig, and Harry G. Levine. 1990. "Crack in Context: Politics and Media in the Making of a Drug Scare." *Contemporary Drug Problems* 16:535–77.

Reiss, Albert J., Jr., and Jeffrey A. Roth. 1993. *Understanding and Preventing Violence*. Washington, D.C.: National Academy Press.

Ro, Ronin. 1996. *Gangsta: Merchandizing the Rhymes of Violence*. New York: St. Martin's.

Rose, Harold M., Anthony Maggiore, and Ellen Hanalon. 1995. *The Milwaukee Homicide Project*. Milwaukee: University of Wisconsin, Department of Geography.

Ryan, Patrick J., Paul I. Goldstein, Henry H. Brownstein, and Patrica A. Bellucci. 1990. "Who's Right: Different Outcomes When Police and Scientists View the Same Set of Homicide Events, New York City, 1988." In *Drugs and Violence: Causes, Correlates, and Consequences*, edited by Mario De La Rosa, Elizabeth Y. Lambert, and Bernard Gropper. Washington, D.C.: National Institute on Drug Abuse.

Sampson, Robert J., and John H. Laub. 1993. *Crime in the Making: Pathways and Turning Points through Life*. Cambridge, Mass.: Harvard University Press.

Sanchez-Jankowski, Martin. 1991. *Islands in the Street: Gangs and American Urban Society*. Berkeley: University of California.

Sanders, Barry. 1994. *A is for Ox: Violence, Electronic Media, and the Silencing of the Written Word*. New York: Pantheon.

Sanders, William B. 1994. *Gangbangs and Drive-Bys: Grounded Culture and Juvenile Gang Violence*. New York: Aldine de Gruyter.

Shaw, Clifford R., and Henry D. McKay. 1942. *Juvenile Delinquency and Urban Areas*. Chicago: University of Chicago Press.

Sheley, Joseph F., and James D. Wright. 1995. *In The Line of Fire: Youth, Guns, and Violence in Urban America*, edited by J. D. Wright. New York: Aldine de Gruyter.

Short, James F. 1990. "New Wine in Old Bottles? Change and Continuity in American Gangs." In *Gangs in America*, edited by C. Ronald Huff. Newbury Park, Calif.: Sage.

———. 1996. "Personal, Gang, and Community Careers." In *Gangs in America*, 2d ed., edited by C. Ronald Huff, Thousand Oaks, Calif.: Sage.

———. 1997. *Poverty, Ethnicity and Violent Crime*. Boulder, Colo.: Westview.

Short, James F., and Fred Strodtbeck. 1965. *Group Process and Gang Delinquency*. Chicago: University of Chicago Press.

———. 1970. "Why Gangs Fight" In *Modern Criminals*, edited by James F. Short. New York: Aldine de Gruyter.

Skolnick, Jerome H. 1990. "The Social Structure of Street Drug Dealing." *American Journal of Police* 9:1–41.

Skolnick, Jerome H., R. Bluthenthal, and Theodore Correl. 1993. "Gang Organization and Migration." In *Gangs: The Origins and Impact of Contemporary Youth Gangs in the United States*, edited by Scott Cummings and Daniel J. Monti. Albany: State University of New York Press.

Slaby, Ronald G., and Wendy Conklin Roedell. 1982. "The Development and Regulation of Aggression in Young Children." In *Psychological Development in the Elementary Years*, edited by Judith Worell. New York: Academic Press.

Spergel, Irving A. 1964. *Racketville Slumtown Haulberg.* Chicago: University of Chicago Press.

———. 1990. "Youth Gangs: Continuity and Change." In *Crime and Justice: A Review of Research*, vol. 12, edited by Michael Tonry and Norval Morris. Chicago: University of Chicago Press.

———. 1995. *The Youth Gang Problem: A Community Approach.* New York: Oxford University Press.

Spergel, Irving A., and G. David Curry. 1995. "The National Youth Gang Survey: A Research and Development Process." In *The Modern Gang Reader*, edited by Malcolm W. Klein, Cheryl L. Maxson, and Jody Miller. Los Angeles: Roxbury.

Spitzer, Stephen. 1975. "Towards a Marxist Theory of Deviance." *Social Problems* 22:638–50.

Stack, Carol B. 1974. *All Our Kin.* New York: Harper Torchback.

Steffensmeier, D. J., and R. H. Steffensmeier. 1980. "Trends in Female Delinquency: An Examination of Arrest, Juvenile Court, Self-Report, and Field Data." *Criminology* 30:136–62.

Sullivan, Mercer L. 1989. *Getting Paid: Youth Crime and Work in the Inner City.* Ithaca, N.Y.: Cornell University Press.

Sutherland, Edwin H. 1934. *Principles of Criminology.* Chicago: Lippencott.

Taylor, Carl. 1989. *Dangerous Society.* East Lansing: Michigan State University Press.

———. 1993. *Girls, Gangs, Women, and Drugs.* East Lansing: Michigan State University Press.

Thrasher, Frederick. 1927/1963. *The Gang.* Chicago: University of Chicago Press.

Thurow, Lester C. 1997. *The Future of Capitalism: How Today's Economic Forces Shape Tomorrow's World.* New York: Penguin.

Tonry, Michael. 1995. *Malign Neglect: Race, Crime, and Punishment in America.* Oxford: Oxford University Press.

Venkatesh, Sudhir Alladi. 1996. "The Gang in the Community." In *Gangs in America*, 2d ed., edited by C. Ronald Huff. Thousand Oaks, Calif.: Sage.

———. 1997. "The Social Organization of Street Gang Activity in an Urban Ghetto." *American Journal of Sociology* 103:82–111.

Vigil, James Diego. 1988. *Barrio Gangs: Street Life and Identity in Southern California.* Austin: University of Texas.

Vigil, James Diego, and Steve C. Yun. 1996. "Southern California Gangs: Comparative Ethnicity and Social Control." In *Gangs in America*, 2d ed., edited by C. Ronald Huff. Thousand Oaks, Calif.: Sage.

Waldorf, Dan. 1993. *Final Report of the Crack Sales, Gangs, and Violence Study*, Study for the National Institute of Drug Abuse. Grant no. 5, R01DA06486. Alameda, Calif.: Institute for Scientific Analysis.

Waldorf, Dan, and David Lauderback. 1993. "Gang Drug Sales in San Francisco: Organized or Freelance?" Alameda, Calif.: Institute for Scientific Analysis.

Weick, Karl E. 1976. "Educational Organizations as Loosely Coupled Systems." *Administrative Science Quarterly* 21:1–19.

West, Candace, and Don H. Zimmerman. 1987. "Doing Gender." *Gender and Society* 1:125–51.

Whyte, William Foote. 1943. *Street Corner Society*. Chicago: University of Chicago Press.

Williams, Terry. 1989. *The Cocaine Kids*. Reading, Mass.: Addison-Wesley.

Willis, Paul. 1981. *Learning to Labor*. New York: Columbia University Press.

Wilson, William Julius. 1987. *The Truly Disadvantaged*. Chicago: University of Chicago Press.

———. 1996. *When Work Disappears: The World of the New Urban Poor*. New York: Knopf.

Wilson, William Julius, and Robert J. Sampson. 1995. "Toward a Theory of Race, Crime, and Urban Inequality." In *Crime and Inequality*, edited by John Hagan and Ruth D. Peterson. Stanford, Calif.: Stanford University Press.

Yablonsky, Lewis. 1966. *The Violent Gang*. New York: Macmillan.

———. 1997. *Gangsters: Fifty Years of Madness, Drugs, and Death on the Streets of America*. New York: New York University Press.

Zatz, Marjorie S. 1987. "Chicano Youth Gangs and Crime: The Creation of a Moral Panic." *Contemporary Crises* 11:129–58.

David P. Farrington

Predictors, Causes, and Correlates of Male Youth Violence

ABSTRACT

Youth who commit one type of violent offense tend to commit others; they also tend to commit nonviolent offenses and have co-occurring problems such as substance abuse and sexual promiscuity. Violent offenders tend to be frequent or persistent offenders. There is considerable continuity from childhood aggression to youth violence. The major long-term predictors are biological factors (low heart rate), individual factors (high impulsiveness and low intelligence), family factors (poor supervision, harsh discipline, a violent parent, large family size, a young mother, a broken family), peer delinquency, low socioeconomic status, urban residence, and a high-crime neighborhood. Immediate situational influences include potential offenders' motives (e.g., anger, a desire to hurt) and actions leading to violent events (e.g., the escalation of a trivial altercation). New longitudinal surveys could measure a wide range of risk and protective factors, study violent careers using self-reports, and focus on types of offenders and offenses.

The focus in this essay is on physical violence by young males that could, in principle, be defined as criminal in North America, Great Britain, or other Western democracies. Youth violence is restricted here to acts committed by persons aged roughly between ten and twenty-one. This age range is chosen to exclude childhood aggression (under age ten) and adult violence (over age twenty-one).

David P. Farrington is professor of psychological criminology in the Institute of Criminology, Cambridge University. For helpful comments on an earlier version of this essay, I am very grateful to Deborah Gorman-Smith, Darnell Hawkins, Sheilagh Hodgins, Clive Hollin, Marc Le Blanc, Rolf Loeber, David Magnusson, Joan McCord, Daniel Nagin, Terence Thornberry, and of course the editors. For excellent secretarial assistance, I am very grateful to Maureen Brown.

The most important violent offenses defined by the criminal law are homicide, rape, robbery, and assault. Assault is commonly divided into the more serious forms of aggravated assault (in North America) or wounding (in Great Britain), compared with less serious simple assaults (in North America) or common assaults (in Great Britain). In the United States, an aggravated assault occurs if the victim suffers knife, stab, or gun wounds, broken bones, or knocked-out teeth; if the victim is knocked unconscious; or if a weapon is used. A simple assault occurs if the victim receives cuts, scratches, bruises, a swelling, or a black eye or if no weapon is used. In Great Britain, a wounding occurs if the victim receives some kind of cut or wound or if the skin or a bone is broken, whereas a common assault occurs if the victim is punched, kicked, pushed, or jostled, with negligible or no injury.

It is not always easy to define an act as violent or nonviolent. For example, there are obvious difficulties in deciding whether a physical fight between two male adolescents in the street (or, even more so, in the home or the school) should be defined as violence committed by both participants. It is easier to count one participant as violent if he strikes the first blow and if he causes significant injury to the other participant.

The most basic definition of physical violence is behavior that is intended to cause, and actually causes, injury. However, many violent criminal offenses involve no physical injury. For example, robberies and rapes may involve only threats, and aggravated assaults may involve only threats with a weapon. Therefore, incidents where there is intentional and threatened injury, but no actual injury, are included as physical violence. Injury in the absence of intention and threat (e.g., in a car accident) is excluded. Governmental or corporate violence (e.g., building a potentially dangerous vehicle), violence between spouses or cohabitees, or by parents against children, and violence committed by "dangerous" or mentally abnormal offenders are also excluded because these types of violence are rarely committed by persons aged ten to twenty-one. Violence against property or animals is also excluded.

It is reasonable to assume that violent offenses, like other crimes, arise from interactions between offenders and victims in certain situations. Some violent acts are probably committed by youth with relatively stable and enduring violent tendencies, while others are committed by more "normal" youth who find themselves in situations that are conducive to violence. This essay aims to explain both the development of violent persons (i.e., persons with a relatively high probability of committing violent acts in any situation) and the occurrence of violent acts. However, the focus is mainly on violent persons. This essay does not aim to explain why some people are disproportionately likely to be victims of violence.

The main focus of this essay is on predictors, causes, and correlates of male youth violence. Most research investigates risk factors for violence. In order to determine whether a risk factor (e.g., school failure, poor parental supervision, delinquent peers) is a predictor or possible cause, the risk factor needs to be measured before the violence occurs. Hence, longitudinal studies are needed. In this essay, I focus on longitudinal studies of large community samples (several hundreds of individuals) containing information from several data sources (to maximize validity). The major longitudinal studies of youth violence are listed in the appendix (see also Farrington 1982), together with their key features (principal investigators, initial sample size, characteristics of the sample, location, time, and follow-up data).

In the interest of throwing light on possible causes of violence and promising prevention methods, I concentrate on risk factors that can change over time. Thus genetic factors that are fixed at birth, such as the XYY chromosome abnormality, are not discussed, but biological factors that can change, such as the resting heart rate, are included. I also concentrate on individual-level studies as opposed to aggregate-level ones (e.g., of rates of violence in different areas). I do not discuss trends over time, substance abuse, gangs, or school factors, which are reviewed elsewhere in this volume.

I offer several main conclusions. First, few studies focus specifically on youth violence (as opposed to childhood aggression or general delinquency). Second, most existing studies are based on police or court records; more research is needed based on self-reports, but this should include detailed information about the nature, circumstances, and timing of offenses and about situational influences. Third, violent youth are versatile in committing other types of offenses and other types of antisocial acts, but there is some specialization in violence; specialized and versatile offenders should be distinguished. Fourth, there is significant continuity from childhood aggression to youth violence and from youth violence to adult violence, but reasons for discontinuity and desistance—and especially protective factors—should be investigated. Fifth, most research compares violent youth with other youth; more research is needed comparing violent delinquents with nonviolent delinquents. Sixth, the major risk factors for youth violence are biological factors (low heart rate), psychological/personality factors (impulsivity, low intelligence), family factors (poor supervision, harsh discipline, violent parents, large families, young mothers, broken families), peer delinquency, low socioeconomic status, and bad neighborhoods. Seventh, risk factors explain why the long-term potential for violence develops; situational factors explain why this potential becomes the actuality of violent acts. Eighth, more research is needed on types of offenders (e.g., those with high violence potential versus those who are situationally influenced) and types of offenses (e.g., assault versus robbery or rape). Ninth, new longitudinal studies are needed that include measurement of a wide range of risk and protective factors and detailed study of violent criminal careers using self-reports.

The organization of this essay is as follows. Section I reviews types of violent crimes, the extent to which offenders are specialized as opposed to versatile, and to what extent violent youth have other co-occurring problem behaviors. Section II reviews the development of violent criminal careers, the place of violent crimes in criminal careers, and developmental sequences from childhood aggression to youth violence. Section III reviews knowledge about changeable risk factors: biological, psychological/personality, family, peer, socioeconomic, neighborhood, and situational. Protective factors are also discussed, although much less is known about them. Section IV reviews theories of youth violence, acknowledging the major problem that most theories are designed to explain delinquency or aggression rather than youth violence. Section V summarizes the main conclusions and identifies gaps in knowledge and priorities for research.

I. Types of Violent Offenders

The most common ways to identify violent offenders are to use police or court records or self-reports, although hospital records could also be used more. Generally, young violent offenders tend to be versatile rather than specialized. They tend to commit many different types of crimes and also to exhibit other problems, such as truancy and school dropout, substance use, lying, and sexual promiscuity. However, there is a small degree of specialization in violence superimposed on this versatility.

A. Classification and Measurement

The most important violent crimes are homicide, rape, robbery, and assault. They can be further subdivided, according to characteristics of the offender (e.g., stranger versus acquaintance versus intimate for rape offenders [Lloyd and Walmsley 1989]), characteristics of the victim (e.g., homicide of children, parents, siblings, spouses, and so on [Daly and Wilson 1988]), the offender-victim relationship (e.g., violence between siblings [Steinmetz 1978]), or characteristics of the offense (e.g., soccer violence, which is an important social problem in Great Britain and Europe [Junger-Tas 1996]). The distinction between assault and robbery mirrors an important distinction in the aggression literature (e.g., Berkowitz 1993, p. 1) between emotional (or angry or hostile) aggression, in which the main objective is to hurt the victim, and instrumental aggression, in which the main objective is to obtain something else.

Homicide is a rare event. Consequently, it is not practicable to investigate risk factors for homicide in prospective longitudinal studies. Instead, retrospective case-control studies need to be carried out, but these are typically based on very small samples. For example, Lewis and her colleagues (1988) compared thirteen juvenile murderers, fourteen violent delinquents, and eighteen nonviolent delinquents; and Busch and his colleagues (1990) compared seventy-one adolescent murderers with seventy-one matched nonviolent delinquents. Most arrested male homicide offenders in the United States (56 percent in 1995 [Federal Bureau of Investigation 1996, table 38]) are over twenty-one, but the highest prevalence of homicide is between ages seventeen and twenty-two.

Rape is also a rare event, particularly in official records, which makes it difficult to investigate risk factors for rape in prospective longitudinal studies. Retrospective studies are more common (e.g., Blaske et al. 1989). However, Ageton (1983, p. 9) studied sexual assault in the U.S. National Youth Survey, which is a longitudinal survey of a nationally representative sample of over 1,700 American youth (see the appendix). Three questions were used (about having sexual relations with someone against that person's will, pressuring someone to do more sexually than he or she wanted to do, and hurting or threatening to hurt someone to get him or her to have sex with you). She found that the prevalence of sexual assault (the percentage of persons who reported doing one or more of those things in the previous year) decreased from 3.8 percent of males in 1978 (average age sixteen) to 2.2 percent in 1980 (average age eighteen). Most arrested male rape offenders in the United States (68 percent in 1995 [Federal Bureau of Investigation 1996, table 38]) are over twenty-one, and the prevalence of rape remains high between ages sixteen and the early thirties. Hence, rape is a youth crime in the sense that it has a relatively high prevalence up to age twenty-one but not in the sense that the majority of rapes are committed by youth aged ten to twenty-one.

Assault and robbery are more common, and they are often measured in prospective longitudinal surveys using official records and self-reports. For example, the National Youth Survey inquired about aggravated assault (attacking someone with the goal of seriously hurting or killing that person), being involved in a gang fight, and robbery (using force or strong-arm methods to get money or things from people; see Elliott 1994, p. 3). Prevalences were surprisingly high. For example, in the first wave of the survey (ages eleven to seventeen in 1976), 31 percent of African-American boys and 22 percent of Caucasian boys admitted a felony assault in the previous year (aggravated assault, gang fight, or sexual assault). At the same time, 13 percent of African-American boys and 6 percent of Caucasian boys admitted robbery (of teachers, students, or others) in the previous year.

The National Academy of Sciences panel on violence (Reiss and Roth 1993, p. 374) argued that, generally, self-report studies of general population samples are not suitable for investigating the occurrence of violent crimes in criminal careers for three reasons: the acts reported (e.g., involvement in gang fights) are not unambiguously violent crimes, many of the most violent people in the population are missing from samples interviewed (because they are disproportionally elusive, uncooperative, not in school, or not at home with their parents [see Cernkovich, Giordano, and Pugh 1985]), and information about the time ordering of different types of offenses is not collected. Strictly speaking, only acts leading to convictions have passed the legal criteria for violence (e.g., having the required intentions and consequences).

In response, Elliott (1994, p. 4) reported that a weapon was used in half of all self-reported serious violent offenses (aggravated assaults, robberies, and rapes) and that some medical treatment was required in two-thirds of cases. Hence, he argued that self-reported violent offenses are at least as serious as those leading to arrests. He restricted his analysis to serious violent offenses (including gang fights) involving weapons or injuries, thus excluding 36 percent of reported acts. Even so, the prevalence of serious violence was remarkably high: at the peak age (seventeen), 36 percent of African-American boys and 25 percent of Caucasian boys admitted a serious violent offense in the previous year. In the light of these figures, it is surprising that the cumulative prevalence of serious violent offenses up to age eighteen was only 40 percent for African-American boys and 30 percent for Caucasian boys.

Self-reports of youth violence reveal many more offenders and offenses than do official records of arrests or convictions (e.g., Le Blanc and Frechette 1989, pp. 58–59). A key issue concerns the validity or accuracy of self-reports. Huizinga (1991, p. 60) reviewed the evidence on this and concluded that the relationship between official records and self-reports was "not strong." Which method was preferable was unclear, since both had advantages and disadvantages. For example, official records greatly underestimate the true number of offenses committed and are limited by biases in police and court processing. However, the greater underreporting of officially recorded offenses of African-American boys compared with those of Caucasian boys was "particularly troubling" (Huizinga 1991, p. 62).

The most recent investigation of the predictive validity of self-reported delinquency in relation to court referrals was carried out in the Pittsburgh Youth Study (Farrington et al. 1996). This is a longitudinal survey of three cohorts, each of about 500 Pittsburgh boys, originally studied at ages seven, ten, and thirteen (see the appendix). The seriousness of self-reported delinquency in the first two waves of the survey predicted later court referrals for Index violence (homicide, rape, robbery, and aggravated assault) for both Caucasian and African-American boys. However, proportionally more African-American boys had court referrals for Index violence at all levels of self-reported delinquency seriousness. We concluded that predictive validity was enhanced by combining self-report, parent, and teacher information about offending.

Assuming that self-reports are tolerably valid, the comparison between self-reports and official records gives some indication of the probability of an offender being caught and convicted. For example, in the Cambridge Study in Delinquent Development (hereafter referred to as the Cambridge Study), which is a longitudinal survey of about 400 London males from age eight to age forty (see the appendix), 45 percent admitted starting a physical fight or using a weapon in a fight between ages fifteen and eighteen, but only 3 percent were convicted of assault between these ages (Farrington 1989b, pp. 404–5). Hence, only 7 percent of self-reported violent offenders between ages fifteen and eighteen were convicted, although 13 percent of self-reported violent offenders between ages ten and thirty-two were convicted. Self-reported violence had predictive validity: 10 percent of those who admitted assaults up to age eighteen were subsequently convicted of assault, compared with 5 percent of the remainder. In the Denver Youth Survey, which is a longitudinal follow-up of 1,500 children initially aged seven to fifteen (see the appendix), 74 percent of self-reported violent offenders were arrested during a five-year period, but only 21 percent were arrested for violence (Loeber, Farrington, and Waschbusch 1998, p. 23).

It would be useful to compare self-report and official record data on youth violence with data from other sources. For example, information about violent offenders is obtained from victims of violence in victimization surveys such as the U.S. National Crime Survey (Hindelang 1981). According to U.S. victims in 1973–77, African-American males aged eighteen to twenty had the highest rates of violent offending, committing forty assaults, thirty-five robberies, and 1.6 rapes per 100 males per year (Hindelang 1981, table 1). It is also possible to investigate violence victims who present themselves for treatment in the accident and emergency departments of hospitals; in a study of this kind, Clarkson and his colleagues (1994) found that there was no relationship between the seriousness of the assault and the probability of an offender being convicted. Interestingly, Shepherd and his colleagues (1993) found that, in Bristol between 1975 and 1990, police-recorded violence increased nine times, while hospital-recorded violence increased six times.

More research is needed on the extent to which valid information about serious youth violence can be collected in self-report surveys. More details about the nature, circumstances, and timing of reported violent offenses should be collected, and this information should be compared not only with police and court records but also with hospital records.

B. Specialization or Versatility in Offending

An important question concerns the extent to which youth who commit one type of violent offense (homicide, rape, robbery, or assault) also commit other types. This is difficult to investigate because of the low prevalence of homicide and rape and because an arrest for homicide or rape usually leads to a prolonged period of confinement during which a youth is not at risk of offending in the community.

The most relevant study is probably that of Hamparian and her colleagues (1978), who identified all 811 youth born between 1956 and 1958 and arrested for violence as juveniles in Columbus, Ohio (see the appendix). These youth were arrested for 2,282 nonviolent offenses and 1,091 violent offenses, including 12 murders, 40 rapes, 255 robberies, and 466 assaults. The murderers had 6.3 arrests of all kinds, compared with 5.6 for the rapists, 5.4 for the robbers, and 4.5 for the assaulters. There was a considerable amount of versatility in violent offending. For example, if we compare the first and second violent arrests, 48 percent of the 52 murder/assault first-arrest cases committed robbery or rape on the second arrest; 42 percent of the 59 robbery first-arrest cases committed murder, assault, or rape on the second arrest; and 57 percent of the 21 rape first-arrest cases committed murder, assault, or robbery on the second arrest (Hamparian et al. 1978, table 5-5). Simon's (1997) review also concluded that most sex and violent offenders were generalists.

A second question concerns the extent to which youth who commit a violent offense also commit nonviolent offenses. Generally, youth are versatile in their offending rather than specialized. The above finding, that violent youth have committed more nonviolent offenses than violent offenses, is typical. For example, in the Cambridge Study, the convicted violent delinquents up to age twenty-one had nearly three times as many convictions for nonviolent offenses as for violent offenses (Farrington 1978, p. 77). In the Oregon Youth Study, which is a longitudinal survey of over 200 boys from age ten (see the appendix), the boys arrested for violence had an average of 6.6 arrests of all kinds (Capaldi and Patterson 1996, p. 215).

In general, violent offenders tend to be persistent or frequent offenders (Loeber et al. 1998). This raises the question of whether violent offenses are essentially committed at random in prolific criminal careers, an issue that was investigated in the Cambridge Study (Farrington 1991). Up to age thirty-two, about 12 percent of all convictions were for violent offenses. Assuming that violent offenses are committed at random in criminal careers, it is easy to specify mathematically (using the binomial distribution) how the probability of committing a violent offense should increase as the total number of offenses increases. To the extent that offenders specialize in violence, the number of violent offenders should be significantly fewer than expected, and each one should commit more violent offenses (on average) than expected. While there was some tendency in this direction, the actual numbers of violent offenders were not significantly different from the numbers expected on the complete versatility model (Farrington 1991, p. 16). However, in a Copenhagen birth-cohort study of over 28,000 males followed up to age twenty-seven (see the appendix), Guttridge and her colleagues (1983, table 11-3) reported a significant difference between expected and actual numbers of violent crimes. This result may be a function of different statistical tests used or of the very low proportion of all Copenhagen crimes that were violent (less than 4 percent); violence was more statistically deviant in Copenhagen than in London.

Specialization in violent offending can also be investigated using transition matrices showing the probability of one type of offense being followed by another. This type of analysis was pioneered in the first Philadelphia birth-cohort study by Wolfgang and his colleagues (1972) in which nearly 10,000 boys were followed up to their eighteenth birthdays (see the appendix). Their average matrix shows some specialization superimposed on a great deal of versatility. For example (as recalculated by Stander et al. 1989, p. 320), the probability of a violent offense being followed by another violent offense was only .14, although this was higher than the probability of a violent offense following any other type of offense (which ranged from .07 to .11). Similar results were obtained by Tracy and his colleagues (1990, p. 124) in a second Philadelphia birth-cohort study of over 13,000 boys born in 1958 (see the appendix) and for self-reports and official records in the Cambridge Study (Farrington 1989b, pp. 413–14).

It is important to quantify the degree of specialization in violent offending. For example, in the Copenhagen birth-cohort study, Moffitt and her colleagues (1989, p. 20) concluded that a first-time violent offender was 1.9 times as likely to commit a violent act among his future offenses as a first-time property offender. The forward specialization coefficient (FSC; Farrington 1986, p. 227) is a simple measure for use with transition matrices ranging from 0 = complete versatility (randomness) to 1 = complete specialization. In a diagonal cell,

$$\text{FSC} = \frac{O - E}{R - E},$$

where O = observed number, E = expected number by chance, and R = row total.

For example, consider a study in which 1,000 offenders made the transition from the first to the second offense. Imagine that 100 of them committed a violent crime on the first offense, 90 committed a violent crime on the second offense, and 20 (of the 100 and of the 90) committed violent crimes on both. The expected number (by chance) committing two violent crimes is

$$E = \frac{100 \times 90}{1,000} = 9.$$

Hence, FSC = (20 − 9)/(100 − 9) = 11/91 = .12. In this example, the degree of specialization is low: only 12 percent of the way from complete versatility to complete specialization.

Forward specialization coefficients in the second Philadelphia birth-cohort study were reported by Kempf (1987). However, the largest study of specialization in juvenile offending was the analysis of nearly 70,000 youth born between 1962 and 1965 and referred to the Maricopa (Phoenix, Ariz.) or Utah juvenile courts (Farrington, Snyder, and Finnegan 1988, p. 478). For males, the FSC was .12 for robbery, .07 for aggravated assault, and .07 for simple assault. It was higher for the Index property offenses of burglary (.16) and motor vehicle theft (.15), but the average of all offenses was .10. Again, these figures show a small but significant degree of specialization in offending superimposed on a great deal of versatility.

Given that violent offenders tend to be frequent offenders, another way of investigating whether violent offenders are different in degree or in kind from other types of offenders is to compare them with those who commit equally frequent but nonviolent offenses. When this comparison was carried out in the Cambridge Study (Farrington 1991), it was concluded that violent offenders and nonviolent frequent offenders were virtually identical in childhood, adolescent, and adult features. These results were replicated in the Oregon Youth Study (Capaldi and Patterson 1996). Hence, it is not clear that violent young offenders are distinctly different from frequent or persistent young offenders.

The bulk of the evidence suggests that there is a great deal of versatility in offending but also some specialization in violence. More research on specialization is needed using self-report methods and also focusing on different types of violence (rapes and robberies as well as assaults). An interesting question is whether specialization is greater or less in self-reports compared with official records. Also, more research is needed, focusing on different types of offenders; perhaps some offenders are specialists and others are generalists (Farrington, Snyder, and Finnegan 1988, pp. 479–81). If so, it is important to investigate the prevalence and characteristics of specialists compared with generalists.

C. Co-occurring Problems

Violent youth have many other co-occurring problems (Huizinga and Jakob-Chien 1998). For example, the National Youth Risk Behavior Survey was a cross-sectional survey of a nationally representative sample of over 11,000 American youth aged fifteen to eighteen (Sosin et al. 1995). About 8 percent of the youth reported that during the previous month they were involved in a fight in which someone was injured severely enough to require medical attention. (Unfortunately, this percentage apparently included youth who were attacked without retaliating.) The prevalence of other problem behaviors was much higher for the fighters than for the remainder. During the previous year, 24 percent of the fighters attempted suicide, compared with 8 percent of all students. During the previous month, 26 percent (vs. 4 percent) carried a firearm, 13 percent (vs. 2 percent) used cocaine, and 39 percent (vs. 17 percent) drove a motor vehicle while drunk. During the previous 3 months, 41 percent (vs. 12 percent) had two or more sex partners, and 45 percent (vs. 29 percent) had sexual intercourse without using a condom.

Many other studies show the co-occurrence of problem behaviors with youth violence. For example, in Project Metropolitan in Stockholm, which is a longitudinal survey of over 15,000 youth (see the appendix), children who were identified by teachers as having conduct problems in school were more likely to become recorded violent offenders (Hodgins 1994, p. 50). Similarly, in a fifteen-year follow-up of over 600 school children in Buckinghamshire, England (see the appendix), conduct problems such as stealing, lying, and destructiveness predicted convictions for violence (Mitchell and Rosa 1981, pp. 24–25). In the Rochester Youth Development Study, which is a longitudinal survey of nearly 1,000 youth originally aged thirteen to fourteen (see the appendix), more of the self-reported violent offenders used alcohol or marijuana, sold drugs, dropped out of school, and were gang members and teenage parents (Thornberry, Huizinga, and Loeber 1995, p. 225). In the National Youth Survey, more of those admitting felony assault or robbery were polydrug users (Elliott, Huizinga, and Menard 1989, p. 60). Also, there is a marked tendency for victims of violence to overlap with violent offenders, both in official records (e.g., Rivara et al. 1995) and in self-reports (e.g., Singer 1986).

Table 1 shows problems co-occurring with youth violence in the Cambridge Study. The court cases are the 10 percent of males who were convicted for violent offenses between ages ten and twenty-one. Violent offenses in court included assault, wounding, robbery, threatening behavior, and possessing an offensive weapon. Offensive weapon cases usually arose from a violent incident. The self-report cases are

TABLE 1

Co-occuring Problems with Youth Violence

Co-occuring problems	Court	Reported
Age 8–10:		
Difficult to discipline	2.5*	1.7*
Troublesome	4.1*	2.0*
Dishonest	1.9	1.8*
Age 12–14:		
Aggressive	4.8*	2.8*
Bully	2.1*	2.2*
Frequent liar	4.0*	1.5
Hostile to police	3.4*	2.8*
Delinquent friends	4.7*	2.2*
Frequent truant	4.6*	2.4*
Early school leaving	3.0*	2.6*
Early sexual intercourse	3.1*	3.5*
Age 18:		
Soccer violence	3.9*	4.2*
Antisocial group member	3.9*	5.3*
Hangs about	2.5*	2.7*
Drug user	5.2*	4.3*
Heavy smoker	3.3*	3.1*
Heavy drinker	6.0*	2.4*
Binge drinker	2.8*	2.5*
Drunk driver	1.6	2.8*
Heavy gambler	1.9	2.3*
Injured	2.7*	2.6*
Sexually promiscuous	2.5*	2.2*
Aggressive attitude	2.0*	4.4*
Antiestablishment attitude	3.0*	2.3*
Low job status	6.9*	3.6*
Unstable job record	4.6*	2.3*
No examinations taken	4.6*	2.9*
Poor relation with parents	4.1*	1.9*

NOTE.—Odds Ratios are shown. These results are based on 411 London boys in the Cambridge Study in Delinquent Development. Court = convicted for violence at age 10–21; Reported = self-reported violence at ages 15–18. For more information about co-occuring problems, see West and Farrington (1973, 1977).

* $p < .05$.

the 45 percent of males who admitted starting a physical fight or using a weapon in a fight between ages fifteen and eighteen.

The measure of strength of association is the odds ratio. For example, of ninety-two boys rated difficult to discipline at age eight to ten by teachers, sixteen were convicted for violence, giving the odds of violence of .211 (16/76); of 316 boys not difficult to discipline, twenty-five were convicted, giving the odds of violence of .086 (25/291). The odds ratio is the odds of violence with the risk factor (.211), divided by the odds of violence without the risk factor (.086), which here comes to 2.45. This is statistically significant, because its 95 percent confidence interval (1.25–4.82) does not include the chance value of one. Basically, the odds ratio indicates the increase in the risk of violence associated with a risk factor. It has statistical advantages over the simple measure of relative risk (here, 16/92 divided by 25/316, or 2.20). An odds ratio of 2 or greater indicates a doubling of risk and hence a strong relationship.

Table 1 shows that official and self-reported violent offenders tended to be identified as troublesome, dishonest, or difficult to discipline as children (ages eight to ten). They tended to be aggressive, bullies, frequent liars, hostile to the police, and frequent truants as adolescents (ages twelve to fourteen). In addition, they tended to have delinquent friends, to leave school early (age fifteen), and to have early sexual intercourse (age fourteen or younger). As teenagers (age eighteen), they tended to be involved in soccer violence, antisocial groups, and spending time hanging about on the street. They tended to be drug users, heavy smokers, heavy drinkers, binge drinkers, drunk drivers, and heavy gamblers, and they tended to be sexually promiscuous. They tended to have had hospital treatment for injury and expressed aggressive or antiestablishment attitudes. They also tended to have low-status jobs, unstable job records, and poor relationships with their parents. They tended not to take examinations. (For previous analyses relating risk factors to violence in the Cambridge Study, see Farrington [1989a, 1991, 1994a, 1997a]; for more information about all the measures and results, see Farrington [1995a]).

II. Violent Criminal Careers

It is difficult to study violent criminal careers using police and court records because most offenders have only one recorded violent offense. However, violent offenses tend to be committed later than property offenses. In general, there is continuity from juvenile to adult violence and from childhood aggression to youth violence. An important question is why there is discontinuity. For example, establishing why some violent juveniles do not become violent adults could have important implications for explanation and prevention. Little is known about this.

A. Onset and Developmental Course

Only a small proportion of offenses in criminal careers are violent: 15 percent up to age forty in the Cambridge Study, for example (Farrington 1997a, p. 54), 9 percent up to age thirty in the first Philadelphia birth-cohort study (Wolfgang, Thornberry, and Figlio 1987, p. 25), and 5 percent up to age twenty-five in the Stockholm Project Metropolitan (Wikstrom 1985, pp. 119–20). Also, at least outside the United States, the majority of officially recorded violent offenders have committed only one violent offense. This was true, for example, of 72 percent of the Stockholm violent offenders (Wikstrom 1985, p. 122), 76 percent of the Copenhagen violent offenders (Moffitt, Mednick, and Gabrielli 1989, p. 18), and 68 percent of the London violent offenders in the Cambridge Study.

In American research limited to the juvenile years, most recorded violent offenders have committed only one recorded violent offense. For example, the average number of violent offenses per violent offender was 1.32 for the first Philadelphia birth cohort and 1.38 for the second Philadelphia birth cohort (Tracy, Wolfgang, and Figlio 1990, p. 64). The same conclusion follows from juvenile offender samples; 83 percent of violent juveniles in Columbus committed only one recorded violent offense (Hamparian et al. 1978, p. 54). However, adult careers of violence can be much more extensive, at least in the United States. In a study of over 1,500 adult violent offenders arrested in Columbus between 1950 and 1976 (see the appendix), 20 percent had five or more arrests for violence, and 53 percent had between two and four such arrests (Miller, Dinitz, and Conrad 1982, p. 68).

The small number of violent crimes in youthful criminal careers makes it difficult to study traditional criminal career features such as age of onset, age of desistance, career duration, probability of persistence, and frequency of offending (Blumstein et al. 1986), at least in official records. Self-evidently, if most violent offenders have only one recorded violent offense, average career durations are very short. However, it is possible to study the place of violent crimes in criminal careers. Generally, the average age of committing violent crimes is higher than for property crimes (see, e.g., Farrington 1986, p. 197;

Tarling 1993, p. 18)—about four years higher than burglary, for example. In the Columbus study of violent juveniles, the average age of the first violent arrest was one year later than the average age of the first arrest of any type (Hamparian et al. 1978, p. 60). In the Cambridge Study, when comparisons were restricted to males with both violent and nonviolent convictions, the violent convictions generally occurred later and had a later age of onset (Reiss and Roth 1993, p. 377).

The large number of violent offenses reported by youth in self-report surveys facilitates the study of violent criminal careers in principle, but it is rare to have information about the relative timing of each offense (as in official records). For example, in the Rochester Youth Development Study, 58 percent of youth admitted a violent offense by age sixteen, and these violent offenders committed an average of nearly ten violent offenses each (Thornberry, Huizinga, and Loeber 1995, pp. 219–20). Similar results were obtained in the Denver Youth Survey; just over half (54 percent) admitted a violent crime by age sixteen, and these violent offenders committed an average of nearly seven violent acts each (Thornberry, Huizinga, and Loeber 1995, pp. 218–20). Studies of careers of violence using self-reports are needed. For example, in their Montreal study of adolescents (see the appendix), Le Blanc and Frechette (1989, p. 117) showed the age of onset of different types of offenses according to self-reports.

Generally, violent males have an early age of onset of offending of all types and a large number of offenses of all types (e.g., Piper 1985; Farrington 1991). Both in official records (e.g., Hamparian et al. 1978, p. 61; Guttridge et al. 1983, p. 222) and self-reports (e.g., Elliott 1994, p. 14; Thornberry, Huizinga, and Loeber 1995, p. 221), an early age of onset of violent offending predicts a relatively large number of violent offenses. It is less clear whether an early onset of violent offending predicts a higher rate of violent offending per year; the earliest onset violent offenders (age six to ten) had only slightly more violent offenses (average 1.4 compared with 1.0) in the Columbus study of Hamparian and her colleagues (1978, p. 61) than later onset violent offenders. However, this analysis is severely limited by the fact that most youth in this project only had one arrest for violence. Research on this topic is needed using self-reports.

At least in official records, recidivism probabilities are lower for violence than for offenses of all types, reflecting the relatively low frequency of violent offending. For example, in the Columbus study of violent juveniles, the probability of committing a second violent crime after a first was only 17 percent, and the probability of committing a third violent crime after a second was only 23 percent (Hamparian et al. 1978, p. 54). These percentages would be higher for follow-up periods beyond age eighteen. In the first Philadelphia birth-cohort study, these probabilities were 38 percent and 49 percent, respectively (Piper 1985, p. 333), compared with the recidivism probabilities for all offenses of 54 percent and 65 percent, respectively (Blumstein, Farrington, and Moitra 1985, p. 210).

Not surprisingly, there is continuity between juvenile and adult violent careers. In the Columbus study, 59 percent of violent juveniles were arrested as adults in the next five to nine years, and 42 percent of these adult offenders were charged with at least one Index violent offense (Hamparian et al. 1985, p. 16). More of those arrested for Index violence as juveniles were rearrested as adults than of those arrested for minor violence (simple assault or molesting) as juveniles: 63 percent compared with 53 percent (Hamparian et al. 1985, p. 20). In the Cambridge Study, half of the boys convicted of violence as juveniles (ages ten to sixteen) were reconvicted of violence as young adults (ages seventeen to twenty-four), compared with only 8 percent of those not convicted of violence as juveniles (Farrington 1995*b*, p. 14). The odds ratio for this comparison was 11.7. It is important to try to quantify the degree of continuity or discontinuity in violence.

B. Developmental Pathways from Aggression to Violence

Laub and Lauritsen (1993, p. 239) concluded that "the stability of aggressive behavior patterns throughout the life course is one of the most consistently documented patterns found in longitudinal research." For example, Olweus (1979) reviewed sixteen surveys covering time periods of up to twenty-one years and reported an average stability coefficient (correlation) for male aggression of .68. Furthermore, this average coefficient decreased linearly with an increasing time interval between measurements. Olweus argued that individual differences in aggressiveness were almost as stable over time as individual differences in intelligence, and similar conclusions were drawn by Cairns and Cairns (1994, pp. 63–64). Unfortunately, these and other studies (e.g., Eron and Huesmann 1990) of the stability of aggression rarely included specific measures of youth violence.

Studies that have compared childhood aggression with youth violence always report significant predictability. For example, in the Orebro (Sweden) follow-up of about 1,000 youth (see the appendix), two-thirds of the boys who were officially recorded for violence, up to age twenty-six, had high aggressiveness scores at ages ten and thirteen (rated by teachers) compared with 30 percent of all boys (Stattin and Magnusson 1989, p. 714). Similarly, in the Jyvaskyla (Finland) follow-up of nearly 400 youth (see the appendix), peer ratings of aggression at ages eight and fourteen significantly predicted official violence up to age twenty (Pulkkinen 1987, p. 206). Also, in the Woodlawn (Chicago) follow-up study of over 1,200 African-American youth (see the appendix), teacher ratings of aggressiveness at age six predicted arrests for violent crimes up to age thirty-three (McCord and Ensminger 1995, p. 10), but not very strongly. Almost half of the aggressive boys were later arrested, compared with about a third of their nonaggressive counterparts.

One possible explanation of the continuity over time is that there are persisting individual differences in an underlying potential to commit aggressive or violent behavior. In any cohort, the people who are relatively more aggressive at one age also tend to be relatively more aggressive at later ages, even though absolute levels of aggressive behavior and behavioral manifestations of violence are different at different ages. There may also be developmental sequences or pathways over time from one type of aggression to another. For example, in the Pittsburgh Youth Study, Loeber and his colleagues (1993) reported that childhood aggression (e.g., bullying) escalated into gang fighting and later into youth violence, and similar patterns have been found in other longitudinal surveys (Tolan and Gorman-Smith 1998, p. 81).

A key question is whether the continuity in aggression and violence is specific or merely one aspect of the general continuity in antisocial behavior over time. This was investigated for bullying in the Cambridge Study (Farrington 1993b, pp. 431–33 and 442–44). It was concluded that both the intragenerational continuity between a man's bullying at ages fourteen and thirty-two and the intergenerational continuity between his bullying at age fourteen and his child's bullying when the man was aged thirty-two held up independently of the general continuity in antisocial behavior. Hence, there seemed to be specific continuity in aggressive behavior over time. More analyses addressing this issue are needed.

III. Changeable Risk Factors

Most studies investigate the prediction of violent youth out of all youth (see also Hawkins et al. 1998). However, this does not make it possible to determine specific predictors of violent as opposed to nonviolent offending, compared with general predictors of offending versus nonoffending. There is also the problem, mentioned above, of disentangling violent offenders from frequent or persistent offenders. A few researchers have compared violent delinquents, nonviolent delinquents, and nondelinquents (e.g., Farrington 1978; Henry et al. 1996) or compared violent delinquents with equally frequent nonviolent delinquents (e.g., Farrington 1991; Capaldi and Patterson 1996), but most studies reviewed in this section are concerned with predictors of violent versus nonviolent youth.

Table 2 presents research on risk factors for violence in the Cambridge Study and the Pittsburgh Youth Study. As in table 1, the London court cases are the 10 percent of boys who were convicted for violence between ages ten and twenty-one, while the reported cases are the 45 percent of boys who admitted starting a fight or using a weapon in a fight between ages fifteen and eighteen. All risk factors were measured at ages eight to ten. The Pittsburgh boys constitute the middle cohort who were first studied at age ten. The court cases are the 12 percent of boys who were petitioned to the juvenile court for Index violence between ages ten and seventeen, while the reported cases are the 39 percent of boys reported by mothers, teachers, or themselves to have committed violence (attack to cause serious hurt, robbery, or rape) between ages ten and thirteen. All risk factors were measured at age ten (see Farrington and Loeber 1998). As before, the strength of each relationship is summarized by the odds ratio. Gaps in the table occur where a particular risk factor was measured in one study but not in the other. Independent or interactive effects of risk factors are not investigated in this essay.

The only risk factor that was measured in both London and Pittsburgh that was a strong and significant predictor of youth violence in both court and reported data was family dependence on welfare benefits (reflecting poverty). Daring, low intelligence, a convicted parent, and low family income were significant predictors of court convictions and reported violence in London but were not measured in Pittsburgh. Low guilt, living in a single-parent female-headed household, and a bad neighborhood were significant predictors of court and reported violence in Pittsburgh but not measured in London. Other results were less consistent.

A. Biological Factors

As shown by detailed reviews prepared for the National Academy of Sciences panel (Reiss, Miczek, and Roth 1994), relationships between

TABLE 2

Explanatory Risk Factors for Youth Violence

Risk Factor at 8–10	London		Pittsburgh	
	Court	Reported	Court	Reported
Biological:				
Pregnancy complications	.3	.9	. . .	. . .
Delivery complications	.5	1.2	. . .	. . .
Individual:				
High daring	4.0*	2.2*	. . .	. . .
Attention deficit	2.3*	1.4	1.1	2.1*
High anxiety	.8	.7	.4*	1.0
Low guilt	. . .	. . .	2.5*	3.3*
Low intelligence	2.6*	1.6*	. . .	. . .
Low achievement	2.4*	1.3	2.7*	3.2*
Parental:				
Convicted parent	2.7*	1.8*	. . .	. . .
Parent substance use	. . .	. . .	1.1	2.2*
Young mother	1.3*	1.2	2.7*	2.0*
Poorly educated mother	. . .	. . .	2.4*	1.4
Large family	2.6*	2.4*	2.4*	1.4
Child-rearing:				
Poor supervision	3.8*	1.5	1.3	1.1
Harsh maternal discipline	3.2*	2.8*	1.1	1.6*
Low parental reinforcement	2.7*	1.8	1.8*	1.1
Parental conflict	2.9*	1.1	1.8	2.0*
Broken family	2.9*	1.3	3.4*	3.1*
Single mother	. . .	. . .	2.0*	2.3*
Socioeconomic:				
Low socioeconomic status	1.4	1.5	2.0*	2.2*
Low family income	3.1*	1.7*	. . .	. . .
Family on welfare	7.5*	2.0*	3.7*	2.0*
Poor housing	2.1*	1.6*	1.1	1.2
Neighborhood:				
Bad neighborhood (C)	. . .	. . .	2.2*	2.0*
Bad neighborhood (M)	. . .	. . .	2.6*	2.3*

NOTE.—C = Census; M = Mother. Odds Ratios are shown. London: results are based on 411 boys in Cambridge Study Delinquent Development. Court = convicted for violence at age 10–21; Reported = self-reported violence at ages 15–18. Pittsburgh: results are based on 508 boys in middle sample of Pittsburgh Youth Study. Court = petitioned to court for violence at ages 10–17; Reported = boy, mother, or teacher report of violence at ages 10–13. For information about risk factors, see Farrington and Loeber (1998).

* $p < .05$.

psychophysiological and hormonal factors, neurotransmitters, and aggression and violence in humans and animals are extremely complex. My modest aim in this section is to review a few of the more important biological factors that may be specifically related to youth violence.

According to Raine (1993, pp. 166–72), one of the most replicable findings in the literature is that antisocial and violent youth tend to have low resting heart rates. This can easily be demonstrated by taking pulse rates. The main theory underlying this finding is that a low heart rate indicates low autonomic arousal and/or fearlessness. Low autonomic arousal, like boredom, leads to sensation seeking and risk taking in an attempt to increase stimulation and arousal levels. Conversely, high heart rates, especially in infants and young children, are associated with anxiety, behavioral inhibition, and a fearful temperament (Kagan 1989).

In the British National Survey of Health and Development, which is a prospective longitudinal survey of over 5,300 children born in England, Scotland, or Wales in 1946 (see the appendix), heart rate was measured at age eleven. A low heart rate predicted convictions for violent and sexual offenses up to age twenty-one; 81 percent of violent offenders and 67 percent of sexual offenders had below-average heart rates (Wadsworth 1976, p. 249). A low heart rate was especially characteristic of boys who had experienced a broken home before age five, but among these boys it was not related to violence or sexual offenses. A low heart rate was significantly related to violence and sexual offenses among boys who came from unbroken homes.

In the Cambridge Study, resting heart rate was measured only at age eighteen, and so it is not shown as a predictor of youth violence in table 2. However, it was significantly related to convictions for violence, and to self-reported violence at age eighteen, independently of all other variables (Farrington 1997b). More than twice as many of the boys with low heart rates (sixty-five beats per minute or less) were convicted for violence as of the remainder. Another interesting result was obtained in the Montreal longitudinal-experimental study, which is a follow-up of over 1,100 children originally selected at age six (see the appendix). Low heart rate at age eleven was significantly associated with teacher ratings of fighting and bullying at the same age (Kindlon et al. 1995).

Neurotransmitters are chemicals stored in brain cells that carry information between these cells. There are many different neurotransmitters, but serotonin is the one that has been most reliably linked to violence. Low serotonin levels in the brain are thought to indicate low cortical arousal, low inhibition, or both; both are believed to be conducive to violence.

The largest investigation of the relationship between serotonin and violence was carried out by Moffitt and her colleagues (1997) in the Dunedin Study in New Zealand. They measured serotonin at age twenty-one in blood samples, finding that men who were convicted for violence, and those who were high on self-reported violence, tended to have high blood serotonin levels. This is in agreement with the theory, since high blood serotonin levels indicate low brain serotonin levels. These relationships held up after controlling for socioeconomic status, intelligence, smoking, drinking, drug use, and other variables.

Hormones are biochemical substances that carry information throughout the body. The hormone that has been studied most in relation to violence is testosterone, which can be measured in blood or saliva samples. Studies of many animal species show that testosterone facilitates aggression between males when animals are reproductively active (e.g., Brain 1994; Turner 1994), leading to the hypothesis that high testosterone levels in boys from puberty onward might be related to violence.

Most studies of testosterone and aggression (e.g., Olweus 1986) have measured verbal aggression rather than physical violence. Results obtained in these studies are inconsistent, although comparisons between violent male prisoners and control groups show the most reliable associations between testosterone levels and violence (Rubin 1987; Archer 1991). In the Montreal longitudinal-experimental study, teacher ratings of fighting and bullying were associated with low testosterone levels (in saliva) at age thirteen but with high testosterone levels at age sixteen (Tremblay et al. 1997, p. 281). These results suggest that high testosterone levels after puberty might be related to youth violence.

Perinatal (pregnancy and delivery) complications have been studied because of the hypothesis that they might lead to neurological damage, which in turn might lead to violence. In the Danish perinatal study, Kandel and Mednick (1991) followed up over 200 children born in Copenhagen in 1959–61 (see the appendix). They found that delivery complications predicted arrests for violence up to age twenty-two; 80 percent of violent offenders scored in the high range of delivery complications, compared with 30 percent of property offenders and 47 percent of nonoffenders (Kandel and Mednick 1991, p. 523). However, pregnancy complications did not significantly predict violence. Interestingly, delivery complications especially predicted violence when a parent had a history of psychiatric illness; in this case, 32 percent of males with high delivery complications were arrested for violence, compared with only 5 percent of those with low delivery complications (Brennan, Mednick, and Mednick 1993, pp. 249–50).

Unfortunately, these results were not replicated by Denno (1990) in the Philadelphia Biosocial Project, a follow-up of nearly 1,000 African American births in Philadelphia in 1959–62 (see the appendix). Because it was part of the larger Collaborative Perinatal Project, this study included extensive data on pregnancy and delivery complications, but they did not predict arrests for violence up to age twenty-two. For males, the only significant biological predictor of arrests was the lead level in the body at age seven. Also, pregnancy and delivery complications did not significantly predict official or self-reported violence in the Cambridge Study (table 2). It may be that pregnancy and delivery complications predict violence only or mainly when they occur in combination with other family adversities.

With the possible exception of low resting heart rate, the evidence linking biological factors to youth violence in community samples is not impressive or consistent. There are a number of reasons for this. In particular, it is difficult to measure biological factors accurately or under rigorously controlled conditions in community samples. Peripheral measures are used (e.g., saliva or blood samples) that do not require very invasive techniques, rather than more direct measures (e.g., using lumbar punctures). Measures of brain functioning (e.g., using brain imaging techniques) are only just beginning to be used. Even in large community samples, the biological analyses may be based on very small numbers; for example, the key analyses of Kindlon and his colleagues (1995) in the Montreal longitudinal-experimental study were based on only forty to fifty boys. Finally, the effects of biological factors may occur primarily or exclusively in interaction with social and psychological factors. The study of such interaction effects is in its infancy (Raine, Brennan, and Farrington 1997).

B. Psychological/Personality Factors

Among the most important personality dimensions that predict youth violence are hyperactivity, impulsiveness, poor behavioral control, and attention problems. Conversely, nervousness and anxiety are negatively related to violence. For example, in the Dunedin (New Zealand) follow-up of over 1,000 children (see the appendix), ratings of poor behavioral control (e.g., impulsiveness, lack of persistence) at age three to five significantly predicted boys convicted of violence up to age eighteen, compared to those with no convictions or with nonviolent convictions (Henry et al. 1996, p. 618). In the same study, the personality dimensions of constraint (e.g., cautiousness, avoiding excitement) and negative emotionality (e.g., nervousness, alienation) at age eighteen were significantly correlated with convictions for violence (Caspi et al. 1994, p. 180).

Many other studies show links between these personality dimensions and youth violence. For example, in the Copenhagen perinatal project, hyperactivity (restlessness and poor concentration) at ages eleven to thirteen significantly predicted arrests for violence up to age twenty-two, especially among boys experiencing delivery complications (Brennan, Mednick, and Mednick 1993, p. 253). More than half of those with both hyperactivity and high delivery complications were arrested for violence, compared to less than 10 percent of the remainder. Similarly, in the Orebro longitudinal study in Sweden, hyperactivity at age thirteen predicted police-recorded violence up to age twenty-six (Klinteberg et al. 1993, p. 383). The highest rate of violence was among males with both motor restlessness and concentration difficulties (15 percent), compared to 3 percent of the remainder.

Similar results were obtained in the London and Pittsburgh studies (table 2). High daring or risk taking at ages eight to ten predicted both convictions for violence and self-reported violence in London. Poor concentration and attention difficulties predicted convictions for violence in London and reported violence in Pittsburgh. High anxiety/nervousness was negatively related to violence in both studies, and low guilt significantly predicted court referrals for violence in the Pittsburgh study.

The other main group of psychological factors that predict youth violence include low intelligence and low school attainment. For example, in the Philadelphia Biosocial Project, low verbal and performance IQ at ages four and seven and low scores on the California Achievement Test at ages thirteen to fourteen (vocabulary, comprehension, math, language, spelling), all predicted arrests for violence up to age twenty-two (Denno 1990, table 3.1). In Project Metropolitan in Copenhagen, a follow-up study of over 12,000 boys born in 1953 (see the appendix), low IQ at age twelve significantly predicted police-recorded violence between ages fifteen and twenty-two (Hogh and Wolf 1983, table 14-4). The correlation between IQ and violence was a remarkable $-.94$, and the link between low IQ and violence was strongest among lower class boys.

Similar results were obtained in the London and Pittsburgh studies (table 2). Low nonverbal IQ at ages eight to ten in London predicted both official and self-reported violence, and low school achievement at age ten predicted official violence in London and court petitions and reported violence in Pittsburgh. The extensive meta-analysis by Lipsey and Derzon (1998, p. 97) also showed that low IQ, low school attainment, and psychological factors such as hyperactivity, attention deficit, impulsivity, and risk-taking were important predictors of later serious and violent offending.

Impulsiveness, attention problems, low intelligence, and low attainment could all be linked to deficits in the executive functions of the brain, located in the frontal lobes. These executive functions include sustaining attention and concentration, abstract reasoning and concept formation, goal formulation, anticipation and planning, programming and initiation of purposive sequences of motor behavior, effective self-monitoring and self-awareness of behavior, and inhibition of inappropriate or impulsive behaviors (Moffitt and Henry 1991, pp. 75–76). Interestingly, in the Montreal longitudinal-experimental study, a measure of executive functions based on cognitive-neuropsychological tests at age fourteen was the strongest neuropsychological discriminator of violent and nonviolent boys (Seguin et al. 1995, p. 620). This relationship held independently of a measure of family adversity (based on parental age at first child's birth, parental education level, broken family, and low socioeconomic status).

C. Family Factors

Numerous family factors predict violence. For example, in her follow-up of 250 treated Boston boys in the Cambridge-Somerville Youth Study (see the appendix), McCord (1979, p. 1481) found that the strongest predictors at age ten of later convictions for violence (up to age forty-five) were poor parental supervision; parental aggression, including harsh, punitive discipline; and parental conflict. An absent father was almost significant as a predictor, but the mother's lack of affection was not significant. McCord (1977, p. 87) also demonstrated that fathers convicted for violence tended to have sons convicted for violence; the odds ratio for this comparison was 3.0. In later analyses, McCord (1996, p. 150) showed that violent offenders were less likely than nonviolent offenders to have experienced parental affection and good discipline and supervision but equally likely to have experienced parental conflict.

Similar results have been obtained in other studies. For example, in the Chicago Youth Development Study, which is a longitudinal follow-up of nearly 400 inner-city boys initially studied at age eleven to thirteen (see the appendix), poor parental monitoring and low family cohesion predicted self-reported violent offending (Gorman-Smith et al. 1996, p. 123). Also, poor parental monitoring and low attachment to parents predicted self-reported violence in the Rochester Youth Development Study (Thornberry, Huizinga, and Loeber 1995, p. 227). Families broken between birth and age ten predicted convictions for violence up to age twenty-one in the British National Survey (Wadsworth 1978, p. 48), and single-parent status at age thirteen predicted convictions for violence up to age eighteen in the Dunedin study (Henry et al. 1996, p. 618).

Harsh physical punishment by parents and child physical abuse typically predict violent offending by sons (Malinosky-Rummell and Hansen 1993). In a follow-up study of nearly 900 children in New York State (see the appendix), Eron, Huesmann, and Zelli (1991, p. 175) reported that harsh parental punishment at age eight predicted not only a man's history of arrests for violence up to age thirty, but also the severity of the man's punishment of his child at age thirty and his history of spouse assault. Interestingly, in the Cambridge-Somerville Study, McCord (1997) found that physical punishment predicted convictions for violence especially when combined with low parental warmth and affection.

In the most famous longitudinal study of abused children (over 900 with nearly 700 controls), Widom (1989, p. 164) discovered that recorded child physical abuse and neglect predicted later arrests for violence independently of other predictors such as gender, ethnicity, and age (see the appendix). The odds ratio for child abuse and neglect predicting juvenile violence was 2.0 (Maxfield and Widom 1996, p. 392). Furthermore, child sexual abuse, child physical abuse, and neglect predicted adult arrests for sex crimes (Widom and Ames 1994, p. 312). In the Rochester Youth Development Study, Smith and Thornberry (1995, p. 463) showed that recorded childhood maltreatment under age twelve predicted self-reported violence between ages fourteen and eighteen, independently of gender, ethnicity, socioeconomic status, and family structure. However, in a retrospective case-control study by Zingraff and his colleagues (1993) in North Carolina, recorded childhood maltreatment predicted court referrals for violence, but not after controlling for other variables such as age, gender, and race.

Large family size (number of children) is a replicable predictor of offending (Fischer 1984). For example, in the Oregon Youth Study, large family size at age ten predicted self-reported violence at ages thirteen to seventeen in a regression equation (Capaldi and Patterson 1996, p. 224). Young mothers (mothers who had their first child at an early age, typically as a teenager) also tend to have violent sons, as Morash and Rucker (1989, p. 63) demonstrated for the prediction of self-reported violence at age sixteen in the Cambridge Study. Interestingly, the relationship between a young mother and a convicted son in this study disappeared after controlling for other variables, notably large family size, a convicted parent, and a broken family (Nagin, Pogarsky, and Farrington 1997, p. 156).

Table 2 shows results obtained with family variables in the London and Pittsburgh studies. Having a convicted parent predicted official and self-reported violence in London, while parental substance use predicted reported violence in Pittsburgh. Having a young mother predicted official and self-reported violence in the Pittsburgh study but not in London, possibly because young mothers were more likely to be married in London. Large family size predicted violence in both studies, and having a poorly educated mother predicted official violence in Pittsburgh. Surprisingly, poor parental supervision predicted only official violence in London. Harsh maternal discipline predicted official and reported violence in London but only reported violence in Pittsburgh. Low parental reinforcement predicted official violence in both cities. Parental conflict and a broken family predicted official violence in both cities and reported violence in Pittsburgh. Coming from a single-parent female-headed household predicted official and reported violence in Pittsburgh.

Table 2 shows that the results obtained with family predictors were not totally consistent. Lipsey and Derzon's (1998, p. 97) meta-analysis of predictors of serious and violent offending concluded that the strongest family predictor was antisocial or criminal parents, followed by parent-child relations (measures of supervision, discipline, or attitude). In contrast, broken families and child abuse and neglect were relatively weak predictors.

D. Peer, Socioeconomic, and Neighborhood Factors

Having delinquent friends is an important predictor of youth violence. For example, peer delinquency was the most proximal influence on serious violent offending in Elliott's causal model (1994, p. 17), and it predicted self-reported violence in the Rochester Youth Development Study (Thornberry, Huizinga, and Loeber 1995, p. 227). In the meta-analysis of Lipsey and Derzon (1998, p. 97), delinquent peers were predictive at ages twelve to fourteen but not at ages six to eleven. The predictability of many risk factors may vary at different ages. What is less clear is the degree to which the link between delinquent friends and delinquency is a consequence of co-offending, which is particularly common under age twenty-one (Reiss and Farrington 1991, p. 372). On the basis of causal models, Elliott and Menard (1996) concluded both that delinquency caused delinquent peer bonding and that delinquent peer bonding caused delinquency. However, there seems to be no information specifically about the link between and relative timing of peer violence and youth violence.

In general, coming from a low socioeconomic status family predicts youth violence. For example, in the National Youth Survey the prevalences of self-reported felony assault and robbery were about twice as high among lower-class youth as among middle-class ones (Elliott, Huizinga, and Menard 1989, p. 38). Similar results have been obtained for official violence in Project Metropolitan in Stockholm (Wikstrom 1985, p. 133), in Project Metropolitan in Copenhagen (Hogh and Wolf 1983, p. 253), and in the Dunedin Study in New Zealand (Henry et al. 1996, p. 618). All three studies compared the socioeconomic status of the family at the boy's birth, based on the father's occupation, with the boy's later violent crimes. The relationship between socioeconomic status and youth violence was weakest in New Zealand.

Table 2 shows the relationships in the London and Pittsburgh studies between socioeconomic factors measured at ages eight to ten and youth violence. Low socioeconomic status, based on the occupation of the parents, predicted official and reported violence in Pittsburgh but not in London. Possibly, occupational prestige in London was not predictive because it did not reflect relative differences between the families in affluence or poverty; many of the manual jobs such as dockers and printers were better paid than nonmanual jobs such as bank clerks. In their meta-analysis, Lipsey and Derzon (1998, p. 97) found that serious and violent offending was predicted by low family socioeconomic status strongly at ages six to eleven but only weakly at ages twelve to fourteen. Low family income and poor housing predicted official and reported violence in London. Possibly, poor housing was predictive in London but not in Pittsburgh because housing conditions were objectively much worse in London. The strongest predictor of official violence in both London and Pittsburgh was family dependence on welfare benefits.

Generally, boys living in urban areas are more violent than those living in rural ones. In the National Youth Survey, the prevalence of self-reported felony assault and robbery was considerably higher among urban youth (Elliott, Huizinga, and Menard 1989, p. 46). Many longitudinal studies of youth violence are based only on urban samples (see the appendix). Within urban areas, boys living in high-crime neighborhoods are more violent than those living in low-crime neighborhoods. In the Rochester Youth Development Study, living in a high-crime neighborhood significantly predicted self-reported violence (Thornberry, Huizinga, and Loeber 1995, p. 227). Similarly, in the Pittsburgh Youth Study, living in a bad neighborhood (either as rated by the mother or based on census measures of poverty, unemployment, and female-headed households) significantly predicted official and reported violence (table 2).

E. Situational Factors

It might be argued that all the factors reviewed so far in this section—biological, psychological/personality, family, peer, socioeconomic, and neighborhood—essentially influence the development of a long-term individual potential for violence. In other words, they contribute to between-individual differences: why some people are more likely than others, given the same situational opportunity, to commit violence. However, another set of influences—situational factors—explain how the potential for violence becomes the actuality in any given situation. They explain short-term within-individual differences: why a person is more likely to commit violence in some situations than in others. Situational factors may be specific to particular types of crimes: robberies as opposed to rapes or even street robberies as opposed to bank robberies.

Much work on describing situations leading to violence has been carried out in Great Britain under the rubric of crime analysis (Ekblom 1988). This begins with a detailed analysis of patterns and circumstances of crimes and then proceeds to devising, implementing, and evaluating crime-reduction strategies. For example, Barker and her colleagues (1993) analyzed the nature of street robbery in London. Most of these crimes occurred in predominantly ethnic minority areas, and most offenders were sixteen-to-nineteen-year-old Afro-Caribbean males. The victims were mostly Caucasian females, alone and on foot.

Most offenses occurred at night, near the victim's home. The main motive for robbery was to get money, and the main factor in choosing victims was whether they had a wealthy appearance.

One of the most influential situational theories of offending is routine activities theory. This suggests that, for a predatory crime to occur, the minimum requirement is the convergence in time and place of a motivated offender and a suitable target, in the absence of a capable guardian (Cohen and Felson 1979, p. 590). In discussing situational factors, I focus on motives of potential offenders, actions preceding violent acts, and characteristics of situational opportunities. Motivation could depend on long-term developmental influences, but it is discussed in this section because of the predominant interest in motives that vary within individuals over short time periods. I do not discuss the situational factors of guns, drugs, and alcohol because they are covered elsewhere in this volume.

In their Montreal longitudinal study of delinquents (see the appendix), Le Blanc and Frechette (1989, table 2.2) provided detailed information about motives and methods used in different offenses at different ages. For example, for violence at age seventeen, the main motivation was utilitarian or rational. For all crimes, however, the primary motivation changed from hedonistic (searching for excitement, with co-offenders) in the teenage years to utilitarian (with planning, psychological intimidation, and use of instruments such as weapons) in the twenties (Le Blanc 1996, p. 161). In the National Survey of Youth, a cross-sectional survey of nearly 1,400 American youth aged eleven to eighteen, assaults were usually said to be committed for retaliation or revenge or because of provocation or anger (Agnew 1990, table 3).

In the Cambridge Study, motives for physical fights depended on whether the boy fought alone or with others (Farrington 1993a, p. 236). In individual fights, the boy was usually provoked, became angry, and hit out to hurt his opponent and to discharge his own internal feelings of tension. In group fights, the boy often said that he became involved to help a friend or because he was attacked, and rarely said that he was angry. The group fights were more serious, occurring in bars or streets, and they were more likely to involve weapons, produce injuries, and lead to police intervention. Fights often occurred when minor incidents escalated because both sides wanted to demonstrate their toughness and masculinity and were unwilling to react in a conciliatory way.

Behaviors leading up to violence have been studied (see e.g., Linaker and Busch-Iversen 1995). Wolfgang (1958, p. 191) classified actions leading to homicide in Philadelphia based on police records. Most commonly, homicides arose from trivial altercations (insults or jostling), domestic quarrels, jealousy, or altercations over money. Similarly, violent offenses in London usually arose from family disputes or quarrels between neighbors or persons working together (McClintock 1963, p. 33). In a typical Swedish town (Gavle), most violent crimes were preceded by arguments, either arising out of the situation or based on existing social relationships (Wikstrom 1985, p. 75). However, in all these studies a minority of violent acts were basically unprovoked attacks or robberies. Pallone and Hennessy (1993) referred to "tinderbox criminal violence," defined as violence occurring between similar types of people, known to each other, ostensibly to settle long-lasting or emerging disputes.

Much is known about the situations in which violence occurs (Monahan and Klassen 1982; Sampson and Lauritsen 1994). For example, in the Swedish study in Gavle, violence preceded by situational arguments typically occurred in streets or restaurants, while violence preceded by relationship arguments typically occurred in homes (Wikstrom 1985, p. 92). In England, stranger assaults typically occurred in streets, bars, or discotheques, nonstranger assaults typically occurred at home or work, and robberies typically occurred in the street or on public transport (Hough and Sheehy 1986, p. 25). Violence in public places could be investigated using systematic observation, for example, recording incidents from closed-circuit television cameras mounted on buildings. More research on situational influences on violent acts needs to be incorporated in prospective longitudinal studies in order to link up the developmental and situational perspectives.

F. Protective Factors

Most research on youth violence seeks to identify risk factors: those associated with an increased probability of violence. It is also important to identify protective factors: those associated with a decreased probability of violence. Protective factors may have more implications than risk factors for prevention and treatment. However, there are three separate definitions of protective factors.

The first suggests that a protective factor is merely the opposite end of the scale (or the other side of the coin) to a risk factor. For example, if low intelligence is a risk factor, high intelligence may be a protective factor. This depends, however, on a linear relationship between the variable and violence. To the extent that the relationship is linear, little is gained by identifying the protective factor of high intelligence and the risk factor of low intelligence.

The second definition specifies protective factors that are free-standing, with no corresponding, symmetrically opposite, risk factor. This especially occurs when variables are nonlinearly related to violence. For example, if high popularity were associated with a low risk of violence, while medium and low popularity were associated with a fairly constant average risk, popularity could be a protective factor but not a risk factor (because the probability of violence was not high at low levels of popularity). To the extent that low popularity indicates nervousness and social isolation, low popularity (like high popularity) could also be associated with a low risk of violence (cf. Farrington et al. 1988).

The third definition of a protective factor identifies variables that interact with risk factors to minimize or buffer their effects (Rutter 1985; Farrington 1994*b*). These protective factors may or may not be associated with violence themselves. In order to facilitate the exposition here, I distinguish between a risk variable (e.g., family income) and a risk factor (e.g., low family income). Interaction effects can be studied in two ways, by either focusing on the effect of a risk variable in the presence of a protective factor or focusing on the effect of a protective variable in the presence of a risk factor. For example, the effect of family income on violence could be studied in the presence of high family cohesiveness, or the effect of family cohesiveness on violence could be studied in the presence of low family income.

Most studies focusing on the interaction of risk and protective factors identify a subsample at risk (with some combination of risk factors) and then search for protective variables that predict successful members of this subsample. For example, Werner and Smith (1982) studied children in Hawaii who possessed four or more risk factors for delinquency before age two but who nevertheless did not develop behavioral difficulties during childhood or adolescence. They found that the major protective factors included being first-born, active and affectionate infants, small family size, and receiving a high amount of attention from caretakers.

Most research on protective factors has focused on the concept of resilient children (Luthar and Zigler 1991). For example, Richters and Martinez (1993) investigated protective factors among African-American children aged six to seven in a low-income, violent neighborhood in Washington, D.C. Adaptational failures were defined as those children who were failing in school and were conduct-disordered. They found that adaptational success depended on living in stable and safe homes. Stable homes were those in which a father was present in the home, the family was not on welfare, and the family did not move frequently, while safe homes were those in which the children did not report seeing guns or drugs.

There has been little research on protective factors for juvenile delinquency or youth violence. In the Pittsburgh Youth Study, all explanatory variables were divided into a risk category (the worst quarter), a neutral category (the middle half), and a protective category (the best quarter), and their relationships with delinquency (rated by the boy, the mother, and the teacher) were investigated (Stouthamer-Loeber et al. 1993). The most common finding was that a variable was related to delinquency both at the protective end (vs. the middle category) and at the risk end (vs. the middle category). A number of variables had risk effects only, but none had protective effects only across all three cohorts.

In the Rochester Youth Development Study, high-risk youth were defined as those with five or more of nine family-based risk factors (poor parental education, parental unemployment, family on welfare, young mother, frequent family moves, etc.). The resilient youth—those who were not serious self-reported delinquents—tended to have good school performance, good parental supervision and attachment, and conventional peers (Smith et al. 1995, p. 232).

More research specifically searching for protective factors against youth violence is clearly needed. Although outside the scope of this essay, the effects of life-course transitions (e.g., marriage) that affect developmental pathways should also be studied.

IV. Theories of Youth Violence

Risk-factor approaches tend to be atheoretical. In order to develop theories of youth violence, it is important to establish how these risk factors have independent, additive, interactive, or sequential effects. Generally, the probability of violence increases with the number of risk factors. For example, in the Cambridge Study, a "vulnerability" score was developed on the basis of five risk factors measured at age eight to ten: low family income, large family size, a convicted parent, low IQ, and poor parental child-rearing behavior. The percentage of boys convicted for violence between ages ten and twenty increased from 3 percent of those with none of these risk factors to 31 percent of those with four or five (Farrington 1997*a*, p. 58). This type of research gives some indication of how accurately violence might be predicted.

A key problem is whether, given the similarity in risk factors between violent and nonviolent but equally frequent offenders, it is necessary or desirable to propose theories specifically for youth violence or for specific types of youth violence (e.g., rape or robbery). A related issue is whether the key underlying construct in a theory should be violence potential or a more general antisocial potential (e.g., a weak conscience, weak bonding to society, or low self-control). An argument in favor of a specific theory of youth violence is that how the potential becomes the actuality of violent behavior is likely to depend on specific situational factors. In this section, I focus on theories of youth violence.

Theories can help to explain how and why biological factors such as a low heart rate, psychological/personality factors such as impulsivity or a low IQ, family factors such as poor parental supervision, peer factors, socioeconomic factors, and neighborhood factors influence the development of an individual potential for violence. For example, living in a bad neighborhood and suffering socioeconomic deprivation may in some way cause poor parenting, which in some way causes impulsivity and school failure, which in some way causes a high potential for violence. Theories can also help in specifying more general concepts that underlie violence potential, such as low self-control or weak bonding to society, and in specifying how a potentially violent person interacts with situational factors to produce violent acts.

A. Theories of Delinquency and Aggression

Unfortunately, there are scarcely any theories specifically of youth violence, although Short (1997) provided a very useful review of the most relevant theories. The most specific is probably the type of causal model tested by Elliott (1994, p. 17). This suggests that the most immediate cause of serious violent offending is peer delinquency, while longer-term causes include stressful family events, early victimization, parental sanctions, and family bonding.

Classic theories of delinquency could be applied to explain youth violence. For example, Gottfredson and Hirschi (1990) would argue that low self-control causes violence as well as other criminal acts, heavy smoking, heavy drinking, accidents, and so on. Moffitt (1993, p. 678) argued that the crimes of "life-course-persistent" offenders were often characterized by overt aggression. Wilson and Herrnstein (1985) would probably argue that people who are poor at considering the future consequences of their actions would tend to be violent. Clarke and Cornish (1985) could argue that people weigh likely costs against likely benefits in deciding whether to commit violent acts. Catalano and Hawkins (1996) would argue that low bonding to society causes violence as well as drug use and other delinquent acts. Violence could be an element of a delinquent subculture (Cohen 1955), caused by the strain between aspirations and actuality (Cloward and Ohlin 1960), or learned by differential association (Sutherland and Cressey 1974).

Theories of aggression could also be applied to explain youth violence. An early theory (Dollard et al. 1939) suggested that frustration caused aggression. Berkowitz (1993) further developed this theory, proposing that hostile (as opposed to instrumental) aggression was activated by unpleasant events such as frustration or insults. Bandura's social learning theory (1973) suggests that aggressive behavior is acquired and maintained through observing models and rewards and punishments received. Patterson, DeBaryshe, and Ramsey (1989) modified this theory into the social-interactional perspective, positing that the development of aggression and antisocial behavior depends on the extent to which parental and other rewards and punishments are consistent and contingent on the child's behavior.

Megargee's (1982) conceptual framework is quite wide-ranging. He distinguished instigators to aggression (internal factors motivating an aggressive response), aggressive habit strength (depending on previous rewards and punishments for aggression), inhibitors of aggression, and situational factors that influenced whether or not an aggressive response occurred. He also reviewed typologies of violent offenders and offenses, distinguishing among people committed to a violent lifestyle, people exposed to provocative or frustrating situations, overcontrolled people who suddenly explode, instrumentally violent people, and biologically or psychiatrically abnormal people.

Felson and Tedeschi's social interactionist perspective (1995) especially aimed to explain instrumental violence. They suggested that people take account of costs, benefits, and moral values when making decisions to be aggressive, in order to achieve interpersonal goals. The main goals are to obtain economic or sexual benefits, to control other people's behavior, to restore justice, and to assert and defend identities.

While the main focus of this theory is on situational influences, motives, and decision making, the authors also considered that individual differences were important.

Recent theories of aggression place most emphasis on cognitive (thinking) processes. Dodge (1991, p. 211) proposed a social information-processing model in which children respond to an environmental stimulus by encoding relevant cues, interpreting those cues, retrieving possible behavioral responses from long-term memory, considering the possible consequences of alternative responses, and selecting and performing a behavior. According to this theory, aggressive children are more likely to interpret cues as hostile, retrieve aggressive alternative responses, and evaluate the consequences of aggression as likely to be positive.

Huesmann and Eron (1989, p. 100) put forward a cognitive-script model, in which aggressive behavior depends on stored behavioral repertoires (cognitive scripts) that have been learned during early development. In response to environmental cues, possible cognitive scripts are retrieved and evaluated. The choice of aggressive scripts, which prescribe aggressive behavior, depends on the past history of rewards and punishments and on the extent to which children are influenced by immediate gratification as opposed to long-term consequences. The persisting trait of aggressiveness is a collection of well-learned aggressive scripts that are resistant to change.

B. The Farrington Theory

The modern trend in criminological theorizing is to try to achieve increased explanatory power by integrating propositions derived from several earlier theories. My own theory of youth violence, shown diagrammatically in figure 1, is also integrative. It is based on my theory of offending (Farrington 1995c, 1996), which is intended to be consistent with existing theories and with knowledge about risk factors.

The theory suggests that long-term influences (biological, psychological/personality, family, peer, school, community, etc.) lead to the development of long-term, fairly stable, slowly changing differences between individuals in their potential for violence. Superimposed on long-term between-individual differences in violence potential are short-term within-individual variations in violence potential. The short-term variations depend on short-term motivating influences such as being bored, angry, drunk, or frustrated, and on situational opportunities, including the availability of potential victims. Faced with an op-

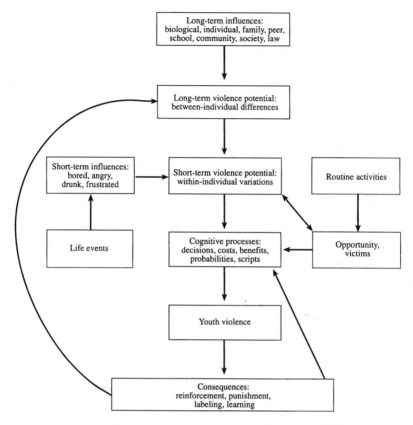

Fig. 1.—A theory of youth violence. Source: Farrington (1995c)

portunity for violence, whether a person actually is violent depends on cognitive processes, including considering the subjectively perceived costs and benefits of violence and their associated subjective probabilities or risks and taking account of stored behavioral repertoires. It is also assumed that the consequences of violence (rewards, punishment, labeling, etc.) can have feedback effects in a learning process (see, e.g., Thornberry 1987; Akers 1990), on long-term violence potential, and on the decision-making process (e.g., by influencing subjective perceptions of costs, benefits, and probabilities).

This theory is of course a simplification of the complex reality. It is an explicit attempt to integrate developmental and situational theories. For example, the interaction between the individual and the environment is seen in decision making in criminal opportunities, which depends both on the underlying potential for violence and on situational factors (costs, benefits, probabilities). Also, the double-headed arrow in figure 1 shows the possibility that encountering a tempting opportunity may cause a short-term increase in violence potential, just as a short-term increase in potential may motivate a person to seek out an opportunity for violence. The theory includes cognitive elements (perception, memory, decision making) as well as the social learning and causal risk-factor approaches.

The theory undoubtedly could and should be developed in more detail, especially in regard to the long-term influences that have been reviewed above. For example, family factors may be more important in childhood, and peer factors in the teenage years. As in most theories, there is insufficient attention to typologies of offenders. Perhaps some people are violent primarily because of their high violence potential (e.g., "life-course-persistent" offenders), while others are violent primarily because they happen to be in violent situations. Or perhaps some people are violent primarily because of short-term influences (e.g., getting drunk frequently) and others primarily because of the way they think and make decisions in potentially violent situations. From the point of view of both explanation and prevention, it would be useful to classify people according to their most influential risk factors and most important reasons for committing violent acts.

My theory also pays insufficient attention to explaining different types of violent acts. Explanations of assault may be very different from explanations of robbery and explanations of rape, and it is not clear that a single dimension of violence potential underlies all these types of acts. Nevertheless, I present it briefly in this essay in the hope that it will stimulate other researchers to develop and test more detailed theories of youth violence.

V. Conclusions, Gaps in Knowledge, and Research Priorities

A major problem in reviewing research on youth violence is that few studies focus specifically on youth violence as opposed to childhood aggression or delinquency in general. More research specifically on youth violence is needed. Youth violence is generally measured using official records of arrests or convictions or self-reports. More research is needed on the validity and relative advantages of both methods and on other measures such as the use of hospital data on intentional injury or information about violence from mothers, teachers, and peers. Systematic observation should be used in studying situational influences.

There is a great deal of versatility in youth violence, although more research is needed on the quantification of versatility versus specificity. People who commit one type of violent offense also tend to commit other types, as well as nonviolent offenses. Violent offenders tend to be persistent or frequent offenders, and there is little difference between violent offenders and nonviolent but equally frequent offenders. Nevertheless, there is some degree of specialization in violence. Violent youth tend to have co-occurring problems such as substance abuse and sexual promiscuity. Often, they might be described as multiple-problem youth. Estimates of the total cost to society of these individuals are useful in assessing the cost-effectiveness of prevention and treatment programs.

Violent offenses tend to occur later than property crimes. However, the small number of violent crimes in official criminal careers makes it difficult to study traditional criminal career parameters such as age of onset, age of desistance, career duration, probability of persistence, and frequency of offending. More efforts should be made to study careers of violence using self-reports. Self-report studies are needed in which detailed information is collected about the nature, circumstances, situational factors, consequences, and exact timing of violent offenses. This will probably require frequent interviewing. One important question is whether an early age of onset of violence predicts a high rate of violent offending per year, a large number of violent offenses, or both. More information is also needed about the probability of persistence in violence, and more efforts should be made to predict the future course of violent criminal careers. These issues have important policy implications.

There is considerable continuity from childhood aggression to youth violence, although more research is needed on the quantification of continuity and stability. One possible explanation is that there are persisting individual differences in an underlying potential to commit aggressive or violent behavior. A key question is whether the continuity in aggression and violence is specific or part of a more general continuity in offending or antisocial behavior over time. It is important to investigate the individual versus the environmental sources of continuity and examine developmental pathways from aggression to violence.

In research on risk factors, more studies are needed contrasting violent offenders with nonviolent offenders and with nonoffenders. It is also important to determine which factors have differential effects on the onset, persistence, escalation, de-escalation, or desistance of violent offending at different ages. The major long-term risk factors for youth violence are biological factors (low resting heart rate), psychological/ personality factors (high impulsiveness and low intelligence, possibly linked to the executive functions of the brain), family factors (poor supervision, harsh discipline, child physical abuse, a violent parent, large family size, a young mother, a broken family), peer delinquency, low socioeconomic status, urban residence, and living in a high-crime neighborhood. Important short-term situational factors include the motives of potential offenders (e.g., anger, a desire to hurt), and actions leading to violent events (e.g., the escalation of a trivial altercation). More research is needed specifically searching for protective factors against youth violence, for example, by investigating why aggressive children do not become violent youth. Protective factors could have important policy implications.

In order to develop theories of youth violence, it is important to establish how risk factors have independent, additive, interactive, or sequential effects. There are virtually no specific theories of youth violence, but theories of delinquency and aggression are relevant. A theory of youth violence was proposed that attempted to integrate developmental and situational approaches. For example, whether a violent act occurred was hypothesized to depend on the development of long-term violence potential, short-term variations in violence potential, and situational factors in opportunities for violence. Key theoretical issues that need to be addressed empirically include why parental violence leads to youth violence, whether and why peer violence leads to youth violence, and whether and why neighborhood violence leads to youth violence. Within-individual designs are useful, investigating, for example, whether a person's violence decreases after he moves from a high-violence to a low-violence area and increases after he moves in the reverse direction.

A key need is for developmental typologies of offenders that specify the developmental pathways of different types of offenders. Different types of offenders may have different types of risk factors and require different theories. For example, some people may be violent because they have a high potential for violence, while others may be violent because of short-term situational influences. The causes of some types of violent offenses may be different from the causes of others, for example in comparing assault with robbery or rape.

In order to investigate developmental and risk/protective factors for youth violence, longitudinal studies are needed. Some questions could be addressed by reanalyses of existing studies, or by collecting additional data in existing studies. However, the designs of many existing studies would not permit key questions to be addressed. For example, existing studies may include too few violent offenders, too few members of ethnic minorities, a too-narrow age range, a too-restricted range of risk/protective factors measured, and too-infrequent data collection.

Many questions about youth violence can be addressed only in new longitudinal studies. Such studies should include multiple cohorts, in order to draw conclusions about different age groups from birth to the teenage years. They should include both males and females and the major racial and ethnic groups. They should measure a wide range of risk and, especially, protective factors (individual, family, peer, school, community, etc.). They should be based on large, high-risk samples, especially in inner-city areas, incorporating screening methods to maximize the yield of violent offenders while simultaneously making it possible to draw conclusions about the total population. They should include long-term follow-ups to permit conclusions about developmental pathways. They should make a special effort to study careers of violence using self-reports and to link developmental and situational data. It will not be easy to mount new longitudinal studies focusing specifically on youth violence, but such studies are needed in order to advance knowledge about predictors, causes, and correlates.

APPENDIX

Major Longitudinal Studies of Youth Violence

Buckinghamshire Survey

Six hundred forty-two children aged five to fifteen in 1961 in Buckinghamshire, England, were rated by their parents. Their criminal records were followed up to 1976. Samples were followed up by interview and mail questionnaires in 1978 (Mitchell and Rosa 1981).

Cambridge-Somerville Youth Study

Six hundred fifty boys (average age ten) were nominated as difficult or average by Cambridge-Somerville (Boston) public schools in 1937–39 and were randomly assigned to treated or control groups. The treated group was visited by counselors for an average of five years and followed up in 1975–80 by interviews, mail questionnaires, and criminal records (McCord 1991).

Cambridge Study in Delinquent Development

Four hundred eleven boys aged eight to nine in 1961–62 were studied. The boys were interviewed eight times up to age thirty-two. Information was also obtained from parents, teachers, and peers. The boys and all their biological relatives were searched in criminal records up to 1994 (Farrington 1995*a*).

Chicago Youth Development Study

Three hundred sixty-two African-American and Latino boys in fifth or seventh grades (ages eleven to thirteen) of Chicago public schools in 1991 were studied. They were followed up yearly with data gathered from the boys, their mothers, and teachers (Gorman-Smith et al. 1996).

Columbia County Study

Eight hundred seventy-five children aged eight in Columbia County, N.Y., were first assessed in 1960 with a focus on aggressive behavior. They were interviewed ten and twenty-two years later (Eron and Huesmann 1990).

Copenhagen Birth Cohort Studies

In the first study all 28,879 men born in Copenhagen in 1944–47 and still alive and in Denmark in 1974 were followed up in police records to 1974 (Moffitt, Mednick, and Gabrielli 1989). The second study examined 216 children born in Copenhagen in 1959–61, with extensive perinatal data. They were followed up in police records to age twenty-two (Kandel and Mednick 1991).

Copenhagen Project Metropolitan

All 12,270 boys born in 1953 in Copenhagen and tested in schools in 1965–66 were studied. Sample of mothers were interviewed in 1968. The boys were followed up in police records to 1976 (Hogh and Wolf 1983).

Dangerous Offender Projects

In the first project all 811 children born in 1956–58 and arrested for violence as juveniles (before age eighteen) in Columbus, Ohio, were studied. They were followed up in adult arrest records to 1983 (Hamparian et al. 1985). The second project studied 1,591 adult offenders arrested for violence in Columbus, Ohio, in 1950–76. Their arrest histories were studied (Miller, Dinitz, and Conrad 1982).

Denver Youth Survey

Fifteen hundred children aged seven, nine, eleven, thirteen, or fifteen in high-risk neighborhoods of Denver, Colo., in 1988 were studied. The children and parents were assessed at yearly intervals, with a focus on self-reported delinquency (Huizinga, Esbensen, and Weiher 1991).

Dunedin Study

One thousand thirty-seven children born in 1972–73 in Dunedin, New Zealand, and first assessed at age three were studied. The children were assessed every two to three years on health, psychological factors, education, and family factors up to age twenty-one. Self-reported delinquency was measured from age thirteen. Convictions were collected up to age eighteen (Henry et al. 1996).

Jyvaskyla Study in Social Development

Three hundred sixty-nine children aged eight to nine in Jyvaskyla, Finland, in 1968 were studied. Peer, teacher, and self-ratings were collected. The children were followed up at ages fourteen, twenty, and twenty-six with questionnaires and up to age twenty-six in criminal records (Pulkkinen and Pitkanen 1993).

Longitudinal Study of Abused Children

Nine hundred eight abused children aged under age eleven were identified in Indianapolis court records in 1967–71, and 667 matched control children were studied. Both samples were followed up in arrest records to 1994 (Maxfield and Widom 1996).

Montreal Longitudinal-Experimental Study

One thousand one hundred sixty-one French-speaking kindergarten boys (aged six) from poor areas of Montreal were assessed by teachers in 1984. Disruptive boys were randomly allocated to treatment (parent training plus individual skills training) or control groups. All boys were followed up each year from age ten, including self-reported delinquency and aggression (Haapasalo and Tremblay 1994).

Montreal Longitudinal Studies

The first study involved a representative sample of 3,070 French-speaking Montreal adolescents. They completed self-report questionnaires in 1974 at ages twelve to sixteen and again in 1976. The second study was of 470 male delinquents seen at age fifteen in 1974 and again at ages seventeen and twenty-two. All were followed up in criminal records to age twenty-five. Males were interviewed at age thirty-two (Le Blanc 1996).

National Survey of Health and Development

Five thousand three hundred sixty-two children were selected from all legitimate single births in England, Scotland, and Wales during one week of March, 1946. The children were followed up in criminal records to age twenty-one. Mainly medical and school data were collected, but samples were interviewed at ages twenty-six, thirty-six, and forty-three (Wadsworth 1991).

National Youth Survey

A nationally representative U.S. sample of 1,725 adolescents aged eleven to seventeen in 1976 was studied. The adolescents were interviewed in five successive years (1977–81) and subsequently at three-year intervals. There was a focus on self-reported delinquency, but arrest records were collected (Elliott 1994).

Orebro Project
One thousand twenty-seven children aged ten (all those in third grade) in Orebro, Sweden, in 1965 were studied. School follow-up data was collected at ages thirteen and fifteen. A mail follow-up occurred at age twenty-six. They were followed up in criminal records to age thirty (Klinteberg et al. 1993).

Oregon Youth Study
Two hundred six fourth grade boys (aged ten) in Eugene, Ore., in 1983–85 were studied. They were assessed at yearly intervals, with data from the boys, parents, teachers, and peers. The boys were followed up in arrest records to age eighteen (Capaldi and Patterson 1996).

Philadelphia Biosocial Project
Nine hundred eighty-seven African-American children born in Philadelphia in 1959–62 and living there between ages ten and seventeen were studied. Extensive perinatal data were related to police contacts up to age twenty-two (Denno 1990).

Philadelphia Birth Cohort Studies
The first study was of 9,945 boys born in Philadelphia in 1945 and living there at least from ages ten to seventeen. A sample was interviewed at age twenty-six and followed up in police records to age thirty (Wolfgang, Thornberry, and Figlio 1987). The second study was of 27,160 children born in Philadelphia in 1958 and living there at least from ages ten to seventeen. They were followed up in police records to age twenty-six (Tracy and Kempf-Leonard 1996).

Pittsburgh Youth Study
One thousand five hundred and seventeen boys in first, fourth, or seventh grades of Pittsburgh public schools in 1987–88 (aged seven, ten, thirteen) were studied. Information from the boys, parents, and teachers was gathered every six months for three years, and then every year, with a focus on delinquency, substance use, and mental health problems (Loeber et al. 1998).

Rochester Youth Development Study
Nine hundred eighty-seven seventh and eighth graders (aged thirteen to fourteen) in Rochester, N.Y., public schools, disproportionally sampled from high-crime neighborhoods, were first assessed in 1988. They were followed up initially every six months and then every year (Thornberry et al. 1991).

Stockholm Project Metropolitan
All 15,117 children born in Stockholm in 1953 and living there in 1963 were studied. They were tested in schools in 1966. A subsample of mothers was interviewed in 1968. The children were followed up in police records until 1983 (Wikstrom 1990).

Woodlawn Project
Information from teachers and mothers of 1,242 children in first grade (aged six) in an African-American Chicago neighborhood in 1966 was gathered. The children and mothers were interviewed in 1975. There was a focus on shy and aggressive behaviors and substance use. Follow-up interviews occurred at age thirty-two (McCord and Ensminger 1997).

REFERENCES

Ageton, Suzanne S. 1983. *Sexual Assault among Adolescents.* Lexington, Mass.: D. C. Heath.
Agnew, Robert. 1990. "The Origins of Delinquent Events: An Examination of Offender Accounts." *Journal of Research in Crime and Delinquency* 27:267–94.
Akers, Ronald L. 1990. "Rational Choice, Deterrence, and Social Learning Theory in Criminology: The Path not Taken." *Journal of Criminal Law and Criminology* 81:653–76.
Archer, John. 1991. "The Influence of Testosterone on Human Aggression." *British Journal of Psychology* 82:1–28.
Bandura, Albert. 1973. *Aggression: A Social Learning Analysis.* Englewood Cliffs, N.J.: Prentice-Hall.
Barker, Mary, Jane Geraghty, Barry Webb, and Tony Kay. 1993. *The Prevention of Street Robbery.* London: Home Office Police Department.
Berkowitz, Leonard. 1993. *Aggression: Its Causes, Consequences, and Control.* New York: McGraw-Hill.
Blaske, David M., Charles M. Borduin, Scott W. Henggeler, and Barton W. Mann. 1989. "Individual, Family, and Peer Characteristics of Adolescent Sex Offenders and Assaultive Offenders." *Developmental Psychology* 25:846–55.
Blumstein, Alfred, Jacqueline Cohen, Jeffrey A. Roth, and Christy A. Visher, eds. 1986. *Criminal Careers and Career Criminals,* vol. 1. Washington, D.C.: National Academy Press.
Blumstein, Alfred, David P. Farrington, and Soumyo Moitra. 1985. "Delinquency Careers: Innocents, Desisters, and Persisters." In *Crime and Justice: An Annual Review of Research,* vol. 6, edited by Michael Tonry and Norval Morris. Chicago: University of Chicago Press.
Brain, Paul F. 1994. "Hormonal Aspects of Aggression and Violence." In *Understanding and Preventing Violence,* vol. 2, *Biobehavioral Influences,* edited by Albert J. Reiss, Klaus A. Miczek, and Jeffrey A. Roth. Washington, D.C.: National Academy Press.
Brennan, Patricia A., Birgitte R. Mednick, and Sarnoff A. Mednick. 1993. "Parental Psychopathology, Congenital Factors, and Violence." In *Mental Disorder and Crime,* edited by Sheilagh Hodgins. Newbury Park, Calif.: Sage.

Busch, Kenneth G., Robert Zagar, John R. Hughes, Jack Arbit, and Robert E. Bussell. 1990. "Adolescents Who Kill." *Journal of Clinical Psychology* 46:472–85.

Cairns, Robert B., and Beverly D. Cairns. 1994. *Lifelines and Risks: Pathways of Youth in Our Time.* Cambridge: Cambridge University Press.

Capaldi, Deborah M., and Gerald R. Patterson. 1996. "Can Violent Offenders be Distinguished from Frequent Offenders? Prediction from Childhood to Adolescence." *Journal of Research in Crime and Delinquency* 33:206–31.

Caspi, Avshalom, Terrie E. Moffitt, Phil A. Silva, Magda Stouthamer-Loeber, Robert F. Krueger, and Pamela S. Schmutte. 1994. "Are Some People Crime-Prone? Replications of the Personality-Crime Relationship across Countries, Genders, Races, and Methods." *Criminology* 32:163–95.

Catalano, Richard F., and J. David Hawkins. 1996. "The Social Development Model: A Theory of Antisocial Behavior." In *Delinquency and Crime: Current Theories*, edited by J. David Hawkins. Cambridge: Cambridge University Press.

Cernkovich, Stephen A., Peggy C. Giordano, and Meredith D. Pugh. 1985. "Chronic Offenders: The Missing Cases in Self-Report Delinquency Research." *Journal of Criminal Law and Criminology* 76:705–32.

Clarke, Ronald V., and Derek B. Cornish. 1985. "Modelling Offenders' Decisions: A Framework for Research and Policy." In *Crime and Justice: An Annual Review of Research*, vol. 6, edited by Michael Tonry and Norval Morris. Chicago: University of Chicago Press.

Clarkson, Chris, Antonia Cretney, Gwynn Davis, and Jon Shepherd. 1994. "Assaults: The Relationship between Seriousness, Criminalization, and Punishment." *Criminal Law Review*, pp. 4–20.

Cloward, Richard A., and Lloyd E. Ohlin. 1960. *Delinquency and Opportunity.* New York: Free Press.

Cohen, Albert K. 1955. *Delinquent Boys.* Glencoe, Ill.: Free Press.

Cohen, Lawrence E., and Marcus Felson. 1979. "Social Change and Crime Rate Trends: A Routine Activity Approach." *American Sociological Review* 44:588–608.

Daly, Martin, and Margo Wilson. 1988. *Homicide.* New York: Aldine De-Gruyter.

Denno, Deborah W. 1990. *Biology and Violence: From Birth to Adulthood.* Cambridge: Cambridge University Press.

Dodge, Kenneth A. 1991. "The Structure and Function of Reactive and Proactive Aggression." In *The Development and Treatment of Childhood Aggression*, edited by Debra J. Pepler and Kenneth H. Rubin. Hillsdale, N.J.: Erlbaum.

Dollard, John, Neal E. Miller, Leonard W. Doob, O. Hobart Mowrer, and Robert R. Sears. 1939. *Frustration and Aggression.* New Haven, Conn.: Yale University Press.

Ekblom, Paul. 1988. *Getting the Best out of Crime Analysis.* London: Home Office Police Department.

Elliott, Delbert S. 1994. "Serious Violent Offenders: Onset, Developmental Course, and Termination." *Criminology* 32:1–21.

Elliott, Delbert S., David Huizinga, and Scott Menard. 1989. *Multiple Problem Youth: Delinquency, Substance Use, and Mental Health Problems.* New York: Springer-Verlag.

Elliott, Delbert S., and Scott Menard. 1996. "Delinquent Friends and Delinquent Behavior: Temporal and Developmental Patterns." In *Delinquency and Crime: Current Theories*, edited by J. David Hawkins. Cambridge: Cambridge University Press.

Eron, Leonard D., and L. Rowell Huesmann. 1990. "The Stability of Aggressive Behavior—Even unto the Third Generation." In *Handbook of Developmental Psychopathology*, edited by Michael Lewis and Suzanne M. Miller. New York: Plenum.

Eron, Leonard D., L. Rowell Huesmann, and Arnaldo Zelli. 1991. "The Role of Parental Variables in the Learning of Aggression." In *The Development and Treatment of Childhood Aggression*, edited by Debra J. Pepler and Kenneth H. Rubin. Hillsdale, N.J.: Erlbaum.

Farrington, David P. 1978. "The Family Backgrounds of Aggressive Youths." In *Aggression and Antisocial Behavior in Childhood and Adolescence*, edited by Lionel Hersov, Michael Berger, and David Shaffer. Oxford: Pergamon.

———. 1982. "Longitudinal Analyses of Criminal Violence." In *Criminal Violence*, edited by Marvin E. Wolfgang and Neil A. Weiner. Beverly Hills, Calif.: Sage.

———. 1986. "Age and Crime." In *Crime and Justice: An Annual Review of Research*, vol. 7, edited by Michael Tonry and Norval Morris. Chicago: University of Chicago Press.

———. 1989a. "Early Predictors of Adolescent Aggression and Adult Violence." *Violence and Victims* 4:79–100.

———. 1989b. "Self-Reported and Official Offending from Adolescence to Adulthood." In *Cross-National Research in Self-Reported Crime and Delinquency*, edited by Malcolm W. Klein. Dordrecht: Kluwer.

———. 1991. "Childhood Aggression and Adult Violence: Early Precursors and Later Life Outcomes." In *The Development and Treatment of Childhood Aggression*, edited by Debra J. Pepler and Kenneth H. Rubin. Hillsdale, N.J.: Erlbaum.

———. 1993a. "Motivations for Conduct Disorder and Delinquency." *Development and Psychopathology* 5:225–41.

———. 1993b. "Understanding and Preventing Bullying." In *Crime and Justice: A Review of Research*, vol. 12, edited by Michael Tonry and Norval Morris. Chicago: University of Chicago Press.

———. 1994a. "Childhood, Adolescent and Adult Features of Violent Males." In *Aggressive Behavior: Current Perspectives*, edited by L. Rowell Huesmann. New York: Plenum.

———. 1994b. "Interactions between Individual and Contextual Factors in the Development of Offending." In *Adolescence in Context: The Interplay of Family, School, Peers and Work in Adjustment*, edited by Rainer K. Silbereisen and Eberhard Todt. New York: Springer-Verlag.

———. 1995a. "The Development of Offending and Antisocial Behavior from Childhood: Key Findings from the Cambridge Study in Delinquent Development." *Journal of Child Psychology and Psychiatry* 36:929–64.

———. 1995b. "The Efficiency of Prediction of Violence." Paper given at the conference on "Mental Disorder and Criminal Justice," Vancouver, British Columbia, April.

———. 1995c. "Key Issues in the Integration of Motivational and Opportunity-Reducing Crime Prevention Strategies." In *Integrating Crime Prevention Strategies: Propensity and Opportunity*, edited by Per-Olof H. Wikstrom, Ronald V. Clarke, and Joan McCord. Stockholm: National Council for Crime Prevention.

———. 1996. "The Explanation and Prevention of Youthful Offending." In *Delinquency and Crime: Current Theories*, edited by J. David Hawkins. Cambridge: Cambridge University Press.

———. 1997a. "Early Prediction of Violent and Nonviolent Youthful Offending." *European Journal on Criminal Policy and Research* 5(2):51–66.

———. 1997b. "The Relationship between Low Resting Heart Rate and Violence." In *Biosocial Bases of Violence*, edited by Adrian Raine, Patricia A. Brennan, David P. Farrington, and Sarnoff A. Mednick. New York: Plenum.

Farrington, David P., Bernard Gallager, Lynda Morley, Raymond J. St. Ledger, and Donald J. West. 1988. "Are There Any Successful Men from Criminogenic Backgrounds?" *Psychiatry* 51:116–30.

Farrington, David P., and Rolf Loeber. 1998. "Transatlantic Replicability of Risk Factors in the Development of Delinquency." In *Where and When: Geographic and Generational Influences on Psychopathology*, edited by Patricia Cohen, Cheryl Slomkowski, and Lee N. Robins. Mahwah, N.J.: Erlbaum (forthcoming).

Farrington, David P., Rolf Loeber, Magda Stouthamer-Loeber, Welmoet van Kammen, and Laura Schmidt. 1996. "Self-Reported Delinquency and a Combined Delinquency Seriousness Scale Based on Boys, Mothers and Teachers: Concurrent and Predictive Validity for African Americans and Caucasians." *Criminology* 34:493–517.

Farrington, David P., Howard N. Snyder, and Terrence A. Finnegan. 1988. "Specialization in Juvenile Court Careers." *Criminology* 26:461–87.

Federal Bureau of Investigation. 1996. *Crime in the United States, 1995.* Washington, D.C.: U.S. Government Printing Office.

Felson, Richard B., and James T. Tedeschi. 1995. "A Social Interactionist Approach to Violence: Cross-Cultural Applications." In *Interpersonal Violent Behavior*, edited by R. Barry Ruback and Neil A. Weiner. New York: Springer.

Fischer, Donald G. 1984. "Family Size and Delinquency." *Perceptual and Motor Skills* 58:527–34.

Gorman-Smith, Deborah, Patrick H. Tolan, Arnaldo Zelli, and L. Rowell Huesmann. 1996. "The Relation of Family Functioning to Violence among Inner-City Minority Youths." *Journal of Family Psychology* 10:115–29.

Gottfredson, Michael R., and Travis Hirschi. 1990. *A General Theory of Crime.* Stanford, Calif.: Stanford University Press.

Guttridge, Patricia, William F. Gabrielli, Sarnoff A. Mednick, and Katherine T. van Dusen. 1983. "Criminal Violence in a Birth Cohort." In *Prospective Studies of Crime and Delinquency*, edited by Katherine T. van Dusen and Sarnoff A. Mednick. Boston: Kluwer-Nijhoff.

Haapasalo, Jaana, and Richard E. Tremblay. 1994. "Physically Aggressive Boys from Ages 6 to 12: Family Background, Parenting Behavior, and Prediction of Delinquency." *Journal of Consulting and Clinical Psychology* 62:1044–52.

Hamparian, Donna M., Joseph M. Davis, Judith M. Jacobson, and Robert E. McGraw. 1985. *The Young Criminal Years of the Violent Few.* Washington, D.C.: Office of Juvenile Justice and Delinquency Prevention.

Hamparian, Donna M., Richard Schuster, Simon Dinitz, and John P. Conrad. 1978. *The Violent Few: A Study of Dangerous Juvenile Offenders.* Lexington, Mass.: D. C. Heath.

Hawkins, J. David, Todd Herrenkohl, David P. Farrington, Devon Brewer, Richard F. Catalano, and Tracy W. Harachi. 1998. "A Review of Predictors of Youth Violence." In *Serious and Violent Juvenile Offenders: Risk Factors and Successful Interventions,* edited by Rolf Loeber and David P. Farrington. Thousand Oaks, Calif.: Sage.

Henry, Bill, Avshalom Caspi, Terrie E. Moffitt, and Phil A. Silva. 1996. "Temperamental and Familial Predictors of Violent and Nonviolent Criminal Convictions: Age 3 to Age 18." *Developmental Psychology* 32:614–23.

Hindelang, Michael J. 1981. "Variations in Sex-Race-Age-Specific Incidence Rates of Offending." *American Sociological Review* 46:461–74.

Hodgins, Sheilagh. 1994. "Status at Age 30 of Children with Conduct Problems." *Studies on Crime and Crime Prevention* 3:41–62.

Hogh, Erik, and Preben Wolf. 1983. "Violent Crime in a Birth Cohort: Copenhagen, 1953–1977." In *Prospective Studies of Crime and Delinquency,* edited by Katherine T. van Dusen and Sarnoff A. Mednick. Boston: Kluwer-Nijhoff.

Hough, Mike, and Kevin Sheehy. 1986. "Incidents of Violence: Findings from the British Crime Survey." *Home Office Research Bulletin* 20:22–26.

Huesmann, L. Rowell, and Leonard D. Eron. 1989. "Individual Differences and the Trait of Aggression." *European Journal of Personality* 3:95–106.

Huizinga, David. 1991. "Assessing Violent Behavior with Self-Reports." In *Neuropsychology of Aggression,* edited by Joel S. Milner. Boston: Kluwer.

Huizinga, David, Finn-Aage Esbensen, and Anne Weiher. 1991. "Are There Multiple Paths to Delinquency?" *Journal of Criminal Law and Criminology* 82:83–118.

Huizinga, David, and Cynthia Jakob-Chien. 1998. "The Contemporaneous Co-occurrence of Serious and Violent Juvenile Offending and Other Problem Behaviours." In *Serious and Violent Juvenile Offenders: Risk Factors and Successful Interventions,* edited by Rolf Loeber and David P. Farrington. Thousand Oaks, Calif.: Sage.

Junger-Tas, Josine. 1996. "Youth and Violence in Europe." *Studies on Crime and Crime Prevention* 5:31–58.

Kagan, Jerome. 1989. "Temperamental Contributions to Social Behavior." *American Psychologist* 44:668–74.

Kandel, Elizabeth, and Sarnoff A. Mednick. 1991. "Perinatal Complications Predict Violent Offending." *Criminology* 29:519–29.

Kempf, Kimberly L. 1987. "Specialization and the Criminal Career." *Criminology* 25:399–420.

Kindlon, Daniel J., Richard E. Tremblay, Enrico Mezzacappa, Felton Earls, Denis Laurent, and Benoist Schaal. 1995. "Longitudinal Patterns of Heart Rate and Fighting Behavior in 9- through 12-Year-Old Boys." *Journal of the American Academy of Child and Adolescent Psychiatry* 34:371–77.

Klinteberg, Britt A., Tommy Andersson, David Magnusson, and Hakan Stattin. 1993. "Hyperactive Behavior in Childhood as Related to Subsequent Alcohol Problems and Violent Offending: A Longitudinal Study of Male Subjects." *Personality and Individual Differences* 15:381–88.

Laub, John H., and Janet L. Lauritsen. 1993. "Violent Criminal Behavior over the Life Course: A Review of the Longitudinal and Comparative Research." *Violence and Victims* 8:235–52.

Le Blanc, Marc. 1996. "Changing Patterns in the Perpetration of Offenses over Time: Trajectories from Early Adolescence to the Early 30's." *Studies on Crime and Crime Prevention* 5:151–65.

Le Blanc, Marc, and Marcel Frechette. 1989. *Male Criminal Activity from Childhood through Youth*. New York: Springer-Verlag.

Lewis, Dorothy O., Richard Lovely, Catherine Yeager, George Ferguson, Michael Friedman, Georgette Sloane, Helene Friedman, and Jonathan H. Pincus. 1988. "Intrinsic and Environmental Characteristics of Juvenile Murderers." *Journal of the American Academy of Child and Adolescent Psychiatry* 27:582–87.

Linaker, O. M., and H. Busch-Iversen. 1995. "Predictors of Imminent Violence in Psychiatric Patients." *Acta Psychiatrica Scandinavica* 92:250–54.

Lipsey, Mark W., and James H. Derzon. 1998. "Predictors of Violent or Serious Delinquency in Adolescence and Early Adulthood: A Synthesis of Longitudinal Research." In *Serious and Violent Juvenile Offenders: Risk Factors and Successful Interventions*, edited by Rolf Loeber and David P. Farrington. Thousand Oaks, Calif.: Sage.

Lloyd, Charles, and Roy Walmsley. 1989. *Changes in Rape Offenses and Sentencing*. London: H.M. Stationery Office.

Loeber, Rolf, David P. Farrington, Magda Stouthamer-Loeber, and Welmoet B. van Kammen. 1998. *Antisocial Behavior and Mental Health Problems: Explanatory Factors in Childhood and Adolescence*. Mahwah, N.J.: Erlbaum (forthcoming).

Loeber, Rolf, David P. Farrington, and Daniel A. Waschbusch. 1998. "Serious and Violent Juvenile Offenders." In *Serious and Violent Juvenile Offenders: Risk Factors and Successful Interventions*, edited by Rolf Loeber and David P. Farrington. Thousand Oaks, Calif.: Sage.

Loeber, Rolf, Phen Wung, Kate Keenan, Bruce Giroux, Magda Stouthamer-Loeber, Welmoet B. van Kammen, and Barbara Maughan. 1993. "Developmental Pathways in Disruptive Child Behavior." *Development and Psychopathology* 5:103–33.

Luthar, Suniya S., and Edward Zigler. 1991. "Vulnerability and Competence: A Review of Research on Resilience in Childhood." *American Journal of Orthopsychiatry* 61:6–22.

Malinosky-Rummell, Robin, and David J. Hansen. 1993. "Long-Term Consequences of Childhood Physical Abuse." *Psychological Bulletin* 114:68–79.

Maxfield, Michael G., and Cathy S. Widom. 1996. "The Cycle of Violence Revisited 6 Years Later." *Archives of Pediatrics and Adolescent Medicine* 150:390–95.

McClintock, Frederick H. 1963. *Crimes of Violence.* London: Macmillan.

McCord, Joan. 1977. "A Comparative Study of Two Generations of Native Americans." In *Theory in Criminology: Contemporary Views,* edited by Robert F. Meier. Beverly Hills, Calif.: Sage.

———. 1979. "Some Child-Rearing Antecedents of Criminal Behavior in Adult Men." *Journal of Personality and Social Psychology* 37:1477–86.

———. 1991. "Family Relationships, Juvenile Delinquency, and Adult Criminality." *Criminology* 29:397–417.

———. 1996. "Family as Crucible for Violence: Comment on Gorman-Smith et al. (1996)." *Journal of Family Psychology* 10:147–52.

———. 1997. "On Discipline." *Psychological Inquiry* 8:215–17.

McCord, Joan, and Margaret Ensminger. 1995. "Pathways from Aggressive Childhood to Criminality." Paper given at the annual meeting of the American Society of Criminology, Boston, November.

———. 1997. "Multiple Risks and Comorbidity in an African-American Population." *Criminal Behavior and Mental Health* 7:339–52.

Megargee, Edwin I. 1982. "Psychological Determinants and Correlates of Criminal Violence." In *Criminal Violence,* edited by Marvin E. Wolfgang and Neil A. Weiner. Beverly Hills, Calif.: Sage.

Miller, Stuart J., Simon Dinitz, and John P. Conrad. 1982. *Careers of the Violent: The Dangerous Offender and Criminal Justice.* Lexington, Mass.: D. C. Heath.

Mitchell, Sheila, and Peter Rosa. 1981. "Boyhood Behavior Problems as Precursors of Criminality: A Fifteen-Year Follow-Up Study." *Journal of Child Psychology and Psychiatry* 22:19–33.

Moffitt, Terrie E. 1993. "Adolescence-Limited and Life-Course-Persistent Antisocial Behavior: A Developmental Taxonomy." *Psychological Review* 100:674–701.

Moffitt, Terrie E., Avshalom Caspi, Paul Fawcett, Gary L. Brammer, Michael Raleigh, Arthur Yuwiler, and Phil A. Silva. 1997. "Whole Blood Serotonin and Family Background Relate to Male Violence." In *Biosocial Bases of Violence,* edited by Adrian Raine, Patricia A. Brennan, David P. Farrington, and Sarnoff A. Mednick. New York: Plenum.

Moffitt, Terrie E., and Bill Henry. 1991. "Neuropsychological Studies of Juvenile Delinquency and Juvenile Violence." In *Neuropsychology of Aggression,* edited by Joel S. Milner. Boston: Kluwer.

Moffitt, Terrie, E., Sarnoff A. Mednick, and William F. Gabrielli. 1989. "Predicting Careers of Criminal Violence: Descriptive Data and Dispositional Factors." In *Current Approaches to the Prediction of Violence,* edited by David A. Brizer and Martha Crowner. Washington, D.C.: American Psychiatric Press.

Monahan, John, and Deidre Klassen. 1982. "Situational Approaches to Understanding and Predicting Individual Violent Behavior." In *Criminal Violence,* edited by Marvin E. Wolfgang and Neil A. Weiner. Beverly Hills, Calif.: Sage.

Morash, Merry, and Lila Rucker. 1989. "An Exploratory Study of the Connection of Mother's Age at Childbearing to Her Children's Delinquency in Four Data Sets." *Crime and Delinquency* 35:45–93.

Nagin, Daniel S., Greg Pogarsky, and David P. Farrington. 1997. "Adolescent Mothers and the Criminal Behavior of Their Children." *Law and Society Review* 31:137–62.

Olweus, Dan. 1979. "Stability of Aggressive Reaction Patterns in Males: A Review." *Psychological Bulletin* 86:852–75.

———. 1986. "Aggression and Hormones: Behavioral Relationship with Testosterone and Adrenaline." In *Development of Antisocial and Prosocial Behavior: Research, Theories, and Issues*, edited by Dan Olweus, Jack Block, and Marian Radke-Yarrow. Orlando, Fla.: Academic Press.

Pallone, Nathaniel J., and James H. Hennessy. 1993. "Tinderbox Criminal Violence: Neurogenic Impulsivity, Risk Taking, and the Phenomenology of Rational Choice." In *Advances in Criminological Theory*, vol. 5, *Routine Activity and Rational Choice*, edited by Ronald V. Clarke and Marcus Felson. New Brunswick, N.J.: Transaction.

Patterson, Gerald R., Barbara D. DeBaryshe, and Elizabeth Ramsey. 1989. "A Developmental Perspective on Antisocial Behavior." *American Psychologist* 44:329–35.

Piper, Elizabeth S. 1985. "Violent Recidivism and Chronicity in the 1958 Philadelphia Cohort." *Journal of Quantitative Criminology* 1:319–44.

Pulkkinen, Lea. 1987. "Offensive and Defensive Aggression in Humans: A Longitudinal Perspective." *Aggressive Behavior* 13:197–212.

Pulkkinen, Lea, and Tuuli Pitkanen. 1993. "Continuities in Aggressive Behavior from Childhood to Adulthood." *Aggressive Behavior* 19:249–63.

Raine, Adrian. 1993. *The Psychopathology of Crime: Criminal Behavior as a Clinical Disorder*. San Diego, Calif.: Academic Press.

Raine, Adrian, Patricia A. Brennan, and David P. Farrington. 1997. "Biosocial Bases of Violence: Conceptual and Theoretical Issues." In *Biosocial Bases of Violence*, edited by Adrian Raine, Patricia A. Brennan, David P. Farrington, and Sarnoff A. Mednick. New York: Plenum.

Reiss, Albert J., Jr., and David P. Farrington. 1991. "Advancing Knowledge about Co-offending: Results from a Prospective Longitudinal Survey of London Males." *Journal of Criminal Law and Criminology* 82:360–95.

Reiss, Albert J., Jr., Klaus A. Miczek, and Jeffrey A. Roth, eds. 1994. *Understanding and Preventing Violence*, vol. 2, *Biobehavioral Influences*. Washington, D.C.: National Academy Press.

Reiss, Albert J., Jr., and Jeffrey A. Roth, eds. 1993. *Understanding and Preventing Violence*. Washington, D.C.: National Academy Press.

Richters, John E., and Pedro E. Martinez. 1993. "Violent Communities, Family Choices, and Children's Chances: An Algorithm for Improving the Odds." *Development and Psychopathology* 5:609–27.

Rivara, Frederick P., Jonathan P. Shepherd, David P. Farrington, P. W. Richmond, and Paul Cannon. 1995. "Victim as Offender in Youth Violence." *Annals of Emergency Medicine* 26:609–14.

Rubin, Robert T. 1987. "The Neuroendocrinology and Neurochemistry of

Antisocial Behavior." In *The Causes of Crime: New Biological Approaches*, edited by Sarnoff A. Mednick, Terrie E. Moffitt, and Susan A. Stack. Cambridge: Cambridge University Press.

Rutter, Michael. 1985. "Resilience in the Face of Adversity: Protective Factors and Resistance to Psychiatric Disorder." *British Journal of Psychiatry* 147:598–611.

Sampson, Robert J., and Janet L. Lauritsen. 1994. "Violent Victimization and Offending: Individual, Situational, and Community-Level Risk Factors." In *Understanding and Preventing Violence*, vol. 3, *Social Influences*, edited by Albert J. Reiss, Jr., and Jeffrey A. Roth. Washington, D.C.: National Academy Press.

Seguin, Jean, Robert O. Pihl, Philip W. Harden, Richard E. Tremblay, and Bernard Boulerice. 1995. "Cognitive and Neuropsychological Characteristics of Physically Aggressive Boys." *Journal of Abnormal Psychology* 104:614–24.

Shepherd, Jonathan P., M. A. Ali, A. O. Hughes, and B. G. H. Levers. 1993. "Trends in Urban Violence: A Comparison of Accident Department and Police Records." *Journal of the Royal Society of Medicine* 86:87–88.

Short, James F. 1997. *Poverty, Ethnicity, and Violent Crime*. Boulder, Colo.: Westview.

Simon, Leonore M. J. 1997. "Do Criminal Offenders Specialize in Crime Types?" *Applied and Preventive Psychology* 6:35–53.

Singer, Simon I. 1986. "Victims of Serious Violence and Their Criminal Behavior: Subcultural Theory and Beyond." *Violence and Victims* 1:61–70.

Smith, Carolyn, Alan J. Lizotte, Terence P. Thornberry, and Marvin D. Krohn. 1995. "Resilient Youth: Identifying Factors That Prevent High-Risk Youth from Engaging in Delinquency and Drug Use." In *Current Perspectives on Aging and the Life Cycle*, vol. 4, *Delinquency and Disrepute in the Life Course*, edited by John Hagan. Greenwich, Conn.: JAI.

Smith, Carolyn, and Terence P. Thornberry. 1995. "The Relationship between Childhood Maltreatment and Adolescent Involvement in Delinquency." *Criminology* 33:451–81.

Sosin, Daniel M., Thomas D. Koepsell, Frederick P. Rivara, and James A. Mercy. 1995. "Fighting as a Marker for Multiple Problem Behaviors in Adolescents."*Journal of Adolescent Health Care* 16:209–15.

Stander, Julian, David P. Farrington, Gillian Hill, and Patricia M. E. Altham. 1989. "Markov Chain Analysis and Specialization in Criminal Careers." *British Journal of Criminology* 29:317–35.

Stattin, Hakan, and David Magnusson. 1989. "The Role of Early Aggressive Behavior in the Frequency, Seriousness, and Types of Later Crime." *Journal of Consulting and Clinical Psychology* 57:710–18.

Steinmetz, Susanne K. 1978. "Sibling Violence." In *Family Violence: An International and Interdisciplinary Study*, edited by John M. Eekelaar and Sanford N. Katz. Toronto: Butterworths.

Stouthamer-Loeber, Magda, Rolf Loeber, David P. Farrington, Quanwu Zhang, Welmoet van Kammen, and Eugene Maguin. 1993. "The Double

Edge of Protective and Risk Factors for Delinquency: Inter-relations and Developmental Patterns." *Development and Psychopathology* 5:683–701.

Sutherland, Edwin H., and Donald R. Cressey. 1974. *Criminology*. 9th ed. Philadelphia: Lippincott.

Tarling, Roger. 1993. *Analyzing Offending: Data, Models, and Interpretations.* London: H.M. Stationery Office.

Thornberry, Terence P. 1987. "Toward an Interactional Theory of Delinquency." *Criminology* 25:863–91.

Thornberry, Terence P., David Huizinga, and Rolf Loeber. 1995. "The Prevention of Serious Delinquency and Violence: Implications from the Program of Research on the Causes and Correlates of Delinquency." In *Sourcebook on Serious, Violent, and Chronic Juvenile Offenders*, edited by James C. Howell, Barry Krisberg, J. David Hawkins, and John J. Wilson. Thousand Oaks, Calif.: Sage.

Thornberry, Terence P., Alan J. Lizotte, Marvin D. Krohn, Margaret Farnworth, and Sung Joon Jang. 1991. "Testing Interactional Theory: An Examination of Reciprocal Causal Relationships among Family, School, and Delinquency." *Journal of Criminal Law and Criminology* 82:3–35.

Tolan, Patrick H., and Deborah Gorman-Smith. 1998. "Development of Serious and Violent Offending Careers." In *Serious and Violent Juvenile Offenders: Risk Factors and Successful Interventions*, edited by Rolf Loeber and David P. Farrington. Thousand Oaks, Calif.: Sage.

Tracy, Paul E., and Kimberly Kempf-Leonard. 1996. *Continuity and Discontinuity in Criminal Careers*. New York: Plenum.

Tracy, Paul E., Marvin E. Wolfgang, and Robert M. Figlio. 1990. *Delinquency Careers in Two Birth Cohorts*. New York: Plenum.

Tremblay, Richard E., Benoist Schaal, Bernard Boulerice, Louise Arsenault, Robert Soussignan, and Daniel Perusse. 1997. "Male Physical Aggression, Social Dominance, and Testosterone Levels at Puberty." In *Biosocial Bases of Violence*, edited by Adrian Raine, Patricia A. Brennan, David P. Farrington, and Sarnoff A. Mednick. New York: Plenum.

Turner, Angela K. 1994. "Genetic and Hormonal Influences on Male Violence." In *Male Violence*, edited by John Archer. London: Routledge.

Wadsworth, Michael E. J. 1976. "Delinquency, Pulse Rates, and Early Emotional Deprivation." *British Journal of Criminology* 16:245–56.

———. 1978. "Delinquency Prediction and its Uses: The Experience of a 21-Year Follow-Up Study." *International Journal of Mental Health* 7:43–62.

———. 1991. *The Imprint of Time*. Oxford: Clarendon Press.

Werner, Emmy E., and Ruth S. Smith. 1982. *Vulnerable but Invincible: A Longitudinal Study of Resilient Children and Youth*. New York: McGraw-Hill.

West, Donald J., and David P. Farrington. 1973. *Who Becomes Delinquent?* London: Heinemann.

———. 1977. *The Delinquent Way of Life*. London: Heinemann.

Widom, Cathy S. 1989. "The Cycle of Violence." *Science* 244:160–66.

Widom, Cathy S., and M. Ashley Ames. 1994. "Criminal Consequences of Childhood Sexual Victimization." *Child Abuse and Neglect* 18:303–18.

Wikström, Per-Olof H. 1985. *Everyday Violence in Contemporary Sweden.* Stockholm: National Council for Crime Prevention.

——. 1990. "Age and Crime in a Stockholm Cohort." *Journal of Quantitative Criminology* 6:61–84.

Wilson, James Q., and Richard J. Herrnstein. 1985. *Crime and Human Nature.* New York: Simon & Schuster.

Wolfgang, Marvin E. 1958. *Patterns in Criminal Homicide.* Philadelphia: University of Pennsylvania Press.

Wolfgang, Marvin E., Robert M. Figlio, and Thorsten Sellin. 1972. *Delinquency in a Birth Cohort.* Chicago: University of Chicago Press.

Wolfgang, Marvin E., Terence P. Thornberry, and Robert M. Figlio. 1987. *From Boy to Man, from Delinquency to Crime.* Chicago: University of Chicago Press.

Zingraff, Matthew T., Jeffrey Leiter, Kristen A. Myers, and Matthew C. Johnsen. 1993. "Child Maltreatment and Youthful Problem Behavior." *Criminology* 31:173–202.

Franklin E. Zimring

Toward a Jurisprudence of Youth Violence

ABSTRACT

Most discussions of legal and social policies that justify different penal treatment for violent acts by adolescent offenders ignore basic substantive issues; youth crime policy has been preoccupied by procedural and jurisdictional matters. Justifications for separate treatment of juveniles can be found both in the principles of the penal law and in social policies that recognize adolescence as an important learning period. Three dimensions of adolescent diminished responsibility stand out—incomplete comprehension of moral duty, deficient capacity to manage impulses, and the vulnerability to peer pressure that is the hallmark of adolescent law violation. Social policy favoring youth development does not require a discounting of penal liability but suggests an effort to avoid using punishments that limit the opportunity of adolescent offenders to survive into normal adulthood. This implies qualitative limits on sanctions rather than quantitative discounts, and it conflicts with retributive minimums for very serious offenses. The challenge is to balance the many relevant dimensions of a youth crime policy in seeking appropriate solutions to key problems: distinguishing high seriousness violence cases for special penal priority in juvenile and criminal courts, constructing coherent firearms policies for youth, and finding just and appropriate outcomes in youth homicide cases.

The three key terms in the title of this essay are rather vague. The pretentious term "jurisprudence," for one, is hardly a model of precision. I use it here to advertise that my concerns are with the basic principles that should govern legal policy toward young offenders who in-

Franklin E. Zimring is William G. Simon Professor of Law and director of the Earl Warren Legal Institute, University of California, Berkeley.

tentionally injure others. The term "youth" is the second inexact usage. I speak of youth violence instead of juvenile violence because I hope to discuss violent behavior that occurs between the onset of adolescence and about age twenty-one. Some of these acts fall within the jurisdiction of juvenile courts. Different jurisdictions divide young offenders in different ways. But the transitional period of adolescence is characterized by very high rates of assaultive violence throughout.

The third ambiguous term is "violence." The problem here is the wide range of harms covered, from the conditional threat of an unarmed robbery through a bloody nose to a fatal injury. All these are violent acts but in very different ways and with widely varying consequences.

This essay thus aims to discuss the basic principles that should govern a wide range of differently dangerous harmful acts that occur in an age range from about twelve through twenty. That is a broad spectrum of policy and behavior. These remarks cannot hope for comprehensive coverage. Instead, what is offered here is usually called "notes toward," in the academic tradition where the author implies that a complete jurisprudence is his next project (but that, of course, never seems to get written).

My version of "notes toward" comes in five installments. Section I discusses the substitution in discussions of youth violence of debates about procedure and court jurisdiction for issues of substantive principle. Section II discusses policy toward youth violence as an extension of legal policy toward crime as well as an extension of legal policy toward youth development. The question is not which of these two perspectives should control thinking about youth violence but how they can jointly determine appropriate responses to particular circumstances. Section III is the heart of this essay, in which an attempt is made to identify two clusters of policies in more detail than previous efforts (Zimring 1979): diminished responsibility and room to reform. Section IV considers whether a good argument can be made that special dispensations toward youth of the types discussed in Section III should not extend to violent youth. The conclusion suggests three specific issues that must be decided in current conditions. The aim of the essay is to provide a framework that can inform the large number of specific questions that a useful youth violence policy must address one by one.

Without doubt, the world would be a simpler place if serious crimes were committed only by fully grown citizens of the republic. That is not the world we inhabit. If there is merit to the notion that immaturity should mitigate the punishment deserved by middle adolescent offenders, this policy should apply in cases of serious violence as well as in cases of lesser seriousness. Further, the law should make substantial efforts to punish youth violence without eliminating an offender's chances to grow into adulthood in near-normal circumstances. This will not always be possible when very serious crime or manifest dangerousness are present.

This view of the goals of legal policy has implications for the procedures used in youth violence cases. If an offender's immaturity is to be taken into account in both juvenile and criminal tribunals, then the border between juvenile and criminal court processing becomes less important. The system can become less preoccupied with waiver to criminal courts and more concerned with identifying appropriate responses to specific problems.

The distinctive patterns of violence in adolescence require special attention in creating punishment policy. Sentencing policy toward young offenders must comprehend group involvement in most cases, and this will require more flexible penalty structures to account for the variety of accessorial responsibilities. Adolescent gun use is a special problem because all the features of youth that support findings of diminished responsibility also make gun possession and use more dangerous. Prohibitions of possession and use of guns seem justified even where adult ownership is not restricted. Homicide cases represent the worst case conflict between youth protection and the punishment of serious crimes. Even if the usual preferences for giving young offenders a chance to mature without interruption must give way in homicide, diminished responsibility should function as an important restraint on the level of punishment of adolescents who kill.

I. Substance versus Procedure

Juvenile violence raises issues for the justice system that involve both the substance and the procedures that the legal system uses to respond to particular acts. The substantive issues include whether punishment is appropriate for particular acts, the degree to which youth and the conditions associated with youth should affect the appropriate punishment in individual cases, and the purposes of punishment that should determine the justice system response to violent acts of varying degrees of seriousness. The procedural issues are whether a particular young person should be referred to a juvenile or criminal court and what procedural provisions should govern in the hearing of particular cases.

To some extent, the choice of court—whether a case is heard in juvenile or criminal court—might determine both the procedures and the substantive principles that will govern a specific case, but this linkage is by no means a matter of logical necessity. In theory, the same principles about responsibility and mitigation could be invoked in both juvenile and criminal courts. In practice, it is widely assumed that these two different court systems employ very different philosophies and standards.

One troublesome feature of the current debate about responding to youth violence is the dominance of jurisdictional concerns. Almost all the policy discussion about the treatment of young violent offenders in the legal system is about which court system—juvenile or criminal—should handle particular types of cases. Political debates and academic discourse are both jurisdictionally focused and most concerned with the procedures that will be used to assign particular cases. Substantive principles are rarely considered as policies that might apply within either juvenile or criminal courts for different kinds of cases or as policies that might be changed to accommodate different circumstances. Instead, the implicit assumption seems to be that each of the court systems has a single stereotyped set of priorities for dealing with all the young offenders before it and, further, that nothing can or should be done to alter this set of mutually antagonistic institutional biases.

Juvenile court is where it is assumed that young offenders are sent to be coddled, reformed, and protected. Criminal courts are assumed to be institutions where the youth of a defendant will be ignored and only considerations relating to the seriousness of the offense and the need for deterrence and incapacitation will control the outcome. If the orientation and outcome in each court is uniform and unvaried, then the only important question to be considered is which court should get jurisdiction.

Such a preoccupation with the issue of which court should try a young person would only make sense if the current legal system for processing young offenders was itself both monstrous and arbitrary—with a single dividing line separating systems with totally inconsistent principles and no capacity to compromise either youth protection or crime control considerations. The juvenile court would pursue one unvarying policy, no matter what the offense, while the criminal court would also be limited to a single policy mode, which would contradict the assumptions and priorities of the juvenile justice system.

Of course, the criminal courts and juvenile courts of the real world are much more complicated and much more subject to variation than the single-sentiment stereotypes of the previous discussion. Punishment and responsibility are not foreign concepts in the modern juvenile court, and diminished capacity as a consequence of immaturity is important in the decisions reached in criminal courts. So there is no sense in which the proper principles for deciding any particular case can be derived from just knowing which court will hear the case. The substantive principles that come into play when considering the appropriate responses are more important than the court that will have jurisdiction, and the discussion of proper substantive principles should also precede any consideration of appropriate form. Rightly considered, the institutions of justice should be servants of substantive principle. That perspective demands prior attention to substance.

The current debate, by stressing only the issue of which court prevails, is not, strictly speaking, putting the cart before the horse. It is instead all cart and no horse. The problem with imagining that the only important issue about youth crime is which court gets jurisdiction is that debate about responding to youth crime can proceed as if the substantive principles are not important in their own right. One reason basic principles get ignored in the current debate is that they are not evident on the agenda. A debate centered on jurisdiction is one important reason principles get ignored. So the current debate is not merely silly, it carries costs. This essay attempts to restore the primacy of substantive issues by first discussing the principles in competition when very young persons inflict serious harm on their victims.

II. Two Standards of Comparison

Sentencing policy toward young offenders is located at the crossroads between legal policy toward youth development and legal policy toward criminal offenders. A sixteen-year-old boy shoots and wounds another youth. The question of the appropriate legal response to this act by this actor is a matter of both crime control policy and youth policy. From the perspective of crime control policy, the question is one of determining the extent to which sixteen-year-olds who shoot and wound should be treated in the same way or differently from older persons who commit the same offense. From the perspective of youth policy, the issue is one of determining whether sixteen-year-olds who shoot and wound should be treated similarly to or differently from other sixteen-year-olds. If policy toward young offenders is properly classified as both youth policy and crime policy, then these two standards should not be thought of as competing to determine which should dominate decision making. Instead, the two perspectives should jointly inform a calculus of policy determination that must take both into account.

From a youth development policy perspective, what separates the sixteen-year-old who shoots and wounds from others his age is the harm of his act and the moral culpability of intention to do an act that causes great harm. Even if youth policy were the only set of principles used to decide legal policy in this case, the harm and culpability associated with the act would justify close to the maximum exertion of social control available to youth policy. One does not need a separate criminal law system to tell the difference between sixteen-year-olds who wound with deadly weapons and other kids. Any youth-serving institution will treat these kids and these acts separately.

From a criminal law perspective, what separates sixteen-year-olds from older persons who shoot is diminished culpability even for intended harms because of immaturity and because of a youth's lessened capacity and experience with self-control. Even if a criminal law perspective were the only tool available for making legal policy in this case, the youth and immaturity of a criminal actor would be relevant to the proper determination of punishment.

So the factors of importance to penal considerations and those that influence youth policy are not mutually exclusive. But there are also policy perspectives that are not shared by these two systems but that should influence policy when they overlap. Youth development policy takes risks with the general public welfare to allow young persons to try out adult privileges like driving even though adolescents are especially dangerous before they become experienced drivers. We take the special risks of this learning period because there is no way to avoid them when the only effective way to learn an activity is by doing it (Zimring 1982, chap. 7). For similar reasons, the system may wish to avoid punishments that inflict substantial permanent harm when dealing with young offenders so that a healthy transition to adulthood is still possible even when harmful mistakes are made.

But the larger dangers of adolescent actions also produce restrictions on the way young persons can behave that are not present for adults.

Activities like drinking, smoking, and purchasing handguns are not available to seventeen-year-olds because of a sense of their larger risk if not restrained. These special limitations of adolescent liberty are based on the same notions of immaturity that reduce the culpability of young persons for criminal acts. I show in the next section that status offenses and diminished penal responsibility are two sides of the same coin.

There is at least some evident tension between the punitive tug of crime control policy and the protective tug of youth development policy when young persons commit serious crimes. Debates about youth crime policy have produced many rhetorical gambits that seek to avoid this tension. The crudest method of seeking to remove young offenders from the coverage of youth protective policy is to rename them. When terms like "juvenile superpredator" and "feral presocial being" are used in debates about youth crime, they have a special rhetorical purpose to set the object of the description apart from other young persons and from the protection of youth development policy. A "superpredator" is posited as something very different from a youth, and the proponent of renaming suggests that thus no special provisions of a youth policy need apply to any person that can be so classified (Bennett, DiIulio, and Waters 1996).

A more reasoned effort to produce the same result can be found in the argument that those young persons who commit very serious crimes should forfeit the protected status of youth. In this view, committing a homicide, for example, is viewed as sufficiently depraved or dangerous behavior so that we would wish to deprive the guilty young person of any special protections extended because of his youth. Loss of the protected status of youth becomes in effect one penal consequence of the forbidden act.

This forfeiture theory is an improvement over the mere relabeling of offenders by using different terms, but it raises serious questions about the appropriateness of the linkage. Is the status of youth just a privilege provided to nice kids, or is it a socially and legally separate stage of development where nice kids and bad kids should alike be governed by distinct rules? Certainly, the law does not prohibit only nice kids from buying liquor under age twenty-one; that is, rather, a prohibition we seek to extend to all kids. Why should some of the protective aspects of a youth policy be less general? There is certainly no logically necessary reason that protective features of youth policy are only for nice kids.

A third device used to restrict the coverage of youth policy attempts to link the intention to commit serious criminal harms with a maturity and commitment to criminal activities that is inconsistent with legal treatment as a youth. In standards providing for waiver to criminal courts, juvenile court judges are asked to decide whether a particular accused is mature. If he is, then he can be punished as an adult (see, e.g., *Kent v. United States*, 383 U.S. 541 [1966]).

The transfer of young persons below the maximum age of juvenile court jurisdiction to criminal court if they are found to be too mature or too sophisticated for juvenile court processing has a history just as long as that of the juvenile court. One year before Judge Julian Mack published his classic polemic in support of a help-oriented juvenile court system, the chief probation officer of the Cook County juvenile court (that was Exhibit A for Judge Mack's optimism) was already suggesting that some delinquents were too far developed for juvenile court treatment (compare Mack [1909] with Circuit Court of Cook County [1907], p. 123).

And saying that the kids who were too much trouble for juvenile justice were mature and sophisticated provided a good jurisprudential rationale for not extending the protection of a youth-oriented policy. If the offenders in the worst cases for a young people's court were significantly more adult in their cognition and behavior than other young offenders and significantly more adult than most youths of the same chronological age, then the reasons justifying special treatment of youth might not apply.

The problem with withdrawing the protections of juvenile justice only when the subject is mature and sophisticated is that the most serious cases are not the most mature offenders. The empirical pattern is, if anything, to the contrary. The most serious acts of violence are probably committed by youth operating with lower levels of educational attainment, less capacity for mature judgment, and less understanding of the world around them than other kids of the same chronological age. The limited number of studies conducted of waiver to adult court suggest that serious violence was always an important prediction of waiver (see Eigen 1981; Dawson 1992; Howell 1996). And the statutes that provide automatic transfer for listed serious crimes of violence for offenders above a particular age further contradict theories that maturity was the animating principle behind transfers to criminal court. This recent tendency to reduce the age for transfer if the offense was sufficiently serious clarifies the priorities that operate generally to withhold juvenile court protections in waiver processes. While some youths who are near the age boundary of juvenile and criminal court may be pushed up because of age, in most cases it is offense severity that is a major influence (Dawson 1992; Howell 1996). Kids who are immature are no less dangerous for that reason. Kids who are dangerous are no older. The traditional language about maturity and sophistication was always largely a cover for pushing the worst-case juvenile offenders into criminal courts. The recent emphasis on serious violence has simply removed the cover.

So there is no persuasive reason available to assume that legal policy toward youth is irrelevant to policy toward violent young offenders. That does not mean that violent youths should be treated no differently from nonviolent youths. It does mean that the reasons the legal system wishes to treat some young people who violate the law differently than older law violators must be surveyed and discussed before proper legal responses to youth violence can be framed.

III. Rationales for Distinctive Penal Policies for Youth

Little has been written about the substantive reasons that support a separate policy toward crimes committed by young offenders for a variety of reasons. As described in Section I, part of the problem is that debate about procedures and jurisdiction crowded out any issues of the substantive content of a youth crime policy. Part of the problem is that juvenile and criminal court issues were usually considered separately, so that there was little pressure exerted to examine the same questions across different procedural settings. A third deterrent to substantive analysis is that separate treatment of children seemed intuitively right in a way that did not invite further scrutiny from its advocates. Of course, kids who violate laws should be differently treated; should we imprison six-year-olds? Legal nuance and complexity might seem beside the point in this context. For all these reasons, no sustained analysis of the factors that justify separate treatment of adolescent offenders is in the literature to measure against the known facts on serious youth violence.

Some years ago, I suggested two general policy clusters that were at work in youth crime policy: diminished capacity due to immaturity, and special efforts designed to give young offenders room to reform in the course of adolescent years (Twentieth Century Fund 1978, pp. 78–81). The issues grouped under the "diminished capacity" heading relate to the traditional concerns of the criminal law, so that these matters tell us why a criminal lawyer might regard a younger offender as less culpable than an older offender. The cluster of policies under the heading of "room to reform" are derived from legal policies toward young persons in the process of growing up. They are the same policies we apply to young drivers, teen pregnancy, and school dropouts.

A. Dimensions of Diminished Responsibility

To consider immaturity as a species of diminished responsibility has some historic precedent but little analytic pedigree. Children below seven were at common law not responsible for criminal acts by reason of incapacity, while those between seven and fourteen were the subject of special inquiries with respect to capacity. But capacity in this sense was an all-or-nothing matter like legal insanity rather than a question of degree. Yet diminished-capacity logic argues that, even after a youth passes the minimum threshold of competence that leads to finding capacity to commit crime, the barely competent youth is not as culpable and therefore not as deserving of a full measure of punishment as a fully qualified adult offender. Just as psychiatric disorder or cognitive impairment that does not render a subject exempt from the criminal law might still mitigate the punishment justly to be imposed, so a minimally competent adolescent should not be responsible for the whole of an adult's desert for the same act.

Despite the universal acceptance of immaturity in doctrines of infancy and the widespread acceptance of reduced levels of responsibility in early teen years, there has been little analysis of what aspects of immaturity should be relevant to mitigation of punishment. Again, the intuitive appeal of the result may have deferred the analysis of its rationale. Yet the specific attributes of legal immaturity must be discovered before judgments can be made about what ages and conditions are relevant to reducing punishment on this ground. Here is an important collaboration for law and the behavioral sciences.

What characteristics of children and adolescents might lead us to lessen punishment in the name of immaturity? An initial distinction needs to be drawn between diminished capacities and the poor decisions such impairments encourage. Most teenaged law violators make bad decisions, but so do most adults who commit major infractions of the criminal law. The Anglo-American criminal law is designed to punish bad decisions full measure. But persons who for reasons not their own fault lack the capacity observed in the common citizen to appreciate the difference between wrong and allowable conduct or to conform their conduct to the law's requirements may be blameless because of the incapacity. Even when sufficient cognitive capacity and emotional control is present to pass the threshold of criminal capacity, a significant deficit in the capacity to appreciate or control behavior would mean the forbidden conduct is not *as much* the offender's fault, and the quantum of appropriate punishment is less.

How might fourteen- and fifteen-year-olds who commit crimes be said to exhibit diminished capacity in moral and legal terms? There are three different types of personal attributes that influence decisions to commit crimes where adolescents may lack full adult skills and therefore also full adult moral responsibilities when the law is violated.

1. *Cognitive Abilities.* First, older children and younger adolescents may lack fully developed cognitive abilities to comprehend the moral content of commands and to apply legal and moral rules to social situations. The lack of this kind of capacity is at the heart of infancy as an absolute defense to criminal liability. This ability to comprehend and apply rules in the abstract requires a mix of cognitive ability and information. A young person who lacks these skills will not do well on a paper-and-pencil test to assess knowledge about what is lawful and unlawful behavior and why. Very young children have obvious gaps in both information and the cognitive skills to use it. Older children have more subtle but still significant deficits in moral reasoning abilities.

2. *Self-Control.* The capacity to pass paper-and-pencil tests in moral reasoning may be one necessary condition for adult capacity of self-control, but it is by no means a sufficient condition. A second skill that helps transform cognitive understanding into the capacity to obey the law is the ability to control impulses. This is not the type of capacity that can be tested well on abstract written or oral surveys. Long after a child knows that taking candy is wrong, the capacity to resist temptation when a taking is the only available route to the candy may not be fully operational.

To an important extent, self-control is a habit of behavior developed over a period of time, a habit dependent on the experience of successfully exercising self-control. This particular type of maturity, like so many others, takes practice. While children must start learning to control impulses at a very early age, the question of how long the process continues until adult levels of control are achieved is an open one. Impulse control is a social skill not easily measured in a laboratory. We also do not know the extent to which lessons to control impulses are generalized or how context-specific are habits of self-control. Kids must learn not to dash in front of cars at an early age. How much of that capacity to self-control carries over when other impulses—say, the temptation to cheat on a test—occur in new situations? The empirical psychology of self-control is not a thick chapter in current psychological knowledge. The developmental psychology of self-control is practically nonexistent. There may also be an important distinction between impulse control in the context of frustration and impulse control in temptation settings. If so, the frustration context may be the more important one for study of the determinants of youth violence.

To the extent that new situations and opportunities require new habits of self-control, the teen years are periods when self-control issues are confronted on a series of distinctive new battlefields. The physical controls of earlier years are supplanted by physical freedoms. New domains—including secondary education, sex, and driving—require not only the cognitive appreciation of the need for self-control in a new situation but also its practice. If this normally takes a while to develop, the bad decisions made along the way should not be punished as severely as the bad decisions of adults who have passed through the period when the opportunity to develop habits of self-control in a variety of domains relevant to the criminal law has occurred. To the extent that inexperience is a condition of reduced capacity, this inexperience is partially excusable in the teen years, whereas it is not usually understandable in later life.

3. *Peer Pressure.* The ability to resist peer pressure is yet another social skill that is a necessary part of legal obedience and is not fully developed in many adolescents. A teen may know right from wrong and even may have developed the capacity to control his or her impulses if left alone to do so, but resisting temptation while alone is a different task than resisting the pressure to commit an offense when adolescent peers are pushing for the adolescent to misbehave and witnessing whether or not the outcome they desire will occur. Most adolescent decisions to break the law or not take place on a social stage where the immediate pressure of peers urging the adolescent on is often the real motive for most teenage crime. A necessary condition for an adolescent to stay law-abiding is the ability to deflect or resist peer pressure. Many kids lack this crucial social skill for a long time.

Figure 1 shows the percentage of juvenile defendants who were accused of committing a crime with at least one confederate in the New York City Family Courts in 1978. These offenders were all under sixteen at the time the act was committed. The percentage of total defen-

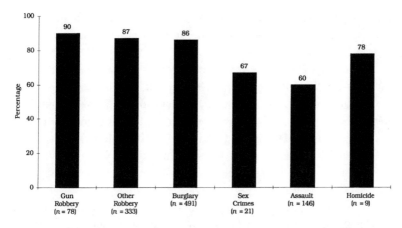

Fig. 1.—Multiple offender cases as a percent of total juveniles charged, by crime, New York City. Source: Zimring (1981).

dants who acted with a confederate ranged from 60 percent for assault to 90 percent for robbery.

The cold criminological facts are these: the teen years are characterized by what has long been called "group offending." No matter the crime, if a teenager is the offender, he is usually not committing the offense alone. When adults commit theft, they usually are acting alone. When kids commit theft, they usually steal in groups. When adults commit rape, robbery, homicide, burglary, or assault, they usually are acting alone. When adolescents commit rape, robbery, homicide, burglary, or assault, they usually commit the offense accompanied by other kids (Zimring 1981). The setting for the offenses of adolescents is the presence of delinquent peers as witnesses and collaborators.

No fact of adolescent criminality is more important than what sociologists call its "group context" (Reiss 1988). And this fact is important to a balanced and worldly theory of adolescent moral and legal responsibility for criminal acts.

When an adult offender commits rape, his motive may be rage or lust or any number of other things. When a teen offender in a group setting commits rape, the motive may well be "I dare you" or its functional equivalent "Don't be a chicken." When an adolescent robs, steals, breaks into a house, or shoots another youth in the company of co-offenders, the real motive for his acts may be the explicit or implicit "I dare you" that leads kids to show off and that deters kids from withdrawing from criminal acts. Fear of being called chicken is almost certainly the leading cause of death and injury from youth violence in the United States.

"I dare you" is the core reason young persons who would not commit crimes alone do so in groups. "I dare you" is the reason that "having delinquent friends" both precedes an adolescent's own involvement in violence and is a strong predictor of future violence (Elliott and Menard 1996; Howell and Hawkins, in this volume).

That social settings account for the majority of all youth crime suggests that the capacity to deflect or resist peer pressure is a crucially necessary dimension of being law-abiding in adolescence. Dealing with peer pressure is another dimension of capacity that requires social experience. Kids who do not know how to deal with such pressure lack effective control of the situations that place them most at risk of crime in their teens. This surely does not excuse criminal conduct. But any moral scheme that gives mitigational recognition to other forms of inexperience must also do so for a lack of peer-management skills that an accused has not had a fair opportunity to develop. This is a matter of huge importance given the reality of contemporary youth crime as group behavior.

I do not want to suggest that current knowledge is sufficient for us to measure the extent of diminished capacity in young offenders or to express in detail the types of understanding and control that are important parts of a normative developmental psychology. We have an awful lot of social psychology homework ahead of us before achieving understanding of the key terms in adolescent behavioral controls relevant to criminal offending.

But it is important to recognize that a substantive criminal law with a broad-spectrum doctrine of diminished responsibility would generate many of the same issues we now confront in juvenile justice. Even if there were no separate youth policy to consult in making decisions about younger offenders, and even if there were no juvenile court, the punishment of young offenders would be a separate problem of complexity for the criminal courts.

B. Room to Reform in Youth Development Policy

The notion that children and adolescents should be the subject of special legal rules pervades the civil as well as the criminal laws of most developed societies. There are a multiplicity of different policies reflected in different legal areas and also important differences throughout law in the treatment of younger and older children. Under these circumstances, to refer to "youth policy" generally risks misunderstandings about both the subjects of the policies and the policy objects of the rules.

The policies I refer to in this section concern adolescence, a period that spans roughly from ages eleven or twelve to about age twenty. This is also the only segment of childhood associated with high rates of serious crime. This span has been described as a period of increasing semiautonomy when kids acquire adult liberties in stages and learn their way toward adult freedoms (Zimring 1982).

At the heart of this process is a notion of adolescence as a period of "learning by doing" when the only way competence in decision making can be achieved is by making decisions and making mistakes. For this reason, adolescence is a period that is mistake-prone by design. The special challenge here is to create safeguards in the policies and environments of adolescents that reduce the permanent costs of adolescent mistakes. Two goals of legal policy are to facilitate "learning by doing" and to reduce the hazards associated with expectable errors. One important hallmark of a successful adolescence is survival to adulthood, preferably with the individual's life chances intact.

There is a currently fashionable theory of the classification of youth crime in legal policy that provides a rationale for a room-to-reform policy. The theory is that the high prevalence of offense behavior in the teen years and the rather high rates of incidence for those who offend are often transitory phenomena associated with a transitional status and life period. Even absent heroic interventions, the conduct that occurs at peak rates in adolescence will level off substantially if and when adolescents achieve adult roles and status. With regard to youth violence, the distinction is drawn between "adolescence-limited" and "life-course-persistent" adolescent violent offenders (Moffitt 1993).

The adolescence-limited assumption may carry three implications. First, it regards criminal offenses as a more or less normal adolescent phenomenon, a by-product of the same transitional status that increases accident risks, rates of accidental pregnancy, and suicidal gestures. This view of youth crime tells us, therefore, that policy toward those offenses that are a by-product of adolescence should be a part of larger policies toward youth.

A second implication of the notion that high rates of adolescent crimes can be outgrown is that major interventions may not be necessary to reorient offenders. The central notion of what has been called "adolescence-limited" offending is that one cure for youth violence is growing up (Moffitt 1993; Howell and Hawkins, in this volume).

Related to the hope for natural processes of remission over time is the tendency for persons who view youth crime policy as a branch of youth development policy to worry that drastic countermeasures that inhibit the natural transition to adulthood may cause more harm than they are worth. If a particular treatment risks severe side effects, it usually should only be elected if failure to use would risk more cost. Those who regard youth crime as a transitional phenomenon see problems of deviance resolving themselves without drastic interventions and thus doubt the efficacy of high-risk interventions on utilitarian grounds. So juvenile justice theories with labels like "radical nonintervention" and "diversion" are a natural outgrowth of the belief that long-term prospects for most young offenders are favorable.

But what about the short term? The current costs of youth crime to the general community, to other adolescents, and to the offending kids are quite large. How would enthusiasts for juvenile court nonintervention seek to protect the community? Is a room-to-reform policy inconsistent with *any* punitive responses to adolescent law violation?

The emphasis in youth development policy is on risk management over a period of transitional high danger. As we have seen, the theory that adolescents are not fully mature allows a larger variety of risk-management tactics than is available for dealing with adults. Minors cannot purchase liquor, acquire handguns, buy cigarettes, or pilot planes. Younger adolescents are constrained by curfews and compulsory education laws. There are special age-graded rules for driving motor vehicles, entering contracts, and establishing employment relationships. Many of these rules are to protect the young person from the predation of others. Many are to protect the young person from herself. Many are to protect the community from harmful acts by the young. So there is a rich mixture of risk-management strategies available to reduce the level of harmful consequences from youth crime.

Does this mix of strategies include the punishment of intentional harms? The answer to this question is yes from all but the most extreme radical noninterventionists, but attaching negative consequences to youthful offenders is good policy in this view only up to a point. Youth development proponents are suspicious of sacrificing the personal interests of a young person in order to serve as a deterrent example to other youth if the punished offender's interests are substantially prejudiced. And punishing a young offender in ways that significantly diminish later life chances compromises the essential core of a youth protection policy. There may be circumstances where drastic punishment is required, but such punishments always violate important priorities in youth development policy and can be tolerated rarely and only in cases of proven need. In this view, punishment begins to be suspicious when it compromises the long-term interests of the targeted young offender.

IV. Categorical Exception for Violent Crime?

Having outlined the principal headings that justify special treatment of adolescent offenders, it becomes necessary to inquire whether any of the considerations in the previous section should be relevant to the legal treatment of youth violence. The argument against extending special youth-oriented policies to violent crime goes something like this: it is okay to allow soft treatment of young offenders when the crimes they commit are kid's stuff, but violent crime is not kid's stuff. There is no room for leniency. Because the harms are so serious, the young offenders who commit them should be treated as if they were adults.

The threshold question to be considered here is whether that reasoning amounts to a principled argument against special youth policies for all violent young offenders. While the rhetoric just summarized sounds much like the denials discussed in Section II, the task of this section is to measure that argument against the specific policies outlined in Section III. The current concern is whether violent acts should be properly excluded from the scope of the policies just discussed.

With respect to doctrines of diminished capacity, there is no logical basis for limiting the scope of a mitigation principle because the harm caused by the criminal act is great. Doctrines of diminished capacity have their greatest effect when large harms have been caused by actors not fully capable of understanding and control. The visible importance of diminished responsibility in these cases comes because the punishments provided are quite severe, and the reductive effect of mitigating punishment is correspondingly large. But if doctrines of diminished capacity mean anything in relation to the punishment of immature offenders, their effects cannot be limited to trivial cases. Diminished capacity is either generally applicable or generally unpersuasive.

The situation with the youth policies served by a room-to-reform perspective is more complicated. A young offender does not become any less young because he pulls the trigger that ends a human life, just as the victim is just as dead as if shot by an adult. The seriousness of harms intended and done may push legal policy in the opposite direction to that which room-to-reform perspectives would usually suggest. But this countervailing force is not the same as suggesting that either violent acts or the young persons who commit them are not suitable candidates for a youth-oriented policy.

To begin with, violent crime is kid stuff as an empirical matter if American criminology is to be trusted. Just under half of all males report being responsible for an assault at some time during their teen years. So a very large proportion of a male youth population crosses the border into violence at least once in adolescence. Further, teenage boys are involved in assaults at annual rates ranging from 10 to 27 percent depending on how the term "assault" is defined and limited. African-American boys reported serious assault involvement rates of 36 percent per year (Farrington 1996, p. 5). At least half these assaults involve weapon use or injury (Elliott 1994).

The empirical literature reports that violence is kid stuff in one further respect importantly relevant to a room-to-reform youth crime policy and discussed in the previous section. Over 75 percent of those in Delbert Elliott's national youth survey who committed a violent offense during their teenaged years did not continue to do so thereafter (see Howell and Hawkins, in this volume). The majority of self-reported youth violence offenders are adolescence-limited. These are the transitional offenders who proponents of a room-to-reform strategy believe will outgrow criminal conduct without drastic intervention. On the evidence from self-report studies, there is no basis for a categorical exclusion of violent offenders.

Official police statistics tell a somewhat different story. A much smaller percentage of the youth population is identified as violent. But the mode in police statistics patterns is for no repeat offense of violence among the ever-arrested, and the desistance probabilities for violence offenders are no worse than for nonviolent offenders (Wolfgang, Figlio, and Sellin 1972, p. 303, table F.2.2). The characteristic patterns of youth crime discussed in this essay are found in most violent offenders. The only real basis for differentiating the violent offender is the seriousness of his crime. Further, using the offense labels that young offenders are arrested for to screen for seriousness of their owners does not work well. Assaults and robberies vary tremendously in seriousness. These two offenses account for 94 percent of all youth violence arrests. Categorical generalizations are therefore a poor basis for policy in a great majority of cases.

Instead, policy discussion should be organized around specific subcategories of violent offenders when measuring the justice and efficacy of particular policy responses. The last section of this essay identifies three of these specific subcategories that are of particular import in the late 1990s. That discussion should also be regarded as my attempt to demonstrate the value of shifting the focus from "juvenile violence" as a general category to smaller policy packages.

One final perspective on youth violence in the context of youth development policy concerns the kinds of harm involved in violence as a possible basis for distinguishing violent crime from other areas where youth protective policies apply. The kind of damage that youth violence sometimes causes means that the stakes are high when formulating policy to respond to it. Life and limb are the largest concerns in criminal justice generally, and life-threatening violence demands the priority concerns of criminal justice policy (Zimring and Hawkins 1997).

But violent crime is not the only dangerous behavior that challenges youth policy in current circumstances, nor is it even the most dangerous. Even though driving privileges are withheld until midadolescence, the "learning period" of unsupervised driving in the United States is associated with high risks of death and injury and large aggregate death and injury losses. From the standpoint of the community at large, the risks generated by drivers aged sixteen to twenty-one are of similar kind and similar magnitude to those associated with intentional injuries.

The analogies between traffic injuries and assaultive injuries in modern American life are instructive if incomplete. In each case, the instrumentalities and values of the larger society play an important role in defining the risk environment associated with youth. Kids must learn to drive to be adult in the United States, and this imperative generates a high transitional risk that cannot be avoided. Yet improvements in the risk environments of driving generally—the kinds of roads, kinds of cars, range of legally required safety precautions—can reduce the death toll produced by youth driving. The nature of American youth violence has similar links to larger social phenomena. Distinctively high rates of lethal violence throughout the age distribution are associated with our high rates of youth violence. Handgun availability in the general society is importantly linked to handgun availability in the youth population, even when we attempt to prohibit acquisition by youths.

Why then are there no serious proposals radically to redefine youth traffic problems, to defer driver's licenses until age twenty-one, or to revoke them when youth drivers have accidents?

The transitional risks associated with young drivers may be regarded as part of the American system, a cost associated with a social process we approve. Youth violence, by contrast, is not believed to be a part of an American system that carries positive benefits. We do not think of high youth homicide rates as growing out of high rates of firearms availability to the general public or out of patterns of male aggression with positive payoffs. Traffic accidents are problems that happen to kids like ours. Youth violence is perceived as a cost imposed on American society from without.

The different social constructions of traffic fatalities and assault fatalities is only one of many differences between highway deaths and homicides. I do not mean to argue that the American public should regard the two problems as equivalent. But it is important to note that in both our history and current affairs, there are contexts other than violence where we are willing to pay the price of adolescent development into adulthood even when community safety is put at risk.

V. General Conclusions and Specific Questions

There are two clusters of reasons criminal acts by immature offenders are treated differently from the same acts committed by adults. Concerns about diminished responsibility come from a criminal law concern about punishment in just proportion to culpability. Concerns about preserving the future life chances of young offenders come from general policies that provide special support to adolescents in the transition to adulthood. Diminished-responsibility doctrines seek to reduce the amount of punishment that is appropriate. Room-to-reform policies address not so much the amount of punishment imposed but the kind of punishment and the kind of consequences that should be avoided. The orientation of these policies is qualitative rather than quantitative.

This essay's next-to-last contribution is a negative one. There is nothing in the known facts about adolescent violence or in other legal policies toward youth that would exclude violent injury categorically from either mitigation or youth protection. These policies will be balanced against other important interests in making decisions on particular topics and in specific cases. The appropriate way to explore the balancing processes is to address specific issues that are raised by recent developments. Identifying some of these specific issues is the final task of this analysis.

The data reported in this volume on the nature of American youth violence and on recent trends in that violence are useful in establishing some important questions that recent developments suggest must be resolved in responding to the 1990s version of violence by the young. Three issues emerge as particularly important:

1. discriminating between serious and less serious forms of youth violence so that special priority programs can be appropriately focused;
2. formulating firearms policies for minors in juvenile and criminal courts;
3. providing punishment processes for young offenders who kill.

Let me briefly discuss why current conditions underscore the importance of these three questions.

1. *Horizontal and Vertical Discrimination.* The increase in youth gun use and youth homicide has produced a demand for making the control of serious violence a priority for young persons in both juvenile and criminal courts. The perceived value of a special focus on serious violence has been widely reflected in mandatory or automatic transfer statutes, mandatory minimum punishments, and special extensions of the punishment powers held by juvenile courts. All of these tactics require capacities to concentrate on serious violence and to define those elements of common offenses of violence that should call for special focus. There are five common youth crimes that involve injury or the threat of injury: homicide, rape, aggravated assault, robbery, and the Uniform Crime Reports "part II" offense of assault (Federal Bureau of Investigation 1996). Homicide and forcible rape are serious offenses by definition. Aggravated assault, robbery, and assault vary widely in seriousness and account for over 95 percent of all youth violence arrests.

Any strategy that brings specially stringent penal policy to serious violence must define in advance what aspects of a crime and what types of participation in a crime are the specially serious grades that deserve the higher sanctions. Raising the penal stakes for serious violence thus also increases the need for coherent distinctions between gradations of seriousness in violent criminality.

A special focus on the most serious classes of violence will require two separate types of distinctions, what I call *vertical* and *horizontal* discriminations of serious individual acts of violence. Vertical distinctions involve deciding which types of attacks and robberies are the most serious and which do not deserve special high priority. Some vertical distinctions are between crime classifications. Homicides are more serious than nonfatal assaults and robbery. Most vertical distinctions will have to make divisions within crime categories, such as separating the most dangerous assaults and robberies from the rest.

Once there is a hierarchy of criminal acts, it is a further necessity to make judgments about the penal priority to be placed on the extent of a particular defendant's participation in a violent act. If a shooting on the street deserves a high penal priority, that decision implies serious consequences for the young offender who fired the gun. What of his (unarmed) friend who drove him to the scene of the assault? What of their mutual friend who, knowing of the pending assault, loaned the shooter gas money? The high level of group involvement reported for all crimes in figure 1 tells us that detailed judgments about the degree of guilt and punishment of accomplices will be a recurrent need for young offenders. Horizontal distinctions between shooters and supporters, as well as between dominant and passive accomplices, are as much a common need as distinctions between serious and less serious offenses.

My suspicion is that no statutory formula or sentencing commission grid can do an acceptable job of defining in advance which acts and actors should be singled out in special priority programs. Judicial waiver proceedings with a high standard of seriousness are the least wasteful way to provide for the occasional exceptionally serious assault or robbery case as a candidate for waiver or other special emphasis programs.

2. Firearms Policy for Minors.   The entire increase in youth homicide over the period 1985–93 was in gun homicide (Cook and Laub, in this volume). This suggests that a special priority for reducing lethal violence by the young is removing guns from kids. There are several kinds of gun-related behavior that can be the subject of special treatment in juvenile and criminal courts. Acquisition and possession of handguns by minors are usually illegal acts, status offenses in the sense that having these weapons are illegal only because of the youth of a subject. There are also laws against carrying concealed weapons and other high-risk uses that apply both to youths and adults. Finally, there are laws that escalate penal liability for some violent crimes if guns are used. All three types of regulation are available for minors, in both juvenile and criminal courts.

There are two questions that should be answered about an emphasis on guns in relation to youth violence, one simple and one complex. The simple question concerns the priority that police, prosecutors, and courts should accord to gun cases. Since changes in gun use are the complete explanation of the troublesome increases in total youth homicide, it would seem that gun availability, carrying, and use by kids are all high-priority issues. The complicated question is which groups of prohibitions should be emphasized in framing a youth gun policy. The broad prohibitions of acquisition and use argue for attempts to prevent gun use before shots are fired. Additional penalties for gun use in crime are also available as policy options, but the upper limits on punishment for gun use are constrained by the system's recognition that immature judgment is to be expected from kids with access to loaded guns. That, after all, is the foundation for the status offense that makes guns unavailable to minors. To then punish misusing minors as if they were as responsible as adults is inconsistent with the central premise of the regulatory scheme. So gun robbery and assault may rightfully generate special penalties, but the lengthy mandatory minimums of several criminal codes contradict the theory of immaturity that is the centerpiece of current youth gun policy.

The status offenses that control youth access to firearms seem, all other things being equal, to be more suitably enforced in juvenile rather than criminal courts. After all, juvenile courts deal with a wide range of age-based prohibitions established because of the higher risks associated with immaturity. Possession of a handgun is near the top of the scale in risk severity for this category of offenses but shares many of the subtleties and peculiarities that are associated with the enforcement of other status offenses ranging from liquor offenses to breaking curfew. When the advanced age of the minor makes a juvenile court referral unavailable, the criminal courts will face difficult and unfamiliar problems. The last thing the system should encourage is the waiver of additional gun status offenses into criminal courts when the defendant is under the maximum age for juvenile court jurisdiction.

3. *The Challenge of Youth Homicide.* Homicide cases are the most serious offenses in Anglo-American criminal law, and the arena where

the retributive pressures generated by a terrible loss clash most power-fully with notions of youth protection and diminished responsibility. The problems associated with cases where young persons kill would be prominent in any environment. The substantial increases in the vol-ume and rate of youth homicide arrests over the years since 1984 make dealing with these worst-case scenarios even more obviously a priority in the 1990s and beyond.

The unfortunate tendency for debates about jurisdiction to crowd out discussion of appropriate substantive principles is nowhere more apparent than for youth homicide. Almost all the discussion of juvenile killers has been in the context of deciding at what age juvenile homi-cide defendants may and must be transferred to criminal courts. Little attention has been paid to the appropriate principles for such cases in juvenile court and very little discussion has concerned what special rules or principles should influence case outcomes in criminal court once a transfer occurs. The implicit assumption has been that the transfer of a juvenile into a criminal court should end any special con-cerns relating to the immaturity of the defendant. Why this might be is not often addressed.

A jurisprudence of youth violence without coherent principles for youth homicide cases is as vulnerable as a house without a roof. But two thin layers of reasoning in death-penalty litigation and conclusory arguments as the background to state legislation are all that is currently available to address these issues. Both legislative debate and the consid-eration of diminished-responsibility questions by state appellate courts in individual cases must provoke the most sustained consideration of these important substantive questions. The proper disposition of ho-micide offenses by middle adolescents will probably require criminal court policies that permit mitigation of punishment on grounds of im-maturity. Transfer to criminal court relocates these difficult problems; it does not resolve them.

REFERENCES

Bennett, William, John J. DiIulio, Jr., and John P. Waters. 1996. *Body Count.* New York: Simon & Schuster.
Circuit Court of Cook County. 1907. *Annual Report of the Circuit Court of Cook*

County, Juvenile Division. Chicago: Circuit Court of Cook County, Juvenile Division.

Cook, Philip J., and John H. Laub. In this volume. "The Unprecedented Epidemic in Youth Violence."

Dawson, Robert. 1992. "An Empirical Study of Kent Style Juvenile Transfers to Criminal Court." *St. Mary's Law Journal* 23:975–1054.

Eigen, Joel Peter. 1981. "Punishing Youth Homicide Offenders in Philadelphia." *Journal of Criminal Law and Criminology* 72:1072–93.

Elliott, Delbert S. 1994. "Serious Violent Offenders: Onset, Developmental Course, and Termination: The American Society of Criminology 1993 Presidential Address." *Criminology* 32:1–21.

Elliott, Delbert S., and Scott Menard. 1996. "Delinquent Friends and Delinquent Behavior: Temporal and Developmental Patterns." In *Delinquency and Crime: Current Theories*, edited by J. David Hawkins. Cambridge: Cambridge University Press.

Farrington, David P. 1996. "The Explanation and Prevention of Youthful Offending." In *Delinquency and Crime: Current Theories*, edited by J. David Hawkins. Cambridge: Cambridge University Press.

Federal Bureau of Investigation. 1996. *Crime in the United States: Uniform Crime Reports, 1995.* Washington, D.C.: U.S. Goverment Printing Office.

Howell, James C. 1996. "Transfers to the Criminal Justice System: State of the Art." *Law and Policy* 18:17–60.

Howell, James C., and J. David Hawkins. In this volume. "Prevention of Youth Violence."

Mack, Julian. 1909. "The Juvenile Court." *Harvard Law Review* 23:107–22.

Moffitt, Terrie E. 1993. "Adolescence-Limited and Life-Course-Persistent Antisocial Behavior: A Developmental Taxonomy." *Psychological Review* 100:674–701.

Reiss, Albert J., Jr. 1988. "Co-offending and Criminal Careers." In *Crime and Justice: A Review of Research*, vol. 10, edited by Michael Tonry and Norval Morris. Chicago: University of Chicago Press.

Twentieth Century Fund. 1978. *Confronting Youth Crime.* Task Force on Sentencing Policy. New York: Holmes & Meier.

Wolfgang, Marvin, Robert Figlio, and Thorsten Sellin. 1972. *Delinquency in a Birth Cohort.* Chicago: University of Chicago Press.

Zimring, Franklin E. 1979. "American Youth Violence: Issues and Trends." In *Crime and Justice: An Annual Review of Research*, vol. 1, edited by Norval Morris and Michael Tonry. Chicago: University of Chicago Press.

———. 1981. "Kids, Groups, and Crime: Some Implications of a Well-Known Secret." *Journal of Criminal Law and Criminology* 72:867–85.

———. 1982. *The Changing Legal World of Adolescence.* New York: Free Press.

Zimring, Franklin E., and Gordon Hawkins. 1997. *Crime Is Not the Problem: Lethal Violence in America.* New York: Oxford University Press.

Author Index

Subject Index